ENLIGHTENMENT

MUSEUM BRITANNICUM;

OR, A DISPLAY

IN THIRTY TWO PLATES,

IN

ANTIQUITIES AND NATURAL CURIOSITIES,

IN

That NOBLE AND MAGNIFICENT CABINET,

THE

BRITISH MUSEUM,

AFTER THE ORIGINAL DESIGNS FROM NATURE,

By JOHN AND ANDREW VAN RYMSDYK, Pictors.

THE SECOND EDITION, REVISED AND CORRECTED
By P. BOYLE.

D E D I C A T E D

(*BY PERMISSION*)

TO HIS ROYAL HIGHNESS

THE PRINCE OF WALES.

LONDON:

PRINTED FOR THE EDITOR, BY J. MOORE, No. 134, DRURY-LANE.
And Sold by T. HOOKHAM, *Bond-Street.*

M,DCC,XCI.

ENLIGHTENMENT

Discovering the World
in the Eighteenth Century

EDITED BY KIM SLOAN
WITH ANDREW BURNETT

THE BRITISH MUSEUM PRESS

IN MEMORY OF ILARIA BIGNAMINI AND MICHAEL KITSON

This book is published to coincide with the opening
in 2003 of the Enlightenment Gallery in the newly restored
King's Library at the British Museum.

The project has been made possible principally
through the great generosity of

THE WOLFSON FOUNDATION

and

SIMON SAINSBURY

Additional support has generously been given by

FRANCIS FINLAY

 Supported by the
Heritage Lottery Fund

THE PIDEM FUND

THE
BRITISH
MUSEUM
FRIENDS

THE JOHN ELLERMAN FOUNDATION
and many others

This book is published with the generous assistance of

HALF-TITLE PAGE: John and Andrew van Rymsdyk,
Museum Britannicum, 2nd edition, 1791, with hand-coloured
engravings. BM, Central Library

FRONTISPIECE: George Scharf (1788–1860), *Staircase of the old
British Museum in Montagu House*, 1845. Watercolour. BM, P&D

TITLE PAGE: *The King's Library*, 1880. Hand-coloured woodcut.
BM, Central Archives

Published by The British Museum Press
A division of The British Museum Company Ltd
46 Bloomsbury Street, London WC1B 3QQ

A catalogue record for this book is available
from the British Library
ISBN 0 7141 2765 5

Set in Minion and designed by Harry Green
Printed in Spain by Grafos

Contents

Preface

The British Museum is an astonishing place. It is the only place in the world where you can see the cultures of the globe gathered together under a single roof. Founded 250 years ago as an encyclopaedia of knowledge – the built equivalent of France's *Encyclopédie* – it has undergone many changes, but its founding ideals remain as valid today as in 1753: that every citizen should have free access to the sum of human understanding.

The universal scope of the Museum's collections, embracing both natural specimens and handmade artefacts, reflected the curiosity of the eighteenth-century Enlightenment in all aspects of the material world. It may be surprising to remember that as well as today's familiar collections of art, ethnography and archaeology, the British Museum also once contained paintings (now largely in the National Portrait Gallery), books and manuscripts (now in the British Library at St Pancras) and natural history (now in the Natural History Museum in South Kensington). Over its 250 years, the British Museum has thus given birth to these other great national institutions. If, in so doing, it has surrendered its eighteenth-century definition of universality, it has developed a new identity as a collection of the cultures of the world, ancient and modern. The Museum remains a unique repository of the achievements of human endeavour, and there is no culture, past or present, that is not represented within its walls. It is truly the memory of mankind.

If the Museum's nature has changed, so has its public. The comparatively small number of people who lived in London and visited its displays in the late eighteenth century have been replaced by the millions who now come every year. That new audience is truly world-wide, both because they come from all over the world and because they include the increasingly cosmopolitan population of London and Britain as a whole. In an age of global citizenship, the Museum offers a unique opportunity for people to sense what has been powerfully described by the writer Ben Okri as the secret one-ness of the world, to participate in the dialogues between civilizations.

If Enlightenment ideas found their intellectual expression in the creation of the British Museum in 1753, they found a visual expression in the Greek Revival architecture of the King's Library, now so beautifully restored. Constructed in 1823–7, the King's Library was created by the architect Sir Robert Smirke to house the royal library of King George III, given to the Museum by his son King George IV. The books now enjoy a new home in the British Library building at St Pancras where they were moved in 1998, once again to a purpose-built space. But the serene and beautiful room was left in Bloomsbury. Now it has a new function.

This room, the finest and largest Greek Revival interior in London, houses a permanent display, entitled *Enlightenment: Discovering the World in the Eighteenth Century*, and this book is published to explain the particular view of the Enlightenment embodied in the new gallery. It is by no means intended to be a comprehensive account of the period or its intellectual achievements. It seeks rather to examine the way people of the time looked at the 'natural and artificial curiosities' being collected from all over the world by scholars and collectors, who then sought to make sense of their past and their present. It tries to evoke how people at that time (roughly dating from the Museum's foundation in 1753 until the 1820s, when the room was built) saw the world – a very different world – through objects then present in the Museum's collection. We hope this will enable the visitors of today to see just how crucial this period was for the development of our present understanding of past and distant cultures. It also provides an intentional contrast with the way the same objects and cultures are understood today and presented in other galleries of the Museum. For example, many people then sought to find and emphasize links, whether in a progressive development of civilizations or in the search for a universal religion. Today perspectives are different, and many prefer to focus on cultural or indeed religious diversity. And in each case, the political implications are considerable. An important message of the *Enlightenment* displays in the restored King's Library is that interpretations do change, and indeed – by implication – that our current perceptions will also be replaced.

Enlightenment: Discovering the World in the Eighteenth Century opens in the restored King's Library in late 2003, the climax of the Museum's 250th anniversary. It is singularly appropriate for this occasion. By encouraging us to reflect on the Museum's past it helps us contemplate our future and explain how we began the voyage of discovery that has, so far, taken 250 years. The new gallery acts in several ways as an introduction to the Museum as it is today, celebrating the breadth and diversity of the collections and drawing together material from every part of them, thereby prompting reflection on the ways in which the universal museum of the eighteenth century can be re-invented as the museum of the world for the twenty-first. The profound social and economic changes of the last decades have revived interest in the way the world works as a whole and the different ways it can be understood. We now have different habits of intellectual address; our social and political concerns are different from those of 1753; but we explore the same subject matter – the unity and diversity of the world that we all live in, which we wish and need to understand.

NEIL MACGREGOR
Director, The British Museum

Contributors

Silke Ackermann is curator of scientific instruments and other medieval and post-medieval collections in the Department of Medieval and Modern Europe at the British Museum.

Peter Barber is head of map collections at the British Library.

Nigel Barley was formerly curator of West African collections in the Department of Ethnography at the British Museum.

Lucilla Burn was formerly curator of Greek antiquities in the Department of Greek and Roman Antiquities at the British Museum and is now keeper of antiquities at the Fitzwilliam Museum, Cambridge.

Andrew Burnett is keeper of the Department of Coins and Medals, project manager for the Enlightenment Gallery and senior keeper at the British Museum.

Clive Cheesman was formerly curator of Roman and Iron Age coins in the Department of Coins and Medals at the British Museum and is now Rouge Dragon Pursuivant at the College of Arms, London.

Tim Clark is curator of Japanese paintings and prints in the Department of Japanese Antiquities at the British Museum.

Jill Cook is curator of Palaeolithic and Mesolithic collections and deputy keeper of the Department of Prehistory and Early Europe at the British Museum.

Joe Cribb is curator of South Asian coins and deputy keeper of the Department of Coins and Medals at the British Museum.

Aileen Dawson is curator of ceramics, sculpture and other post-medieval collections in the Department of Medieval and Modern Europe at the British Museum.

Brian Durrans is curator of Asian collections and deputy keeper of the Department of Ethnography at the British Museum.

Jessica Harrison-Hall is curator of Chinese ceramics and Vietnamese art in the Department of Oriental Antiquities at the British Museum.

Robert Huxley is head of collections in the Department of Botany at the Natural History Museum.

Graham Jefcoate was formerly head of early printed collections at the British Library and is now director general of the Berlin State Library.

Ian Jenkins was formerly senior curator in the Department of Greek and Roman Antiquities and is now keeper of presentation at the British Museum.

J. C. H. King is curator of the North American collections in the Department of Ethnography at the British Museum.

Tim Knox is head curator at the National Trust.

Jennifer Newell is curator of Polynesian collections in the Department of Ethnography at the British Museum.

Thorsten Opper is curator of ancient sculpture in the Department of Greek and Roman Antiquities at the British Museum.

Judy Rudoe is curator of engraved gems and other post-medieval collections in the Department of Medieval and Modern Europe at the British Museum.

St John Simpson is curator of ancient Iran, Arabia and the Alexander to Islam periods in the Department of the Ancient Near East at the British Museum.

Kim Sloan is curator of British drawings and watercolours in the Department of Prints and Drawings and principal curator of the Enlightenment Gallery at the British Museum.

Luke Syson was formerly curator of medals in the Department of Coins and Medals and a curator of the Enlightenment Gallery at the British Museum and is now curator of Italian painting 1460–1500 at the National Gallery.

Jane Wess is curator of science at the Museum of Science and Industry.

Jonathan Williams is curator of Roman and Iron Age coins in the Department of Coins and Medals at the British Museum.

Acknowledgements

This book is published to mark the opening in 2003 of the new Enlightenment Gallery in the restored King's Library in the British Museum. We would like to pay tribute here to the people who were principally influential on the early intellectual development of the project: Jessica Rawson, former Keeper of the Department of Oriental Antiquities, and Ian Jenkins and Luke Syson, who are also contributors to this book. The professionalism, support and patience of the King's Library project designer Caroline Ingham and project manager Satvinder Jandu provided constant reassurance when the book ate into project time.

We are grateful to all the contributors for their excellent chapters, which often entailed an approach quite different from that normally required in their fields of expertise, but particularly Jill Cook and Rob Huxley, of whom we asked more than anyone else. Other curators who did not write chapters but made valuable contributions were Sheila Canby, Frances Carey and Richard Parkinson. It is worth noting that, in keeping with the general intention of this book to convey Enlightenment objects and ideas through eighteenth-century eyes, we decided to retain the use of 'mankind' and 'men' rather than 'humankind' and 'men and women' where appropriate.

A new view of the Enlightenment required a great deal of new photography and we are extremely grateful to all the Museum's photographers for the beautiful images which are a vital part of this book. We are also grateful to the contributors and departmental museum assistants for their help in organizing the objects for photography. Brendan Moore showed extraordinary energy in co-ordinating the work of the Museum's departmental photographic officers, curators and hard-pressed photographers, who all worked extremely hard to meet our demands, while Beatriz Waters at British Museum Press kindly gathered all the photographs from external sources. Brendan also co-ordinated the photography from the institutions lending to the new display. The curators and photographers there were also generous with their time and assistance, especially John Goldfinch of the British Library, Jane Wess of the Museum of Science and Industry, Emily Winterburn of the National Maritime Museum and Lorraine Cornish, Alan Hart, Rob Huxley, Vicki Noble, Kathie Way, Frank Steinheimer and Jo Cooper of the Natural History Museum. Elaine Paintin, formerly of the British Library, generously tracked down long-lost images. We would also like to thank other major lenders to the display for their kind support and assistance: Dora Clark and Priscilla Baines of the House of Commons Library, Gina Douglas and John Marsden of the Linnean Society, Bernard Nurse and Dai Morgan Evans of the Society of Antiquaries, Sir Hugh and Lady Roberts of the Royal Collections, Arthur MacGregor of the Ashmolean Museum and Neil Chambers of the Banks Research Project of the Natural History Museum.

We are very grateful to Emma Way, former head of British Museum Press, for agreeing to the idea of this book and helping to steer its initial direction. Alasdair MacLeod honoured her commitment and in difficult times found just the right American partner to co-publish the book: we were thrilled with the enthusiastic response of the Smithsonian Institution Press. Nina Shandloff has been an efficient and calm editor, always willing to negotiate to find a solution to any crisis, while John Banks has been the perfect copy editor. The designer, Harry Green, was a dream to work with, as always. Finally, the study of many aspects of the art and culture of the Enlightenment was enhanced by the work of two scholars especially, Ilaria Bignamini and Michael Kitson, and it will suffer greatly at their untimely deaths. This book is dedicated to their memory.

KIM SLOAN AND ANDREW BURNETT
April 2003

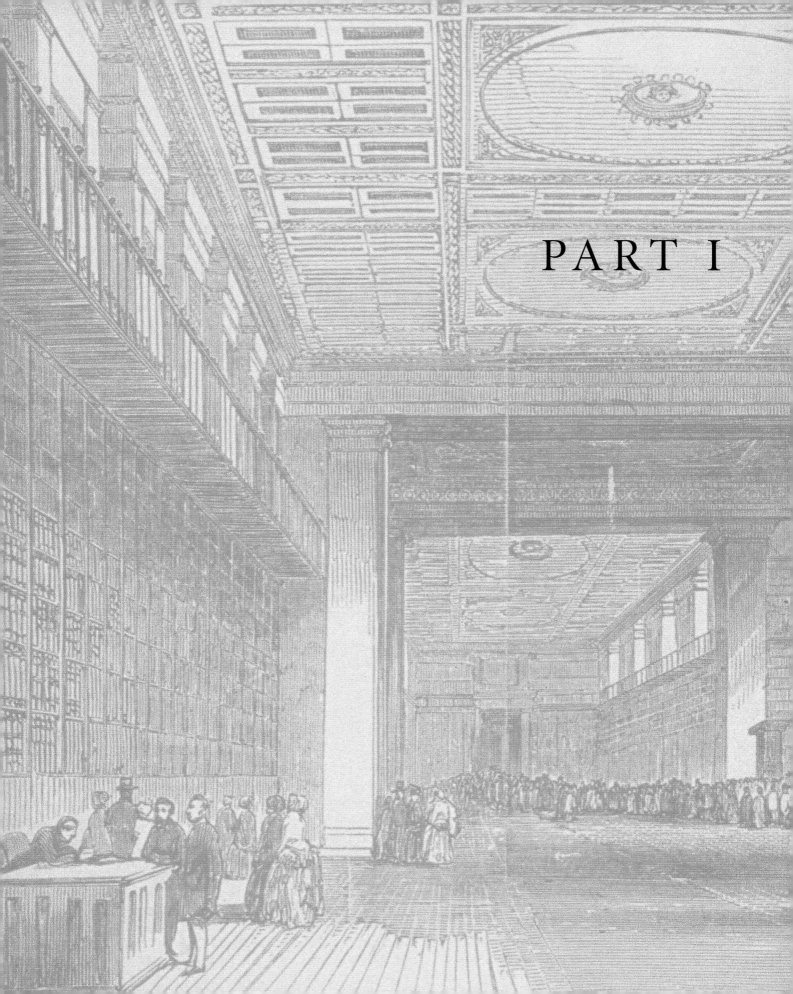

PART I

The 'Universal Museum'

1 A view of the King's Library in the British Museum, from the *London Illustrated News*, 1851. Engraving. Archives

1

'Aimed at universality and belonging to the nation': the Enlightenment and the British Museum

KIM SLOAN

Nature and Nature's Laws
lay hid in Night.

God said, *Let Newton be!*,
and all was *Light*.[1]

Thus in 1730 Alexander Pope summed up the eighteenth-century view of Sir Isaac Newton's achievements. All the diverse streams of activity that made up the scientific revolution seemed to flow together in Newton: in his *Encyclopédie*, Diderot declared Newton's *Principia* an 'Immortal work, and one of the finest that the human mind has ever produced'.[2] No learned society or public institution was without a plaster bust of the great man and the British Museum was no exception (fig. 2). As Pope implied, to many Newton was the personification of the Enlightenment.

Sir Francis Bacon had sown the seeds nearly a century earlier when he had claimed that 'Men have been kept back, as by a kind of enchantment, from progress in the sciences by reverence for antiquity, by the authority of men accounted great in philosophy, and then by general consent'.[3] Bacon argued that truth and knowledge did not come from such authority alone, but instead were the fruit of observation and inductive reasoning. Through the seventeenth century much still remained in darkness, but after Newton's discoveries about gravity and light seemed to unlock God's own laws of the universe, and after John Locke set forth his own empiricist doctrine emphasizing the importance of experience in the pursuit of knowledge, 'it seemed reasonable to hope that human effort would eventually penetrate every corner of the universe'.[4] Indeed, in 1702 the earliest of the French *philosophes*, Bernard le Bovier de Fontenelle, predicted that the coming century would be 'more enlightened day by day so that all previous centuries will be lost in darkness by comparison'.[5]

'RETHINKING ALBION'S ENLIGHTENMENT'

The Enlightenment appeared throughout the Western world, with philosophers, scientists and writers in Britain, America and all over Europe all making fundamental contributions. Its proponents were known by the French term *philosophes*, and the German Immanuel Kant was one of the first to use the word 'Enlightenment' to describe the age;[6] but it is Britain's contribution that will largely concern us here.

There have been many attempts to define the term 'Enlightenment', and certainly its meaning and the dates it covers have been reinterpreted frequently over the years. According to the *Oxford English Dictionary*, to 'enlighten' is to instruct or inform a person on a subject; used poetically it means to shed light on an object or give light to a person, but it can also indicate freeing a person from prejudice or superstition – hence 'enlightenment'. Although the word was used occasionally in the late eighteenth century, the Victorians employed it to describe a dull age of reason in contrast to the imaginative age of romanticism, and it has had many academic definitions since. The horrors of the first half of the twentieth century made its legacy of science and reason as guiding principles especially vulnerable to question, and Marxist critical theory has not only questioned but often rejected this legacy.[7] The late Roy Porter, the most prolific writer on the Enlightenment, noted that Michel Foucault considered it to be about control and domination rather than emancipation and quoted Eric Hobsbawm who wrote in 1997: 'These days the Enlightenment can be dismissed as anything from superficial and intellectually naive to a conspiracy of dead white men in periwigs to provide the intellectual foundation for Western imperialism.'[8] Porter himself thought these readings 'wilfully lopsided' and found Enlightenment thinkers to be broad-minded and tolerant, valuing knowledge, education and opportunity yet at the same time full of contradictions. In the end, as Norman Hampson wrote in 1968 in the first English history to bear the title: 'Within limits, the Enlightenment was what one thinks it was.'[9]

Recent trends have been towards a reinterpretation of the Enlightenment as a lived experience rather than simply a set of great ideas, and have studied its social and institutional sites.[10] It was not an event but a way of thinking, a desire to re-examine and question received ideas and values and explore new ideas in new ways. Through an empirical methodology, guided by the light of reason, one could arrive at knowledge and universal truths, providing liberation from ignorance and superstition that in turn would lead to the progress, freedom and happiness of mankind. Of course some form of enlightenment can be found during most periods. But as the new

2 Sir Isaac Newton (1642–1727), after Michael Rysbrack, h. 54.4 cm. This plaster bust from Sir Hans Sloane's collection was based on a terracotta bust of 1739 in Trinity College, Cambridge. MME.

approaches to it indicate, when it is described as the 'age of Enlightenment' it refers to a time when these ways of thinking and behaving permeated all aspects of life – the interlacing pattern of history, arts, science, philosophy, politics and religion all reacting upon each other and in turn affecting people's attitudes to them.[11] It was a period when the culture of the educated person was thought to take in the whole of human knowledge, a time of polymaths, when philosophy and science could not be divorced from theology, when men, and to an increasing extent women, did not specialize but instead could be artist, scientist, historian and philosopher all in one.

The period covered by the age of Enlightenment is frequently described by historians as 'the long eighteenth century', which encompasses several political, historical, social and artistic movements, each with its own equally difficult to define labels. The furthest extent it has been considered to cover runs from the Restoration of the British Monarchy in 1660 to the Great Reform Act of 1832. The Restoration, Glorious Revolution, the Scientific Revolution, the age of Reason, the Augustan age, the Hanoverian period, the Gothic Revival, the age of Revolution, neoclassicism, the Georgian age, the Regency and even early Romanticism are in themselves terms devised to help us make sense and order of an incredibly rich and fertile period in British arts, science, commerce and politics – in fact a period when the principles of classification, taxonomy itself, came into their own. 'Truth', 'freedom', 'liberty' and 'progress' were words alluded to in nearly every work of art, public speech and publication.

It is a period which currently supports an international society and hundreds of national and regional societies whose thousands of academic members are prolific authors of publications which cross the normal boundaries of disciplines.[12] Yet in Britain, where its achievements were most varied and profound, the age of Enlightenment is the period of its history about which the general public seems the least knowledgeable: it does not appear on the national school curriculum, and even in North America and France it is covered only as the period in which their great Revolutions occurred. Ask any schoolchild and many adults about the Vikings, the Tudors, the Civil War, the American and French Revolutions, the Victorians or the World Wars and they will have some response, but chances are that the Hanoverians, the Georgians, the Enlightenment or even the eighteenth century will draw a blank. There is indeed a need for changing this situation – for 'rethinking Albion's enlightenment and shedding light on the "black hole"'.[13] This book and the project that prompted it are, it is hoped, a step towards this goal.

'A PALACE FULL OF ALL GOOD THINGS'

The foundation of the British Museum was one of the most potent acts of the Enlightenment.

In his will of 1749 the physician and collector Sir Hans

Sloane had written that 'being fully convinced that nothing tends more to raise our ideas of the power, wisdom, goodness, providence, and other perfections of the Deity ... than the enlargement of our knowledge in the works of nature, I do Will and desire that for the promoting of these noble ends, the glory of God, and the good of man, my collection in all its branches may be, if possible kept and preserved together whole'.[14] In order to achieve this, it was offered to the nation at his death in 1753 for £20,000, and Parliament agreed, knowing that its true value was estimated to be nearer to £100,000. The proceeds of a national lottery provided enough for the purchase not only of the collections but of a building to house them – the late-seventeenth-century mansard-roofed Montagu House with its painted hall and ceilings and large gardens in Bloomsbury (figs 3–4). There was just enough left over to provide money for the installation of the collections and the Sloane, Cotton, Harleian, Edwards and early Royal libraries, and for the salaries of the staff.[15]

The dominance of the libraries over the intellectual content and physical space of the Museum was clear from the staffing arrangements which continued into the following century. A Principal Librarian was in overall charge of three Under Librarians who headed the Museum's three departments: Printed Books (including Prints), Manuscripts (including Coins and Drawings) and Natural and Artificial Productions (everything else). The Department of Antiquities was not created from the latter until 1807.

In January 1759 the British Museum was opened free to 'all persons desirous of seeing and viewing the [collections] ... that the same may be rendered as useful as possible, as well towards satisfying the desire of the curious, as for the improvement, knowledge and information of all persons'.[16] It was the first public national museum and library in the world, its foundation and later collections formed not just for its original creators but for other scholars and 'the curious', for the improvement of the knowledge and good of the nation, and dedicated to the glory of God and the good of mankind. The British Museum Act of 1753, the Act of Parliament with which it was founded, drew on the universalist ideas of the Enlightenment to proclaim that all arts and sciences had a connection with each other and that the Museum was founded for the advancement and improvement of all branches of knowledge. As an early donor noted in an address to the overseers of 'the great and noted treasury called the British Museum', 'they have built a tower for them all [the arts and sciences] and a palace full of all good things.'[17] The British Museum was thus a universal museum in every sense of the word – a true product and even embodiment of the Enlightenment, and certainly one of its greatest achievements.

As such, a virtual encyclopaedia of the state of the knowledge of the world as it stood in the eighteenth century, the British Museum collections and the men and women who formed, guided and curated them provide us with an ideal portal into the Enlightenment. But the spirit of enquiry that motivated them to 'discover the world' was enhanced by the moral imperatives of the age, which encouraged them not only to seek knowledge but also to share it and thus to contribute to the progress, freedom and happiness of mankind and of course also to the glory and prosperity of the British nation. Discovery was not limited to new ideas, which indeed resulted in laying the foundation for many of the 'modern' disciplines with which we organize and utilize knowledge today; discovery also included new lands and cultures which were not 'new' at all to those who already inhabited them, and in those instances 'discovery' led to struggles for power and domination, the repercussions of which continue today. But by studying the microcosm of the world as represented in the British Museum in the long eighteenth century and how it reflected the ideas and ideals of the Enlightenment, we are better equipped to understand and rediscover our own world.

A NEW GALLERY FOR THE ENLIGHTENMENT

In 2003, to mark the 250th anniversary of the Museum's foundation, the new permanent display devoted to the Enlightenment was inaugurated in the room known as the King's Library in the British Museum. This grand and elegant room 'provides a vista of neoclassical magnificence that is unequalled in London' (see ch. 4). It was designed and built in 1823–7 by Robert Smirke to house the library of George III (1738–1820), presented to the nation by his son, George IV, in 1823. It was the first wing of what was eventually to comprise four long blocks around a central courtyard, with a colonnaded front resembling a temple, to house the new British Museum and replace the crumbling, damp and overstuffed seventeenth-century Montagu House. The books of King George III's Library filled the bookcases the entire length, breadth and height of the new room, and a number of large free-standing presses holding portfolios, boxes and atlases stood down the sides (see fig. 1). It was not permanently opened to the general public until 1857, when the bookcases were glazed and new display cases were added, but it has remained a public space ever since. The books themselves were all removed with the music, maps and manuscripts when the British Library, a separate national institution from 1973, moved to its new home at St Pancras in 1998. The room has been restored to its original condition in order to house a portion of the House of Commons library on long-term loan to the Museum[18] and a permanent display of objects selected from the rich stores of the Museum (fig. 5), arranged in

3 South front (main entrance) of Montagu House, the original home of the British Museum. Pen, ink and wash drawing by Joseph Buckler, 1828. P&D.

4 East wing and colonnade of Montagu House, from the quadrangle. Pen, ink and wash drawing by Joseph Buckler, 1828. P&D.

an exhibition devoted to discovery and learning in the age of George III, titled *Enlightenment: Discovering the World in the Eighteenth Century*.

Like the new display, this book is intended to provide a view of the Enlightenment through the windows of the British Museum of Montagu House and through the eyes of its visitors, curators and librarians, as well as its collectors, patrons and trustees, during the long eighteenth century. It has been written for the most part by some of its current curators, and encompasses, in addition to objects from the Museum's present collections, objects from the natural history, science, painting, book, map, manuscript and maritime collections nearly all once housed in the British Museum but now in public museums and separate institutions such as the Natural History Museum and the British Library which have sprung from it. None of the contributors is a specialist in the Enlightenment, but they have been asked to take their own modern disciplines and special fields of expertise and examine them in the light of how they were perceived and understood from the late seventeenth century, through the developments of the Enlightenment and on into the early nineteenth century, by which time many of their disciplines were much closer to the way we understand them today. In this respect, the general approach of this book is therefore an unusual one – contextual, in that it is inspired by but not limited to the eighteenth-century contents of the Museum, and prosopographical, reflecting the men and women connected with it and the imperatives and ideas that drove and inspired them.

LIBRARIES AND NATURAL
AND ARTIFICIAL RARITIES

This book is arranged in five parts in order to reflect five issues of the Enlightenment most relevant to the Museum's collections. Part I examines the philosophical and cultural context of the Enlightenment by describing the Museum's early collections of commemorative portrait busts and paintings, sculptural antiquities and libraries and their relationship to Montagu House and to the first part of the new Smirke building, the King's Library. This elegant and imposing neoclassical room, with its allusions to Athena, goddess of learning, and her Greek city-state, then considered to be the height of political, social, artistic and cultural achievement, was designed not only to house a library formed by George III in order to provide an encyclopaedia of all human knowledge, but also to house a national gallery of paintings on its upper floor, making clear the Museum's intention to be a Universal Museum.

John Locke argued that we must understand a thinker's terms in the sense he uses them, and not as they are appropriated by each man's particular philosophy.[19] In our efforts to understand the sections of the Museum's original collection which are the subject of Parts II and III of this book, the natural and artificial rarities, and what they tell us of Enlighten-

ment thought and the contributions their owners made to it, we must try to understand the way they were perceived, understood, described and utilized at the time.

But this often requires a great leap of imagination on our part. The Enlightenment commenced in an era when the physician Sir Hans Sloane's *materia medica* still included ground Egyptian mummies' fingers as 'proper for contusions' and ground amethyst for drunkenness, and nephrite (jade) to be placed against the skin for kidney disease.[20] At the time when he was collecting natural history specimens, during his own voyage to Jamaica and from other travellers around the world, a myth persisted that birds of paradise never landed but slept on the wing – a myth which arose from the practice of those trading in

6 Bird of paradise and humming birds, probably from Sloane's collection, by John van Rymsdyk. Watercolour, later engraved as illustration for John and Andrew van Rymsdyk's *Museum Britannicum*, 1778. P&D.

5 An impression of the new permanent display in the King's Library in the British Museum. The floor press on the left is one of the original ones that furnished the King's Library, and held the General Atlas drawings of the King's Topographical Collection (see ch. 15). The sloping top was added later in the 19th century to display books and manuscripts.

their skins simply cutting off the birds' feet to facilitate the transport of the all-important feathers (fig. 6). Even by the end of the century, Sir Joseph Banks, who had travelled to Australia with Captain Cook, was refusing to believe in the existence of the platypus until provided with a preserved specimen.[21]

It was a time when, like the 'cabinets' of all private collectors, the Museum's collection was divided into Natural and

7 Dr John Dee's (1527–1608) large wax disk (the 'Seal of God') (h. 23 cm) on which his crystal 'shew stone' stood, a gold disk engraved with a vision and two wax disks. The obsidian mirror on the left was used for calling up spirits and visions. The crystal 'shew stone' now in the Museum is probably not the one once owned by Dee or Sloane. MME.

Artificial Rarities – natural products of the earth and the products of man. But understanding of some of these specimens was based not only on empirical knowledge, but also on historical and theological authorities; as a result the division between the two was frequently not as we might place them now. One of Sloane's and thus the Museum's greatest curiosities was a crystal sphere, one of the 'shew stones' of the great Tudor mathematician, astronomer, astrologer and navigator John Dee, possibly the one reportedly given to him by God through a medium on 21 November 1582.[22] Revered during his own time, by the eighteenth century Dee was better known as an alchemist and practitioner in the occult sciences. His great 'speculum', also known as 'The Devil's Looking Glass', was actually an Aztec piece of polished black obsidian (fig. 7). It was one of the greatest treasures of Horace Walpole's eclectic collection in his gothic confection at Strawberry Hill. Walpole's description of it in the 1784 catalogue of his collection illustrates the eighteenth century's rational approach to sixteenth-century mysticism: 'A speculum of kennel-coal, in a leathern case. It is curious for having been used to deceive the mob by Dr Dee, the conjuror, in the reign of Queen Elizabeth.'[23]

The natural rarities were the greatest strengths of Sloane's collection, and our view of Montagu House reveals much about the Enlightenment's changing attitudes towards and knowledge

of the history of the earth and the history of man. Natural philosophy was God's own instrument for the revelation of truth and thus both the earth and man, as objects of nature, could be explained by its principles. Sloane's collections revealed a belief in a God who could act as he chose, in a way unintelligible to helpless mankind, but which man might move towards understanding through Newton's and Locke's principles of observation and experience. Gathering as many examples together from as wide an area of the earth as possible, and organizing, naming and classifying them, particularly with regard to their medicinal relationships, was Sloane's main underlying purpose in his collecting of plants, minerals and animals.

The world of the Enlightenment was a small one, and Sloane's life was long: he knew Newton and Locke personally, as well as the great classifiers of his age, Ray and Linnaeus. His own collection gradually incorporated the finest of his time: the natural history and antiquities belonging to William Courten (fig. 13),[24] the entomologist and conchologist Petiver, the botanists Catesby and Herrmann, the buccaneer Dampier, the traveller Kaempfer and the gardener Miller (who oversaw the Chelsea Physic Garden). These were in addition to his own collections from Jamaica and the West Indies and thousands of individual gifts and purchases from myriad other travellers and correspondents (fig. 8).[25]

THE BIRTH OF THE MUSEUM

The proliferation of private and public collections – 'the birth of the museum' – was one of the most significant features of the British Enlightenment, and the British Museum was to continue to benefit through the century from the growth of

8 A Surinam crocodile (Spectacled Caiman) and pipe snake, by Maria
Sibylla Merian (1647–1717). 306×454 mm. Two albums of drawings
of the flora and fauna of Surinam, from the artist's voyage with her
daughters in 1699–1701, belonged to Sir Hans Sloane and were placed
at the top of the stairs in Montagu House for visitors to look through
(see also fig. 68). P&D.

both. [26] The chapters in Part II consider the collections of the
Duchess of Portland, Sir William Hamilton and his nephew
Charles Greville, Thomas Pennant, Sir Joseph Banks, William
Smith and countless others who contributed to the natural rarities in the Museum – all either through donation or purchase
of entire collections, or through donation of smaller groups of
items. The collections of Dr Richard Mead, Horace Walpole,
Sir William Hamilton, the Reverend C. M. Cracherode,
Richard Payne Knight, Charles Townley, George III, Claudius
James Rich and Robert Ker Porter were to become key components of the artificial rarities in the British Museum, their
names recurring in Parts III and IV of this book. Part V considers what we would now describe as ethnographic material
collected on voyages of trade and discovery to parts of the
world previously unknown in the West; Sir Ashton Lever (see
fig. 86) and William Bullock (see fig. 209) opened private
museums or put on public exhibitions for which they

charged entrance. Such enterprises were often short-lived,
their collections were sold and dispersed, and many objects
from them eventually came to the British Museum (fig. 9).[27]
A chronological table is appended to this book outlining the
respective dates of many of these collectors and museums in
the context of historical events and major publications of the
Enlightenment.

But the discussions in the chapters of this book are not
limited to a consideration of the founding collections of the
British Museum as the summary above might imply. The
philosophies of the Enlightenment and the Museum acted
upon each other in both subtle and overt ways that were
mutually influential, if not always beneficial.

Some of the reasons for the rapidly expanding role of
museums in Britain in the eighteenth century were much the
same as the reasons for the increasing numbers of visitors to
them today – changes in social patterns and attitudes towards
education. Francis Bacon and others had advised on the setting up and use of collections for gentlemen, and, in 1650,
John Drury noted that the most useful form of education
came from visiting collections. He recommended visits to
Tradescant's 'Ark' in London (eventually to form part of the
Ashmolean in Oxford), but he also advocated the formation
of collections in schools.[28] Locke's promotion of more

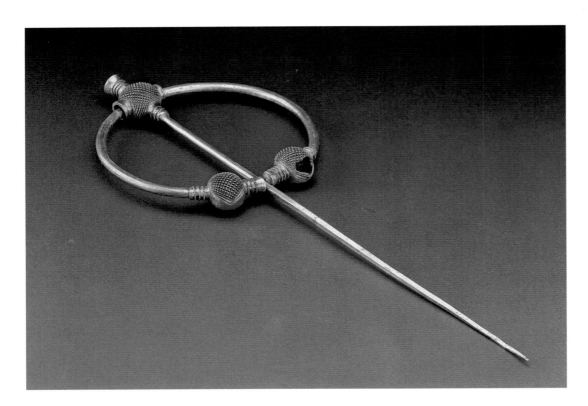

9 Penannular silver thistle brooch, Irish-Viking, 1st half of 10th century, l. 51.2 cm. Found in a field near Penrith in 1785, it was displayed in the Leverian Museum where it was drawn by Sarah Stone (see fig. 86). Her drawings and the brooch were later acquired by the British Museum. MME.

'modern' and useful subjects, including natural philosophy, rather than the existing near-total reliance on the classics, had far-reaching repercussions throughout the century, receiving a further boost from the progressive 'natural' theories of Rousseau after the publication of *Emile* in 1762.

Women too were encouraged in the study of natural history, particularly botany and 'natural curiosities'.[29] In the late seventeenth century the Duchess of Chandos had organized and catalogued her father's collection, and visited the collection Courten had left Sloane, as well as 'Mr Flamstead and his astronomical instruments at Greenwich'; Evelyn took the Countess of Sutherland to see Courten's collection, and in 1695 Ralph Thoresby complained that his own visit was interrupted by 'an unfortunate visit from the Countess of Pembroke and other ladies from the Court'.[30] In the eighteenth century the moral and educational precepts of Locke and Shaftesbury filtered their way through to the female members in some families and by the second half, although 'bluestockings' were mainly literary figures and increasingly socially ridiculed,[31] a number of women managed to enter what had previously been a mostly male preserve. The Duchess of Portland (who was responsible for the Harleian manuscripts coming to the Museum) and Sarah Sophia Banks (sister of Sir Joseph) were themselves the creators of two collections which were the largest and perhaps finest of their kind in Europe. The Duchess collected natural history specimens, particularly plants and shells, much of it catalogued by Solander or drawn by Ehret and the Duchess's companion, Mary Delany (see fig. 75), but also some artificial rarities

(see fig. 76), many of which, including the Portland Vase, eventually found their way to the British Museum.[32] Sarah Banks collected coins, medals, tokens and ephemeral material (visiting and shop cards, trade bills, etc.), creating a kind of 'ethnography of Britain' with direct parallels to her brother's collections. Her material all came to the Museum and now provides an invaluable source of information about otherwise lost aspects of social and commercial life in the eighteenth century.[33]

ANTIQUARIES, ARCHAEOLOGISTS AND ANCIENT CIVILIZATIONS

There are no extant visual representations of the interiors of the galleries containing the collections of the Museum in Montagu House. There are, however, written records from the time of the Museum's first plan of 1756, through the *General Contents* published in 1761, van Rymsdyk's privately published *Museum Britannicum*, 'synopses' published periodically from 1808, and the accounts of individual visitors.[34] There are plans and views of the new wing begun in 1803 to accommodate the Townley, Hamilton and other antiquities collections, and the temporary room erected for the Elgin marbles in 1817.[35] George Scharf's views of the Entrance Hall and staircase (see fig. 18 and frontispiece) give some clues to the visual impact on the visitor, but for this we have to rely mainly on the written descriptions.

From these it is clear that the library and natural history collections filled the majority of the rooms in Montagu

House, while antiquities, works of art and 'instruments, habits, indian curiosities etc.', which we would now term ethnographic collections, were mainly confined to two or three rooms, the basement and small rooms off the back stairs. This reflected the Enlightenment's emphasis on the classification and ordering of knowledge of the natural world. The sheer quantity of new information in the eighteenth century, and, indeed, the sheer quantity of objects from the natural world in the Museum, threatened chaos – the diversity had to be pulled into order, leading to new developments in classification and their repercussions as discussed in Part II.[36] But the imposition of order on the natural world and the understanding of the laws that governed it invariably affected the way people perceived and organized 'artificial' rarities. As described in Part III, new methods were devised to order, classify, examine and utilize collections of coins, gems, vases, scientific instruments, maps and other antiquities from the ancient and modern world, with repercussions that were felt not only in the British Museum but by collectors, historians and philosophers throughout the world.

Visits to the British Museum and other collections throughout the eighteenth century are well documented, the numbers and social classes swelling with increased ease of admission, longer hours of opening and new acquisitions of what were once termed artificial rarities but had come to be known as antiquities and artefacts. Townley's ancient sculptures, Banks's and Cook's Pacific materials, monuments from Egypt, the Elgin Marbles, and objects from Ross's expedition to the Arctic and Rich's discoveries at Babylon and Nineveh, all acted as public 'attractions' to compete with the increasingly popular privately operated ones. In 1810 only 120 people a day passed through the Museum's doors, but, after the 1835 Parliamentary Select Committee's recommendations for longer hours and easier access, the first opening on a public holiday, Easter Monday 1837, saw 23,895 visitors fill the building and push its still mainly seventeenth-century fabric to its limits. As an MP had put it earlier: 'the public paid for the Museum and therefore had a right to insist on every facility of ingress'.[37]

But the shifting of balance in the British Museum, away from natural history and towards antiquities and objects representing ancient and contemporary cultures from all over the world, closer to the Museum we know today, began only very slowly from 1772 with the acquisition of the collection formed in Naples by Sir William Hamilton. Eventually to become a trustee who advised on the disposition of antiquities, he typifies this shift in Enlightenment thinking from a focus on natural history towards a wider approach, since his own first connections with the Museum were through his gifts of examples of the productions of nature – lava from Vesuvius and fish and shells from the Bay of Naples.[38]

Hamilton's first gift was accompanied by a letter explaining that he merely wished to provide, in true Enlightenment fashion, 'facts for those more versed in natural philosophy to interpret', hoping that they might lead to useful discoveries by those 'learned in natural history'.[39] Observation was the key, and its recording and presentation were imperative. Hamilton sent his publications and further examples of the rocks to the British Museum and to his nephew, the Honourable Charles Greville. He, in turn, amassed a collection of minerals that was purchased by the Museum after his death, providing it with the foundations to become one of the finest in the world.

Sloane, Hamilton, Banks, Hollis and many others were members of the Royal Society, delivering their papers at meetings and publishing them in the Society's *Philosophical Transactions*. Similar societies existed for Antiquaries, Dilettanti, the Encouragement of Arts, Manufactures and Commerce, Asian studies, and, from 1788, even for Linnaeus (see the chronological chart on p. 276). Societies and clubs were a prominent feature and one of the most crucial elements of the Enlightenment, providing a public forum and like-minded audience for the reception of factual observations and discussion of new ideas, and many members belonged to several. Morally minded disciples of Shaftesbury's and Locke's civic humanism, who believed it was their innate duty to act publicly for the greater good of mankind and the British nation, were not only members of such societies but also trustees of the British Museum and sat on boards of governance for hospitals and trading companies. This peculiarly British notion of 'public spirit' and trusteeship of the future combined with 'clubability' ensured the fast spread of new ideas and at the same time ensured that these ideas crossed disciplines amongst the polymathic members – developments in natural history were soon informing how one thought about history, antiquities, art, commerce and one's fellow man.

As is made clear in Parts III and IV, such interrelationships assisted in the evolution towards modern historical methods. Historians traditionally dealt with tracing political events, heavily reliant on the accounts of the classical authors and writers considered to be contemporary with the events. Antiquaries, on the other hand, in their 'learned curiosity' described all aspects of life, systematically, through the evidence provided by language, literature, custom and the material remains of the past, ruins and relics. In the eighteenth century, historical writing gradually shifted from the one to the other: as Addison observed, 'It is much safer to quote a medal than an author for in this case you do not appeal to Suetonius or to Lampridius, but to the emperor himself or to the whole body of a Roman senate.'[40] The result was the reinvigoration of historical method, the rejuvenation of the antiquary and the attendant birth of archaeology, thus combining classical knowledge with new advances in understanding the history of the earth and stratigraphy.

Lively debates ensued. An iron buckler we now know to

have been made in the sixteenth century was believed by its owner, the renowned Cambridge physician and collector Dr John Woodward, to be a Roman shield contemporaneous with the greatest events in Roman history as related by Plutarch and Livy, when the Gauls' invasion of Italy reached the gates of Rome (fig. 10). Public and published discussions about Dr Woodward's shield instigated the great literary 'War of the Books'.[41] Anglo-Saxon cremation urns found by seventeenth- and eighteenth-century English antiquaries such as Sir Thomas Browne and William Stukeley were believed to be Roman until the more 'scientific' excavations of Hoare and Douglas at the end of the century. Prehistoric monuments such as Stonehenge and Avebury were thought to be Druid temples, and indeed debate concerning their true

10 'Dr Woodward's Shield', an embossed iron buckler, made in France c. 1540–50, dia. 35.5 cm. Believed to be a Roman antiquity, it was acquired by Woodward from the apothecary John Conyers (see p. 183). It was bequeathed to the Museum by Dr John Wilkinson in 1818. MME.

origins has continued ever since. Increasing knowledge of British medieval history, through manuscripts recently made publicly available, coins and seals in the British Museum supplemented by new finds and the writings of antiquaries such as Richard Gough and J. T. Smith, enabled new histories of Britain to be written in concordance with the newly invigorated sense of nation (see ch. 17). But one of the most important discoveries that resulted from these new historical methods concerned the early history of Italy and its connections with Greece. Sir William Hamilton's 'Etruscan' vases were not made by Etruscans at all but, as he himself came to realize, were imported from Greece, and such studies soon led to a new interest in Grecian art and civilization that was to have a major impact on the art and civilization of nineteenth-century Europe.

The progressive 'Great Chain of Being' in natural history theory found a parallel echo in new ideas about an equivalent 'Great Chain of Art': Roman ideal sculptures were thought to be Greek originals by Phidias and considered by British collectors (following the lead of Winckelmann) to be the height of artistic achievement. The so-called 'primitive' arts of India and South America provided a chronological and stylistic foundation for the beginnings of art and civilization that then 'progressed' upwards through Persia and Egypt towards the achievements of the Greeks, while the remains of Roman, early Christian and medieval gothic cultures were all evidence of a steady decline and fall until the rebirth of classicism in the Renaissance (see ch. 16 and fig. 164). Collections of gems such as the Reverend Cracherode's, and coins and medals such as his and George III's, were as much the sign of an eighteenth-century gentleman as his collections of natural history, sculpture, drawings and painting – enabling him, with his extensive knowledge of the classics, to reconstruct ancient history through the coins and to picture its gods and heroes through the gems and commemorative medals which, although they are little collected or appreciated today, were then recognized as the sculptural equivalent of the exquisite art of painting in miniature.

During the Enlightenment the search for the origins of writing, monotheism and biblical sites led to vast collections of figures and drawings of gods, written and material evidence of their worship, and the re-examination of inscriptions on coins and monuments and increased attempts to transcribe and decipher them. Increasing numbers of travellers, amateur and professional antiquaries, well-informed about the value of such historical evidence, presented the Museum with their observations and finds, or made do with transcriptions, rubbings and casts when the inscription or sculpture itself proved impossible to remove or transport. Iconography led to new comparative studies of religions, and epigraphy led to the decipherment of many previously untranslatable scripts, providing the keys with which to unlock the secrets of ancient civilizations.

For all these men, and some women, publication was the main medium for transmitting their carefully garnered observations *and* collections. Indeed the 'print revolution' – the invention of new and often cheaper processes for both words and images – was as vital a constituent of the Enlightenment as the information the publications conveyed. The authors often presented copies to the Museum as well as to the King, and thus George III's library included most of these publications, in both pamphlet and journal, as well as lavishly illustrated and beautifully bound book form. From 1823 the King's Library combined with and complemented the Museum's own and helped to interpret the knowledge that could be gleaned from the collections.

George III's library was open to all serious scholars while it was still located in Buckingham House: a universal library eventually to be housed in a universal museum.[42] His fascination with scientific instruments (see ch. 14) mirrored that of Hamilton and many of his compatriots, who ordered the latest electricity machine, air pump or telescope as soon as they were created by London instrument-makers, some of the finest in the world. The King's involvement with the navy led to great advances in navigation, building upon the work of the Board of Longitude which had led to the invention by John Harrison of a timepiece which could accurately measure longitude at sea. This crucially important advance in turn made possible the expeditions of men such as Sir Joseph Banks and Captain James Cook, and the resulting explosion of knowledge about cultures previously unknown to Europeans – a wealth of exotic natural and artificial rarities soon entered the British Museum and many other collections.

DISCOVERY AND TRADE

Sir Hans Sloane and Sir Joseph Banks stand at either end of the long eighteenth century: both were natural historians first of all, Presidents of the Royal Society, and both were concerned with improving British economy and trade – Sloane in cochineal and chocolate, Banks in breadfruit and merino sheep, amongst innumerable other ventures. They travelled and collected in parts of the world relatively unknown to their contemporaries, ensuring that they brought back specimens to enlighten those who could study them in person and publishing them for those who could not. Although they collected and organized such objects from the differing perspectives and rationales of the opposite ends of the century, both also made significant contributions to the ethnographic collections of the Museum and consequently to their contemporaries' knowledge of foreign cultures and customs, setting an example and encouraging and supporting others in their own travels and observations.[43] Historians began to understand that study of contemporary cultures often provided insight into their ancient histories.

But this was the same period that saw the rise in importance of national trading companies. As nations began to compete and expand their power internationally, trade became a vital part of this global competition. Trading companies gave governments a foothold on foreign soil while the companies in return gained government support for their activities. Their intervention in local affairs – social, political and economic – grew stronger as increasing national support came not only in diplomatic but also often naval and military

form. Thus while the Museum's natural history and ethnographic collections and British understanding of their history and cultures grew as the result of the activities of the East India, Hudson's Bay, Turkey and Russia Companies and their officers, so the growing level of intervention by British and other foreign governments often ensured a concordant alteration in those same cultures. As Kant declared in 1784, this was the age of Enlightenment, but not an enlightened age.[44]

Nevertheless, it was also an age of liberty, freedom and revolutions. It was governed by a general intellectual spirit of opposition to prejudice, superstition and fanaticism, but the search to understand their origins and places in other cultures[45] did not always lead to seeing them in one's own. Thomas Hollis, a republican and fervent supporter of the American Revolution, was one of the Museum's most significant patrons in its early years. He donated antiquities and works of art from classical civilizations (fig. 11); but to Harvard University he presented a collection of the works of Milton, inscribed with the warning: 'People of Massachusetts ... When your country shall be cultivated, adorned like this country, and yr shore become elegant, refined in civil life,

12 Anti-slavery medallion, produced in jasper by Josiah Wedgwood, to be worn as a button or brooch. Enlarged; actual size 3 cm. The image was modelled in 1787 after the seal of the Slave Emancipation Society founded that year; Wedgwood was an active member. MME.

11 Red wax model (h. 53.5 cm) of the Laocoon, a Roman sculpture in the Vatican, believed by many Enlightenment scholars to represent the height of Greek artistic achievement. Presented to the British Museum by Thomas Hollis in 1758. MME.

then – if not before – " 'ware your liberties!".'[46] Civilization and progress did not necessarily go hand in hand with freedom, liberty and equality. The outlawing of slavery in Britain came long before the final abolition of the slave trade – Enlightenment ideals may have been universal, but economics, history and power militated against these ideals being applied universally (fig. 12) (see chs 21 and 22).[47]

However, it cannot be denied that commerce, the search for information about past and present civilizations from their artefacts rather than relying on written sources, and the unceasing desire for progress led to new discoveries and apparently limitless knowledge. By 1815 the new edition of the *Encyclopaedia Britannica* ran to twenty volumes, Montagu House contained antiquities and natural history collections to match the size of its libraries and was bursting at the seams, and George III's library filled more than three large rooms at Buckingham House. When the library was installed in Smirke's new King's Library in 1828, one could indeed 'discover the world' in Britain's universal museum.

The foundations had also been laid for a host of modern specialist disciplines, soon reflected in new displays and departments. As the Museum itself evolved, so London was to see the emergence of other great museums until, later in the nineteenth century, the portrait paintings of the British Museum were removed to the National Portrait Gallery and its extensive natural history collections to the Natural History Museum. This process of dispersal continued with the removal of the library to St Pancras a century later. The universal museum of the Enlightenment, filled to overflowing, spilled over to create the more limited specialized institutions of the modern age. Meanwhile, in presenting itself as a collection of world cultures, the British Museum continues to embrace the globe as it did in the time of its own creation.

From 2003 the British Museum represents Enlightenment knowledge, once contained within the books of the King's Library, through the artefacts and antiquities gathered and studied through the long eighteenth century – the empirical data that provided the foundations of that knowledge. Like the present book, this display is intended to chart the voyage of intellectual discovery by permitting the objects and their collectors to speak for their century as the books on the shelves once did. It makes possible a new way of seeing the Enlightenment: not with hindsight, from the modern philosophical, historical, economic or scientific point of view, but, as far as possible, by attempting to experience the objects, collectors and their ideas through eighteenth-century eyes. The viewer is also challenged, however, to consider – and especially with reference to the rest of the Museum's displays – how modern ideas of the knowledge that the same objects can convey has changed since the eighteenth century. Using reason to understand the ways in which these differ from our own, we can progress in our knowledge of the past and use it to shed light on the way we understand these objects and cultures today.

2

Collectors and commemoration: portrait sculpture and paintings in the British Museum

AILEEN DAWSON

The memory of great men and ancestors has been enshrined in painted or sculptural portraits from ancient times. One of the earliest 'museums' in the world was the Greek *pinakotheke* established in the fifth century BC on the Acropolis in Athens to house paintings honouring the gods; commenting on sculpted portraits in Athens, Pliny the Elder noted 'the rooms and halls of private houses became so many public places, and clients began to honour their patrons in this way'. In the Roman world painted and sculpted portraits were often intended to evoke their subjects' virtues and inspire emulation in their descendants, an idea revived in Italy during the Renaissance, spreading from thence to the most distant parts of Europe, including Britain.[2] The Papal physician and historian Paolo Giovio (1483–1552) assembled a collection of four hundred painted portraits of poets, philosophers, writers, craftsmen, popes, kings and generals at his villa near Lake Como. By thus honouring the great men of the past, Giovio hoped not only to emulate and be inspired by them but even to invite comparisons with them.[3] His 'museum', as he called the building that housed them, was renowned and served as a model for other collectors such as the scholar and poet Giovanni Della Porta of Naples and his brother, who set aside two rooms in their home as a study and museum. By Giovanni's death in 1615 it contained five complete portrait statues, seventeen classical heads in niches and thirty-three smaller marble figures and heads placed on a ledge running around the room. In addition, there were medals kept in a walnut desk, forty-two painted portraits of kings of Spain and various saints, and a few more of contemporary figures such as Galileo, hung on the walls. This collection of portraits, as well as those from Giovio's earlier museum, was used to illustrate Della Porta's treatise on portraiture as an indication of character: *De humana physiognomia* (1586).[4]

In England Lord Chancellor Clarendon (1608–74) owned portraits of Erasmus and Cardinal Wolsey and of monarchs from Queen Elizabeth I to King James I, as well as of contemporaries he had known personally. He seems to have intended to use them for his own *History of the Rebellion* (published posthumously, 1702–4). Although he was unable to illustrate his own publication, many of those who owned it interleaved, or 'extra-illustrated', their copies with engraved portraits, or 'heads' as they were described by printmakers who throughout the following century published portraits specifically intended for this purpose, as well as for framing and hanging on walls. As Jonathan Richardson noted in 1715: 'Painting gives us not only the Persons, but the Characters of Great Men. The Air of the Head and Mein [*sic*] in general, gives strong Indica-

13 William Courten (1642–1702) as a young man, oil painting by an unknown artist. His 'museum' in the Middle Temple was celebrated as one of the finest cabinets of natural and artificial rarities in Europe. It was bequeathed to his friend Sir Hans Sloane and was thus one of the foundation collections of the British Museum. Trustees' collection.

14 Matthew Maty MD, FRS (1718–76), oil painting by Berthélemy Dupan (1712–63). Maty was responsible for buying the Roubiliac busts from the sculptor's sale after his death in 1762 and immediately presenting them to the Museum. Trustees' collection.

tions of the Mind and illustrates what the Historian says more expressly and particularly.'[5]

Many European collections of naturalia made during the period preceding the establishment of the British Museum also embraced portraits of kings and eminent men, as well as landscape paintings. At least some of these were princely assemblages, intended to glorify the ruler, and, in turn, his country or region. There were pictures, for example, in the first room of the Dresden *Kunstkammer* of the Elector Augustus of Saxony (reigned 1553–86),[6] and an engraving by Daniel Marot in 1702 of a library probably designed for King William III of the Netherlands, shows busts and globes on top of bookcases. Another by F. Ertinger (engraver to King Louis XIV) from a series of 1688 depicts a cabinet of curiosities where a hierarchy is established of monarchs, whose large portraits hang in the upper register, with smaller portraits of philosophers and saints (including Aristotle, Erasmus and St Thomas Aquinas) hung on the wall below with landscape paintings.[7]

Not generally known, however, is the fact that from its foundation the British Museum embodied notions of memory and the commemoration of great men and of its own servants in three substantial collections of portraits – painted, sculpted and engraved. Like the collections of natural and artificial rarities, they were intended to 'illustrate

to the advancement of the Glory of God, the honour and renown of his country and history and ancient times … to the no small promotion of knowledge and useful arts' – Sir Hans Sloane's description of the purpose of Sir William Courten's collection which formed the backbone of Sloane's own.[8] The portraits in Sloane's own collection were also intended to illustrate history through the representation of its key figures. But, as we shall see, the portraits were not limited to rulers: like Sloane, the patrons and employees who were responsible for the growth of the British Museum's portrait collection over the next half century ensured that the contributions of philosophers, scientists, collectors and patrons provided a history typical of the Enlightenment – one that was not only 'universal' but at the same time British and provided a kind of 'family' history of the institution itself.

This chapter considers the largely unpublished history of how these busts and paintings came to be in the British Museum – an institution originally known mainly for its libraries and collections of natural history and antiquities. Throughout the period when ideas associated with the Enlightenment were current, the Museum's paintings collection continued to grow. It was closely connected with the building of the King's Library which enshrined the literary remains of the sitters, and was an important keystone in the foundations of the National Gallery and National Portrait Gallery. Finally it answers the question of why those portraits that remain in the Museum are scarcely known outside it, having been removed from the public gaze and thus from the eyes of those whom they were originally intended to benefit.

'IMMORTALIZING GREAT MEN':
ANCIENT AND MODERN WORTHIES

The founding collections of the British Museum reflected Sir Hans Sloane's particular interests in medicine, natural history, travel and history. Like many other collectors before him he also owned paintings and sculpture.[9] There were 471 items in his *Catalogue of Miscellanea*, in a section entitled 'Pictures &c, Pictures & drawings in Frames'.[10] These included studies of birds, reptiles, insects, anatomical studies, mosaic pictures, and a number of portraits in a variety of materials: medals, drawings, oils, prints, miniatures and cut-paper, as well as in wax, silver, lead and brass, turned honestone and even carved walnut shells.[11] The portraits appear to have been an attempt by Sloane to construct a history of Britain through objects and images and, as with many of the Renaissance and early

British collectors mentioned above, the artistic quality of the image and its historical accuracy were less important than the representation itself. A recent comment on Sloane's print collection applies equally to his pictures: 'He was no art collector, and did not buy to decorate his walls. Everything that he acquired was intended to serve his scholarly and scientific interests.'[12]

In his account of his visit to Sloane on 26 May 1748 the Danish scholar Per Kalm (1715–79) noted 'a room in which a number of paintings hung on the wall' and another in which 'we saw a number of representations of kings, learned men & others. Among them was a portrait of Mr John Ray, which must be the only one of him to be found in England.'[13] John Ray FRS (1627–1705) (fig. 20) made three botanical journeys in England, Wales and Scotland, describing and cataloguing many hundreds of species (see ch. 6). A life-long correspondent of Sloane's, Ray was his greatest friend and earliest mentor, encouraging his trip to Jamaica and the publication of his findings there. Amongst the other portraits on Sloane's walls were several other contemporaries who, like Ray, were friends and fellow collectors, from whom he acquired specimens for his collections. They included a portrait of the navigator and buccaneer Sir William Dampier (1651–1715) (see fig. 71),[14] who kept careful accounts of the natural history of the countries he visited while harassing the Spanish shipping in the South Seas and presented many specimens to Sloane, who also owned manuscript accounts of his journeys (see ch. 7). The portrait described as 'Mr Courten when young' was of William Courten (1642–1702) (fig. 13), a merchant and lifelong friend of Sloane, who inherited a considerable collection from his father and added to it from his own travels, eventually establishing a museum in his rooms in the Middle Temple, London. He bequeathed the entire contents to Sloane as his residuary legatee and sole executor and it was in this way that many treasures entered Montagu House, including the magnificent Nicholas Robert volumes depicting flora and fauna that sometimes stood open for visitors to consult at the top of its grand staircase (see frontispiece).[15] Sloane's gratitude to his friend caused him to erect an altar-tomb to Courten in Kensington churchyard, designed by Grinling Gibbons.[16]

Amongst the sculpture which came to Montagu House in 1753 with Sloane's collections were a death mask of Cromwell and a relief portrait of Charles II, both part of his collections representing the history of Britain, but he also had two portraits of his friend who had preceded him as President of the Royal Society, Sir Isaac Newton. One was a plaster bust perhaps after

15 Sir Hans Sloane PRS (1660–1753), terracotta bust by Michael Rysbrack, about 1737, h. 68.5 cm. The bust, presented by the sitter's daughters, Lady Cadogan and Mrs Stanley, in 1756, greeted the visitor on arrival in Montagu House. MME.

Michael Rysbrack (1694–1770) (see fig. 2)[17] and the other was an oval fired clay plaque with a gilt relief portrait of Newton on a black painted ground (fig. 16).[18] This unusual object by an unknown artist had been given to Sloane before 1751 by his friend Batty Langley (1696–1751), architectural writer and inventor of an artificial stone composition; it was probably intended to be incorporated into an architectural setting, but was noted in the Sloane Catalogue as 'in Library with Dr. Maty'.[19]

The terracotta bust of Sloane by Rysbrack of c. 1725 (fig. 15)[20] presented by his daughters in 1756 was the third item of contemporary sculpture to enter the Museum. Its status was clear in the first published guide to the Museum, printed two years after it finally opened to the public in 1759: 'As you go up Stairs, the Busto of *Sir Hans Sloane*, on a Pedestal, presents itself immediately to your view.'[21] It seems always to have been kept on view in the Museum.

It was entirely appropriate that the bust of Sir Isaac Newton, Alexander Pope's embodiment of the Enlightenment, was in the library with Dr Maty, who has been described as a 'French Apostle of English Letters'.[22] Matthew Maty MD, FRS (1718–76) (fig. 14), a French Huguenot who was born and brought up in Holland, arrived in London aged twenty-two before the end of 1740. He had studied medicine at Leiden University and was probably making a good living treating wealthy patients when he became a Fellow of the Royal Society in 1751. He was appointed an under-librarian of the British Museum on 19 June 1756 and, even though he was not a collector, his role, as we shall see, was enormously

important in establishing the institution as a repository of portraits of monarchs and learned men and women.

There were relatively few women in intellectual circles in mid-eighteenth century Europe, but one, the writer, poet and translator Anne-Marie Le Page, Madame Fiquet du Bocage (1710–1802), whose quotation on the English as collectors of busts began this chapter, was as energetic as her male counterparts in travelling and meeting fellow authors and poets. On her visit to London in 1750 she encountered Maty and other members of his circle including Lord Chesterfield and Dr Mead.[23] Maty wrote verses to her and apparently requested her portrait for the Museum.[24] Her terracotta bust (fig. 17) was duly presented on 1 August 1766, but its location in Montagu House remains unrecorded until it was depicted in a watercolour of the Entrance Hall in 1843 (fig. 18). It is shown there on a bracket near the full-length marble statues of Shakespeare by Louis-François Roubiliac (1702–62),[25] which had arrived in the Museum in 1823 from David Garrick's widow as part of the actor's bequest to the Museum, and the seated figure of Sir Joseph Banks by Sir Francis Chantrey,[26] presented by the Linnean Society in 1826. It is suggested that the acquisition of these two life-size sculptures was the occasion for a new arrangement of the Front Hall in which the terracotta bust of Madame du Bocage was rather unhappily fitted. But it also indicates that from a relatively early stage in the Museum's history a pantheon of modern worthies, even if on a reduced scale, greeted the visitor on entry to the premises.

The most significant acquisition in the decade after the establishment of the Museum was the group of terracotta portraits by Louis-François Roubiliac purchased by Maty at the sale held in May 1762 at the sculptor's studio after his death. These included 'Socrates, *Plato*, *Demosthenes* & *Tully* from the Antique, *Marcus Aurelius* from a cast brought from Rome,[27] King Charles the first, Oliver Cromwell and Shakespear Models in Terra Cotta, Milton, Pope, Dr Mead [fig. 19], Mr Folkes [see fig. 105] and Ld Chesterfield Casts in Plaister, Ray [fig. 20], Willoughby, Dr. Barrow and Dr. Bentley original models in Terra Cotta[28] from which the Marble Busts in Trinity college Cambridge were executed'[29] as fine a group of 'ancient and modern worthies' as might be desired to grace any eighteenth-century library (see ch. 5).[30] Like Newton, Milton and Pope were well-known figures in any contemporary pantheon; but Maty had known the collector Dr Richard Mead personally, publishing his biography in 1755,[31] and was probably Chesterfield's physician, addressing verses to him and publishing a *Life* of him in 1777.[32]

The Trustees expressed their gratitude to Maty for this 'considerable donation' and ordered 'that he do place them in his department in such a manner as he thinks proper with suitable inscriptions'. The busts appear, therefore, to have joined the relief bust of Newton with Maty in the Library at Montagu House. Shown in an etching dated

16 Sir Isaac Newton PRS (1643–1727), fired clay plaque, painted and gilt, modeller unknown, about 1730–51, h. 48.5 cm. Presented to Sloane by the architect and gardener Batty Langley, this bust hung in various libraries in the Museum. MME.

17 Anne-Marie Le Page, Madame Fiquet du Bocage (1710–1802), terracotta bust by Jean-Baptiste Defernex, signed and dated 1766, h. 60.2 cm. The terracotta was presented by the sitter in 1766 and was for long displayed in the Entrance Hall to Montagu House. MME.

18 Entrance Hall of Montagu House by George Scharf I, watercolour, 1845. The full-length statues are of Sir Joseph Banks by Chantrey (now Natural History Museum) and Shakespeare by Roubiliac, with the bust of Madame du Bocage above the latter. The main staircase can be seen through the doorway, and warding staff are wearing the Windsor Uniform. P&D.

19 Dr Richard Mead MD FRS (1673–1754), plaster bust by Louis-François Roubiliac, about 1756, h. 61.5 cm. Dr Mead, physician to King George I, King George II and Sir Isaac Newton, allowed visitors to examine his collection of coins, gems, drawings and sculpture at his purpose-built gallery in Great Ormond Street. MME.

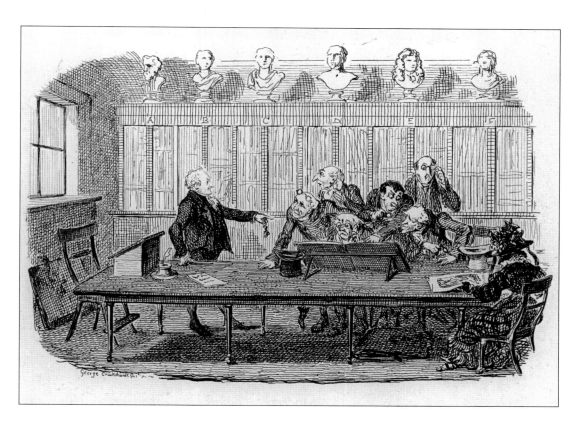

22 The first Print Room (Montagu House), etching by George Cruikshank, 1728. The Keeper, J. T. Smith, shows an album of drawings or prints to a group of connoisseurs. The busts on the tops of the cases are probably those given by Dr Maty, but are not easily identified. P&D.

20 John Ray FRS (1627–1705), terracotta bust by Louis-François Roubiliac, about 1751, h. 58.5 cm. Ray was known as the father of natural history in Britain. The sculptor modelled the bust from an oil portrait of Ray from Sloane's collection (now in the National Portrait Gallery). MME.

21 Sir Robert Bruce Cotton Bt (1571–1631), terracotta bust with partly painted surface by Louis-François Roubiliac, about 1756, h. 63.1 cm. The bust, the model for the marble in Trinity College, Cambridge, was purchased in 1924 from the Harvey family who commissioned the marble. MME.

1828 by G. Cruikshank on top of the presses of the first Print Room (fig. 22), these magnificent busts have always graced the Museum's libraries, reading rooms and offices and probably never have been displayed in the Museum public galleries as a group since their acquisition. Nevertheless the historical commemorative intention of their donor, admirer and friend of Roubiliac for many years,[33] has always been clear.

Another terracotta by Roubiliac joined the others in the Museum collection only in 1924.[34] It depicts Sir Robert Bruce Cotton (1571–1631), the collector, antiquary and bibliophile (fig. 21).[35] Cotton himself was interested in the commemoration of famous men, and paid for several tombs and epitaphs to be erected to his ancestors, and to medieval Scottish princes from whom he claimed descent, in All Saints, Conington, Huntingdonshire. The inscriptions and other Roman stones he collected on gathering trips with his teacher and fellow antiquarian William Camden were arranged in a summerhouse in his garden.[36] Subsequently neglected, they passed through the last of the Cotton line to Trinity College, Cambridge, only three years before the establishment of the British Museum, which through various historical accidents had acquired Cotton's outstanding library (now in the British Library), a group of family portraits attributed to Cornelius Jonson and John Hayls which now hang in the anteroom to the Museum Trustees' Board Room, and bronze busts of twelve Roman emperors and two of Cleopatra and Faustina (now all lost) which had surmounted the book presses containing Cotton's own library.

Not long after Maty had made the gift of the Roubiliacs, 'A bust of Mr. Fontenelle from Dr. Maty' was received from him by the Museum in 1767.[37] Maty had admired and longed to meet Bernard le Bovier de Fontenelle (1657–1757), scientist and man of letters and cousin of the playwright Pierre Corneille (whose portrait Sir Hans Sloane had owned as a pair to Molière's). Fontenelle was an important early figure in the French Enlightenment; indeed, Voltaire thought him the most universal genius of his age. Maty dedicated a long lyric poem entitled 'Vauxhall' to him, published in an early number of his *Journal Britannique* in April 1750, but Fontenelle died in 1753 before Maty finally made his trip to Paris in 1764.

Towards a 'universal history': 'Portraits of Illustrious Personages'

The collection of ancient and modern portrait busts at Montagu House continued a European tradition dating back to classical Greece and Rome; but the collection of oil portraits in the Museum reflected a comparatively recent and essentially British tradition. From the time of Queen Elizabeth I, portrait painting had dominated British art, from miniatures to life-size group portraits and every size and

23 François-Marie Arouet, called Voltaire (1694–1778), oil painting by Theodore Gardelle. Voltaire visited Sir Hans Sloane at his house in Chelsea. Trustees' collection.

24 Sir Hans Sloane PRS (1660–1753), oil painting attributed to John Vanderbank, depicting the sitter as President of the Royal Society with its mace on the table beside him. Trustees' collection.

variation in between. During the eighteenth century a taste for portraiture, whether it was important patrons and heroes in the hall, divines and poets in the library, or family and friends in private spaces, expressed a sense of social and civic responsibilities. Traditional images of honour and heroism found public expression in British portraits rather than in history paintings as found in contemporary painting on the continent: 'They spoke forcefully to a public which, by dint of more than two centuries of conditioning, understood, it would seem instinctively, their meanings and purpose.'[38]

We have noted above that Sloane's founding collection included painted portraits of his friends John Ray, William Dampier and William Courten; and, like Sloane, Maty owned several portraits in oil, which he presented to the Museum. One of the most remarkable, for its subject rather than the skill with which it is painted, is a three-quarter-length portrait of Voltaire by Théodore Gardelle,[39] which has for many years hung in the Museum Director's office (fig.23). Among other portraits presented by Maty to the Museum were an unfinished sketch of Locke after Kneller,[40] and a portrait of

25 Sir Joseph Banks PRS (1743–1820), oil painting by Sir Thomas Lawrence (1769–1830), depicting the sitter as President of the Royal Society with its mace on the table beside him and wearing the Order of the Bath. Trustees' collection.

26 King George II (1683–1760), oil painting by John Shackleton (d. 1767), with gilt wood frame by Thomas Black. Both the picture and the frame were commissioned by the Museum Trustees, a unique occurrence in the 18th century. Trustees' collection.

the seventeenth-century essayist Saint-Évremond.[41] His bequest of a half-length portrait of himself, by Barthélemy Dupan (fig. 14), is part of a series of portraits of Principal Librarians and Directors today kept in the Museum's Trustees' Board Room.

The earliest Museum guidebook of 1761 notes 'there are many Portraits of illustrious Personnages, hung up in the several Departments of this *Museum*; they are all Presents, and continually increasing in Number: I choose to give my Reader the Names of the chief of them in this Place'.[42] The list, too long to give in full here, comprises eleven British monarchs, three foreign rulers, Oliver Cromwell, five English nobles of note, two English bishops and an Italian cardinal, and twenty-four philosophers, statesmen, lawyers, writers, antiquaries and other learned men. Besides painted portraits, busts of Homer, Sir Thomas More and the Reverend Dr Samuel Clarke are mentioned: the Homer must be the bronze head once in the collection of Dr Mead and now called *Sophokles*;[43] the Thomas More was presented by Thomas Hollis and appears to have been made by the engraver to the Society of Antiquaries, George Vertue, who is otherwise unknown as a sculptor;[44] while the bust of the philosopher and theologian Samuel Clarke, presented by Maty in February 1760 together with a picture of Shakespeare,[45] has disappeared from view.

The British Museum commemorated monarchs, churchmen, scientists and intellectuals, not only in marble, terracotta and even bronze, but in a considerable collection of portraits which numbered over one hundred by the time of the first printed list in 1838. This list of 'Portraits in the British Museum' apparently compiled by the printer George Smeeton (fl. 1800–28), who considered it to be 'probably the largest collection of portraits in the kingdom',

noted that they hung in the 'long or mineral gallery (situated over the King's Library)', the upper floor of which had indeed been designed by Smirke specifically to incorporate them (see fig. 58). Smeeton's list, based on a report in *The Times*, which in turn was based on an official list compiled by the Chief Librarian, Sir Henry Ellis,[46] was a kind of *catalogue raisonné* and reveals how many of the portraits arrived in Montagu House within the first two decades of the Museum's existence. Amongst the additions in the 1750s and 1760s, besides those already mentioned above, was an entire series of ten British historical portraits presented by the

Assistant Librarian and numismatist Dr Andrew Gifford (1700–84).[47] Further royal portraits followed, including two portraits of Queen Elizabeth I,[48] King Edward VI,[49] and a supposed portrait (then attributed to Van Dyke) of Charles I when prince.[50] The Reverend Andrew Planta (1717–73), Assistant in the Department of Printed Books, presented portraits of King Charles XII of Sweden, King Louis XIV of France and another identified as Augustus the Strong of Poland,[51] three kings widely considered as particularly important rulers. Dr Gifford ensured that the British Museum's pantheon included a selection of ten sixteenth- and seventeenth-century statesmen including Lord Burghley and Chancellor Bacon, and divines such as Archbishop Ussher who had been responsible for establishing the date of creation as 4004 BC (see ch. 17).[52] The 1838 list also included antiquaries such as Dr John Ward, whose portrait was given by Thomas Hollis in 1759.[53] The portraits of Robert and Edward Harley, first and second Earls of Oxford, the great bibliophiles, were presented by the second Earl's daughter, the dowager Duchess of Portland, in 1768 to hang with the Harleian library, acquired shortly after the Museum's foundation.[54] Fittingly, Sloane, who owed his fortune to his successful medical practice, owned a portrait of Vesalius, once attributed to Sir Antonio More, which still remains at Bloomsbury[55] and another, of the naturalist Ulysses Aldrovandi (1522–1607), whose renowned cabinet of curiosities must have provided an inspiration for Sloane's own and for William Courten, from whom Sloane had inherited the portrait.[56] Portraits of artists included James Rousseau (1630–93) who with Monnoyer and La Fosse had the ornamented the staircase of Montagu House.[57] Museum Trustees and other prominent public figures presented portraits of their own illustrious ancestors, patrons and friends. Sir Thomas Robinson presented a portrait by Allan Ramsay of the fourth Earl of Chesterfield along with a medal and a marble bust of him by Wilton.[58] A 'Hunting Piece' signed by J. B. Weenix,[59] and a landscape by Richard Wilson, presented by Thomas Hollis, were also included in the list.

This is no place for a detailed art-historical study of these portraits, but mention must be made of a group of five formal portraits, three of which were painted specifically with display in the British Museum in mind. The first is the full-length portrait of Sloane, acquired in 1767 from the widow of Dr Horsman and traditionally attributed to Godfrey Kneller, although it is now attributed to John Vanderbank (1694–1739) (fig. 24). Holding a letter and seated in a chair surmounted by the coat of arms of the Royal Society, its mace on the table beside him, he is depicted in a dark green velvet coat, wearing the same magnificent wig seen in his bust by Rysbrack, with his classical statue of the Roman god of healing Asclepius in the niche in the background. Recently dismissively described as a 'pompous and vacuous affair and certainly conservative in taste',[60] in fact it represents a splendid example of early eighteenth-century British portraiture commemorating public figures. It presided over his collections in the British Museum in the same manner David Allan intended his elegant and striking full-length of the diplomat and collector Sir William Hamilton to preside over his collection of vases and other antiquities acquired by the British Museum in 1772. Sir William himself commissioned a further full-length portrait of himself from Sir Joshua Reynolds ten years later – depicting him less in the role of a diplomat and more as a member of the group of Dilettanti distinguished for their love of the Antique – to hang with the Hamilton collection which had been increased in size in the interval (see fig. 161).[61] In 1834 the antiquary the Reverend Daniel Lysons presented Sir Joseph Banks's portrait by Lawrence showing him also seated in the chair of the President of the Royal Society, with its mace and *Proceedings* on the table before him (fig. 25). These portraits hung either in the rooms in which their collections were displayed or in the Long, or Mineral, Gallery above the King's Library: all except the Reynolds of Hamilton now hang in the Hartwell Room, used for special Museum functions. The room is dominated by the full-length oil of King George II, by John Shackleton (fig. 26),[62] the only portrait 'painted for the Trustees' during the eighteenth century, its splendid frame specially commissioned from Thomas Black, who had succeeded Arthur Pond as the Museum's picture restorer and framer. In the 1808 edition of the *Synopsis of the Contents of the British Museum*,[63] the portrait is listed as 'Over the chimney' in 'The Saloon'. The Grand Staircase from the Entrance Hall led directly to this imposing room. In 1828 it was moved to the new Long Gallery over the King's Library as part of the 'national collection of pictures'.[64]

The library Banks bequeathed, now in the British Library, was for many years in the Banksian Room near the North end of the King's Library, together with a bronze bust of him by the Hon. Anne Seymour Damer presented by herself in 1814 with instructions that it be placed on a pivot (now missing). This bronze was originally placed in a prominent position on the landing of the great staircase of Montagu House, presumably near Sloane's bust, but it was removed after only fifteen years.[65]

A 'UNIVERSAL HISTORY' AND ITS FATE

The later history of the portrait busts and oil paintings in the British Museum is now as little known as its development during the first fifty years of its existence. A brief outline of what became of various parts of the collection is given below, which may serve to explain why the National Gallery has few national portraits and no department of prints and drawings, and why the national collection of works on paper is in the British Museum and the national collection of British por-

traits is housed in a building behind but not connected to the National Gallery.

As discussed in the first part of this chapter, Sir Hans Sloane and successive keepers and patrons had ensured that the British Museum had a collection of portrait busts and paintings of great men and women, of both the past and the present, representing a 'universal history'. These were in addition to a fine collection of portrait prints and drawings from Sloane and others, a rather more motley collection of prints, drawings and paintings of natural history and genre subjects and a handful of Old Masters. This is no place to examine the growth of the collection of drawings, which has been relatively well documented,[66] nor the attempt made by Sir William Hamilton to begin a collection of Old Master paintings.[67] It is worth noting, however, that Hamilton complained in 1776 that 'the old dons do not so much as thank me when I send a work of art. They are delighted with a spider or shell and send me many thanks for such presents',[68] indicating that the bias of the Museum was still towards libraries, natural history and antiquities.

The early years of the new century saw a shift in emphasis towards the visual arts and classical sculpture, no doubt reflected in the choice of Museum Trustees such as the artist Sir Thomas Lawrence (1769–1830) and collectors such as Richard Payne Knight (1751–1824), Sir Charles Long (1760–1838) and Sir George Beaumont (1753–1827). All these men felt a growing public responsibility (not to mention a desire for public admiration and approval and a monument to their generosity) to provide a public place for the permanent display of their collections. The manoeuvres of Sir George Beaumont in particular, which have been fully discussed elsewhere,[69] were intended to transform the British Museum into a museum with a picture gallery attached. In 1822 he added a codicil to his will leaving all his paintings to the British Museum, believing 'the one service he could perform for his country was to help the British public towards the appreciation of works of art, with the establishment of a national gallery ... where they would be "not merely toys for connoisseurs but solid objects of concern to the nation"'.[70] In 1823 Parliament approved money for the construction of a building at the Museum to house the King's Library with the provision of rooms above as a 'fit receptacle' for any pictures which might be donated.

However, between 1824 and 1826 moves by the Treasury, in the person of Lord Liverpool, effectively scotched the idea of creating an institution encompassing antiquities, natural history, a library and a picture gallery. Although the British Museum Trustees were made Trustees of the newly established National Gallery founded through the purchase of the Angerstein collection, and remained the nominal owners of Beaumont's gift of pictures to the nation until 1861,[71] plans for a new picture gallery, ultimately located in Trafalgar Square, were unstoppable, and meant the separation of the Museum's paintings from Montagu House for ever. In addition, all but a small group of portraits ultimately left Bloomsbury as a result of moves initiated by Noel Desenfans, a picture dealer, in 1799, as a consequence of a need felt to commemorate military heroes during the period of the Napoleonic Wars. Desenfans's plan 'to preserve portraits of characters of England, Scotland and Ireland'[72] lay fallow until the middle of the century. In 1857 George Scharf borrowed for exhibition in Manchester a number of the 150 portraits noted two years earlier by the *Athenaeum* as in the Museum's collection,[73] and in 1859 the National Portrait Gallery came into being. The large collection hanging over the Zoological Collection in the Long Gallery over the King's Library (fig. 58) was dismembered in two phases: seventy British portraits were transferred in 1879, and the formal handover, which included paintings from the Museum in the National Gallery, was approved in 1888. The Museum was left with foreign sitters and those 'of family interest to the British Museum'.[74] In 1946 a remaining group of portraits was transferred to the Ministry of Works for the nominal sum of £1 each and these now form part of the Government Art Collection, decorating various government offices.

Thomas Carlisle's belief, articulated in 1840, that 'Universal History, the history of what man has accomplished in this world, is at bottom the History of Great Men, those great ones; the modellers, patterns, and in a wide sense creators, of whatsoever the general mass of men contrived to do or attain'[75] no longer has wide currency. However, from its foundation and for three-quarters of a century afterwards, the British Museum represented this 'universal' view of history, which was enshrined in its great collections of natural history, antiquities, works of art and in particular its representations of great men. In the second half of the nineteenth century its paintings went to Trafalgar Square, its natural history collections to South Kensington. At the end of the twentieth century its great libraries have gone to St Pancras. Of its once fine collections of art, only those on paper in the Department of Prints and Drawings remain.

But the initial impulse to include paintings, especially portraits, in displays in British Museum galleries has never entirely disappeared. A handwritten gallery plan of the King Edward VII Gallery dated September 1939[76] reveals that its walls were hung with portraits. Several were eighteenth-century donations kept by the Museum, including the portrait of Cardinal Sforza Pallavicini presented by Smart Lethieullier and Sloane's painting of Mary Davis, called the 'horned woman',[77] exhibited as part of this miscellaneous group of curiosities and ancient and modern worthies.

Today, high up on the walls of the 'Europe 1400–1800' gallery display completed in the early 1990s, are hung portraits of historical figures. These have all been borrowed from the National Portrait Gallery and bear no relationship to the collection assembled in earlier centuries, while other formal portraits with important connections to collections in the

Museum, such as Sir William Hamilton's, have had to be borrowed back on long-term loan for the private function spaces of the Museum, so reinstating its 'family history'. Some paintings have been lent to the British Library for display on a long-term basis and three busts have been transferred there, as they commemorate donors and librarians associated with that institution. In general, however, the commemorative function of the portrait sculpture has never been forgotten, despite the temporary loss of identity of some of the busts and various attempts to transfer others. Both paintings and portrait sculpture have, and have had since the mid nineteenth century, an ambiguous status within the Museum. Not formally collected, their numbers still continue to increase, although slowly. Busts of collectors, such as the marble of Charles Townley by Christopher Hewetson (fig. 27),[78] are acquired by departments for their collections, and paintings and busts of past directors, such as the bronze bust of Sir John Pope-Hennessy by Elisabeth Frink,[79] and the Allen Jones painted portrait of Sir David Wilson, are acquired by the Trustees for their Board Room. Two and a half centuries from its foundation, the Museum continues to commemorate collectors and its own; but, instead of a 'universal' history for the promotion of knowledge and improvement of the public, the remaining portraits provide a 'family' history, mainly in the Museum's private spaces for its staff, trustees and patrons.

27 Charles Townley (1737–1805), marble bust by Christopher Hewetson, 1769, h. 57.5 cm. This bust was made in Rome, which Townley first visited in 1767 when he began his collection of classical sculptures (see figs 51, 162–3) which were eventually purchased by the Museum after his death. MME.

3

'Most curious, splendid and useful': the King's Library of George III

GRAHAM JEFCOATE

28 King George III (reigned 1760-1820), marble bust by John van Nost the Younger, 1767. Van Nost made several busts of George III; this one is inscribed 'from the life by van Nost, 1767'. Victoria & Albert Museum, on loan to the British Museum.

In 1828 the British Museum received one of the most generous donations in its history: the Library of George III (1738–1820, reigned 1760–1820). The Library, itself one of the most significant collections of the Enlightenment, was accommodated at the Museum in a gallery designed especially for it by Robert Smirke, 'one of the noblest rooms in London'[1] (see ch. 4). Both Smirke's gallery and the collection it housed came to be known as the 'King's Library'. Since its transfer with other collections to St Pancras, the new London home of British Library (the national library of the United Kingdom, founded in 1973), George III's library has once again been accommodated in a purpose-built space, this time a six-storey glass tower conceived by the Library's architect Sir Colin St John Wilson (b. 1922) which it shares with the equally splendid library of Thomas Grenville (1755–1846), bequeathed to the British Museum in 1847.

GEORGE III AS BOOK COLLECTOR

When George III (fig. 28) succeeded to the British throne in 1760 he found no royal library in the true sense of the term. His grandfather and predecessor George II had presented the so-called 'Old Royal Library', which had accumulated since the fifteenth century, to the newly founded British Museum in Montagu House in 1757. Although the Royal Library had possessed the right to receive copies of new English publications since the seventeenth century, it had been neglected for many decades. The house of Brunswick-Lüneburg appears to have made do with reading matter in its own private collections.

Though scarcely a scholar, George, Prince of Wales, heir presumptive since 1751, had received a well-rounded education, covering not only music and theology but also art and history, mathematics, natural history and geography (see ch. 15).[2] His best-known tutor was John Stuart, third Earl of Bute (1713–92). Although Bute's political advice was later to prove disastrous, Bute instilled the young prince with a genuine regard for learning. George was particularly interested in architecture, later making his architectural tutor William Chambers (1726–96) his court architect.[3] Although he never travelled abroad, not even to his German electorate, he read and conversed in several languages (including German, of course). With his Queen, Charlotte of Mecklenburg-Strelitz, whom he married in 1761, he enjoyed both the theatre and music (in which their tastes, however, were rather conservative). The King was well read in both English and foreign literature. His interest in astronomy is well attested. That he made pseudonymous contributions to periodicals on topical matters relating to husbandry is also well known, his practical interest in agriculture earning him the sobriquet 'Farmer George'.[4]

BUILDING THE COLLECTION

George pursued a vigorous collecting policy almost from his accession, acting at first through Richard Dalton (d. 1791), his librarian as Prince of Wales, who was retained in post.[5] In 1762 he acquired for £300 the so-called 'Thomason Tracts', a collection of broadsides and pamphlets made by the London bookseller George Thomason (d. 1666) during the Civil War and Commonwealth periods, 1640–60.[6] In January 1763 he spent £10,000 on the outstanding collections of Joseph Smith (c. 1674–1770), British consul in Venice, which included many important early printed editions, being especially strong in Italian literature and history (fig. 29).[7] The King also bought paintings, prints and drawings; indeed, with the Smith collections, he acquired significant works of art as well as books.

With his educational background, it is scarcely surprising

30 Sir Frederick Augusta Barnard (1742–1830), George III's Librarian, oil painting by John Prescott Knight RA. Trustees' collection, on loan to the British Library.

29 A vellum-bound book from the collection of Joseph Smith, British consul in Venice. The collection was purchased by George III for the King's Library in 1763. The British Library.

31 Octagon Library in Buckingham House, built in 1766–7. The arrangement of book cases on the floor and the gallery was followed in Smirke's King's Library (see fig. 41). Coloured lithograph by R. Reeves after a watercolour by J. P. Stephanoff, 1818. From W. H. Pyne, *The History of the Royal Residences*, 1819. P&D.

that the young king resolved to create a new royal library. Moreover, he was prepared to spend considerable sums for the purpose. From about 1767, what can be described as a more systematic policy of collection building appears to have begun, annual expenditure on books rising in that year to £1,459 5s. 7d.[8] By 1769 the collection already held about 10,000 volumes. In the decades that followed, the King's agents were active on his behalf at book sales and auctions throughout Europe. Sir Frederick Augusta Barnard (1742–1830), the King's librarian from 1774 (fig. 30),[9] was authorized to spend up to £2,000 annually on new acquisitions. In the years 1768 to 1771 Barnard visited booksellers in France, Germany, Italy and the

Low Countries in search of potential acquisitions to add to those that the King was making through the London trade.[10] The King's London bookseller, George Nicol of Pall Mall (1741–1829), also played a key role in the process of collection building. By the time of George III's death in 1820, around a fifth of his private income (£120,000) was spent on the Library, not including personnel costs.[11]

It was noteworthy that the King was acquiring material in subject areas where the fledgling library of the British Museum was known to be weak, including English literature, early English printing, philosophy and the classics, Italian, French and Spanish literature, geography and topography, architecture, painting and sculpture. Books on subjects reflecting the King's private interests were also collected, including of course agriculture, astronomy and the natural sciences (see ch. 14).[12] All ancient and modern languages were represented, although, unexpectedly for a royal house of German origins, there are more Italian than German books.[13] Whole collections continued

32 The King's Library in Buckingham House. Coloured lithograph by J. Baily after a watercolour by J. P. Stephanoff, 1817. From W. H. Pyne, *The History of the Royal Residences*, 1819. P&D.

to be added, as well as, during the 1770s, the most important items in the libraries of Anthony Askew, James West and John Ratcliffe.[14] The acquisition of the collection of the Danish philologian Grimr Jonsson Thorkelin (1752–1829) alone brought some 2,085 works on Danish, Norwegian and Icelandic literature, philology and history into the Library.

In contrast with other noble collectors and contemporaries, the King tended to avoid bibliographical curiosities for their own sake, with the arguable exception of first editions. Nevertheless, the King's Library includes innumerable fine editions and presentation copies.[15] Few can be described in detail here, but his Gutenberg Bible (Mainz, c. 1455)[16] and the incomparable collection of English incunabula (books printed before 1501), including Caxton's edition of Chaucer's

Canterbury Tales (Westminster, c. 1476, now known to be the first book printed in England) should at least be mentioned.

By the time it was donated to the British Museum the Library contained some 65,259 printed books, representing the 'most encyclopaedic of pre-Panizzi accessions'.[17] Supplementing the books were periodicals and a collection of some thirty thousand pamphlets covering the period from about 1550 to 1810 and concentrating on English and French affairs. The King was a less enthusiastic collector of manuscripts[18] (the British Museum already held the finest collections in Britain in the Cottonian and Harleian libraries) but he built very considerable collections of prints, drawings, musical scores, maps and topographical drawings (see ch. 15) and coins and medals (see ch. 11).[19]

THE USE OF THE COLLECTION

The Library was conceived from the beginning as a working library and, like the libraries in the British Museum, it was generally accessible on request to all *bona fide* scholars. As early as 1767 the Library was known and used by men of letters.[20] Even those of whom the King personally disapproved were given access, including the scientist Joseph Priestley (1733–1804), whose theological and political radicalism were anathema to George III. Former enemies of the King such as the American revolutionary John Adams (1735–1826) were admitted. Hardly an admirer of the King, Adams reported of his visit in 1783 that the Library had been assembled 'with perfect taste and judgement' and wished that he had more time to read in it:

> The King's Library struck me with admiration; [...]
> The books were in perfect order, elegant in their
> editions, paper, binding, etc. but gaudy and extravagant
> in nothing. [...] every book that a king ought to have
> always at hand, and as far as I could examine, and could
> be supposed capable of judging, none other.[21]

During his reign the King's Library was accommodated in a number of rooms at Buckingham House (later to become Buckingham Palace) and especially in the four designed for the purpose by Chambers in the years 1762 to 1773. These were grouped around a two-storey octagon built in 1766–7, which was fitted out with bookshelves (fig. 31). This arrangement allowed the King direct access to the Library from his private apartments and it was not unknown for private scholars to meet him there. Contemporary illustrations (fig. 32) suggest that the Library's appearance was not dissimilar to other scholarly libraries.[22]

The King's books were placed on the shelves by subject and format although their precise arrangement at Bucking-

ham House is unknown. The King maintained a bindery there, which he occasionally visited in person. The generally fine but not extravagant work of the Buckingham House bindery can be seen to good effect through the glass of the King's Library Tower in the British Library today (fig. 33). Between the years 1812 and 1820 Barnard prepared a classified catalogue of twelve manuscript volumes. An author catalogue was issued as *Bibliothecæ Regiæ catalogus* by Bulmer and Nicol between 1820 and 1829.[23] Although this was never formally published, copies were presented to major libraries at home and abroad and to foreign potentates.[24]

THE KING'S LIBRARY AS AN ENLIGHTENMENT COLLECTION

From this brief outline of the King's Library it should be clear that George III and his librarians were following clear principles in building the collection. This royal library was certainly not intended as a cabinet of bibliographical curiosities in the manner of certain early modern princely libraries, which often served their owners as theatres for baroque display. What, then, were the principles upon which the collection, indeed the whole rationale of the King's Library, was built?

That Samuel Johnson (1709–84) advised the King on the acquisitions he should make is well known. Johnson discussed the world of letters and scholarship with the King personally when they met in the Library in February 1767. In a

33 A selection of books showing bindings from the King's Library. The British Library.

34 View of Göttingen University Library in the former Paulinerkirche (after 1812). Städtisches Museum, Göttingen.

letter of 28 May 1768 to Barnard, a personal friend, who was preparing to leave on a book-hunting expedition on the continent, Johnson suggested that, of published books, the Library should acquire 'at least the most curious edition, the most splendid, and the most useful'. He recommended the acquisition of material in the classics, literature, law and topography as well as exemplars of early printing.[25] The purchase of whole libraries should be avoided in order to avoid unnecessary duplication, advice that was generally followed after the initial period of collection building.

Valuable as Johnson's guidance clearly was, the development of George III's library needs to be considered, as it rarely has been, in its wider, European context. The historian Jonathan Israel has recently underlined the importance to the Enlightenment enterprise of the development of 'universal libraries'.[26] This concept had first been developed in print in the early seventeenth century by the young French scholar Gabriel Naudé, whose *Advis pour dresser une bibliothèque* (Paris, 1627) is regarded as one of the first treatises on the

principles of librarianship. The *Advis* was widely influential, translations appearing in most major European languages, including an English version by John Evelyn: *Instructions Concerning Erecting a Library* (London, 1661).

In the *Advis* Naudé argued for a collection that was as comprehensive as possible, including not only all the major and canonic authors, ancient and modern, but also minor and more recent authors in every branch of science and the arts. As translated by John Evelyn, Naudé tells us:

And therefore I shall ever think it extreamly necessary, to collect for this purpose all sorts of books, (under such precautions, yet, as I shall establish) seeing a Library which is erected for the public benefit, ought to be universal; but which it can never be, unless it comprehend all the principal authors, that have written upon the great diversity of particular subjects, and chiefly upon all the arts and sciences; [...] For certainly there is nothing which renders a Library more recommendable, then when every man findes in it that which he is in search of. [pp. 19–20]

Scholars using Naudé's 'universal library' were to be able to range freely across genres, languages, periods and subjects, making new connections and, with fresh insights based upon them, adding to the sum of knowledge. Most importantly, this 'universal library' was to include works by members of the ideological opposition, heretical Protestants, Jews, Muslims and even freethinkers. It was not the role of the librarian to confine the scholar's researches or anticipate his conclusions by restricting the evidence. Naudé advises against the inclusion only of the most trivial, vulgar or derivative works.

Underlying Naudé's dedication and the first chapter of the *Advis*, 'Why establish a library?', is the assumption that a great library will be founded by a man of wealth and substance. One of the functions of great libraries was to emphasize and make visible the support of a patron or polity for serious scholarship. By implication this would place them in a better light than empty manifestations of baroque display. This theme was taken up by others during the latter part of the seventeenth century, notably by Richard Bentley (1672–1742), the young Cambridge scholar, who had been entrusted with the care of the (old) royal library. In 1697 Bentley published his *Proposal for Building a Royal Library and Establishing it by Act of Parliament* in which he argued on patriotic grounds (in section XI) for the creation of a well-funded library with some two hundred thousand volumes:

> And since the writings of the English nation have at
> present that great reputation abroad, … 'tis easie to
> foresee, how much glory will be advanced, by erecting
> a free library of all sorts of books, where every foreigner
> will have such convenience of studying.

The cost of the library would be offset by the 'publick interest and profit' that would accrue from the greater visibility, accessibility and prestige of English scholarship (section XII).

If Bentley's vision remained unrealized in England during the seventeenth and early eighteenth centuries, then 'universal libraries' began to develop quite rapidly on the continent. In Germany court libraries were founded or greatly expanded after the end of the Thirty Years War in 1648, including the famous Bibliotheca Augusta of the Dukes of Brunswick-Lüneburg at Wolfenbüttel, the Electoral (later Royal) Libraries at Berlin and Dresden, and the Court Library itself at Vienna.

The most celebrated Enlightenment theorist of universal libraries after Naudé was Gottfried Wilhelm Leibniz (1646–1716) who, on his appointment as Director of the Bibliotheca Augusta in 1691, prepared a memorandum for the Duke setting out a comprehensive programme for the development of an encyclopaedic collection based on a regular purchase fund, a comprehensive catalogue and an open access policy for scholars. Leibniz's scheme remained unrealized (indeed unpublished until after his death), but his ideas certainly contributed to the theoretical background for Europe's first truly modern, universal research library, the Library of the University of Göttingen (fig. 34).

The University of Göttingen was founded in 1737 under the patronage of the King's grandfather, George II, as the 'national' university of his Hanoverian electorate.[27] As far as I am aware, a detailed comparison has not yet been made between the development of the King's Library in London and the Library of the University of Göttingen. Nevertheless, the connections and parallels are striking. The University's founder, Gerlach Adolph von Münchausen (1688–1770), Hanover's chief minister, saw the Library from the beginning at the heart of its work in teaching and research. Münchausen paid close personal attention its development, ensuring it received the kind of regular and generous funding that both Bentley and Leibniz had proposed (and also frequent 'extraordinary allocations' from fiscal surpluses). Like George III, Münchausen pursued an active acquisitions policy across Europe, closely involving even the Hanoverian diplomatic service.[28]

By 1760 Göttingen's Library had already grown to rival some of Europe's largest research libraries. In 1763 the classical philologian and librarian Christian Gottlob Heyne (1729–1812) was appointed to a professorship at Göttingen and entrusted with the direction of the University Library.[29] A letter from the Hanoverian Privy Council to George III recommending Heyne's appointment and George III's reply of 17 March 1763[30] confirming his appointment as professor of eloquence and librarian are not the only evidence for a close connection between the two. Despite his reluctance to visit his German electorate, George III took a close interest in its affairs and in those of its University. He received senior Göttingen professors when they visited London (although Heyne was not among them). In the late 1780s he despatched three of his younger sons at once to study at Göttingen, a measure of his personal regard for Heyne, who was by this time the University's leading figure. Although I am unaware of direct evidence of contacts or correspondence between Heyne and Barnard, it must be assumed that the King's librarian was fully apprised of Heyne's work at Göttingen and its significance.

On his appointment as University Librarian Heyne initiated a rapid expansion of the collections. By 1800 some 133,200 volumes had been accumulated. In that year alone, some 2,069 books were acquired.[31] A notable visitor to Göttingen at this time (1801) was Johann Wolfgang von Goethe, who found he needed the research materials available there to complete work on his *Farbenlehre*. Goethe was assisted in this by Heyne's future successor, Jeremias David Reuss, later describing the Library as a 'great investment ["Capital"], that silently repays an incalculable interest'.[32]

Despite this evidence for a systematic and effective collection policy, Heyne's first and only detailed statement of its principles was made in 1810, two years before his own death in office. The Library would acquire, he tells us,

> continually and systematically from the daily accretion
> of native and foreign literature only that which, in the
> perpetual progress of scientific culture, was necessary
> for a library that was instituted with a scientific

intention, not after the predilection of individual disciplines, not with a love of splendour, not for the sake of outward appearances, but as comprehensive collection of the most important writings of all times and all nations in all branches of learning ... As a rule, only those books are sought and selected in which human knowledge scientific, technical or practical has progressed or been advanced, if only by a single step; and, in particular, those works which contain either the sources of systems, or improvements, enlargements, and corrections in form or in substance, and do not consist in repeating, reproducing and compiling what is already known or even trivial.[33]

This statement places Heyne's vision firmly in the tradition of the Enlightenment 'universal library', a comprehensive repository of the materials required for serious research. It also provides us with a clear blueprint for the development of the King's Library itself. An example can be found in Heyne's and Barnard's policies of acquiring imaginative literature. In both cases contemporary novels were often acquired only when the authors had gained respectability through a collected edition. Some were never acquired at all. If Barnard, who remains a rather shadowy figure, left no statement of his own collection policy, the evidence for it can be found in the collection itself.

Although the King founded the Library on his own initiative and built the collection entirely from funds supplied from his privy purse, it was clear that he regarded it as a 'national resource'.[34] We can only assume that he understood and supported Barnard's determination to build a collection that met the criteria laid down for a scholarly universal library.

THE ACQUISITION OF THE COLLECTION BY THE BRITISH MUSEUM, 1823–8

George III's successor, his eldest son George IV, who succeeded to the throne in 1820 having been Prince Regent since 1810, shared few of his father's personal interests. In March 1822 rumours appeared in the press that he wanted to sell his father's collection. The *Morning Chronicle* reported, for example, that he was considering a sale of the books to the Russian Tsar. Although these rumours were quickly denied, they may have been originated quite deliberately in the King's own inner circle, an early example of 'news management'. George IV probably saw advantages in his negotiations with the government if he announced he was prepared to present the library to the nation rather than selling it overseas. The King required a large quantity of ready money in order to pay for his ambitious building plans, money the government was understandably reluctant to provide. Apart from this, the library occupied a space in Buckingham House that his architect, John Nash (1752–1835), had chosen as the location of a new kitchen.

On 15 January 1823 George IV wrote to the Prime Minister informing him he had resolved to 'to present the most valuable and extensive library collected by his father, the late King, to the British nation'. Although it was to be housed at the British Museum, the collection was not to be dispersed among the Museum's existing books but rather 'kept entire, and separate ... in a repository to be appropriated exclusively for that purpose'.[35]

THE KING'S LIBRARY TODAY

The donation of George III's library effectively doubled the British Museum's collection of printed books. Throughout its history, and in each of its locations, it has remained very much a working collection, an essential element in the national collection of rare and early printed books in the British Library. The King's Library Tower stands at the heart of the new national library building at St Pancras, a monument not only to the very special significance of this great Enlightenment library but also to a conscientious librarian and to the taste and foresight of its royal founder.[36]

4 The King's Library and its architectural genesis

TIM KNOX

35 Sir Robert Smirke (1780–1867), architect of the King's Library and the new British Museum (knighted in 1835). Marble bust by Thomas Campbell, 1845, h. 72 cm. MME.

It was George IV who decreed the gift of his father's library to the nation, expressing his intention, in a letter dated 15 January 1823 to his Prime Minister, Lord Liverpool. The offer was duly recorded in the Treasury Minutes of the following day: 'His Royal Majesty has been graciously pleased to inform him that he has resolved to present the most valuable and extensive library collected by his father, the late King, to the British nation'.[1] The House of Commons was consulted and the gift was accepted, although not without some dissent, the British Museum being settled upon as the institution best suited for the reception of the vast collection. In 1823 the British Museum already possessed a considerable library, comprising not only its foundation collections of Sir Hans Sloane's books and the Harleian and Cottonian manuscripts but also the old royal library which George II had presented in 1757 and an important collection of English Civil War pamphlets donated by George III in 1762. Thus, by making his gift to the British Museum, George IV was carrying on a tradition established by his father and grandfather – although spiteful rumours circulated that the library had in fact been secretly sold to the nation for £180,000 to prevent its sale to the Tsar of Russia.[2]

But the British Museum, then housed in old Montagu House, was overcrowded and could not possibly accommodate such a huge influx of books. Moreover, the accommodation at Bloomsbury was hardly ideal – even in 1829 the Museum's manuscripts were kept amidst the superannuated splendour of one of the former state rooms on the first floor of the house: 'ornamented with real fluted composite columns, in pairs, which have an elegant carved entablature and festoons between the capitals', with a ceiling 'richly painted, with Jupiter hurling his lightning at Phaeton'.[3] Another reading room, according to a critic of 1835, was 'situated in an obscure corner of the premises, and approached by a labyrinth, leading along a gutter and over two drains'.[4] In any case George IV's gift was accompanied by the proviso that his father's library be 'kept entire, and separate from the rest of the Library of the Museum, in a repository to be appropriated exclusively for that purpose'. A new building was therefore inevitable, and Parliament voted £40,000 for its construction.[5]

The architect chosen to build the new library was Robert Smirke (1780–1867), the most reliable and businesslike of the three 'attached architects' to the Office of Works – the others being Sir John Soane and John Nash. Robert Smirke (fig. 35) had a reputation for sound construction and coming in on estimate, and he was also the favourite architect of the Tory establishment then in power. Moreover, he had carried out work for the British Museum before, repairs and additions – including a temporary gallery for the Elgin Marbles – in 1815–16 (fig. 36).[6] Indeed, an ambitious series

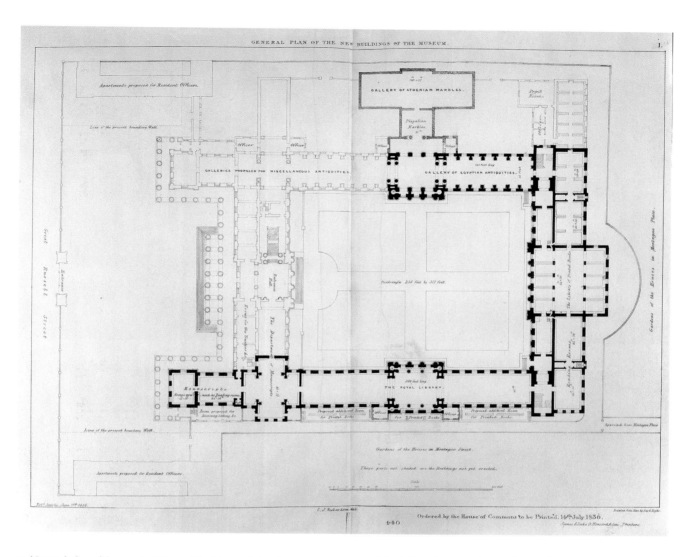

36 'General Plan of the new buildings of the Museum', showing
the ground-plan of the new King's or 'Royal Library'. Lithograph by
C. J. Richardson after Sir Robert Smirke, 1836. Archives.

of extensions of the Museum had been planned as long ago as
1802, and in 1819 there was a plan to demolish Montagu
House altogether and build a new museum in Waterloo
Place.[7] In 1820 Smirke was instructed to draw up plans for
extensions to the old buildings, proposing to the Treasury, in
February 1821, two parallel wings projecting from the back of
Montagu House, the first stage of a grand Greek Revivalist
design that was eventually intended to encompass the entire
Museum, rebuilding it as a great rectangular quadrangle
fronted by a huge portico flanked by colonnades (fig. 36).[8]
The late King's books were allocated the eastern wing of the
two proposed ranges – on a site on the north-east corner of
old Montagu House, balancing George Saunders's Townley
Gallery of 1804–8. This was the first of the new buildings to
be embarked upon, and its internal arrangements were
accordingly revised to serve its new purpose.

Much has been written about the novelty of Smirke's
colonnaded design for the front of the British Museum, for
it actually predates Schinkel's Altes Museum in Berlin
(1823–8), its closest continental counterpart.[9] However, this
façade, with its distinctive 'redundancy of columns'[10] (itself
perhaps inspired by Jean-Nicholas-Louis Durand's ideal
design for a museum published in 1808 in his influential
Précis des leçons d'architecture (1802–9)),[11] was not begun
until 1841 and was completed only under the direction of
his younger brother, Sydney Smirke (1798–1877) in 1848
(fig. 37). Therefore it forms no part, strictly speaking, of the
story of the accommodation of the King's Library. The
exterior of the new east range was plain, as befitted a sub-
sidiary section of a much larger design. It took the form of
a plain rectangular range of eighteen bays, ornamented in
the centre of its western flank by an attached portico of
Ionic columns. It was built of grey stock brick faced with
Portland stone, and the severe and pristine new building
must have looked odd projecting from the decrepit late
seventeenth-century fabric of Montagu House (fig. 38).

37 The entrance façade of the new British Museum showing Smirke's colonnade. Lithograph after Sydney Smirke, 1851. Of the sculpture shown, only that shown in the tympanum of the pediment was executed, by Sir Richard Westmacott in 1851. P&D.

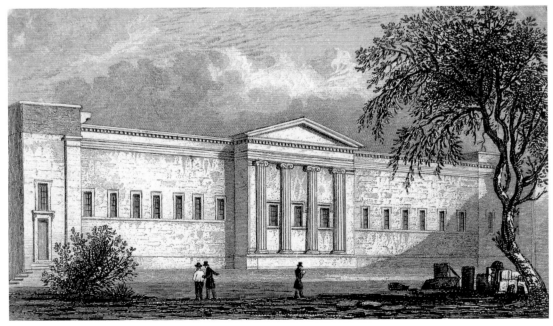

This contrast increased as the other sides of the new quadrangle began to be erected. J. Timbs, writing in 1865, recalled how 'strange it was to see the lofty pitched roof, balustraded attic and large-windowed front of "the French manner" giving way to the Grecian architecture of Sir Robert Smirke's new design'(fig. 39).[12]

The choice of the severe Grecian style for the new British Museum was significant; it was both daringly novel and harked back to the glorious, rational civilization of ancient Greece, so memorably represented in the Museum's collections by the newly arrived Elgin Marbles. Grecian motifs had

38 'The East Wing of the New Building containing the Royal Library. British Museum', engraving, c. 1828. The façade of the King's Library, the first portion of Smirke's new British Museum to be completed, is now once again visible on the east side of the Great Court in the centre of the Museum. P&D.

been popular since the publication of the first volume of James 'Athenian' Stuart and Nicholas Revett's *Antiquities of Athens* for the Society of Dilettanti in 1762 (see ch. 16). But as the eighteenth century had progressed, so too had an enthusiasm for the notion of the pure and simplified Greek ideal, not only in aesthetics and culture but in society and political life as well, as the only way for people and nations to become truly great. Its greatest apologist, Winckelmann, located the

greatest achievements of Greek art and civilization during the era of the free city state of Periclean Athens, so that neoclassicism became associated in Britain with the revival of liberty and the arts – 'the culminating, revolutionary phase in that great outburst of human enquiry known as the Enlightenment'.[13]

But the new Library owed more than its style to the Age of Enlightenment. Advances in steam engines and iron foundry

39 The Western Colonnade of Smirke's new British Museum rising above the outbuildings of Old Montagu House. Watercolour by George Scharf the Elder (1788–1860), 1845. The artist was a Bavarian *émigré*, who made many drawings and watercolours of Montagu House and of the construction of the new British Museum. Archives.

40 Engraved view of the interior of the King's Library showing the columns and plasters of the central tribune and the relationship between the coffered ceiling and the parquet floor. A drugget of matting runs down the centre of the room, which is almost completely unfurnished. Engraving by Henry Shaw, 1834. P&D.

during the preceding century had laid the foundations for the Industrial Revolution and provided new technologies which might be utilized in architecture. Like its glorious Grecian prototypes, the new library was solidly built; C. W. Pasley, reviewing the construction in his *Course of Practical Architecture* (Chatham, 1826), noted how the walls were laid six bricks deep, with an especially lime-rich mortar and grouted with cement. Great care was taken to protect them from taking up damp, the building being raised upon a series of capacious vaulted cellars, used for storage and the heating system, running off a central spine corridor.[14] Unusually, the roof of the building was sheathed in copper, possibly on account of its reputed efficacy against lightning.[15] This was laid by Messrs Kepp, a firm Smirke used throughout his work of rebuilding. 'The material is so rarely used', the architect later told the Commissioners of Woods and Works, 'that I do not know of any other tradesman employed in such work except upon a very small scale'.

Internally, the ground floor of the new range was to contain one vast double-height room, with a gallery running around it at first-floor level, lined with bookcases (figs 40, 41). The room was 300 feet long and 41 feet wide, with a columned bay or tribune in the centre dividing it into three. It was also some 31 feet high, its ceilings supported on great cast-iron beams of extraordinary size and novel construction, produced by the ironfounder John Raistrick of Foster,

Raistrick & Co. of Stourbridge. At first Smirke hesitated over bridging the void with beams cast in one section, and proposed trussed girders composed of sections of cast and wrought iron, but he was reassured by Raistrick, who developed beams of flanged section up to 50 feet long. Rastrick later informed a Parliamentary Committee that they were 'the first beams that were ever introduced into London of so great a length and with large openings through the web of the beam'. Between the beams was laid a fireproof ceiling formed of arched plates of steel, 1/8 inch thick.[16]

On the floor above Smirke built a suite of smaller galleries which were originally intended to house the pictures from the Beaumont and Angerstein collections, the nucleus of the National Gallery (see ch. 2). In the end, however, these were diverted to Trafalgar Square and the empty rooms were reallocated for the display of the Museum's mineralogical and geological specimens with the Museum's collection of portrait paintings hung above. The upper floor was accessed by a staircase at the northern end of the range. Work on the construction of the new Library began in late 1823. The building took five years to complete and cost £130,000, just over Smirke's estimate of £129,200.[17]

The internal fitting-up of the King's Library was accomplished in the same spirit of imposing but austere magnificence as the external fabric of the building. The chief extravagance was the installation of four colossal columns of

41 The interior of the King's Library, looking north from the south balcony. Photograph by Donald Macbeth, 1912. Archives.

42 A view of the central tribune of the King's Library showing the tall exhibition case installed by Sir Antonio Panizzi at the time of the Great Exhibition. This was the first time the Library was opened to the general public. Many of the display cases are still in use today. Watercolour by Eugene A. Roy, Museum Assistant, Printed Books, c. 1851, recently presented to the Museum. Archives.

pinkish-grey Aberdeen granite whose role was to demarcate the central bays of the tribune (fig. 40). The shafts were purchased cheaply enough at £15 apiece, but the cost of polishing the monoliths – a laborious undertaking before the introduction of steam-powered polishing machines later in the century – raised the expense to £2,400.[18] This put paid to Smirke's original idea of having eight additional granite columns in four pairs projecting into the room and separating the two halves of the Library.[19] After toying with the idea of replacing them with pillars of exposed cast-iron, Smirke eventually decided upon pilasters – the four nearest the columns were faced with slabs of granite while the outer ones were revetted with white marble – handsome enough but hardly compensation for the proposed peristyle of gleaming

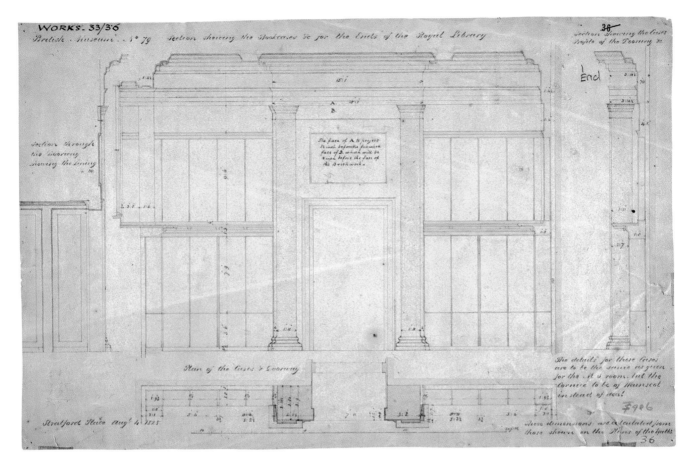

43 Design for the doorcase, commemorative inscription and bookcases at the north end of the King's Library, by Robert Smirke's office, 1825. Public Record Office.

granite shafts. Despite these economies, both the columns and the pilasters had Corinthian capitals carved from white Derbyshire alabaster and these, together with the yellow scagliola (resembling sienna marble), with which the walls between the pilasters were sheathed,[20] made the central tribune of the Library into a marmoreal setting of truly Roman grandeur (fig. 42).[21]

The two great halls that lay on either side were dominated by the tall bookcases of polished oak which rose from floor almost to the ceiling, broken at first-floor level by a gallery. The gallery balustrade was of polished brass and bore the sprightly wings or *talaria* of Hermes, messenger of the Gods, upon its reeded uprights (fig. 42). These elements were gilded and resemble a *caduceus*, the snake-twined wand of Mercury, which symbolized diligence and in modern times has become associated with the medical professions. To Smirke and his contemporaries, however, the *caduceus* bore another meaning, entirely appropriate to a room embodying the ideals of Greek simplicity and civilization designed to house the King's Library. To eighteenth-century scholars of ancient Athens, the *caduceus* was an attribute of the goddess Athena, symbol-

izing eloquence, one of the arts necessary to civilisation which had been her gift to the city which bore her name.[22]

Another masterful touch was the framing of the bookcases between the windows on the gallery with pilasters so as to make them appear like a vista of projecting *aedicules* or temple-fronts. Above each bookcase was a panel of yellow scagliola, continuing the theme established in the central tribune. At each end of the room were two imposing doors, 'ornamented with bronze, of a size commensurate with the grandeur of the room', each framed by consoles supporting a rich architrave (fig. 43).[23] These were dignified by surrounds of white marble enclosing gilded dedicatory inscriptions and were flanked by pilasters faced with white marble.

Smirke concentrated the decoration on the ceiling: the central tribune had the most elaborate plasterwork, a large circular panel with the crown and monogram of George IV forming the central boss, set within a monumental framework incorporating sunken panels of scrolling acanthus and other ornaments. The *caduceus* appears here yet again in the spandrels around the central panel (see fig. 42). The room was given a frieze and cornice of the richest description. The side gallery ceilings were slightly simpler, with plain circular panels surrounded by massive, sunken coffering. The floor followed the hierarchical arrangement of the ceiling plasterwork, the oak boards in the central tribune being laid in a lozenge-pattern parquet, while a simpler pattern prevailed in the wings, divided and bordered with inlaid mahogany stringing (see fig. 40). Smirke's intention must have been to call to mind the vast and elegant interior of an ancient Greek temple, perhaps even the Parthenon itself. There Athena the warrior, in the form of Phidias's towering chryselephantine statue, protected the treasury of the city: here in Smirke's great room, Athena the wise presided, rather more discreetly, through a myriad of *caducei*, the symbol of her gift of eloquence, over a vast temple of learning.

The books of the King's Library were originally shelved behind grilles of brass trellis, which, according to the *Gentleman's Magazine* for 1834, were equipped with 'locks of a new and singular construction by Barrow. The key which locks each case, shoots at the same time bolts above and below the "door".[24] It was only increased public access to the King's Library, and the dirt and dust of London, that necessitated the introduction of glazed doors in the 1850s. Originally there were few other furnishings in the room. The description of 1834 noted 'Down the sides of the room are placed at intervals large tables in which the maps are kept, some in rolls the length of the table, and others as long as the table's breath [*sic*] and also other atlases, charts and plans preserved in 125 immense portfolios' (see fig. 1).[25] This restraint in furnishing seems to have been deliberate, emphasizing the architectural qualities of the room that from the first was conceived as a showplace for the Royal gift, an exhibition of bibliomaniacal bounty for important visitors, rather than a working library. Gradually the great room accumulated additional furnishings, at first desks for the librarians and then exhibition cases, being opened as an exhibition space on a permanent basis only in 1857 at the insistence of Antonio Panizzi. E. Edwards, writing in 1870, asserted 'The floor cases and heavy tables – very needful, no doubt – have since detracted not a little from the architectural effect and elegance of the room itself'.[26]

All the ornamental plasterwork of the King's Library was painted a plain, uniform cream. At first only the central boss of the tribune ceiling and the inscriptions on the marble tablets over the doors at either end of the room were gilded; the gilded *caducei* and the burnished brass balustrade to the gallery that ran around the room must have struck an additional touch of opulence. In any case, when the late King's books were installed in the summer of 1828, the gilt lettering and tooling on the spines of George III's magnificent volumes must have handsomely made up for any deficiency in that respect. Indeed, the gilding, the subtle tints of the calf and morocco bindings of the books, together with the new-polished oak bookcases and joinery, the yellow scagliola and the pinkish granite, made this a 'golden gallery' – a characteristic still recognizable today and worthy of the encomium bestowed upon it by the *Gentleman's Magazine*: 'the encadrement of one of the most precious jewels ever attached to the Crown of England'.[27]

The King's Library has been described as Sir Robert Smirke's masterpiece, the only one of his works that has 'proved almost immune from criticism'.[28] Architecturally unexciting outside – and until recently almost wholly invisible thanks to the filling up of the British Museum courtyard with Panizzi's Round Reading Room and surrounding bookstacks – the lofty and dignified interior of the King's Library provides a vista of neoclassical magnificence that is unequalled in London. But it is also difficult to pin down its architectural antecedents, for, although simple in conception – it is, after all, a long, rectangular, galleried room divided into three sections – the King's Library bears no close resemblance to its nearest counterparts in England, the great university libraries in Cambridge and Oxford (see ch. 5).[29] It has been asserted that contemporary continental museums inspired Smirke's overall plan for the British Museum, notably Leo von Klenze's Glypothek in Munich (1816–30), and Karl Friedrich Schinkel's Altes Museum in Berlin (designed 1823, built 1825–8), but they can have had only limited influence on the interior of the King's Library, the earliest portion of the new museum to be realized (1823–7). Smirke himself, responding to questioning by the Select Committee on the British Museum in 1836, admitted examining the designs of other libraries and museums during the preparation of his own plans in 1821–3, but stated:

> there are none of the same description … in regard to the extent and variety of the collections …, and some of the best were not then built. The great buildings in Berlin and Munich were not then erected … The only Library I had seen possessing any character of architectural importance was the Imperial Library at Vienna, which is a room about 230 ft. long and more expressive and magnificent in its decoration than any room in the museum here.[30]

The Imperial Library – better known as the Hofbibliothek – is a great Baroque library, erected by J. B. Fischer von Erlach between 1722 and 1726. Although it may have encouraged Smirke to adopt the idea of a longitudinally planned library with naves flanking a central tribune, divided by screens of columns, it cannot be the sole prototype of the King's Library.

The origins of the King's Library must lie closer to home, in the architecture of the British age of Enlightenment. The chief, and most obvious, source of inspiration available to Smirke was the former home of George III's books at Buckingham House – then known as the Queen's House and what is now the present-day Buckingham Palace. Buckingham House was acquired by the Crown in 1762 for the accommodation of the young George III and his burgeoning family.[31] Works were almost immediately put in hand to update the stately, old-fashioned house, which had been built by William Winde for John Sheffield, first Duke of Buckingham, between 1702 and 1705. The architect entrusted with the job was William Chambers, then joint Architect of the Works and the

King's favourite architect and drawing master. In enlarging and modernizing Buckingham House, Chambers's main task was 'largely a matter of keeping pace with the King's insatiable bibliomania', which initially took the form of a southern extension comprising a 'Great' or 'West' Library, which was begun in 1762 (see fig. 32).[32] This lofty and imposing ground-floor room, which could be entered only via the King's bedchamber and thus remained very much within his personal domain, was completed in 1764. Though grandiose in scale, it was a simple room, at first fitted up with bookcases made by William Vile for William Kent's Queen's Library at St James's Palace, economically adapted 'with many Additions and Alterations'.[33] In keeping with 'Farmer George's' plebeian tastes, the plasterwork of the vaulted ceiling was also restrained, as was the chimneypiece. Over it, serving as an overmantel, was an ingenious wind dial by Benjamin Vulliamy, which enabled the King to 'follow what parts of the world are affected if a heavy gale is sweeping England … [and] conjecture how his fleet is faring'.[34]

As the King's book collection increased in size, so did its accommodation, and between 1766 and 1767 Chambers added two more capacious rooms to Buckingham House, the South and Octagon Libraries (see fig. 31). These followed the same austere architectural character of the Great Library and projected from it at right angles. Finally, in 1772–3, the single-storey East Library was inserted into the gap between the South Library and the main block of the house, being extended a year later by an additional floor, the 'Marine Gallery', to accommodate the King's collection of models of British ships and fortresses. Once again, the King personally supervised the planning and fitting-up of these rooms, even providing rough sketches to his architect of his requirements.

Later, the old Kentian bookcases in the Great Library were replaced with the simpler, floor-to-ceiling presses which are visible in James Stephanoff's watercolour of the room, and this is how Smirke, as heir to Chambers's post of Architect to the Office of Works, would have known it. Stephanoff's views of the Great and Octagon Libraries, reproduced as aquatints and published in W. H. Pyne's *History of the Royal Residences* (the first volume of which appeared in 1819), form a valuable record of the original home of the King's Library in Buckingham House, before it was swept away by John Nash's rebuilding of 1825–30. They show well how Smirke reproduced their essential character in the internal arrangements of the King's Library, and strongly suggest that they must have been an influence on the architect when it came to the planning of a new setting for the late King's books in Bloomsbury.

But there were also other, rather more potent, sources of inspiration available to Smirke for his new King's Library. Smirke had, as a young man, received his architectural training from the pioneering neoclassical architect George Dance the younger, acquiring a taste for the megalomaniac schemes of Giovanni Battista Piranesi and his contemporaries – including

Boullée and Durand – as well as for Dance's own brand of stripped-down classicism.[35] Indeed, this early exposure to sophisticated architectural ideas belies Smirke's reputation as a dull and conventional architect, who owed his reputation more to his reliable and meticulous business methods than to brilliance of invention. George Dance must have inherited a fondness for monumental halls from his father, the architect George Dance Senior, who built the Mansion House in London between 1739 and 1742, with its columned 'Egyptian Hall' after Palladio and Lord Burlington. In 1763, during his own architectural training in Italy, the younger Dance produced a design for 'a Public Gallery for Statues, Pictures, etc.' for which he won the Gold Medal from the Accademia di Belli Arti at Parma.[36] This design, with its severe exterior and succession of differently shaped halls within – rectangular, square, circular and cross-shaped, flowing into one another 'with screens of columns as intermediaries' – is said to have been an influence on Robert Adam's design for the third Earl of Bute's Library in Berkeley Square, London, the following year. This magnificent room, in its myriad incarnations, can almost certainly be counted as the germ of Smirke's King's Library.

John Stuart, third Earl of Bute, the friend and mentor of the young George III, and his unpopular chief minister from 1761 to 1763, was a great bibliophile – indeed, it was probably he who first fostered in the young prince a love for books and learning. In 1761, at the height of his political powers, Bute purchased a site off Berkeley Square on which to build a splendid townhouse.[37] He engaged as architect, Robert Adam, a fellow Scot, for whom he also procured one of the two newly created posts of Architect of the King's Works – the other going to Chambers. By 1764, plans for the house were well advanced and took the form of an elegant square house with a 'Great Library' extending out in a wing to the north to accommodate Bute's extensive and valuable collection of books. Adam's plan shows the Library as three large rooms, two octagonal pavilions flanking a three-bay rectangular core, linked by paired columned screens, while his beautiful coloured section shows full-height bookcases divided by pilasters, a gallery, and coved and domed ceilings enlivened with coffering (fig. 45).[38] It cannot be coincidental that at precisely the same time as Adam was engaged on designs for Bute's Great Library he was also working at Buckingham House, carrying out minor alterations in his capacity as joint Architect of the King's Works with Chambers. Adam's octagonal pavilions for Bute House are surely the inspiration for the Octagon Library erected by Chambers for George III in 1766–7. The tripartite form of Bute's Library may also have influenced the triple divisions (reversed as a central tribune flanked by galleries) later introduced in Smirke's design for the King's Library.

But Adam's Great Library was never executed for in 1765, by now disgraced and obliged to retire from London, Bute sold the site in Berkeley Square, together with Adam's design for the house, to William Petty, second Earl of Shelburne. Bute retired

44 *Design for a Library at Lansdowne House,* by Joseph Bonomi, in
pen, ink and watercolour, 1786. Bonomi's design would have combined
Lansdowne's famous collection of books and manuscripts with full-
scale ancient marbles supplied by the excavator and dealer Gavin
Hamilton. Gerald Goldie, Esq.

to Luton Hoo, his new estate in Bedfordshire, where he con-
soled himself commissioning Adam to devise yet more ambitious schemes for the accommodation of his enormous library,
all based on the sequence of interlocking rooms at Berkeley
Square.[39] At first Shelburne, also a bibliophile, persevered with
the scheme he had inherited for the huge Library behind the
house, and had Adam produce a second set of his coloured
design drawings for it.[40] However, in 1771 he went abroad to get
over the death of his wife and there became infected with a
passion for Antique statuary. Under the influence of Gavin
Hamilton, Lord Shelburne was persuaded to abandon the idea
of a library in favour of a great sculpture gallery, and designs
were supplied by the Italian architect Francesco Pannini on the
model of the Farnese Gallery in Rome.[41] In 1774 Shelburne
reverted to the Library scheme and a fresh design by Charles-
Louis Clerisseau was considered – but was also set aside. Years
later, in 1779, another Frenchman, François Belanger, proposed
a Sculpture Gallery, but again inanition prevailed. In 1786,
Shelburne, by now first Marquess of Lansdowne, returned to
the idea of a library and commissioned new designs from

Joseph Bonomi, a former assistant of Adam, whose perspective, exhibited at the Royal Academy in that year, shows a tripartite library divided by screens of Corinthian columns and
stocked with books and Antique sculpture (fig. 44).[42] This
scheme too came to nought. Finally, in 1792, Smirke's master
George Dance was commissioned to produce another proposal
for the library which followed the triple divisions of all the earlier schemes, taking the form of a barrel-vaulted rectangular
hall, apsed at both ends like some ancient Roman bath, with a
boldly coffered ceiling, its walls articulated with niches and
pilasters (fig. 46). It was this design that was eventually built,
for the third Marquess of Lansdowne in 1819, with modifica-
tions to transform it into a sculpture gallery after the sale of
the Lansdowne Manuscripts to the British Museum in 1807.[43]
The task of carrying out Dance's design was entrusted to his
rising disciple, Robert Smirke.

Smirke's Sculpture Gallery at Lansdowne House (fig. 47) –
which survived the demolition of that house in 1935 and
now lurks, mutilated and stripped of its statuary, at the back
of the present Lansdowne Club in Stratton Street – was very
much a dress rehearsal for his design for the King's Library
in the British Museum, begun four years later. The two
rooms share a common architectural character, and certain
motifs – notably the monumental coffered ceiling and the
restrained pilasters separating the triple divisions of the room
– occur in both interiors. These are combined with elements

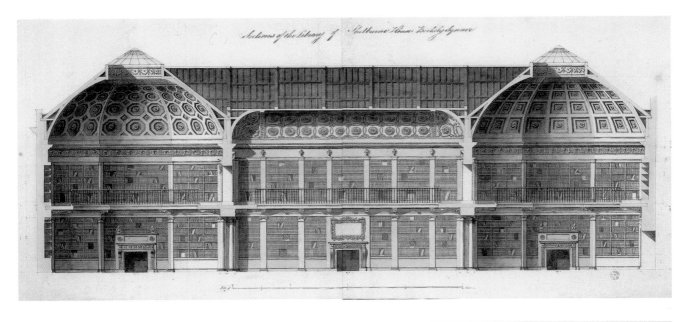

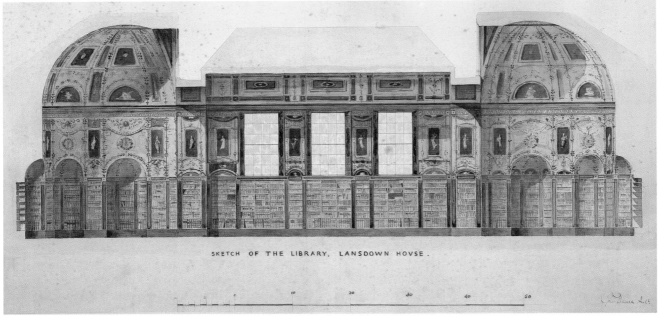

SKETCH OF THE LIBRARY, LANSDOWN HOVSE.

that might well have been culled from the other, unexecuted schemes for the library-sculpture gallery at Lansdowne House by Adam, Bonomi and the others that Smirke doubtless had access to amongst his patron's papers while carrying out the commission. Even if he did not consult the copies of the magnificent design for Bute's 'Great Library' that Adam executed for Lord Shelburne in 1765, Smirke must have seen the original presentation set at Luton Hoo where he worked for the second Marquess of Bute from 1816 onwards. It is almost as if Smirke has rearranged Dance's design, squaring it off and amplifying its scale, to provide maximum accommodation for the royal books. What is certain that only four years separates the execution of the Lansdowne House

45 Section of the 'Great Library' of Bute, later Lansdowne House, Berkeley Square, London, by Robert Adam, c. 1764. This magnificent design was never executed, but may have influenced George III's Octagon Library at Buckingham House (1766–7), the former home of the King's Library. Sir John Soane's Museum.

46 Design for the Library at Lansdowne House, Berkeley Square, London, by George Dance the Younger. A successor to Adam's scheme, which converted it into a Sculpture Gallery, was built by Robert Smirke in 1819 (fig. 47), almost a trial run for the King's Library, begun four years later. Sir John Soane's Museum.

47 The Sculpture Gallery at Lansdowne House, Berkeley Square, London, as executed by Robert Smirke in 1819. Photographed before the sales and mutilation of 1935. English Heritage: National Monument Record.

Gallery and the King's Library, and one must have influenced the other. Smirke's coyness over his sources of inspiration to the Select Committee in 1836 was probably due to the very proximity of its true origin, as well as to his master, Dance's, involvement in its design. Smirke's discretion was perhaps understandable, given the way John Nash had been hauled over the coals by no fewer than three Select Committees between 1828 and 1830, but it was unwarranted. The King's Library, whatever its dependence on the gallery at Lansdowne House, percolated through the filter of Adam, Clerisseau, Bonomi, and Dance, and distilled by the whims and indecision of Bute and Lansdowne, government parsimony and Smirke's own tendency towards 'urbane banality', is a noble and inspiring achievement of English neoclassicism and remains 'A perpetual monument of the munificence, judgement, and liberal taste of the Royal Founder'.[44]

The dual role of the gallery at Lansdowne House as a receptacle for both books and sculpture also helps explain the fitness of the King's Library for its new use as an exhibition gallery to illustrate the genesis of the varied collections of the British Museum. The architectural predecessors of the King's Library – notably the designs by Bonomi and Dance for libraries and sculpture galleries – all show large statues as an integral, if not essential, part of the proposed building, but at its inception Smirke's great Library housed nothing but books – the very tables upon which to consult them being admitted only on sufferance. This may have been because of George III's will, which strictly enjoined that his books be 'kept entire, and separate … in a repository to be appropriated exclusively for that purpose'. Gradually, however, additional furniture was introduced and then, probably after the Library was thrown open to the public in 1857, portrait busts of eminent men were added, culminating in the arrival of Roubiliac's statue of *Shakespeare* in recent times (see ch. 2). If something of the empty clarity of Smirke's grand vista was lost in the process, the King's Library gained a sculptural element it had formerly lacked. Libraries have, after all, traditionally been the setting for the display of sculpture and curiosities, from the profusely stocked *wunderkammer* of a Renaissance prince to the plaster busts and dusty Etruscan urns that adorned the bookrooms of countless English country houses (see ch. 5).[45] It is therefore not inappropriate that the former home of the King's Library, in its new incarnation as the dynamo of the British Museum, is again populated by sculpture – not only busts of illustrious men but Graeco-Roman gods, a brace of fantastical marmoreal confections by Giovanni Battista Piranesi, scientific instruments and massed displays of objects – natural and artificial – that illustrate every facet of the encyclopaedic aims and collections of this great institution.

5 Ancient glory and modern learning: the sculpture-decorated library

THORSTEN OPPER

It occurs to me, however, that a library may be ornamented with statues and busts so as to form something elegant and beautiful.[1]

48 The courtyard of the Palazzo Sassi, Rome, drawing by Marten van Heemskerk, c. 1535. The sculpture on the right was once thought to be the Hermes now in the British Museum. Kupferstichkabinett, Staatliche Museen zu Berlin – Preussischer Kulturbesitz.

A defining characteristic of the Enlightenment was the vastly increased output of books and the greatly enlarged reading public. Books and journals became the prime media for scholarly debate and the dissemination of knowledge. At the same time the number of readers reached unprecedented heights and encompassed a much wider social spectrum than ever before.[2] Inevitably, this had a profound effect on libraries, which in some aspects can be regarded as key venues of Enlightenment culture.

Existing collections, particularly of the universities, were considerably expanded to cope with the massive influx of books, often prompting the introduction of new decorative schemes. More importantly, this period saw a vast increase in the number of private libraries: they now became standard, indeed mandatory, in the houses of nobles and other gentlemen and soon were focal points of social interaction within the house.[3] It was in the libraries, therefore, that important statements about social status or aspirations were made, and both an individual's and an institution's place within enlightened society was negotiated. The number and quality of books was only one element within this process; suitably grand furnishings and a carefully conceived iconographic programme built around paintings and statuary were of almost equal importance.

Formulated first by grand institutions and wealthy patrons, certain patterns for appropriate styles soon emerged and were effortlessly passed down the social ladder. As a result, most libraries during the eighteenth century contained sculpture of some sort: portraits of famous ancients or contemporaries and, increasingly, specimens of antique sculpture in the form of originals or copies such as casts. It was a truly European phenomenon, and a visitor to any library in Britain, France, Germany or any other country would have encountered familiar principles of decoration.

If the Age of the Enlightenment thus produced some of the most splendid and ornate libraries ever built, this was only the culmination of a long and dynamic process in which the relationship between books and sculptures was continuously redefined. After the rigorous clear-out advocated in the seventeenth century, Britain perhaps pioneered the fashion for reintroducing the display of ancient marbles in library spaces, just as it led the way in the vogue for ancient sculpture in general, fuelled by that most British of institutions, the Grand Tour. Whereas earlier sculpture usually had played a subservient role to books, it was now that some amateur scholars had their libraries built around their statues both in a physical sense and in terms of the selection of books that chiefly served to illuminate the ancient context of their prized marbles. After all, this was the epoch that made an instant best-seller of such books as Joseph Spence's *Polymetis: or An Enquiry Concerning the Agreement Between the Works of the Roman Poets, and the Remains of the Antient Artists: Being an Attempt to Illustrate them Mutually from One Another* of 1747. In Britain Spence's treatise sold more copies than Winckelmann's epochal 1764 *History of the Art of Antiquity*, written, perhaps not coincidentally, when the latter was employed as librarian by the foremost collector in eighteenth-century Rome, Cardinal Albani.[4]

The prominent display of ancient sculptures and eighteenth- or early nineteenth-century portrait busts in the former King's Library in the British Museum is ideally suited to reflect the depth and variety of Enlightenment attitudes to libraries as spaces reflecting both a certain social order and the generation of knowledge. The following survey aims to set out briefly the role of sculpture in libraries over a wider period. Through some of the institutions and personalities involved, this has a direct bearing on the changing perceptions of ancient sculpture from the seventeenth to the early nineteenth century and on the collections of the Museum itself.

LIBRARIES AND SCULPTURE FROM ANTIQUITY TO THE EIGHTEENTH CENTURY

The idea of displaying sculpture in libraries was of course by no means new. Its beginnings go back to classical antiquity, where libraries had developed out of the annexed porticoes of sanctuaries that were rich in statuary.[5] Pliny the Elder, writing in the first century AD, stated that 'likenesses ... are set up in the libraries in honour of those whose immortal spirits speak to us in the same places'. This innovation he attributed to Asinius Pollio, founder of the first public library in Rome under the Emperor Augustus. The practice may already have been common long before in the greatest libraries of the ancient world, those at Alexandria and Pergamon. To the Pergamene library its modern excavators have assigned a colossal statue of the goddess Athena, together possibly with images of writers and thinkers of which some remnants have been found. The sanctuary itself was decorated with sculptures in great number, sometimes described as a veritable 'museum' of classical Greek statuary assembled by Pergamon's Hellenistic kings through purchase or booty. Although much of this is open to debate, the key elements can certainly be found later in libraries of the Roman world. There a statue of Athena (Roman Minerva) or the founder, be it an emperor or local magnate, would invariably dominate the reading room, and portraits of literary worthies must have been common.

In the West this tradition was largely broken through the dominance of the church. The Vatican Library, unsurprisingly, is decorated with fresco cycles extolling the lives of the saints, not pagan statues. Only in the *studiolo* or *wunderkam-*

mer of the Renaissance scholar or prince did sculptures and books come to be reunited in one room again. It was the rarity of both that lent them their character as curiosities, most suitably displayed together. When books and ancient marbles increased in number, they were invariably divided and transferred to designated libraries and galleries. The nobles of Renaissance Rome set the tone, displaying antique sculpture in the courtyards and gardens of their palaces as their ancient predecessors had done (fig. 48). Wealth was the decisive factor, for a spatial division was necessary only where both books and sculptures were acquired in quantity, and often sculpture galleries and libraries would be immediately adjacent. The Republic of Venice, crucially important as Europe's gateway to the East, eventually displayed its public collection of ancient sculpture, the *Statuario Pubblico*, in the antechamber of the Serenissima's main library.[6]

In Britain this process lasted well into the seventeenth century, for even in the 1650s books in private households were few in number and often kept in chests.[7] In spite of this gradual break-up of the old-style cabinet, the newly furnished libraries often did retain some form of sculptural decoration, for which humanist scholars sought to formulate some basic rules with recourse to ancient writers. The earliest treatise of this kind is Justus Lipsius's *De bibliothecis syntagma* of 1602. Essentially written to induce a local duke to make his valuable book collection the nucleus of a new academy open to scholars for study, it examines all the evidence on ancient libraries preserved in written sources, with one chapter devoted entirely to the display of sculpture.[8] Lipsius particularly recommended the use of images of writers and thinkers, as attested by Pliny and others, to serve as a visual cue to a library's holdings and an inspiration to readers.

A telling example of this rigorous abolition of the old *wunderkammer* concept in the wake of increasing wealth and specialist scholarly interest is the collection of the Cardinal Giulio Mazarin in the early seventeenth century. Although he was of humble background and initially not able to indulge his taste for expensive books, paintings and antiques, the steady advancement of his career eventually allowed him to gather an amazingly varied collection in his house in Rome. The library, consisting of more than five thousand beautifully bound volumes, was kept in ornate gilded cupboards surmounted by a plethora of vases, busts and other antiques. With Mazarin's move to Paris and the important role he played within the French political hierarchy, a much different mode of display was called for. The sculptures were gathered in a grand gallery, while under the stewardship of the scholar Gabriel Naudé the library was massively expanded and opened to the public. On the basis of this experience Naudé wrote his *Advis pour dresser une bibliothèque* (1627), a set of basic instructions for the running of a library aimed at wealthy collectors that contains important comments on the use of sculpture in such a space.[9] For both Naudé and like-minded specialists, books and their contents were the most important, that is, the quality of their editions, the breadth of the subjects covered, not ornate bindings or grand furnishings. Sculpture ought to play a subordinate role. Naudé thus wrote explicitly: 'nor is there any point in seeking out and amassing in a library all the pieces and fragments of odd statues since it is enough for us to have good copies carved or cast of those which portray the most famous literary men'. Other manuals, such as Claude Clément's *Musei sive bibliothecae extructio* of 1635, followed in the same vein: images of literary worthies were to complement what could be gauged from their writings, and were meant to spur on the audience to achieve similar merit, while the display of other sculpture was to be eschewed. Thus a canon of worthy subjects was established, among them Homer, Hippocrates, Aristotle, Pindar, Virgil and Cicero. Soon rulers were added to this list, first Roman Caesars and then contemporaries. In Britain Robert Cotton, whose choice collection of important manuscripts eventually found its way into the British Museum, had his book presses surmounted by portraits of the Caesars along with Faustina and Cleopatra.

The sculpture-decorated library of the Enlightenment evolved gradually out of these seventeenth-century predecessors. Portrait sculpture continued to be of great importance, and it speaks for the profound confidence of the new 'Augustan Age' that the established canon was now expanded to include contemporaries considered equal in stature to their ancient predecessors. Within a short space of time in the middle of the eighteenth century, when the British Museum was founded, three colleges of famous universities in the British Isles put in place ambitious iconographic programmes in their libraries, all containing a mixture of established ancients, a new canon of contemporaries and individual founders, patrons and fellows. These were the library of Trinity College in Dublin, the Codrington Library at Oxford, and the Wren Library of Trinity College, Cambridge, perhaps the most grandiose example.[10] Busts of men such as Newton and Locke proudly staked the university's claim to important scientific discoveries of the recent past and the promotion of modern thought, and served to visualize the college's own institutional history.

This specific use of portrait sculpture is now exactly paralleled in the display of images of the founding figures of the British Museum in the former King's Library, the busts of Hans Sloane and Robert Cotton chief among them. Indeed, this is the first time that all these busts have been be found together in the finest room of the Museum (see ch. 2).

Individuals similarly could express their intellectual affiliations through the choice of portrait sculpture in their libraries. Alexander Pope, bard of the English Enlightenment and famed for his translation of Homer, adorned his library with busts of Homer, Newton, Spenser, Dryden, Milton, Shakespeare, Inigo Jones and Palladio. Pope's own portrait,

carved in stone by the leading portrait sculptors of the eighteenth century in Britain, M. Rysbrack and L.-F. Roubiliac, soon became a staple of library sculpture itself.

THE IMPACT OF THE GRAND TOUR

Much more dramatic, however, was the ever-increasing influx into Britain of ancient marbles during the eighteenth century, fuelled chiefly by the Grand Tour. This transformed particularly the private libraries of those involved and provided a clear break with the principles proposed only a century before.

Collecting of ancient sculpture had started late in Britain, and its first phase in the early seventeenth century proved short-lived, centred as it was on the Catholic court of Charles I. Still, it set the precedent for what was to follow on a massive scale in the following century.[11] Thomas Howard, Earl of Arundel and Surrey (1585–1646), later described by Horace Walpole as the 'Father of Vertu' in England, built up a large collection closely modelled on Italian fashions of display, but with sculpture gathered by special agents from the entire eastern Mediterranean. Henry Peacham, under the fine example set by the virtuoso collecting of his patron Arundel, felt obliged to add a section on antiquities, statues, and medals to the second imprint of his treatise, the *Compleat Gentleman*, in 1634. His book proved highly influential over the next two centuries and marks the beginning of the English aristocracy's passion for ancient sculpture.

The golden age of British collecting followed in the eighteenth century. One of the pioneers of this phenomenon was Thomas Coke, Earl of Leicester.[12] After inheriting a grand Norfolk estate, at the age of fourteen he embarked on a Grand Tour to Italy that lasted for six years. After his return work began on Holkham Hall, his Norfolk country seat, built in Palladian style by Matthew Brettingham the Elder. The architect's son, the younger Brettingham, was sent to Rome to acquire further marbles which eventually were displayed at Holkham in state rooms and a grand sculpture gallery that rivalled the palaces of Roman nobles. The library at Holkham did not fall behind, for under the guidance of his tutor, an avid manuscript collector, Leicester had acquired books and manuscripts on his grand tour as well as antiques. At Holkham, casts of sculptures representing Venus, Cybele, a Vestal Virgin and Alexander Pope surmounted the book presses in the Long Library. The South Tribune, adjacent to the statue-filled Sculpture Gallery and North Tribune, had book presses added in its niches that were surmounted by marble busts of Roman emperors and their families. The presses held beautifully bound folios mostly on antiquities and the sites of ancient Rome, 'for use in company', for here one would retreat for learned discussion of the marbles next door.

If the imperial imagery in the South Tribune was not unusual, then the use of casts of ancient ideal statuary in the Long Library pointed to an important new development, and

49 *Sir Rowland and Lady Winn in the Library, Nostell Priory*, oil painting by Hugh Douglas Hamilton, 1767. Designed by Robert Adam in 1766, the library with its books on classical monuments and plaster copies of ancient sculpture is intended to evoke the Grand Tour. By kind permission of the Winn Family and the National Trust.

we are fortunate to have archival material that elucidates the matter. With keen business acumen, the Brettinghams had sensed a market in the supply of appropriate busts to Grand Tourists who after their return home wanted to decorate their houses with visible tokens of their exploits. Casts of ancient statuary from the main collections, such as the Tribuna in Florence and the Belvedere in Rome, rather than being merely ornamental, provided physical proof of the intellectual conquest of antiquity, in theory at least the main premise of the Tour. After initially buying sets of finished casts, the younger Brettingham then, at considerable difficulty and expense, acquired moulds for twelve antique statues and sixty antique portrait busts, many of them of Greek philosophers and poets and thus suitable for libraries. Hence the Brettinghams thought to supply the burgeoning English market.

One of their (as it turned out very few) customers was Nathaniel Curzon at Kedleston Hall, his country seat designed by Robert Adam. While full-length casts of famous statues were shown in a sculpture gallery, seven busts were put on library shelves. The library design at Kedleston is typical of Adam's work in the 1750s and 1760s, and can be encountered similarly in a number of other houses.[13] A painting by H. D. Hamilton of 1767 depicting Sir Rowland and Lady Winn in the Library at Nostell Priory (fig. 49), illustrates how the classical past was conjured up through casts of famous sculptures that one would have encountered on the Grand Tour.[14] Alternatively, one could display original marbles acquired in Italy, as did the second Lord Berwick in his library at Attingham Park.[15]

By contrast Horace Walpole's famous gothic library in his house at Strawberry Hill is usually considered the model for an important alternative mode of library decoration at the time. Dominated by book presses that imitate the sombre forms of medieval Nordic architecture, it is decidedly non-classical in character (fig. 50). Yet even this space was not entirely without ancient sculpture, for on the floor

between the presses there are Roman cinerary chests, chosen undoubtedly for their strong geometrical quality and obvious architectural character, that subtly complement the bookcases.

By the latter half of the eighteenth century the admiration of ancient art had effectively become a shared language that transcended political and cultural boundaries. In Rome Pope Pius II vigorously built up the Vatican's collection of ancient marbles in the newly founded Museo Pio-Clementino that proved highly influential in its methods of display.[16] It was on this shared classical ground that foreign sovereigns, among them many northern Protestants, were received. With this sort of Papal sanction, the clerics of the Chapter of Cambrai in France could put classical reliefs as well as a statue of the pagan goddess Athena in the centre of their library without causing offence.[17]

British libraries in the Adams' style were fairly standard in that the sculptures consisted mostly of busts, chosen from a well-established canon, that were surmounted on the book presses. Quite a different matter was the library of the serious collector, Charles Townley. A Catholic educated mostly in France, Townley had embarked on his first Grand Tour of Italy in 1767–8.[18] The top-lit library in his new house in Park Street, Westminster, served as the focal point of his extensive collection of ancient sculptures. This was not the usual gentleman's collection of books but a veritable research apparatus. Johann Zoffany's well-known painting shows Townley in

50 *Horace Walpole in the Library at Strawberry Hill*, engraving after a watercolour of 1756 by J. H. Muntz. Walpole pioneered the gothic style of library decoration, but his library also contained some ancient sculpture, including the sepulchral chests seen here. Courtesy of The Lewis Walpole Library Print Collection, Yale University.

51 Charles Townley (right), Baron d'Hancarville (centre), Charles Greville and Thomas Astle (both standing) in the Library of Townley's house in Park Street, oil painting by Johann Zoffany, 1781–98. Zoffany introduced key sculptures from other rooms (see figs 162–3) into this image of Townley's library to stress its function as intellectual centre for antiquarian research. Townley Hall, Burnley, Lancashire.

the circle of his friends discussing ancient sculpture in the library (fig. 51). Many of the sculptures represented in the painting were in fact displayed in other parts of the house but depicted by Zoffany in the library to underline the central importance of this room as the prime venue for scholarship and learned debate. Central in the group is the Baron d'Hancarville, a brilliant if controversial scholar employed by Townley for a while as librarian. In was in this environment that d'Hancarville wrote his *Recherches sur l'origine, l'esprit et les progrès des arts de la Grèce* (see ch. 16). Townley's house was open to the public by appointment, and soon became one of the main attractions in London.

At the time Townley built up his stock of ancient marbles in Park Street, yet another collector, the Earl of Shelburne, later first Marquis of Lansdowne, set out to acquire marbles in great style. His aim was, in the words of his agent at Rome, Gavin Hamilton, to gather 'a collection that will make Shelburne House famous not only in England but all over Europe'.[19] Hamilton, of course, also supplied Charles Townley, who proved to be a far more discerning client than Shelburne. The first designs for Lansdowne House (see figs 45, 46) envisaged a sculpture gallery very closely modelled on the famous Renaissance Gallery in the Farnese Palace, Rome (fig. 52).[20] Two ancient statues from the Farnese collection, a Hermes (fig. 53) and a Faun with infant Bacchus (fig. 54), were acquired by the British Museum in the nineteenth century and are now among the marbles on display in the former King's Library. The fact that original statues of the highest quality appropriate for a grand overall decorative scheme were required for Lansdowne House led to long delays in the realization of the project. Hamilton had to wait to see if his excavations in the vicinity of Rome would yield something suitable, for which he then needed an export licence from the Papal authorities. In the meantime Shelburne had acquired a large collection of books and manuscripts, so that the plans had to be changed in order to accommodate the marbles in what was now predominantly to become a library.[21] A beautiful design was drawn up by Joseph Bonomi (fig. 44). Ironically, Bonomi also worked on proposals for Townley, who for lack of space in his town

Veduta della Galleria dipinta da Annibale Carracci e suoi Scolari

52 *Interior of the Farnese Gallery, Rome*, engraving by Giovanni Volpato after Annibale Carracci. Designed in the 1580s, the gallery integrated choice specimens of ancient sculpture with specially commissioned paintings into a powerful iconographic programme. The statue in the first niche to the left is the Faun in fig. 54; the Farnese Hermes (fig. 53) stood in the fourth niche. P&D.

53 Farnese Hermes, marble, 2nd century AD, h. 201 cm. Many sculptures from the Farnese collection were brought to Naples in the 18th century where they would have been seen in the royal collection by numerous Grand Tourists. GR.

54 Faun with the infant Bacchus, marble, 2nd century AD, h. 171 cm. This sculpture and the Farnese Hermes were purchased from the King of Naples in the 19th century. GR.

house – the sculptures had spilled over from the library to all parts of the house (see figs 162–3) – considered the transfer of his marbles to a designated sculpture gallery to be built at his country seat. Bonomi's design for Lansdowne was not executed, and after the sale of Lansdowne's manuscript collection (acquired by the British Museum in 1807) it became redundant. In the end the plan reverted to a pure sculpture gallery, executed between 1815 and 1819 by Robert Smirke, the British Museum's chief architect (see fig. 47). Bonomi's design lives on in the former King's Library, for Smirke's grand concept and fine detailing are clearly not entirely uninfluenced by it, and this uncanny similarity is now heightened through the prominent display of sculptures.

While Townley and Lord Lansdowne brought together their collections in London, the evolution of classical archaeology from the private pursuit of the wealthy dilettante into a serious academic discipline found its first formal expression at Göttingen, the main university of King George's German Electorate of Hanover. There, three years after the publication of Winckelmann's *History*, Christian Gottlob Heyne in 1767 held for the first time his *Academic Lecture on the Archaeology of Art in Antiquity*. Director since 1763 of Göttingen's famous University Library – the prototypical universal library of the Enlightenment (see ch. 4) – Heyne now began to acquire casts of classical sculptures to complement his lectures. These were held in the library, where the casts, among them the Laocoon and pieces from Townley's collection in London, as well as a few originals, were exhibited (fig. 34).[22]

A similar arrangement of sculptures in an important library space almost came about at Oxford. In the 1750s Sir Roger Newdigate had given casts of the Belvedere Apollo and the Medici Venus to the Bodleian Library.[23] In 1777 two marble candelabra, acquired by Newdigate on his second Grand Tour two years before, were installed in Wren's Radcliffe Camera in Oxford. They had been excavated by Gavin Hamilton in 1769 and restored by Piranesi. They are grand decorative pieces of the sort that found a ready market in England, and similar pieces can also be found in the new displays in the former King's Library (fig. 55). Crucially, however, it seems that this was only part of a wider plan on Newdigate's part to create a veritable museum of ancient sculpture in the Tribuna-like ambience of the Radcliffe Camera. Remarkably, this would have included the remnants of the Arundel marbles, which had come to Oxford via the collection of Lord Pomfret. In the end the university declined, no doubt prompted by the fragmentary state of many of the Arundel pieces that went against contemporary fashion. Equally problematic was their eastern Mediterranean origin, for among them were many Greek originals rather than the copies of established classical works that came to light in the environs of Rome and dominated contemporary taste. Only a generation later was the plan for a library-cum-gallery in the Radcliffe realized. From 1818 a pair of benefactors, the

55 The Piranesi Vase, marble, 2nd century AD, with 18th-century additions, h. 271.8 cm. Piranesi's workshop specialized in decorative sculptures, often made up of both ancient and modern elements, for the Grand Tour market. GR.

Duncan Brothers, gave marble busts and casts to be displayed there. These were fully in accordance with the established canon, as a guidebook of 1828 indicates: among them could be found the Laocoon, Apollo Belvedere, Diana and the Fawn, and several pieces from the Townley collection, namely his Venus, Clytie and Discoboulus (fig. 56).[24]

The Townley Marbles were prime examples of the sort of Roman works after famous classical Greek originals that had graced the villas of Rome's elite particularly in the first and second centuries AD. But in the British Museum, and indeed in British taste, they were soon to be eclipsed by the advent of the Parthenon sculptures. Brought from Athens by Lord Elgin and acquired for the nation in 1816, these original fifth-century BC works of the highest quality provoked an intense debate about their relative value as art and ultimately led to the devaluation of the Roman marbles brought to Britain in the previous century. Casts of the Elgin marbles that challenged the traditional canon were notably absent in the library at Oxford, but in Göttingen the new discoveries were readily embraced. The loose display of sculptures throughout the library eventually proved unsatisfactory for teaching purposes. As a result, in 1823 one room was divided off from the rest of the library and fitted as a designated gallery for the entire cast collection. To this were proudly added the casts of the Elgin marbles donated to the university by George IV in 1830.

THE BRITISH MUSEUM

In conclusion it may be useful to remember that the British Museum itself had started out essentially as a grand library, with a miscellany of antiquities and natural history specimens added to the collection of books – fittingly, the Director's official title for a very long time was that of 'Principal Librarian'.

As early as 1697 Richard Bentley had proposed a scheme for a *Free Library* based on the royal collection and adorned 'with marbles ... ancient inscriptions, basso-relievos etc.',[25] and in 1707 Hans Sloane projected a public library based on the libraries of Sir Robert Cotton, the Society of Antiquaries and the Royal Library. Nothing came of these plans, but when the British Museum was finally founded in 1753 it very much consisted of the libraries of Cotton, Robert Harley, first Earl of Oxford, and the collection of Sir Hans Sloane himself. The entire ground floor of old Montagu House, the Museum's first home, was reserved for books, drawings, maps etc., while the upper floor was equally divided between manuscripts, medals and coins on one side, and 'natural and artificial productions' on the other, reflecting the Museum's three original departments. The few antiquities of the original collection were thus displayed among the natural history specimens, and as a consequence the entire Museum resembled an old-style library with adjacent curiosity cabinet, albeit on a grand scale. It was only gradually that the balance between antiquities and items of the natural world changed. In 1772

Sir William Hamilton's magnificent collection of ancient vases and other antiquities was acquired, in 1802 Egyptian sculptures arrived from Alexandria, followed after Charles Townley's death in 1805 by the Townley marbles.[26] To house

these treasures the Townley Gallery, an extension to old Montagu House, was built and a new Department of Antiquities founded. Yet in spite of this the Museum's character as a national library with added art collections was to remain for much longer: in 1823 George IV donated his father's library to the nation, and Robert Smirke built the King's Library as first wing of the new Museum building.

56 *Interior of the Radcliffe Camera, Oxford,* engraving by John Keux after drawing by F. Mackenzie, for James Ingram's *Memorials of Oxford,* c. 1835. The Radcliffe Camera combined Grand Tour marbles with casts of famous classical sculptures in a library setting. Bodleian Library.

57 *Interior of the Queen's Library at Frogmore,* coloured aquatint by W. J. Bennett after watercolour by C. Wild, from W. H. Pyne's *History of the Royal Residences,* 1819. Unlike the King's Library which occupied four large rooms designed for the purpose in Buckingham House, the Queen's private library at Frogmore was decorated with busts on plinths and on top of the cases. P&D.

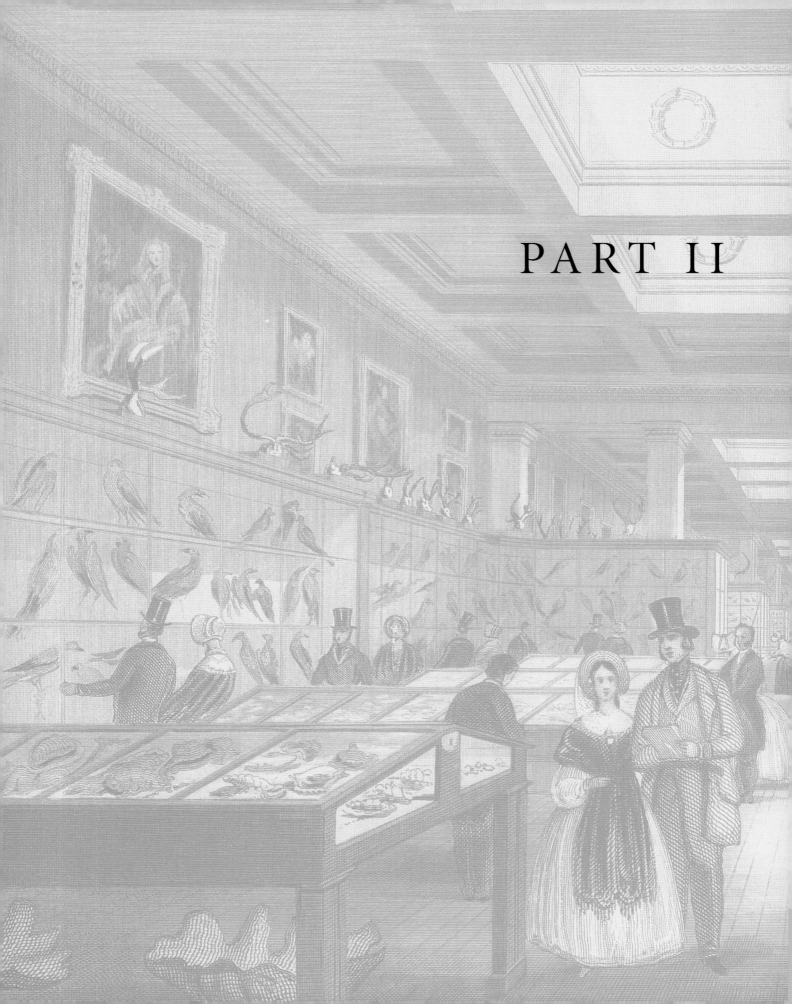

PART II

The Natural World

6

Challenging the dogma: classifying and describing the natural world

ROBERT HUXLEY

Order is Heaven's first law.

Alexander Pope

59 Copy of the Greek physician Dioscorides's *De materia medica*, used as the standard medical work up to the Middle Ages. This copy, made in 1460, is from the collection of Sir Joseph Banks. Natural History Museum, Library.

This and the following three chapters consider the explosion of interest in the natural world in Britain during the Enlightenment. By the second half of the seventeenth century the received wisdom of the ancients such as Aristotle and Pliny was being challenged by experimentalist followers of philosophers such as Francis Bacon and René Descartes. The long eighteenth century's burgeoning interest in the natural world, and the discovery of many new species of animals and plants during increasingly wide-ranging voyages to new parts of the world, resulted in a period dominated by the description and collection of natural objects – the creation of a vast empirical 'database' – which gradually shifted in its emphasis towards explaining as well as describing the diversity of life, past and present. By the nineteenth century, firm ground had been laid for the modern sciences of classification and description – taxonomy and systematics[1] – and the main elements that led to the first credible theory of evolution. Two strands flowed concurrently throughout: first, natural history collecting and its social and scientific context and, second, theorizing about and understanding the natural world. The interests of individual collectors and natural scientists of the time were very wide and covered many disciplines from botany to zoology, geology and mineralogy; indeed, it was during this period that the foundations for such modern specialist disciplines were laid.

Chapter 6 discusses the ways in which the living world was described, named and classified during the Enlightenment. The focus is largely, though not exclusively, on botany, the one field in which much useful groundwork had already been laid by earlier students of natural history, and the one in which some of the greatest advances were to be made during this period. Chapter 7 considers the social, scientific and increasingly profitable activities associated with collecting and preserving living objects, and the men and women whose collecting led to the creation of the British Museum (part of which eventually became the Natural History Museum). Chapters 8 and 9 look at early Enlightenment ideas on the origin and age of the earth and the attempts to classify and understand the underlying structure of minerals and fossils – the birth of the scientifically based disciplines of geology and palaeontology.

ARISTOTLE AND THE FIRST NATURAL HISTORIANS

The first natural scientists in the modern sense were ancient Greeks. Despite their limited use of scientific methods of theory and experiment and without the body of knowledge that we have inherited, they arrived at some conclusions not far from those we accept today. Aristotle's (384–322 BC) writings were to condition western thinking well into the eighteenth century. He firmly believed that the way to understand the universe was through observation, describing and classifying the animals of his Mediterranean world and, through the collecting of his pupil, Alexander the Great, the exotic faunas and floras of more distant lands. He believed that animals fell into natural groups, roughly equivalent to our genus and species. He used what he called 'essential traits' to form these groups much as today we would define species and genera. This philosophy, in which all objects are perceived to have a defining essence and which could best be understood by reasoning rather than experimentation, was to condition future western scientific thought and hold back scientific development well into the eighteenth century.

The tradition of Aristotle was followed by the Romans Dioscorides (AD 40–c. 90) (fig. 59) and Pliny the Elder, whose thirty-seven-volume *Natural History* attempted to summarize all knowledge of the natural world. But after the fall of Rome and the turbulent times that followed, religion became more influential and important than the study of what would now

history became a mish-mash of misinformation, mythology, fabrication and, only occasionally, accurate observation. With the decline of the ancient world and the loss of the Greek texts on which Pliny had so heavily depended, his *Natural History* became a substitute for a general education in the European Middle Ages.

Dioscorides' text was also a standard, but it was far too detailed and impenetrable for the average herbalist who really needed a simple guide to identifying relevant plants, their locations and properties. From this need arose the herbal, a collection of plant illustrations with text outlining the plants' uses with its legendary and magical properties.

By the end of the sixteenth century a number of works had been published describing the form of plants and animals, such as Conrad Gesner's *Historiae animalium* (fig. 60) – but scepticism was increasing and one critic complained that his contemporaries might argue about how many teeth a horse had from consulting the ancient texts when all they had to do was look in a horse's mouth! It was in this environment that

60 Rhinoceros, woodcut engraving (based on a print by Dürer) from Conrad Gesner's *Historiae animalium*, 1601, p. 953. Gesner established the importance of illustrations and actual specimens to make clear precisely what organism a name was being applied to. Natural History Museum, Library.

be regarded as science. Original thought was effectively stifled until the fifteenth century. The scholars who kept alive the traditions of Aristotle were firmly bound by the Church's doctrine, and attempts to consider the 'why and how' were answered with mystical or religious explanations. Scientific enquiry was treated with gravest suspicion and its practitioners risked being accused of necromancy or lunacy. Natural

natural scientists began to study plants and animals for their own properties rather than for their usefulness to humans.

One of the most significant botanical publications of the century was the Italian botanist Caesalpino's (1519–1603) *De plantis* (1583), in which some fifteen hundred plant species were classified. Some of his plant groupings are basically the same today. Caesalpino followed Aristotle, however, in assuming an *essence* to connect a group and mainly used a limited set of reproductive structures, which he believed best expressed the essence, as a basis for grouping plant species.

OBSERVATION AND EXPERIMENT:
TAXONOMY IN THE SEVENTEENTH CENTURY

The English statesman and philosopher Francis Bacon (1561–1626) believed that the only scientific method for understanding the world was to amass observations and to theorize on the basis of these – 'putting the question to nature' – rather than repeating the works of Aristotle and others. He also saw the value of gathering negative results to disprove a theory. Bacon was a practical man as well as a theorist and carried out experiments himself on seed germination and the uses of manure.

There were practical as well as philosophical problems presented by the inadequacy of descriptions of the living world, and this was exemplified by the considerable controversy of the time regarding quinine and its effectiveness against malaria. Much of the confusion was probably due to misidentification of the cinchona tree from which quinine is extracted. It is self-evident that without an adequate description one could not be sure that one was using the right tree. This kind of problem and the ability of taxonomists to assist remains a strong justification for the existence of taxonomy to this day.

The challenge then to the natural historians of the seventeenth and eighteenth centuries was to bring order not only to the known living world but also to the vast numbers of new species being discovered by voyages of exploration. In 1600 there were around six thousand known plant species but by 1700, at the dawn of the great age of exploration, it had doubled to twelve thousand. This influx of new species and genera that required systematic description was a spur to the development of a universal and workable system of classification and taxonomy.

In *The New Atlantis*, Bacon's blueprint for a Utopian society, he proposed that scientific research should be a collaborative effort, and academies soon sprang up all over Europe, especially in Italy. But during the first half of the seventeenth century in Britain the hazards of travel, the way that scientists generally worked on their own and political instability made the formation of such societies difficult. However, in the 1650s, during the Commonwealth period, a group of scientists began to meet informally in Oxford and London at colleges, taverns and private homes. In 1660 this group became more formal, meeting regularly at Gresham College in London, and in 1662 received a charter from Charles II as the Royal Society for the Improvement of Natural Knowledge. The Fellows met weekly to discuss scientific topics and witness experiments, and several members used the society and its publications as a means of spreading the philosophy of 'mechanisms'.[2]

Robert Hooke (1635–1703) had been appointed Curator of Experiments of the Society with responsibility for presenting experiments and demonstrations at meetings. His major contribution to natural history was his *Micrographia* (1665). Ostensibly a publication relating to his microscopic observations, it also outlined 'mechanism' – a philosophy which saw the world as a pocket-watch-like machine put together by God, 'the Great Mechanic', and which had its roots in the writings of Galileo and others of more than a century before.

Hooke saw evidence of mechanisms in the smallest things: '[in animals] we shall find, not only most curiously compounded shapes but most stupendous mechanisms and contrivances'.[3] His most famous microscopical discovery was the honeycomb structure of the cork plant, and he coined the word 'cell' to describe the little chambers that he saw, which he likened to monks' cells. He was also an excellent illustrator, and the engravings after his drawings of a flea or the eye of a fly are still familiar images today. In this manner, Hooke and his famous contemporary, the Dutch microscopist Antonie van Leeuwenhoek, revealed yet more new things to be described and classified by inadequate systems of the time.

NATURAL VERSUS ARTIFICIAL
CLASSIFICATION SYSTEMS

The turn of the eighteenth century sits at a crucial point in the development of taxonomy as it was during this period that a major debate arose on the methodology of classification of animals and plants which was to persist in various forms to the present day.

Classification systems fall broadly into two main categories, natural and artificial. Natural classifications are based on many characteristics and tend to group together plants and animals with genuine affinity. They tell us something about the relationships of living things and furthermore allow a degree of prediction. The *Solanaceae*, or potato family, for instance, is made up of some 2,800 plant species. Being closely related, they share a number of common characteristics; for example many members of this family contain poisonous alkaloids at least in their green parts. When a new species is recognized as belonging to this family by virtue of, say, its flower structure, it is reasonable to predict that it will share many of the other characteristics of its relatives, including their poisonous nature. Artificial classifications such as those used in the early herbals are usually based on only one or two characteristics such as the number of stamens or even alphabetical order of names. As they group together plants that are not necessarily related, it is not possible to predict reasonably characteristics of new additions to the group.

These arguments are strongly related to Aristotle's belief that groups of similar things have an *essence* that eternally and unchangingly links them. Caesalpino, for instance, believed that a limited set of flower characteristics could represent the

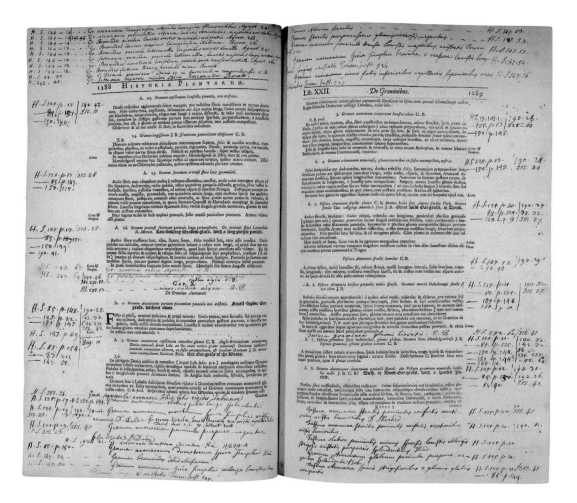

61 Sir Hans Sloane's annotated copy of John Ray's *Historia plantarum*. Copies of Ray's work in its original edition are still used as an index to Sloane's plant collections. The Natural History Museum, Botany.

essence of a particular group of plants. Against these 'essential' characteristics were ranged so-called 'accidental' characteristics which might distinguish individuals but did not relate to the *essence,* for instance flower colour in sweet peas. As an element of the thinking of the ancient world, this came under fire from philosophers such as John Locke (1632–1704), who considered that reliance on a few essential characteristics was doomed to failure as the human senses could not be guaranteed to perceive this so-called *essence* accurately. He went on to say that classifications are a mere human construct and do not necessarily exist in Nature: 'I cannot see how it can properly be said, that Nature sets the boundaries of the species of things; … we ourselves divide them, by certain obvious appearances, into species, that we may the easier under general names communicate our thoughts about them.' [4]

John Ray – the English Aristotle

Locke's ideas were to be reflected to some degree in the work of John Ray (1627–1705) (see fig. 20), an important figure in the break from the classical tradition and the development of systematic classification. He was born in Essex, the son of a successful blacksmith, and was able to study at Cambridge University, quickly becoming an expert in mathematics and languages, being made a Fellow in 1649. From an early age however, perhaps partly thanks to the influence of his herbalist mother, he had shown an interest in the natural world, his main pursuit in later life. Ray was very much a man of the Commonwealth, puritan in his religious beliefs and encouraged by the new attitude and status of science during that period.

Ray travelled widely, collecting and describing thousands of plants in his magnum opus, *Historia plantarum* (1686–1704), a general account of plants from Britain and Europe as well as many of the new species collected on recent voyages of exploration (fig. 61).

Ray's puritan views followed those of Francis Bacon in that he thought the best way to understand God's works was by planned experiment and observation. He recognized that the study of plants and animals was greatly facilitated by dividing them into basic groups and went further to recognize that there is a basic unit, which shared a number of characteristics that would always be perpetuated in the plant or animal's offspring, the species, noting that: 'no matter what variations occur in the individual or the species, if they spring from the seed of the one and the same plant, they are accidental variations and not such as to distinguish a species'.[5]

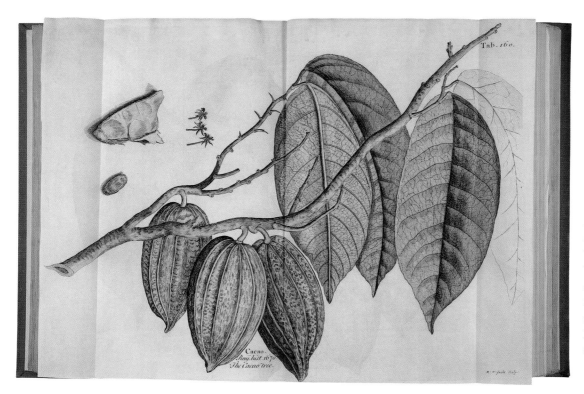

62 Sir Hans Sloane's *Natural History of Jamaica*, plate 160, depicting a cocoa plant. The two volumes of this book were illustrated with engravings by Michael van der Gucht after drawings by Edward Kirkius, not only of botanical specimens but also birds, fish and other animals Sloane observed and collected. House of Commons Library.

He noted also that environmental conditions affected characteristics such as height, and he preferred to use consistent characteristics such as the position, form and number of flower parts which would always be the same in plants of the same species.[6]

Although Ray's ideas of species and his taxonomy were possibly the most logical and useful of the time, his method was neither quick nor easy to apply. After his death, Ray's system was used by other naturalists, but it was not developed further. It remained cumbersome in part owing to his use of 'polynomials' or phrase names – strings of Latin words to identify each species uniquely. But what the botanists and zoologists of the day wanted was a universal system of classification that could be quickly applied and universally recognized. This major development, which would turn out to be a mixed blessing to the science of systematics, was to emerge later from Sweden, in the prolific and influential work of Carl Linnaeus.

SLOANE AND THE NATURAL HISTORY OF JAMAICA

While Ray was describing and devising classificatory systems for plants, his friend and protégé Sir Hans Sloane was well on his way to making his mark as one of Britain's greatest collectors and describers of the living world.[7] Trained as a physician, he was also a capable natural historian in his own right. His exact descriptions of the plant and animal species were competent and are still useful today, and his attitude towards naming new species was advanced and lacked the egotistical competitiveness of his contemporaries.

His major descriptive work was the result of a fifteen-month visit to Jamaica in 1688 as physician to the island's Governor, *A Voyage to the Islands Madera, Barbados, Nieves, S. Christophers, and Jamaica, with the Natural History of the Herbs and Trees, Four-footed Beasts, Fishes, Birds, Insects, Reptiles, &c. Of the last of those ISLANDS* (referred to in short as *The Natural History of Jamaica*). The first volume appeared in 1707 and the second in 1725. This work contains accurate and very readable descriptions of the plants and animals he encountered and also how natural resources were used by the islands' inhabitants. In addition, Sloane was careful to provide a good pictorial record (fig. 62), as many specimens lost their colour or decomposed before they could be transported to Britain. Sloane's entire Jamaican plant collection, and the drawings associated with it, formed part of the foundation collections of the British Museum and are now housed in the Botany Department of the Natural History Museum (figs 63, 64).[8]

Sloane did not devote much time to classification systems; however, in 1735 he had been given a copy of a new publication, *Systema naturae* by the Swede Carl von Linné (Linnaeus,

63 Drawer of bark samples from Sloane's Vegetable substances collection. Sloane's handwritten labels still survive on these drawers from his original cabinets in which they remained after they came to the British Museum. Natural History Museum, Botany.

64 Volumes from Sir Hans Sloane's herbarium and two boxes from his collection of Vegetable substances. His manuscript catalogue lists the thousands of glazed boxes and drawers of seeds, fruit, bark, roots, gums, etc. that made up his collection of *materia medica*. Natural History Museum, Botany.

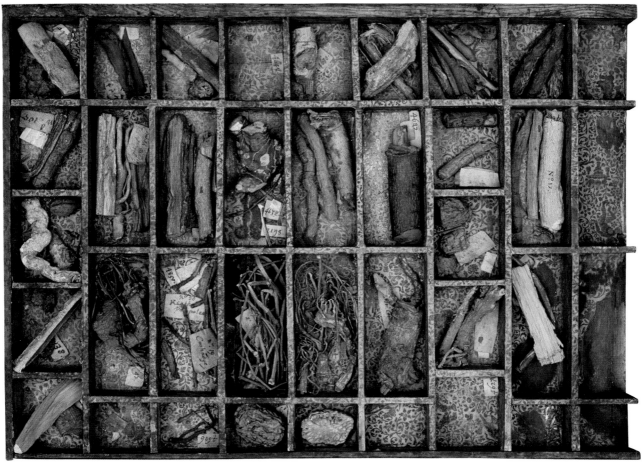

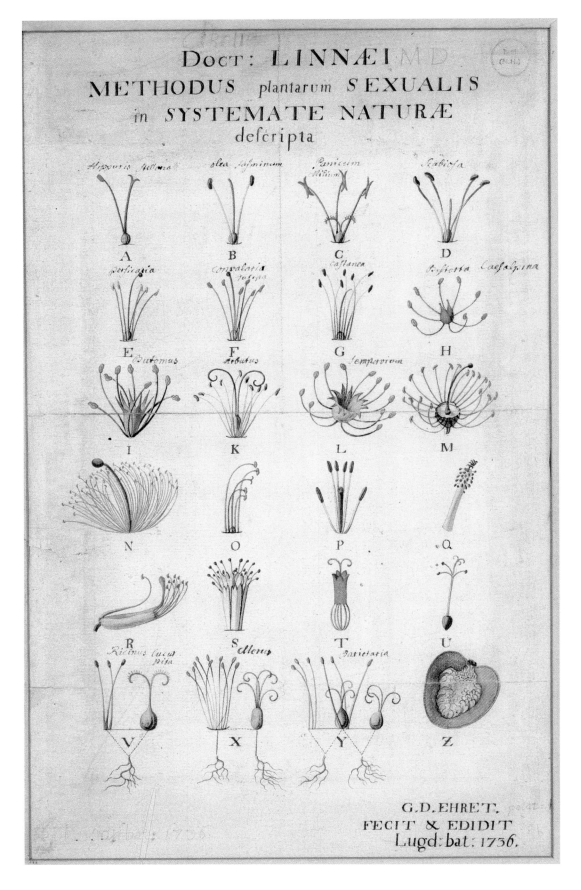

65 Georg Dionysius Ehret's 1736 hand-coloured engraving illustrating Linnaeus's *Methodus plantarum sexualis* as described in the *Systema naturae*. Linnaeus's book was originally published without illustrations in 1735, and Ehret published his print explaining the system a year later. Natural History Museum, Library.

1707–78), who was to be known later as the father of modern taxonomy. In the *Systema*, Linnaeus laid out classifications of animals and minerals and a 'sexual system' for the classification of plants. Sloane commented honestly that he was too set in his ways to accept this. The following year Linnaeus arrived on a visit to England, and one of the first people he was to meet was Sloane, but it was not the marriage of minds that some might have expected. A letter of introduction from the great Dutch botanist Boerhaave had been tactless, and perhaps language difficulties and his apparent arrogance did not endear him to Sloane. It has been suggested that this was partly the reason why Linnaeus failed to stay in Britain. Linnaeus did indeed think that Sloane's collection was chaotic.[9]

THE LINNAEAN REVOLUTION

Like many natural historians of his time Linnaeus gained his formal education as a physician, studying medicine first at Lund and then closer to his Swedish home at Uppsala before moving to Holland where he obtained an MD in 1736. Whilst like Ray, Linnaeus believed that a natural system of classification would tell more about the relationships of the living world ('The Natural Method is the ultimate end of Botany'[10]), he realized that this would be a time-consuming and complex task and instead he produced what was intended to be a stop-gap system – the sexual system. This artificial method used just a few arbitrary characteristics selected for convenience to divide the plant world into manageable groups.

His system was hierarchical, with three kingdoms subdivided into classes within which were orders and within those genera and species. For plants he used a simple set of characteristics relating to flower structure such as numbers of stamens and styles (fig. 65). All flowering plants were divided into twenty-three classes based on the number and length of stamens: thus *Monandria* (one stamen), *Diandria* (two stamens) and so on. Plants with apparently no flowers, such as mosses, he assigned to his twenty-fourth class, *Cryptogamia*. The classes were subdivided into orders based on the female organs: *Monogynia*, with one style or sessile stigma, *Digynia*, with two styles or sessile stigmas, and so forth. Although this system worked well to identify plants already known, Linnaeus acknowledged that it was an artificial system and did not necessarily put genuinely related plants in the same group. For example, the snowdrop would fall into class *Hexandria*, order *Monogyna*, exactly the same as the distantly related lily.

As is often the case, a temporary solution was taken up by many natural historians and became the norm from the 1750s to the early nineteenth century, particularly in Holland and Britain but less so in France. Much of the criticism of Linnaeus came from that country, and especially from Georges Louis le Clerc Compte de Buffon (1707–88). He began the thirty-six volumes of his *Histoire naturelle* in 1749 with descriptions of animals and plants, including speculation on

their origin. Most classifications, he argued, as had Locke nearly a century earlier, were the product of the human mind and did not take into account the continuous variation shown by living things.

Buffon was the inspiration to others, in particular Jean Baptiste de Monet, chevalier de Lamarck (known as Lamarck; 1744–1829), and Michel Adanson (1727–1806). Linnaeus's system was gradually replaced by systems such as these and that of the French botanist Antoine-Laurent de Jusssieu (1748–1836), which bear more resemblance to the natural system of Ray. Linnaeus had provided a neat means of pigeon-holing plants and a useful key to plants from a limited area, but his system was not natural and failed when applied to the vast numbers of new species returning to Europe from the new world and elsewhere. His classification of animals was to stand the test of time better than that for plants, and many of his groupings are close to today's (for example, Mammals and Birds); others are only approximate, and amphibians are

66 *Leonotis leonurus,* from the Clifford herbarium. Despite their differences, Linnaeus received a good collection of plants from Philip Miller to take back to his patron George Clifford in Haarlem. Beautifully mounted, Clifford's herbarium was acquired by Joseph Banks in 1791. Natural History Museum, Botany.

included with reptiles in *Amphibia*. Linnaeus's names of most insect orders survive to this day, such as *Lepidoptera* (butterflies and moths) and *Hymenoptera* (bees and ants, wasps etc.).

Although much of his classification system has been abandoned, one Linnaean innovation was to provide the simple and eminently practical means of naming organisms that is used to the present day. Natural historians of the seventeenth century were partly hampered in their work by use of polynomials, the long and unwieldy names used to identify new species. Linnaeus's two-word name (binomial) divorced the need to put a label on an organism from the need to describe it. The binomial name for the dog violet is then simply *Viola canina* – *Viola* representing the larger more general classification, the genus, and *canina* the more particular species.

When Linnaeus visited the Chelsea Physic Garden, its Superintendent, Philip Miller, pointed out the various plants giving them their Latin phrase names (fig. 61). Linnaeus later wrote:

> I remained silent, with the result that he said next day, 'this botanist of Clifford's doesn't know a single plant.' This came to my ears, and when he again began using these names I said, 'Don't use such names; we have shorter and surer ones', and gave him examples. He grew angry and scowled at me.[11]

Interestingly, it was to be Miller who would pioneer the use of the binomial names in the eighth edition of his *Gardener's Dictionary* of 1768.

LINNAEUS AND NATURAL HISTORY IN BRITAIN

Although Linnaeus's system of classifying plants was quickly adopted in Holland, in Britain its impact was felt more slowly. The first guide to British plants that used his system was Hudson's *Flora anglica* of 1762. However, once accepted, its popularity was to persist long after other countries had returned to natural systems. In the entomological world the first substantive work to use the system was Moses Harris's *The English Lepidoptera* of 1775.

The popularity of Linnaeus's system in Britain was to some extent connected with the arrival of Daniel Solander (1733–82) (fig. 67), one of Linnaeus's pupils, in 1760.[12] Solander was to become well known as Joseph Banks's friend and fellow naturalist on Captain James Cook's noteworthy first voyage (see ch. 7). He was occasionally employed by the Duchess of Portland (see fig. 76) and others to give scientific names to and classify their collections, for which he naturally used the Linnaean system. The popularity of the Linnaean method no doubt assisted in Solander's appointment to a post in the British Museum in 1763, and in 1773 he became Keeper of the Department of Natural History. A popular and highly competent natural scientist and promoter of Linnaeus, he was much lamented on his premature death in 1782.

Whilst there were critics of Linnaeus and others who partly accepted his ideas and attempted to modify them, his system had made its mark and would not go away. A significant aristocratic patron of natural history, John Stuart, third Earl of Bute (an early tutor of George III and later his First Minister), wrote his own botanical text in which he expressed his dissatisfaction with elements of Linnaeus's system, describing it as a poor mix of natural and artificial systems. Unlike the Duchess of Portland, who employed others to carry out the scientific work, Bute had trained with the great Boerhaave in Leiden and was a competent botanist himself. It is interesting

67 Wedgwood cameo portrait in blue jasperware of Daniel Carl Solander (1733–82), made as pair to one of his friend Joseph Banks. They were issued as part of Wedgwood and Bentley's series of portraits of eminent men. MME.

that his book was partly intended to encourage botany as a suitable occupation for young women, writing: 'the contemplation of Nature's works gradually leads to the omnipotent architect, of nature, God.'[13] The example set by such esteemed promoters was 'to raise the prestige and public recognition of an area of knowledge [botany] which had been frequently dismissed as being of little or no scientific importance'.[14] Bute could hardly have done more for natural history in Britain than his encouragement and training in botany of his pupil the future George III, the patron of that hothouse of Enlightenment activity, the Royal Botanic Gardens at Kew.

Others, like the Welsh traveller, collector and natural historian Thomas Pennant (1726–98), remained critical of Linnaeus even after his general acceptance. Pennant wrote that he was 'not generally smitten with the charms of Linnaeus … as in Ornithology he is too superficial to be thought of …[and] in fossils abler judges than myself have found him incompetent. His fort[e] is Botany; & in that you may perhaps edify from his instructions.'[15] He found Linnaeus's classification of man with other primates difficult to accept, as did many in the religious climate of that time. He did however see the value of his binomial naming system and used it in his major work *Synopsis of Quadrupeds* (1771).

Whilst Linnaeus's system continued to be regarded as having some practical value as a means of organizing collections well into the nineteenth century, its limitations were being recognized (as indeed they are today).[16] Even Sir Joseph Banks (see ch. 7), a former supporter of Linnaeus and close friend of Solander, was encouraging the manager of his collections, his librarian and protégé Robert Brown, to use the more natural system of the French de Jussieu. Brown, a skilled botanist who was to become the first Keeper of Botany at the British Museum, could also see flaws in de Jussieu's system but considered it the best available at the time and his support was instrumental in promoting it over the Linnaean system in Britain.

Some continued to defend Linnaeus, notably the Scottish botanist Sir James Edward Smith (1759–1828); perhaps not surprisingly as in 1788 he had founded the Linnean Society based around Linnaeus's collections which he had acquired after Linnaeus's death.[17]

On the whole, the eighteenth century is not perceived as a dynamic period in natural history in contrast to the scientific revolution of the previous century and the new specialist disciplines that led to the three-age system and to the theory of evolution in the following century. This was in part due to the fact that after Newton the physical sciences overshadowed natural history, especially in the minds of fellows of the Royal Society. In the eighteenth century the main advances of the British Enlightenment lay not in the creation of schemes of classification but in important publications, many of them beautifully and usefully illustrated, and in the creation of collections that, once classified, formed a huge 'database' of information on which nineteenth-century students of natural history could build. The abandonment of the total reliance on classical authors and the new reliance on observation, experimentation and empirical data, the foundation of societies, and growing numbers of collectors, enabled the realization of Bacon's utopian dream of the exchange of information between like-minded people in Britain and abroad in a truly international community. In addition, they were convinced that if they could use observation and classification to unravel the mysteries of the natural world, the knowledge and the methods used to achieve it could also be applied to the human and economic worlds for the benefit of mankind, as Bacon had predicted a century earlier.

From Ray through to Linnaeus, the emphasis had been on describing the increasing diversity of life, but by 1830 a significant change was taking place in how the living world was studied. More thought was being given to the 'why?' behind the patterns and apparent affinities of species that could be observed. A crucial new dimension was added to the debate – time. Did the diversity of living things reflect some change through time? Had birds come to be different from reptiles and mammals through a gradual process of change? Lamarck and others raised the questions, and Darwin provided the explanation for a credible mechanism. From that point onwards to the present day, systematics has studied the evolutionary relationships of different groups of organisms, most recently and controversially through a methodology known as cladistics which relies heavily on evolutionary theory. The process started by Aristotle and built on by Ray, Linnaeus and others enables us to prioritize parts of our world for conservation, to recognize the insect carriers of deadly diseases and to provide guides for plant and animal identification for use by many others worldwide.

7

Natural history collectors and their collections: 'simpling macaronis' and instruments of empire

ROBERT HUXLEY

Censure would be his Due,
who should be perpetually heaping
up of Natural Collections, without
Design of Building some Structure
of Philosophy out of them,
or advancing some Propositions
that might turn to the Benefit and
Advantage of the World.
This is in reality the true and only
proper End of Collections,
of Observations, and Natural
History: and they are of no manner
of Use or Value without it.

John Woodward[1]

The previous chapter examined new developments in classifying and describing the living world from the mid seventeenth century to the end of the eighteenth. The raw materials for much of this classification were the collections of natural objects being amassed not only from the immediate world of the collector but from the new lands being opened up by voyages of trade and exploration. The reasons for collecting and preserving great assemblages of plants and animals were by no means exclusively academic. The period from 1660 to 1830 witnessed a variety of motives, including the social prestige of owning such a collection, purely practical uses such as teaching aids, or personal, even national economic benefit.

CABINETS OF CURIOSITY

From the Renaissance to the seventeenth century, natural history specimens formed part of the *wunderkammer* or cabinets of curiosities that proliferated all over Europe, such as that of Fernando Cospi of Bologna, depicted by Mitelli in 1667 (fig. 91). These collections of 'natural and artificial rarities' were intended partly as a representation of the world and of creation. In earlier cabinets the collector placed natural history specimens amongst artefacts such as vases and coins and, in parallel with the earlier texts describing animals and plants, included items relating to mythical animals and plants, such as unicorn horns or the vegetable 'lamb of Tartary'.[2] A German visitor to the Tradescant collection in 1628 observed, all displayed together in the same cabinet:

> a piece of wood, an ape's head, a cheese, etc.; all kinds of shells, the hand of a mermaid, the hand of a mummy, a very natural wax hand under glass, all kinds of precious stones, coins, a picture wrought in feathers, a small piece of wood from the cross of Christ.[3]

Curiosity and a desire for knowledge had driven the British virtuosi of the seventeenth century to collect. One of the finest cabinets of natural and artificial rarities in Europe was the 'Museum' of the virtuoso William Courten (1642–1702).[4] A modest man (fig. 13), Courten himself had inherited part of his collection from his merchant father and amassed the rest himself on his many trips to the continent. His collection in his rooms in the Middle Temple in London was never catalogued, but focused on natural history and books, pictures and manuscripts (including albums of drawings by Nicholas Robert and others which formed a 'paper museum' of natural history, expanded later by Hans Sloane with works by Maria Sibylla Merian: figs 8, 68).

For men such as Courten, or the John Tradescants, Elder and Younger, Elias

68 Maria Sibylla Merian (1647–1717), life cycle of a frog, one of the series of watercolours made by her in Surinam in 1699–1701 (see also fig. 8). From the collection of Sir Hans Sloane. P&D.

69 Lower molar of a mastodon, *Tetrabelodon angustidens*, from the Royal Society Collection. It was catalogued and illustrated by Nehemiah Grew as a 'Petrifyd Tooth of a Sea Animal' in 1681. The Society's collection was presented to the British Museum in 1781, but little of it remains. Natural History Museum, Palaeontology.

Ashmole who purchased their collections for his Ashmolean Museum in Oxford, John Woodward at Cambridge (see ch. 9), or Ralph Thoresby in Leeds,[5] their collections were a sign that they understood Francis Bacon's notion that knowledge in itself was a virtue. But by the end of the seventeenth century, some virtuosi who formed such collections but did nothing to learn from them, apart from displaying them to others, began to be criticized: 'He Trafficks to all places, and has his

Correspondents in every part of the World; yet his Merchandizes serve not to promote our Luxury, nor encrease our Trade, and neither enrich the Nation, nor himself.'[6]

However, the role of a cabinet of curiosities could change greatly when it passed into new ownership. The collection of the Royal Society (fig. 69),[7] which aimed to be comprehensive and was formed by encouraging collectors to donate items to it, was in fact based on the cabinet of curiosities of Robert

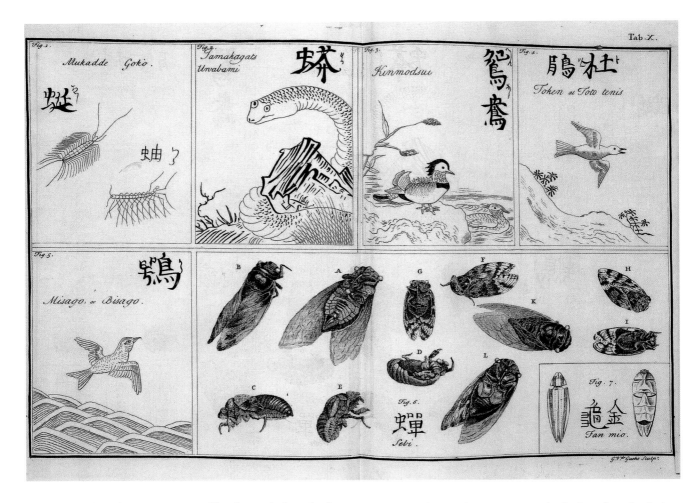

70 Birds and insects from Japan. Engraving by Gerard van der Gucht based on drawings and specimens from Kaempfer's collection that Sloane acquired and published after his death. Engelbert Kaempfer, *The History of Japan*, 1727, plate X. JA Library.

Hubert purchased in 1666. But, unlike the majority of collections at this time, it was available to all the members of a public society and was thus one of the first attempts at a scholarly approach to organizing, acquiring and housing such collections in Britain. The collection was there to be employed for 'considerable Philosophical and useful purposes',[8] to elucidate the similarities and differences between plant and animal specimens and was in keeping with the Baconian tradition of groups of scientists working together to understand the natural world, 'to find likenesse [*sic*] and unlikenesse of things upon a suddaine'.[9]

A COLLECTOR OF COLLECTIONS: SIR HANS SLOANE AND NATURAL HISTORY COLLECTING

Like the Royal Society's collection, Sir Hans Sloane's collection was made up partly of material he collected himself, but also from parts of some virtuosi collections of his contemporaries. It was one of the first to display some of the characteristics which might be considered to define collections informed by the Enlightenment. Certainly many objects had curiosity value alone, but others were collected to inform and improve his own work and the work of other physicians; most was carefully

classified and catalogued; and much of it might be seen to have been intended to 'increase trade, enrich the Nation [and indeed] himself'. Bacon, whose imperative this was, had not only indicated that knowledge in itself was a virtue, but he also believed that sciences such as natural history could be used to endow human life with 'new discoveries and power',[10] and provide a means to achieve 'the relief of man's estate'.[11]

The formation of Sloane's collection illustrates the surge and changes in the activity of natural history collecting in the late seventeenth and first half of the eighteenth centuries. His collection at his death in 1753 contained large numbers of specimens put together from significant and pioneering expeditions.

On his departure for Jamaica in 1687 Sloane had taken with him a list of specimens required by his friends John Ray, Martin Lister and others, and, as might be expected, he put together a fine collection of Jamaican plants, molluscs, insects, fish and many other specimens, most of which survive as the historical core collections of the Natural History Museum. On his return to Britain, Sloane continued to acquire collections by purchase, exchange or gift from his friends and acquaintances. Many were members of the Temple House Coffee Club, which had served as a focus for much collecting and discussion of natural history in the late seventeenth century.

Sloane acquired many other collections such as that of William Courten, but undoubtedly the major natural history collection he acquired was that of James Petiver (1658–1718), an apothecary who taught himself sufficient botany to be considered one of the greatest experts on oriental and other exotic plants of the time. He named many new species and was elected to the Royal Society in 1695, publishing extensively on plants with details gathered on collecting trips around the British Isles.[12] Petiver encouraged others to make collections and gave detailed instructions for ships' crews and others travelling abroad, including a list of:

> things to be taken with you when you go abroad, viz.
> Collecting books etc
> A Quire or tow of Brown Paper
> A Flagg Baskett
> Two or 3 Cloath or Linnen Baggs for Shells
> Several wide mouth'd Vialls or Glasses
> A box for insects
> A pincushion and Pins
> brandy or spirits for preserving fleshy worms etc.[13]

Petiver's collection, kept in his apothecary shop, grew to the size of a small museum and on his death Sloane 'bought Mr Petiver's collections, books etc for a considerable sume.'[14] While very large in scale, Petiver's collections were poorly organized and labelled and it is difficult to locate specimens in the collection today, although they are organized according to John Ray's system of classification.[15] But many specimens were of lasting importance to natural history, and Linnaeus described many new species from them, by then with others in Sloane's extensive herbarium.

In contrast to Petiver, the distinguished botanist Leonard Plukenet's (1642–1706) collections were most orderly. Superintendent of the gardens at Hampton Court, Plukenet bore the title of Queen's Botanist and corresponded and met Sloane and Petiver regularly,[16] and Linnaeus – unlike John Ray – held him in high regard and described many species from his specimens which by then were also with Sloane's. Although principally a botanist, Plukenet also formed a collection of insects, which like his plant specimens he preserved by pressing and gluing on to paper, a surprisingly effective method since the colour of Plukenet's specimens is still well preserved

Another significant collection from a very different part of the world came to Sloane from the German natural historian Engelbert Kaempfer (1651–1716). Kaempfer trained in law and medicine but, like many others with this background, he had a keen interest in natural history and collected plants from several countries. His most notable expedition was to Japan, a country then closed to foreigners with the exception

of limited access by the Dutch East India Company (see ch. 24). Kaempfer sailed as a ship's surgeon, arriving in Japan in 1691. Although no geographical, cultural or topographical observations were allowed, the Japanese were pleased to support his botanical activities and he was to become the first

71 William Dampier by Thomas Murray, c. 1697–8. The buccaneer and circumnavigator collected widely, and many of his shells eventually came to Sloane, who also owned this portrait. National Portrait Gallery.

European to make extensive botanical collections there. His collections are well preserved and annotated with the Latin phrase names as well as the Japanese names. He described and published these new plants in his major work *Amoenitatum exoticarum* (1712).

Sloane was most interested in Kaempfer's work and was able to buy his collection and manuscripts from his nephew after his death. He had the manuscripts translated and published the *History of Japan* (1727), illustrated with engravings of objects from his collection, which included, in addition to plants, shells, insects (fig. 70) and some animals, a number of Japanese artefacts and medical instruments.

Although naturalists were not specifically employed on early voyages, the enthusiast could travel under his profession and indulge his interest as a sideline. Perhaps one of the most extreme examples of mixing natural history with other occupations was William Dampier (1651–1715) (fig. 71), a remarkable man who combined the roles of pirate, explorer and natural historian. His *A New Voyage around the World* (1697) is a fascinating, at times highly disturbing, and amusing account of his voyages.[17] Dampier was the first European to collect and describe the natural history of Australia, landing on the north-west coast some seventy years before James Cook and Joseph Banks sailed into Botany Bay. His first visit in 1688 was as a result of a detour to avoid British and Dutch shipping after a mutiny. On landing in what was then known as New Holland, Dampier made extensive descriptions of the vegetation and wildlife. On his second visit to Australia in 1699 he made extensive botanical collections, which, like their collector, were lucky to survive the return journey. They were forced to abandon their heavily leaking ship near Ascension Island in the south Atlantic and were marooned in harsh conditions for five months. Dampier managed to save his plant specimens, some shells, his journal and little else. He presented the shells from his second voyage to Sloane, who had lent his support.[18]

RECORDING THE ASSETS OF THE NEW WORLD: MARK CATESBY IN THE CAROLINAS

It was this need to chart and record the natural resources of new territories that drove the activities of a number of natural historians and collectors in the American colonies of the eighteenth century. Hans Sloane sponsored one such collector, the highly productive, in terms of specimens, descriptions and illustrations, Mark Catesby (1682–1749), who had left Britain for expeditions to the Virginia colonies in North America, first in 1712 and then again in 1720. His second trip

was sponsored by Sloane and other influential Royal Society fellows including the incoming Governor of Carolina, Colonel Francis Nicholson. The latter offered Catesby £20 a year to 'Observe the Rarities of the Country for the uses and purposes of the Society'. Sloane received two volumes of plants with many new plant species and type specimens.[19] Catesby was a systematic collector, covering a large area of the Carolina territory as well as Florida and elsewhere, being careful to visit places at times of the year when the fauna and flora would be different. His major work *The Natural History of Carolina, Florida and the Bahama Islands* was published in 1747 (fig. 72).[20] Unlike many of his contemporaries, Catesby was aware of the associations and interrelations of species in their habitats and in the *Natural History* he often illustrates and describes both plant and associated fauna.

As well as plants, Sloane made a significant collection of shells while in Jamaica and later added to this with donations from others (fig. 74).[21] Shell collecting crosses the boundary between the cabinets of curiosities of the sixteenth century and the more scholarly collections of the following three centuries. While plant collecting had obvious relevance for apothecaries and doctors, many collections of shells were made for their intrinsic beauty, but conchology, the study of shells, became established as a discipline in the late seventeenth century and one of its most important early disciples was Sloane's friend Martin Lister (1639–1712).[22] He made contributions to the knowledge and description of spiders and speculated on fossils, which he did not believe to be of living origin, but his first and last love was conchology and

72 The crested or blue jay, *Pica cristata carulea*, and the Bay-leaved Smilax, pl. 15 from Mark Catesby's *Natural History of Carolina*, 1747. Catesby etched his own prints: volume I was devoted to birds and volume II to fish, reptiles, mammals, insects and plants. Natural History Museum, Library.

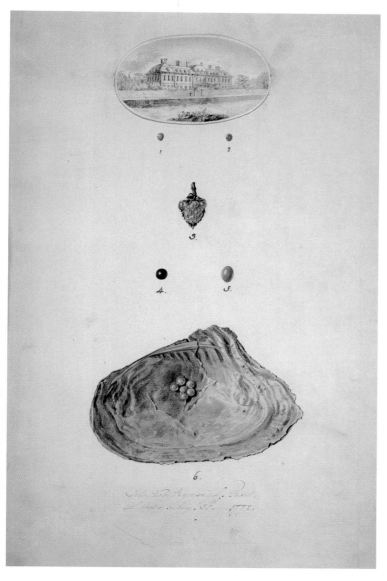

73 Examples from Sloane's collection of pearls with a vignette of Montagu House above, from John and Andrew van Rymsdyk's album of original watercolours for the illustrations for their *Museum Britannicum*, 1778. P&D.

his major work *Historia conchyliorum* (1685–92) remains a masterpiece of description and illustration. It contains nearly a thousand plates, all the work of his daughters, Susanna and Anna (fig. 74).

Sloane's collection included over a thousand birds and eggs, over fifteen hundred fish and nearly two thousand quadrupeds as well as other fauna. But 'skins' are particularly vulnerable to decay and pests; nearly all these specimens have perished and only a handful of skulls and horns survive.[23] Initially, soft-bodied invertebrates and fish were pressed and dried like plants if they were preserved at all. A revolution came with the use of Spirits of Wine (the product of repeated distillations of wine) as a preservative, a practice devised by

Sloane's friend Robert Boyle (1627–91), and used by many others, including Sir Ashton Lever in his museum (fig. 86). The basic methodology has changed little: in the Darwin Centre of the Natural History Museum in London today there are some 22 million specimens ranging from fishes to fly larvae, preserved in jars of alcohol.

FROM VIRTUOSI TO AMATEURS AND FROM CONNOISSEURS TO ENTREPRENEURS

One of the most significant characteristics of the study of the natural world during the age of the Enlightenment was that it was pursued mainly by amateurs, and it was they who were to a large extent responsible for the vast 'database' that was created. John Ray was a clergyman, Sloane and Lister were physicians and Petiver an apothecary. George III and Queen Charlotte were keen botanists, as were many of their courtiers, including the third Earl of Bute, the Duchess of Portland and her friend Mary Delany (fig. 75). If one excludes Sir Hans Sloane's museum, none in Britain to that date could compare in scale or magnificence with the Portland Museum (fig. 76).[24] The diplomat and connoisseur Sir William Hamilton was also a keen vulcanologist, his nephew Charles Greville collected minerals, and the zoologist Thomas Pennant, the collector C. M. Cracherode, and Sir Joseph Banks were all landed gentry first, and natural historians second.

Even by the middle of the eighteenth century, apart from the Ashmolean, Royal Society and British Museum, collections were mainly in private hands. There had been a shift in

74 Sloane's specimen of *Cassis (Phalium) strigata*, with Anna and Susanna Lister's engraving prepared from the specimen for their father Martin's *Historiae conchyliorum* (1685–92), vol. iv, pl. 1014, species 78. Natural History Museum, Zoology, Molluscs.

Pancratium Maritinum
Sea Daffodil

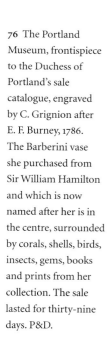

75 *Pancratium maritinum* (sea daffodil) by Mary Delany (1700–88). In her seventies Mrs Delany made over a thousand 'paper mosaics', based on real flowers from the Royal Gardens at Kew, the Duchess of Portland's garden at Bulstrode or given to her by friends such as Joseph Banks or the Earl of Bute. She classified them according to Linnaean principles. P&D.

76 The Portland Museum, frontispiece to the Duchess of Portland's sale catalogue, engraved by C. Grignion after E. F. Burney, 1786. The Barberini vase she purchased from Sir William Hamilton and which is now named after her is in the centre, surrounded by corals, shells, birds, insects, gems, books and prints from her collection. The sale lasted for thirty-nine days. P&D.

Executed under the direction of J. Bell, Book-seller to His Royal Highness the Prince of Wales, London April 8th 1786.

emphasis in collecting and study towards individual collectors. The earlier, often reviled, 'virtuoso' who collected for collecting's sake, evolved into the amateur – wealthy, often aristocratic men and women with the means to indulge in travelling, collecting and carrying out scientific experiments. The old Baconian imperative of the acquisition of knowledge for 'the relief of man's estate' was translated in the first half of the eighteenth century through Locke's and Shaftesbury's advocacy of civic humanism into a search to find something of use to the general improvement of mankind and the nation in such activities. Natural history also revived in the second half of the eighteenth century with the swift adoption in Britain of Linnaeus's systems of classification of animals and plants.

Wealthy collectors entered the field with varying degrees of interest in the science – for some amassing a high-quality collection was enough in itself. The Duchess of Portland and

77 Shells from the collection of the Reverend C. M. Cracherode, bequeathed to the Museum in 1799, including the thorny oyster, *Spondylus americanus*. Some of his shells had been purchased at the Duchess of Portland's sale. Natural History Museum, Zoology, Molluscs.

the Reverend Clayton Mordaunt Cracherode (1730–1799) exemplify this type of collector. Cracherode was a shy recluse who had inherited a small fortune, which enabled him to purchase fine books, prints, coins, gems and other minerals (see chs 9, 11–12) and shells (fig. 77), often for record sums, through an agent.[25] His only publications were some Latin verses, and his curiosity appears to have been limited – the *Dictionary of National Biography* records that 'so slight was his curiosity that he never saw, except in a drawing, a celebrated chestnut tree on his own estate in Hertfordshire.'[26] His collecting criteria were clearly those of a connoisseur but Cracherode's collection of shells is worthy of special note, since when his collection came to the British Museum at his death in 1799 it was the first addition to Sloane's founding collection of invertebrates. The British Museum at this time had little purchasing power compared to the wealthy virtuosi, and many collections from newly discovered territories or from Cook's voyages went directly to private collections such as that of Cracherode, so his bequest instantly improved the breadth of coverage of the collections. Cracherode's shells were displayed in Room IX of Montagu House in their own case.[27]

JOSEPH BANKS: THE 'FLY-CATCHING MACARONI'

Hans Sloane and Joseph Banks, spanning the Age of Enlightenment, are exemplars of the final type of collector to be

discussed – the collector 'entrepreneur'. Both searched in their own ways to improve man's estate through new discoveries in natural history – Sloane through medical improvements and Banks through ways of benefit to the nation's economy. As an individual, Sloane benefited financially from his voyage to Jamaica where he was introduced to the nauseous, bitter and hard-to-digest cocoa used by the native peoples (see fig. 62). After experimenting by boiling it and adding milk, he found it more palatable and enjoyable as a drink which he believed aided the digestion. On his return he passed his recipe to apothecaries for production and they marketed it for its restorative powers. Soon 'Sloane's milk chocolate' was being sold all over London, the recipe eventually passing to Cadbury's. Sloane made a considerable sum from chocolate, and also from his promotion of cinchona bark whose active ingredient quinine was an effective treatment for malaria.

The economic, scientific and political forces behind many collecting expeditions in the later eighteenth century are exemplified by the work of Joseph Banks – botanist, collector and promoter of the natural sciences (fig. 78). As a high-profile virtuoso, Banks exposed himself to the ridicule of the satirists of his time who labelled him a 'macaroni', an increasingly derogatory term for a well-to-do and fashionable young person apt to indulge in whims such as collecting.[28] But science of the late eighteenth century was very much applied, and Banks represented this in his desire to use science and natural history in particular to discover new species and manipulate them for the benefit of mankind and particularly of Britain and its trading empire.

Banks was born in London in 1743 into a well-to-do, land-owning Lincolnshire family and attended Harrow and Eton before going up to Oxford. He left without a degree, determining to continue his education through practical experience. Eschewing a Grand Tour, he instead signed on as naturalist aboard HMS *Niger* for an expedition to Labrador and Newfoundland. On his return in 1767 he had already been elected a fellow of the Royal Society, at the age of twenty-three. The plant collections he made there were to form the core of his extensive herbarium, now held at the Natural History Museum.

Soon after he returned from this voyage, the Admiralty was organizing a scientific expedition to the South Seas under the command of Captain Cook (see ch. 23): the drive for this expedition was largely economic; accurate observation of the transit of Venus would enable improvements to navigation, which, in turn, would strengthen the navy's ability to protect British trade routes; but there was also need for a naturalist among the scientific personnel. Cook also had secret orders to search for the rumoured southern continent for possible future exploration and exploitation.

Banks was determined to go and he paid a considerable sum to fund his party of natural historians, which included his friend Solander, two artists, four servants and an amanuensis. Of these only Banks, Solander and two of the servants were to return.

The expedition sailed aboard HMS *Endeavour* in August 1768, visiting Madeira, Tierra del Fuego and Rio de Janeiro with a four-month stop in Tahiti. The naturalists collected as much as they could at each landfall, filling the Great Cabin of the ship, normally reserved for the captain. After several months charting the coast of New Zealand, then thought to be a promontory of the 'Great South Land', they landed in what was to be known as Botany Bay in Australia on 28 April 1770. Despite hostility from the native people, they managed to amass one of the most significant natural history collections ever made. The adventures of the expedition have been well documented,[29] and on their return to England in 1771 Banks and Solander were feted by the London public (fig. 79). From his position in the British Museum, Solander helped Banks to organize, catalogue and study the material they had brought back, regarding the collections as tools of science rather than collections for their own sake (fig. 80).

One of the greatest works of scientific recording to come out of the *Endeavour* voyage was the collection of natural history drawings, mainly done in pencil, some with colouring, by the young artist Sydney Parkinson, who died on the return journey. In England Banks employed a number of other artists to complete Parkinson's work using the herbarium specimens and Parkinson's own notes as reference material. At Banks's considerable personal expense, 743 plates were engraved, of which all but five survive, but their publication was never realized during Banks's lifetime (fig. 81).[30]

Banks was to be the instigator of several other ventures to make use of plants and animals, including attempts to transplant them from one part of the world to another. The government had identified the need for a cheap and nutritious food source to support the expanding slave population of the West Indies. In Tahiti Banks had observed a tree whose abundant fruit provided a staple diet for the islanders. It could be eaten cooked or raw and, once fermented, stored well for many months. Both Banks and Cook saw the potential of this fruit in the West Indies, and the ill-fated HMS *Bounty* under the command of Captain William Bligh was sent out to transport breadfruit trees from the south seas to the Caribbean. Mutiny on the return meant that this expedition ended in disaster, but Bligh successfully completed a second voyage and breadfruit became well-enough established in the West Indies to provide a staple food for slaves; unfortunately they found it unpalatable (see ch. 21).

Banks played a more successfully instrumental role in promoting the introduction of tea from China to India and merino sheep to Australia, and was involved in the African

78 Sir Joseph Banks by Anne Seymour Damer (1749–1828), bronze, h. 56 cm. The sculptor was a friend of Banks and presented this bust to the British Museum, where Banks was a trustee, in 1814. MME.

The great South Sea Caterpillar, transform'd into a Bath Butterfly.

Description of the New Bath Butterfly, taken from the Philosophical Transactions for 1795. " This Insect first crawl'd into notice from among the Weeds & Mud on the Banks of the South Sea; & being afterwards placed in a Warm Situation by the Royal Society, was changed by the heat of the Sun into its present form — it is noticed & Valued solely on account of the beautiful Red which encircles its Body, & the Shining Spot on its Breast; a Distinction which never fails to render Caterpillars valuable. —

79 *The Great South Sea Caterpillar, transformed into a Bath Butterfly,* hand-coloured satirical engraving by James Gillray, 1795. Sir Joseph Banks had been elected President of the Royal Society in 1779 and in 1795 was invested as a Knight of the Bath. P&D.

Association and innumerable other ventures. And, while he could not be described as a leading scientist himself in any significant sense, he was an enthusiastic promoter of science and the applied value of natural history to human health and wealth for Britain and its empire. 'I may flatter myself that being the first man of scientific education who undertook a voyage of discovery and that voyage of discovery being the first which turned out satisfactorily in this enlightened age, I was in some measure the first who gave that turn to such voyages.'[31] With little formal training in natural history, nevertheless his education 'exposed him to the values of a society where science, and rational discourse generally were accorded respect as natural allies of the cause of true religion and sound government'.[32]

BUILDING ON THE LEGACY

The early nineteenth century saw a clearer distinction develop between the collectors who collected for study, usually professional collectors and natural scientists, and the increasing and often destructive army of amateur 'fad' collectors. Many a cabinet of curiosities had an artistically arranged shell collection as its centrepiece, and from the late eighteenth century other groups of organisms began to attract this kind of attention, in particular ferns and seaweeds, easily collected on the shore, which might be used as 'foliage' in artistic arrangements then fashionable with female amateurs.[33] This interest in seaweeds by women was to put the science of phycology (the study of algae including seaweeds) ahead of some other branches of science. However, the sheer number of collectors and the amounts of marine algae collected on the favoured shores of Devon and Cornwall had devastating effects on the flora.

By 1830 collecting had become an organized and respectable profession and was firmly tied in with the expanding empires of the European countries. As the British national collection, the British Museum grew and outshone individual collections. Fulfilling its original Enlightenment intention of becoming a universal collection, a virtual 'encyclopaedia of the world', it weakened the cult of the 'cabinet of

curiosities' and of the virtuosi collectors that had helped to create it. Developments such as Linnaeus's classifications system provided a commonly agreed means of filing the products of the natural world into an orderly and rational system, investing the activities of the natural historian and virtuoso collector with the dignity of a true science.[34] Just as the virtuoso's study of antiquities was at the same time being transformed into the disciplines of archaeology, art history and even anthropology (see Parts IV and V), the polymathic and eclectic gentlemen (and women) amateur collectors of natural history in the eighteenth century were replaced by the scientific specialists of the nineteenth – professional botanists, mineralogists, zoologists, entomologists and palaeontologists.

81 *Gardenia taitensis*, annotated 'Gardenia florida', watercolour by Sydney Parkinson, made during Cook's first voyage with Joseph Banks, 1768–71, and later engraved for Banks's intended *Florilegium*. Natural History Museum, Picture Library.

80 A tray of shells from Sir Joseph Banks's collection, catalogued and organized by Solander, in boxes based on a type invented by Linnaeus. Natural History Museum, Zoology, Molluscs.

8 The nature of the earth and the fossil debate

JILL COOK

Copernicus and Galileo dealt a blow to human pride in revealing that the earth was not the centre of the universe. Two centuries later, the Victorians had to adjust from belief in a magnificent genesis to bacterial origins in a primordial soup followed by millennia of dinosaur disorder and ice ages. In between, the natural philosophy of Francis Bacon encouraged the late seventeenth-century founding fellows of the Royal Society to investigate nature by observation and experiment providing revelations about the natural world as new facts accumulated. By the end of the eighteenth century, the classification and use of information accumulated in this way brought the realization that the earth had a far greater antiquity than human or any other form of life, as well as awareness that its natural history could be traced as a pattern of dynamic events and that organisms could become extinct. This knowledge was crucial to the development of modern geology and evolutionary biology.

THEORIES OF THE EARTH

Histories of geology tend either to ignore theories of the earth or hold them up for ridicule in the belief that they demonstrate how religion held back the development of empirical science. However, as may be seen from the work of writer and divine Thomas Burnet (c. 1635–1715), in the eighteenth century theories of the earth, although not science as we know it, were widely read, influenced empirical investigations and actually helped to loosen the hold of doctrinaire views because of their non-conformist approach.

At the end of seventeenth century the god of the English was the god of the Bible rather than the philosophers.[1] However, the influence of natural philosophy had made the investigation of nature almost a form of worship, celebrating the ingenuity of the Creator and his purpose through natural laws. Within the Anglican Church there were clerics who were convinced that such investigation would replace blind faith with proof of Christianity. Most of these so-called Latitudinarians emerged from the University of Cambridge. The most influential of them was Burnet, Master of Charterhouse, London, and, briefly, chaplain in ordinary and Clerk of the Closet to King William III. In 1671 Burnet accompanied the Earl of Wiltshire on a Grand Tour and was so moved by the sights of the Alps and the Apennines that he resolved to give 'some tolerable account of them'.[2] This he did in a volume first published in Latin in 1681 and subsequently enlarged before its publication in English in 1690 as *The Sacred Theory of the Earth*.

Burnet was impressed by the rugged terrain of the mountains because they gave such dramatic emphasis to the fact that nothing in nature could now be described as pristine which was surely the way God would have made it. He realized that the landscape had been changed by natural processes that had operated in cycles over long periods of time, thereby establishing the germ of a principle fundamental to geology.[3] Using the narrative of Genesis, the prophecies of Peter and the Book of Revelation he envisaged the history of seven cycles of transformation illustrated in his frontispiece.[4] Starting from an earth without form and void God created Paradise, pristine with a smooth surface, uninterrupted by the chaos of mountains, ravines and oceans. Noah's Flood modified this landscape to its present form and this in turn would be consumed by the fires of the apocalypse before the original world could be reformed on a smooth surface, only to be subsumed at the Last Judgement to become a sun or star in another part of the universe.

Although not geology as we know it, Burnet's theory establishes complementary concepts of time that have supported geological theory ever since: a linear history moving through stages from a beginning to an end, as well as repeating but distinctive cycles bringing destruction and renewal. The former subsequently accommodated the sequence of strata and differing forms of life essential to the concept of evolution whereas the latter provided a model for the way in which the earth had been modified to its existing state replacing biblical processes with those observed in the field such as erosion and deposition, uplift and collapse.

Although unscientific in a modern sense, Burnet's work found support from both Newton and his rival the German philosopher and mathematician Gottfried Leibniz (1646–1716), as well as reaching a wider circle through essays in the *The Tatler* and *The Spectator*. There was criticism. Both naturalist John Ray (1627–1705) (see ch. 6) and fieldworker Edward Lhwyd[5] (1660–1709) denounced such theories as premature when there was still so much to collect and observe,[6] but Burnet's work was as much a product of natural philosophy as theirs because it insisted that the world was knowable by reason and observation. Unlike Newton, Burnet was unwilling to attribute things he could not explain to divine intervention. His mind was as open as those of the empirical observers who also adhered to the authority of the Bible, and he encouraged research by declaring that nothing that could be discovered could be an enemy of religion because: 'Truth cannot be an Enemy, God is not divided against himself; and therefore we ought not on that Account to condemn or censure what we have not examined or cannot disprove.'[7] Furthermore, Burnet's opinions about Genesis opened the debate on the date of origin of the earth which, on the basis of biblical chronology, was at this time believed to be 4004 BC (see ch. 17) and offered a new approach to reconciling the known world with scripture. He considered the biblical account of Creation to be an allegory given to Moses so that ordinary people might understand and have faith. The educated needed to read between the lines and realize that the days might represent much longer periods. Here was a divine giving permission to investigate the nature and age of the earth in the belief that there could be no such thing as heresy.

This new-found freedom of expression, albeit couched in devout beliefs, provided the philosophical framework for research on the nature of the earth for the century that followed. While interest remained speculative for some, others began using empirical observations based on rocks and fossils to explore Burnet's *Theory*. Among them was Burnet's younger contemporary John Woodward (1665–1728), Professor of Physick at Gresham College in London. Woodward had travelled throughout Britain collecting minerals which at this time incorporated all types of rock as well as fossils. His observations and carefully curated collection led him to a theory of the earth that dealt with one of the most controversial issues in natural philosophy: the origins of fossils.

FOSSILS

Up to the end of the seventeenth century the word 'fossil' was used to refer to anything that might be dug up. This term is now restricted to the remains of formerly living organisms preserved in stone. Three hundred years ago such relics were classed as minerals, amongst which they were distinguished as 'formed' or 'figure stones' of unknown origin. Woodward's curiosity about formed stones began on a visit to Sherbourne, Gloucestershire, in 1689 when he found a fossilized shell lodged in rock in Sir Ralph Dutton's vineyard and whole beds of shells in the nearby fields. Although for Woodward this was 'the first fossil shell I ever found',[8] such finds had long been a matter of debate among natural historians. Most regarded their resemblance to living organisms as fortuitous and assumed they had been created in and by the earth. This view was entirely consistent for its time. The origins of the earth were then understood from the biblical account of creation which states that all plants and animals were created at once. Formed stones could not be the remains of formerly living organisms because field observations and collections showed that they have a different distribution from extant species, being found on the tops of mountains and down into the depths of the earth. Furthermore, they included many examples unknown from the modern context and excluded others, particularly plants such as grass and roses. Such differences between the empirical and textual evidence were sufficient to cause opposition and equivocation among fellows of the Royal Society who were well aware of the proposition that formed stones were the remains of formerly living organisms. Their own thoughts on the matter had been thrown into contention by the publication of researches of the Danish anatomist Niels Stensen (1638–86), known as Steno,[9] and the Sicilian artist, collector and naturalist Agostino Scilla[10] (1619–1700), as well as from the work of the Royal Society's Curator Robert Hooke[11] (1635–1703).

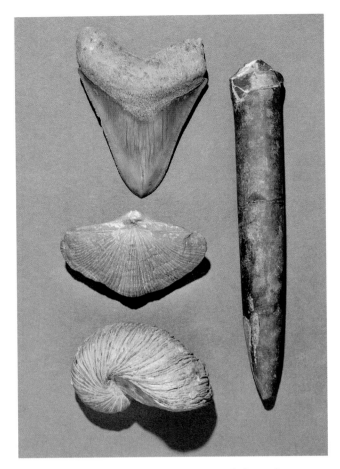

82 Fossils from Thomas Pennant's collection, including a *glossopetra* (top), known as a 'tongue stone' until the 18th century, with examples of extinct molluscs, including a brachiopod or 'lamp shell' (centre), a *Gryphaea* or 'devil's toenail' (bottom) and a belemnite. Natural History Museum, Palaeontology.

While working as physician to the Grand Duke of Tuscany, Steno was called upon to dissect the head of a shark. In so doing he realized that the animal's teeth were identical to the *glossopetrae* or tongue stones commonly found embedded in rocks (fig. 82, and see ch. 17, fig. 166) and concluded that these were the fossilized remains of animals that had died in the distant past. His sensational idea was brought to the attention of the Royal Society in 1667 and appeared as an abstract in the *Philosophical Transactions*. In the same year Hooke took up the theme in a series of lectures on earthquakes and 'what reasons may be given for the frequent finding of shells and other sea and land petrified substances, scattered over the whole terrestrial superficies'.[12] In these lectures he made the crucial distinction between minerals, which he identified by their crystalline form which varies according to their chemistry, and figured stones which he called petrifactions. He argued that the particular and varied shapes of petrifactions were not determined by the substance forming them like minerals, but were moulds and casts. Listing what was known about petrifactions he noted that they most resembled plants and animals and, following a series of propositions matched with proofs, concluded that this must be their origin. Against the objection that many fossil shells bore only a passing resemblance to modern forms such as had been raised by leading conchologist Martin Lister (1639–1712), Hooke insisted that the similarities were more important than the differences. He illustrated this by showing how the detailed structure of 'serpent stones' (ammonites) (fig. 83) found in rocks on Portland, Dorset, was like that of the living *Nautilus* and concluded that these molluscs must have been similar. Both are now known as cephalopods, which also include squid, octopus and cuttlefish and have been shown to be descended from the straight-shelled belemnite. The absence of ammonites in the modern ocean was attributed to a failure to discover them or to their extinction. John Ray was equivocal and Lhwyd[13] had his own theory, but Woodward stole the thunder by synthesizing the ideas of Scilla, Steno and Hooke into a theory like that of Burnet.

In *An Essay Towards a Natural History of the Earth*, first published in 1695, Woodward accepted that formed stones were once living creatures and advocated fossil shells and geological formations as the key to understanding the ancient history of the earth.[14] In the introductory dissertation to his history Woodward explains that:

> Bodies which consist of Stone, of Spar, Flint and the like, and yet carry a *Resemblance* of Muscles, Cockles and other Shells were originally formed the *Cavities* of Shells of these Kinds which so resemble these Shells have served as *Matrices* or *Moulds* to them; the Sand, Sparry and Flinty matter, being then soft, or in a *State* of *Solution*, and so, susceptible of any Form, when it was thus introduced into these: and that it consolidated or became hard afterwards.[15]

Like Hooke he did not think it a problem that many fossil shells were of unknown species: 'it being evident from the *Relations* of *Dyvers*, and *Fishers* for *Pearls*, that there are *many*

83 An ammonite from upper liassic strata. Commonly called 'serpent stones', these were once believed to be snakes turned to stone by St Hilda. Their value as index fossils useful for distinguishing strata was recognized by William Smith at the turn of the 19th century. Natural History Museum, Palaeontology.

Kinds of *Shell-fish* which lye perpetually *concealed* in the *Deep* screened from our Eyes by that vast World of Water'.[16]

Despite insisting on the importance of reliable evidence, Woodward hypothesized that Noah's Flood could explain all observed phenomena. He conjectured that the whole world had been dissolved by the deluge and the present earth had reformed from the mass of material, including animal and plant remains, settling into strata according to their specific gravity with the heaviest particles at the bottom. However, such gradation with 'the heavyer Shells in Stone, the lighter in Chalk and so the Rest' was contrary to what could be observed and failed to explain how animal and plant remains had survived dissolution. Woodward's theory was quickly under attack. He was accused of plagiarizing the work of Scilla[17] whose collection he had acquired, and the mathematician Dr John Arbuthnot (1667–1735) calculated that the quantity of water required to dissolve the earth would have stood some 450 miles above its present surface. However, no one doubted the organic origin of fossils and, despite criticism at home, the theory gained recognition on the continent only to wane as evidence gathered that drew the effects of the Flood and the biblical timescale into question. This development took place as the subject developed during the early Hanoverian period. Woodward's collection rather than his theory and a book by Edward Lhwyd contributed significantly to this process.

THE MUSEUM COMES TO THE FIELD

Lhwyd was the son of impoverished gentry and on going up to Oxford in 1682 took a job as assistant to Dr Plot at the Ashmolean Museum in order to make ends meet. He was to live and work there until his death. Under Plot's tutelage his first task was to catalogue the mineral collection which included formed stones and he was soon scouring the quarries around Oxford for new specimens. He believed that these were facts from which the earth would eventually be understood and advocated travel and fieldwork as the key method. To this end he endeavoured to collect an example of every type of fossil in Britain. Having planned an inventory, he undertook long journeys to fulfil this ambition. The outcome of this research was his *Lithiphylacii Britannici ichnographia* published in 1699.

Literally translated as 'a map of British cabinets of stones', *Lithiphylacii* is in modern terms a field guide to British minerals and fossils. It makes no reference to the Bible or any other textual sources. The specimens are divided into twelve classes in which the crystalline minerals and corals are separated from the formed stones as suggested by Hooke. The fossil classes are named by their resemblance to plants and animals but Lhywd did not presume an organic origin. Lhwyd's classes were for the purpose of identifying specimens rather than classifying them. Instead of 'shells' he distinguishes

spiral shells, bivalves and vermicular (wormlike) shells so that collectors could easily look up the forms they found. Using these classes 1,766 specimens are described, each with a provenance, and an illustration of an example of every form was included. It was a format that was to be used in scientific catalogues well into the twentieth century, produced in a handy pocket size so that it could be carried into the field. The guide was sought after and influential despite the fact that it was hard to obtain because only 120 copies were officially printed. However, a pirate edition appeared in the same year and a second edition in 1760. Lhywd's guide was followed by Woodward's attempt at a systematic mineralogy in his 1728 *Fossils of All Kinds Digested into a Method*, followed, posthumously, in 1729 by his *Catalogue of the English Fossils in the Collection of John Woodward*. Collecting had become a scientific pursuit.

CABINETS OF FACTS

Woodward's geological collection was unusual for its time. It was not confined to rare or exotic specimens nor was it eclectic. His objective was 'to get as compleat and satisfactory information of the whole Mineral Kingdom as I could possibly obtain'.[18] To this end he travelled around England carrying out systematic field investigations to collect specimens. He also had a wide network of correspondents who supplied him with geological information and material. His purpose was to collect facts from which he would understand the earth in order to advance 'some Propositions that might turn to the Benefit and Advantage of the World. … the true and only proper End of Collections, of Observations and Natural History.'[19]

Woodward bequeathed his two cabinets of British fossils to the University of Cambridge and endowed a lectureship stipulating that the post holder should show the collection 'to all curious and intelligent persons as shall desire a view of them for their information and instruction'. The university purchased his other two cabinets of foreign specimens from the executors for £1,000 before they went to auction.[20] In total there were nearly ten thousand items collected over thirty-five years, carefully numbered and organized in purpose-built burred walnut cabinets. His British material was divided between two cabinets: one containing minerals and rocks catalogued as 'native fossils', the other containing fossilized organic remains referred to as 'extraneous fossils'. The foreign collections were similarly divided and the terms 'extraneous' or 'exotic' were used to distinguish 'minerals' or 'fossils' (things dug up) as of organic origin until the nineteenth century when the word *fossil* assumed its current meaning. Every specimen was labelled and given a registration number and the entries record the provenance and context of the finds.[21] Woodward's collection has been maintained in its original cabinets and may be seen in the

Sedgwick Museum, Cambridge to this day.[22] The first Wood-wardian Professor, Charles Mason, increased the collection from his extensive foreign travels and a fifth cabinet was added. At the same time a similar process of augmentation and reorganization of the mineral collections was in progress at the Ashmolean Museum and the Royal Society. Lhywd and Woodward had shown a way forward from what had begun as cabinets of eclectic curiosity. In the process, the organic origin of fossils had become an established fact.

THE SLOANE COLLECTION

Collecting rocks, minerals and fossils for practical, aesthetic, scientific and monetary purposes was fashionable throughout the eighteenth century but, unlike Woodward's, few collections have survived intact. Some were not well curated and had nothing but intrinsic interest; others became obsolete as scientific advances in systematic classification were made or better specimens were discovered. This process, which reflects not decline or stagnation but change, is well documented for the Sloane collection.[23] Hans Sloane (1660–1753) was a physician. He collected throughout his life but few of his two hundred thousand specimens were of his own discovery. Although the collection was

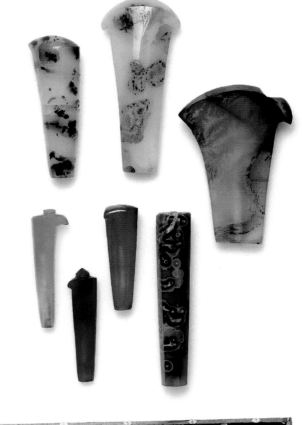

84 A variety of mocha stone, agate, carnelian and jade handles from Sloane's large collection of cameos, spoons, bowls, cups and other artefacts which showed to advantage the lovely colours, translucency and other properties of these minerals. Natural History Museum, Mineralogy.

85 Minerals and fossils from Sloane's pharmaceutical collection, in their original drawer which still bears his labels. He kept a manuscript catalogue identifying the specimens and recording their use and how he acquired them. Natural History Museum, Mineralogy.

86 A copy of Sarah Stone's watercolour of Sir Ashton Lever's Museum with natural history specimens kept in spirit jars on the left, and including shells, birds, large mammals and other animals. Ethno Library.

not specialized like that of Woodward and covered all aspects of natural history, it was well organized and reflected his broad scholarly interests (fig. 84).[24]

Sloane liked to record his own material, and his catalogues show that he separated the fossils or formerly organic remains from the inert components of the earth: crystals, metals and sediments.[25] He used broad categories for his cataloguing and was consistent in his identifications. In listing specimens he used the long descriptive phrases in Latin that were usual in pre-Linnean classifications (see ch. 6). As the chemical constituents that would make possible further classification of minerals were as yet unknown, his classes for these were as good as they could be for the time. He also kept a collection of material of pharmaceutical interest (fig. 85).[26] This included examples of ancient remedies such as jet for toothache, nephrite for kidney problems, amethyst for drunkenness and belemnite for kidney stones. History does not relate his opinion of them but his interest in the prophylactic properties of plants brought from newly discovered areas of the world suggests that he favoured a more modern pharmacopoeia in his practice and kept his collection for historical interest.[27]

Sloane did not use his mineral and fossil collection for original research but the foundation of the British Museum on his death in 1753 made it available free of charge to any member of the public in the first publicly owned museum in Europe. In this context it represented contemporary knowledge and the practice of curation that could be admired, studied, emulated and improved upon. However, in the diary of his visit to London in 1793, the Scottish naturalist Robert Jameson (1774–1854) records that it was difficult to use the collection because of 'very absurd and antiquated' regulations. He further recounts that: 'All the fine collection of Insects & Shells & Minerals are locked up and not shewn', there being only fish and Amphibia on display '… as these are not apt to attract the attention of the vulgar'.[28] For Jameson, Sir Ashton Lever's Leverian Museum opened by the impresario and entrepreneur to a paying public in Leicester Square, then Leicester Fields, was of greater interest.[29] Its coverage was eclectic, including all aspects of natural history, plus antiquities and ethnographic material from Captain Cook's second and third voyages. Cabinets of fossils and minerals can be seen in a painting by Sarah Stone (c. 1760–1844) (fig. 86) that shows the neat organization of the displays, confirming contemporary accounts of how Lever was energetically engaged in its curation. Stone was commissioned by Lever to record some of the outstanding items in the collection and completed some nine hundred drawings and watercolours.[30] These beautiful illustrations also show that each specimen was labelled with its identification and provenance. As a result it was most instructive for the young Jameson and many others who used it but, like so many collections at this time, it was expensive to maintain and was ultimately dispersed in a sale in 1806.

The success of private collections open to a paying public has been taken to indicate that by the turn of the nineteenth century the Sloane collection at the British Museum was in a state of decline and deterioration due to neglect and a general lack of progress in natural history.[31] However, by the turn of the nineteenth century the Museum was rather the victim of its success in terms of attracting visitors and needed to modernize the collections because there had been so many developments in natural history during its first forty years.[32] Within the field of geology, this included new discoveries, classifications and theories. In 1799, the Museum formed a committee of experts to evaluate the Museum's material and recommend new acquisitions to reflect some of the scientific changes that had occurred.

Modernizing collections

The collection of least scientific value acquired by the British Museum following the recommendations of the committee was that of one if its members, the Honourable Charles Greville (1749–1809), Vice Chamberlain of the Household to George III and nephew of Sir William Hamilton. Greville was a connoisseur and his collection consisted of beautiful artefacts and gems which were purchased following his death in 1809 for £13,727. The average wage of a labourer at this time was about £20 a year but Parliament approved the huge sum despite the fact that the country was at war against Napoleon. It certainly added magnificent material for exhibition and had some scientific value in that many of the specimens had been drawn by the artist and collector James Sowerby (1757–1822) to illustrate his *British Mineralogy* (fig. 87), published in eighty-four parts forming five volumes, between 1804 and 1817, as well as his two-volume work *Exotic Mineralogy* (1811–17).[33] These works provided an enormous stimulus to collecting and identifying minerals and fossils throughout Britain. The availability of the published specimens in the museum would have been useful for comparative purposes especially as Sowerby's own collection was broken up. Furthermore, Sowerby followed the important trend of describing and organizing fossils according to the strata in which they were found. This practice was to provide a means of determining the relative age of layers of rock, as well as revealing the extinctions and changes indicative of evolution.

Other acquisitions, including the collections of the Reverend Clayton Mordaunt Cracherode (1730–99) and the eminent chemist Charles Hatchett (1765–1847) acquired in 1799, reflect late eighteenth-century trends more aptly. Cracherode was a Trustee of the British Museum. The small mineral collection he bequeathed was classified following the Linnaean system (see ch. 6). The method of classifying rocks that Linnaeus (1707–78)[34] included in his *Systema naturae* (Leiden, 1735) was the least enduring part of his great work. The manner in which it applied what was known about the properties of rock was in accord with the knowledge of times but his use of the

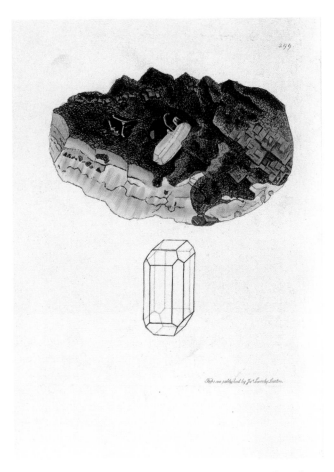

87 Illustration of the sample of Plumbum carbon-muriate from the collection of Charles Greville in James Sowerby's *British Mineralogy*, vol. IV. Sowerby also illustrated books on botany and shells, written by him and by others. His hand-coloured engravings were realistic, accurate and usually life-size. Natural History Museum, Library.

sexual system on inorganic material was not entirely successful although the concept did enable Linnaeus to take some steps in recognizing the significance of crystal forms. Steno had described the mechanical growth of crystals in his *Prodromus*, and Linnaeus took from this the idea that salts were the 'fathers' of stones and recognized that crystal forms varied according to the type of salt from which they developed.

These forms were diagnostic. For example, nitre forms a hexagonal prism whereas alum produces an octahedral configuration. Species of these genera could then be recognized by the way in which the edges or angles of the generic crystal form were truncated. As diamonds and amethyst have a modified octahedral form they were considered as species of the alum genus and could be given a characteristic Linnaean binomial such as *Alumen adamos* for diamond.[35]

Although the Linnaean system of classifying minerals still had its advocates in the late eighteenth century, by this time English collectors were beginning to favour alternatives such as the method of identification advocated as 'oryctognosy' (study of things dug up) by Abraham Gottlob Werner (1749–1817), Inspector of Mining and Instructor of Mineralogy at the Freiburg Mining Academy in Saxony. His chief protagonist in Britain was the Scot, Robert Jameson, who founded the University of Edinburgh collection. Werner's method certainly systematized the teaching of mineralogy by advocating that minerals should be identified by their colour, lustre, form, streaking and specific weight and provenance.[36] However, in his theory on the origins of the earth published in 1791,[37] Werner advocated a new version of the Woodwardian view that all rocks and minerals had been laid down from solution in a primeval ocean. The aqueous origin of rocks proposed in this so-called Neptunist theory opposed new 'Plutonist' ideas developing in Britain and on the continent which advocated that rocks had formed by fusion caused by great heat at the centre of the earth and had been forced upwards. This debate, described in chapter 9, revealed an ignorance of the actual nature of rocks that turned some collectors to investigate their chemical composition.

By the end of the eighteenth century several collectors were showing an interest in the chemical characteristics of minerals. One member of the British Museum's evaluation committee, Charles Hatchett, had actually collected minerals and earths in order to investigate their chemical properties and published several papers on the subject, as well as discovering a new metal which he named columbium, subsequently renamed niobium, in a North American mineral. Indeed, his reputation was such that the mineral substances hatchettite, discovered in Australia and hatchettolite found in North Carolina were named after him. Unfortunately, Hatchett gave up chemistry to take over his father's coach building business but his collection, consisting of about seven thousand specimens, was purchased by the British Museum in 1799 for £700 and reflected state-of-the-art research that was also receiving some influence from Europe despite political instability and war.

Hatchett's classification of his material under nine headings reflects an increasing understanding of both the nature of rocks and the significance of the order in which they were laid down. It included: 'bituminous substances, ores, volcanic products, systematic strata of rocks, strata of rocks of the Hartz arranged by Lasius, strata of rocks arranged by Voight [*sic*], and strata of rocks of Transylvania collected by Fichtel'.[38] The rocks arranged by the German mining consultant Johann Voigt (1752–1821) who included the poet Goethe amongst his pupils, may have been one of the teaching packs he prepared for students in 1785. These consisted of a set of labelled specimens to help the beginner prepare a collection and understand the terminology, as well as notes on types of rocks. An opponent of Werner, he made important observations on the effects of tectonic movements of the earth's crust and volcanism.[39] Johann von Fichtel (d. 1791) had similar interests and was convinced on the basis of field observations that granite was volcanic in origin. Such evidence and the arguments surrounding its interpretation were of considerable interest in Britain, where understanding of the nature of rocks and new theories about their age were emerging. The original Sloane mineral collection was obsolete for this purpose. The new acquisitions, reorganization and display in a room above the King's Library by Kee per Charles Koenig (1774–1851) brought the science of specimens up to date, making it relevant to contemporary debate on the origin of rocks and the age of the earth.

EMERGING DEFINITION

The word 'geology' was first used to distinguish the study of the earth as a topic of interest in a definition of natural philosophy in 1735.[40] Within twenty years it was defined with concise elegance as 'knowledge of the state and nature of the earth' and listed separately under G in Samuel Johnson's *Dictionary of the English Language*. By this time there was a web of co-operative investigators that extended beyond Oxford, Cambridge and London. Their discoveries through fieldwork, mapping and the exchange of mineral and fossil specimens were gradually transforming an aspect of natural philosophy into a subject in its own right. Although there had been no particular peaks of achievement with great names attached to innovative theories that encompassed and surpassed all existing ideas, the early Hanoverian period (1714–75) had established a normal pattern of accumulative investigation independent of genius. Much had changed. The organic origin of fossils was accepted, the nature and origins of minerals were under consideration and the earth was widely regarded as more than six thousand years old. Attention now turned to rocks and the forces that shaped their modern appearance.

9 Rocks, fossils and the emergence of palaeontology

JILL COOK

From the late seventeenth century fieldwork had been directed at collecting minerals and fossils. By the 1750s the collection of these facts had initiated some new understanding of their nature and origins but there had been no comparable development in the understanding of the rocks that incorporated the collectibles. God had created the earth, and Woodward's idea that rocks had re-formed as a result of dissolution following Noah's Flood had not been improved upon in print. However, observations on volcanoes and the effects of earthquakes made on the continent changed this, stimulating research on rocks, land forms and structures that were to substantiate new theories on the origins and age of the earth.

EARTHQUAKES AND VOLCANOES

In 1748 the Reverend Richard Pococke (1704–65), known for his writings on Egypt and the Near East, published a paper in the *Philosophical Transactions* of the Royal Society describing a visit to the Giant's Causeway on the north coast of Ireland, where dramatic cliffs are formed by vertical prismatic columns of basalt. He had made a drawing of the site that he published with a map and notes on other basalt outcrops in the area. Later, on his second journey to Scotland in 1772, the Welsh naturalist, traveller and scholarly collector Thomas Pennant (1726–98), recorded the same type of structure at Fingal's Cave on Staffa in the Hebrides. He published his description in his highly successful book *A Tour of Scotland and Voyage to the Hebrides* (1772) but, like Pococke, he could only speculate on the nature of the rock and cause of the formation. An English diplomat in Naples was to provide the answer.

Sir William Hamilton (1730–1803) (see fig. 161) arrived in Naples in 1764 with no knowledge of natural history or geology yet he was immediately fascinated by Mount Vesuvius and started to record its activity.[1] When it began to erupt in 1765 he spent days and nights observing. He sent his observations for publication in the *Philosophical Transactions* of the Royal Society and, recognizing the importance of continuous direct observation, kept up his work until 1790. He collected every sort of erupted matter and sent them to the British Museum. In 1769 he visited Sicily to observe Mount Etna and noted the vast tracts of land that successive lava eruptions had created. Eight years later he recognized the characteristic rocks and structures of an extinct volcanic landscape in the Rhineland, south of Cologne. By this time he had published one of the most lavish, original and informative books of the eighteenth century. Entitled *Campi Phlegraei*, it appeared in 1776 with fifty-four plates drawn by the artist Pietro Fabris, with a supplement in 1779 (fig. 88). In his text Hamilton

88 Frontispiece by Pietro Fabris for the 1779 supplement of Sir William Hamilton's *Campi Phlegraei*, addressed to the Royal Society in London. The first volumes had been so well-received, and the volcano was still so active, that Hamilton issued this supplement. British Library.

demonstrated that volcanoes built up the land rather than destroying it and suggested that they proved the great age of the earth. He also observed how lava flowed in great masses cooled and solidified to form basalt. Combined with accounts of earthquakes such as that which destroyed much of Lisbon in 1755, a new awareness of forces of nature which were both constructive and destructive had to be absorbed into new theories of the earth.

NEW THEORIES ON THE ORIGINS AND AGE OF THE EARTH

In the late eighteenth century, four broad categories of rocks were recognized: the Primary hard rocks of upland regions, the Secondary soft rocks of lower-lying areas, Volcanic rocks of all ages and superficial Alluvial sediments such as unconsolidated silts, sands and gravels.[2] Following the work of Steno, it was generally acknowledged that massive Primary rocks formed the earth's crust and were overlain by the Secondary rocks. However, these categories were too wide to incorporate the diversity of rocks being recorded in different regions and through individual layers in quarries and mines. In Saxony, Werner developed the idea of the 'formation', a complex of more or less similar rocks or sediments sharing the same origins that could be distinguished from others by distinct boundaries.

Werner, being a deist, made no mention of Noah's Flood in presenting his theory and extended the history of the earth back to about one million years without commenting on the biblical chronology that allowed only a six-thousand-year timespan. However, his theory was linear: the world was being eroded away towards its end and no allowance was made for the effect of movements in the earth's crust (tectonics) interrupting or altering the chain of events, although his students were taught to recognize the structures these produced within and at the boundaries of formations. In Britain this scheme was advocated by Robert Jameson, doyen of the University of Edinburgh who had attended Werner's lectures in Freiburg. However, Werner's theory had its opponents. The wealthy landowner James Hutton (1726–97), who had studied medicine in Edinburgh, Paris and Leiden, realized that Werner's concept of denudation without replenishment would eventually bring an end to the living world. As a modernizing farmer he had studied soil and knew that it was formed by the destructive forces of erosion. This he believed was counterbalanced by tectonic uplift of new rocks formed by the deposition of sediments eroded from older rocks. He considered that new rocks were formed by heat and fusion not water; uplifted they formed new land which was in turn denuded. His earth history was a constant process of recycling in which he could envisage 'no vestige of a beginning – no prospect of an end'.[3]

Hutton had discovered geological time: the earth was no longer six thousand years old but infinitely older. Realizing the theological implications of his conclusion, he wrote of his opposition to scriptural geology but emphasized that his theory was 'not in any way concerned with the period at which Man was made' and did not 'in any respect interfere with the chronology of the Old Testament',[4] thereby suggesting that the biblical chronology related only to human history (see ch. 17) which was not his concern. This did little to assuage the fundamentalists, and the full version of Hutton's theory published in 1795 also came under attack by proponents of the Wernerian theory led by Jameson, as well as those geologists who needed the catastrophe of the Flood to explain evidence for the extinction of large vertebrate animals known from fossils.

Hutton's theory was dismissed as speculative and lacking in empirical evidence. There was some justice in this.[5] Hutton's 1785 paper to the recently formed Royal Society of Edinburgh, published in the *Transactions* for 1788, was not based on firsthand field observations, and his book published in 1795 relied heavily on lengthy quotations from other works. This is surprising because he had found proof for several cycles of deposition and uplift, as well as evidence that granite was of volcanic origin rather than being a petrified water-lain sediment of the greatest age, as suggested by the Wernerians or 'Neptunists'.[6] Instead it was Hutton's friend the Presbyterian minister John Playfair (1748–1819), Professor of Mathematics at the University of Edinburgh, who clarified these matters making Hutton's work more readable in *Illustrations of the Huttonian Theory of the Earth*, published in 1802.

Playfair's exposition of Hutton did not answer all reservations. In his theory Hutton attributed change to processes he could see in action in the modern world. His cycles required no miracles or catastrophes such as Noah's Flood. Others denied that there could have been uniformity through time because there was geological evidence against it. In the absence of glacial theory, the only explanation for rocks dumped far from their original formation ('erratics'), massive spreads of boulder clay and bedded drift deposits was catastrophic flooding. Furthermore, the constancy implicit in Hutton's theory did not allow for the climatic changes implied by discoveries such as that of the fossilized remains of a hippopotamus at Chatham, Kent, by James Douglas in 1785[7] and later by Dean William Buckland (1784–1856). Nevertheless, the idea that the earth must have a much greater age than that allowed by scripture was spreading.

FOSSILS AND STRATIFICATION

Although fossils had been collected throughout the century, their relevance to geology had not been fully appreciated. Referred to as 'extraneous' or 'exotic' minerals or fossils following Woodward (see ch. 8), they were not used for any scholarly purpose but were generally just enjoyed for their intrinsic interest. Attention focused on Primary rocks that lacked fossils but contained valuable mineral veins that could be exploited for economic purposes.[8] The observations of a surveyor supervising the digging of a canal through Secondary rocks changed this.

William Smith (1769–1839) was the son of an Oxfordshire blacksmith brought up on his uncle's farm following the death of his father. He attended the village school and was apprenticed to a Gloucestershire surveyor in 1787 before setting up in his own practice in Bath in 1791. While working on drainage and other land improvement projects he obtained a shareholding in a coal mine near his home at High Littleton in north Somerset. During the summer of 1792, he descended the mine shaft many times and noticed that the strata were not horizontal but sloped to the east, extending unseen for hundreds of miles. He reasoned that by following the slope it would be possible to predict where and at what depth that same rock would be found in other places. Furthermore, he learned from the miners that every seam of coal had particular characteristics and occurred in a predictable sequence wherever a pit was dug. He guessed that this might mean that a similar arrangement of strata might be found in all the rocks of Britain but he needed to see cuttings across a long transect to prove his theory.

The opportunity for this came with the proposed construction of the Somerset Canal on which Smith went to work as a supervisor. Every day he surveyed, cut and recorded sections and collected fossils. In doing this he found that the fossils found in layers of sedimentary rock were always in a certain order from top to bottom and, as a tour around England in 1794 showed him, this order could be seen again and again. Rocks at different locations could be correlated by their fossils and mapped. He had established the principle of faunal succession, and, although there was scarce acknowledgement of his achievement in years ahead, his work might have circulated and been absorbed more quickly had he immediately published his discovery in print form.[9]

After his dismissal from the Canal project in 1799, Smith devoted himself to producing a geological map of England and Wales. While travelling hundreds of miles on business he recorded numerous sections, all of which were used to compile the map which was finally published in 1815. The endeavour ruined Smith financially and he had to sell his collection to the British Museum in 1816. It contained some three thousand carefully provenanced specimens, and in the catalogue published as *The Stratigraphical System of Organized Fossils* in 1817 Smith coined the term *stratification* to refer to a sequence of strata. He had added the vital third dimension to geology. The study of stratification would reveal the chronological relationships between rocks; biostratigraphy would provide correlations between regions and across continents. Smith had made an important breakthrough.

Smith's work had an enormous if delayed impact. By 1837 Buckland was able to publish an ideal section through the earth's crust showing the relationship between stratified sedimentary and massive, unstratified rocks such as granite.[10] The old terminology had gone. Stratigraphic successions or 'systems'

with particular characteristics were given the names such as Silurian, Carboniferous and Cretaceous by which they are still known, eventually to be put in order on a geological timescale. Hutton's conclusion that the unstratified rocks were of volcanic or 'igneous' origin was incorporated and the plants and animals found as characteristic fossils in particular parts of the stratification are shown above the section. The history of the earth was starting to be written from evidence rather than theory. Systematic work on the fossils was important to this.

Smith was exceptional in bringing the fossil succession together with the concept of a map but he published only two short works describing his method.[11] These were not published until after his map. By then the connection he had made been fossils and strata was widely known and others with interests in fossils began taking a more analytical approach to the study of palaeontology.

ADVANCES ON SMITH'S WORK

In London the political pamphleteer and surgeon James Parkinson (1755–1824), renowned for defining Parkinson's disease, had built up a fine collection of fossils (fig. 89).[12] His collecting led to his work *Organic Remains of a Former World* (1804–11), which has been described as an 'outstanding event in the history of our scientific knowledge of British fossils'.[13] However, it is transitional rather than revolutionary in its contribution. Through the course of three volumes it is evident that Parkinson was refining his ideas. In addressing the general reader he structured his text as a series of letters between the expert and the beginner. After presenting a history of the ideas relating to fossils, the first volume deals with vegetable fossils and describes the impressive array of chemical analyses he used to discover their nature. Having correctly concluded that bitumen, amber, jet, coal and peat were all of vegetable origin, he wrongly ascribed the cause of coal and peat to cataclysmic flooding. The second volume concentrated on corals, sponges and crinoids, and the third on starfish, sea urchins, arthropods and vertebrates.

Parkinson's approach was thoroughly descriptive but he did not use Linnaean or any other nomenclature to define his specimens, stating that 'Even to one who possessed the necessary qualifications, success, in the present state of our knowledge, could not be assured'.[14] In this respect, *Organic Remains* might just be regarded as an updating of Lhwyd's *Lithophylacii*. Despite his political radicalism, Parkinson was a scriptural geologist. Considering the palaeontological evidence for extinctions he proposed a sequence of creations with humans coming last, eschewing emerging ideas on the transmutation of species such as that of Erasmus Darwin (1731–1802) that allowed for the progression of animal forms into more complex types. This necessarily made Parkinson a catastrophist. Summoning up floods to destroy the forests fossilized in coal, he inevitably rejected Hutton's eternity of

89 Whale barnacles like this fossilized one live embedded in the skin of whales. When Parkinson illustrated this specimen in his book in 1811, he thought this species still existed, but it was later studied by Charles Darwin who recognized it as from the extinct species *Cornula barbara.* Natural History Museum, Palaeontology.

repeating cycles. In modern minds these ideas might seem conservative, even counter-revolutionary, but for the fact that volume three included a statement of the principle of faunal succession proved by describing the fossils characteristic of twenty-three rock units covering a vast period of geological time. This invaluable framework provided a key reference for collectors and geologists well into the nineteenth century. Although it did not acknowledge Smith, it undoubtedly disseminated knowledge of his discovery.

Parkinson did not know Smith and must have become familiar with his ideas through his acquaintance with other geologists. It is possible that he added this final letter in the knowledge that Smith's friend, John Farey (1766–1826) was about to publish a survey of Derbyshire commissioned by Sir Joseph Banks (1743–1820). Recognizing the predictive value of Smith's discovery, Banks employed Farey to carry out a survey of the county in which he had both agricultural and mining interests. The result was the first geological section across England and a description of the soils and succession of strata in his *Survey of the County of Derbyshire,* published in 1811.

Farey's work seems to have influenced that of William Martin, who published his *Petrificata Derbiensa* in four parts between 1794 and 1809. *Petrificata* describes fossils collected in that county with much insight. It was followed by *Outlines of an Attempt to Establish Knowledge of Extraneous Fossils on Scientific Principles* which could be described as the first palaeontological textbook. In this work Martin uses Linnaean nomenclature and emphasizes that a fossil should never be named and described from a single example because 'In many instances, it is only by collating a number of specimens, that we are able to acquire that knowledge of a species, which is sufficient for the purpose of discrimination'.[15] He also

stresses the importance of recording the strata in which fossils have been found because Farey 'has well pointed out to me the utility as well as the practicability of distinguishing the various strata in a soil, or series of strata, by their organic contents'. Like James Sowerby's works on *Mineral Conchology of Great Britain* (seven volumes, 1812–46) and *Genera of Recent and Fossil Shells* (two volumes, 1821–34), completed by his sons, Martin's publications are important to the development of systematic classification of fossils. They also show that Smith's insight was spreading and being effectively adopted. Larger fossils were also starting to cause a stir.

DINOSAURS

During the seventeenth and eighteenth centuries large fossilized animal bones were occasionally found both in rocks and in unconsolidated deposits. They were a mystery. In 1758, Mr Wooller reported the remains of what looked like a crocodile found in cliffs near Whitby on the Yorkshire coast to the Royal Society. He compared it with living crocodiles from Bengal, noted differences and declared it to be older than Noah's Flood or 'antediluvian'.[16] Similar chance finds became well known,[17] but they remained unexplained novelties for which there was little comparison until some remarkable finds were made in Dorset at the turn of the century.

The cliffs of Lyme Bay on the Dorset coast were a well-known source of invertebrate fossils, particularly ammonites and belemnites, in the late eighteenth century. To supplement their income during a period of poverty and starvation during the Napoleonic war, the inhabitants of Lyme Regis collected these curiosities from the cliffs and sold them as souvenirs to travellers. Amongst them was the Anning family whose discoveries were to start a new branch of palaeontology.[18] In 1810 Joseph Anning discovered the skull of what appeared to be a crocodile and showed his sister Mary (1798–1847) where he had found it. Mary, who had regularly collected fossils with her late father, watched the place for nearly a year and eventually discovered the creature's body. The fossil was sold to the local lord but news of it spread and Buckland visited Lyme. The animal was unlike anything seen before and took ten years to publish. The description was done by Buckland's friend the Reverend William Conybeare, who noted that the skull was similar to a crocodile but differed in important detail while the body was more like that of a fish. He named it *ichthyosaur* or fish-lizard (fig. 90). Mary continued searching the cliffs often in the company of geologists and added a plesiosaur (a marine reptile) and a pterosaur (flying reptile), as well as numerous invertebrates, to the ark of new animals now known to have existed from about two hundred million to sixty-five million years ago. Spurred on by these finds Dr Gideon Mantell (1790–1852) was exploring quarries in Sussex where he discovered and described the giant lizards, megalosaurus and iguanadon.

90 Skull and lower jaw of an ichthyosaur, *Ichthyosaurus platyodon*, collected by Mary Anning from the Blue Lias of Lyme Regis, Dorset, in 1821. She was the first person to find a complete ichthyosaur, the year previously, and later was to discover a plesiosaur (1824) and a pterodactyl (1828). Natural History Museum, Palaeontology.

These extraordinary animals, which Richard Owen later named 'dinosaurs' meaning terrible lizards, opened up a new branch of palaeontology and further controversy about the age of the earth. Dinosaur remains were found stratified in ancient rocks. Their distant world was evidently pre-human and lasted a long time. They obviously became extinct. All this could be dealt with by reasoning that the pre-human world was represented by the six days of biblical creation being an allegorical representation of vast geological time. However, there was also an increasing awareness of mammal bones being discovered in caves and superficial deposits in Germany and France. These were clearly much more recent than those of the dinosaurs but included extinct species such as mammoth and woolly rhinoceros, as well as animals such as hyena and hippopotamus that no longer occur in Europe. Such fauna suggested climatic change and raised the question of whether they were contemporary with human life. Interest in the problem led to the excavation of British sites notably by Buckland who, finding no evidence for such contemporaneity, concluded that a catastrophe, Noah's Flood, had caused the extinction of what are now known to be Ice Age faunas (one million to ten thousand years old). Once again science and the Bible were reconciled. Artists such as Francis Danby (1793–1861) and J. M. W. Turner (1775–1851) painted dramatic scenes of the Deluge, but the way ahead for Lyell, Owen, Darwin and Agassiz had been also been opened.

EMPLOYMENT AND PROFESSIONALISM

In the late seventeenth century the community of natural historians interested in finding out about the earth was vigorous but small. Most of its members had a clerical or medical background and were connected by the universities of Oxford and Cambridge. Although the foundation of the Royal Society in 1660 and the regular publication of its *Philosophical Transactions* did much to reduce the intellectual isolation of the natural historians, private correspondence was still the main means of exchanging ideas. The subjects embraced by natural theology or history were not taught; the self-educated in these matters might have had no successors had it not been for the popularity of the theories of the earth published by Burnet and Woodward. General interest in these books probably relates to changing attitudes towards religion. The religious strife of the seventeenth century had divided families, altered fortunes and blighted lives. The toleration brought about by the accession of William and Mary in 1689 enabled people to express their faith through natural theology in quiet rejection of the politics of the established churches. By the end of the eighteenth century this mood had found obvious expression as the nonconformist, dissenting movements emerged. Excluded from formal education in grammar schools and universities, rational dissenters, among them many Quakers, found an alternative culture in practical scientific pursuits. This enabled them to find employment in new trades often related to science such as chemistry, plating and engraving, instrument making, surveying and geological consultancy. Opportunities in these fields arose from agrarian reform and industrialization.

Enclosing pasture and arable land to prevent the exercise of common rights so that fields could be more profitably and efficiently managed began in about 1750. Enclosure and improvement required surveyors. As ditches were cut and hedges planted, the surveyors became familiar with soil and rock types, as well as finding fossils and minerals. Both Farey and Smith were among the many who earned their living in this way. Although such men were cut off from the conceptual developments of the Oxbridge and London elite and knew little about contemporary discoveries, their unrivalled empirical knowledge based on fieldwork influenced the metropolitan institutions. The need to exploit other natural resources for profit also encouraged the developing middle-class professionalism.

Banks's employment of Farey on his Derbyshire estate was brought about by the desire to prospect for minerals that might be exploited commercially. He was not atypical. When the Askesian Society was founded in 1796 its members took an entirely utilitarian view of mineralogy.[19] They carried out chemical analysis of soils and minerals received from farmers, coal owners and industrialists throughout country, as well as publishing notes on metallic oxides, gilding, malleability and the chemistry of mineral waters. Dissenters formed a high proportion of the membership of the Askesian Society, and anybody could attend meetings of the Literary and Philosophical Society of Newcastle-upon-Tyne founded in 1793, where practical local geology based on local knowledge of coal mining and lead working were frequent topics of discussion.

Radical energy, religious or otherwise, also played an important role in the achievements of some members of the Lunar Society of Birmingham founded in the 1760s. The Society included a mix of Dissenters, gentlemen and industrialists. Amongst them were scientists, engineers and thinkers such as James Keir, James Watt, Matthew Boulton, Joseph Priestley, Josiah Wedgwood and Erasmus Darwin. The interaction of their needs and skills encouraged the development of geology for the exploitation of mining and industrial processes. Keir (1735–1820), a soldier turned chemist, experimented with minerals in investigations to improve glass making, in the course of which he produced a pioneering paper on mineral crystallization.[20] He also assisted his friend Josiah Wedgwood (1730–95) to find the materials he needed to make a fine white body for his pottery. They collected materials in Derbyshire and carried out over five thousand experiments with feldspar, moorstone, spaths and barium carbonate to develop jasper that would not crack in the kiln.[21] Watt was also testing spars for his Glasgow pottery works, and Boulton's geological researches, instigated by pot-making interests, led him to exploit the Blue John mines to make high quality ornaments from its beautiful radix amethyst that had formed along the boundary between the limestone of the Peak District and the granites, sandstone and millstone grit of the Pennines. Further north, the highly profitable exploitation of sal ammoniac on the Scottish estate of James Hutton who visited the Lunar Society and numbered several of its members amongst his friends and supporters, is a reminder that many of those writing about geology were still landed gentlemen and, strictly speaking, amateurs.[22]

Supplying such gentlemen with specimens and assisting them with the cataloguing and illustration of their collections was also a gainful occupation for men and women. In Wales, the Morris brothers, Lewis, Richard and William, supplied natural history specimens of all kinds to Thomas Pennant (see fig. 82) and others. In Cornwall William Borlase (see ch. 17) not only supplied minerals and fossils as cabinet specimens to Pennant and other wealthy collectors in order to supplement his meagre income as a parson, but also sent three or four tons of minerals to decorate a grotto in the garden of the poet and essayist Alexander Pope.

In Dorset, Mary Anning was sought out for her expertise in finding and extracting the fossils that were her business although she, like other women, would not be admitted to scientific societies and never contributed her knowledge to a journal. Contemporary literature also acknowledged women's interest in minerals, as when in Jane Austen's *Pride and Prejudice* Elizabeth Bennett contents herself with a visit to the Peak District instead of the Lakes because there she might at least find 'a few petrified spars'. Illustration was a source of pleasure and employment for women, as shown by the work of Sarah Stone at the Leverian Museum without which there would be but a scant record of the Lever collection (see fig. 86). Other women worked on illustrations to accompany articles in books and encyclopaedias but at the time there was little acknowledgement of their work and their skills were not allowed to develop.

CONCLUSION

Conceived in the age of Enlightenment, geology had come of age by the turn of the nineteenth century. In 1807 a dining club called the Geological Society was set up by thirteen geologists with modern practical interests. The club expanded rapidly, founding its own collection and library, circulating questionnaires to elicit records and setting up a committee to standardize nomenclature by selecting appropriate terms and eliminating colloquial names. By 1809 its sphere of influence was increasing. Independent of the Royal Society, it absorbed both the Mineralogical and Askesian Societies and began publishing its own *Transactions*.[23] Geology was being taught at the universities of Oxford and Cambridge, discussed in the salons and societies of gentlemen and practised by middle-class professionals. From a wide, co-operative network, by slow accumulative activity, it had acquired a conceptual, systematic and empirical basis that was to be the foundation of the nineteenth-century transformation of science. Geological debate was also influencing the romantic aesthetic of contemporary poetry and art in revealing the majesty and antiquity of the earth, exploring slow but profound processes, imagining great catastrophes and subterranean depths, all of which were 'a geological way of seeing'.[24]

PART III

DITA HÆC ARTIS ET NATVRÆ   MACHINAMENTA AD EXCITANDAM ANTIQVITATIS MEMORIAM FE

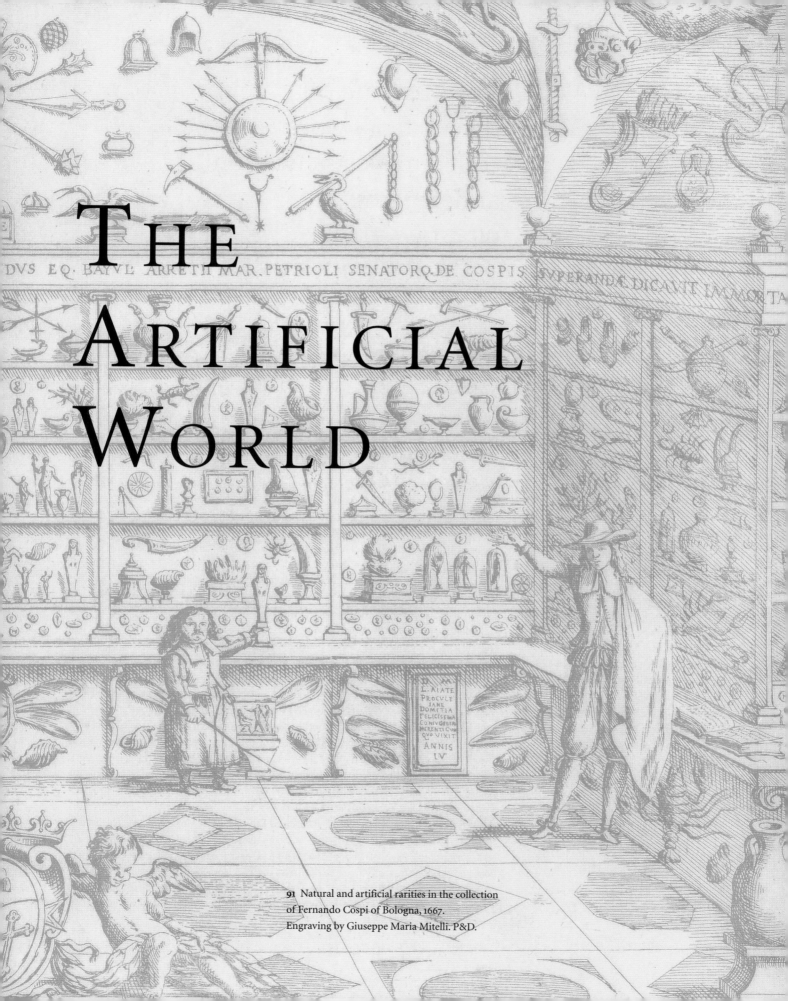

THE
ARTIFICIAL
WORLD

91 Natural and artificial rarities in the collection
of Fernando Cospi of Bologna, 1667.
Engraving by Giuseppe Maria Mitelli. P&D.

10

The ordering of the artificial world: collecting, classification and progress

LUKE SYSON

92 Watercolour of Charles Townley's *cista* (engraved bronze container), 3rd century BC, supposedly found in a shrine at Palestrina c. 1786, with a group of other 'Ancient Bronze vessels and instruments of sacrifice'. The group is now known as Townley's *cista mystica* and was probably found in a tomb. GR.

P art II of this book looked at the development of the discipline 'natural history', in a period when the study of 'natural curiosities' was beginning to be seen as distinct from the interpretation of 'artificial curiosities'. But the world of the Enlightenment was not the world of the highly specialized scholars of today, and the same people often had an interest in and studied and collected artefacts as well as the products of nature. The way that the collection, study and classification of 'artificial curiosities' developed is the theme of Part III, and it will become clear how developments in one area can be paralleled in the other.

A collection of objects should rarely be seen as a matter of neutral accumulation. In the seventeenth and eighteenth centuries, just as now, collections were built up to make points about the character, wealth, intellectual pursuits and status of the collector, about the universe in which he or (less often) she lived and about his or her place in it. Fundamental to our understanding of these purposes are the organizing principles which guided the listings, catalogues and publications of collections and which lay behind the ways in which objects were displayed together (fig. 91). By analysing these different methods it becomes possible to determine the perceived functions and uses of particular collections.

This chapter concentrates on the man-made or 'artificial' as opposed to the 'natural' world and is intended to provide a broad intellectual background to the more specific studies in the following chapters (chs 11–15) of the collections – of coins, maps, gems, vases and other antiquities – amassed by Charles Townley (fig. 92), Richard Payne Knight, William Hamilton and George III. It will demonstrate that it was because of changes in antiquarian method that the aims and ambitions of the collections formed in the second half of the eighteenth century in Britain, including those in the British Museum, were substantially different from those formed in the first half of the century and at the end of the seventeenth century, such as that of the long-lived Sir Hans Sloane, for example, the main founding collection of the British Museum. The Enlightenment imperative to give a philosophical and scientific dimension to antiquarianism, a development that received as much impetus from continental European scholars as from the British, or more, connects this shift with that in another area of collecting – that of scientific instruments themselves. The fact that their primary value lay increasingly in their capacity to demonstrate 'new' scientific principles and their practical application, rather than in their antiquarian interest, was ultimately to ensure that these types of material were institutionally divided, one from the other, in Britain and elsewhere (see ch. 14).

93 Greek vases from Sir William Hamilton's collection and one of
d'Hancarville's illustrated volumes describing the collection, with a
selection of casts, antique gems and bronzes. GR.

COLLECTIONS, MUSEUMS AND GALLERIES

It has been argued that by the beginning of the nineteenth
century the British Museum aspired to display its antiquities
collections in such a way as to illustrate evolutionary notions
of human artistic progress, at the heart of which lay a belief
that increasing or decreasing adherence to a naturalistic aesthetic was a signal of man's spiritual state (see ch. 16).[1] By
institutionalizing such a scheme, the British Museum, and
other European museums and galleries at much the same time,
could be said to be drawing physical parallels between evolved
ancient Greek perfection and the current 'enlightened'

94 John and Andrew van Rymsdyk, *Museum Britannicum*, 2nd edition, 1791. A hand-coloured aquatint depicting a piece of stone that looks like landscape and an agate pendant from Sloane's collection (reversed). Central Library. Beside it is the agate pendant: 'here again nature has drawn in it … an eclipse of the sun and the moon'. MME.

regimes under whose auspices the collections were built up and displayed.[2] The message was often carefully reinforced by the Greek revival architecture of their settings; this was certainly the case with Smirke's chosen architectural idiom for the reconstructed British Museum and the placement of Richard Westmacott's relief of the *Progress of Civilisation* on its pediment (see ch. 4 and fig. 208).

However, that is not to say that such a progressive sequence was ever fully achieved in Bloomsbury. In part this failure, if so it can be counted, was caused by a flood of incoming material from all over the world which limited the possibilities for such disciplined displays; in part because display policies in most institutions lagged a little – sometimes quite considerably – behind avant-garde thinking in other areas of intellectual endeavour. Thus the British Museum at

the beginning of the nineteenth century was fully the product of earlier epistemological approaches to objects, natural and artificial (fig. 93), systems of thought and belief which, in some instances, significantly predate the Museum's foundation, going back to the late seventeenth century when Sir Hans Sloane started his collecting activities.

The founding collection of the British Museum could be regarded as typical, in its aims and universal scope (though perhaps not its great size), of any European cabinet of curiosities. Sloane's was a collection which set out to make manifest the wonders of God's universe to mankind, to stimulate enquiry, provoke or satisfy curiosity and, by an emphasis on the rare, the exotic and the exceptional, to encourage speculation on the mysteries of nature and the ingenuity of humankind at its centre. The approach was essentially connective; similarities were as important as differences. Thus any attempt to reorganize the collection along evolutionary lines would have not only required the physical rearrangement of artefacts but implied a wholesale rejection of this earlier thinking.

Sloane made distinctions between his treatment of his natural history specimens (in which he was certainly more interested) and his artefacts, but it was essential to this microcosmic approach that both could be seen together (fig. 94). Indeed their necessary proximity goes some way to explaining why, even after antiquarianism and natural history had become more distinct disciplines, a certain parallelism of method and approach developed in the eighteenth century between them. An examination of Sloane's catalogues, as well as accounts of the arrangement of his collections, illuminates the functions of a cabinet of curiosities such as the one he had built up. His many catalogues of natural history specimens were followed by two other main categories: 'Miscellaneous Things not comprehended with the foregoing [natural history specimens], both Natural and Artificial' (2,098 curiosities) and 'things relating to the Customs of antient Times, or Antiquities, Urns, Instruments, &c.' (1,125 objects).[3] He formed separate listings of his 'mathematical instruments' (55), for hardstone vessels and gems (700) and for 'Medals, antient, as Samarian, Phaenician, Greek, Consular, Roman &c. and Modern, and Coins in all Metals' (some 23,000).

However, it is clear that some of the distinctions maintained in his catalogues were not reflected in the objects' displays. Saveur Morand in 1729 described a great jumble of things: Egyptian antiquities were sited just before nearly four thousand different insects and a Surinam toad; shoes of different nations (fig. 95) and 'Indian clothes' were arranged between fossils and pearls. And the 1748 account of the Swede Per Kalm indicates that artefacts were arranged with *naturalia* – so that petrified objects including wood were stored in the same place as a Lapp drum and 'strange tobacco pipes', carved from stone, a mummy (fig. 96) with anatomical objects. Apart from polished and engraved gems, included presumably because of the minerals they were carved from, his description does not include classical antiquities. These displays were less higgledy-piggledy than they might seem today. Sloane was interested not just in natural phenomena but in the ways in which natural 'productions' could be transformed by human hand. Thus his classifications, like those of Pliny the Elder, were frequently based on materials, placing like with like, whether worked or unworked, and craftmanship taking precedence over style. Moreover a 1748 newspaper account of the visit of the Prince and Princess of Wales to Sloane's cabinet mentions not only coins and medals but also

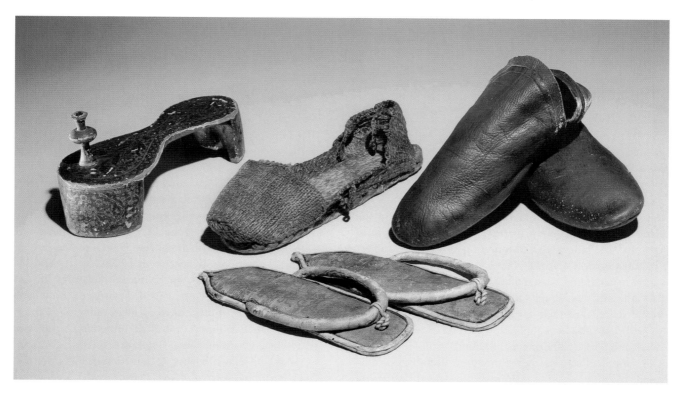

95 A group of shoes from Sloane's collection acquired through a wide variety of contacts from the Coromandel Coast of India (left), the Spanish Pyrenees, Morocco and Japan. Ethno.

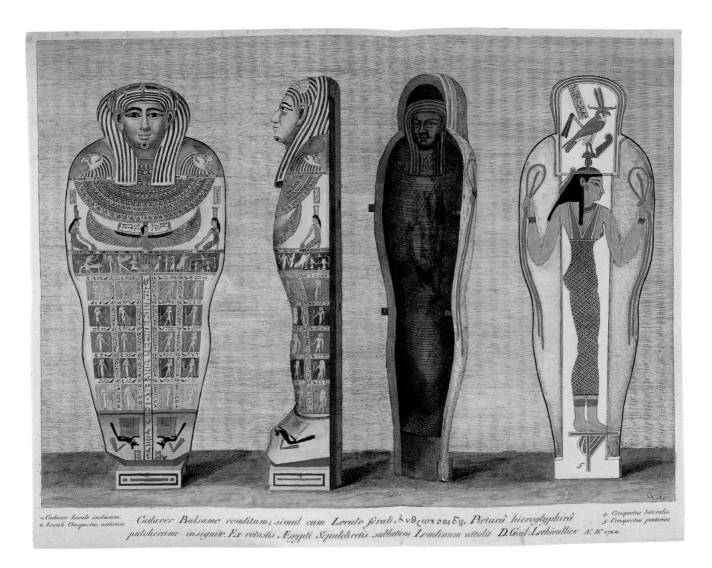

96 William Lethieullier's mummy and coffin, bequeathed to the British Museum in 1756. Hand-coloured engraving by C. Vandergucht, 1737. Sloane's mummy no longer survives. AES Library.

'the most precious and remarkable ornaments used in the *habits* of men, from Siberia to the Cape of Good Hope, from Japan to Peru', indicating a classification of objects by subject and function which could embrace and organize archaeo-logical material and contemporary exotica. This description also indicates that Sloane's antiquities were kept separately 'below stairs': described as from 'Egypt, Greece, Hetruria, Rome, Britain and even America', these objects were listed as 'relating to the Customs of antient Times'.[4]

Sloane's collections might therefore usefully be com-pared to that of Elias Ashmole in Oxford, to Ralph Thoresby's in Leeds, or to other collections in Europe, such as Pierre Borel's (1620–71) in Castres. His *Antiquitez, raretez, plantes, minéraux et autres choses considérables de la ville et du comté de Castres* included a 'Catalogue des choses rares'

in the author's own 'museum'.[5] The introduction was addressed to 'the curious' and he described his museum as a microcosm, which included not only the works of God and nature but also liberal, mechanical and chemical arts – that is, the works of peoples from all over the world. This hierarchy was indicated by the catalogue where objects were arranged into standard categories: first, the 'Raretez de l'Homme' (anatomical specimens), then a sequence of quadrupeds (mammals), birds, marine creatures, insects and serpents, and plants (divided up into roots and branches, leaves, gums, seeds, fruits), minerals ('firstly stones'), petrified things and other minerals – a reversed Aristotelian 'Chain of Being' – followed finally by antiqui-ties and 'Choses artificielles'. It can be seen therefore that Sloane's cabinet shared many characteristics with other museums in this period; they were deliberately expansive 'compendia of the universe' whose broad remits were intended to encompass all the wonders of God's creation, whether animal, mineral or vegetable.

But is evident even in these early collections that classical antiquities and artificial curiosities were to some extent separated out. This was a trend that was to continue at the beginning of the eighteenth century with increasingly distinct classifications applied to different parts of what had previously been unified collections. Cabinets of curiosities were broken up into different spaces and categories and placed in the care of specialists: numismatic collections were separated from other antiquities, and self-contained collections of scientific instruments, prints and drawings, artificial treasures, paintings and natural history were established. Thus different classification methods were applied at different times. The study of the 'habits of man' proved influential on thematic physical displays of artificial objects, contemporary artefacts collected all over the world as well as antiquities. The antiquarian scholar Marchese Scipione Maffei (1675–1755), for example, was largely responsible for (re)creating the museum of sculptures and inscriptions in his home town of Verona.[6] This was made up of local pieces as well as Greek, mainly Hellenistic, sculptures and Etruscan, Hebrew, Arab, and Christian medieval monuments and inscriptions. These groups, and especially the large body of Roman material, were then broken down into subdivisions – sections which dealt with the sacred, imperial, matters relating to senate, magistracy and so on. In 1732–6 he also advocated the reorganization of the antiquities in Paris in such a way that they could be studied to reveal 'certainty and truth about the customs, the opinions and the learning of ancient times'.

Indeed, displays of sculpture according to subject and function became almost standard; parallels can be adduced at the Villa Albani and the Museo Pio-Clementino in Rome, and, just as Maffei urged, at the Louvre.[7] In Turin in 1764 Edward Gibbon (1737–94) was able to admire the arrangement of antiquities in the royal cabinet of curiosities, housed on the ground floor of the university.[8] There the pieces were arranged in eight glass-fronted cases, each dedicated to one of the Roman gods. The case devoted to Bacchus, for instance, contained antiquities related to theatrical performances – images of actors, masks and so on – while the vitrine given to Hercules had a bas-relief depicting the rescue of daughter of the king of Troy which led on to a display of 'Trojan' and Roman objects.[9] Its curator was one Giuseppe Bartoli, a disciple of Maffei.

When Sloane's curiosities went on show in Montagu House, the 1762 guide indicates that in certain respects this method of arrangement by subject – already implicit in the division of the catalogues – had become more central and organized.[10] Although it is true that the ordering of Sloane's coins and medals by subject, the 'lasting monuments of historical facts', was lost during their move, what little is known

about the arrangement of the Museum's classical antiquities, mostly Sloane's, suggests that they were classified by theme and object type rather than chronologically – drinking vessels, for example were displayed together, as were so-called sacrificial instruments.[11] And, once again, this method was extended, as perhaps it had always been, to material which we would now term ethnographical. 'We may see', says the guide, 'the progress of Art in the Different Ages of the World, exemplified in a Variety of Utensils each Nation in Each Century has produced.' There was a comparative display of idols, supposedly revealing similarities between Egyptian and American idols to illustrate the peopling of the Americas from Europe.

Paintings were usually treated separately, and it was in displays of fine art that the progressive advance of the arts of the kind later proposed for classical antiquities was first publicly expressed, most notably in Vienna.[12] The catalogue of the imperial paintings collected together at the Belvedere by their curator Christian von Mechel (1737–1817) was published in 1781. In the catalogue he outlined the principles behind the rearrangement and new groupings of pictures by chronology and school – calling it a 'depot de l'histoire visible de l'art', with an emphasis on instruction. His treatment of the paintings can be compared to the new arrangements of the imperial natural history and coin collections, which now formed distinct areas of study, no longer parts of a standard *wunderkammer*.[13]

It took a little longer before other artefacts, whether ancient or modern, were displayed to demonstrate chronological 'progress'. Alexandre Lenoir (1761–1839) opened his Musée des Monuments Français in Paris to the public in 1795, filled with contents of churches which had been sacked during the Revolution. Its longest gallery showed sculptures from the sixteenth and seventeenth centuries (with some earlier material), arranged in a rough chronology to encapsulate what Lenoir viewed as progress and decline.[14] But a chronological scheme for the display of classical antiquities was adopted by the architect Leo von Klenze (1784–1864) only in 1816–30, for the sculptures in Ludwig of Bavaria's Glyptothek in Munich, where the Aegina marbles were treated as the perfect nub of a developmental sequence leading from Egypt to Rome to the revival of the arts under Ludwig.[15]

ANTIQUARIES AND PHILOSOPHERS

Such displays represent a substantial epistemological shift from the end of the seventeenth century to the beginning of the nineteenth. At the beginning of this period chronological divisions were to some extent collapsed so as to explore connections between the habits of man. Investigations of antiquity of this kind established connections between cultures which could be extended into scholars' and collectors' own day. Thus classifications derived from the establishment of these connections were not necessarily period-specific. By the nineteenth century such concerns were combined with or overlaid by others, which laid more stress on change over periods of time and within different cultures or societies. Some aspects of this newer treatment of *artificialia* reflect Enlightenment investigations of other kinds, especially in the fields of history and natural history.

Certainly by the beginning of the eighteenth century, in Britain and elsewhere in Europe, the image of the antiquary was more than a little tarnished, and the study of ancient artefacts had become somewhat discredited. Sloane himself wrote in his *Natural History* published in 1707: 'the Knowledge of Natural-History, being Observations of Matters of Fact, is more certain than most Others, and in my slender Opinion, less subjected to Mistakes, than Reasonings, Hypotheses and Deductions are' and he insisted upon the distinction between 'Matter of Fact, Experiment, or Observation, and what is Hypothesis'.[16] Antiquarian endeavour was not always seen as meeting these expectations. In his 1728 *Dunciad* Alexander Pope used familiar terms (and deliberately archaic language) in his portrait of the notably conservative Oxford historian Thomas Hearne (1678–1735), whose work was based mostly on his reading and cataloguing of medieval manuscripts in the Bodleian Library:

> But who is he, in closet close y-pent
> Of sober face, with learned dust besprent?
> Right well mine eyes arede the myster wight,
> On parchment scraps y-fed, and Wormius hight.[17]

Hearne, in other words, was one kind of dunce (and Pope created a whole taxonomy) because of his exaggerated and indiscriminate preoccupation with the material fragments of the past, studying recondite irrelevancies while shut away from the great matters of the present world.

Although this kind of investigation of the past had achieved a legitimacy and an authority by the efforts of English antiquaries from the late sixteenth century onwards to construct a national history, it was now all too often perceived as an end in itself. The broader moral purpose of historians was sometimes viewed as lost within a mass of minutiae, the study of objects seen as of dubious merit from the point of view of its lack of utility in a modern Britain. Its findings were also distrusted because of the perceived incompetence or downright dishonesty of the so-called experts. Pope described Sir Andrew Fountaine (1676–1753), another kind of antiquarian dunce, as 'false as his gems and cancer'd as his coins'.

This was the traditional meat of the satirical jibes that were long aimed at the antiquary in the early eighteenth century. But Pope's criticism was of a kind which was slowly underpinned by more serious intellectual challenges; seventeenth-century antiquarian methods had been found increasingly inadequate and inaccurate by a whole gamut of French *philosophes* and their British, German and Italian equivalents.

Almost all antiquaries of this period employed an epistemology inherited from their Renaissance forebears; their study of objects was essentially text-led and certainly text-driven. With only very few exceptions, their histories were constructed by quarrying the writings of the ancient Greeks and Romans, which dominated their analysis of material remains. Thus surviving material evidence was interpreted and contextualized chiefly by reference to a set of well-read classical texts. Artefacts were therefore employed to illuminate these texts – descriptions of religious practice, domestic life and so on – and were only rarely studied in themselves. Antiquaries therefore concentrated almost exclusively on subject matter or iconography, and on inscriptions, which could be used to identify or date a piece.

These priorities ensured the central position of numismatics – the study of ancient coins. These were objects which usefully combined word and image – they could be dated and they bore images relating to a whole range of 'customs' and thus were seen as key to traditional antiquarian investigations of the classical (and, latterly, national) past. Very little attention was paid to the period or cultural styles of objects, and almost none to their original find-spots. Small wonder that the interpretation of artefacts was sometimes fanciful, and that it was criticized as overly dependent on an accretion of received knowledge, frequently myopic in its concerns and essentially flawed in its conclusions.

Antiquarian methods faced their primary challenge from a new breed of philosophic, chiefly narrative, historians.[18] In 1744, for example, Voltaire (1694–1778), wrote scornfully of the ways in which historians studied the distant past. His mention of 'medals' suggests that it was the works of antiquaries that he had particularly in mind:

> Dealing with history is simply a matter of compiling a handful of truths with a mountain of lies. This type of history can only be useful in the way a fable is, where major events become the constant subject of our pictures, poems and conversations, and allow us some moral or other. We are taught about Alexander's exploits in the way we are about the labours of Hercules. All in all, I see the relationship between modern and ancient history as being the same as that between old medals and today's currency: the former are shut away in private collections, while the latter circulates freely in the world for the benefit of man's commerce.[19]

Modern history, he argued, was the superior discipline because it was simply more easy to establish facts from which to draw (or which could be drawn into) moral arguments and conclusions. And it was especially important that Voltaire's 'science de l'histoire' was designed as an exploration of that enormous subject, the human spirit, rather than as merely the exposition of sterile facts and dates, the kind of data which could be gleaned, for example, from ancient coins.[20]

In fact some antiquaries had already realized that they needed to find a 'scientific' basis for study of artefacts from the past that would place it on the same intellectual standing as the philosophical study of history. They had to turn their dry-as-dust, semi-fictional investigations of often-unconnected detail into a sustained philosophical enquiry, based on established facts through which they could arrive at truths. To do either they often chose to employ or adapt those epistemological models established for other philosophical disciplines in the previous century, ones that were generally recognized as establishing the bases for the breakthroughs that made up the 'scientific revolution'. They stressed the need to disregard authorities and were distrustful of traditional forms of 'curiosity', promoting instead systems of methodical research, often through systematic classification.[21]

Although the term continued to be widely used, 'curiosity' was increasingly regarded as an outmoded way of thinking about the world. The 'curious' were defined by French dictionaries in the eighteenth century as those who desire 'to know or to learn everything', not without some of the unpleasant moral connotations associated with the word today. 'Curiosities' were therefore those objects that were collected by figures such as Sloane and his precursors to satisfy or stimulate a type of enquiry that was both legitimately all-encompassing and necessarily arbitrary. Their interpretation was often founded on many of the received ideas that the early *philosophes* were so anxious to condemn. The French philosopher René Descartes (1596–1650), in his dialogue *Search after Truth*, published only in 1701, had been one of the first to posit an opposition between the 'healthy mind' and undesirable 'insatiable curiosity'. Concentration on the most unusual and exotic of the products of God, Nature and Man encouraged error, and a panoply of disparate facts only encumbered the memory. Instead, importantly, he advocated the study of the common and ordinary rather than the exceptional and strange.

While Descartes advocated methodical research within relatively restricted fields, there remained questions as to what might constitute that underlying method. Cartesian rationalism was a deductive process – a method working from general principles, theories or hypotheses to the particulars that could be used as evidence to prove them. This was *a priori* reasoning; starting with abstract notions or propositions, 'innate' ideas rather than received views were to be employed to explain things – events, objects, phenomena – which were perceived as their consequences. Eighteenth-century scholars were faced with another option: the inductive, empirical method pioneered by Francis Bacon (1561–1626). This was a thinking that prioritized experience and experiment, observation and record, from which could be derived 'aphorisms'. These were then to be 'collected', if possible, into generalizations – explanatory

theories of particular phenomena that might be disproved by negative instances.

Here was a method that went even further in its rejection of established authorities, and it was also the epistemology that found most favour in Britain.[22] In the late seventeenth century Bacon became a hero, not merely for his conclusions but for his whole system of thought. His writings were regarded as paradigmatic by the nascent Royal Society and his method was adopted by the two philosophers who were probably the most celebrated in eighteenth-century Britain, and indeed abroad – John Locke and Isaac Newton (see ch. 1) – as well, as we have seen from his views on the solid foundations of natural history, as by Sir Hans Sloane. Locke especially was explicit and influential in his rejection of Cartesianism, particularly of the much-discussed notion that ideas were innate, in his *Essay concerning Human Understanding* of 1690. Instead he proposed that 'ideas' arose from external material things – provoking first sensations, then reflections that involved an 'idea'.[23]

However, it would be wrong to pretend that this methodological choice was absolute, or that Cartesian rationalism and Baconian or Lockean empiricism were mutually exclusive or contradictory. Despite their often self-consciously polarized rhetoric, many scholars of the period realized that the best method of arriving at a truth was through a combination of experiment (or observation) and hypothesis. Moreover the interpretation of empirical data might be affected, as before, by certain givens. Some 'innate' ideas and other empirical interpretations were unavoidably affected by, or set within, long-held beliefs (then as now), such as the existence of a Christian god, the creationist notion of prehistory and the assumption, particularly crucial in this context, of the inherent superiority of an established western European classical and neoclassical aesthetic. And in the case of antiquaries, as with others, it would not, of course, be correct to state that at a certain moment in time, or as a unified group, they all abandoned traditional methods of working. But some at least attempted to graft these newer epistemologies on to their established approaches. And it is also the case that antiquaries became ever more conscious of the need to make empirical observation central to their theories.

CLASSIFICATION

The considered arrangement of information derived from observation or experiment was usually seen as paramount whether it was then interpreted deductively or inductively. By attempting to link material according to different criteria, scholars could develop theories that might explain those links. But just as there were disparate philosophical models, so too were there alternative approaches to classification. In his *Systema naturae* of 1735 Linnaeus promoted an 'artificial', tabulatory system based on empirical observation whereby 'every note should be a product of number, of form, of proportion, of situation',[24] intended as no more than a way of ordering plants and other natural phenomena in such a way as to provide the foundations for further study (see ch. 6).[25] Such similarities and differences as he noted were not supposed to reveal hidden truths; instead, this focus on utility was empiricism in its purest form and Linnaeus's tables were an armature on which to build.

His system was, however, vociferously opposed by the champions of 'natural' methods of classification. Chief among his opponents was Georges-Louis Leclerc, Comte de Buffon (1707–88), whose forty-four-volume *Natural History* started appearing in 1749. Another self-proclaimed empiricist, Buffon condemned Linnaeus's method on the basis that his classifications did not reflect natural laws – essentially God's laws. Buffon accused Linnaeus of nominalism; a paper taxonomy, he believed, should be more than just giving names to things, it should be organized according to an overarching system. He himself chose to organize his data according to an adaptation of the long-standing notion of the 'chain of being', a model which derived in the first instance from Aristotle and described an unbroken progress from the lowest to the highest forms of creation, that of humanity, then decline. Thus his method stressed just those elements of truth and time that were absent from Linnaeus's.

Antiquaries, like other 'scientists', were therefore faced with choices, and especially were confronted by the challenge of whether or not to systematize in the way that might seem to be demanded by the imperatives of historians. Moreover they continued to be affected by their own pre-eighteenth-century traditions of classification. Many of these, as well as their perceived limitations, are suggested by the first section of the *Dialogues upon the Usefulness of Ancient Medals* by Joseph Addison (1672–1719) which, approved by Pope, were published posthumously in 1721. He starts with an attack on 'Medallists' and virtuosos, who are dubbed 'Critics in Rust' by one of his interlocutors and seen as obsessed with value, authenticity and the merely illustrative nature of the material in question. The respondent confesses: 'the knowledge of Medals has most of those disadvantages that can render a science ridiculous, to such as are not well versed in it', but goes on to state that this could be said of almost any science, and then lists the possible approaches to ancient coins. He points out that it can be 'amusing' to look at the faces of the emperors to try to divine their characters as they are described in texts – faint praise directed at traditional chronological arrangements of coins in order of emperor. He goes on, more positively, to advocate their physical arrangement by subject – as illuminating habits and dresses, instruments of war, sacrificial items and religion and customs in general – in accordance with numismatic tradition going as far back as the Renaissance.[26] Even

here however he has his doubts, which again make a distinction between curiosity and knowledge:

> Should I tell you gravely that, without the help of coins, we should never have known which was the first of the emperors that wore a beard, or rode in stirrups, I might then turn a science into ridicule. Yet it is certain that there are a thousand little impertinancies of this nature that are very gratifying to curiosity, tho' perhaps not very improving to the understanding.[27]

Abbé Bernard de Montfaucon (1655–1741), however, was in the ten volumes of his *L'Antiquité expliquée et représentée en figures*, which appeared between 1719 and 1724 (fig. 97), to develop the method of classification of artefacts on thematic principles in such a way that it might begin to satisfy empirical demands. He too expressed his frustration with existing antiquarian literature, although his own observations mostly depended on his thirty to forty thousand prints and drawings of ancient and early medieval art and artefacts, rather than generally on objects themselves. Scipione Maffei broadly subscribed to Montfaucon's traditional classification system but gave himself a much narrower remit.[28] His *Verona illustrata*, a history of his native city, was published in eight volumes in 1731–2 and, as discussed earlier, he too arranged the objects he described and illustrated by their subject matter. However since his field of research was largely local he could, unlike Montfaucon, afford to insist on the use of primary visual sources, which he cited in his writings.

These schemes were essentially tabulatory rather than systematizing; there was no grand scheme. Buffon-like systems were also roundly spurned by the aristocratic Anne-Claude-Philippe de Tubières-Grimoard de Pestels de Lévis, the Comte de Caylus (1692–1765), who published his seven volumes of *Recueil des antiquités* between 1752 and 1767.[29] The range of material that he considered was broad – Egyptian, Etruscan, Greek, Roman and Gaulish objects, mostly in his own collection and those of his friends. He evidently examined objects closely and at first hand, preferring the ordinary to the extraordinary, and made great play of his view that antiquarian research should be compared to that of the scientist, expressing the Baconian view that one new fact could dispose of a whole elaborate hypothesis. As such, he explained that his arrangement was deliberately unsystematic. He would not (or could not) arrive at chronological criteria for their organization. Indeed he stressed his unwillingness to submit to an overriding theory: 'the antiquary should shun every kind of system; I look upon them as an illness of the spirit'. However he was not afraid to emphasize, for example, the value of household objects as evidence of the 'progress and resources of the human spirit'. Thus, very significantly, he can be differentiated from his immediate predecessors by his evident belief in the notion of human progress. Moreover it is clear that he also believed in the

moral connotations of artistry. The arts, he wrote, 'present a picture of the morals and spirit of a century and of a nation; it is possible to deduce from them, if not actual proof, at least solid conjectures regarding history, the character of rulers, and changing systems of government'.

We have seen above that these approaches of the first half of the century failed to satisfy Voltaire, and he was not alone. The frustrations for Voltaire and those who thought similarly were caused especially by a lack of unifying theories that might explain this vast body of material from the past, especially in reference to that monumental Enlightenment project, the investigation of the human spirit. Nevertheless, the introduction by Caylus of the notion of progress in the arts pointed the way to the introduction of just such a systematic doctrine. It required another ingredient, however, to pull it together – the capacity to measure that progress 'scientifically'.

CONNOISSEURSHIP AND PROGRESS

The notion of human progress and, sometimes, decline was central to the writing of 'universal history' (as opposed to the histories of particular eras or places) that was such a feature of the Enlightenment. This was not a term which had a stable meaning, but its ingredients might include a view of global history founded on a scheme of the succession of world empires, which could be related to the concept of a passing on, or 'translation', of the arts and learning – the notion of progress from barbarism to civilization.[30] If antiquaries were to meet the approval of the *philosophes*, this was one of the criteria which they had to build into their system of study; here was a scheme on which they might base a taxonomy. The notion of artistic progress and decline was not new; it is enshrined, for example, in Giorgio Vasari's mid-sixteenth-century *Lives of the Painters, Sculptors and Architects*. But this was hardly a universal system. The criteria of artistic progress were based on autonomous rules of art which centred on colour and design, which were not easily applicable to antiquities. To achieve a convincing universality, scholars needed to demonstrate that their approach was more disinterested, and that the laws of taste, by which quality could be defined and progress therefore assessed, were integrated, natural and definable.

In one of his celebrated *Tatler* essays Addison suggested that the arts should 'deduce their Laws and Rules from the general Sense and Taste of Mankind, and not from the Principles of those Arts themselves'.[31] Earlier Anthony Ashley Cooper, third Earl of Shaftesbury (1670/1–1713), in his posthumously published treatises on art, *Second Characters or the Language of Forms*, had fostered the notion that the arts flourished under political liberty.[32] Implicit in these statements is the belief that the analysis of art need not be self-referential and, more, that style can be read as an indicator of the state of civilization.

97 A group of votive 'hands of Sabazius' (a wine god associated with Dionysus and Mithras). Engraving from Bernard de Montfaucon's great pictorial encyclopaedia of antiquity, *L'Antiquité expliquée* (1722–4), vol. II. GR Library.

ARCHAEOPHILORVM . SODALITIO . LONDINENSI .
GVGL . HAMIL . TONVS . BAL . ORD . EQVES .
D. D. D.

98 The opening of a tomb at Nola, engraving after a drawing by C. H. Kniep (1748–1825), used as the frontispiece to J. H. W. Tischbein's publication of Sir William Hamilton's second vase collection in 1793. Connoisseurship was used to classify such collections. GR Library.

99 Portrait of Johann Joachim Winkelmann (1717–68) holding a copy of Homer's *Iliad*, by Raphael Mengs (1728–79). The Metropolitan Museum of Art, Harris Brisbane Dick Fund, 1948 (48.141).

Their near contemporary the painter and collector Jonathan Richardson (1665–1745) suggested a method by which quality could be determined empirically, even if his exertions were in the service of modern, rather than ancient art. It was Richardson who made the first serious efforts to suggest that the connoisseurship of the visual arts could be regarded as a science. He published his theories in two *Discourses* published together in 1719 – *The Connoisseur: An Essay on the Whole Art of Criticism* and *An Argument on Behalf of the Science of a Connoisseur*, which were translated into French in 1728. His science of 'connoissence' was based on a self-proclaimed Lockean empiricism.[33] 'To be a connoisseur,' he wrote, 'a man must be as free from all kinds of prejudice as possible; he must moreover have a clear and exact way of thinking and reasoning, he must know how to take in, and manage just ideas and, throughout, he must have not only a

solid, but unbiased judgement.' He proposed that connoisseurship required logical demonstration: 'We must examine up to first principles, and go on step by step in all our Deductions, contenting ourselves with that degree of light we can thus strike out, without fancying and degree of assent is due to any proposition beyond what we can see evidence for … If the nature of the thing admits no proof, we are to give no assent.' He divided the science of looking into eight parts: composition, colouring, handling, drawing (all formal aspects), invention, expression, grace (elements that spoke of feeling) and greatness; and added three more criteria for judgement: advantage, pleasure and the sublime.

In this way the scholar – and in particular the collector – could empirically classify objects in a collection, on the basis of a visual taxonomy of style which, Richardson argued, could be considered 'certain'. He stated the need for proper application to achieve these ends. Thus, rather than emphasize curiosity and variety, this eighteenth-century connoisseur stressed quality and authenticity, assuming all aspects of style to be intentional (fig. 98). And in all of this there was evidently an underlying belief, reinforcing Shaftesbury's notion, that the quality of art could be read as an index of society: 'Arts and politeness have a constant rotation'.[34] Moreover he proposed that a new history of humankind could thus be written in this spirit:

> Methinks it should be worth the while of some one duly
> qualified for such an undertaking, instead of the
> accounts of revolution in empires and governments and
> the means or accidents whereby they were effected,
> military or political, to give us the history of mankind
> with respect to the place they hold among rational
> beings; that is a history of the arts and sciences wherein
> it would be seen to what heighths [sic] some of the
> species have risen in some ages and some countries,
> while at the same time on other parts of the globe, men
> are but one degree above common animals; and the
> same people, who in this age give a dignity to human
> nature in another state is sunk almost to brutality, or
> changed from one excellency to another.[35]

That he considered the visual arts could be treated in this way is demonstrated by the more-or-less traditional account of rise and decline which followed:

> the arts of design, painting and sculpture were known
> in Persia and Egypt long before we have any accounts of
> them amongst the Greeks; but then they [the Greeks]
> carried them to such an amazing height, from whence
> they afterwards spread themselves into Italy, and other
> parts, with various revolutions, till they sunk with the
> Roman empire and were lost for many ages.[36]

No one was to take up his suggestion immediately, and there were certainly those who were sceptical of this 'science'. However, by the mid eighteenth century it was believed that connoisseurship, understood as a scientific, even philosophical

system, might become an essential ingredient in arriving at a system for mapping the past. Indeed traditional chronological arrangements or displays of the portraits of the Roman emperors, whether on coins or, better, in bust form, were reread in this light. By 1722, for example, a display of the busts and statues of the Roman rulers could be visited at the Uffizi in Florence – from Julius Caesar to Gallienus, as complete as possible and based on a traditional numismatic classification. Charles-Louis de Secondat, baron de Montesquieu (1689–1755), realized that such a chronological sequence of emperors also revealed a chronological development of artistic styles – and, predictably, he traced a decline of art. Edward Gibbon too followed the 'progress and decadence of the arts' by looking at the Roman emperors in the Uffizi.[37]

Johann Joachim Winckelmann (1717–68) (fig. 99) was the first to attempt a history of art (and mankind) of the type envisaged by Richardson. His *Geschichte der Kunst des Alterthums* appeared in 1764, containing an arrangement of the arts of the ancient world into a chronological, dynamic sequence. Winckelmann stated explicitly that his history of art was to be 'no mere narrative of the chronology and alterations of the art', but rather an attempt 'to provide a system'.[38] His stylistic analysis, based on detailed and evocative description, resembled that of Caylus; but Winckelmann, unlike Caylus, organized his close observations into a scheme.[39]

He divided the history of art into four periods that constitute his taxonomic divisions. His first epoch was defined by the severe, 'straight and hard' lines of the archaic period – of Egyptian and Etruscan art, which represented different stages of archaism, and of early Greek art which alone was to progress. He divided his flowering of arts, his perfection, into two, seeking to encompass but distinguish the arts that he found were most highly praised by Pliny into, firstly, a high period when sculptures were 'grand and square', an era of Phidian austerity, the fifth century BC, and, secondly, a period of 'flowing beauty' which was summed up by the idealized naturalism of Praxiteles and his contemporaries under Alexander the Great. Lastly he identified an era characterized by its imitative and decadent copying of nature – the decline of the arts under Rome.

Winckelmann's system, as has now often been pointed out, is broadly consistent with the ages of man outlined by Gian Battista Vico (1668–1744) in his 1744 *New Science*: 'the character of nations is first rude, then severe, then benign, then delicate and finally dissolute'. Although no definitive contact between Vico and Winckelmann can be discovered, this view quickly became pervasive.[40] But it is equally important to point out the parallel with Buffon's model.[41] Winckelmann in his early career had taken an interest in natural history,[42] and it is therefore not really surprising that his scheme should be a 'biological' one of the life-cycle, divided into distinct periods. As he said himself, what he was doing was providing a system into which empirical evidence could

100 A selection of Sir William Hamilton's gems arranged according to d'Hancarville's principles of classification, including an uncarved amethyst pendant (centre), Etruscan and 'Pelasgian' intaglios, a scaraboid (18th-century forgery, top left) and 'Persian' and Egyptian scarabs. GR, MME and AES.

be fixed. This was not intended as simply an autonomous history of art – this was indeed the history of the human spirit, as it expressed itself through art. It is probably no coincidence that it was Buffon who in 1753 expressed the now famous thought that 'these things (knowledge, facts, discoveries) are outside man, the style is the man himself'.[43] And just as Addison had long before proposed, Winckelmann argued that the predominant style of a period was a reflection of the general sense and taste of humankind.

Thus Winckelmann followed Shaftesbury in his view that the arts flourished under political liberty. But neither Winckelmann's connoisseurial eye (formed by his devout neoclassical ideology) nor his system was disinterested. His scheme was also, not untypically, restrictive and distorting. He had problems explaining the perfection of art under Alexander,

hardly a libertarian. And, for his taxonomical system to function, he was forced to devise appropriate dates for objects that he particularly admired – sculptures such as the celebrated Belvedere torso in the Vatican or the colossal head of Antinous, now in the Louvre, which he classed as works belonging to periods of Greek 'liberty' which were either somewhat spurious or which significantly skewed the actual dates of the works.[44] In fact his 'system' received early challenges from, for example, the German artist Raphael Mengs and the scholar Christian Gottlob Heyne (1729–1812), and would look theoretically outmoded with the introduction of modern archaeological techniques in the nineteenth century. Nevertheless his progressive and libertarian interpretations became commonplace and, as with the classification methods of Montfaucon and Caylus before him, were, as we have seen, to have considerable impact on arrangements and displays of collections around Europe, transforming cabinets of curiosities, such as Sloane's into museums with different, but no less universal, ambitions.[45] His influence became pervasive in many fields, being applied (as the next chapters show) not only to the organization of vases, coins or gems (fig. 100), and other 'artificial' objects but to entire civilizations.

11

'The King loves medals': the study of coins in Europe and Britain

ANDREW BURNETT

'I will tell you something; the King loves medals,'[1] wrote Horace Walpole in 1760, the year of the accession of George III. When his son George IV gave the British Museum his library in 1823, it came with his collection of over fifteen thousand medals and coins (the term 'medals' at that time covered both coins and medals), as well as the numismatic books in the library itself. How and why did people collect and study coins in the eighteenth and early nineteenth centuries?

EARLY STUDIES

Since the Renaissance, ancient, and in particular Roman, coins had been collected for two reasons, as moral exemplars and as sources of information about the classical past. Both aspects can be illustrated by the Italian poet Petrarch, who presented some coins with portraits of Roman emperors to the emperor Charles IV, and encouraged him to gaze upon the features of those he had succeeded and wished to emulate. Petrarch and other scholars had also used coins to help their understanding of classical texts and their reconstruction of the classical world. We know of large collections in the fifteenth century belonging to members of the Italian elite such as Barbo or the Medici. But coin collecting was not the prerogative of princes and scholars; every aristocrat or gentleman came to have a collection, as an obligatory sign of culture. The production of contemporary medals as a way of commemorating the great figures of the Renaissance and later periods was a natural extension of this activity, and they were collected alongside ancient coins. Until the nineteenth century, both were regarded primarily as 'monuments of historical facts'.

The growth of coin collecting was matched by developments in their study and publication. The first important books on coins were written in the 1510s. Guillaume Budé published his philological masterpiece – much admired by Erasmus – *De asse et partibus eius* (*On the As and its Parts*) in 1514, and in 1517 Andrea Fulvio's *Illustrium imagines* (*Images of the Famous*) used mostly Roman coins as a source of imagery for rulers from antiquity to the early Middle Ages. Thereafter enormous care was devoted to the study of numismatics in the sixteenth and seventeenth centuries, and the flood of works on weights and measures (metrology) and the imagery of coins has recently been recognized as 'one of the greatest (but most neglected) achievements of Renaissance scholarship'.[2] A particularly rich period was the 1550s, a decade which saw the first handbook on coins, by Enea Vico. His *Discorsi … sopra le medaglie de gli antichi* (*Discourses on the Medals of*

101 H.Goltzius, *Fastios magistratuum et triumphorum romanorum* (Bruges, 1571), p. 166 (detail). Goltzius attempted to reconstruct the chronology of Roman Republican history by using coins and inscriptions. This page refers to the years 81–79 BC and the coin on the lower left has been given an imaginary inscription, referring to Sulla's return to Rome. C&M Library.

Wolfgang Lazius promised a future volume that would, he claimed, comprise a detailed description of seven hundred thousand coins! Not surprisingly his ambition met scepticism from his contemporaries, and more modest ambitions prevailed. Adolf Occo's *Impp. Romanorum numismata* (*Coins of the Roman Emperors*) (1579) gave a succinct list of the coins made by the Roman emperors, and his work remained a standard text for almost two hundred years,

102 Joseph Eckhel (1737–98), from 1775 professor of antiquities and numismatics at the University of Vienna and curator of the Austrian imperial collection of coins. Anonymous engraving, made for A. von Steinbüchel, *Addenda ad Eckhelii Doctrinam numorum veterum* (Vienna, 1926). Kunsthistorisches Museum, Vienna.

the Ancients) was first published in 1555 and is full of information about matters such as the inscriptions and designs on Roman coins, forgeries, denominations and the metals from which they were made.

Vico was not alone, and during the seventeenth and eighteenth centuries many books were published. Italy, Germany, France and the Low Countries held the best and most numerous collections, as the list of more than eight hundred collections visited in the 1550s by the scholar Hubert Goltzius indicates.[3] They were also the main places for numismatic research, resulting in a growing literature on the study of coins, metrology, iconography and catalogues of collections. Some catalogues were more systematic than others, and many used various different ways of classifying the coins they contained. In addition, aspirations to produce a systematic corpus and a systematic treatment of ancient coins were not infrequently expressed. As early as 1553 Jacopo Strada had declared the intention to publish a four-volume work with a description of every coin produced by each Roman emperor, and only a few years later

being revised in 1601, 1683 and finally 1730. Occo's book was a great achievement and made a remarkable attempt to arrange the coins in the chronological order of their production within each emperor's reign, rather than the alphabetical order favoured by others.

ECKHEL AND THE SYSTEMATIC STUDY OF COINS

The aim of producing a complete corpus resurfaced in the eighteenth century, and there were undertakings on a more ambitious scale, especially in France where the enormous collection of the king of France provided a stimulus to other collectors and to scholars. However, the production of corpora began to be realized only in the very early nineteenth century, spurred on by the publication in Vienna during the 1790s of the bible of numismatics, J. Eckhel's *Science of Ancient Coins* (written in Latin as *Doctrina numorum veterum*) (figs 102, 103).

Eckhel's approach mirrors developments in other fields,

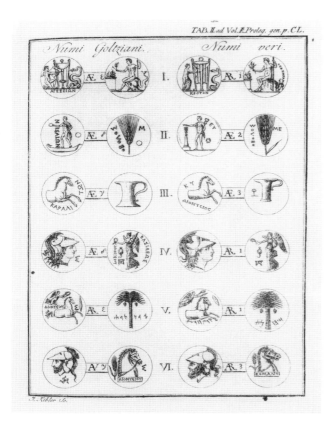

103 J. Eckhel, *Doctrina numorum veterum* (Vienna, 1792), vol. 1, plate facing p. 150. The engraving illustrates and compares falsely described coins on the left (*numi Goltziani*) with correctly described ones on the right (*numi veri*). C&M Library.

for example natural history and language, even though he does not explicitly acknowledge any debt, and it would not be a flight of fancy to compare his procedures with those of Linnaeus or Johnson. Firstly, Eckhel had an empirical attitude to the material, insisting on starting with the actual objects: 'there will be no place in this work except for coins which I myself have seen or which I have found, or which I have found accepted by trustworthy authors',[4] he says, having a particular dislike of what he called *numi Goltziani*, coins which were implausibly recorded by Goltzius and his followers (fig. 103; see also fig. 101). The insistence on this starting point is reminiscent of Samuel Johnson's *Dictionary of the English Language* (1755), with its significant subtitle: *in which the words are deduced from their originals, and illustrated in their different significations, by examples from the best writers*. Both Eckhel and Johnson shared in the common insistence of the later Enlightenment on autopsy, in its eighteenth-century sense of personal examination. From this starting point Eckhel developed criteria for establishing a universal framework for all ancient coins, much as Linnaeus had taken the sexual system as the basis of classifying the whole family of plants.

The next stage was the use of a geographic arrangement. He reviewed the way coins and coin collections should be organized in his chapter on *How museums should usefully be organized*, discussing a number of different methods of arrangement and summarizing their strengths and weaknesses. It was important to get it right, he emphasized, 'because a good arrangement creates many opportunities for scholars'. He favoured the arrangement of Roman coins by chronology and of Greek coins by geography. The geographical system had first been introduced by Joseph Pellerin in his superb *Receuil des médailles de peoples et de villes* (*Collection of Coins of Peoples and Cities*) (Paris, 1763–7), and it replaced the alphabetical system used by earlier seventeenth-century writers,[5] soon becoming almost universally adopted. 'The system established by Pellerin and perfected by Eckhel in his fine work' remained current for a hundred years, and even in the late nineteenth century catalogues would still explicitly acknowledge their debt to Eckhel.[6]

Within the geographical arrangement, Eckhel then established criteria to create five families, or as he called them periods (*epochae*), of ancient coins. The five periods are described in his chapter *On determining the date of coins*:

1 From the beginnings to Alexander I of Macedon (462 BC)
2 From 462 to the early years of Philip II, and lasting for about the next hundred years
3 From then to the overthrow of the Roman Republic (the end of the first century BC), about three centuries 'which is thought to be the golden age of Greek art'
4 From then to the reign of Hadrian (AD 117–38)
5 From the Antonines to the reign of Gallienus (AD 253–68).

These were not recognized divisions of ancient history but 'natural' ones created by Eckhel as an overall classification which resulted from his application of five criteria, which together combined to characterize each of these periods and its products. The criteria were:

a metal (e.g. mostly bronze for period 5)
b inscription (e.g. the names of magistrates were often added in period 3)
c letter forms (e.g. the adoption of long vowels in Greek inscriptions in period 3)
d fabric (e.g. coins were more spherical in period 1 than 2)
e style (*stilus picturae*) (e.g. the art of coins in period 3 was at its greatest).

The most important aspect of these groupings is that they illustrate Eckhel's concern to make the coins work historically. To that end, Eckhel's procedure really seems to have had two main aspects. The first was to make sense of the material. The second was to use it to help advance the understanding of the ancient world. Again the comparison with Linnaeus is relevant. He wanted both to understand the system of plants and thereby help advance the understanding of the natural world. Of course

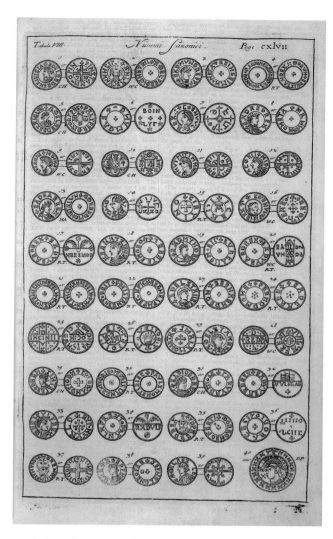

104 A plate of engravings of Anglo-Saxon coins from the Cotton collection in the 1695 edition of Camden's *Britannia*. C&M Library.

there are differences. The natural world was constructed from observation, but the ancient world was, for Eckhel, constructed from texts, which explains the constant references to books and texts that occur on every page of Eckhel.

Eckhel was concerned to explain coins by texts and vice versa, but he did not enter into the debate of the relative reliability of coins (or other physical remains) versus texts, a debate which had emerged in the late seventeenth century, notably in the works of Ezechiel Spanheim, and was taken up by many authors in the eighteenth century, notably Gibbon. Indeed the 'numismatists' tended to study their subject on its own, leaving it to others to place it in a more general intellectual context.[7]

A system such as that of Linnaeus was more enduring, whereas a number of Eckhel's views later became victims to changing fashion. For example, by the late nineteenth century Eckhel's five periods for classifying coins, which anyway

seem rather idiosyncratic, had been replaced by a more predictable seven, even though they were still ones dominated by the fourth-century sculptor Praxiteles rather than his fifth-century predecessor Phidias, and art itself had, in good nineteenth-century fashion, replaced the other criteria as being the most significant:

1 Period of Archaic Art (700–480 BC)
2 Period of Transitional Art (480–415 BC)
3 Period of Finest Art (415–336 BC)
4 Period of Later Fine Art (336–280 BC)
5 Period of Decline of Art (280–146 BC)
6 Period of Continued Decline of Art (146–27 BC)
7 Imperial Period (27 BC – AD 268).

These and other changes and developments all took place very much within the debate which Eckhel had established. The influence of Enlightenment thinking is readily apparent: an interest on a systematic and all-embracing account, or the insistence on empiricism, looking at the coins themselves and working out the system of classification that best suited them. Thanks to Eckhel, it was the years around 1800 that saw the study of ancient numismatics finally put on a systematic and complete basis and which set the framework for its development for the next two centuries.

BRITAIN

Where was Britain during all this time? In numismatic terms Britain had remained something of a backwater, with few collections and very little publishing. We know of almost no collections at all in England until the early seventeenth century, and then they are very few. Only two were of importance. Henry, Prince of Wales and the son of King James I (r. 1603–25), was 'fond of antiquities and the arts, and a favourer of learning' and acquired part of a continental collection in 1609, but he died in 1612 aged only eighteen. His collection passed to his brother, the later King Charles I, who 'could judge of medals whether they had the number of years they pretended to',[8] but the collection was lost later in the century. Sir Robert Cotton, the great humanist and collector (1571–1631) (see fig. 21), had been a close associate of Prince Henry and may have influenced him to take up the collecting of antiquities, including coins. Cotton himself had a good collection of English coins, some of which were published in William Camden's great *Britannia* (fig. 104). Cotton had been a pupil of Camden's, and Camden included illustrations of his coins from the edition of his work published in 1600, referring, as he did so, to the collection of Cotton 'who hath begunne a famous cabinet whence of his singular courtesie he hath often times given me great light in these darksome obscurities'. Cotton may rightly be recognized as the 'father of numismatics' in Britain, initiating in these ways the royal collection and the significant use of coinage for writing the history of Britain.

There were also other aristocrats' or antiquarians' collections, but these were not many and were not well known. Perhaps typical examples are provided by the small collections of the antiquarian Elias Ashmole or the great classical scholar Meric Casaubon (1599–1671). Casaubon was a canon at Canterbury cathedral, and remarkably his collection of about three hundred pieces is still preserved in the cathedral today. The ancient coins are mostly Roman silver and bronze coins in moderate condition, but as a whole the collection compares poorly with the great collections which we hear about on the continent. Indeed, a hundred years later in the early eighteenth century, it could be observed that 'so many Books have been already published concerning the cabinets of *Italy, France, Germany, Holland, Flanders,* and other parts. *England* alone remained unsearched by Antiquaries, or, to speak more properly, the hidden Treasures of this happy Island have never yet been made publick: This Consideration induced me [Nicola Haym] to examine some of the most celebrated Cabinets in *London*.'[9] The reason was simply a lack of material.

There were indeed few books either, and few English translations of books written on the continent. Haym himself, for example, was an Italian, and his work was published in Italian for an Italian audience, as well as English. Otherwise, works such as John Evelyn's *Numismata – A Discourse of Medals, Ancient and Modern* (1697) and Joseph Addison's *Dialogues Upon the Usefulness of Ancient Medals: especially in relation to the Latin and Greek Poets* (1726) are few, and the latter, at least, is a work of only limited scholarship, despite the poet Alexander Pope's praise in his *Epistle to Mr Addison*. Perhaps the most important work to be published in the period was in fact in another field, that of English numismatics. The absence of a good treatment of the English coinage was a matter of concern to the antiquarians of the early eighteenth century, and the gap was eventually filled by Martin Folkes's work on the English coinage (fig. 105), his *A Table of English Silver Coins from the Norman Period to the Present Time* (1745), a book which was revised very extensively by Andrew Gifford, an assistant librarian at the British Museum, for its republication in 1763.[10]

A good sense of the lack of activity in Britain can be gained from considering Eckhel's authoritative survey of earlier writing on numismatics. He named over fifty great books published since the Renaissance, but only three of them were British. Much the same conclusion can be drawn from the books in George III's own library; the number of books published in England is small, even though the bulk of the library consists of books published in the eighteenth century.[11] The three British books mentioned by Eckhel were all published in the eighteenth century, and it was in that century that Britain began to catch up with the rest of Europe, especially with the formation of important coin collections. The three books were the volume by Nicola Haym of engravings of coins in the collection of the Earl of Pembroke, published in 1726; the catalogue of the coins in the Bodleian Library in the University of Oxford, written by Francis Wise in 1750; and the catalogue of part of William Hunter's collection by Charles Combe, published in 1782. The last book was praised both for the 'learning, brilliance and accuracy' of its text and also for its plates. It suited its subject, for the finest collection in Britain at that time was indeed that of William Hunter (still preserved in its entirety in the Hunterian Museum in Glasgow). Hunter (1718–83) was a brilliant doctor who collected coins, books, manuscripts and ethnography, as well as anatomical and pathological specimens. His coin collection was described by Eckhel as a 'prodigy'. It was very large for

105 The antiquarian Martin Folkes (1690–1754), plaster bust by Louis-François Roubiliac, h. 61.5 cm. Folkes was president of both the Royal Society and the Society of Antiquaries of London. His *A Table of English Silver Coins from the Norman Period to the Present Time* was published in 1745. The bust is one of a group presented by Dr Matthew Maty in 1762. MME.

its day, and contained coins of exceptional rarity and fine preservation, all the more remarkable since it was put together in only just over a decade at the end of his life.

KING GEORGE III'S COLLECTION AND THE BRITISH MUSEUM

The Charles Combe who published the catalogue of the Greek coins in Hunter's collection was the father of Taylor Combe (fig. 106), and both played important parts in the numismatics of the period. Charles both catalogued Hunter's collection in 1782 and wrote the manuscript *CATALOGUE of the Several Series of Modern Medals & Coins in HIS MAJESTY's Collection* (1771, revised 1814) and the *CATALOGUE of the Ancient Coins in HIS MAJESTY's Collection* (1814) (fig. 107). Taylor worked at the British Museum and produced its first coin catalogue, *The Coins of Ancient Peoples and Kings Preserved in the British Museum*, in the same year, 1814.

The manuscript inventories of George III's collection of over fifteen thousand ancient and European coins and medals are preserved in the British Museum. They reveal that the King's passion for 'medals' meant that his medal collection was, and still is, the single largest acquisition of medals made by the British Museum. However, the means by which the King acquired his collection of coins and medals (figs 108–11),

106 Taylor Combe (1774–1826), who from 1803 was responsible for the coins in the British Museum (in the Department of Manuscripts), and became the first Keeper of Antiquities after the creation of that department in 1807. Medal made to mark his death, aged fifty-two, by W. J. Taylor, after Benedetto Pistrucci. C&M.

107 C. Combe, *Catalogue of the Ancient Coins in His Majesty's Collection* (1814, manuscript, f.7, detail). This page lists the gold coins of Philip II of Macedon (see fig. 108). The red line and the red number 5 at the top left of the page denote the relevant drawer in the cabinet (see fig.112). C&M Library.

108 Greek coins from George III's collection: gold coins of Philip II, king of Macedonia (359–336 BC), and of Alexander the Great (336–323 BC), dia. 1.8 cm. C&M.

109 Roman coins from George III's collection: gold coins of the emperors Augustus (27 BC – AD 14), Tiberius (AD 14–37), the deified Augustus under Caligula (AD 37–41), and Claudius (AD 41–54), dia. 1.9 cm. C&M.

of which the 'modern' part at least was already largely complete by 1771, are not clear. It was presumably a combination of the coins casually acquired by previous monarchs with a collection put together more carefully in George's own early years, some at least coming from Andrew Gifford and others from the Earl of Bristol. The ancient coins, however, were not of as high a quality as other contemporary collections, and modern study has revealed a relatively large number of pieces which are now regarded as false, many more than those gold pieces that were already recognized by Charles Combe and catalogued as such (*nummi auri fictitii*). Nor was the collection particularly large. It consisted only of about 4,500 Greek and Roman coins, compared with the 6,000 in Sir William Hamilton's collection, the 30,000 beautiful pieces in the Hunter collection and the 23,000 in Sir Hans Sloane's collection. Most of George III's were Roman, with a relatively high proportion of early imperial gold.

One of the most valuable aspects of the Combe inventories is that they show how the coins and medals were organized, since they describe the contents drawer by drawer. The drawers are presumably parts of the cabinet made in about 1750, and of which two parts survive today in the Victoria & Albert and Metropolitan museums (fig. 112).[12] The arrangement of the Greek coins is alphabetic. At first sight this is surprising for a work dated 1814, twenty years after Eckhel's great work, but the coins and their catalogue were probably originally organized earlier when the new cabinet was acquired, and

only written out in 1814. The year 1814 also saw the publication by his son Taylor of the first catalogue of the Greek coins in the British Museum, and Taylor explicitly acknowledged the change that had by then come over the subject, since he stated in his foreword that he was following Eckhel's system (*juxta systema Eckhelianum*). The passing from one Combe generation to the next neatly reflects the revolution in the subject.

George III's collection was deposited in the British Museum on 28 May 1825. By that time the museum's own collection was well established, though still in its early development compared with those in Paris and Vienna. The basis had been formed by Sir Hans Sloane's collection (so large that the list filled ten volumes) and the English and Anglo-Saxon coins from Robert Cotton.[13] Additions were rapidly made, some from people who had collected them in Italy or Sicily, such as George Tatem (the British consul in Messina), Brownlow Cecil (ninth Earl of Exeter) or Sir William Hamilton. British coins were also acquired, from hoards such as that found on Tiree in 1780 or at Tealby in 1807, or from collectors such as Samuel Tyssen of Narborough. Spectacular additions, however, were few, one of the most significant being the bequest made in 1799 by the Reverend C. M. Cracherode of Greek, Roman and English coins and medals of outstanding beauty 'which could hardly be provided with adequate praise'.[14] The collection was, however, still modest compared to those of Paris or Vienna, and indeed the publication of Taylor Combe's catalogue in 1814 was lamented by another collector because it was detrimental to national pride.[15]

The acquisition of George III's collection shows well how the Museum's collection developed during the nineteenth century. It represented a great acquisition of medals and European coins and a good, though not a spectacular, acquisition of ancient coins. It provides an excellent illustration of the way that the sustained accumulation of numerous substantial collections, all good but none of enormous size, meant that by the end of the century the Museum had established a preeminent role in the systematic study of the coinage.

The Enlightenment period thereby marked a shift in the use of coins by British authors. Before the nineteenth century coins had been used primarily by antiquarians as part of their

reconstruction of local British history, following the example set by Camden's use of Cotton's coins in his *Britannia*. From 1800 this tradition continued, for example with J. T. Smith's *Antiquities of London* or *Westminster*, but was accompanied by a growing literature which came to form an ever more

110 Gold medal, from the collection of George III, commemorating the coronation of the English king Edward VI in 1547 (1546 old style), the first coronation medal made in England, with the Latin inscription 'Edward VI by the grace of god King of England, France and Ireland, defender of the faith and the supreme head on earth of the Church of England and Ireland, crowned 20 February 1546 at the age of ten years'. The same inscription appears in Greek and Hebrew on the other side. Dia. 6.1 cm (greatly enlarged). C&M.

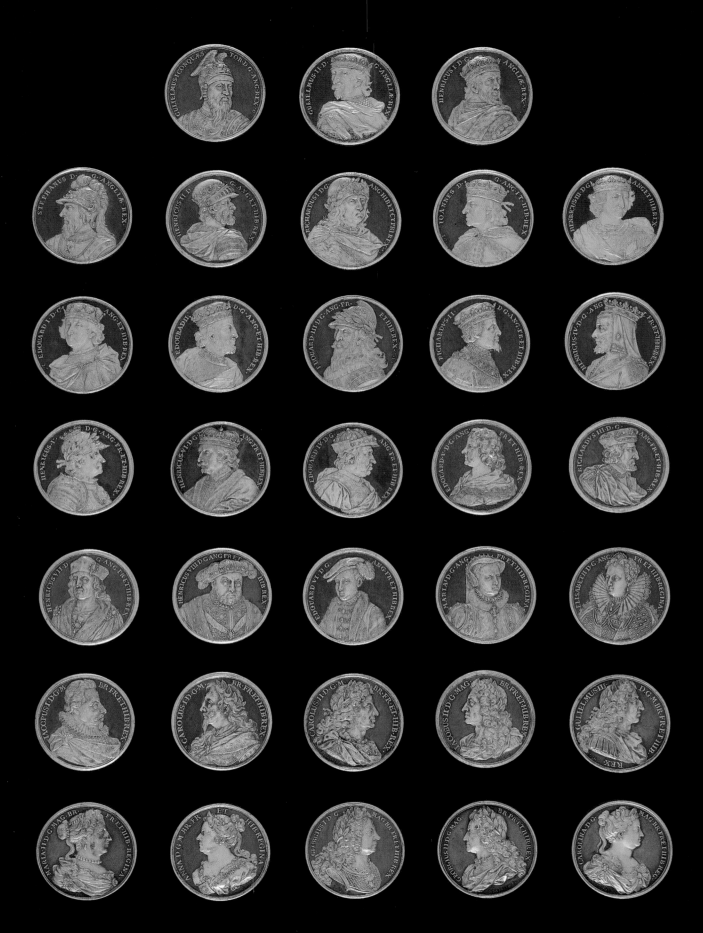

significant part of the international literature on the study of the coins of all places and periods.

The British Museum itself had played and was to play an increasingly important role in this development of numismatics in Britain. Beginning with the efforts of Andrew Gifford on Folkes's book on English coinage and Taylor Combe's work on ancient and medieval coins in the Museum's collection, the foundation was laid for the leading inter-national role attained in the later nineteenth century. The *British Museum Catalogue of Greek Coins*, a series running to many volumes, was launched in 1873. The steady growth of the Museum's collection so alarmed the Duc de Luynes that he gave his collection to the Paris cabinet in 1862 'to help the Cabinet of France maintain itself in the first rank which it has for long occupied in Europe and which English gold is taking away'. The years around 1800 were crucial both for the system-atic development of the classification of coins and for the full adoption of the study of coins in Britain, a development in which the young British Museum played a principal part.

111 Medals from George III's collection: imaginary portraits of the English kings from William I (1066–87), by the Swiss medallist Jean Dassier (1676–1763), who came to England in 1728 and three years later issued this medallic series of English monarchs. Dia. 4.2 cm. C&M.

112 Part of 'His Majesty's Grand Medal Case', 1755. This superb mahogany cabinet can be identified with a series of entries in the Royal Accounts for 1760/1, recording bills from William Vile and John Cobb for alterations which were made to it. Victoria & Albert Museum.

12 Engraved gems: the lost art of antiquity

JUDY RUDOE

Small-scale images cut into gemstones, whether in relief (cameo) or below the surface (intaglio), are known as engraved gems. With a few exceptions, they fit easily into the palm of the hand and many are no bigger than a thumbnail. Interest in them today is limited to a handful of specialists, but during the eighteenth century they were held in high regard not only as works of art but also for the knowledge they provided about the ancient world. As one of the great categories of art from the classical world that had survived, they were collected with passion by scholars of the antique who used ancient intaglios as their own personal letter seals and paid huge sums for them. When the young English aristocrat George Grenville of Stowe paid £400 in 1774 for the cameo bust of the Athenian general Phocion that had belonged to

113 Onyx cameo from the collection of the 4th Duke of Marlborough (1739–1817) depicting two members of the imperial family as Jupiter Ammon and Juno or Isis. Roman, c. AD 35–50, w. 22 cm. This is one of only five large cameos to survive from antiquity. GR.

the Great – and during the Middle Ages rulers such as Charlemagne and Frederick II Hohenstaufen encouraged the art. From the fifteenth century engraved gems were assiduously sought by the humanists of the Italian Renaissance, the most celebrated collection being that of the Medici in Florence. This was followed in the sixteenth century by other great continental cabinets, such as the French royal collection in Paris or the Habsburg gems in Vienna, both of which held classical and contemporary gems. Britain had no comparable collection at this time. It was not until the early seventeenth century that Charles I formed the nucleus of the present royal collection, and his collection was far superseded in numbers by that of Thomas Howard, Earl of Arundel (1585–1646). In the eighteenth century other English noblemen, most notably the Dukes of Devonshire and Marlborough and the Earl of Carlisle, assembled outstanding collections (fig. 113). It was George III, bibliophile and patron of the arts, who was to turn the royal gems into a collection of note with his purchase in 1762 of the entire collection, including gems, of Joseph Smith (c.1674–1770), British Consul in Venice.[1]

Smith was one of many collectors who acted as agents as well. His friend and fellow Venetian Anton Maria Zanetti (1680–1757) played a similar role; ostensibly a collector, he had no qualms in selling if the price was high enough. Many of these collectors had their collections published to make them visible; Zanetti's and Smith's were catalogued in 1750 and 1767.[2] Such books, often called *dactiliothecae* (literally, cabinets to keep rings, but which came to mean gem cabinets because gems were frequently set in rings), contained prints of the gems, greatly enlarged, which were often works of art in their own right and occasionally issued separately. One of the more exquisitely produced books was the Polish Baron Philip von Stosch's ground-breaking book on engraved gems of 1724 (fig. 115).[3] Stosch (1691–1757) was among the many colourful characters in the gem world: his book was written while spying for the English Crown on the Stuart Pretender, James Edward, in Rome. His own collection of engraved gems was then the biggest ever assembled, comprising 3,444 intaglios; the catalogue produced after Stosch's death by the German antiquary J. J. Winckelmann provided a model for the way gems were classified in the late eighteenth century.[4] There were eight sections: Egyptian (combined with a few 'Persian' gems); Greek, Etruscan and Roman gods; legendary Greek history including the Trojan war; recorded history; games and festivals; marine subjects; animals, and lastly gnostic or magical gems of the Christian era combined with examples of the modern revival of gem-engraving. In this way Winckelmann gave both an analysis of style and a subject index.[5]

Although the vast majority of ancient gems were found in Italy, Paris and London were also major centres of collecting and learning. In Paris the key figure was Pierre-Jean Mariette

114 Still life painting of a collection of antiquities by Hendrik van der Borcht. Dutch, early 17th century. Van der Borcht had visited Italy and collected engraved gems and medals. The left foreground shows a group of carved hardstone cameos amongst coins and medals. Worcester Art Museum, Massachusetts.

the art-loving Cardinal Albani, the news reverberated round Europe. What made engraved gems such a talking point? They were seen as an essential element, alongside coins and medals, in the understanding of classical history (fig. 114); they could be arranged in series to illustrate classical mythology, legendary history, gods, heroes or Roman emperors. They were part and parcel of a classical education, like knowledge of Latin and Greek. This account places the British Museum's gem collection, which, like many other parts of the Museum, is a collection of collections, in the context of the eighteenth-century perception of gems as illustrations of the ancient world.

COLLECTING GEMS IN THE EIGHTEENTH CENTURY

If the age of George III was the great age of gem collecting, it has a long and distinguished history. Engraved gems were highly prized in antiquity – we learn from Pliny that one of the first gem collections or cabinets was owned by Pompey

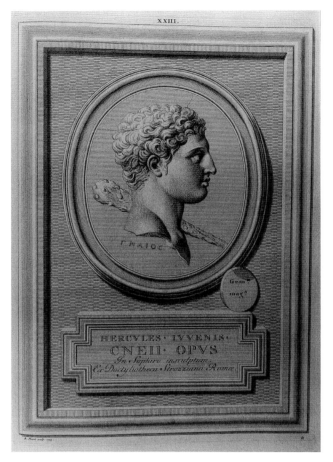

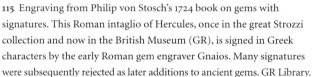

115 Engraving from Philip von Stosch's 1724 book on gems with signatures. This Roman intaglio of Hercules, once in the great Strozzi collection and now in the British Museum (GR), is signed in Greek characters by the early Roman gem engraver Gnaios. Many signatures were subsequently rejected as later additions to ancient gems. GR Library.

116 Seventeenth-century pen, ink and wash drawings of engraved gems in the collection of Cassiano dal Pozzo. The drawings passed to Cardinal Albani and were later acquired by Charles Townley. Enlarged drawings were an important kind of visual record of gems. GR.

(1694–1774), scholar, collector, agent and author; his *Traité des pierres gravées* of 1750 is still a standard account of the history and technique of gem-engraving.[6] It was from Paris that Catherine the Great assembled much of her astounding collection from around 1780 to 1795. She bought earlier collections such as that of the Duc d'Orléans in their entirety while her agents scouted out the best of what was available, whether antique or modern, in London and Rome as well, to feed her voracious appetite. She was, in her own words, 'gripped by a gluttonous greed' for engraved gems.[7]

Like most serious collectors, Catherine also owned casts or impressions of engraved gems in other collections. Such casts, usually made of plaster or sulphur, made possible the dissemination of huge quantities of images, far exceeding those published in books (see fig. 124).[8] For ease of study, they were always in relief, whether the originals were cameos or intaglios, the latter being intended as seal stones and so difficult to see without a cast. The most famous maker of casts after engraved gems was James Tassie of Edinburgh, who used

coloured glass, imitating the colour of the original gemstone. In 1781–2 Catherine the Great had ordered a complete set of Tassie's stock which then numbered 6,076 subjects.[9] With her patronage, Tassie gained access to all the gem cabinets of Europe and eventually produced 15,800 casts.[10] These were catalogued in 1791 by R. E. Raspe, who adopted Winckelmann's stylistic approach for the initial series of Egyptian, Persian, Indian etc., but for the Graeco-Roman gems turned to an arrangement by subject matter.

Casts were accurate, but, being life-size, still small-scale. Another kind of visual record was to have enlarged drawings made, a tradition going back to the early seventeenth century that complemented the prints after gems. Rubens was bowled over by the Gemma Tiberiana, one of the largest cameos to have survived from antiquity, when he first saw it in Paris in the 1620s; he drew it, and planned to publish the most beautiful surviving cameos.[11] Cassiano dal Pozzo had his entire collection drawn to create a 'paper museum' (see ch. 16). Some of Cassiano's drawings of gems were later acquired by

Charles Townley (1737–1805), who then had many of his own gems drawn in the 1780s. Both seventeenth- and eighteenth-century drawings are now in the British Museum (fig. 116).[12]

SIR HANS SLOANE'S GEM COLLECTION

The Townley gems were among several distinguished collections assembled by British collectors in the late eighteenth or very early nineteenth century, often from British dealers resident in Rome, and which entered the British Museum *en bloc*. One such collection was that of Sir William Hamilton; it was formed in Naples, where he was British ambassador from 1764 to 1799, and was acquired by the British Museum in 1772.[13] It comprised 149 gems, mostly intaglios, including some rare Egyptian and Etruscan scarabs as well as Near Eastern seal stones (see fig. 100). After the Hamilton gems, there was a gap of some twenty-five years, until 1799 when the Reverend C. M. Cracherode (1730–99), a Trustee of the British Museum, bequeathed his collections of books, coins and medals, prints and drawings, engraved gems numbering 83, and shells and minerals. Then came Charles Townley's collection of 511 engraved gems, purchased in 1815, followed by Richard Payne Knight's 111 gems, bequeathed in 1824.

The eighteenth-century interest in the antique produced

117 Engraved gems from the collection of Sir Hans Sloane, demonstrating his taste for fine stones. Cameos: Minerva in pink sardonyx (h. 2.7 cm); 'African' heads in dark brown agate and layered onyx; female heads with veils cut in the different layers of the stone; female bust in garnet and tiny animals cut in appropriate coloured stones. Intaglios (in centre): Cupids flanking a tree (sardonyx) and Cupid standing before a tree (both stones have beautiful natural markings but they are opaque and so the images are hard to see). MME.

collections which are very different from the foundation collection of the British Museum, that of the physician and botanist Sir Hans Sloane (1660–1753).[14] Most of his collecting was done over about forty years from the late 1680s to the 1720s. This makes it in spirit a seventeenth-century collection not an eighteenth-century one; it emerges not from the world of the scholar of the antique but from the world of science. Nevertheless, we should consider it briefly, for it established that both ancient and modern gems were collected by the Museum from the start. Sloane's purpose in collecting gems was not for their quality (though some are very fine) but as specimens of the natural and artificial world. His 550 intaglios and cameos can be understood only when studied in the context of other parts of his collection such as the agates, precious stones, crystals, shells, fishes, birds and

118 Shell cameos from the collection of Sir Hans Sloane. The Three Magi on the right (h. 2.8 cm) is cut from a shell of at least four layers so that each head is in a different colour. The double heads are cut from a protrusion on a helmet shell which allowed a greater depth, but its pointed shape dictated the contorted positions. MME.

119 Amethyst intaglio of Cupid bound to a trophy with the Greek signature AULOS (h. 1.6 cm). Carlisle acquired it as ancient but Dalton catalogued it as 'indisputably modern' in 1915. It is now generally thought to be a work of classical antiquity with a signature that may have been added later. MME.

quadrupeds. These were split from his antiquities when the Natural History Museum was established in 1880.

Firstly, the variety of stones is enormous – lapis lazuli, garnet, emerald, bloodstone, rock-crystal, amethyst, etc. – and they are always meticulously noted in Sloane's own manuscript lists of his gems. Secondly, the subjects include, in addition to many that are classical, biblical or taken from recent authors, the different human races and species of animal, from tiny cameos with exotic animals and birds, such as quails, tortoises, bears, dromedaries and elephants, cut in stones of appropriate colour, to 'African' heads cut in dark brown agates[15] (fig. 117). Often the stones are so beautiful or the layers so well exploited that they could equally well be placed with his plain polished specimens of each stone, or his comprehensive series of agate knife handles (see fig. 84).[16] Most of Sloane's cameos are agates, varieties of the mineral quartz; these include chalcedony, carnelian and jasper, together with onyx and sardonyx, the names given to banded agates with parallel bands of red and grey (sardonyx) or white and grey (onyx). The coloured layer is porous and is usually stained to achieve the characteristic bands of black and white associated with onyx cameos.[17] Sloane also owned a number of shell cameos, notable both for their quality and for their use of the natural layers of the shell (fig. 118).[18]

The Carlisle, Cracherode, Townley and Payne Knight gem collections

But none of Sloane's gems, either cameos or intaglios, bears an engraver's signature, whether classical or modern. The artists were not his prime concern and in this his collecting differs completely from that of his eighteenth-century successors such as Henry Howard, fourth Earl of Carlisle (1694–1758). Although it was purchased by the British Museum only in 1890, the Carlisle collection, comprising 170 items, classical and post-classical, was put together between

about 1739 and 1758. Thus in its period of assembly it immediately follows the collection of Hans Sloane, but, unlike Sloane's, it reflects the development in the study of engraved gems, in particular Baron von Stosch's influential publication of 1724, which set out to establish that the signatures on seventy fine gems were the signatures of the artists responsible.[19] Scholars at this time hoped to build up a systematic history of ancient art from such signatures, which often corresponded to names mentioned by classical authors, especially Pliny. Carlisle was above all concerned to acquire gems with signatures, and this marks him out as an eighteenth-century scholar interested in the art of gem-cutting itself, as opposed to Sloane, the scientific collector of specimens. With his two agents, Ficoroni in Rome and Zanetti in Venice, Carlisle amassed a number of signed gems that may or may not be ancient, though he certainly bought them as such (fig. 119).[20]

The collecting of gems reached a peak in the 1770s and 1780s. Cracherode, Townley and Payne Knight were all collecting at this time. Cracherode never travelled to Italy; his gems were acquired in England, only a few were sent from Rome. He was educated in classics at Oxford and, although trained in the

120 Cameos from the Cracherode and
Carlisle collections. The sardonyx lion was
once owned by Lorenzo de' Medici and was
Cracherode's most valued ancient gem; he
thought it ancient, but it was later catalogued
as 15th century. The 16th-century Nereid and
Hippocamp and the 17th-century bust of
Minerva (h. 4.8 cm) are both from the
Carlisle collection. MME.

121 Collecting contemporary work: six red
sulphur impressions of carnelian intaglios
by Nathaniel Marchant (1739–1816),
purchased by Cracherode in the 1780s.
The head of Minerva (top right) (h. 3.3 cm)
and Achilles mourning for Patroclus (below
centre) were destroyed in an air raid in 1941.
In Cracherode's inventory, the former was
valued at £50, a very high sum for a
contemporary work and the same as his lion
from the Medici collection shown in fig. 120.
The impressions are mounted on squares of
coloured wood. MME.

Church of England, he did not practise as a clergyman but led a reclusive life, spending his inherited fortune on his collection.[21] His was the first comprehensive bequest since Sloane's of 1753. Like Sloane he also collected shells, minerals and uncarved hardstones. He had written his will leaving his collection to the British Museum by 1772 and from then on he was collecting for the public as much as himself, especially after he had become a Trustee of the British Museum in 1784. He was extremely select about his purchases; he added them one by one, weighing each of them up beforehand. The arrangement of his gems seems to follow Winckelmann, to judge by the set of casts that accompanied them. Interestingly, these casts bear the numbers of Raspe's catalogue and many are annotated 'Mr Cracherode', suggesting that it was Tassie who made them. A manuscript inventory drawn up after his death records the 'supposed' cost of the gems and makes startling reading: the antique gems cost him on average from £2 to £10, with three exceptions costing £40 or £50: one of these was a cameo of a lion from the collection of Lorenzo de' Medici (fig. 120), a gem which has not previously been recorded as Cracherode's.[22] In terms of prices paid, the real surprise comes at the end: his modern gems comprised two by Pichler, one by Edward Burch, and no fewer than six intaglios by the great English master Nathaniel Marchant, whom he knew intimately;[23] the Marchants cost him between £25 and £50 each (the present-day equivalents would be £1,500 and £3,000). This meant that the sixty-six listed ancient gems had cost him £466 while the nine modern ones had cost him £220, almost half as much.[24] The modern gems are all classical subjects and included what was undoubtedly Marchant's masterpiece: Achilles mourning the death of Patroclus (fig. 121).[25]

Charles Townley is best known for his classical sculptures, purchased by the Museum immediately after his death in 1805. His gem collection was not purchased till 1814. He bought in large quantities, often twenty to thirty at a time. He was primarily interested in their subject matter and collected gems as a visual record, which explains his commissioning of drawings discussed earlier. A set of casts of his gems made in 1804 came with the collection. Townley's arrangement was largely by subject, within loose cultural and chronological divisions. The largest sum he gave was for a large cameo of Minerva which he bought in Rome in 1768 for £150; he returned it to the dealer, Thomas Jenkins, in 1774 and it was eventually purchased by Catherine the Great.[26] In 1773 he spent £100 and £50 respectively on two intaglios with the signatures of Roman gem-engravers: an intaglio of Cupid and Psyche signed Pamphilus and one of Venus and Cupid signed Aulos (fig. 122). Townley thought all his gems ancient and a large proportion are still considered so.[27] There was one exception: a head of Pericles signed 'Brown' for Charles or William Brown, after the marble bust in Townley's collection. This was his only modern gem.[28]

Payne Knight's gem collection was much smaller than Townley's, comprising only 111 gems. He bequeathed it with his collection of antiquities, in 1824. He had become a Trustee

122 Ancient versus modern: the intaglio of Venus and Cupid (h. 2.3 cm), and the cameo of a Satyr and Maenad were acquired by Charles Townley as ancient, catalogued as 18th century in 1915, but are now thought classical once more. MME.

of the British Museum in April 1814. Two months later he changed his will in order to leave his collections to the British Museum. He said he wished them to join those of his late friends, Cracherode and Townley. Like Townley's, it contained many ancient gems, but there were two significant differences. Firstly, it was acquired with an eye to quality and, secondly, he acquired two modern gems as works of art in their own right: a female head signed by Girometti and a cameo of Augustus. The latter is unsigned but described by Payne Knight in his own manuscript catalogue of his gems as a masterpiece by the celebrated Italian gem-engraver and medallist Benedetto

123 Richard Payne Knight's cameo head of Flora (h. 2.3 cm). Cut in carnelian breccia, this is an exquisite use of a layered stone for the wreath of flowers in the hair. It was sold to Payne Knight in 1812 as ancient, but was later claimed by Benedetto Pistrucci (1784–1855) as his own work. MME.

Pistrucci.[29] Payne Knight also owned one of Pistrucci's most famous gems, a cameo of Flora in carnelian breccia (fig. 123).[30] Like the head of Augustus the Flora cameo is unsigned but was purchased in London in about 1812 as ancient. Pistrucci subsequently claimed it as his own work, carved in Rome as a forgery.[31] This episode may explain why, in his manuscript catalogue, Payne Knight tried to prove his gems ancient by devising abstruse and lengthy interpretations of them, derived from classical texts and written entirely in Latin.

When the Cracherode bequest arrived in the British Museum in 1799 it was given its own room, the Museum Crachrodeanum, which remained intact till around 1807.[32] During the first half of the nineteenth century engraved gems, both classical and post-classical, were held in a single Department of Antiquities. A manuscript catalogue done around 1830 suggests that the various collections were arranged in a single chronological sequence. In 1861 this by then enormous department was split into four, including a Department of Greek and Roman Antiquities and a Department of Coins and Medals; the gem collections were allocated to the Greek and Roman department. Nevertheless they were displayed in the Gold Ornament Room together with coins and medals, in the eighteenth-century tradition of keeping gems with coins and medals as illustrations of ancient history. In many continental cabinets the gems, coins and medals have remained together, irrespective of date; there is an added logic to this as many gem-engravers, from the Renaissance onwards, were also medallists. In the British Museum the classification of gems as antiquities meant that when the Gold Room was dismantled in 1919 the gems were physically divided into classical and post-classical groups and are now housed between two separate departments. Some initial sorting was done at the time of the first published catalogue by A. H. Smith in 1888.[33] This summary text had at the end a small section of twenty-three gems definitely thought modern, while others are indicated as of doubtful authenticity.

During the nineteenth century scepticism had gradually crept in. By 1913, when O. M. Dalton was preparing his 1915 catalogue of post-classical gems, all that mattered was whether the gem was ancient or modern.[34] Huge numbers of gems were, rightly or wrongly, given to the post-classical collections. Even as late as the Second World War, it was the modern gems that were thought expendable and placed on display during the blitz of 1941, only to be destroyed. The eighteenth-century view of the art of gem engraving may have been lost in the present-day arrangement of the collections, and much work remains to be done from surviving documentation.[35] But thanks to the survival of contemporary late eighteenth- or early nineteenth-century sets of impressions made of Cracherode's, Townley's and Payne Knight's gems, it is still possible for scholars of the future to study these collections as a single continuum (fig. 124).

124 This set of red sulphur impressions enables the whole of Richard Payne Knight's collection of 111 engraved gems to be seen in its entirety (originals now in MME and GR). The arrangement follows Knight's manuscript catalogue apart from the larger gems which are placed in the second tray. Two of the gems were destroyed in the Blitz of 1941, but, thanks to these impressions, a three-dimensional record is still available. GR.

13 Words and pictures: Greek vases and their classification

LUCILLA BURN

125 A south-Italian (Apulian) red-figured bell-krater in Cassiano dal Pozzo's 'Paper Museum': both the shape and the scene are sympathetically and convincingly drawn. GR.

Greek vases were relative latecomers to the world of collectors and collecting. Before the eighteenth century, if represented at all in cabinets of curiosities or other collections, they were probably not highly esteemed. This may have been in part because there were simply not enough of them around to awaken the attention of the scholarly community until excavations around the Bay of Naples had begun to gather pace in the eighteenth century and bring more significant numbers of them to light – and even then the excavations of the great Etruscan cemeteries of Vulci, the source of many of the finest vases in present-day collections, did not start until the late 1820s.[1] But a more substantial impediment to the earlier recognition of Greek vases was that, unlike coins or inscriptions or marble portraits, vases could not readily be related to ancient Greek or Latin texts – they are virtually never mentioned by ancient Greek authors, and Roman references are generally ambiguous. In the scholarly world of the Renaissance onwards, therefore, where learning was dominated by, or even equated with, a knowledge of classical texts and, through these, the events and personalities of Greek and Roman history, there was no obvious way into such largely uninscribed documents of the past, no method of determining their value or significance. This is not, of course, to deny that some vases were collected and, perhaps, examined or admired. Occasional glimpses of vases or motifs taken from them in late medieval and early Renaissance paintings, combined with extremely sparse documentary evidence, suggests that they did attract the attention of a few,[2] but we know nothing about how they were perceived or interpreted, and it seems unlikely that there were any serious attempts at classification of any kind.

Between the Renaissance and the nineteenth century, interest in Greek vases on the part of collectors and antiquaries gradually expanded and branched out in several different directions. For some collectors, vases served a purely decorative function, assisting in the elegant furnishing of a library or study. Other groups of scholars or intellectuals – by insisting on their Etruscan origins – forged vases into political ammunition for the promotion of the ancient culture of modern Tuscany. The counter-argument, that they were Greek, was pursued with energy by another group, while yet others concentrated on iconography, quarrying the scenes on the vases for information on ancient mythology, ritual and religion. It is the development of some of these ideas that this chapter will explore.

The first, very gradual growth in the status of Greek vases can be perceived in the course of the late sixteenth and seventeenth century. Included in a book of water-colours that once belonged to the French antiquary Nicolas-Claude Fabri de Peiresc (1580–1637), for example, are paintings of ten black- and red-figured vases, very accurately and intelligently rendered; the vases may have been de Peiresc's own, or they may be ones he had seen in other collections in either Italy or France.[3] Similarly Cassiano dal Pozzo (1588–1657) included a few drawings of vases in his 'Paper Museum', some very accurately and others less convincingly designed (fig. 125).[4] What seems significant in both cases is that both de Peiresc and dal Pozzo at least thought vases worthy of consideration, if less important than, say, sculpture, gems or bronzes. The earliest work of scholarship known to devote space to any sort of discussion of vases was Thomas Dempster's *De Etruria regali*, written in 1619–20 though published only a century later by Filippo Buonarroti and Giovanni Bottari. Dempster's text includes a short chapter that is essentially a compilation of quotations purportedly about vases from Latin authors; Buonarroti added about thirty plates of engravings of vases in the collections of the Grand Duke of Tuscany and Cardinal Gualtieri in Rome. *De Etruria regali*, written under the patronage of the Dukes of Tuscany, takes it very much for granted that all painted vases are Etruscan in origin.

In the late seventeenth century there is a little evidence for a growing interest in the imagery of painted vases; a handful were, for example, illustrated both in Bernard de Montfaucon's encyclopaedic *L'Antiquité expliqué* (see chs 10, 16), and in M. A. de la Chausse's *Romanum museum*. From the same period we start to hear the names of various Italian collectors who numbered vases among their possessions; and, as Clare Lyons has shown, Naples, through its proximity to the main sources of vases, became an important centre for their collection and study.[5] Among the earliest and most assiduous of the Neapolitan collectors was Giuseppe Valletta (1636–1714), many of whose fine vases, dispersed after his death, went ultimately (via the Cardinal Gualtieri) to form the basis of the Vatican's collection. It was probably the relative cheapness of vases, as opposed, say, to sculpture or architectural fragments, that made them an attractive acquisition prospect not just for the nobility but also for the wealthier members of the professional classes: Valletta, for example, was a lawyer.

In contemporary England, although there were by this time active collectors of classical antiquities, among them the Earl of Arundel (1585–1646) and Dr Richard Mead (1673–1754), vases were probably few and far between. A few examples were, however, included in the collection of the physician and founder of the British Museum, Sir Hans Sloane (b. 1660). Ian Jenkins has clearly demonstrated that antiquities, vases among them, were not of any intrinsic interest to Sloane, who collected them simply as one individual element in the kaleidoscopic microcosm of the natural and artificial universe that he aimed to recreate.[6] Thus in Sloane's house, at 3–4 Bloomsbury Place, vases rubbed shoulders with fossils, shells, crystals, zoological exhibits, shoes, clothing and many other categories of 'natural and artificial rarities'. Despite the several extant eye-witness accounts of

visits to the house (which include such references as 'a collection of instruments of the ancients, urns, lachrymatories, etc'),[7] we have little idea of how or where the antiquities were set out; the governing principle seems to have been that like was placed with like, with little or no apparent concern for aesthetics. The main significance of Sloane's collections in the present context must be that vases were included at all among the objects in his 'house museum', an enterprise that anticipated by roughly a century the more sophisticated experiments of Charles Townley, Thomas Hope or Sir John Soane.

GREEK VASES IN THE EIGHTEENTH CENTURY: MASTRILLI AND HAMILTON

In the course of the eighteenth century Greek vases gradually began to play a more significant role in the scholarly appreciation of classical antiquity, perhaps both fostered by and fostering the slow emancipation of the study of the surviving monuments of antiquity from text-based learning. The idea of the progress of the arts through one civilization to another, analogous to the scientific 'chain of being', was expounded by more than one learned eighteenth-century author. The French scholar, teacher and antiquarian the Comte de Caylus, in his monumental *Recueil d'antiquités* (Paris, 1761–7), argued that a 'chain of art' led from Egypt through the Etruscan civilization to that of Greece; his work included many illustrations and discussions of Greek vases – which he firmly maintained were Etruscan (fig. 126). Much of Caylus's theory was, however, rejected by the most influential theorizer of the time, J. J. Winckelmann (see figs 99, 159), a believer in the theory of progress who nevertheless maintained that the superlative artistic developments of the Greeks were autochthonous and owed nothing to the Egyptians. Winckelmann's primary field of interest lay in sculpture, and it was largely on a close analysis of sculptural style that his arguments depended. Yet as has been pointed out, while vases are quite summarily treated (and placed in the category of 'Art of the Etruscans and their neighbours') in the first (1764) edition of his monumental *History of the Art of the Ancients*, in the revision of 1776 vases are admitted to be Greek – and compared with the drawings of Raphael. Winckelmann's 'conversion' has been directly attributed to the visit he paid to Naples in 1767 and to his acquaintance with Sir William Hamilton.

During the eighteenth century, important progress in the understanding of Greek vases was made in Naples. For the notable Neapolitan collection of the Marchese Felice Maria Mastrilli (c. 1694–1755) we are fortunate in the survival of both eye-witness accounts of its arrangement and a manuscript, *Spiega di vasi antichi*, which presents drawings and commentaries by various scholars on a number of the individual vases.[8] In the Marchese's Palazzo di San Nicandro the vases were very deliberately displayed as art objects; attached

126 Comte de Caylus, *Receuil d'antiquités égyptiennes, etrusques, grecques et romaines*, Paris, 1752–67, vol. 1, pl. XXV, an Athenian red-figured *skyphos* and *hydria*, with the figured scenes 'unrolled' above and below. The Greek legend on the *skyphos*, *opaiskalos* ('the boy is beautiful'), is plainly visible, yet Caylus firmly championed the Etruscan origin of such vases. GR Library.

to the walls of the room were a dozen oval gilded picture frames, with brackets fitted above, below and to the sides, and on these stood the smaller vases, while the larger pieces stood on bases on the floor of the gallery, interspersed with busts of Roman emperors and other notables; in the same room were marble tables holding bronzes and other pieces of sculpture. This thoughtful and integrated display must have bestowed upon the vases a very different status from that which they generally enjoyed in the collection of such predecessors or contemporaries as Giuseppe Valletta or the Duca di Noia, where they would have been ranged along the tops of bookcases so that little beyond the elegance of their shapes could be appreciated: it may be significant that Winckelmann visited Mastrilli's collection on more than one occasion. *Spiega di vasi antichi*, with other documentary evidence that includes letters between Mastrilli and A. F. Gori, a leading Neapolitan antiquary of the time, reinforces the impression that Mastrilli believed vases might be a more significant and more fruitful field of scientific enquiry than had hitherto

been supposed. The drawings in the manuscript are careful representations of the shapes and designs of the vases, inscriptions are accurately transcribed and marginal notes are impressively technical in their reports of dimensions and their notes on the colour of the clay, the quality of the black glaze and the presence of polychrome details. The detailed commentaries suggest that the principal interest for contemporary scholars was their iconography and the evidence it could be made to yield for ancient rituals and beliefs. Mastrilli himself, however, was particularly interested in the inscriptions on some of the vases – Lyons indeed has suggested that he went out of his way to acquire inscribed examples, perhaps because in an intellectual climate that gave such primacy to texts he believed that vases on which texts and images were combined could more easily be made to contribute to an understanding of the past. Although this fondness for inscribed vases may well have encouraged unscrupulous dealers to add false inscriptions to some of the vases offered to Mastrilli, his specialization did in the end bear fruit, as it was the sensible and perceptive interpretation (by A. S. Mazzochi) of the inscriptions on five Mastrilli vases that provided some of the initial impetus for the theory that the vases were Greek, rather than Etruscan.[9]

Many of the interests and pursuits of the well-to-do in late eighteenth-century Naples, in particular their enthusiasm for scientific and antiquarian studies, were eagerly and instantly entered into by Sir William Hamilton when he arrived there in 1764 to take up the position of His Britannic Majesty's Envoy Extraordinary to the Court of Naples. Hamilton rapidly became an obsessive collector of Greek vases; he bought partly from other collectors (for example at the sale of the Mastrilli and Porcinari collections in 1766) and partly from local dealers and suppliers who soon heard of his interest and hastened both to feed and to profit from it. Hamilton's huge contribution to the greater admiration, appreciation and influence of Greek vases has been very thoroughly canvassed in recent years.[10] Yet his importance in the context of the early collections of the British Museum is such that the most significant elements of his achievements in this area must briefly be summarized here.

First among these was the direct physical legacy of his collecting activities. The sale to the British Museum in 1772 of his first collection of vases, some 730 pieces (see fig. 93), gave the British nation for the first time in significant quantity and quality a class of object that had previously been only rather sporadically collected and casually displayed by members of the nobility. They were arranged in eye-level cabinets in the 'Hamilton Room' in Montagu House in the strong natural light requested by their former owner,[11] and early museum visitors were invited to view the vases as objects deserving of interest and inspection in their own right: this was a major advance in their status and one that must have contributed a great deal towards their wider appreciation in Britain. Nor were the vases in the British Museum the sole Hamilton vases to reach Britain. The sale in 1801 to Thomas Hope of the part of Hamilton's second vase collection that escaped the wreck of HMS *Colossus* off the Scilly Isles in 1898 resulted in the concentration of a second major group of vases displayed with the utmost care and thought in London, this time in Hope's Duchess Street mansion (see below).

But, in addition to this major role in physically increasing the stock of vases in Britain, Hamilton had more subtle parts to play in furthering their influence. The two great publications of his two vase collections form a tangible and highly visible testimony to the strength of his feeling that these objects were as deserving of recognition as, say, the architectural remains of ancient Greece or Rome. The text of both works was undoubtedly important to Hamilton, who, modestly aware of his own lack of expertise, took pains to engage the best authorities that he could find for the task. The author of the first publication, Pierre-François Hugues, better known as the 'Baron' d'Hancarville, was determined to rival and if possible outdo Winckelmann's great *History*. Since a large proportion of the text bears no relationship at all to the illustrations of the vases, there are few grounds for claiming that d'Hancarville's text made any great contribution towards the methodology of Greek vase studies. Where vases come into the text at all it is for the evidence they can provide for ancient religious beliefs and practices, or for their place in d'Hancarville's theory of the rise and development of the arts. He was, however, aware of contemporary views and what seem today among the more lucid passages of his text are those where he argues for the Greek, as opposed to the Etruscan, origin of the vases, which he, in common with Hamilton and most of the Neapolitan scholars, believed had been made by the Greeks who settled in southern Italy and Sicily. And in this belief Hamilton and his friends were largely right, for although it is now recognized that the great majority of black-figured vases and some of the finest of the red-figured in Hamilton's collection had in fact been made in Athens, where the techniques originated, many of the red-figured vases, including some of the largest and most ornate, were indeed products of the Greek colonies in southern Italy and Sicily.

D'Hancarville's arguments for Greekness were based on his and others' reading of the Greek inscriptions on so many vases, and he also tried to use the letter forms to suggest a relative chronology for some of the vases. It was, however, Hamilton himself, in the preface and a postscript to the first volume and in 'Additional Remarks' at the end of the second volume of the publication of the second collection, who quietly brought further and conclusive proof of Greekness by drawing attention to vases exactly like some of his own found in a tomb on Melos.[12] The text of the second publication was generally more closely related to its ostensible subject, with descriptions, largely of the subjects of the figured scenes, by Hamilton's friend Count Italinski; few of his interpretations would be accepted today, and Valerie Smallwood has shown that Hamilton's own contributions are of more objective and perhaps more lasting value, consisting as they do of notes on find-spots and comparisons with vases in other collections and in his own first collection. There are also descriptions of some of the tombs in which vases had been found, their content, and even detailed observations on techniques, including notes about the preliminary sketch lines he had noticed on some vases.[13]

It was, however, through their illustrations rather than their texts that both the Hamilton publications were significant and influential. It is largely because of these that the four folio volumes devoted to the first collection, *Antiquités etrusques, grecques et romaines* (*AEGR*), are generally considered as one of the most beautiful publications of the eighteenth century (figs 127, 128). The magnificent coloured plates with their richly bordered engravings of the 'unrolled' scenes from the vases, are works of art in their own right; less conspicuous but equally well drawn are the measured drawings of the

127 The dedication plate of the first volume of d'Hancarville's publication of the first collection of Hamilton's vases. The dedication is to Hamilton's sovereign and childhood friend, George III; the handsome design is a richly symbolic blend of Greek, Roman and Etruscan elements. GR Library.

128 'Unrolled' view of the upper figured zone of the 'Meidias hydria', one of the most admired and influential of the Hamilton vases, from *AEGR*. Many elements of its figured scenes were selected for reproduction by late eighteenth- and early nineteenth-century potters, painters, silversmiths and furniture-makers. GR Library.

shapes of individual pots. The beauty of the books as vehicles for the wider appreciation of the beauty of his vases was undoubtedly highly satisfactory to Hamilton, who, despite his antiquarian instincts for the significance of origins, and his concern for archaeological accuracy, was primarily interested in the vases from an aesthetic point of view. But a further deep-rooted concern, and a paramount reason for desiring to publish his vases, was Hamilton's wish to improve contemporary standards of art and design. Already in 1755 he had become one of the earliest members of the Society for the Encouragement of Arts, Manufactures and Commerce (the Society of Arts): and despite the success of *AEGR*, when it came to the publication of the second collection, Hamilton's concern that it should be rather less lavish in design was prompted not only by the desire to keep his own costs down but also by his very sincere determination (attested by remarks both in private correspondence and in the text itself) to make the books more affordable to artists and artisans.[14]

The illustrations for the publication of the second collection were supervised by Wilhelm Tischbein and they take the form of simple line drawings (fig. 129): less immediately attractive than the coloured engravings of *AEGR*, they were

undoubtedly influential in their day, as evidenced, for example, by the at times very similar-looking outline technique adopted by John Flaxman for his *Odyssey* illustrations. In fact both publications had enormous impact on late eighteenth- and early nineteenth-century style. As Ian Jenkins remarks, 'From fireplaces to papier mâché boxes, and from wall paintings to tapestry, the influence of his publications could be seen everywhere.'[15] The effect on the potter Josiah Wedgwood must surely have surpassed even Hamilton's expectations. Wedgwood, who received copies of some of the plates of *AEGR* (including the 'Apotheosis of Homer' scene[16]) before their full publication, was quick to acknowledge the benefit he had derived from Hamilton's vases (figs 130, 131). But when in 1786 he wrote to Hamilton that 'The collection of Etruscan vases in the British Museum will ever be resorted to for the finest models of elegant and simple forms, it is a source from which you will know how greatly I have profited', he might more accurately have stated that it was rather to the publication of the vases, from which he and his designers and potters actually worked, that he owed the greater debt.

Greek vases into the
nineteenth century: Thomas Hope

While Sir William Hamilton was undoubtedly the most influential in terms of making Greek vases better known, he was by no means the only collector to bring vases back to Britain in the late eighteenth or early nineteenth century. Quite rapidly a lively British market for vases came into being, as

129 The scene on a south-Italian (probably Apulian) figured vase, as drawn in W Tischbein, *Collection of Engravings from Ancient Vases …*, 1793–1803, vol. 2. The simple, linear style adopted for this publication was designed to promote more accurate study and appreciation of the style of the paintings. GR Library.

130 Red-figured *calyx-krater* (wine bowl) from Hamilton's first collection, showing the victorious performer in a musical contest. The subject was identified by d'Hancarville as 'The Apotheosis of Homer'; Hamilton himself was more circumspect, suggesting it might rather represent 'some celebrated poet'. GR.

131 Jasperware plaque, *The Apotheosis of Homer*, made at Wedgwood's Etruria factory after a design by John Flaxman. The composition is taken from the engraving of the Hamilton vase shown in fig.130, which Wedgwood and Bentley were shown before publication. MME.

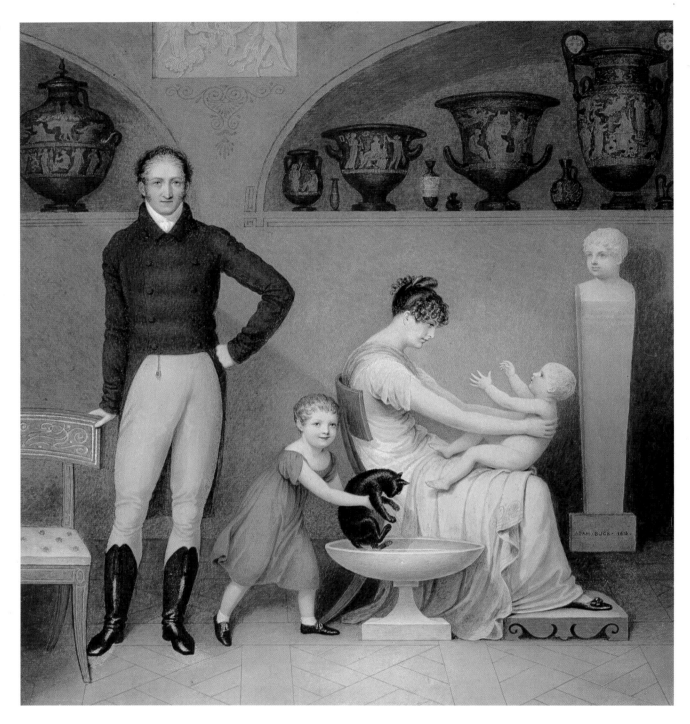

several of the earliest collections, such as that of the 1st Baron Cawdor, were sold soon after their arrival in Britain; moreover, the resumption of hostilities with France following the temporary peace of 1802 severely restricted opportunities for travel and the acquisition of antiquities in Italy. Thus the first decades of the nineteenth century saw collectors eagerly buying from one another, a situation dramatically described by Richard Payne Knight to Lord Aberdeen in a letter of 1812: 'We collectors have been preying upon each other's spoils

132 *Portrait of the artist's family with the bust of a deceased child*, watercolour by Adam Buck, 1813. The vases on the far left and second from the right (see fig. 130) were star items in Hamilton's first collection, in the British Museum from 1772. New Haven, Yale Centre for British Art, Paul Mellon Collection.

133 The library in Sir John Soane's house in Lincoln's Inn Fields; placed on the tops of the bookshelves or on specially contrived ledges and brackets the main functions of the vases are to contribute to the overall decorative effect and the scholarly ambience. Sir John Soane's Museum.

lately like cray fish in a pond, which immediately begin sucking the shell of a deceased brother.' Ian Jenkins, in discussing the work of Adam Buck, has illustrated the contemporary vogue for including vases in fashionable portraiture (fig. 132), and he has also drawn attention to the fact that even those collectors whose primary interests lay elsewhere, like Charles Townley, Richard Westmacott, Sir John Soane or Payne Knight himself, still felt the need to own a few vases if only to bestow upon their libraries the proper ambience of scholarship and culture.[17] Indeed, Soane's use of vases as library ornaments was surely one of the few conventional aspects of the decoration of his eccentric house-museum in Lincoln's Inn Fields: apart from the massive 'Cawdor vase', a south-Italian volute krater that must always have demanded special treatment, his vases are generally small in scale and placed either on the tops of the bookcases, on specially designed wall-brackets or else in 'columbarium niches' (fig. 133), a fashionable device that he may have borrowed from Thomas Hope.

In the deliberate harnessing of Greek vases, along with other antiquities, to the shaping and 'improving' of contemporary art and taste, it was the Dutch banker Thomas Hope who was to prove Sir William Hamilton's natural successor.[18] As he was a great deal richer, and probably more single-minded, than Hamilton, he was able to devote himself more fully and energetically to the cause – by producing and publishing his own designs, derived from those of antiquity, by patronizing the products and designs of others, and, most spectacularly, by collecting works of ancient art and displaying his collections for the enjoyment and edification of others. In the development of what was to become known as the 'Hope style', Greek vases played a major role, because in contrast to monumental sculpture or architecture they seemed to afford a direct and immediate link with aspects of the private life of the ancients, from tableware to costume and furniture, that might most readily be admired and emulated by contemporary artisans and their patrons.

Hope's enthusiasm for and use of vases is very clear in his own publications, including *Costume of the Ancients* and *Household Furniture and Interior Decoration Executed from Designs by Thomas Hope*, both of which present designs taken or derived almost exclusively from vase paintings. Many examples of the actual furniture and table wares that he either designed himself or commissioned from others still survive and testify to how rich a source of inspiration he found vases to be, while contemporary accounts report the enthusiasm with which 'Grecian' fashions of dress were adopted by society ladies.[19]

In the history of the development of the display of Greek vases the well-documented arrangement of Hope's own collection in his Duchess Street mansion is of particular interest. As already mentioned, in 1801 he had bought the surviving part of Hamilton's second vase collection, probably around

750 items. He subsequently sold some of these and bought others at various sales, so that the exact numbers in his possession at any one time are not entirely clear. However, it is estimated that at least five hundred were generally on display in the three vase rooms of his house, which, like the rest of the 'public' rooms, with their displays of paintings, Egyptian and Indian art, are discussed and illustrated by engravings in *Household Furniture* (fig. 134). It seems likely that the practical usefulness of the vases for contemporary design, combined with their aesthetic qualities, was what chiefly appealed to Hope, and Richard Westmacott's comment on the vase rooms suggests that these aspects were what Hope tried to emphasize to visitors: 'Independent of their great variety, and varied elegance of forms, they are doubly valuable as specimens of ancient history and costume, every object presenting some new and highly instructive design, tending to correct and refine the taste, and direct the student to the purest style of Greek art.'[20] At the same time Hope was sympathetic towards the contemporary interest in the perceived religious and funerary symbolism of vase iconography, and he tried to create settings for the display of his vases that would evoke these associations: thus the first vase room was fitted out with columbarium-style niches (more correctly used for Roman funerary urns by Charles Townley at Park Street or Sir John Soane in his 'Catacombs'), and the furnishings of all three rooms were adorned with a wealth of Dionysiac symbols from masks of the god to swags and staffs wreathed in vine and ivy leaves. The engravings that show the three rooms suggest that the message behind this arrangement may not have been immediately apparent. Although the furnishings, in the form of long shelves supported on scrolling brackets above low wall cabinets, are extremely elegant, the ordering of the vases is oppressively symmetrical, consisting for the most part of long rows of massive bell kraters alternating with small jugs or oil flasks. The rather repetitive effect of the arrangement was certainly mocked by one irreverent critic who wrote in an issue of the *Monthly Review or Literary Journal, Enlarged* in 1809 that the vases were 'well adapted for the furniture of a Museum; but in their present mode of arrangement, they excite rather the idea of an apothecary's shop on a very grand scale' – an unfortunate effect not easy to avoid when dealing with large numbers of similarly shaped vessels![21]

GREEK VASES AFTER HOPE

The flamboyance of Thomas Hope's approach to vases and the fashion for owning and displaying them that he did so much to foster, in addition to his relentless quarrying of their designs and motifs as sources of inspiration for contemporary art and craft, did much to make vases more widely known in early nineteenth-century England. Yet Hope contributed virtually nothing towards their scholarly under-

134 View of the third vase room in Thomas Hope's house in Duchess Street, from *Household Furniture and Interior Decoration*, 1807. Hope's arrangement was designed to evoke what he perceived as the funerary and Dionysiac symbolism of the vases. British Library.

standing or classification. By this time others, including Thomas Burgon, Edward Dodwell and of course Lord Elgin, were visiting Greece, discovering vases there in tombs that were exactly like those found in Italy, and gradually bolstering the conviction that they were Greek; but still no system had evolved for dating or otherwise sorting out the vases and the often far-fetched interpretation of their scenes was still the main concern. In the late 1820s and 1830s the discovery and excavation of the great Etruscan cemeteries at Vulci and elsewhere brought a dramatic flood of large numbers of high-quality and predominantly Athenian black- and red-figured vases on to the European markets. The British Museum managed to acquire a notable collection from the sale of the Chevalier Durand in 1836 [22] and other private collectors also benefited: even William Beckford, not generally noted as a collector of classical antiquities, acquired a couple of small vases from this source towards the end of his life: they are now in the British Museum.[23] The Vulci excavations were also

significant in that they provided the impetus for the foundation of the Istituto di Corrispondenza Archeologica in Rome; and, although the original focus of research was still interpretation of the iconography, gradually, and perhaps as a response to the positivist philosophical theories sweeping through mid-nineteenth-century Europe, 'objective facts' such as measurements and precise descriptions of shapes and subjects began to drive out interpretation. Slowly a few steps were taken towards establishing a relative chronology of wares and painting styles, and thus was the path cleared for the two great and in some ways complementary initiatives of late nineteenth-century vase studies, the establishment of the (still on-going) *Corpus vasorum antiquorum*, a series of publications which aimed to establish a precise and objective record of every known vase, and the development of attribution studies, the gathering together of vases whose painting could be attributed to an individual hand.[24] While both these lines of enquiry continue to flourish, recent years have also seen a revival of interest in iconographic studies, and even a renewed sympathy for chthonic and Dionysiac interpretations of the scenes on vases: thus, two hundred years on, the interests of the age of Enlightenment are once more among the concerns of classical scholarship.

14 Between antiquarianism and experiment: Hans Sloane, George III and collecting science

SILKE ACKERMANN AND JANE WESS

This is a tale of two sciences: natural history in its widest sense, and experimental philosophy. The collections of scientific instruments of Sir Hans Sloane and King George III, as they have come down to us, invite comparisons between the differing approaches of the two men. Both were wealthy, educated, well-versed in the culture of their respective times, and able to indulge in their interests without restraint. However, the way they perceived what we would now term 'science', and the way they interacted with their collections, was quite distinct. While personal preferences played a part, in many ways the two men illustrate a changing attitude towards the subject, and in particular its instruments, which was taking place in the eighteenth century.

In the previous century the study of the natural world which we now call 'science' was generally known as natural philosophy. While mathematics and medicine were established disciplines taught to would-be practitioners, natural philosophy had not yet reached that maturity. In England there were no courses to follow, and the study of the natural world was largely left to gentlemen who built up collections of natural history and curiosities. Sir Hans Sloane exemplifies this attitude, which is admirably illustrated through his collection.

However, the situation was gradually changing. In Italy a more experimental attitude was emerging towards the natural world with a small group of dilettantes undertaking experiments on mechanics, heat and air pressure. In 1660 the Royal Society took up the banner of the new 'experimental philosophy' and became its central focus in England. Robert Boyle, a leading member, devised many experiments using an air pump. Isaac Newton's influential work of 1687, usually known simply as 'the *Principia*', set out his ideas concerning mechanics. The Newtonian doctrine was taken up at the university of Leiden where the first courses in experimental philosophy were taught to students. In 1704 Newton's *Opticks*, his second book, discussed many optical phenomena. By the start of the eighteenth century there was a growing body of experiments which could be combined to form a course suitable for a wider audience.

Initially, the subject matter treated varied considerably depending on the lecturer, and could be in any order. After 1720 the courses became more standardized, partly owing due to the work of Jacob 'sGravesande at Leiden. As the courses became standardized so did the instruments, which could now be bought from established makers by gentlemen for their private collections. In 1760, when George III came to the throne, he commissioned a substantial set of instruments from George Adams, a leading London maker. King George III's collection exemplifies the aristocratic collecting of contemporary scientific instruments.

What we now call scientific instruments were classified into 'philosophical', which

were used in experimental philosophy, 'mathematical', which were used in astronomy, timekeeping, navigation, surveying, gunnery, carpentry, gauging, and other trades requiring mathematics, and 'optical' which included telescopes, microscopes and spectacles. Philosophical instruments were essentially for demonstration. They in their turn could be classified into mechanics, which often included magnetism, pneumatics (air and gases), hydrostatics (water pressure, syphons etc.), optics and astronomy. In the second half of the century electrostatics began to feature in the courses, and electrical machines became extremely popular.

The changing expectations of what constitutes science, and how it should be represented in a collection in the late eighteenth century, is well illustrated by a letter supposedly written by Matthew Bramble, one of the main protagonists of Tobias Smollett's novel *The Expedition of Humphry Clinker*, first published in 1771:

> Yes, Doctor, I have seen the British Museum; which is a noble collection, and even stupendous, if we consider that it was made by a private man, a physician, who was obliged to make his own fortune at the same time ... I could wish ... the whole of the animal, vegetable and mineral kingdoms completed, by adding to each, at the public expense, those articles that are wanting ... I could also wish, for the honour of the nation, that there was a complete apparatus for the course of mathematics, mechanics, and experimental philosophy; and a good salary settled upon an able professor, who should give regular lectures on these subjects.

King George III was just fifteen in 1753, the year Hans Sloane died at the age of ninety-three. Their differing attitudes to collecting 'science' and what that science entailed can be accounted for to some extent by this generation gap. Sloane could have chosen to embrace the new experimental philosophy, especially as he was in contact with its most vigorous proponents at the Royal Society, but adhered to the antiquarian collecting style to which he had been exposed in his youth. Similarly, George III's collection of scientific instruments reflects early influences on his life; as Prince of Wales in 1754, under the supervision of Lord Bute, he attended a course of experimental philosophy by Stephen Demainbray, an itinerant lecturer. Both types of collecting co-existed in England and on the continent during the eighteenth century, after which it was the newcomer, the dynamic and immediately useful experimental philosophy, which disappeared from the libraries and studies of gentlemen, eventually to be sited in institutions and evolving into physics and chemistry.

The two strands of scientific endeavour can be seen entwined in a sometimes uneasy relationship from the very founding of the Royal Society in the early 1660s. The Royal Society was the central focus for the fledgling interest in 'experimental philosophy', having been set up in the early 1660s with the express purpose of 'promoting Physico-Mathematical Experimental Learning'. However, it also championed the natural historical approach of observation and ordering. Sir Hans Sloane subscribed to the aims of the Society as stated by Thomas Sprat in 1663:

> To make faithful Records of all the Works of Nature or Art, which can come within their reach, that so the present Age, and posterity, may be able to put marks on the Errors, which have been strengthened by long prescription: to restore the Truths that have lain neglected ...

Thomas Birch, historian of the Royal Society, described Sloane's altruistic activities as follows:

> It was not a trifling or vain Inclination of merely getting together a great Number of uncommon things, that induced him to spend £50,000 in purchasing the rarities which every country produced. His constant endeavour was to employ them to the best purposes, by making himself acquainted, as far as possible, with the Properties, Qualities and Uses, either in Food, Medicine, or Manufacture of every Plant, Mineral or Animal that came into his possession.

OBSERVATION AND ORDERING

Sloane's few scientific instruments appear to have been collected within the framework of a natural historian's outlook. The majority seem to have been seen as cultural artefacts, revealing aspects of a particular trade or activity, not as apparatus. As with his other specimens, many were gifts, and their various countries of origin tell not only of his foreign contacts but of a desire to represent the encyclopaedic nature of human achievement. Sloane spent a great deal of time ordering and classifying his collections; but, because the instruments were not for demonstration, observation by the viewer was the primary method of learning.

It is perhaps revealing that not all of Sloane's instruments are grouped together in his inventories. The major part, fifty-seven, are listed under the heading 'Mathematicall Instruments &c.' in his own hand in the 'Miscellanies' catalogue, now kept in the British Museum's Department of Ethnography. These are instruments for time-measurement, such as astrolabes, sundials and nocturnals, but also fortification and surveying instruments, 'opticall tubes', old microscopes and objects for general measurement such as rules and protractors. This mixture is quite interesting, since strictly speaking mathematical and optical instruments should have formed distinct groups as explained above and should not have fallen under the same heading.

One of the earliest and finest European astrolabes known to have survived is amongst these objects. Described in the inventories as 'A brasse astrolabe made at London for the latitudes of Rome, London, &c. with a perpetuall almanack

136 The 'Shah Husain astrolabe'. This extraordinarily beautiful, silver inlaid Persian astrolabe was made in AD 1712 for Shah Husain, the last ruler of the Safavid dynasty. Unfortunately, it is not known how it came into Sloane's collection. OA.

137 Two telescope tubes, made by the famous 17th-century Italian maker Eustachio Divini. The lenses have not survived. MME.

upon it', it is undated, but likely to have been made in about 1300 in England (fig. 135). On the other side of the historical and cultural spectrum stands the fabulous Persian 'Shah Husain' astrolabe (fig. 136), made in Sloane's lifetime for the last of the Safavid rulers, but still in the same medieval tradition as the earlier European instrument.

Not all the instruments are of such splendour, and many of the entries are very short, such as 'A protractor' or 'A gnomon', and, curiously, 'Many nails &c.'. The brevity of these entries makes it sometimes rather difficult to identify the objects in the collections if their connection with Sloane was lost at some point in the Museum's early history. However, amongst the instruments described in greater detail we find sundials and a fortification instrument by Michael Butterfield, the well-known English maker living in Paris at the end of the seventeenth century, and instruments 'bought of [Henry] Wynne' (died 1709). It is interesting to note that at least one

of the latter's instruments seems to have been previously in the possession of the Duke of Albemarle, whose physician Sloane had once been.

Of the types listed in this group, but mentioned separately in other parts of the same catalogue under the heading 'Miscellanies', are 'A small perspective glasse made by [the seventeenth-century Italian maker Giuseppe] Campani at Rome' and two abaci: one from seventeenth-century England and the other a Roman type, but now thought to be from the same period. It is interesting to note that some of the objects seem to have been acquired in a condition which would have made it impossible to use them properly, had Sloane ever intended to do so: there are several sets of telescope tubes amongst the 'mathematical instruments', two listed as made by the seventeenth-century Italian maker Eustachio Divini (fig. 137) – rather battered and without the lenses, which were apparently kept separately and have subsequently not survived.

But there are other types of instruments to be found scattered amongst the 'Miscellanies': contemporary 'working' instruments such as a newly invented German hygrometer, thermometers, and 'a sett of microscopes made by Mr. Musschenbroek of Holland'. A very small number of these one might call 'philosophical' instruments, such as an artificial eye or a balance to establish specific gravity. However, the catalogue gives prices only for instruments which would have been connected directly with Sloane's professional work, such as the microscopes and a set of surgical instruments, while the

majority of the objects appears to have been given to him and do not bear evidence of systematic acquisition. Although Sloane is known to have had at least one copy of a trade catalogue by the Dutch maker Jan van Musschenbroek in his library, probably annotated by his own hand, there is no evidence that he bought any of the instruments listed in the catalogue, nor does he appear to have done so on earlier occasions when contemporary instruments were shown to him.

At no point does Sloane seem to have had the intention of building up a 'modern' instrument collection. As a collector, he was interested in how things worked in the past in a variety of cultures, not in the latest discoveries of the present – these were worth knowing, not collecting. The instruments potentially used for his professional work appear to be randomly listed in his catalogue of miscellaneous objects. Nowhere is any obvious attempt made to classify the objects as 'optical' or 'philosphical' instruments and the term 'mathematical instruments' is used in a rather inaccurate way as we have seen. As such, the majority of Sloane's instruments are 'antiquities', not 'scientific instruments' in the modern sense of the word.

It is interesting to note that although Sloane knew Newton, succeeded him as President of the Royal Society, and indeed owned two portraits of him and possessed his seals, he did not concern himself with the experimental philosophy in which Newton was engaged. This is reminiscent of Queen Caroline, wife of George II and grandmother of George III, who in 1731 had a hermitage erected in Kew Gardens in which she had busts of Newton and Boyle installed. Caroline certainly took a lively interest in natural philosophy; however, when George III took over Kew in the 1760s, the hermitage was swept away and an observatory built in a clear statement of the move to active involvement with scientific instruments.

EXPERIMENTAL LEARNING

The other strand in the aims and ambitions of the Royal Society, as already mentioned, was that of experiment. In 1662 Robert Hooke was appointed as Curator of Experiments, being expected to provide three or four demonstrations for each weekly meeting. While many of these experiments concerned what we would now call physics or chemistry, many also were biological. While Sloane and his fellow natural historians would passively observe living animals and plants, and collect dead specimens for a static display, the experimental philosophers actively interfered with nature at every level to investigate the processes of life. It was a difference of attitude rather than one of subject matter.

The initial years at the Royal Society were full of enthusiastic experimental activity. Robert Hooke, Robert Boyle and their contemporaries led the discussions on a wide variety of topics, such as the velocity of sound, the freezing of water in constricted spaces, the burning of lamps underwater, and the design of weathercocks to name but a few. However, by the time that Sloane became a fellow in 1685, the experimental ingredient of the Fellows' diet had diminished and the Society was in general decline. In 1696 Sloane took on the considerable task of publishing the *Philosophical Transactions*, the Society's principal publication, which had been allowed to lapse, and he was largely responsible for revitalizing the entire endeavour. However, he had his critics, as under his stewardship the *Transactions* reflected his natural historical and antiquarian leanings, accepting diverse and miscellaneous contributions which did little to further the progress of knowledge through experiment. When Isaac Newton became president in 1703 all this was to change again. Experiment was again on the agenda with lines of enquiry being pursued which had originated with the work of Hooke and Boyle. Others on capillarity, gravity and magnetism were also introduced.

By the start of the eighteenth century the stable political climate and increasing wealth, combined with a proliferation of coffee houses and availability of newspapers, made London the perfect seedbed for the new ideas. Unlike mathematical training, the experimental demonstrations were not directly applicable to any existing trade; scientists and engineers did not yet exist. However it was widely recognized that this information was beneficial, both socially and economically. One catalyst for the introduction of experimental philosophy to a wider urban public was the combination of Newton and Francis Hawksbee, the new Curator of Experiments, at the Royal Society. In 1704 Newton's *Opticks* was published, with the tantalizing *quaeries* appended, giving rise to a number of optical demonstrations. These could be added to the pneumatics experiments contrived by Boyle, and the various hydrostatical and mechanical experiments previously devised at the Society, to form a course. In 1705 the first public lectures were given by James Hodgson, who used the services of Francis Hawksbee and his magnificent air pump.

While the English experimental philosophy revolved around the London coffee houses in the early eighteenth century, the Dutch were quick to absorb the experimental methods into their university curricula. In Leiden the inspiring teacher Jacob 'sGravesande put together a course of natural philosophy which opened up Newton's indigestible *Principia* to hundreds of students. His textbook, *Mathematical Elements of Physicks, Proved by Experiments; being an introduction to Sir Isaac Newton's philosophy* which was published in 1720, became a standard, and his instruments, experiments, and the overall framework of his course were copied shamelessly for most of the century. He too worked with a talented instrument maker, Jan van Musschenbroek. The sixth edition of this work, translated from the Latin by John Theophilus Desaguliers and published by his son in 1747, appears to have been widely disseminated; it provided much of the material for George III's course on mechanics.

While the lecturers spread the word of experimental philosophy to a wider urban public, the aristocracy and country

138 Orreries, models of the Copernican solar system, were mainstays of the astronomy sections of the courses. This example, dating from about 1750, includes all the then known planets and is similar to that in the well-known painting by Joseph Wright of Derby. Science Museum.

gentry began to assimilate their private collections. Although few of the instruments in the King George III collection were collected by previous generations, there are some outstanding items that were, and there is evidence of significant interest and contact with the new philosophy on behalf of the royal family. In 1716 George I attended lectures by Desaguliers, a leading figure in English experimental philosophy, who took over from Francis Hawksbee as curator of experiments at the Royal Society. His son George II had the magnificent grand orrery enlarged and improved in 1733 (fig. 138). Caroline, George II's queen, acted as the go-between in a dispute between Newton and Gottfried Wilhelm Leibniz over the decline of natural religion in England, with Newton visiting Caroline to discuss his philosophy. Both she and George II were friends and neighbours of Samuel Molyneux, an astronomer and performer of optical experiments. Prince Frederick, George III's father, was even more closely involved, having Desaguliers and his collection installed in 'a large room fitted up at the top of the house'. During 1737 Frederick attended daily lectures. A beautiful armilliary sphere by Jonathan Sisson, made in 1731, is testimony to his interest. Perhaps more importantly for George III's future involvement, Lord Bute, his adviser and close friend of his mother after Frederick's death, had a substantial private collection.

At the beginning of the eighteenth century Hawksbee worked with Newton as an instrument maker and technical adviser. Van Musschenbroek had served the same function for 'sGravesande. The instruments produced were uniquely 'bespoke'. However, by the 1730s the courses and the instruments had become standardized, and instrument makers in London began to produce them routinely in larger numbers. Thus, when George III came to the throne in 1760, a substantial collection of what were known as 'philosophical' instruments could be commissioned for him from a leading instrument maker, George Adams, at Tycho Brahe's Head, Fleet Street. George III had a collection just as Sloane had, but he had not collected them as such. Much of Sloane's energy, expertise and discernment had gone into the process of collecting. George III's knowledge and expertise would develop only after he had reaped the benefit of seeing his collection in action.

The King George III collection embodies this new approach, which departed from the earlier natural historical attitude towards objects of interest in a number of ways. While the new philosophical instruments were still kept by gentlemen in their private houses as beautiful treasures, both to stimulate conversation and demonstrate their wealth and learning, these objects had an additional role. These newly designed artefacts did not represent knowledge in themselves, but were used as active tools, merely apparatus, to tease out the underlying principles of nature. The natural world was interrogated through a series of experiments, not simply reflected by passive specimens. A knowledge of these underlying principles could then be used to explain a whole range of other phenomena and be applied in a whole range of applications. The Enlightenment confidence in man's ability

139 Apparatus for demonstrating elasticity of a spring or wire, made in 1762 by George Adams (1750–95), instrument maker to King George III. Science Museum.

140 The whirling tubes, also part of the mechanical apparatus made by Adams in 1761/2, were rotated round a vertical axis so that heavy objects such as lead balls rose to the top of the tubes while light objects sank. Science Museum.

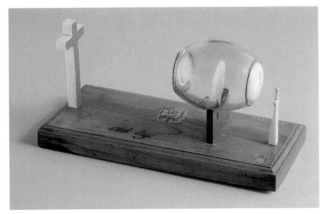

141 In 1752 Demainbray added a set of 'machines', in this case ray diagram models, to illustrate optical phenomena. This model shows the long-sighted 'old eye'. Science Museum.

to control and order nature was inherent in these experiments, as was the desire to provide useful knowledge for the benefit of humankind.

The apparatus commissioned for George III supported two courses, one in pneumatics and one in mechanics. Electricity was intended to be covered, but although some instruments appear to have been made during the 1760s this course was not completed. The courses were described in two manuscript books and illustrated by drawings of the instruments. The pneumatics course centred on a large double-barrelled air pump which was completed by Adams in 1761. Some of the experiments performed are well known today: the bell in a vacuum, the Magdeburg hemispheres, the cohesion disks. Others would now be considered part of chemistry, such as the temperature changes during chemical reactions and the purification and mixing of 'airs'. The tall bell jar in the King's Library is part of this set of apparatus.

The second course, completed in 1762, was on mechanics and centred on the 'philosophical table': a large rectangular table with a pillar at one end for pendulum experiments, and attachments at the other for collision experiments. Various instruments could be placed on the centre of the table, such as the apparatus for demonstrating elasticity (fig. 139) which can now be seen in the King's Library. The tubes for whirling (fig. 140) were attached to the central forces machine which in turn was fixed to the table. A windlass and capstan showed how the fundamental laws were related to real-life situations.

George III had been exposed to experimental philosophy in his youth through courses given by the itinerant lecturer Stephen Demainbray and by seeing electrical demonstrations by William Watson. In 1762, having installed his collection, George III was reported to be extremely busy with a course of experimental philosophy, and his interest appears to have continued for a few years. In 1763 Joseph de Lalande, the French astronomer, records being shown the double-barrelled air pump which George Adams was called upon to operate. Adams continued making instruments for the King during the 1760s; a magnetic toy is dated 1765 and a magnificent pair of globes (fig. 142) was described in 1766. The most ambitious project by far was accomplished in 1769 when the King had an observatory built at Richmond, now known as Kew Observatory, to observe the transit of Venus of that year.

In 1769 when the Observatory was complete, the King's collection was amalgamated with that of Demainbray who, having taught George when he was Prince of Wales, had eventually been successful in obtaining patronage in the form of a position as superintendant. His collection covered the standard subject area, including the standard classifications of mechanics, astronomy, hydrostatics, pneumatics, and optics, and his course emphasized the practical applications of knowledge gained by experiment. Demainbray had lived in the house of Desaguliers, to whom many of his instruments appear to have belonged. Some of the instruments now on

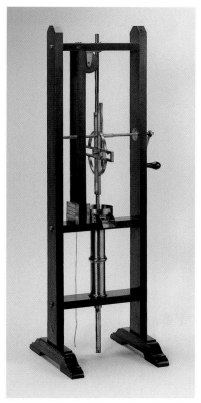

143 This model sucking pump was made by Jeremiah Sisson in 1756 and used by Demainbray in his lectures. When the handle was turned it lifted water from a trough placed between the feet to the spout. Science Museum.

142 Terrestial and celestial globes, made by George Adams c. 1766 for George III. The terrestrial globe shows the route of Admiral George Anson's (1697–1762) voyage round the world 1740–4 (see fig. 251). Science Museum.

display in the King's Library have been drawn from this part of the collection so as to represent the types of experiment being demonstrated to a wider audience (figs 141 and 143).

Summary

Whereas Sloane treats his material as a cabinet of curiosity, revealing past and distant civilizations, George III's instruments have to answer precise, businesslike questions about the underlying laws of nature. The objects are merely tools, however elegant, in imparting useful knowledge.

This comparison throws light on the differences, both straightforward and subtle, between antiquarian, natural historical collections and collections of experimental philosophy. Although both types of instrument would be today classed as scientific, in fact the intentions of the collector and the uses to which the instruments were put were quite distinct. Both Hans Sloane and King George III have left us magnificent collections, and a comparison of their 'scientific' content reveals the shift which took place during the age of the Enlightenment and had consequences for the further development of science into the next century and beyond.

15 King George III's topographical collection: a Georgian view of Britain and the world

PETER BARBER

Among George III's multifarious interests few seem to have been stronger than geography.[1] As a child in 1749 he was depicted by Richard Wilson (fig. 144) with his tutor, Dr Ayscough, and his brother, the Duke of York, sitting next to a globe and in another, painted by George Knapton in 1751, he was shown holding a map of Plymouth Harbour.[2] As a parent he saw to it that his own children were educated in geography from an early age, using the most advanced teaching aids, in the form of some of the earliest recorded jigsaw puzzles, in the process.[3] He himself had received a liberal education along the lines recommended by the philosopher John Locke and followed by those who believed in using the powers of observation to begin to know and understand the world, rather than learning by rote. From his tutors, particularly the Earl of Bute, he inherited a great love of learning and curiosity evidenced most of all in the great library he formed (see ch. 3). As a future king, he had been trained in military fortification and its concurrent skill, architectural drawing. It is no surprise, therefore, to learn that a contemporary observed in about 1770 that 'topography is one of the King's favourite studies: he copies every capital chart, takes models of all celebrated fortifications, knows the soundings of the chief harbours in Europe and the strong and weak sides of most of the fortified towns'.[4]

To an extent such an interest could be said to have been in his blood. His uncle, William, Duke of Cumberland, the victor of Culloden, had accumulated a large collection of maps and plans, and his grandmother, the highly cultivated Queen Caroline, had acquired a number of manuscript maps, plans and atlases, some of them – an atlas of military plans of about 1660 dedicated to the Dutch-born seventeenth-century military engineer Sir Bernard de Gomme, and two volumes of fortification and battle plans assembled by the Venetian Molino family in the second quarter of the seventeenth century – gifts from the library of the founder of the British Museum, Sir Hans Sloane, himself.[5] Moreover considerable numbers of atlases, maps, charts and plans that had formed part of the working libraries accumulated by the Stuart sovereigns and their consorts since 1660 were still lying scattered on shelves and in drawers through the royal palaces.

From the mid-1760s George energetically set about building on these foundations. In this he seems to have been guided by the existing organization and by the nature of his uncle's collection which included not only military maps and plans but also views of Scottish castles such as Glamis by John Elphinstone or Stirling by Thomas Sandby[6] and architectural plans, such as those of Holkham Hall by its architect Matthew Brettingham.[7] Of still greater importance, however, were the

144 *Francis Ayscough with the Prince of Wales (later George III) and the Duke of York and Albany*, oil painting by Richard Wilson, 1749. The globe and what may be an atlas (right) occupy a prominent place. National Portrait Gallery, Beningborough Hall.

recommendations made to George III's librarian Frederick Augusta Barnard by Samuel Johnson in a letter of 28 May 1768 which emphasized that, as well as collecting general medium- and small-scale maps and atlases, and trying wherever possible to purchase large, ready-made collections:

> It will be of great use to collect in every place [that Barnard was to visit in his forthcoming European tour] maps of the adjacent country and plans of towns, buildings and gardens. By this care you will form a more valuable body of Geography than can otherwise be had. Many countries have been very exactly surveyed, but it must not be expected that the exactness of actual mensuration will be preserved when the Maps are reduced by a contracted scale and incorporated into

a general system ... This part of your design will deserve particular regard because, in this your success will always be proportionate to your diligence.[8]

The emphasis on 'exactness of actual mensuration' very much reflected the spirit of the age of Enlightenment. This saw the disappearance of the ancient notion of the map as a visual encyclopaedia where measurement was but one of the elements and its replacement with the notion that a 'good' map was primarily a functional expression of mathematical precision in the measurement of the earth's surface. Allegorical decoration all but disappeared, except, perhaps, around the title cartouche, being replaced (if at all) by depictions, on charts, for instance, of coastal views and on county maps by text panels giving official and commercial information which would be of real use to the intended purchasers. In this spirit, in 1714 the Board of Longitude had been set up to award prizes for the discovery of a means of determining longitude at sea, a skill essential for navigation and thus trade and exploration; its positive results were being felt on navigation by the third quarter of

145 *Surveying party near Loch Rannoch,* watercolour by Paul Sandby, 1749. The great survey of Scotland (1747–55) organized by William Roy with Sandby as principal draughtsman was to provide a model for the first Ordnance Survey maps. British Library.

the century, owing in no small part of George III's support for the clockmaker John Harrison. In 1762 the Royal Society of Arts in a similar spirit and as a counter to the British government's perceived lack of interest in high-quality mapping, instituted a prize of £100 for 'an accurate survey of any county upon a scale of one inch to the mile'. A mixture of security considerations and Enlightenment principles led the Board of Ordnance to map the Highlands in considerable detail (fig. 145) after the defeat of 'Bonnie Prince Charlie' at the Battle of Culloden (1746) and eventually to survey other countries of vital importance to Britain's trade or security such as India or Ireland.[9] Commercial considerations lightly overlaid by Enlightenment principles caused the government to offer prizes for the discovery of a North-West Passage through North America to the Far East and similar routes, and it assisted with the funding of other voyages of discovery which contributed to the knowledge of the globe. By the end of the eighteenth century, thanks to Captain Cook and his successors, *Terra Australis nondum cognita* on most globes was more precisely mapped as Australia and New Zealand. Books, many of them illustrated, describing travels at home and voyages abroad in Europe and more exotic lands, were extremely popular and George III's library expanded with them in parallel to his geographical collections. But above all, it is worth recalling the Eurocentric nature of all of these maps, descriptions and views – even the names of these 'new found lands' and cities reinforced Britain's ownership and control, most

notably Georgia, Georgetown, King George's Sound and numerous Forts William, Henry, Augustus and George all over the world.

THE GROWTH AND ORGANIZATION OF GEORGE III'S GEOGRAPHICAL COLLECTIONS

The status of George III's geographical collections appears to have been ambiguous from the first. A part of it seems to have been regarded as being related to his 'King's' library which was intended to be available to the public. Some handsome printed and manuscript atlases were housed with volumes from this library on shelves in the Queen's House (eventually with a dual numeration system that continues to cause problems for readers), and George's librarians sought maps and atlases in bulk from private collections, from printsellers and at auction in the same way as they looked for printed books. This accounts for instance for the presence of portions of the Albani collection including volumes and single items from the Cassiano del Pozzo collection, five drawings of Lucca by Bernardo Bellotto which are assumed to come from the Consul Smith collection[10] and large numbers of architectural plans by Hawksmoor ultimately stemming from the sale of his effects in 1740.[11] Single maps and atlases that were formally presented to the King by his subjects and by the occasional foreign visitor were eventually incorporated into his geographical collections in a similar fashion to presentation volumes in the King's Library.

George however seems clearly to have felt that most of his geographical collections formed an essential part of his private working library intended for his personal use alone. He intervened far more actively in their development than he did in the growth of the King's Library. In particular he seems regularly to have retained material that had been sent to him

in the course of his business as monarch. This accounts for the presence of the original drawings by James Cook of the survey of St Pierre and Miquelon, undertaken for the Lords of the Admiralty between 1763 and 1767.[12] Later, when an attractive set of topographical ink and wash drawings of the convict colony at Port Jackson by the Spanish court artist Fernando Brambila crossed his desk in 1793 as enclosures to a dispatch from the Lieutenant Governor to the Home Secretary, he simply retained them for his own collections (fig. 146).[13] He regularly diverted Board of Ordnance maps and plans of military installations at home and abroad that were sent to him for inspection and – it must have been assumed – return. Moreover he retained the highly confidential 'Red-Lined Map', presented to him by the secretary of legation, Richard Oswald, showing the ultimate concessions that the British had been prepared to make in negotiations with the American delegation in Paris in 1782–3.[14]

In the same way he retained the original large-scale manuscript surveys, executed between 1764 and 1790, of his electorate of Hanover and of the neighbouring bishopric of Osnabrück of which his second son Frederick was titular bishop. Though the original survey of Hanover was sent to Hanover in the 1820s, and is now in the Staatsbibliothek in Berlin, the related papers and the reductions from the large-scale maps are still in the British Library. Not only that, but in an interesting sidelight on the links between culture and politics, one of George's Hanoverian surveyors, Ludwig Hogrewe, was sent to map the canals that were being created through-

out England, no doubt for the benefit of the King's Hanoverian administration, and a set of these canal plans is now in the King's Topographical Collection. In addition to these official documents George seems also to have added personal communications that struck him as interesting. Thus when the Commander-in-Chief, Lord Amherst, invited him to his

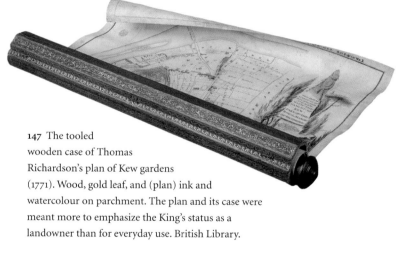

146 *View of Sydney in 1793*, ink and wash drawing by Fernando Brambila. The first view of Sydney by a professional artist shows a Spanish ship in front of where the Opera House now stands. The depiction of natives was copied from sketches by a convict, Thomas Watling. British Library.

147 The tooled wooden case of Thomas Richardson's plan of Kew gardens (1771). Wood, gold leaf, and (plan) ink and watercolour on parchment. The plan and its case were meant more to emphasize the King's status as a landowner than for everyday use. British Library.

home, Montreal House in Kent, in 1778 George saw to it that the written instructions for getting there and the accompanying watercolour plan were incorporated in his collections.[15] Similarly there are a considerable number of maps and plans relating to the royal parks in Windsor and in Kew that were presented to or commissioned by George in his role as landowner (fig. 147).

The lack of surviving Privy Purse accounts between 1772 and 1811 makes it difficult to reconstruct the geographical collections' pattern of growth. It seems clear, nevertheless, that there was a steady increase on the basis of the acquisitions in the 1760s of the Cumberland, Consul Smith and Albani collections. George and his librarians and agents seem to have been particularly busy in the 1790s, and this continued over the next decade. Enormously increased funding for the geographical collections as part of the King's Library became available after 1811 and continued until the moment when the Library and the geographical collections were donated to the British Museum by George IV in 1823.[16] The acquisitions were impressive in terms of technical and artistic quality, with numerous volumes of beautifully coloured aquatints and of lithographs joining ever more precise printed maps. Though the personal, somewhat quirky element, and the inflow of secret government mapping diminished after 1800 as a result of George III's withdrawal from active involvement as his eyesight degenerated into total blindness and his mental state grew ever more precarious, the principles that he had established as interpreted by the faithful Barnard continued to inform the growth of the collection.

By the 1790s when a listing seems to have been created, the geographical collections may already have been organized along their present, geographical lines in a series of 'volumes'. It is impossible to say whether these 'volumes' were physical entities with each being represented by a guardbook or (probably more likely) by a box or portfolio of loose items, or whether the arrangement was notional. The first volume was devoted to astronomy, proceeding to the terrestrial and then to particular parts of the globe within a hierarchical geographical framework, with smaller areas being subordinated to the larger until single buildings were reached. Within each area the material was arranged chronologically. Each volume was identified by a Roman numeral and each category of place by an arabic numeral, with individual pieces within that arrangement receiving a letter of the alphabet. The geographical hierarchy of the Topographical Collection is based on the divisions of Europe as they existed before 1772, again suggesting that George III took over the structure of the collection from his uncle. Such a structure necessitated the dismemberment of numerous manuscript and printed atlases and books of views. Atlases and books were, however, kept entire where they illustrated the appropriate theme, whether the world, a country or a region. As a result the same maps or views are sometimes to be found in different parts of the collection.

By 1810 the detailed arrangement in 'volumes' and their accommodation must have been under severe strain because of the enormous growth of the collections since 1790. In these years large, folio-sized boxes or 'portfolios' were created for the medium and small loose items. The maps and views were placed in the boxes in folders, each folder having a descriptive title on the front. The large items were placed in map tables and the atlases and other volumes on shelves with references to them on dummy sheets placed in the appropriate place in the boxed sequence. There were originally 150 such boxes.[17] In 1824, when they were seen by one M. Duchesne, a visiting Frenchman, while still in 'the Queen's house' (Buckingham House, the predecessor of Buckingham Palace), they were all labelled 'General Atlas', as are the spines that are to be seen in the King's Library gallery in the British Museum which are likely to be survivors from the time when the collection was in the Queen's House (see fig. 5).[18] This suggests that as of 1811 there may have been only one geographical collection, perhaps known interchangeably as the 'General Atlas' or the 'Geographical and Topographical' Collection, with various subdivisions such as the 'Scotch Topography' referred to by Barnard in his letter to the Earl of Buchan of October 1786.[19]

It was in the years after 1811 that the existing divisions within the geographical collections were created and that the contents were catalogued in detail: a process that continued until the late 1820s.[20] The geographical collections were subdivided into three parts: the far smaller King's Military collection, consisting predominantly of manuscript and printed plans of marches, encampments, sieges and military engagements from the earliest recorded times, totalling about four thousand items; the King's Maritime Collection, consisting of manuscript and printed charts and maritime atlases totalling about three thousand items; and, dwarfing them with about fifty thousand images, the King's Topographical Collection. Each of these collections was divided up into volumes, each corresponding to one of the new boxes or 'portfolios', with 124 (including a supplement of then unidentified items) for the King's Topographical Collection and totalling 150 for all three collections and the three boxes of Hanoverian items that were later sent to Germany.

A mirror of Georgian Britain

It was the King's Topographical Collection that finally, and after some considerable administrative battles, came to the British Museum in 1828. The King's Maritime Collection has been coming to the British Museum and later the British Library in drips and drabs since 1844 from the Admiralty where it had been deposited in 1828. George IV managed to retain the King's Military Collection, and it still forms part of the Royal Library in Windsor.

The King's Topographical Collection can be viewed as an example of the eighteenth-century west European craze for collecting maps and topographical prints and drawings of the world, of which the van der Hem collection, now in the Austrian National Library, and the 113-volume collection, assembled between 1719 and 1749 by the Bristol-born London bookseller John Innys (1695–1778), now in Holkham Hall, Norfolk, are other outstanding examples.[21] As far as the British Isles are concerned, the King's Topographical Collection has close affinities with the 49-volume

148 *Caerphilly Castle,* pencil and ink wash drawing by Archibald Robertson, a military engineer. British Library.

Gough collection of British topography, assembled by the antiquary Richard Gough, now in the Bodleian Library in Oxford, and with the so-called 'Green Frog' dining service, commissioned by Catherine the Great from Josiah Wedgwood in 1773 and now in the Hermitage Museum, St Petersburg. The original 944 pieces of the 'Green Frog' service were adorned with 1,222 views of British towns, gardens and natural and improved landscapes.[22]

The pictorial sources for the British sections of the King's Topographical Collection, and of the Gough collection and the 'Green Frog' dining service are, to a significant extent, the same. Prints, drawings and watercolours of the antiquaries William Stukeley, Bernard Lens II, the Bucks and Francis Grose, artists such as the Sandbys, Anthony Devis and Jean-Baptiste Chatelain, cartographers such as John Rocque and Hermann Moll, local artists such as Thomas Smith of Derby and William Green and etchings, engravings and aquatints published by John Boydell, are much in evidence (fig. 148).[23] They also share a common ideological programme. Far from being simple accumulations of maps and views, the collections are an expression of *British* and not simply English patriotism, assembled in a period when the industrial and agricultural revolutions, the fame of its political and economic theorists, its balanced political constitution, its evident and growing prosperity, its (relative) political liberty and its growing military, commercial and imperial might were making Britain a world leader and a source of emulation and envy abroad. In the same period Britain was also becoming the largest and arguably technically the most skilled producer of maps and prints in the world.[24] Thus the contents of the collections in them-selves demonstrated British superiority – all the more so through the numerous engraved, etched and particularly the aquatinted views of places beyond its shores, published in Britain, that are to be found in the King's Topographical and the Holkham Hall collections.

The collections alluded to the uncorrupted antique valour of the Briton through the numerous depictions of the (particularly Gothic) ruins of monasteries and castles (fig. 149) and of other antiquities, such as brasses and medieval stained glass that were to be found throughout the land (though in the case of the King's Topographical Collection, depictions and plans of Roman antiquities by Stukeley, the Lens family, Grose and William Roy were also included). The 'natural' landscape of the newly discovered Lake District, and the Irish, Welsh and Scottish mountains, was also well represented in aquatints and watercolours, as were examples of 'improved' landscapes, agricultural and industrial (fig. 150). There was an emphasis on the horticultural through views and garden plans, especially those engraved by John Rocque (fig. 151) and the vignette views engraved by John Peltro after drawings by the landscape gardener Humphrey Repton that appeared in the successive annual editions of the *Peacock's Polite Repository*, an almanac. For, with its abandonment of the formality typical of French gardens of the previous century, the English landscape garden became a visual exemplar of the love of liberty and opposition to despotism and tyranny that were supposedly embodied in the eighteenth-century British constitution.[25]

Beyond these categories – which Catherine the Great had stipulated should be included in the 'Green Frog' service[26] – the King's Topographical Collection, like the Gough, the 'Green Frog' and Innys collections, contains numerous town plans and panoramas, particularly by Kip, Kniff and the Bucks, and plans and views of the churches that had recently been built in and around London and the great houses that were then being created by the aristocracy and gentry throughout the land. Printed and manuscript, these plans reinforced the message of British civilization implicit throughout the collection.

At a rough estimate, maps and views of the British Isles represent about 40 per cent of the total collection (England alone occupies just over 30 per cent of the whole). Britain's colonies represent only about another 7 per cent (or 10 per cent including the United States of America). By contrast, no less than about 33 per cent is taken up with the western European countries particularly associated with the Grand Tour. France, the Netherlands, Germany and Italy are strongly represented, with Switzerland depicted, through numerous maps and views, as a bastion of Rousseauan simplicity and liberty and as a kind of newly discovered foreign Lake District.[27] Paris and Rome are covered in five and four volumes respectively. New York City is the only other city

149 *View of the entrance to the Archbishop of York's palace,* watercolour by Michael Angelo Rooker. A leading watercolourist, Rooker began his career as a scene painter and its influence can be seen here. The border is typical of watercolours in the King's Topographical Collection. British Library.

150 *Coal mine near Neath,* aquatint by J. Hassell, 1798. The coal mine is shown in what to modern eyes may seem the bizarre setting of a picturesque landscape. British Library.

that has a volume dedicated to it. The rest of the world is very sparsely covered.

Like the Gough and the van der Hem collections, though not the 'Green Frog' service, the King's Topographical Collection extends back in time to the mid sixteenth century, being particularly strong in Italian printed maps of these years and in seventeenth-century Dutch atlases. It also included the Jacques du Cerceau watercolour depictions of French royal chateaux dating from the same period, which are now in the

British Museum's Department of Prints and Drawings (fig. 152). Perhaps uniquely, however, King George III's Topographical Collection is distinguished by the strong presence of manuscript material with a governmental provenance – principally military and generally but far from exclusively British, with maps of European and American theatres of war and plans of fortresses, barracks often with the related written reports. So strong is this element that King George III's geographical collections rival the holdings of the Public

Record Office, and can shed significant light on events in British military and political history.

An additional dimension is added to the King's geographical collections by the ephemeral material that was tipped in if it contained topographical views or information. Thus British eighteenth-century civilization can be experienced not only through accomplished watercolours, aquatints, engravings, lithographs, maps and plans but also through the advertisements, annual reports, broadsides, bills, amateur watercolours, sketch maps and printed propaganda that formed the warp and weft of everyday life during the age of the Enlightenment. The King's Topographical Collection may owe its origin to the geographical interests of a monarch, but it breathes the interests, activities and attitudes of his people.

151 *A Plan and Views of the Builings and Garden at Rest* (i.e. Wrest Park, Bucks), engraving by John Rocque, 1737. Garden plans and views are one of the great strengths of George III's Topographical Collection. The cartographer John Rocque began his career as a garden designer. British Library.

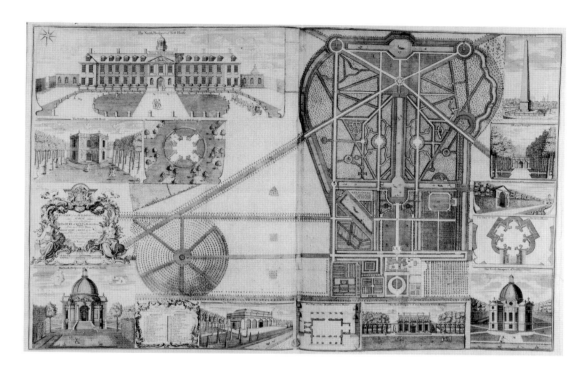

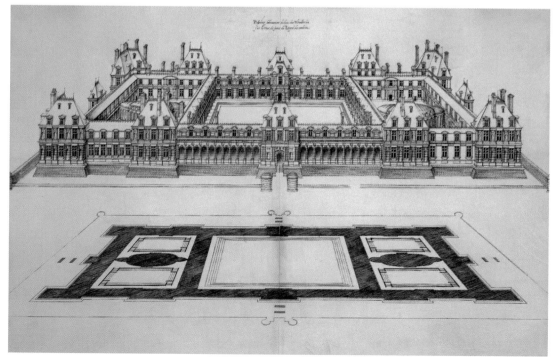

152 Jacques du Cerceau, watercolour of the Palais des Tuilieries, one of a series of 122 views of French Royal chateaux, c. 1570. Transferred to British Museum's Department of Prints and Drawings in the early 1970s shortly before the separation of the British Library from the British Museum. P&D.

PART IV

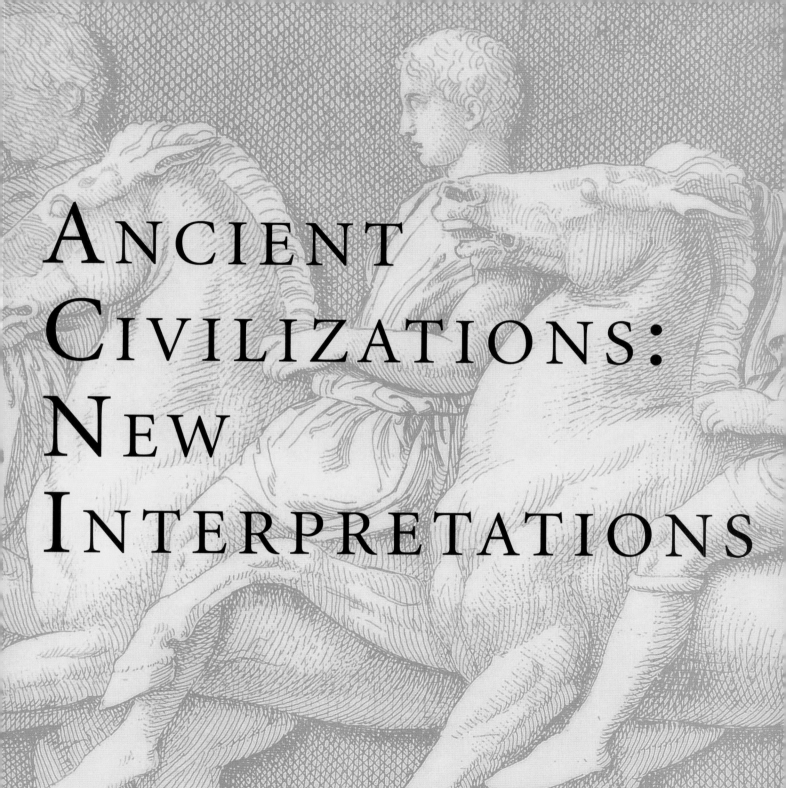

ANCIENT CIVILIZATIONS: NEW INTERPRETATIONS

153 Figures from the Parthenon frieze, engraving
by Thomas Stothard (1755–1834), based on a drawing made
on the spot by William Pars (1742–82) in 1765. P&D.

16 Ideas of antiquity: classical and other ancient civilizations in the age of Enlightenment

IAN JENKINS

To the Enlightenment of the eighteenth century, written history largely comprised the chronicle of ancient military and political events narrated by the Greek and Latin authors; philosophy was determined by the treatises of Plato and Aristotle; poetry was dominated by the legacy of Greece and Rome, principally the works of Homer; and art theory was discussed in the light of the aesthetic response of Roman writers to the sculpture and painting of Greece. All human creative expression, indeed all that one said and did in polite society of the eighteenth century, was informed by the classics.

Latin was the *lingua franca* and could carry the traveller through a European community of common culture. This Republic of Letters, as it was sometimes called, was a place where acquaintances were maintained through correspondence. Class and inherited wealth were natural qualifications of membership, but poor men of talent could also join. Among those who wrote about antiquity in the eighteenth century, some were responding to the demands of enforced leisure, while others were acting out of financial necessity. The Comte de Caylus was from the highest nobility, while Pierre-François Hugues, self-styled Baron d'Hancarville, and Johann Joachim Winckelmann (see fig. 99) were both sons of tradesmen. Intellectual brilliance, such as theirs, combined with a lust for social self-improvement, was to be a driving force of Enlightenment culture. At their most ambitious, the new men could even topple the old order, as in the American War of Independence and in the French Revolution. Athens and Rome had both been republics, and free-thinkers found there a ready source of rhetorical parallels for their own political aims.[1] Classical antiquity was not merely an ornament in eighteenth-century society, it could also be a powerful model of utopian dreams.[2]

The classical past was all things to all men: the farmer in his fields could find in Hesiod's *Works and Days* a source of good husbandry; a horseman could read with instruction the equestrian treatises of Xenophon; Vitruvius's *De architectura* was the handbook of architects; Hippocrates and Galen had set out the principles of medical science. The Greeks had been the first systematically to discover their world and to classify what they found there. The very word *museum* comes from the Greek *mouseion*, meaning a sanctuary of the Muses, that is to say a place presided over by the various Muses, each with her own responsibility for the arts and sciences. Famous *mouseia* in antiquity were the great libraries of Pergamum and Alexandria, nurtured in the Hellenistic kingdoms of the Attalids and the Ptolemys. There were deposited copies of all the great works of classical literature amidst displays of artworks reflecting the learning contained in them. Thus at Pergamum were to be found busts of poets,

154 Bronze lamp with Jupiter and a dog, with a detail of the suspension chain. Drawing from dal Pozzo's 'Paper Museum'. The lamp is now in the British Museum and the drawing attributed to Pietro Testa (1612–50). GR Library.

dramatists and thinkers, including images of figures who, like Homer, had lived before the age of naturalistic art and of whom portrait types had to be invented. The ancient library, with its books and sculpture, found a modern echo in the British Museum's own endeavour to capture universal knowledge.

The Greek legacy to Rome was *knowledge*, on the one hand, and a disconcerting sense of Greek intellectual superiority, on the other, which impelled Romans to preserve the Greek achievement, but also to revive and emulate it. This imperative led Roman writers to record their own past, weaving together narratives that embraced Roman, Etruscan, Greek and, further back still, Trojan chronicles.[3] Greek *archaiologia* (knowledge of the past) was absorbed and adapted to become Roman *antiquitates*, and no one was more diligent in collecting these than the Roman antiquary Varro (116–27 BC).[4] He was a prolific author, whose writing

made up in quantity for what it lacked in style. He is best known for his *Libri antiquitatum*, which have not survived, but about which enough is known to make it possible to reconstruct the outline. Varro distinguished between human and divine matters, devoting twenty-five books to *Antiquitates rerum humanarum* and sixteen books to *Antiquitates rerum divinarum*. Varro's *Antiquitates* were not restricted only to material things but also included accounts of people, places, past times and actions.

THE CLASSICAL TRADITION

Ancient 'lore' is perhaps in our terms a more accurate description of Varro's survey of facts and beliefs than the narrower definition associated with our word 'antiquities'. His system of classifying the past, and in particular the division

155 J. B. Oudry (1686–1755), *Composition aux Livres*. The fame of Montfaucon's encyclopaedia merited this painted 'portrait' of his book. Musée Fabre, Montpellier.

into secular and sacred, was to become influential to Renaissance scholars and their successors. One such was Flavio Biondo (1392–1463), who in 1457–9 crowned a life of antiquarian pursuits when he published his great survey of Roman civilization, *De roma triumphante*, in ten books arranged under five headings: *antiquitates sacrae, publicae, militares, privatae* and *triumphi*.

Another Renaissance antiquary in the Varronian tradition was the Neapolitan architect and painter Pirro Ligorio (1513–83), who compiled a vast pictorial archive of antiquity in many volumes, illustrated by himself.[5] This in turn greatly influenced the seventeenth-century antiquary Cassiano dal Pozzo (1588–1657).[6] He was at the heart of an important circle of humanists in Rome gathered around the court of Pope Urban VIII. Cassiano corresponded with such distinguished figures in the seventeenth-century Republic of Letters as the French antiquary Nicolas Fabri de Peiresc (1580–1637) and the Flemish painter Peter Paul Rubens (1577–1640). Cassiano's collection of drawings comprised a great encyclopaedia of antiquity arranged by division into *res humanae* and *res divinae* (figs 125 and 154). His 'Paper Museum', as it came to be called, did not enjoy the influence it might have done if it had been engraved. The drawings, however, have largely survived as a collection, passing into the library of the eighteenth-century Cardinal Alessandro Albani, where they were curated and studied by Winckelmann, before they were purchased in 1762 by the architect James Adam for King George III. They are now mostly in the Royal Library at Windsor Castle and in the British Museum.[7]

Already before Cassiano's drawings left Italy, his vision of

156 An imaginary monument dedicated to Caylus from d'Hancarville's publication of Sir William Hamilton's vase collection, *Antiquités, étrusques, grecques et romaines* 1767–76, volume 3. GR Library.

a great pictorial encyclopaedia of antiquity had been antici-pated in the fifteen printed volumes of Bernard de Montfau-con (1655–1741), entitled *L'Antiquité expliquée et représentée en figures* (1719–24) (see figs 98, 155).[8] This work can be seen as the culmination of a two-millennia-long tradition of interest in the classification of knowledge about the classical past. 'Here', wrote Montfaucon, 'is all antiquity.' By this he meant not only the material objects but also the literary sources that accom-panied them. Montfaucon's volumes are heavy with citations of the Greek and Latin authors. Even where a subject existed in literature but had left no physical trace, Montfaucon did not neglect to include it. *L'Antiquité expliquée* attests to the primacy of classical literature in the antiquarian tradition that descended from the texts of Varro and Pliny.

The collecting and arrangement of coins in particular was strongly motivated by the desire to illustrate the histories of the Greek and Latin authors.[9] Suetonius's *Lives of the Emper-ors* could be laid out in the obverses of coins struck by the imperial mints, and coin collections were seen as appendages to the library, wherein the deeds of the Roman rulers were told in books. There were, however, aspects of coins that were more independent of literature.[10] In Roman coins there were, for example, the many and varied devices for decorating the reverses; Greek coins, moreover, were difficult to classify as linear history. Often there was no royal portrait minted upon them to indicate authorship and date. Instead, origin had to be deduced from the place where a coin was found and from the device upon it, symbolizing the city, while date could be inferred from the style of that device.

Such non-textual research would illuminate the history of times and regions not charted by the ancient authors. The development of what we would today call archaeology opened up new vistas on the ancient world. Prehistoric Wiltshire along with much of Europe had escaped inclusion in the chronicles of classical authors. To residents of these regions, however, their past was no less interesting for all that, or indeed physically evident. There was, it is true, an inevitable tendency among antiquaries interested in undocumented monuments to relate them to biblical or classical phenomena. So Stone-henge to the early writers on the antiquities of Wiltshire tends to be a Tacitean Druids' temple. Nevertheless, by looking closely at the megalithic monuments and by comparing one with another, John Aubrey and William Stukeley in the seven-teenth and eighteenth centuries, and William Cunnington and Richard Colt Hoare in the early nineteenth, were to lay the foundations of forensic archaeology (see ch. 17).

Archaeological discovery not only illuminated cultures without written history but also enlarged knowledge of those civilizations known to the ancient authors. Renaissance humanists in Italian cities outside Rome gathered objects and deciphered inscriptions to supplement their recorded history.[11] During the eighteenth century, culminating in the Napoleonic invasion, knowledge of the ancient civilization of Egypt was to

increase, while diplomatic and mercantile missions to the Near East led to greater interest in the surviving monuments of those peoples and places that were recorded in the Bible (see ch. 18). The decipherment of hieroglyphics and, later, of cuneiform enlarged the written record of these peoples beyond that handed down by the classical authors and led to a more system-atic study of language (see ch. 19). The combination of new texts, images and objects, particularly those found in tombs, led to new perceptions and interpretations of ancient and modern religions and raised questions about common sources and sys-tematic progression from one state of development to another (see ch. 20). The mass of new evidence prompted the more sys-tematic study that was needed to make sense of it all.

Among the first to try to chart and chronicle the civiliza-tions of antiquity was the greatest of all eighteenth-century antiquaries, Anne-Claude-Philippe de Tubières-Grimoard de Pestels de Lévis, Comte de Caylus (1692–1765) (see fig. 156 and p. 116).[12] Between 1752 and 1756 he published in seven volumes his *Recueil d'antiquités égyptiennes, étrusques, grecques, romaines et gauloises*. Caylus in his preface emphasizes the primacy of the object over texts:

I am restricted to publishing in this collection only those monuments that belong to me or were once owned by me. I have had them drawn with the greatest accuracy ... Objects can explain particular practices, they clarify customs that are obscure or badly described by the authors, they bring the progress of the arts to our attention and serve as models for those who cultivate them. But antiquaries have seldom seen them thus; they have regarded them only as the supplement to and the proof of history, or as isolated texts requiring elaborate commentary.[13]

Caylus's intention was to use objects to construct a narra-tive, leading the reader through the ancient civilizations of Egypt, Etruria, Greece, Rome and not forgetting Caylus's own native France. His grand vision of the interconnectedness of the cultures of antiquity, for example the dependence of Greece on Egypt, cut across the subject-based classification of antiquity favoured by Varro and Montfaucon and introduced a dynamic that would prove very influential in the formation of the early British Museum.[14]

Before settling down to compile his *magnum opus*, Caylus had been French ambassador to the ancient city of Constan-tinople (Greek Byzantium) and had travelled in Asia Minor. He was one of the few of his day who had first-hand knowl-edge of the remains of Greek antiquity outside Italy. Diplo-matic links with Turkey had brought earlier travellers to Asia Minor in search of antiquities. They include agents acting on behalf of the seventeenth-century British collectors, notably King Charles I, George Villiers, first Duke of Buckingham and Thomas Howard, second Earl of Arundel. In the later seven-teenth and early eighteenth centuries British representatives at the trading post of Smyrna on the Aegean coast continued to

J. Stuart delin. _Published by James Stuart Oct 27, 1767, according to Act of Parliament._

157 James Stuart sketching the Erechtheum. Engraving from _Antiquites of Athens_, volume 2, 1787. GR Library.

158 The east front of the Parthenon, the Elgin Marbles still in place. Watercolour by William Pars, 1765. It was also engraved for the same volume. P&D.

bring home portable antiquities, including some of the first Greek specimens to reach the British Isles.[15] There was no systematic attempt, however, to survey the architectural monuments which lay in ruins along the western shores of Turkey and, indeed, across the Aegean in the Turkish dominion of mainland Greece, until the Society of Dilettanti expeditions.[16]

THE GREEK REVIVAL

The Society of Dilettanti was founded in 1734 as a dining club for aristocrats who had been on the Grand Tour and had visited Italy. From the beginning, therefore, it had a scholarly and artistic bias, but its focus became increasingly Hellenic when in 1750–3 it sponsored the expedition to Greece of the architects James Stuart (1713–88) and Nicholas Revett (1720–1804). Their drawings, the first accurate and systematic records of the principal monuments in Athens, were to be engraved and published with explanatory texts in four folio volumes entitled *Antiquities of Athens*, the first of which appeared in 1762 (fig. 157). The great success of this venture prompted a second expedition directed at the monuments of Asia Minor. The travellers this time were Richard Chandler (1738–1810), an expert in deciphering inscriptions who had already published the Arundel Marbles that were in Oxford, Nicholas Revett and the painter William Pars (1742–82). They reached Smyrna by September 1764 and spent a year in Turkey before travelling back through Greece (fig. 158), where Pars made a detailed series of drawings from the sculptures of the Parthenon (fig. 153). In 1769 a volume entitled *Ionian Antiquities* appeared. It was later revised and re-published as part of a four-volume series entitled *Antiquities of Ionia*, wherein a third Dilettanti expedition was also published. This took place in 1812 and was led by the topographer and draughtsman William Gell (1777–1836).

The Greek project of the Society of Dilettanti was the quintessential Enlightenment enterprise in the search for antiquity. Foreign lands were visited, ancient monuments explored and drawn, the results transferred to copper plate (fig. 153) and turned into books which are themselves beautiful and monumental works. These were to have a profound influence on a burgeoning Greek taste in contemporary architecture and, indeed, would instruct and inspire Robert Smirke in creating his Greek Revival British Museum (see ch. 4).

One of the most important of all eighteenth-century antiquaries, who never went to Greece, but who was to become the high priest of Hellenism, was Johann Joachim Winckelmann (fig. 159).[17] His life story is as remarkable as his writing. Born at Stendal in Prussia in 1717, he was the son of a cobbler, and rose to hold the post of Papal antiquary in Rome, before his cruel murder. He had over the winter of 1763–4 published his great work *A History of Ancient Art Among the Greeks*. This was the first history of its kind, presenting a coherent account of the rise and supremacy of Greek art that was deeply influenced by the moral thinking of Plato. For Winckelmann the claims he

made for the superiority of Greek art were not merely a matter of taste. His Hellenism with its ideas of Greek political and spiritual freedom was a prescription for the human soul. By imitating the Greeks, he thought, we could discover our own best selves. Winckelmann wrote in a clear, bright style which was to have great influence upon the development of the new German literature associated with Lessing, Goethe and Schiller. Winckelmann's prose is both didactic and poetic. The great

159 Winckelmann, engraving by M. Blot after an oil by Raphael Mengs (see fig. 99). P&D.

set-piece descriptions of principal works such as the Apollo Belvedere of the Vatican are enlivened by the tension of his own homoeroticism. His sexuality was to be his undoing when he died at the hands of Francesco Archangeli on 8 June 1768 in the north Italian sea port of Trieste.

Working in Rome, Winckelmann traced in the sculptures he knew there the development of Greek style. Observing Roman copies of lost Greek works, he described the rise and fall of Greek art from its rigid, archaic origins, through the full-blown beauty of the classical style which he associated with the sculpture of Praxiteles, to the decline of Greek taste in what he called the Macedonian (Hellenistic) period. This model for the study of Greek art had considerable influence

and was to be adopted as a standard by subsequent generations of Hellenists. One of the first was Richard Payne Knight
(1751–1824), whose connoisseurial publication of fine bronzes
for the Dilettanti Society, *Specimens of Ancient Sculpture* (1809)
borrowed heavily from Winckelmann's aesthetic (fig. 160).[18]
Naturally there had to be adjustments to Winckelmann's
scheme when the appreciation of originals from Greece itself
rendered the works Winckelmannn had admired in Rome
somewhat obsolete. Nevertheless, his essential idea for the
development of Greek art survived, and still today, and especially in Germany, he is revered as the founding father of
modern classical archaeology.

In the spring of 1768, shortly before his death, Winckelmann
took Sir William Hamilton (1730–1803) (fig. 161) around the
sights of Rome. Hamilton was then the British diplomatic representative in Naples. Already in autumn 1767, Winckelmann
had made Sir William's acquaintance when he journeyed south
to see his collection of so-called Etruscan vases. Hamilton, with
the assistance of another great antiquary of the age, Baron
d'Hancarville (1719–1805) (see fig. 51), was in the process of
publishing his vases in four sumptuous volumes that are perhaps the most beautiful books of the Enlightenment (see fig. 93
and ch. 13).[19] The British Minister would have liked Winckelmann to have written all the descriptions for the plates, but he
was himself engaged in another publishing project and had no
time. The task fell instead to d'Hancarville, who sought to use
the opportunity to outrival the great German scholar. His text
lacks Winckelmann's clarity and concise direction, but is none
the less a remarkable achievement, and notable for its engage-
ment with the role that vases were fast assuming as primary
subjects for the discovery of Greek art.

Hamilton's vases, along with the many other parts of his
first collection of classical antiquities, came to the British
Museum in 1772. Their acquisition was a major event in the
development of the early Museum. The founding collection of
Sir Hans Sloane had contained antiquities, but there was nothing special about them, his interests being more in other
areas.[20] The incorporation of Sir William's collection was to set
the course for the Museum's becoming the great repository of
art and antiquity that it is today. It acted as a magnet drawing
other collections to it. In 1802 came Egyptian sculptures and
inscriptions, including the Rosetta Stone, presented to the
Museum by George III after its capture from the French at the
battle of Alexandria. In 1805 the Museum purchased Charles
Townley's (1737–1805) collection of Roman sculpture (figs 162
and 163) and in 1814 acquired his vases, bronzes, terracottas and
other antiquities. In 1815 the sculptured frieze of the Temple of
Apollo at Bassae in western Greece arrived as the first great
body of original Greek sculpture. Then in 1816 Parliament purchased the Elgin Marbles for the Museum. This was the single
most important event in the history of the Museum's collections since its foundation. The Marbles were to become the
centrepiece of its collections of ancient art. The sculptures of

the Parthenon, in particular, were presented as the highpoint
of human achievement in antiquity (fig. 164). In the subsequent physical arrangement of the Museum's ever-increasing
collections, all other works were seen to lead up to or away
from the one supreme moment in ancient art. Winckelmann's
system was appropriated and adjusted to take the crown from
Praxiteles and award it instead to Phidias, and new gods were
found for worship at the old altar of Hellenism.[21]

CONCLUSION

In the European Enlightenment two major ideas dominated
the interpretation of antiquity: on the one hand, there was the
tradition of classification by subject, whereby ancient human
experience, sacred and secular, could be presented as an infinite encyclopaedia of independent topics; on the other hand,
there was the approach that applied a deterministic theory of
the finite development of ancient art, in which the Athenian
achievement of the classical period represented fulfilment.
Both ways of looking at the past had been current in antiquity

160 Statuette of Zeus or Neptune, one of the Paramythia bronzes. From
Richard Payne Knight, *Specimens of Ancient Sculpture*. GR Library.

161 *Sir William Hamilton Seated with the Publication of his Vases.*
Joshua Reynolds (1723–92). National Portrait Gallery, London.

162 The Townley Marbles in the Entrance Hall of 7 Park Street, Westminster. Watercolour by William Chambers. 1794. P&D.

163 The Townley Marbles in the Dining Room of 7 Park Street, Westminster. Watercolour by William Chambers. 1794. P&D.

164 *An Assemblage of Works of Art in Sculpture and Painting from the earliest period to the time of Phydias,* watercolour by James Stephanoff, 1845, based on the collections of the British Museum. P&D.

itself: the one was exemplified by the lexicographical cataloguing of the polymath Varro; the other was found in late-Hellenistic and Roman interest in the development of earlier Greek art and rhetoric.[22] At its founding in 1753 the former approach was the norm in the British Museum but, under the influence of Winckelmann and other forces, the Museum came more and more to adopt the aesthetic that privileged Greek over all other art. The encyclopaedic approach was by no means abandoned; indeed it was revived in 1908 in the permanent exhibition of Greek and Roman life where the collection is still displayed according to subjects similar to

those of Varro and Montfaucon.[23] Nevertheless during the nineteenth century all the civilizations of the past tended to be appointed a place in an evolutionary scheme that judged aesthetic merit in relation to the absolute standard of Greek art. Today some of those ideas are alive in contemporary archaeological discourse, while others have gone out of fashion. Whatever their status, however, all contribute to the essential identity of the Museum as a place of variable thinking and changing values. The objects in its collections are 'bearers of meaning'[24] that can remain constant or can change to offer new relevance to new audiences.

17

The discovery of British antiquity

JILL COOK

Hindsight rather than history is often used to describe the practice of archaeology in Britain before the nineteenth century. Hindsight is a wonderful gift. It allows us to look back and judge the past from a modern perspective. In the footsteps of Charles Darwin, we search for signs of inevitable progress towards our current state of knowledge, producing narratives which place our theories and criteria at the top of the evolutionary tree. Where progress towards our opinions and theories cannot be found, stagnation, relapse or even failure may be identified. From this position we may then criticize, ridicule or view with amazement those who did not know what we do, just because they lived then and we live now. Needless to say, this 'progressivist' approach does not help us understand the criteria by which past scholars worked, or the ideas, principles and methods through which their parameters were developed. This is a drawback with many of the histories of archaeology which cover the period from 1660 to 1830.[1] Most of these separate the subject and its practitioners from the intellectual milieu of the time and tell an apparently unbroken story from a patchwork of individual, often disconnected achievements. In this chapter the work of those curious about the past is reviewed in the context of their beliefs and the chronology they accepted.

THE INTELLECTUAL BACKGROUND

Although the term archaeology or *archiology* was in use by about 1660 and, was defined in 1726 as consisting of 'Monuments ... still subsisting',[2] those who studied the material remains of the past, or antiquities, referred to themselves as antiquaries. It was not until the twentieth century that the title antiquary was replaced by that of archaeologist. Archaeologists also study the material remains of the past but their criteria are different from those that formed the bases for investigations prior to the late nineteenth century. This separation of the modern, scientific order of archaeologists from antiquaries reflects the differing parameters governing their research. Unfortunately, this distinction often assumes a pejorative sense, implying that antiquarian work was hopelessly constrained by theological dogma, hindered by classical texts and, consequently, failed to recognize the length of human antiquity and its subdivisions so obvious to us.[3] This is far from an accurate reading.

Eighteenth-century interest in British antiquities was nurtured away from the universities amongst men of varied social and educational background. Antiquaries included gentlemen trained and practising in, amongst other things, law, theology, medicine, philology, classics, mathematics and physics, as well as shoemakers, apothecaries and dealers in books, prints, curiosities, wool and wine. They were not distinguished from the practitioners of other forms of enquiry and their subject was not separated from other areas of knowledge let alone distinguished as a discipline taught in universities. This is emphasized by the fact that many were Fellows or frequent guests of the Royal Society of London, formally founded in 1662. At its meetings antiquities were discussed along with philosophy, astronomy, mathematics, physics, zoology, botany, geology and chemistry, as well as other practical subjects which were to emerge as the several disciplines named and eventually described collectively as 'science' in the nineteenth century.[4] The Society's full title included the words 'For the Promotion of Natural Knowledge'[5] and suggests the criteria that stimulated and informed antiquarian research.

NATURAL KNOWLEDGE

The concept of natural knowledge or philosophy made possible progress in most fields of intellectual endeavour during the late seventeenth and eighteenth centuries. The idea that God could be revealed in his works, not his word, encouraged the investigation and understanding of all things in 'nature' or the sphere of natural light.[6] There was a gradual acceptance of the idea that it was proper and possible to deduce the existence and nature of the Creator from his creation. Nature was awaiting the human mind to recognize God's work and express it. The idea that antiquities were to be regarded as part of this nature was clearly expressed by Robert Plot (1640–96), Keeper of the Ashmolean Museum and Professor of Chemistry at Oxford University, when, in his 1686 account of Staffordshire, he justified the inclusion of: 'Medalls, Ways, Lows,[7] Pavements, Urns, Monuments of Stone, Fortifications, &c. of the Ancient Britans [sic], Romans, Saxons, Danes or Normans', but not 'pedigrees, descents and religious houses' on the grounds that the former, 'being all made out of Natural things, may as well be brought under a Natural History as any thing of Art',[8] whereas the latter were about persons and actions. Similarly, Martin Lister's remarkable account of the Roman kilns unearthed in York, which includes a discussion of the types of pottery found and their distinctive fabrics, was published in the *Philosophical Transactions* of the Royal Society because of 'the relation they may have to the advancement of Natural Philosophy and Art'.[9]

Nature was also considered to be the force implanted in things by God and the law by which all things proceeded along their paths.[10] The philosophers Francis Bacon (1561–1626) and René Descartes (1596–1650) influenced the way in which this law, God's work, might be discovered in nature. Both Bacon and Descartes promoted a secular approach to knowledge, doubting assumptions based purely on traditional scriptural or historical authority and promoting questioning and observation as a means to discovery and understanding. During the seventeenth century this encouraged experimentation, as well as the practice of recording first-hand observations of natural phenomena and organizing them to determine any pattern which might lead to their interpretation. The empirical approach encouraged by Bacon's natural philosophy gradually spread amongst those investigating the world around them and was promoted further by the Royal Society, which adopted Bacon as its figurehead. By 1724 William Stukeley (1687–1765) could declare in the preface of *Itinerarium curiosum* that it was 'an account of places and things *from inspection*, not compiled from other's labours, or travels in one's study',[11] although the biographer and antiquary John Aubrey (1625–97)[12] recalls that this change in approach had begun earlier, in about 1649.[13]

For some historians of archaeology, particularly Piggott,[14] this application of empirical techniques in the late seventeenth to early eighteenth century is viewed as a great leap forward in method but an advance which failed, stagnated or relapsed because the evidence collected was 'fancifully' interpreted on the basis of biblical and classical writings. This judgement stems from a modern secular perspective which recognizes the method but not the purpose of the research. In the context of the time the recording, description, ordering and interpretation of British antiquities was the investigation of God's work. Although natural philosophy had instilled the idea that the history of the Earth, as well as human life, could be discovered and was worth knowing, the literal truth of the Bible was impossible to dismiss without evidence to substantiate alternative possibilities. These would take time to develop, although misgivings about the Biblical account were already being expressed.[15] Meanwhile, the material evidence of the human past had to be assessed within the available theoretical framework provided by the Bible. The results are now often harshly judged by those with an understanding of evolution and a chronology which encompasses millions of years.

Throughout the seventeenth and much of the eighteenth century the world was thought to be no more than six thousand years old. The only chronological frameworks available were those of the Bible and the written records of the Greek and Roman worlds. In order to provide a date for a British monument or artefact it was necessary to make a connection with a written record. This was usually an account of Britain by a classical historian or a document such as the *Notitia dignitatum*[16] but, as the physician and collector John Woodward (see ch. 8) recognized in his dating of the Roman walls of London by means of an excavated coin,[17] it could also include artefacts with inscriptions. There was no concept of unknown, extinct peoples, or periods of unwritten time, and, consequently, no concept of human *prehistory*.[18] All human time was history because of the account of it given in the Bible and pre-human time was regarded as short because without people the earth had no purpose.

BREAKING THE TIME BARRIER

Before the nineteenth century most people believed in God who created the world as a suitable habitat for humanity. Literal belief in the Book of Genesis determined that the earth and humanity were created within five days of each other. The history of the earth and of humanity were thus essentially the same. However, the biblical account of history from Adam to the birth of Christ is incomplete[19] and during the seventeenth century, as before, much scholarly effort was directed at synthesizing all historical knowledge, from both biblical and classical sources, to achieve a chronological history which, incidentally, provided a date for the Creation.

One such date was that of 4004 BC calculated by James Ussher (1581–1656), Archbishop of Armagh and Primate of All Ireland, in his history of the world,[20] and quoted in the margins of the King James Bible for over two hundred years. Both Ussher and his calculation of the age of the world have often been ridiculed for showing a dogmatic belief in the infallible Word of God rather than regarded as a great scholarly work.[21] Isolating the date and making it seem the absurd product of religious dogma has also led to the assumption that it hindered the development of archaeology.[22] However, this does not bear close scrutiny: the date of the Creation made no difference to the study of Roman and Saxon antiquities in Britain and even the relatively short biblical chronology allowed some two thousand years from the time of the Flood and the peopling of the earth by Noah's descendants to the invasions of Britain by Julius Caesar (55 BC) and Claudius (AD 43). In this respect chronology is not significant in the development of archaeology in the Enlightenment and becomes a critical issue only in the early nineteenth century when it was the accumulation of stratigraphic evidence in the fields of geology and palaeontology rather than antiquarian study that demanded a longer timescale (see ch. 9).

This does not mean that Genesis was not questioned at an earlier stage.[23] Sir Hans Sloane's friend the botanist and philosopher John Ray (1627–1705) had misgivings about the literal interpretation of the Biblical account which were shared by writer and divine Thomas Burnet (?1635–1715), Master of Charterhouse, who was removed from his theological position after suggesting that Genesis should be read as an allegory.[24] As an alternative to the theological approach, the astronomer Edmund Halley (1656–1743) suggested that the age of the earth might one day be ascertained empirically, by measuring the amount of salt contained in the oceans and calculating the rate at which saltiness had increased through time.[25] However, it is important to realize that these ideas

were strictly concerned with the creation of the earth: the five days before the creation of Adam. The subsequent six thousand years of human time were still regarded as fixed, whatever the arguments about the pre-human epochs.

Such opinion persisted well into the nineteenth century. By the end of the eighteenth century the mapping of different rock types, observations on the stratigraphy of fossils and greater understanding of the dynamic geomorphological processes which had shaped the Earth in the past led to some acceptance of a longer chronology for the formation and transformation of the world.[26] However, a greater length for human antiquity was still doubted. When antiquaries such as Woodward and the engineer soldier turned Anglican clergyman James Douglas (1753–1819)[27] discussed and wrote dissertations on the longer chronology of the earth, they did not address the question of a greater length for human antiquity but rather whether people might have existed in Europe before the Flood. As late as the 1850s, Charles Darwin was sceptical about the contemporaneity of stone artefacts and the remains of animals now extinct in Europe which had been found in the Somme valley, France, by Jacques Boucher de Perthes (1788–1868), whose discoveries were not vindicated until 1863.[28] Curiously, the blame for such general scepticism is often laid at the door of Dean William Buckland (1784–1856), who became the first reader in Geology at Oxford University after holding an appointment in Mineralogy. Buckland's presumed dogmatism stands accused of holding up progress towards a longer chronology at the turn of the nineteenth century. This was not the case.

Buckland realized that he needed stratified evidence to deal with the possibility of human occupation in Europe before the Flood and with the questions posed by the discovery of the bones of animals now extinct from Britain, such as those of hippopotamus discovered by Douglas in the gravels of the River Medway, Kent,[29] and now recognized as indicative of the warm last interglacial period about 120,000–100,000 years ago. In the true spirit of the period he decided to observe occurrences in place by excavating through the deposits in a series of caves in south Wales and Yorkshire and comparing them with the evidence similarly achieved in Germany and France. He published his results with illustrations of finds in 1823 in *Reliquiae diluvianae*. This title, *Remains of the Flood*, identifies the cause of his vilification as a biased cleric in modern times. However, Buckland's conclusions were the product not of religious dogma but of the evidence he found in the caves. At Kirkdale Cave, Yorkshire, he found only animal remains and, by careful examination of their condition, was able to suggest how they had accumulated in the site by means of natural processes, correctly identifying the gnawing and breakage caused by hyenas.[30] Where he did find human remains and artefacts at Paviland, Glamorgan, he was cautious, rejecting an association between

165 Plan and section through the deposits in Goat Hole, Paviland, lithograph from Dean William Buckland's *Reliquiae diluvianae* (1823). The position of the human skeleton led him to believe that the grave had been dug into the ancient sediments and could not be contemporary with the fossilized bones of animals now extinct in Europe which he thought had been wiped out by Noah's Flood. Ethno Library.

SECTION OF THE CAVE CALLED GOAT HOLE.
In the Sea Cliffs 15 Miles West of Swansea.

the archaeology and the remains of mammoth because he believed that there had been disturbance of the deposits which may have caused items of differing age to be mixed (fig. 165).[31] This does not mean that he was blinded by clerical bias. Like Buckland, the French palaeontologist Georges Cuvier (1769–1832) and the English geologist Charles Lyell (1797–1875)[32] could find no convincing evidence and they also emphasized the need to understand how things were deposited before accepting their association and contemporaneity. In a later work Buckland reiterates these points and acknowledges that, had he found evidence of stratified human remains, 'there would have been great difficulty in reconciling the early and extended periods which have been assigned to the extinct races of animals with our received chronology'.[33]

Buckland felt it necessary to err on the side of caution and rightly distrusted material from disturbed contexts where natural and human processes might have caused mixing. Lyell concurred, writing that: 'It is not on such evidence that we shall readily admit either the high antiquity of the human race, or the recent date of certain lost species of quadrupeds'.[34]

History has treated the two men differently. Although it might be said that, in stressing the importance of understanding how things have come to be buried, Buckland was asserting a principle of vital importance to archaeology, as a cleric he has been branded as dogmatically opposed to a longer human antiquity. Lyell, his pupil and a geologist not in holy orders, has been regarded in the perspective of his times. In their day Buckland's views were also considered reasonable and acceptable. Eventually in the 1860s they were proved wrong by the discovery of the evidence he himself had looked for but not found. This should not be taken as failure: the chronology Buckland defended on the basis of empirical investigations was that of the previous centuries when it had been no obstacle to gaining an understanding of the past through its artefacts and monuments.

STONE TOOLS AND CLASSIFICATIONS

The discovery of stone tools did not take place until the end of the seventeenth century. This does not mean that they were unknown: they were simply not understood as the products of human manufacture. Despite biblical references to stone implements,[35] as well as knowledge of the use of such tools by native North Americans,[36] distinctively shaped stone objects continued to be categorized as fossils in the early seventeenth century. Ole Worm (died 1655), who formed a famous museum in Copenhagen and recorded many Danish monuments, particularly the megalithic tombs, illustrates some perforated stone axes alongside a variety of non-precious, semi-precious and precious stones in the 1655

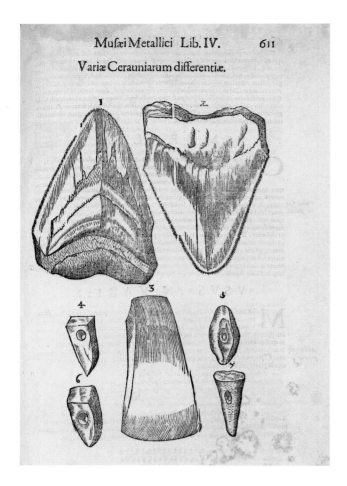

166 Different types of thunder stones as illustrated in the catalogue of Ulysses Aldrovandi's Museum Metallicum, 1648. At this time fossils were not recognized as the remains of once living organisms, and there was no knowledge of prehistoric tools. Consequently, a shark tooth and group of stone axes are shown together in the belief that they had a common origin from the sky. Society of Antiquaries Library.

167 Polished stone axe correctly identified as a tool made by 'native Britans' by Sir William Dugdale in *The Antiquities of Warwickshire*, 1656, engraved by Wenceslaus Hollar. The axe is now understood to be about six thousand years old. PEE Library.

catalogue of his collection. In the text he groups them under the Latin name *ceraunia* or thunder stones, explaining the belief that they may have fallen from the sky as meteorites were known to do. He carefully describes their colour, texture and shape but is ultimately indecisive about their nature whereas earlier, in 1648, Ulysses Aldrovandi,[37] describing his Musaeum Metallicum in Bologna, illustrates one polished and four perforated stone axes which may be the same examples shown by Worm, purposefully catalogued amongst an impressive array of shark teeth (fig. 166). In an earlier chapter[38] a tanged stone arrowhead hides between the teeth of other animals classed as *glossopetrae* or tongue stones.

Given the supposed mystery of the thunder stones and the superstitions attached to them, it is almost surprising to find a carefully drawn engraving of a polished stone axe described without any reference to *ceraunia* in Sir William Dugdale's book on the antiquities of Warwickshire published in 1656 (fig. 167).[39] In Dugdale's description of the axe the power of simple observation over received wisdom shines through. He states that 'divers Flint stones' had been found by ploughing on the north part of Oldbury fort and then describes their size and shape. From this he goes on to conjecture that:

Considering there is no flint in all this part of the
Countrie, nor within more than XL miles from hence,

they being at first so made by the native Britans, [*sic*] and put in a hole, board [*sic*] through the side of a staff, were made use of for weapons inasmuch as they had not then attained to their knowledge of working iron or brass to such uses.[40]

The inscription on the engraving states that the axe was in the Ashmolean Museum. However, the Ashmolean was not founded until 1683, by which time the axe had been lost in the fire of 1679 that destroyed Elias Ashmole's apartment in the Middle Temple, London.[41] Today the axe is understood as Neolithic, made some six thousand years ago by people who did not know the use of metal. Dugdale had observed well.

In similar vein but using what would now be called ethnographic evidence, Edward Lhwyd (1660–1709), Keeper of the Ashmolean Museum, wrote in 1699 that the arrowheads often ascribed to 'elfs or fairies ... are just the same chip'd flints the natives of New England tip their arrows with at this day: and there are also several stone hatchets found in this kingdom, not unlike those of the Americans'.[42] This echoes Robert Plot's advice that his readers could see how stone tools might have been 'fastened to a helve' by looking at Indian (North American) examples in the Ashmolean Museum.[43]

By the end of the seventeenth century stone tools were generally recognized as stone tools, distinct from fossils

168 Handaxe found in the 1690s with the remains of an elephant in Gray's Inn Lane, London and later acquired by Sloane. Recognized as a 'British Weapon', it was attributed to the period of the Roman invasion in AD 43 when the Emperor Claudius brought elephants to Britain. It is now considered to be about 350,000 years old. PEE.

which, following the proposals of the Danish anatomist Nicolaus Steno (1638–94), were now understood as the remains of ancient living organisms. Examples were sought after and collected, as in the case of a distinctive form discovered in the 1690s, in Gray's Inn Lane, London, by John Conyers (1633–94), apothecary (fig. 168). Conyers 'made it his chief business to make curious observations and to collect such Antiquities as were daily found in and about London'.[44] Little remains of his work, but a manuscript in the Sloane collection about Roman kilns and pottery found during the digging of foundations for St Paul's Cathedral shows him to be a keen observer, aware of the importance of the stratigraphic context and associations of finds.[45] The axe he discovered was not the familiar polished kind with an evenly weighted, tapering shape, but a pointed tool, flaked on both sides, thicker and heavier towards the bottom. It was easily recognized as a 'Weapon very common amongst the Ancient Britains' who did not have 'the use of Iron or Brass as the Romans had',[46] but it was more difficult to explain the remains of an elephant which were found nearby.

The report of Conyers's Gray's Inn Lane find is the first record of an artefact found in association with the remains of an animal now extinct in Europe. At the time there were only two possible explanations: the elephant was either the victim of Noah's Flood, or had been brought to Britain during the invasion led by the Roman Emperor Claudius where it died a casualty of war. John Bagford (1650–1715), a shoemaker who succeeded in an antiquarian career dealing in books, prints and curiosities, published the find following Conyers's death and opted for the latter. A century later, in *Archaeologia*, the journal of the Society of Antiquaries, similar handaxes, discovered at Hoxne, Suffolk, by John Frere, were referred to 'a very remote period indeed: even beyond that of the present world' (fig. 169).[47] This was not the first reference to pre-Roman times as a 'very remote antiquity'. Earlier papers in *Archaeologia* had used the phrase in relation to both Neolithic and Bronze Age antiquities,[48] reflecting the gradual acknowledgement of a longer pre-Roman period which was developing from the accumulating evidence provided by observations on the context and stratigraphy of pre-Roman artefacts. Although many of these were casual by modern standards, they were starting to form a more coherent picture capable of interpretation without recourse to written sources. Similar work by geologists and palaeontologists also began to undermine confidence in the six-thousand-year biblical timescale. In 1700 there had been no basis for that change and the consequent overthrow of the immense scholarship particularly in Hebrew, Greek and Latin, which had been devoted to the biblical chronology.

Once stone tools had been recognized, it was gradually acknowledged that they had preceded the use of metals. Proper survey and description of monuments revealed differences in the tools and pottery associated with them. As early as 1740 the French antiquary Mahudel[49] described the chronological sequence of stone – bronze – iron on the basis that in ancient European graves the urns which were the most decayed were frequently associated with bronze tools whereas more recent pots tended to be found with iron. Following him, the Cornish clergyman and antiquary William Borlase (1696–1772)[50] observed that the most ancient weapons had been tipped with stone, bone and ivory which had been followed by the use of copper then brass (bronze).[51] Having observed this from the material remains he had recorded, he then used evidence from the inscriptions on the Arundel marbles in the Ashmolean Museum to date the introduction of iron to 188 years before the war of Troy, about the thirteenth century BC, but noted that the use of bronze continued longer in Britain owing to

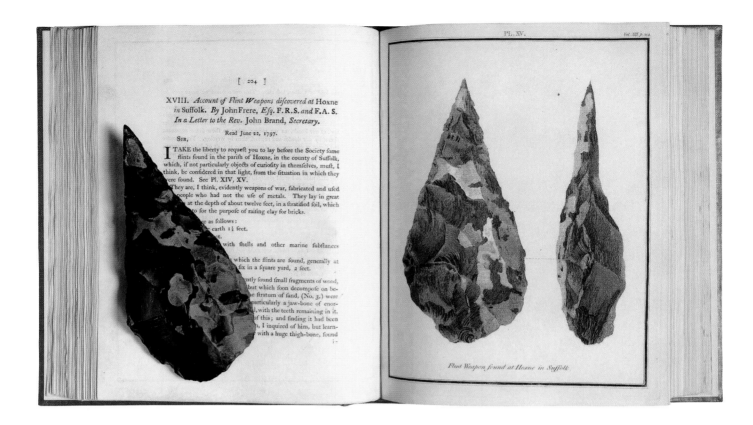

the scarcity of iron in Britain noted in Julius Caesar's description in his *Commentaries on the Gallic Wars*. Bishop Lyttelton also wrote that stone tools were used 'before ... brass or iron' by people who 'had no knowledge at all of these metals'.[52] By the end of the eighteenth century there was tacit acceptance of a pre-Roman sequence in which stone tools were succeeded by copper and bronze then iron. This was not only the case in Britain. Application of the scheme in the organization of the collections of the Copenhagen Museum by C. J. Thomsen and J. J. A. Worsaae in the mid nineteenth century subsequently formed the basis of the 'Three Age' system of classification that still underpins our thinking today.[53] Its development was based on the evidence accumulated during the eighteenth century and, later, excavation of field monuments.

RECORDING MONUMENTS

The recording of antiquities, particularly ancient monuments, had begun to emerge in Britain with the appointment of John Leland (c.1503–52), Royal Chaplain and librarian to King Henry VIII, as the King's Antiquary in 1533.[54] Leland collected miscellaneous facts about antiquities, as well as topographical features, folklore, family histories and details of estates, from the libraries of monasteries, colleges and great houses. These were intended to connect the recorded history of Britain with the world of the classical writers, and

169 Handaxe from Hoxne, Suffolk, with John Frere's report on his finds published in *Archaeologia*, 1800. The flint implements were referred to 'a very remote period' suggesting that antiquaries, as well as geologists were increasingly of the view that the earth must be older than the six thousand years allowed by the biblical chronology. The Society of Antiquaries on loan to PEE.

beyond that, the Bible. The purpose of such an anthology was to describe the kingdom, serving political purpose and evoking notions of what it was to be British by definition of customs and a sense of place.[55] Leland did not finish his *De antiquitate Britannica*. The material he had collected was used as a basis for William Camden's *Britannia*. Camden (1551–1623) was educated at Oxford and initially became a schoolmaster before his antiquarian interest led him to travel all over Britain visiting antiquities which he recorded and published with the benefit of Leland's unpublished notes. First published in 1586, the *Britannia*[56] went through five Latin editions before being published in English in 1610. The availability of such a large amount of information in English undoubtedly stimulated further collections of local history and antiquities up and down the country but by the end of the century libraries were not the only source of material. Antiquaries such as Dugdale, Aubrey, Lhwyd and Stukeley were reporting first-hand observations without trying to relate them to written sources and force them into quasi-historical narratives. Aubrey, for example, made a proper plane table survey of Stonehenge and noted the circle of fifty-six filled pits which showed up as surface depressions inside the bank and ditch. These were not described again until they were excavated in the twentieth century.[57] His unpublished work *Monumenta Britannica*[58] incorporates illustrations and notes which show that the book was to be organized in sections. The first dealt with what he described as temples of the Druids including Stonehenge and the first written description of the much bigger monument at Avebury with its stone circles surrounded by a massive bank and ditch. This account later stimulated Stukeley's interest in the site that culminated in its publication in 1743.[59] The notes and drawings for Aubrey's other sections concentrated on pre-Roman and Roman camps, barrows, burials, pottery and earthworks, as well as medieval buildings. Considering the latter, he discussed how they might be dated by features which identify the architectural style of a particular period. Subsequent work by Lhwyd and Stukeley followed similar lines.[60]

endorsed in a recent reconsideration of Avebury which states that 'fresh scrutiny of the manuscript records and draft illustrations ... made by William Stukeley revealed new facts about the state of the site in his time' which 'in the light of subsequent destruction and of the inevitable incompleteness of the archaeological testimony... are indispensable to any attempt to understand the site'.[63] However, although Piggott[64] regarded all these descriptions as important to the development of modern archaeology he also suggested that, after 1730, Stukeley lapsed from an empirical approach as he developed his interpretation of henges as Druidical temples. Piggott saw this as the result of religious bias or mental breakdown following Stukeley's marriage and ordination into the Anglican church, noting a similar dichotomy in early and later works of the mathematician and physicist Sir Isaac Newton (1643–1727), and a general mid-century decline in empirical scholarship.[65] Both suggestions are difficult to sustain.

Stukeley was an Anglican living in an age of religious

Prospect of STONEHENGE *from the Southwest.*

170 Illustration from William Stukeley's *Stonehenge: A Temple Restor'd to the British Druids* (1740), a work (see also fig. 200) which inspired many artists to depict the monument, including John Constable, who chose the same south-west prospect for a series of sketches and watercolours. House of Commons Library.

Stukeley's fieldwork has been admirably recounted by Piggott,[61] who extols his recording of the monuments of Stonehenge (fig. 170) and Avebury, the stone avenues and barrows situated around them and his discovery of cursus monuments which he recognized as long parallel banks with ditches on the outside and enclosed ends and considered contemporary with the barrows and henge sites.[62] This is

innovation which challenged the orthodox.[66] To assume that the motivation for his antiquarian research was ever driven by a desire to understand antiquities purely for their own sake is probably mistaken. Like many of his contemporaries, antiquaries and fellows of the Royal Society, he was a Freemason[67] and therefore committed to the study of an occult philosophy which leads the initiate by stages taught by allegory to a truer understanding of God and the essence of religious thought. The influence of, and perhaps on, masonic caballa, as well as Stukeley's interest in the Druids (fig. 170) and ancient Egypt (fig. 171),[68] may be seen mixed together in his interpretation of the inner circles at Avebury as representative of the Sun and Moon which he regarded as the 'principal

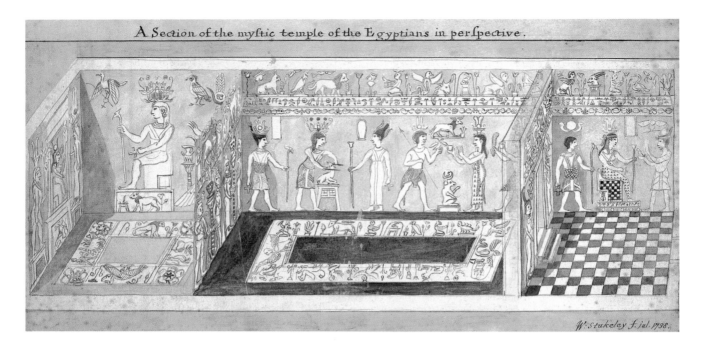

A Section of the mystic temple of the Egyptians in perspective.

W. Stukeley f. jul. 1738.

171 Stukeley's 1738 three-dimensional interpretation of the Temple of Isis, grey wash and watercolour, based on Montfaucon's engraving of the Mensa Isiaca bronze relief in Turin (then thought to be Egyptian). EAS Library.

agents or instruments of the soul and of the world the father & mother, one furnishing heat and the other moisture whence all generation, the Liber & alma Ceres of Virgil'.[69] Within the masonic lodge the major posts have similar allegorical significance. The Master symbolizes King Solomon or the deity, masculinity or the Sun which controls life and his role is balanced by the Senior warden who represents the Moon, Mother Earth and femininity. Just as the brotherhood promotes the belief that dissimilar religious systems are united by the expressed belief in God, so Stukeley found that the Druids were 'of Abraham's religion intirely [sic] ... and worshipped the Supreme Being in the same manner as he did'.[70] Making this assertion also provided a connection with the biblical account of the peopling of the earth after the Flood by the descendants of Noah and a basis for claiming the continuity of his own Christian faith with that of the Patriarch, establishing it as a true religion. For Stukeley at least, this justification was a blow against deism. The deists believed that God the Creator had no interest in the moral choices of men who were born with an innate ability (reason) to know the deity but were subverted by religions.[71] This was anathema to Stukeley and for him it must have been important to contradict the views of the leading contemporary proponent of deism, the freethinker John Toland (1670–1722), who had developed seventeenth-century ideas on Druids in works which were known to Stukeley (see also ch. 20).[72]

Although Stukeley's elaborate doctrinal arguments may have had little influence on contemporary religious debate

(see ch. 20), they do show that his antiquarian research never stemmed simply from a desire to discover the past through objective empirical methods, and there is no dichotomy between his earlier and later work.[73] Just as modern archaeological interpretations often reflect contemporary concerns, so did Stukeley's. He was the product of his time, not ahead of it. This view reflects the continuing value of his field records, as well as the contemporary influence of his work on the Druids, along with that of Toland and others,[74] on how the British past was represented in art and literature.

ANCIENT BRITONS

In his 1670 preface to his description of north Wiltshire, Aubrey invites his readers to 'imagine the kind of countrie this was in the time of the Ancient Britons'. Using what he knew from classical sources, he describes their warfare, coracles and use of iron. From his fieldwork he adds stone circles and earthworks and concludes with a reference to the latest ethnographic evidence that the Britons were 'two or three degrees ... less savage than the Americans'.[75] There were few depictions of these people at this time. Like the antiquaries, topographical artists such as the master etcher Wenceslaus Hollar (1607–77), who had drawn the Tradescant collection and worked on antiquities for Dugdale (fig. 167) and Francis Place, were beginning to see and appreciate the countryside thanks to signposting, turnpike roads and other improvements in travel.[76] Landscapes came from the background to the foreground of pictures, sometimes including melancholy ruins but usually unpeopled and uncivilized. It was the Druids and their kin who populated them and inspired popular imagination as the century faded.

172 Antiquarian research inspired popular imagination. In this typical aquatint from S. R. Meyrick and C. H. Smith, *The Costume of the Original Inhabitants of the British Isles*, 1815, a robed Druid decorated with Irish Bronze Age ornaments is shown with a harp, mistletoe and mystical snake. P&D.

From the late seventeenth century throughout the eighteenth century images of cloaked and bearded patriarchs with staff and mistletoe represented the pre-Roman Briton both in the works of antiquaries such as Stukeley and those for popular enjoyment (fig. 172).[77] By the turn of the nine-

teenth century, in the wake of the anti-slavery movement, the American and French revolutions and the Napoleonic Wars, works of the Romantic period were reflecting a noble aboriginal patriot (fig. 173), fighting courageously for liberty, patriotic against the Roman aggressor, wise at the feet of St Paul or

173 *A Maxtada and Caledonian, with cromlech in background*, from Meyrick and Smith (see fig. 172). Their torcs and weapons were based on newly discovered finds. P&D.

in awesome, repressive counter-revolutionary stance in William Blake's *Jerusalem, The Emmanation of the Giant Albion* (1804–20).[78] Stonehenge inspired works by many artists including Thomas Girtin, John Flaxman and John Constable whilst pseudo-cromlechs, stone circles and Druid's cells featured in many of the great landscape gardens of the period.[79] In all of these representations antiquities were used allegorically, reflecting the contemporary concerns which must also have influenced the discussion of antiquities in the clubs and societies which sprang up all over country after the Glorious Revolution of 1689 ended the reign of James II and brought greater tolerance and freedom of thought.

THE SOCIETY OF ANTIQUARIES

By the late seventeenth century antiquarian studies lacked a formal focus. Although several antiquaries were fellows of the Royal Society[80] or attended meetings as its guests, its initial interest and promotion of antiquarian research quickly declined and, after the publication of Sir Isaac Newton's *Mathematical Principles of Natural Philosophy* in 1689, there seems to have been a backlash against study that, for some, appeared to

bring no advantage to humankind. The Presbyterian minister and antiquarian John Horsley (1685–1732), who also experimented in the field of mechanics, responded to this when he wrote in the preface to his *Britannia Romana* that antiquities enrich and cultivate the mind, providing a more rounded picture of the world in the same way as theorems in mathematics and natural philosophy that some might also say 'were not worth knowing'.[81] To fill this gap, in 1707 the Anglo-Saxon scholar Humphrey Wanley met with others at the Bear Tavern in the Strand, London, to propose a society the business of which would be 'limited to the subject of antiquities and more particularly to such things as may illustrate and relate to the History of Great Britain'.[82] An important feature of the Society was its determination to maintain correspondence 'with the Learned and Curious Men in each county and the most eminent persons abroad'. This statement reflects the expansion of clubs up and down the country. In Spalding, Lincolnshire, Maurice Johnson, Fellow of the Royal Society and member of the Society of Antiquaries, formed the Spalding Gentlemen's Society in 1710, and similar bodies developed in other counties. These clubs have been described as 'beacons of urbane improvement to the neighbouring countryside',[83] although both Stukeley and Johnson noted the limited numbers of local people who could be encouraged to attend meetings.[84]

In London membership of the Society of Antiquaries continued to grow. The Society was reconstituted in 1717 and purchased its charter from King George II in 1751.[85] In 1770 it began to publish the papers read at its meetings in *Archaeologia* and, although some have denigrated the quality of its early content,[86] the availability of a journal dedicated to antiquities was an important improvement in the dissemination of knowledge and information. Early contributions cover a variety of topics ranging from finds of stone and bronze artefacts and Roman remains to Welsh castles, the Alfred jewel, the tomb of Edward the Confessor and the Irish Rebellion, as well as papers on classical antiquities found outside Britain. The number of papers available, as well as the Society's role in publishing major works, suggests that there was a sustained interest in antiquities from which early nineteenth century developments arose.

DECLINE OR CONTINUATION?

The assertion that antiquarian research declined during the mid eighteenth century[87] is difficult to sustain given the work of antiquaries such as Richard Gough (1735–1809),[88] editor of the 1789 edition of Camden's *Britannia*, who developed his own expertise on sepulchral monuments and Anglo-Saxon antiquities, General William Roy on Roman antiquities in Scotland, James Douglas on pre-Roman and Saxon sites in Kent and Borlase on pre-Roman and Roman material in Cornwall. Their work suggests that the death of empirical methods has been exaggerated.

Borlase took to the study of Cornish antiquities because his clerical living did not permit him the luxury of travelling to Greece and Italy.[89] Encouraged by Jeremiah Milles (1714–84), later president of the Society of Antiquaries, and Charles Lyttelton (1714–68), an expert in the Cornish language, both of whom were senior to him in the church, he learned Cornish and started to record ancient monuments, in some instances by digging them, as in the case of the barrows at Bosavern Rôs. These excavations informed his discussion of urn burials in which he distinguished between Roman and earlier interments, carefully describing and illustrating the deposition of the human remains, as well as the differing constructions of barrows,[90] dismissing theories that they were anything but pre-Roman and sepulchral. From Karn-Brê (Carn Brea) he recorded pre-Roman coins, carefully describing each one[91] before going on to discuss socketed bronze axes from the same site. His sober, well-argued opinions undoubtedly influenced future surveys and excavations.

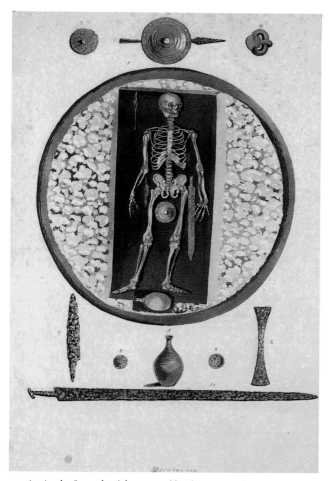

174 An Anglo-Saxon burial excavated by the Reverend James Douglas on the Chatham Lines, Kent, published in aquatint in his *Nenia Britannica*, 1786. The high status of the man is shown by his weapons and the Frankish wine flask at his feet. House of Commons Library.

William Roy developed his interest in Roman antiquities when employed on a military survey of Scotland between 1747 and 1755 (fig. 145, see ch. 15). Following the example set by Horsley in his careful recording of Hadrian's Wall, as well as his accurate work on inscriptions which has contributed so much to Romano-British scholarship,[92] Roy used his skills to produce a map of Roman Scotland and the Antonine Wall, as well as plans of the many camps he visited.[93] All of these were bequeathed to the Society of Antiquaries, which acknowledged their importance and paid for their publication in 1793.[94] Although its text is flawed by the inclusion of material from the false documents attributed to a fourteenth-century monk, Richard of Cirencester, the maps and drawings form a remarkable and enduring record of these antiquities, showing their distribution and relationship with the topography of Scotland. Roy also proposed that there should be a National Survey: this was implemented shortly after his death in 1791. The survey was conceived for practical and military purposes but the subsequent inclusion of sites and monuments on Ordnance Survey maps has proved invaluable to archaeologists to this day.

Excavation

In the last quarter of the eighteenth century, other antiquaries, following Borlase, extended their work from simply recording monuments to excavating them. In 1786 the Reverend James Douglas,[95] working in Kent, produced his *Nenia Britannica*:

> an account of some hundred sepulchres of the ancient inhabitants of Britain. Opened under a careful inspection of the author ... tending partially to illustrate the history of Britain in the fifth century ... to which are added observations on the Celtic, British, Roman and Danish Barrows ...[96]

The book is important because Douglas correctly and unequivocally describes many of his finds as Anglo-Saxon rather than Roman. The quality of the material belied Aubrey's conclusion that the Saxons had lived 'sluttishly in poor houses'[97] and opened up a new field of archaeological research. The early sections of *Nenia Britannica* describe and illustrate what Douglas saw in his excavations and are followed by systematic inventories of glassware, objects found only in the graves of women, jewellery and iron weapons. He goes on to discuss types of pottery, the uses and limitations of coins for dating burials and the value of comparing similar objects from different places. His attention to the systematic illustration of his sites and finds, often in more than one view and sometimes showing cross-sections, also set a new standard for archaeological reporting with a more specialized form of drawing also apparent in Borlase. Antiquaries often employed artists to illustrate their material[98] but Douglas drew his own, bringing new details as evidence in a volume

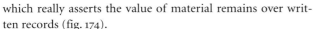

175 & 176 Frontispiece and title page of Sir Richard Colt Hoare's *Ancient Wiltshire*, 1812–21, showing a Bronze Age collared urn inverted (as it was found) bordered by amber and jet beads and two flint arrowheads emblematic of the finds he had excavated from barrows with William Cunnington. The archaic spelling suggests a romantic view of the past despite the author's declaration of a factual approach. Frontispiece (left) engraved by H. Meyer after Henry Edridge, 1821; title page (right) engraved by James Basire after P. Crocker, Hoare's draughtsman. House of Commons Library.

which really asserts the value of material remains over written records (fig. 174).

This assertion is reiterated in the subsequent publication of the Wiltshire excavations of William Cunnington (1754–1810), a wool merchant in Devizes for whom the investigation of monuments became the object of the physical exercise deemed necessary for his health, and his patron Sir Richard Colt Hoare, who, being unable to travel in Europe because of the Napoleonic wars, turned his interests to English antiquities.[99] In publishing their joint endeavours Hoare declared: 'We speak from facts not theories' (figs 175, 176).[100] This emphasis on facts is also apparent in the work of some late eighteenth-century antiquaries working on Roman Britain such as Samuel Lysons (1763–1819).[101] Lysons's interest in Roman remains had begun in Bath, where he studied law, and continued in London when he left the bar to become Keeper of Records at the Tower of London and concentrate on his antiquarian research. His work with his brother Daniel (1762–1834) on the *Magna Britannia*[102] was in the earlier tradition, harking back to Camden's county-by-county record of antiquities of all periods, whereas his excavations on Roman sites were without precedent (fig. 177). In his monograph[103] on the Roman villa excavated at Woodchester, Gloucestershire, in 1793 he reported not just the magnificent Orpheus mosaic but everything he found, showing an awareness of stratigraphy and its significance and drawing interpretations

from the evidence of the material remains rather than Latin authors. Lysons summarized his work at Woodchester and other Roman sites in *Reliquiae Britannico-romanae*,[104] a concise and innovative view of Roman Britain that has led to him being described as the founding father of Romano-British archaeology.[105]

Piggott[106] refers to the work of the Lysonses as a revival but it is clearly a continuation of the type of research begun by Gordon, Horsley and Roy, as well as many local antiquarians who contributed notes on their finds to *Archaeologia*. As the nineteenth century dawned, although there had been no change in the pre-Roman chronology subsequently regarded as so important, motivation had changed. Antiquaries now wanted to build up a picture of the past, a vision of Albion, by investigating antiquities rather than just recording them,

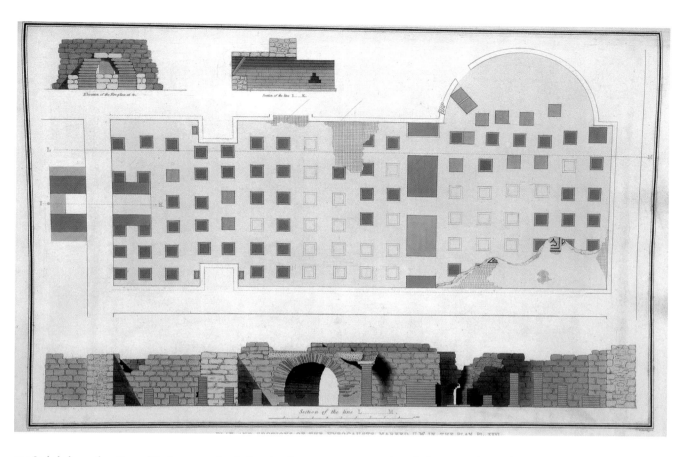

177 Scaled plan and sections of the hypocaust (underfloor heating system) of the large room of the Roman villa excavated at Bignor, Sussex, drawn by H. Weddell for Samuel Lysons's *Reliquiae Britannico-romanae*, 1813. Such accurate drawings of excavated buildings and finds were an important step forward in the recording of archaeological remains. PEE Library.

assuming their age and proving connections with classical texts or theological convictions, as they had done earlier.

Overview

Like so many disciplines, British archaeology emerged from the patchwork of intellectual endeavours which characterized the Enlightenment. There is no true progression towards its emergence and it is often difficult to connect the efforts of individual scholars. Their type of investigation necessarily developed away from the universities which concentrated on the classics. Although they sometimes associated together at meetings of the Royal Society and the Society of Antiquaries, and often corresponded, their practices, principles and purpose were highly individual, reflecting their own beliefs. Most believed in a benevolent God whose greatest work was the creation of humanity. Their implicit purpose in investigating the material remains of the past was to reveal God through his works. Whilst they were prepared to debate the age of the earth, the length of human history was believed to be fixed at six thousand years. In all these respects the criteria which drove their investigations were utterly different from those of the present but it cannot be denied that they established the use of antiquities as a valid approach to studying the past, as well as helping to define a sense of national identity and patriotism in an era marked elsewhere in Europe and America by political change, social upheaval and wars.[107]

18

From Persepolis to Babylon and Nineveh: the rediscovery of the ancient Near East

ST JOHN SIMPSON

The fragments collected by Mr. Rich were subsequently placed in the British Museum, and formed the principal, and indeed almost only collection of Assyrian antiquities in Europe. A case scarcely three feet square inclosed all that remained, not only of the great city, Nineveh, but of Babylon itself.[1]

emarkable sixteenth- and seventeenth-century travellers' tales of wondrous ruins and desolate sites in Iran and Mesopotamia tempered with an intimate knowledge of the Bible and classical sources mark the beginning of the European rediscovery of the cultures of the ancient Near East. The weakening of the Ottoman empire by the end of the eighteenth century opened lucrative new markets in the eastern Mediterranean: following first the loss of its American colonies and then the threat posed by Napoleon's Egyptian campaign (1798–1801), Britain became particularly concerned about safeguarding the two routes to India which ran via Egypt and the Red Sea, and Mesopotamia and the Persian Gulf. This is therefore a story strongly shaped by the professional duties of civil servants, diplomats and soldiers, many of whom served the East India Company and for whom antiquarian pursuits were a minority hobby in an overwhelming environment of heat, disease, boredom and excessive drinking.[2]

NAPOLEON, EGYPT AND THE HOLY LAND

On 19 May 1798 Napoleon Bonaparte (1769–1821), then a general in the French Revolutionary army, secretly sailed from Toulon at the head of a fleet. His aim was to found a colony in Egypt, control the markets of the Levant and dominate the Red Sea route to India. Within months the plan had begun to go wrong with the English destruction of the French fleet at Abu Qir bay; despite regular the French victories over Mamluk and Ottoman forces their army was forced to make an ignominious retreat from Acre and finally capitulate at Alexandria in September 1801.

Nevertheless, the creation of a French academic institute in Cairo in 1798 had made possible the first serious exploration of Egypt and Palestine, the survey teams including scholars and the artist-diplomat Dominique-Vivant Denon (1747–1825). Standing monuments were exhaustively catalogued and drawn, although the copies of the inscriptions were not particularly accurate owing to unfamiliarity with the script; the savants retained their notes and drawings when the French were defeated and the results were published in a twenty-volume series, the *Description de l'Egypte* (1809–28) (fig. 178). The most important discovery during this period was the Rosetta stone, a fragmentary stela inscribed in hieroglyphic, demotic and Greek scripts, which was discovered by chance in July 1799 during the reconstruction of the fortifications of Fort St Julien at el-Rashid (Rosetta) on the bank of the River Nile (see ch. 19). Soon after the French defeat the French Consul-General in Egypt, Bernardino Drovetti (1776–1852), began

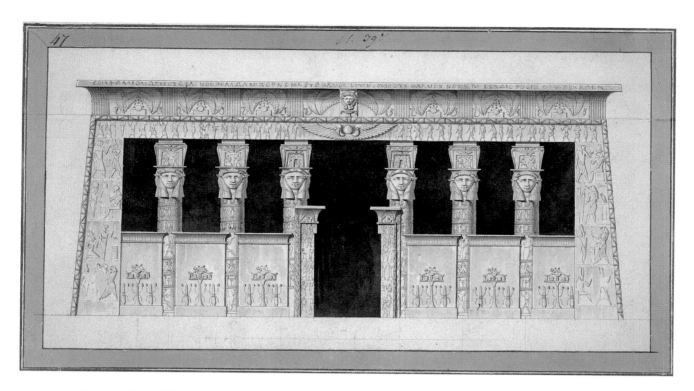

178 The temple of Hathor at Dendarah, constructed between 125 BC and AD 60, one of the best-preserved temples in Egypt. Drawing by Dominique-Vivant Denon. P&D.

179 Group of Egyptian antiquities collected by Henry Salt and Giovanni Belzoni, including a painted limestone shabti figure of Nefertiti (right) said to have been 'found in the Mummy Pits at Thebes'. AES.

searching for portable antiquities, which in turn triggered the so-called 'war of the consuls' as different national agents scrambled for objects. On the British side these included the diplomat Henry Salt (1780–1827), the traveller-collector William John Bankes (1786–1855) and the one-time circus performer Giovanni Belzoni (1778–1823), each of whose collections greatly contributed to the burgeoning collections in the British Museum (fig. 179) and about which much has already been written.[3]

The discovery of the Rosetta stone developed the expectation of further multilingual inscriptions which might allow the decipherment of other unknown eastern scripts. Bonaparte's Egyptian venture also had several side effects on the European rediscovery of the Orient. One was an improvement in official British Ottoman relations followed by the lifting of travel restrictions in parts of the Ottoman empire; another was the British desire to gain better first-hand intelligence about the geography, resources and routes of the Near East, usually through military officers of the East India Company (see ch. 24).

THE MYSTERY OF PERSEPOLIS AND THE PERSEPOLITAN SCRIPT

Before the travellers began to describe and sketch great ruined monuments in the Near East, European scholars and artists were forced to rely on passages in the Bible and classical historians for an appreciation of the ancient Near East. The first archaeological site to capture the attention of a western readership was Persepolis, capital of the Achaemenid empire and situated on the Iranian plateau near the city of Shiraz.[4] The romance of the ruined columned palaces with their sculptured façades, coupled with their accessibility, rendered them a frequent place of visit by Political Residents, official delegations and merchants. Influential publications by the Italian scholar Pietro Della Valle (1586–1652) and others, notably Engelbert Kaempfer (1651–1716), Jean Chardin (1643–1713) and Cornelius de Bruijn (1652–1726/7), illustrated not only delegations on the sculptured façades but also inscriptions in a curious 'arrowheaded' writing giving rise to the terms 'Persepolitan', 'cuneatic' or 'cuneiform' ('wedge-shaped').

Although copies of these inscriptions were published by Della Valle it was Karsten Niebuhr (1733–1815), the first traveller to spend serious time at the site and whose objective was to produce better copies of the inscriptions, who recognized the existence of a sign list of forty-two letters. A decade later William Francklin stated that:

the old inscriptions discernible on the walls, and other parts of the palace, may be reckoned among the greatest curiosities, as they have never yet been deciphered, either in the East or in Europe; and what is very extraordinary, the most learned and curious in the

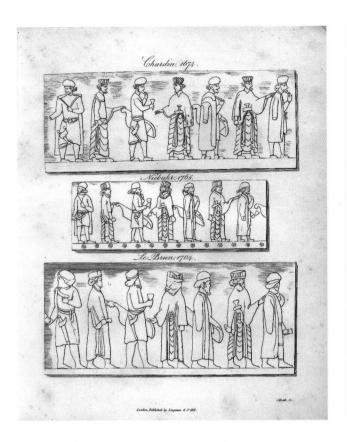

Oriental languages have been baffled in every attempt made to learn their meaning: – like the hieroglyphics of Egypt, they remain buried in an impenetrable mystery.[5]

However, just as copies of the Rosetta stone and other inscriptions allowed Jean-François Champollion (1790–1832) to offer the first decipherment of Egyptian hieroglyphs in 1824, Niebuhr's publication enabled Danish and German scholars gradually to determine that the Persepolitan inscriptions were also trilingual. The Old Persian version of these was alphabetic; it was further realized that the inscriptions were read from left to right, and that they included the names of the Achaemenid rulers Darius I (521–486) and Xerxes (485–465), which provided the first secure date for them.[6]

On 23 June 1818 the wealthy and celebrated painter Sir Robert Ker Porter (1777–1842) (fig. 181) reached Persepolis with the intention of making more accurate drawings of the sculptures themselves, which had hitherto not attracted rigorous attention or very good copies (fig. 180).[7] During a period of eighteen days he also copied most of the visible inscriptions, drew the reliefs at Naqsh-e Rustam and Naqsh-e Rajab and was the first author correctly to identify the tomb of Cyrus at Pasargadae. At the same site he copied the now-destroyed trilingual inscription of Cyrus on Gate R which he sent to Georg Friedrich Grotefend (1775–1853) for translation. In his travel account he commented, wistfully yet partly sarcastically, that 'it is much to be lamented that none of the

180 Detail of sculptured façade of the north face of the Apadana at Persepolis as drawn by Chardin (1674), Niebuhr (1785) and de Bruijn, reproduced together for comparison by Ker Porter in *Travels in Georgia*. ANE Library.

181 Sir Robert Ker Porter, mezzotint by W. O. Burgess after a portrait by George Harlowe. P&D.

British ambassadors, all of whom have passed through these ruins (at least, so their names on the walls would testify), did not set their numerous followers to work, to clear away some large portions of the collected matter, which buries so many valuable documents of antiquity'.[8] Ker Porter chose not to add his own name as a graffito on the Gate of All Nations or Palace of Darius (fig. 182); yet seven years earlier Sir Gore Ouseley's (1770–1844) mission to the court of Persia had stopped in Persepolis and indeed conducted the first trenches in May and July 1811.

Ker Porter's plea for excavation was taken up again in 1825 by the East India Company Resident at Bushire, Lieutenant-Colonel Ephraim Gerrish Stannus (1784–1850), who excavated 'a number of sculptured stones, capitals of columns etc.' and successfully made moulds of a large number of the exposed sculptures on the Apadana, winter palace of Darius and the Hall of a Hundred Columns (fig. 183). This was a remarkable achievement and a forgotten landmark in the history of using moulds to record sculptures too difficult to remove and which had already been the subject of different artists' attempts. Excavations were enthusiastically re-adopted the following year by Colonel John Macdonald [-Kinneir] (1782–1830), then British East India Company Envoy Extra-ordinary to the Shah.[9] Macdonald, his wife and eleven members of his delegation left their names as graffiti but two of this party died within a fortnight. The hardships of travel and the threat of disease or robbers continued to pose serious obstacles to research and exploration.

THE SEARCH FOR BABYLON

The major sites of ancient Mesopotamia were less accessible: large tracts of Iraq were too loosely controlled by the Ottoman authorities to be safe for travel and the very location of ancient cities described in the Bible was uncertain. The same applied also to much of the Levant, leading one modern writer to claim that between the end of the Crusades and the beginning of the nineteenth century fewer than two dozen Europeans had travelled more than a hundred miles inland.[10] The fact that brick rather than stone was employed as the principal building material in Mesopotamia effectively committed these structures to oblivion until excavation, since sun-dried clay bricks simply eroded into unrecognizable mounds mistaken by some travellers for natural hillocks. More substantial buildings constructed from fired brick were subjected to heavy robbing for reuse in later construction.

182 Partly buried sculpture of guards, one carrying a shield, inside one of the portico doorways of the Palace of Darius at Persepolis. Engraving after drawing by Sir Robert Ker Porter from *Travels in Georgia*. ANE Library.

183 Persians at Persepolis. Cast from a mould made by Stannus along the still unexcavated lowest register of the Apadana, Persepolis. ANE.

This was in complete contrast to Persepolis or temple and tomb ruins in Egypt, Greece and Italy, and one writer commented on the 'vast succession of mounds of rubbish of such indeterminate figures, variety, and extent, as to involve the person who should have formed any theory in inextricable confusion'.[11]

On 19–20 June 1625 Della Valle, travelling via the so-called Desert Route from Basra to Aleppo, became the first European to visit the ruins of the ancient city of Ur, where he acquired several bricks stamped with cuneiform inscriptions, the first to be brought to Europe.[12] Most educated travellers and collectors attempted to procure similar pieces as examples of an undeciphered script which was nevertheless recognized as related to that used on the Persepolis sculptures. Della Valle also suggested that the mound of Makloubé (also known as the Mujelibé or Babil) – which he visited in 1616 – was the site of the Tower of Babel, which had been fancifully depicted by scores of artists on the basis of passages in the Bible and classical authors (fig. 184). The exact location of this monument was hotly disputed: other suggestions ranged from the high mounds near Falluja on the Euphrates to the ruined ziggurat at Aqar Quf (now recognized to be the Kassite capital of Dur Kurigalzu).[13] However, Della Valle's proposal was supported by Niebuhr, who visited the nearby town of Hilla in 1765 where he observed the large number of inscribed bricks and noted the fact that the classical authors specified that the Hanging Gardens were next to the Euphrates and that the surrounding area was still known in Arabic as 'the land of Babylon', although he agreed that the ziggurat at Birs Nimrud – an hour's ride away – was also a strong contender.[14]

The breakthrough in the identification of Babylon finally came in 1813 with the publication of a memoir by Claudius James Rich (1787–1821) (fig. 185), who was the first to describe the physical topography of the Babil area. Counter-arguments by the formidable Major James Rennell induced Rich to return to Babylon in 1817 and publish a second memoir the following year, confirming his earlier identification and inspiring Lord Byron (1788–1824) to write:[15]

Because they can't find out the very spot
Of that same Babel, or because they won't
(Though Claudius Rich, Esquire, some bricks has got,
And written lately two memoirs upon't)'.[16]

184 *Fall of Babylon*, mezzotint by John Martin. A romantic reconstruction combining pre-archaeological perceptions of the 'Tower of Babel' and the 'Hanging Gardens' (right). P&D.

185 Claudius James Rich, portrait by Thomas Phillips, RA. Trustees' collection, on loan to the British Library.

Rich had been granted a military cadetship in the East India Company in 1803, soon converted to a writership in Bombay. However he was first appointed as secretary to the British Consul-General for the Mediterranean in Cairo, where he finally arrived after a circuitous journey involving shipwreck, three months' stay in Naples and fifteen months of travel in Turkey and the Aegean. Four years later, having arrived in Bombay dressed as a Mamluk (a mode of dress commonly adopted by early European travellers as it was more practical and attracted less attention), he was appointed at the age of twenty-one to be the East India Company's first Baghdad Resident. This post was created to counter possible French designs on the overland route to India and, according to one traveller, 'Mr. Rich was universally considered to be the most powerful man in Bagdad, next to the Pasha'.[17] His youth was deceptive as Rich was fluent in Turkish, Arabic and Persian, and familiar with Syriac and Chinese as well as French, Greek, Latin and Hebrew. These languages gave him a tremendous advantage not only in his business negotiations but also, like Sir Gore Ouseley, in developing an important collection of manuscripts during the course of his Residency.[18] Rich's linguistic abilities also allowed him to compare classical, Jewish and Arabic geographers' accounts as historical sources for reconstructing a skeletal Mesopotamian historical geography.

Rich's first visit to Babylon in December 1811 – a journey of a day and a half from Baghdad – was occasioned by the visit of his sister-in-law Kitty and lasted ten days; they were accompanied by his young wife Mary, Dr John Hine,[19] representatives of the Pasha and local sheikhs, a troop of twelve Indian sepoys, a light artillery piece and some seventy baggage mules. During this and subsequent trips he collected a few inscriptions, objects and unusual fragments which caught his eye, such as 'a large black stone, with figures and inscriptions on it' and 'a ram of a black stone, pieces of which are plentifully found among the ruins' (fig. 186).[20] His fascination with natural phenomena and the biblical prophecy that the Tower of Babel should become 'a burnt mountain' (Jeremiah 51.25) may have led him to keep a piece of glass production waste, probably found at Babylon or Birs Nimrud.

At the Mujelibé Rich deployed his sepoys to excavate the so-called 'Serdaub' where a wooden coffin had reportedly been unearthed four years before.[21] Among their finds were a glazed jar, a reused amulet in the form of the Mesopotamian demon Pazuzu, a 'little brass ornament that was found with a skeleton in a coffin'; 'a round stone which they found under the head of the coffin' and 'a brass bird, which, from being hollow on the other side, seems to have been fixed to the coffin as an ornament'.[22] Contradicting Della Valle, Rich concluded that this could not be the Tower of Babel as its size did not correspond with the classical descriptions and it appeared to be the site of multi-period buildings rather than a single construction, an argument finally confirmed through excavations at the close of the nineteenth century by the Deutsches Orient Gesellschaft.[23]

In addition Rich's men re-excavated the Lion of Babylon, or 'Idol' as it was locally known, although this proved too heavy to remove and Rich was disappointed that it was not 'the statue of a man with inscriptions' which he had hoped for.[24] They also briefly excavated a trench in the side of the mound of Tell Ibrahim Khalil near Birs Nimrud in an unsuccessful search for the 'petites inscriptions de terre grasse cuite' which Niebuhr found here and thought to be the legendary Chaldean astronomical observations.[25] These attempts at excavation were rare however, as Rich normally relied on 'curiosity-hunters' such as Delli Samaan, a Syrian Christian he employed for several years, to procure finds.[26] This must have been relatively easy at Babylon as the Kasr and Mujelibé were being quarried for reusable bricks and the nearby town of Hilla was 'the general depot for antiques found throughout all this country, especially on the banks of the Euphrates, from Raka to Samawa'.[27] In common with other antiquarian collectors, Rich also collected coins and seals. 'No Babylonian money has ever, to my knowledge, been discovered; but numbers of Greek, Roman, and Coufic coins are procured at Hellah, among which I found one of Alexander in good preservation.'[28] However, precious metal objects were scarce as these tended to be rapidly melted down after discovery. Thus

186 Antiquities collected by Charles Rich in Babylonia, ranging from a carved stone and small bronze figures of animals to a fragment of glass furnace waste. ANE.

when a hoard of over two thousand Athenian silver coins and up to seven hundred silver bar ingots was found near Humania by boatmen collecting wood for sale in Baghdad, Rich was able to acquire only a small number as the remainder were melted down and the site itself reinvestigated by the Ottoman authorities.[29]

Rich's comment that 'the execution ... as of all the Babylonian sculptures, is indicative of a very barbarous taste' perhaps explains the presence in his collection of two fake terracottas which were loosely inspired by Hellenistic or Parthian models.[30] These were not the only fakes which he unwittingly acquired, as his collection also included fake tablets and cylinders made by impressing real Neo-Babylonian economic tablets into solid lumps of clay. Nevertheless, although he was unable to read the inscriptions, Rich remarked that 'the written bricks form perhaps the most curious article of the Babylonian antiques, both on account of the form of the letters inscribed in them, the difficulty of accounting for their use, and the very great abundance in which they are found'.[31]

RICH AND 'THE CURIOSITIES OF NINEVEH'

After a spell of rest in Europe the Richs returned to Baghdad from 1816 to 1821. During this time Rich employed as his secretary Karl Bellino (1791–1820), a talented young Orientalist whom he had met in Vienna.[32] Bellino soon turned his mind to the cuneiform brick inscriptions but his promising career was brought to a premature end as he died from a fever in Mosul in November 1820. Earlier that year the Richs, Bellino and Dr Bell (Hine's surgeon successor) made a journey from Baghdad to Mosul via Kurdistan, with regular excursions or 'ruin-hunting expeditions' to quote Mary Rich.[33] This was an exceptional journey for the period; many of the sites which Rich considered to be Sasanian have not been surveyed since, and he was the first to identify correctly a Late Sasanian form of pottery decorated 'with pictures of deer or cows in small circular compartments'.[34] The Richs stayed in Mosul for four months, during which time Claudius Rich produced the first measured plans of the mound of Kuyunjik on the opposite bank and correctly argued that it must represent the remains of the citadel of the ancient city of Nineveh.[35]

At the site of one of the city gates he picked up a small fragment of stone near the spot where a few years previously local residents had discovered – and later smashed – 'an immense bas-relief, representing men and animals, covering a grey stone of the height of two men'. It was probably at Kuyunjik itself, where he mentions finding pottery, bricks and a fragmentary cylinder 'of the finest kind, yellowish, with a polished or hard surface',[36] that Rich picked up the first sherd of a third-millennium BC pottery type now known as Ninevite 5, tiny worn chips of Assyrian sculptures and a moulded Seljuk sherd. Delli Samaan also obtained for him a Neo-Assyrian cylinder seal 'in the mound of Koyunjik'. The nearby mound of Nebi Yunus, the Assyrian arsenal of Nineveh, was the provenance for the so-called Bellino cylinder, 'a small earthen vase covered with cuneiform writing', an historical account of Sennacherib (fig. 187), as well as several more inscribed bricks belonging to Assyrian rulers; the Museum Trustees were reminded at acquisition that 'the antiquities from Nineveh are the first ever brought to the West'.[37] Meanwhile, at the earlier Assyrian capital of Nimrud, situated a few kilometres downstream of Nineveh, Rich 'was delighted to find scattered about fragments of burnt bricks with cuneiform inscriptions on them. I immediately sent to the village to try to procure a whole one, and was successful. I obtained a brick covered with cuneiform writing on the face and the edge; the writing was larger than at Babylon, and not

Wood and James Dawkins, whose publication *The Ruins of Palmyra otherwise Tedmor in the Desert* (London, 1753) helped create the Neoclassical movement. During his stay in Baghdad Buckingham remarked on antiquities in Rich's collection, a large portion of which was later sold by his widow to the British Museum for £7,500, the equivalent of a healthy annual income from an estate.[42] Buckingham was guided by Bellino on his trips to Aqar Quf , Babylon, al-Ukhaimir (Kish), Birs Nimrud and the remains of the Sasanian palace at the Taq-i Kisra near Ctesiphon, although he followed Rich's advice not to bother crossing to the opposite bank, beyond which Buckingham claimed to have espied the broken diorite statue of the seated King Gudea.[43] Two years later Sir Robert Ker Porter spent six weeks in the Richs' company, again travelling with Bellino to Aqar Quf, Babylon,

187 The so-called Bellino cylinder, a fired clay barrel-shaped document with a 64-line cuneiform inscription referring to the late Assyrian ruler Sennacherib (704–681 BC). ANE.

in the centre of the brick, but covering the face; the bricks thicker than those at Babylon, and indeed much resembling the Nineveh bricks.'[38] 'The prospect of one day seeing these inscriptions decyphered and explained, is probably not so hopeless as it has been deemed.'[39]

ROMANTIC TRAVELLERS AND ARTISTS

In Baghdad the Richs played host to a number of important passing travellers including James Silk Buckingham (1786–1855) who stayed with them for over a month during the summer of 1816 before continuing on to Bombay.[40] Buckingham had previously travelled across Egypt and Syria where he had met Jean Louis Burckhardt (1784–1817), the Swiss explorer who recorded the first Hittite hieroglyphic inscriptions at Hama in 1812 and who rediscovered the Nabataean city of Petra shortly afterwards.[41] He also met Lady Hester Stanhope (1776–1839), the celebrated English reclusive romantic and favourite niece of William Pitt, who became one of the first Europeans to visit the ruins at Palmyra after the pioneering stay in March 1751 by Robert

Birs Nimrud and al-Ukhaimir. Ker Porter's artistic talents allowed him to record these ruins through drawings later illustrated as engravings in his own account.[44] He was also fascinated by the building materials used at these sites and at Aqar Quf, which he – like some of his predecessors – mistook for Babylon on account of the ziggurat (fig. 188). Here he extracted 'a large quantity' of reeds 'and found many of them two feet in length'.[45]

In the spring of 1821 a threatening confrontation with Dawud Pasha, the Governor of the Province of Baghdad, obliged Rich to leave and temporarily close the Residency. He was offered in consolation a new appointment as Member of Council in the Bombay government. Although his wife continued on to Bombay from Bushire, Rich decided to make a brief inland detour and visit Persepolis. He arrived at the site on 22 August and pitched his tent close to the Gate of All Nations, where he added his name as a graffito. He spent several days here, wandering over the ruins in the moonlight, hiring three workmen to 'clear out the south face of the platform ... as there are three inscriptions on it, and a row of figures very perfectly preserved, from their having been under the rubbish' and copying all but one of the visible Old Persian inscriptions for which he commended the use of the system of Grotefend, who had arranged the signs in tabular form 'for any one who may wish to attempt the task of decyphering them'.[46] Rich condemned the destruction of exposed sculptures at the site 'by the passion for possessing curiosities' and returned on 30 August to Shiraz, where he was obliged to stay because of a cholera outbreak that had spread from Bushire. He used this time to make fair copies of the inscriptions (published posthumously by his wife)[47] but sadly died of cholera in Shiraz on 5 October.

EPILOGUE

The European rediscovery of the ancient Near East was at the hands of a small number of remarkable travellers and political residents spanning the seventeenth to early nineteenth centuries. Rich had blazed a trail for future scholars of Mesopotamian topography and his publications were an essential point of reference for future travellers, most of whom contented themselves with observations on standing remains. Over the next two decades travels by James Baillie-Fraser (1783–1856), who had been beside Rich when he died, led to the discovery of several important sites in southern Iraq.[48] More exceptional were the wide-ranging reconnaissances conducted from 1826 to 1828 by Captain Robert Mignan (died 1852), commander of the Baghdad Residency escort. He regularly excavated test trenches at sites and was the first European to excavate near the Taq-i Kisra and the Sasanian city-site at Kifri where he discovered a number of coins and seals.[49] It was also from the late 1820s that the Anatolian plateau began to be explored, firstly with the copies of Urartian cuneiform inscriptions in the Van region by Charles Schulz between 1827 and 1829 and then the discovery of the Hittite capital of Hattusha by Charles Texier in 1839.

In Egypt and the Levant improved accessibility and security under the rule of Muhammad Ali, Pasha of Egypt (1805–48), encouraged travellers and artists to travel more widely during the late 1830s. In 1838 the American scholar Edward Robinson (1794–1863), accompanied by the missionary Eli Smith, conducted a thorough survey of Palestine and identified many biblical sites on the basis of their surviving names;[50] in the same year the Scottish artist David Roberts began a lengthy eastern journey which culminated in the publication of monthly instalments in 1842–9 of his lithographs *The Holy Land, Syria, Idumaea, Arabia, Egypt and Nubia*.[51] This and the work of the English watercolourist William James Müller (1812–45) marked an important watershed in the popular European perception of the Holy Land, although the romance of the Cairo bazaar and the upper Nile continued to be the main focus of the Orientalist painters.

Within the Grand Central Saloon (later Central Egyptian Saloon) of the British Museum the cabinet of Rich's finds was displayed beneath Roman sculptures and the Ouseley sculptures and Stannus casts from Persepolis from 1825 until about 1851.[52] It was this display which inspired Julius Mohl, secretary of the French Asiatic Society, to instruct the new French consul in Mosul, Paolo Emilio Botta (1802–70), to initiate serious excavations at Kuyunjik in 1842. These and the subsequent archaeological expeditions led by Austen Henry Layard (1817–94), Victor Place (1822–75) and Hormuzd Rassam (1826–1910) belong to the next major phase when excavation became the norm in Mesopotamia, triggering a scramble for antiquities by archaeologists from Britain, France, Germany, America and Turkey, an Assyrian revival and the development of museum collections in those countries.[53] The discovery of thousands of cuneiform tablets in Assurbanipal's (668–627) library and sites across Babylonia likewise unlocked the archives of ancient Mesopotamia, leading one American scholar to write that 'It is the written tablets in the British Museum, and not the large and showy slabs and bulls, which make that Museum the school where men of every nation must go to study Assyriology'.[54]

188 Babylonian brick, mortar and bitumen fragments in the original box presented to the British Museum by Sir Robert Ker Porter. ANE.

19

'The curse of Babel': the Enlightenment and the study of writing

CLIVE CHEESMAN

When we think of advances made in the study of writing we tend, nowadays, to think of the decipherment of forgotten and unintelligible ancient scripts. Indeed this process may well seem the classic Enlightenment story. By the faithful application of scientific principles, the liberal exchange of ideas in the blossoming intellectual (though not necessarily academic) community, and – not least – a large element of trial and error, a path was beaten out of the esoteric fantasy world of the Renaissance to a position where the lost scripts could be read for what they were, and vast new vistas opened up on the societies that produced them.

But to see the eighteenth-century study of alphabets and writing systems purely in these terms would be to miss much of its interest and indeed its point. It would also be deeply disappointing, since, despite the calibre of the minds involved, only depressingly small advances in decipherment were made until the end of the century, and the first really impressive breakthroughs came only in the early nineteenth century. Many came much later still. What we see instead is a much richer range of thought about the nature and origins of writing, passing through a process that might be mirrored in other areas of Enlightenment thought: demystification, classification, practical application and finally the beginnings of a subtler and less categorical appreciation.

ESOTERICISM AND SCEPTICISM

So the story is not only, or even principally, the story of decipherment. But it certainly opens as the search for understanding, for enlightenment. Let us start where the tale usually begins, in the Renaissance fantasy world referred to above. For the Renaissance, as for later ages, the unintelligible script of the ancient world *par excellence* was the Egyptian system called hieroglyphics. This was well known to scholars of the period not from trips to Egypt but from its survival on many prominent antiquities in the heart of Rome, where they had been transported in the days of the Empire. Some, such as the obelisk erected by Hadrian in memory of Antinous in AD 130, may have even been made and inscribed for display in Rome. But hieroglyphs and the way they functioned had been very imperfectly understood by the ancient Greek and Latin writers whom the humanists of the Renaissance studied so closely, and some misleading notions were accordingly received. Chief among these was that propounded by Plotinus, the neo-Platonist philosopher of the third century AD, namely that the symbols making up hieroglyphics were signs representing not real language but philosophical and esoteric ideas.[1] They were, in short, a picture language for the direct

189 All the obelisks in Rome came under Athanasius Kircher's scrutiny. The fine example in the Piazza del Popolo (engraved here for Kircher by John Blaeu), and originally at Heliopolis in Lower Egypt, was possibly one of the sources for Manetho, one of the few ancient writers on hieroglyphics. EAS Library.

communication of concepts. A later text (late fifth century), transmitted under the name 'Horapollo', was probably compiled partly on the basis of native Egyptian word-lists in hieroglyphic, as well as its derivative cursive scripts, 'hieratic' and 'demotic'; but it consciously emphasized the emblematic and figurative nature of the symbols and thus did nothing to undermine the account given by Plotinus.[2] Translated by the great humanist Marsilio Ficino in 1492, Plotinus's version was taken up by many other scholars, especially in the late Renaissance world of the Counter-Reformation, when some of the greatest talents were channelled into the obscure fields of neo-Platonism and Hermetic philosophy.

The apogee of this approach was reached with the famous German Jesuit polymath, Athanasius Kircher (1601–80). Kircher was a talented linguist who was acquainted with Near Eastern tongues, both living and dead, and knew what it was to be able to read a non-Roman script.[3] However, with regard to Egyptian hieroglyphs he was content to interpret them in the way proposed by Plotinus. They contained the ancient wisdom of the Egyptians, an enticing Hermetic storehouse of forgotten insights which could be coaxed out of them by a considerable amount of *a posteriori* reasoning and externally inspired interpretation. An example of what this produced is Kircher's reading of the hieroglyphs making up the name of

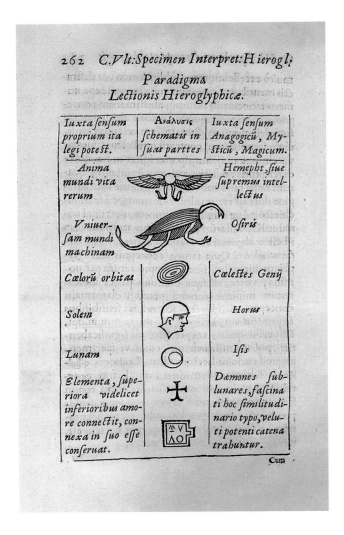

190 A sample page illustrating the interpretation of hierglyphics from Athanasius Kircher's *Prodromus Coptus sive Aegyptiacus* (Rome, 1636). Kircher offers two levels of meaning for each sign: the 'proper' or literal, and the 'mystical' or 'magical'. EAS Library.

the pharaoh Psammetichus on the obelisk in the Piazza della Minerva in Rome: 'The protection of Osiris against the violence of Typho must be elicited according to the proper rites and ceremonies by sacrifices and by appeal to the tutelary Genii of the triple world in order to ensure the enjoyment of the prosperity customarily given by the Nile against the violence of the enemy Typho' (fig. 189).[4]

It may seem surprising that Kircher and his learned predecessors, all highly literate men, each at home in several languages and acquainted with several more, could have seriously 'translated' hieroglyphic texts in the way they did (fig. 190). It is one thing, for example, to interpret a helmet as the sign for protection, or even a bull (for reasons too obscure to go into here) as indicating 'acuity of hearing'; but it is quite another thing to get from these roped-together

abstractions to a sentence, complete with subject, object and finite, parsable verb – all the things, in short, which make language intelligible.

This, however, misses the point. Kircher and his fellows would have responded that the chief characteristic of the hieroglyphic texts was that they did not employ language. As Plotinus had described them, they did away with the need for any linguistic stage in the communication of ideas from the writer to the reader. In writing their *own* books, of course, Kircher and his predecessors had to resort to language, if they were to claim to have translated or interpreted the symbols at all. In doing so they would have to plump for specific verbal tenses and moods, particular nominal cases and so forth. But they did *not* claim that these were hidden away in the hieroglyphs; they claimed that they were simply not needed there, where the interplay of basic philosophic and religious ideas was unencumbered by the mechanisms of linguistic expression and could be grasped, non-linguistically and directly, by the initiated. In this, of course, they were wrong. It is impossible to communicate in any useful way merely by the visual representation of abstractions.

A reaction was bound to set in. It is most visible in the reception that other unintelligible ancient scripts had in the West, especially the varieties of 'cuneiform' writing used in the Near Eastern empires of Assyria, Babylonia and Persia (Iran). The first news of cuneiform inscriptions was brought back by travellers to Persepolis in the early seventeenth century, who were mostly satisfied that they were true writing and, if ever deciphered, would surely be found to 'conceale some excellent matter' (to quote Thomas Herbert, who was there in 1626).[5] From the later 1600s reports were also being received of another unknown script at Persian sites such as Naqsh-e Rustam; this is now known to be Sasanian. However, even though accompanied by (admittedly bad) drawings of the Sasanian inscriptions, these reports failed to arouse much interest at home, save for the contemptuous remarks of those who rejected the possibility that these curious marks could be writing at all. Chief proponent of this view was Thomas Hyde (1636–1703), Regius Professor of Hebrew and Laudian Professor of Arabic at Oxford, who in 1700 dismissed Sasanian as ' "travellers" ' graffiti ... late, insignificant and scarcely worth the bother of solving'. The cuneiform inscriptions of Persepolis were clearly less ephemeral, but Hyde was convinced that they were purely decorative.[6] His condemning remarks stifled serious attempts at decipherment for half a century.

The Origins and Classification of Writing Systems

But, as stated earlier, decipherment was not the burning issue it was later to become. Of greater interest was the history and origins of the western, Greek-derived alphabet, and – linked with this – the origins and theoretical capabilities of writing itself. Discussions of the history and the theory of writing were for a while closely intertwined, and it is no surprise in 1755 to find the *Encyclopédie* of Diderot and d'Alembert saying, before embarking on its account of the origins of writing, 'c'est un beau sujet philosophique'.[7]

The theoretical and historical account that the *Encyclopédie* then gives is principally that expounded by William Warburton (1698–1779), bishop of Gloucester, in his many-sided work *The Divine Legation of Moses*, first published in 1740 and much expanded in the next two decades.[8] Warburton argued that early writing was essentially ideographic, in that it sought to represent not words but the things 'behind' the words; his name for this approach was, precisely, 'hieroglyphic', which he applied to a broad range of early writing

systems at different stages of development. The first stage was simple picture writing, represented for him (as for most Europeans in the eighteenth century) by the scripts of central America. In the case of Aztec glyphs (fig. 191), this was not so far off the mark, but Maya writing was in fact a sophisticated combination of signs for words and syllables, representing the sounds of the writers' spoken language; true writing, in other words (fig. 192). Those Europeans who had first come into contact with it in the sixteenth century, such as the Franciscan priest Diego de Landa (1524–79), had witnessed it in use, but had assumed it was basically an alphabetic script like their own.[9] The Enlightenment made the opposite error, treating it as a primitive (and indeed wholly impractical) form of suggestion by imagery.

The second stage was exemplified by Egyptian hieroglyphs

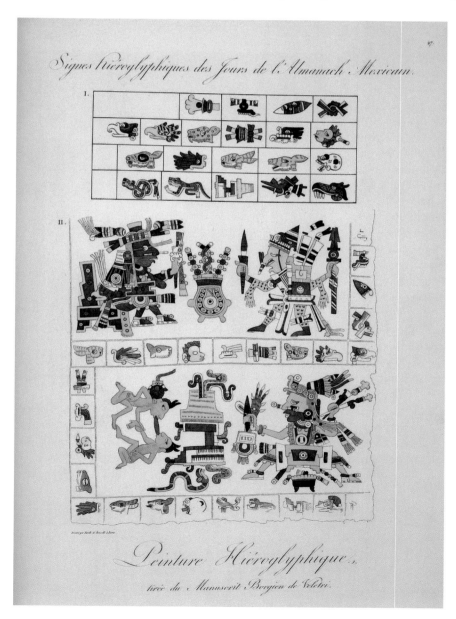

192 Lithograph by J. F. Waldech of a Mayan relief from Palenque, in Mexico, with glyphs. Plate 13 from *Description of the Ruins of an Ancient City* (London, 1822).
This illustrated translation of an official report on Palenque made in 1787 by a Spanish cavalry officer, Antonio del Rio, was the first published book to show Maya carved writing. Ethno Library.

191 Hieroglyphs as illustrated in Alexander von Humboldt's *Vue des Cordillères, et monuments des peuples indigènes de l'Amérique* (Paris, 1810), plate 27.
The twenty signs at the top represent the names of the days used by the Aztecs and Mixtecs. Ethno Library.

themselves. Warburton characterized this method as representing objects and concepts allusively and economically, 'by analogy or symbols'. Arguing from the fact that hieroglyphs were so widely and so visibly displayed on all varieties of monument, he concluded that, far from the obscure, conceptual code Plotinus had represented them as, they must in origin have been readily comprehensible to large numbers. Certainly, the interpretations of specific symbols offered by Horapollo did not always assist the notion of transparency, and Warburton held that with time the general comprehensibility of the hieroglyphs had diminished until it was restricted to a priestly caste. But he also argued that, by their nature, even the 'public' form of hieroglyphs were allusive and suggestive, rather than directly representational; this was what distinguished them from mere picture writing.

The third and final stage of 'hieroglyphic' writing for Warburton was the designation of objects and concepts by arbitrarily instituted symbols, which in no way resembled or recalled them. An example, to all intents and purposes, was provided by Chinese characters, which he believed had passed through the first two stages and now had lost all visible relationship with the things they originally depicted. Like many in the West in his day, Warburton was wedded to the view that Chinese writing was cleanly detached from the many different languages and dialects used in China, and yet equally comprehensible to the whole population (fig. 193). It thus qualified (albeit within a limited area and in a cumbersome, unphilosophical form) as a sort of universal writing, and as such a remedy for 'the curse of Babel'.[10] It was this detachment from spoken language that categorized it as 'hieroglyphic' in his analysis. In this he differed from others who regarded Chinese writing as fundamentally non-hieroglyphic because its symbols were arbitrary rather than figurative.[11] Warburton tended to accept instead Kircher's testimony that Chinese characters were in fact originally pictures of the things they stood for, but he held that, regardless of whether or not this was true, they were hieroglyphs in that they did not stand for words in the spoken language; and although Chinese writing, as he put it, was 'on the very border of letters', this non-linguistic character was fundamental.

Warburton's position and the weaknesses in it emerge more clearly from his lengthy response to a critique of his argument made by the Arabist and traveller Richard Pococke (1704–65) in his *Description of the East*. Pococke, bishop of Ossory in Ireland, had written that Egyptian hieroglyphs 'stand not for things alone, but as words, for sounds *and* things'. Warburton regarded this as internally contradictory.[12] His theory did not separate out 'logograms' (symbols standing for specific, entire words in a language) from 'ideograms' (symbols standing for objects or concepts). A graphic symbol, whether arbitrary or figurative, that stood for an item in the world should not be confused or associated with the item's spoken name.

Logically it was a tenable view. However Pococke's description of hieroglyphs was closer to practical reality. In fact the symbols in use in Egyptian hieroglyphics *were* in part multi-functional, and could be loosely said to stand for both sounds and things. They are figurative representations which were used to record the sounds of the spoken names for the objects they designated. Some had a logographic function in regard to those objects, but were also read as syllables or letters in other words. Some signs might also be used as 'determinatives', unspoken written elements representationally clarifying or classifying a word spelled out with other signs.

It was a long time before the complexities of this system were grasped or even conceived; arguably, not until after the Enlightenment was over. But Warburton's approach to Egyptian hieroglyphs, although not directed towards their decipherment, was none the less a great step forward, and was recognized by the later decipherers as such. He was the

193 Two Chinese seals collected by Sir Hans Sloane. The left-hand seal, of quartz crystal (h. 5.6 cm), shows a 'dog of Fo' (a Buddhist lion dog); the other, of red soapstone, has seal characters for long life. Seal script evolved from inscriptions on bronzes and is markedly different in form from Chinese handwriting. OA.

first to argue convincingly that hieroglyphs were intended to be read and understood by all educated Egyptians, and that they should be included in a general evolutionary account of writing. Furthermore, despite the importance of the distinction he was drawing between 'hieroglyphical' and 'alphabetical' writing systems, he was certain that the latter could develop from the former. He contended that when public hieroglyphs had evolved into arcane sacerdotal symbols, whatever writing system was then developed for general use was extremely likely to have taken over, at least in part, the now disused hieroglyphic signs. He also felt it likely that this had happened with Coptic, relying here to some extent on Kircher's account of that language and its script, and that Cadmus the Phoenician, who for the ancients had been the inventor of the Greek alphabet, had also plundered the hieroglyphs for his letter forms. Indeed, he added, the Hebrew alphabet was likely to have had a similar origin, being brought back by the Jews when they left Egypt; Moses did not, after all, invent it or receive it direct from God, for Holy Scripture should certainly have informed us if that were so.[13]

Warburton's arguments were extremely influential, at home and abroad. The vindication of ancient testimony with regard to Cadmus and the ready acceptance of Egyptian paternity for all western alphabets, including the Hebrew, were typical of the age; as was the fact that this should be achieved in the context of a lengthy dissertation in support of true, revealed religion. Scholars were now encouraged to think of hieroglyphics as a writing system like any other, and this had two effects. First attention turned to those other writing systems; and, secondly, serious thought began to be given to the unpicking of the Egyptian hieroglyphic script itself.

One individual whose work chimed particularly happily with that of Warburton was the abbé Jean-Jacques Barthélemy (1716–95), a distinguished classicist and numismatist with an interest in Near Eastern languages. Apart from demonstrating in 1752 that demotic script did indeed include symbols derived from hieroglyphics, and thereby proving one of Warburton's chief hypotheses, Barthélemy started to look at other writing systems of the Near East and their interrelationship.[14] His decipherment of Palmyrene writing in 1754, working from the plates in the newly published *Ruins of Palmyra* by Dawkins and Wood, had importance for him in this context, not as a particularly great feat of intellectual bravura; indeed for one who knew various Semitic languages and now had reliable pictures of bilingual Greek and Palmyrene inscriptions to work from, it had not been especially hard. The Oxford don John Swinton (1703–77) had found it just as easy and almost beat Barthélemy to the post.[15]

The first forays into these areas were not always surefooted. Thus the fifth plate illustrating the entry 'Alphabets anciens' in the *Encyclopédie* shows an alphabet labelled 'Egyptian' taken from a stela at Carpentras in France; this is in fact a north Semitic script, related to Phoenician and probably dating to the fifth or fourth century BC, but it was thought to be Egyptian because it was found on a monument with hieroglyphs.[16] The optimistic belief in a connection between Semitic script and hieroglyphs had exceeded its bounds somewhat, and when Barthélemy's close examination of hieratic and demotic revealed that they could not possibly be simply alphabetic in structure (there were far too many different symbols in each), the reaction was one of disappointment. The ancient belief in a hieroglyphic paternity for Phoenician and therefore Greek letters was abandoned, though revived in more sophisticated form by the nineteenth-century scholars Emmanuel de Rougé and Isaac Taylor;[17] the more durable view proved to be that of the great Near Eastern epigrapher Wilhelm Gesenius (1786–1842), who argued that Phoenician letters originated in symbols representing the objects designated by their names: *aleph* an ox's head, *beth* a house, and so on.[18] A synthesis of these two views is now held by many scholars, according to which awareness of Egyptian hieroglyphics prompted and guided the birth of the Semitic consonantal alphabet.[19]

AUTOPSY AND RECORD

None the less, despite the occasional faltering steps and disillusionments, the breadth and richness of the epigraphic record was now receiving proper attention, and it was at last understood that inscriptions needed to be seen, either directly or through the medium of a proper illustration, if they were to be understood or in any way studied. This desire for autopsy and faithful record was one motive for the rise in scholarly travel to parts where inscriptions in obscure or unknown scripts could be found. Dawkins and Wood's work at Palmyra, though their chief interests were architectural and decorative, was (as we have seen) a beneficial early example. The next great name in the field was Karsten Niebuhr (1733–1815), a Holsteiner who travelled widely in Egypt and the Near East and produced accurate drawings of inscriptions which he then dissected in order to isolate the individual signs used.[20] His list of distinct hieroglyphic symbols (which as a class he carefully distinguished from the larger, purely figurative elements of Egyptian relief sculpture) was by far the fullest yet seen. Many other travellers not only attempted to make faithful transcripts of inscriptions they saw but brought back movable inscribed objects – such as coins, seals, baked bricks and pottery – which played their part in increasing familiarity with ancient Near Eastern scripts (see ch. 18). Cuneiform writing, barely mentioned in the *Encyclopédie*, became a frequent if still far from comprehended sight in the museums and collections of Europe; and cuneiform tablets, like all sought-after objects, were subject to forgery (fig. 194) (much as codices containing the still undeciphered Maya glyphs were in the twentieth century).

Other factors were the scholarly publication of ancient texts such as the *Zend Avesta*, edited by Anquetil-Duperron in 1771, and the newly scientific interest in language, partly born from the influential rediscovery (scarcely a discovery) of the relationship between languages such as Latin, German and Sanskrit, announced by Sir William Jones in 1787 (see fig. 204).[21] Ancient Persian could now be examined directly,

194 Fake cuneiform tablets acquired in Babylon by Claudius Rich (1786–1821), indicating an unusually early local response to the new demand for cuneiform inscriptions, despite scholars' inability to decipher them. ANE.

195 The Rosetta Stone. The lower part of a large stela displaying three copies (in hieroglyphic and demotic Egyptian, and in Greek) of a decree relating to the cult of Ptolemy V Epiphanes, king of Egypt 205–180 BC. EAS.

Certain aspects of the decipherment of the stone indicate the continuing hold of Enlightenment ideas.[24] Though the stone was handed over to the victorious British in 1801, its first impact was in France, where Sacy set to work on it in a methodical and sensible manner. But he was hampered by the persistent beliefs, fostered by Warburton's theories, that the demotic text on the stone, though derived from the hieroglyphs, would itself be alphabetical in character, and that the hieroglyphs would have nothing phonetic or linguistically grounded about them. Both ideas were wrong.

The first partial breakthrough on this point came with regard to the proper names in the inscription, which had been the initial focus in any case as it was rightly held that they would be roughly the same in all three texts on the stone. Sacy took up a suggestion made first by Barthélemy and then by Georg Zoëga (1755–1809), Warburton's main successor as theorist of Egyptian writing, that the hieroglyphs in the oval 'cartouches' were royal names; as the royal name in question, Ptolemy, was Greek rather than Egyptian, Sacy pointed out that it would probably have to be spelled out phonetically and not ideographically. This showed that hieroglyphics *could* in certain circumstances be used phonetically, and Sacy held that the function of the cartouche was to indicate that they were being so used.[25]

In fact the cartouche merely indicates a royal name, whether Egyptian or Greek in origin, and implies nothing about the nature of the hieroglyphs it contains. Sacy's idea was none the less suggestive in the way it began to break down the rigid divide between ideographically and phonetically based writing, and it may be no coincidence that in the same year (1811) as Sacy's proposal, a pupil of his, Abel-Rémusat, published findings showing that the Chinese often used their characters in a phonetic way, overturning the basic western view of Chinese writing held for two centuries.[26]

The reciprocal conclusion – that the demotic script was not alphabetical – was drawn with great reluctance and dismay by Thomas Young (1773–1829), the English polymath of astounding talents who corresponded with Sacy and had important insights into the way that hieroglyphs might work.[27] Less dismayed, however, was Jean-François Champollion (1790–1832). It was Champollion, of course, who was the real decipherer of the two Egyptian texts on the stone, and he was superbly qualified in late Enlightenment terms

rather than through Parsee texts of a later date, and, with the gradual development of a science of comparative philology from Jones's insight, reasonable conjectures made about the forms that words would take in other, related languages. The value of this work had an early confirmation when Silvestre de Sacy (1758–1838), Professor of Arabic in Paris, using his familiarity with the Persian language and with Greek texts about ancient Iran, and working from Niebuhr's accurate copies, showed that the '"travellers'" graffiti' at Naqsh-e Rustum were royal inscriptions set up by the Sasanian rulers and, at length, deciphered them.[22]

The great breakthrough in hieroglyphics, when it came, was no less a result of these trends. There is no need to rehearse here the well-known story of the discovery of the Rosetta Stone in 1799 (fig. 195).[23] It suffices to say that, while its discovery may have been by chance, its salvage and the rapid recognition of its importance was not, for the French presence in Egypt at this time had, in part, the character of a vast scholarly expedition under arms. The occupying force of *savants*, engaged in the systematic reduction of the country into the vast tomes of the *Description d'Égypte* which emerged in 1809 were a very real embodiment of confident Enlightenment principles.

for the task: a pupil of Sacy, he was intimately acquainted with Coptic and learned in Arabic and Persian. But he was more than ready to break down the over-rigid categories that the Enlightenment had set up. His first decisive steps towards decipherment were in the field of non-Egyptian proper names; looking not only at the Rosetta Stone but at other monuments too such as the Bankes obelisk at Kingston Lacy, and a bilingually inscribed vase held by the

196 Champollion's chart of phonetic signs from demotic and hieroglyphic, with Greek equivalents, as it apeared in his *Lettre à M. Dacier* of 1822. EAS Library.

French collector the Comte de Caylus, he worked out the hieroglyphic transcriptions of a great many names, including that of the Persian king Xerxes, which showed that these 'phonetic hieroglyphs', as Champollion called them, had a long history. It need scarcely be emphasized how bizarre a concept that of 'phonetic hieroglyph' would have seemed to

Warburton. But Champollion had read Rémusat and knew the phonetic role played by Chinese characters; the concept of 'pure' ideographics was one he was ready to drop. The proof of his method came when he found that his ability to transliterate the hieroglyphic names of the kings of Egypt did not cease when he got back before the period of foreign rulers; he was able to continue in triumph back to the pharaohs of the eighteenth Dynasty (1550–1295 BC). From here he was able to use his Coptic to identify royal titles and start to unravel the whole structure of hieroglyphic writing and its derivative forms (fig. 196), not to mention the grammatical and syntactical nature of the language they preserved.[28]

If the decipherment of cuneiform writing was longer in coming than that of Egyptian hieroglyphs, it none the less followed a similar path, although the rigid categorizations and fallacies that dogged comprehension of the latter were not all present; in particular the confusing and misleading concepts of 'hieroglyphic' was blissfully absent. Niebuhr's fine copies of cuneiform inscriptions at Persepolis were used by the Göttingen teacher G. F. Grotefend in conjunction with Sacy's work on Sasanian and Duperron's edition of the *Avesta*, and in 1805 he published a partial identification of the proper names and titles, reading versions of the names of Darius and Xerxes.[29] This was a great achievement but for twenty years no further advance was made until the Dane Rasmus Rask, who had himself travelled in the Near East, applied a much more developed linguistic understanding to the problem, making full use of the nascent science of comparative philology.[30] This approach was pursued with still greater success by Christian Lassen, in Bonn, in the 1830s,[31] it becoming clear that the Persian cuneiform texts were syllabic, rather than alphabetic; another distinction that would have left Warburton cold. The good linguistic understanding that was developed now only lacked a large body of text to be applied to, and this was provided by the energetic and indefatigable Henry Rawlinson (1810–95), who was stationed in the Near East as a British political officer between 1827 and 1849, and most spectacularly copied the vast cliff-face inscriptions at Bisitun, yielding a quantity of writing which both he and the Dublin clergyman Edward Hincks (1794–1866) were able to decipher (fig. 197).[32]

EPILOGUE

With Rawlinson and Hincks we finally leave the Enlightenment behind and enter a new age. Like Champollion they were heirs of eighteenth-century learning (Hincks literally, as son of the Professor of Hebrew in Belfast), but by specialization and sophistication they helped move matters on. The decipherment of Persian cuneiform opened up other languages written in the same, or similar, script, the majority of them Semitic and thus not related to Persian at all. It also led to a still subtler appreciation of how writing could work, particularly when adopted by language-groups other than those who had invented them. The concept of the 'xenogram', for instance, a foreign word read as a word in one's own language, was to become familiar in the cuneiform scripts of ancient Mesopotamia;

than their original ones, or rejected. The question became suffused (especially in the works of Isaac Taylor) with a form of Darwinian evolutionism; a very different interpretation of descent from the patrimonial one current in the eighteenth century.

Not that the new-found subtlety and sophistication of ideas was universal or immediate. The study of Mayan writing had not benefited directly from the Enlightenment much. The phase of autopsy and record, performed by intrepid travellers (though in the hostile environment of central America they tend to be called explorers), really begins only with Alexander von Humboldt in 1810; the fact that his brother Wilhelm was one of the principal champions of Champollion's decipherment of hieroglyphics emphasizes the temporal disjunction. And though Champollion was to

197 Elamite detail from the trilingual (Old Persian, Elamite and Babylonian) cuneiform inscription of Darius I (521–486 BC) at Bisitun. ANE.

it would have been just as hard to fit into Warburton's scheme as the hieroglyphic 'determinative' was. Less dramatically, notions of the transmission or 'descent' of alphabets were refined, it being appreciated that an alphabet did not need to be taken over wholesale, and that individual letters might be adopted, turned to uses other

be the addressee of an open letter on the analysis of Mayan glyphs from the eccentric adventurer Constantine Rafinesque (1783–1840), this was a conscious and unrequited piece of wishful emulation on the latter's part; Mayan glyphs remained undeciphered until the last two decades of the twentieth century.[33] The reasons are unfortunately all beyond the scope of this chapter, but it is fair to say that it was partly because this branch of the study of writing had its own phases of demystification, classification, application and sophistication to go through.

20

Sacred history?
The difficult subject of religion

JONATHAN WILLIAMS

Claiming to be wise, they became
fools, and exchanged the glory
of the immortal God for images
resembling mortal man, or birds,
or animals, or reptiles.

St Paul, Epistle to the Romans 1.22–3

Until the late seventeenth century, Christian Europe tended to resort to the biblical account of mankind's wilful rejection of the God of Israel to explain the apparent diversity of human religious practice.[1] Two developments opened the way to a new way of thinking. The ferocity of the various religious wars, including the English Civil War, which ravaged Europe during the early seventeenth century provoked a widespread horror of zealotry. This in turn encouraged a more sceptical attitude towards Christian tradition and established forms of belief. Secondly, an ever-increasing amount of information was being published by colonists and travellers about the pagan religions of the Americas, Africa, Asia and the South Seas. This prompted speculation on the question of how they had come to be, and how, if at all, they related to Christian monotheism.

A new generation of religious sceptics set about questioning the accepted traditions of Bible and Church and comparing them, sometimes unfavourably, with other religions. Biblical fable and Christian priestcraft were revealed as having unsettling affinities with paganism both past and present, and little in common with highminded notions of the worship of the one, true God. Free-thinking philosophers also began to develop radical ideas on the origins and nature of religion within their works of social and political theory. As writing on this and all subjects of sceptical inquiry became increasingly specialized, the history of religion itself became a focus for learned speculation, often within the context of a wider historical debate about the origins of humanity and the subsequent peopling of the world. The idea took off that the practices of contemporary primitive societies might provide a window on to the mind and customs of prehistoric peoples, and thus on to the early history of religion.

Despite these profound changes in attitude, nobody in our period was truly able to think or write about the subject of religion without reference to Christianity. Some radicals, such as Voltaire (1694–1778), were willing to jettison the authority of Church and Bible forthwith. Others, like the great British orientalist Sir William Jones (1746–94), tried to reconcile new linguistic evidence for early human history with the traditional framework of biblical narrative. But try as he might to save the sacred uniqueness of Christian tradition from the universal acid of secular rationalism, Christianity could not escape consideration within comparative general accounts of human culture and history.

The British Museum presented one such account to its early visiting public when it opened in 1759. In one of the rooms of the Department of Natural and Artificial Productions were displayed antiquities, Etruscan, Egyptian and Roman, together

198 Pair of wooden portable Buddhist shrines, c. 17th century, brought from Japan by Kaempfer and acquired with his collection by Sir Hans Sloane. JA.

199 Group of Islamic amulets, from the collection of Sir Hans Sloane, inscribed with texts mostly from the Qur'an. The register of his collection reveals that he had them translated into Latin. The Qur'an had recently been translated into Latin by Ludovico Maracci (1698) and into English by Sir George Sale (1734). OA.

with a variety of more recent artefacts including religious objects from around the world. The Museum's first guide book, published in 1761, describes 'American idols' from South and North America, pointing out their similarity to Egyptian figurines as evidence of the supposed peopling of America from the Old World. Japanese pagodas are likened to Roman household shrines (fig. 198). There was also a display of Islamic charms with Arabic inscriptions: 'In these Superstitions the *Mahometans* have great Faith' (fig. 199). Also exhibited were some early Christian amulets, 'with which some superstitious or artful People in the first Ages of Christianity pretended they could cure all diseases'.[2] The inclusion of evidence for superstition even within Christianity is remarkable, and indicative of the new universal scope of the times. Yet superstitious Christianity of the sort represented by the amulets on display was effectively consigned either to antiquity or to the contemporary Roman Catholic world, and thus rendered as alien to the religion of Protestant Britons as that of any pagan from the ancient world or the South Seas.[3]

FROM RELIGIOUS POLEMIC
TO PHILOSOPHICAL SCEPTICISM

For the most part, however, the study of religion was a literary pursuit, based on the evidence of texts, whether ancient scriptures or contemporary travel accounts, rather than arte-facts. In England and France anti-clericalism and rationalism inspired the earliest attempts at formulating general theories that did not simply expand upon biblical tradition. An important early figure in this movement was the Irishman John Toland (1670–1722), who argued in his controversial work *Christianity not Mysterious* (1696) that the baleful influence of priests had caused a primitive monotheism, which he proposed as the original, pure religion of humankind, to decline into paganism. He and others who wrote in the same spirit were collectively known as Deists. Toland favoured a rationalized form of Christianity cleared of fable and mystery, which differed from the established version:

But if any should wonder how Men cou'd leave the direct and easy Path of Reason to wander in such inextricable Mazes, let him but consider how in very many and considerable Regions the plain Institution of JESUS CHRIST cou'd degenerate into the most unintelligible Doctrins, absurd Jargon, ridiculous practises, and inexplicable Mysterys: and how in almost every corner of the world Religion and Truth cou'd be turned into Superstition and Priestcraft.[4]

French writers of the period could be even more bracing in their criticisms of sacred tradition. Pierre Bayle (1647–1706), in his *Dictionnaire historique et critique* (1697, published in English 1710) inveighed against a wide range of religious traditions, both Christian and pagan, revealing the blatant absurdities and immoralities in myths associated with such characters as the Roman god Jupiter and, more boldly, the biblical figure of David. Widely anathematized as an atheist, he was certainly a radical sceptic, even rejecting the Deists' idea of a primitive monotheism in favour of the notion that early man was non-religious. He also argued for religious toleration, even towards atheists, for which he was deprived of his Rotterdam professorship. Voltaire was perhaps less sceptical but more explicitly anti-clerical. Regarding the religious traditions of the East as earlier than those of Israel and Greece and morally superior, in the *Dictionnaire philosophique* (1764) he compared Christianity and, to a lesser extent, Islam, unfavourably with other religions on account of their peculiar propensity for sectarian violence. Like many a later rational humanist, Voltaire attempted in the same work to rescue the person of Jesus himself from Church tradition. In a moving dialogue with the author, Jesus portrays himself as a simple teacher of morality and good-natured monotheism (Voltaire's preferred creed) whose intention was never to found a new religion, yet was cruelly murdered by priests and judges.

This distinction between a primeval monotheism, simple, sublime and ethical, and the various later forms of degenerate priestcraft, both pagan and Christian, would be fundamental to both religious polemic and the writing of the history of religion in the eighteenth century. In an interesting and characteristically idiosyncratic twist, the druidical enthusiast William Stukeley (1687–1765) identified the Deists' notion of an ancient monotheism with the patriarchal religion of Abraham and his descendants (see ch. 17). This, he argued, was in fact true Christianity, brought to and uniquely preserved within England first by the Druids (to whose agency he famously attributed the building of Stonehenge) (fig. 200),[5] and later by the Church of England which was thereby transformed into the unique inheritor of the 'ancient and true religion'.

The great Enlightenment philosophers also weighed into the debate on the nature of religion and exploited the new ethnographic evidence in support of their positions. John Locke (1632–1704), in his *Essay Concerning Human Understanding* (1690), argued that all knowledge is acquired empirically through personal experience, and that the mind is not born supplied with certain ideas and ethical truths, as many believed at the time. He cited evidence for the huge diversity of human custom and religion as evidence to controvert the notion of universally innate knowledge.

It is familiar among the Mingrelians, a people professing Christianity, to bury their children alive without scruple … The virtues whereby the Tououpinambos believed they merited paradise, were revenge, and eating abundance of their enemies. They have not so much as a name for God, and have no religion, no worship. The saints who are canonized amongst the Turks, lead lives which one cannot with

200 Frontispiece and title page to chapter 1 of William Stukeley's *Stonehenge: A Temple Restor'd to the British Druids* (1740), showing his vision of an ancient Druid (see also fig. 170). House of Commons Library.

modesty relate … Where then are those innate
principles of justice, piety, gratitude, equity, chastity?
Or where is that universal consent that assures us there
are such inbred rules?[6]

An increased awareness of the endless variety of religious
practice and opinion married with a new-found suspicion of
Christian 'enthusiasm' (what might now be called dogmatic
fundamentalism) was also productive of religious tolerance.
Like his contemporary Bayle, Locke argued strongly against
official imposition of religious orthodoxy and in favour of
toleration (though not apparently for treacherous Roman
Catholics or faithless atheists), while Toland wrote in support
of the naturalization of the Jews.[7]

In his *Natural History of Religion* (1757) David Hume
(1711–76) deployed the universal occurrence of polytheism
observed among the primitive peoples of the world against
both orthodox Christian and Deist positions. For, he argued,
as there was no positive evidence from present experience of
idolatrous tribes in Africa, America or Asia, it was difficult to
maintain the idea that ancient peoples were natural
monotheists. It was rather unlikely that 'while they were
ignorant and barbarous they discovered truth: But fell into
error [i.e. polytheism] as soon as they acquired learning and
politeness'.[8] His final judgement on the ultimate cause of
human religion was that it 'arises chiefly from the anxious
fear of future events'; and, witheringly, on humankind's religious principles, that it was hard to regard them as other than
'sick men's dreams', or 'the playsome whimsies of monkeys
[*sic*] in human shape'.[9]

WRITING THE HISTORY OF RELIGION:
EXPLAINING VARIETY

Out of religious polemic and the theorizing of philosophers
developed the historical study of religion as a pursuit in its
own right. Among the earliest of its students was the important French savant Bernard Fontenelle (1657–1757), who
wrote extensively on the origins of myths and the evolution
of religious ideas. As he argued in *De l'origine des fables*
(1724), the simple minds of early men were so impressed by
natural forces more powerful than themselves that they made
up fabulous stories and superhuman personalities, gods, to
explain them. This, he argued, was a universal phenomenon
characteristic of all primitive societies with the exception of
the chosen people of Israel. Fontenelle's universal picture of
human mental development also allowed him to draw new
comparisons between Greek and indigenous Peruvian myths
to shed light on the development of early religion. The
Greeks, he argued, had once been as primitive as the natives
of Peru were on their discovery by the Spanish, while the
Peruvians might have become as sophisticated as the Greeks,
had they had the chance. Another early student of the comparative ethnographic method of a different cast of mind was

Joseph Lafitau (1670–1740), a Jesuit missionary in Canada,
who wrote a detailed first-hand account of the religious customs of various native American peoples.[10] His aim was to
discover traces of early monotheism remaining among them,
and to challenge the argument sometimes used by sceptics
and atheists alike that, as primitive people lacked religion, so
religion must be a later human invention and not natural.

The later eighteenth century saw the elaboration of a variety of different theories about the nature and origins of
primitive religion as ethnographic literature increased its
range. French *philosophe* Charles de Brosses (1709–77) proposed that its earliest stages consisted in the worship of inani-
mate objects and animals, fetishes, in his influential work *Du
culte des dieux fétiches* (1760). Comparing the rites and beliefs
of contemporary Africans with what was known of animal
worship among the ancient Egyptians, he argued that this
was a universal phenomenon among primitive peoples. For
him, as for Hume, primitive man was simply savage, and
unable to be saved by the Deists' appeal to an early state of
monotheistic grace. The French scholar and politician
Charles Dupuis (1742–1809) ascribed all religion to nature
worship in his *Origine des tous les cultes* (1795). Adducing
comparative evidence taken from travel literature, Dupuis
interpreted Jesus, along with the Greek heroes Jason and Hercules, as a sun-god. He loathed priest-ridden Christianity and
all forms of religion beset by scriptures and rituals which, he
argued, were merely inventions of fraudulent priests attempting to conceal the truth.

Two English collectors and connoisseurs of antiquities,
both intimately connected with the British Museum in its
early years, Sir William Hamilton (1730–1803) and Richard
Payne Knight (1751–1824) (fig. 201), published works proposing priapism, the worship of the phallus as an emblem of the
creative principle, as the root of all human religious thought,
including Christianity. They were prodigious collectors of
Greek and Roman antiquities amongst which the promi-
nence of sexual symbolism was impossible to ignore, especially since the recent publication of the antiquities recovered
from Herculaneum. Contemporary descriptions and illustrations of similar motifs in Asian, and especially Indian, cults
had prompted speculation on their role in non-classical religion as well.[11] In 1781 Hamilton confirmed in a letter to Sir
Joseph Banks that he had witnessed a survival of the cult of
Priapus on a visit to Isernia in southern Italy. Wax phalli,
dedicated to the local saints by the women of the town, were
brought back to London by Hamilton and given to the
British Museum. These then formed the illustration for the
frontispiece of Knight's *Account of the Remains of the Worship
of Priapus*, published in 1786 (fig. 202).

Knight used the evidence of his collections as the basic
source for his theories, turning only to literary material for
corroboration. This was remarkable for its time. His thesis
was understandably controversial, both because of its content

201 Sir Thomas Lawrence, *Richard Payne Knight*, 1794. The bronze vessel to the right may have been given to him by Charles Townley as it was allegedly found with his Etruscan cista (see fig. 92), which he believed to be connected with an ancient religious ceremony. Whitworth Art Gallery, University of Manchester.

202 Frontispiece to Richard Payne Knight's *An Account of the Remains of the Worship of Priapus … and its Connection with the mystic Theology of the Ancients*, 1786.

and his tendency to what then would have been considered extraordinarily blasphemous opinions. He even suggested that the Christian cross was a phallic symbol. In his characteristically enlightened manner Knight assaulted 'artificial decency' which branded the 'organ of generation' as a 'subject of shame and concealment', defending it as 'a very natural symbol of a very natural and philosophical system of religion'.

Knight also took a variety of other ancient religious symbols which he observed on coins in his collections (fig. 203), including eggs, horns, bulls and goats, as referring to the same principle of reproduction and regeneration:

The incubation of the vital spirit is represented on the colonial medals of Tyre by a serpent wreathed around an egg; for the serpent, having the power of casting his skin, and apparently renewing his youth, became the symbol of life and vigour, and as such is always made an attendant on the mythological deities presiding over health.[12]

Somewhat more fancifully, Hamilton attempted to interpret the Greek coin design of a butting bull as symbolizing the divine power of creation:

The creator, delivering the fructified seeds of things

203 Two Greek coins from Knight's collection with a butting-bull design, and a third-century AD bronze coin of Tyre. The design shows a serpent wrapped round a sacred rock, not an egg as Knight thought. C&M.

from the restraints of inert matter by his divine strength, is represented on innumerable Greek medals by the Urus, or wild Bull, in the act of butting against the Egg of Chaos, and breaking it with his horns. It is true, that the egg is not represented with the bull on any of those which I have seen; but Mr d'Hancarville [French antiquary, 1719–1805, see ch. 13] has brought examples from other countries where the same system prevailed which ... prove that the egg must have been understood, and that the attitude of the bull could have no other meaning.[13]

However implausible the idea, its use of material evidence from Greek and other traditions was unusual for the period.[14] In this Knight diverged significantly from the philological trend of the comparative study of mythology and religion in the late eighteenth and early nineteenth centuries, which drew fresh impetus from the discovery, translation and fabrication of ancient religious texts from Asia and Europe.

New scriptures from antique lands

The publication in 1771 of a French translation of the Zoroastrian *Zend Avesta* by Abraham Hyacinthe Anquetil-Duperron (1731–1805) marked the first arrival of a non-biblical, non-classical religious text in Europe.[15] It was followed by a rapid increase in familiarity with Asiatic languages and translations of Asiatic religious and other texts. In 1784 the Asiatic Society of Bengal was founded at Calcutta to foster oriental studies, and in the next year Sir Charles Wilkins published a translation of the *Bhagavad Gita*, the first Sanskrit text ever translated entire into a European language.[16]

The increased availability of Asiatic religious texts provided new material for those seeking to write the history of early religion and to trace the ultimate origins of all mythological systems. The most brilliant of these was perhaps Sir William Jones (fig. 204), whose expansive and brilliant mind is nowadays best remembered for having first proposed a linguistic relationship between Latin, Greek and Sanskrit. He

204 Sir William Jones (1746–94), stipple engraving by Evans after A. W. Devis, 1798. P&D.

was also among the first to pursue the comparative, philological approach to the study of religion.

Jones became convinced that European and Indian languages shared a common ancestor. So too did the various heathen mythologies of Greece, Italy, India, Egypt, the ancient Near East, and even 'some of the southern kingdoms and even islands of America' which all sprang from a common root 'at the time when they deviated, as they did too early deviate, from the rational adoration of the only, true GOD'.[17] Although he attempted to preserve the distinctiveness of Christianity, in Jones Christian tradition found a defender whose work merely served to undermine it.

In 1810 a comprehensive and illustrated account of Indian deities was published in English by Edward Moor in his *Hindu Pantheon* (1810) (figs 205–206).[18] However, the cult of India as the original cradle of religion really took off in Germany. Friedrich Schlegel (1772–1829), pupil of Herder (see below), was the first German scholar to undertake the study of Sanskrit, and he wrote one of the first detailed studies of Indian philology and mythology.[19] Another crucial figure in the exaltation of India in the German imagination was Friedrich Majer (1772–1818), who worked extensively on Indian religious material and began composing a general

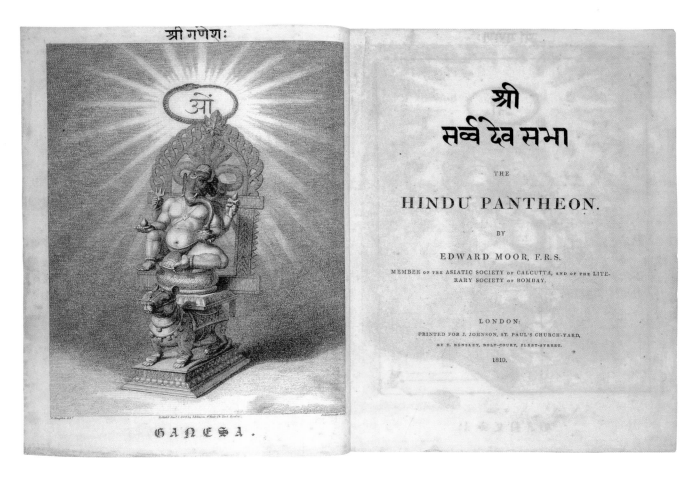

श्री गणेशः

GANESA.

श्री
सर्वे देव सभा

THE

HINDU PANTHEON.

BY

EDWARD MOOR, F.R.S.

MEMBER OF THE ASIATIC SOCIETY OF CALCUTTA, AND OF THE LITE-
RARY SOCIETY OF BOMBAY.

LONDON:
PRINTED FOR J. JOHNSON, ST. PAUL'S CHURCH-YARD,
BY T. BENSLEY, BOLT-COURT, FLEET-STREET.
1810.

mythological lexicon, which was originally intended to collect together the myths of all the peoples of Europe, Asia, America and even Australia.[20]

A further new source of comparative material for the late eighteenth-century student of religion came from the north of Europe. Paul Henri Mallet, a Swiss by birth, was a professor at the University of Copenhagen. In 1756 he published an exposition of the mythology of the Nordic world of the *Eddas*, and introduced its gods, including Odin, Thor and Loki, to a wider European audience.[21] For the first time a mythology from antiquity had been made available which northern Europeans could feel attached to, and even patriotic about. Mallet's work in turn stimulated one of the most important fabrications in the history of European literature, James Macpherson's 'translated' Gaelic epics purportedly by Ossian, first published in 1760. Macpherson claimed to have found the poems, intended as a vindication of Highland culture in the wake of the disastrous Jacobite Rebellion of 1745, preserved in ancient manuscripts and oral tradition. Despite some scepticism as to their authenticity, they were hailed as the north European equivalent of the Greek epic poems of Homer until their final debunking in the late nineteenth century. Translated into several languages, Ossian's literary influence throughout Europe was vast, and its supposed antiquity widely regarded as providing an important new source for natural, pre-institutional religion.[22]

205 Edward Moor, *The Hindu Pantheon*, 1810. The copious illustrations were based on examples from his own collection and others from Charles 'Hindoo' Stuart and the Museum of the East India Company, London. Most eventually came to the British Museum. OA Library.

206 Wooden carving of Krishna, 18th century, south Indian, one of a group of similar carvings owned by Townley and acquired with his collection by the British Museum in 1805. Payne Knight and Ashton Lever also had Indian art in their collections. OA.

Similar religious and poetical forgeries in honour of a freshly minted Welsh antiquity were produced by Edward Williams (1747–1826). This remarkable autodidact and itinerant stonemason both collected and manufactured an ancient literary heritage for the Welsh language. Adopting the bardic name Iolo Morganwg, much as Stukeley had once styled himself Chyndonax the Archdruid, he set about 'reviving' druidic ritual in the form of the Eisteddfod, an open-air meeting of the self-proclaimed Gorsedd ('throne') of bards which first convened within a ready-made stone circle on Primrose Hill in London in 1792.[23] But Williams's druids were rather different from Stukeley's. His were invented in the cause of establishing a distinctively non-Christian, libertarian tradition within Welsh culture (Williams himself was a Unitarian), and they had little in common with Stukeley's proto-Anglican

207 'A Grand Conventional Festival', aquatint. Druids at Stonehenge as imagined by Meyrick and Smith in *The Costume of the Original Inhabitants of the British Isles*, 1815. P&D.

monotheists. Yet Stukeley and Williams were alike in searching for survivals of a prehistoric religion and culture within more recent tradition. They had no other option of course, as there was no authentically ancient evidence for the druids, and the gap between the deep past and the present had to be filled by speculation and invention (fig. 207).

DIFFUSIONISM AND DIVERSITY

The explanatory model generally adopted in universal histories of religion in the eighteenth and early nineteenth centuries still had its roots in the biblical myth of the Tower of Babel. It was widely accepted that the infinite variety of human cultures, languages and religions could be traced back to a single common origin from which, through migration and mutual separation, they had diverged over the course of time. In theory, therefore, the exact location of this origin could be identified through the careful collection of apparent affinities between dissimilar cultures and the establishing of a comparative chronology for their development. India became a popular option for many, especially in Germany, as exem-

plified by the work of Joseph Goerres (1776–1848) and Friedrich Creuzer (1771–1858), both of whom were enthusiastic and influential Indophiles.[24]

More nuanced views and emphases began to develop in opposition to the 'diffusionist' approach. Johann Gottfried von Herder (1744–1803) stressed the distinctness and particularity of different folk traditions rather than their common origins. In 1778 he published an important collection of *Volkslieder* (*Folksongs*) in which he included German, Italian, Estonian, Lettish, Eskimo and Inca folksongs, among many others. In this he was followed by the Brothers Grimm, Jacob (1785–1863) and Wilhelm (1786–1859), whose collection of Germanic folklore (including their famous fairy tales) was intended to establish the uniqueness of Teutonic tradition.

The study of religion based on sound historical and philological evidence emerged as a discipline in its own right in the person of the brilliant German scholar Karl Ottfried Mueller (1797–1840).[25] In his work on Greek mythology and religion he argued against Indic origins and primordial monotheism. Instead Mueller properly located the origins of Greek religion within the development of Greek society.

In Britain Thomas Keightley (1789–1872), a prolific Irish writer on religion and mythology, inveighed most judiciously against the naive diffusionism of a previous age:

I will freely confess, that I see little strength in the arguments for the original unity of mankind, founded on a similarity of manners, customs and social institutions; and am inclined to reject these arguments, when brought forward in proof of migrations and colonization ... There were Vestals at Rome, and Virgins of the Sun at Cuzco; yet it does not follow from thence that Peru derived its religion from Asia, or that, as I have seen it asserted, Rome was founded by a colony of Gypsies from India.[26]

Yet the Enlightenment view of the early history of religion lingered on long enough to imprint itself permanently on the fabric of the new British Museum, in the form of the sculpted figures on the pediment over the main entrance. Executed by Richard Westmacott and installed in 1851, the tableau is entitled *The Progress of Civilization* (fig. 208). Westmacott described his work thus in words later expanded by Sir Henry Ellis, Principal Librarian of the British Museum (1827–56):

> Commencing at the Eastern end ... man is represented as emerging from a rude savage state, through the influence of religion. He is next personified as a hunter, and a tiller of the earth ... Patriarchal simplicity then becomes invaded and the worship of the true God defiled ... Paganism prevails and becomes diffused by means of the Arts ...[27]

By the time the sculptures were in place, the view of human history which they represented was becoming obsolete.

CONCLUSION: AFTER ENLIGHTENMENT

Later nineteenth-century scholars tended to abandon the notion that human nature is essentially the same everywhere and at all times, and side-stepped the quest to derive religious and cultural variety from an illusory original unity. They were more given to pluralist accounts of the early history of religion, and to concentrating on the folklore of their own lands, thereby implicitly rejecting the comparative approach, at least in its diffusionist form. Furthermore, the gradual recognition over the nineteenth century that human history actually went back much further than the six thousand years or so offered by traditional biblical chronologies interposed a new gulf between Genesis and the present. This made most recent learned attempts at sketching humanity's cultural genealogy look rather jejune. It took the rise of archaeology to provide a new way into the deep past of human mental and material development. Yet the elusive quest for ancient origins and lost connections underlying human cultural diversity still lives on in the writings of such modern luminaries as Thor Heyerdahl and Graham Hancock.[28] Their books and films on submarine civilizations and ancient explorers enjoy a popularity far outstripping the works of academic archaeologists and prehistorians. The scholars have proceeded into learned obscurity, but the general public is still happily basking in the afterglow of Enlightenment.

208 *The Progress of Civilization*, watercolour design for the sculptures in the pediment over the main entrance to the British Museum, by Richard Westmacott, 1851. P&D.

PART V

VOYAGES OF DISCOVERY

209 William Bullock's 'unique exhibition of ancient Mexico',
in the Egyptian Hall, Piccadilly, 1824, lithograph of the interior
after Augustin Aglio (detail). Large plaster casts of Aztec
monuments dominate the space, and copies of codices are hung
around the walls. Many of the smaller antiquities were purchased
for the British Museum in 1825. Ethno Library.

21 Venture to the exterior

BRIAN DURRANS

Everyone now living inherits an ancestry as long and illustrious as anyone else's, no matter whether or how it is recorded. In the making or the telling, history was never a monopoly of Europe; and travellers' tales, whatever their claims to objectivity, were no more value-free than the narratives or impressions of their hosts. Those whom Europeans met on their expeditions also met Europeans.

The last chapters in this book detail several such encounters from various parts of the world. They do not just refer to non-European viewpoints but also remind us that those who, at different times and in different places, 'represented' Europe, or particular European countries, were themselves individuals as well as historical agents. If Europeans and non-Europeans are unlikely to have had such ideas uppermost in their minds as they negotiated with each other, it is perhaps equally unlikely that none of them ever registered that such an encounter worked both ways. Longer and better acquaintance taught that, regardless of attributes shared with those of their background culture, other people were also individuals with distinctive personalities of their own.

PEOPLE STUDYING PEOPLE: A CHANGING AGENDA

Academic disciplines are often suspicious of subjective experience, and it is only from the mid-1980s that insights of this kind have started to become incorporated into mainstream anthropological or ethnographic thinking. In the hands of Enlightenment intellectuals the concrete, reflexive or reciprocal aspects of such encounters were bypassed in favour of grand theory about humanity's place in nature. Rather than 'the European encounter with the Other', specialists (who include a growing number from former colonies, whether calling themselves anthropologists, sociologists or cultural historians) now study more closely what actually happens when people meet across cultural boundaries.

With this shift of focus – itself prompted by geopolitical change – has come the reinvention of ethnography as an academic pursuit with implications for other means to cultural knowledge. Once largely a description of distinctive and traditional cultural facts based on 'participant-observation' fieldwork among a group of people in a particular place, ethnography still values objective reporting but is now more alert to the constructed and contested character of 'facts'; the personal experience of the enquirer and of informants (who are increasingly acknowledged as collaborators); local change and globalization as factors transforming or redefining tradition; and cultural understanding as only ever provisional because based on incomplete evidence.

Linked to this is a growing awareness that, however provisional they are and whether published in an academic paper, book, television programme, exhibition or lecture, the results of ethnographic enquiry should not be treated as the exclusive property of the ethnographer but are also of legitimate interest to those in the community concerned and their co-citizens and representatives. It is now increasingly necessary (and often more rewarding intellectually) for fieldwork and its outcomes to be conducted as part of a planned, collaborative programme from which all participants can expect definable benefits – a radical contrast to the conditions for philosophical speculation in eighteenth-century Europe.

Like any other discipline, ethnography approaches its subject – the different ways of life of human societies – with a mixture of objectivity and self-interest. We tend to think of eighteenth-century European views of the world as responses to unprecedented new discoveries, and so they were; but they were still limited by gaps in knowledge, of less familiar or unknown regions, of local communities and the lower orders of complex societies less easily discerned through trade, missionization or conquest. In that setting, what could Ethnography amount to? Enlightenment minds, like any others, traded in categories by means of which order and therefore meaning was imposed on the apparent chaos of facts. Stock images took significance not from their accuracy as representations of how people actually were, but rather from how well they suited their inventors. And yet this was also an age of self-conscious rationality and of new contacts abroad. Literary figures slowly and casually began to be compared with graphic images, with an increased variety of reported and recorded observations made at first hand (fig. 210),

210 Sir Joseph Banks, mezzotint by J. R. Smith after Benjamin West, 1773. Here Banks displays some of the items he collected on Cook's first voyage on the *Endeavour*. He described the taniko border of the Maori cape as being woven with 'an ingenuity truly surprising'. The Tahitian ceremonial headdress to his left was donated to the British Museum during the 18th century, perhaps by Banks himself. Ethno.

211 A selection of objects associated with Cook's Pacific voyages: a stone pounder for breadfruit and an adze from the Society Islands, a wooden hand from Rapa Nui (Easter Island), bone fish-hook, feather lei and sample of decorated barkcloth from Hawaii. The Maori handclub on the right was made in New Zealand of basalt. On the left is a brass replica made for Joseph Banks (see ch. 23). Ethno.

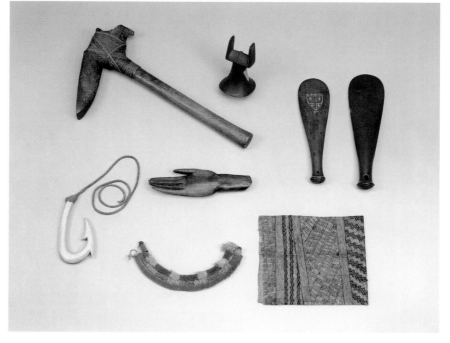

and sometimes with actual individuals brought back, perhaps inevitably, as curios. Vastly expanding the documentation of elsewhere were multiplying descriptions and images of objects, and of objects themselves; and these, whether or not they were thought wonderful (as many indeed were), served as sober evidence of other ways of life (fig. 211). This did not mean that some objective Truth was suddenly revealed, for the older assumptions about differences of culture and moral worth, set in feudalist terms, were being nudged aside by newer versions which spoke of rights and freedoms, terms more appropriate to the consumer society then taking shape in western Europe which would then be in the vanguard of a model of economic and moral progress in which others were assigned their appropriate places. Perhaps not surprisingly, the objects of others neither supported nor denied the constructions of such propaganda; neither the objects nor their original makers spoke for themselves but were at every turn interpreted. However attractive such items were – advertising the expansive interests of their (new) owners – owners and networks, exhibitors and audiences, did not necessarily see them in the same ways. Here at last, and on an expanding scale, was a body of material evidently made by, and therefore representing, formerly mythologized others, regardless of what scholars or collectors or propagandists might have to say.

Such polarities as we/them, explorer/discovered, nation/tribe, urban/rural, literate/oral, centre/periphery, east/west mask shared participation in expanding relationships and processes (fig. 212). Misleading they may be but, by guiding or rationalizing action, the influence of such categories is real enough. Orientalism is perhaps the clearest example of them all. Its core dogma – that east and west are measured on different scales (in Kipling's phrase, 'never the twain shall meet') – is flawed by the fact that except for abstract ones on maps, most borders are porous, whether on the ground or, to which Kipling was probably alluding by way of metaphor, in the mind. Those living on opposite sides of a border usually have more in common with each other than either has with compatriots further away. If the cultural borderline between east and west is hardly the Greenwich meridian, an alternative through the Bosphorus is no less arbitrary. Most people – east or west, north or south – tend to interact with others for their own reasons, even if not in circumstances of their own choosing. Kipling was right, metaphorically: the whole point about east and west as cultural labels – that is, as cultural constructs of the mind – is the contrast between

212 Geisha, watercolour by Kawahara Keiga (dates unknown), who produced hundreds of images of Japanese plants, animals, genre scenes and portraits in the 1820s. The strongly western-influenced style of Keiga reflects the fact that he was commissioned and tutored by Philipp Franz von Siebold (1796-1866), an influential German-born Japanologist active in the middle of the 19th century. JA.

them; bring them together and the contrast collapses since, as the experiences of translocated peoples repeatedly prove, in such matters nothing is so liable to change as 'essential' or 'immutable' human nature. Ideas of change undermine claims to authority even in the religious idiom where the intentions of the Almighty are subject to lively debate. If the world is no one's chessboard, it is no longer legitimate to play chess on it. When individuals, classes or nations no longer owe privilege to God or Nature, their critics become more assertive. The pretence of English exclusivity, for example, has rarely been more savagely attacked than by Daniel Defoe in 1703:

> Thus from a mixture of all kinds began
> That heterogeneous thing an Englishman …
> We have been Europe's sink, the jakes where she
> Voids all her offal outcast progeny …
> Fate jumbled them together. God knows how;
> Whate'er they were, they're true-born English now.[1]

When privilege follows pedigree, and pedigree is shown to be a matter of historical jumbling, then privilege becomes historically determined and therefore open to amendment. What then of appeals to destiny, whether God-given or 'natural', or of the rhetorical personalization of nations or groups of nations ('Britain'; 'The West') as if such complex identities can behave as single individuals?

SELF AND OTHERS; WINNERS AND LOSERS

Abstractions aside, it is only ever particular individuals who make and sustain (or break) contact with each other, and only through their agency that we can imagine institutions, cultures, peoples, nations, continents or hemispheres doing so. Such meetings, like the images which they endorse or initiate, tend to be neither neutral nor primordial. Stereotypes unquestioned in one age are often rejected in another. Brief encounters are followed sooner or later by more prolonged contact. Strangers are almost always moving in next door. Outsiders covet your land, your labour, your soul. You may want their exotic objects as much as they want yours. Europeans may once have been a novelty in your part of the world, but for your predecessors they were seldom the first strangers anyway. Practically everywhere discovered by Europeans in the last few hundred years had already been discovered, usually much earlier, by someone else.

After our distant ancestors left their African homeland, few groups ended up in complete isolation, and in favourable environments secondary expansions reintegrated peoples as well as redistributing them. However extensive your social network, there are usually strangers to be reckoned with along trade routes or in the next town or village or temporary encampment. Rules for dealing with familiar outsiders, whether real or imagined, are then applied to less familiar ones, including, in due course, Europeans, who returned the compliment by fitting non-Europeans into pre-existing templates

213 'Smoking god from Palenque', lithograph from Viscount Kingsborough's *Antiquities of Mexico* (1831–48), pl. 40. The artist has 'westernized' the original Mayan style of these reliefs by adding three-dimensional shading and altering the anatomy and figures. Ethno Library.

of their own (fig. 213). If past actions in favourable circumstances cumulatively benefit my group rather than yours, I may be inclined to explain my good fortune by denigrating your group's achievements and perhaps also by claiming some innate superiority. History as a dominant account of the past is written by winners. This makes it hard to imagine what 'history' might look like to those judged to be losers.

From a European view, Asia participates in such encounters sooner than the Americas, north Africa before central and south Africa, and all of these before the Pacific. Yet such a view is misleading in several respects. Whether or not they wrote about it, cultures of the ancient world expanded, contracted, coalesced or fragmented according to their circumstances. All through the medieval period and the Renaissance up to the Enlightenment, while Europe imagined itself as discovering new parts of whatever it understood as the world, cultures elsewhere were simultaneously discovering or rediscovering each other. This they did both in their own backyards and across greater or lesser domains through trade, warfare or religious conversion, linking areas and regions in some cases earlier and more widely than European newcom-

ers were first able to do. Like those within Europe, and between Europe and non-European others, the relations which peoples in all continents developed among themselves were sometimes more, sometimes less stable, and included every variety of asymmetry and approximate equality. For most of the world, the record of such relations, if available at all, is preserved in the ground (and sometimes in museum collections) rather than in written history. Something of it can also be glimpsed, if problematically, in the languages, cultural patterns and biological signatures of contemporary populations. Although each kind of evidence of past interactions between peoples needs its own kind of interpretation, taken together they undermine the self-image of Europe as discoverer of the world.

Europe itself was far from a single entity either before or after the European 'age of discovery'. No single political interest was ever able to dominate the continent wholly or for very long, although the Romans and later perhaps the Vatican were the most successful in both respects. If Europe's constituent nation states were relatively autonomous, each of them was also divided internally by region, religion or class. Wealth and power motivated relations within and between states but always with reference to norms and categories that defined humanity or citizenship, and therefore the behaviour considered appropriate towards particular groups. Exploitation and interpretation were part of the same process of encountering particular peoples, whether close to hand or further afield. The general task of religion or philosophy was to provide respectable justification for what soldiers, politicians or entrepreneurs wanted to do, although there was sometimes a degree of objective reporting and, more rarely, dissent. Julius Caesar's notes on the customs of the British or the Gauls went beyond military necessity, and Tacitus wrote a reasonably dispassionate ethnography of at least some of the German tribes in the northern part of the Roman empire. From the fifteenth century onwards, as leading European powers began to look overseas for commercial advantage, models for how to deal with and interpret newly encountered others were to be found in Europe itself. Britain's earliest colonization of Ireland, for example, generated stereotypes no less dehumanizing than those later used in reference to Africans, while the expulsion of the Moors from the Iberian peninsula and the prolonged eradication or assimilation of the indigenous Guanches of the Canary Islands, were a rehearsal for the Spanish conquest of the Americas.

But such models could keep pace with neither new encounters abroad nor the changing political and intellectual milieu of Europe itself. In the eighteenth century, European views of Asia, for example, were subject to massive revision. Up to the end of the seventeenth century, most British and European interests in Asia were focused on the Near East (figs 214–15). Intellectual enquiry was constrained by excessive reliance on biblical and classical sources, which were of course preoccupied with this part of the world, and therefore by the delusion that most of its present condition could be explained by reference to books. A century later this notion was turned on its head. During the eighteenth century, as the British and the French encountered and began to come to terms with the almost wholly unfamiliar cultures of India, it became apparent that new and systematic observation, rather than books alone, would be the necessary basis for a durable administration. Not even the translation and scholarly study of classical Indian texts could account for the complexity of Indian society. With the need came the means. The level of British involvement in the subcontinent, together with local labour, provided the bureaucratic infrastructure for gathering social and economic data on an unprecedented scale, the use of which helped, at least in the short term, to strengthen British control. Different approaches were necessary in China, where Europeans had to contend with a single, hierarchical state which restricted them as far as possible to the status of trading

214 & 215 'Sultan Moradbax [Moradbakhsh]' (left) and 'Mahmud Edelshar [Adilstah], King of Vilapur [Bijapur]' (right), from Sloane's album of Indian (*Deccani*) miniatures, acquired to provide information on costumes and customs of people from other parts of the world, much as he collected specimens that would provide him with information on the natural history of the world. OA.

partners (figs 216–17). No network of on-the-spot observations could be developed as it had been in India, but if European stereotypes of Indians were just as insulting, they were at least less monolithic than those created for the Chinese.

There was no simple expansion of 'Europe' into the rest of the world. Several European countries sought to advance in foreign trade what they or at least some of their citizens saw as their short- or longer-term interests. The agents who carried their own and others' changing demands and interpretations beyond their homelands operated in competition with others, each within a more or less circumscribed territory. Up

216 Chinese porcelain serving dish (c. 1715–22) with *famille verte* enamels showing the coat of arms of Lord Archibald Hamilton, the father of Sir William Hamilton who is known to have used this service while Ambassador to Naples (1764–1800). OA.

217 Pair of covered *en grisaille* enamel and gold painted cups showing the arms of Sir Joseph Banks, probably commissioned after Banks came into his parental fortune in 1764 and before he married in 1779. The shape of the cups derives from English silverware and the arms are copied from a printed bookplate. OA.

to the mid nineteenth century, national and commercial interests increasingly converged as competition between rival European nations intensified, creating the colonial system as a more or less integrated and territorially based commercial and political enterprise. But such interests came together earlier in the establishment of chartered companies, mainly from the beginning of the seventeenth century.

FROM CHARTERED COMPANIES
TO IMPERIAL POWER

A chartered company was essentially a joint stock company (a group of traders operating as a unit with shared finances) granted monopoly privileges by the state. Subject to government supervision, it might be allowed to colonize a certain territory as well as to sign treaties, make laws and enforce them by independent military means. Such outfits were largely free to conduct their own business, but their very emergence hinted at rivalry between their sponsoring nations in the pursuit of foreign trade. Although in some ways anticipating the modern transnational corporation in its flexible cross-border operations, the chartered company was still ultimately dependent on a particular nation state. This is illustrated by the readiness with which governments took over companies which were either failing commercially or no longer served the interests of their sponsors – as happened, for example, to a number of British, French and Dutch chartered companies in the Caribbean and eastern North America. Conversely, companies were free to make deals which would have been inappropriate between governments. In the later seventeenth century, for example, the Royal Africa Company entered into long-term contracts with the Spanish for supplying African slaves to the Caribbean even though the slave trade itself was commercially uncertain and for this reason often combined with smuggling of goods. Attracted by the prospect of Spanish silver, the British and French governments could afford to conduct such business at arm's length, transferring risk to their chartered proxies.

The (British) East India Company was originally created to end the Dutch monopoly on the Indonesian spice trade but concentrated on India after the Dutch killed British merchants at Amboina in 1623. Once a nation (or its chartered company) enjoyed a substantial advantage over its rivals in pursuing and consolidating its overseas trade – as the British had over the French by the end of the eighteenth century, for example – the balance could not be redressed by commercial competition alone. Napoleon's military occupation of Egypt in 1789 was designed to block trade routes and, in due course, to displace the British from India. That attempt was short-lived but makes the point that, once they became established, trade monopolies sometimes gave rise not to trade wars but to real ones. It was also in the last quarter of the eighteenth century that James Cook explored the Pacific. Although he

was alert to economic opportunities, the voyages themselves were undertaken not by or for a commercial company but on behalf of the Admiralty or the state. At least in one respect, commercial nous in the form of market testing could have saved considerable wasted effort (and subsequently delayed Marlon Brando's rise to stardom). As President of the Royal Society, Joseph Banks, one of Cook's most distinguished travelling companions, proposed introducing recently discovered Polynesian breadfruit to the Caribbean as food suitable for slaves. Ironically, after William Bligh successfully transferred the plant from Tahiti to the West Indies (his first attempt, on the *Bounty*, ended in the famous mutiny immortalized by Hollywood), those for whom it was intended found it not to their taste and for half a century it was fed instead to pigs. In this venture, as with the establishment in 1778 of the British penal colony in Australia at Botany Bay, government did not rely on trading companies, even with charters, to conduct its business. Indeed, at this point, 'national interest' was not yet clearly formulated and was still developing through arguments in which commerce did not always have the loudest voice.

The first chartered companies were established by the British and Dutch and later by the French. Among the more important of the British companies were: the Royal Africa Company (founded in 1672), the East India Company (1600), the Russia (Muscovy) Company (1553), and the Hudson's Bay Company (1670). The Dutch East India Company was established in 1602, the French East India Company in 1664 and the Russian American Company in 1799. Finding faster (and therefore more profitable) routes between Europe and Asia was a key motive in founding the Hudson's Bay and Muscovy Companies. The latter failed to find the elusive North East passage from Europe to Asia but helped establish overland trade routes to Persia. The Hudson's Bay Company was more successful in finding the North West passage but concentrated on controlling trade and colonizing in the Hudson Bay area itself.

In Britain the conduct of chartered companies was regularly criticized in parliamentary debate, in the press and in taverns and coffee-houses. Through their chartered (and therefore public) status private companies were enabled not only to make profits but crucially also, by investing in infrastructure and local politics, to ensure their future profitability in competition with European rivals, a risk-management gambit tending towards a monopoly of trade. Some were simply eclipsed by international deals or out-manoeuvred by their rivals but most were wound up once the cumulative investment in a colonial territory required the more substantial resources of the nation state to defend it. The legacy of chartered companies was sometimes loftily impugned by those pleased to redeploy it on behalf of formal empires. Thenceforth, until the nemesis of old-style colonialism in the mid twentieth century, the main way for an existing power to increase its colonial profits (apart from applying more efficient technology) was to take over the colonies of another. By that time, however, immediate economic advantage was not always guaranteed, and colonial relations became increasingly an arena of political debate in which strategic calculations – sometimes posing as national pride – might overshadow and even contradict economic ones.

Once superior trade routes were opened up and entrepots established, they had to be defended. Such thinking later made growing appeal to patriotic sentiment. National interest in colonial policy was buttressed, and later sometimes almost completely displaced, by wider or vaguer justifications, such as serving God, fulfilling destiny, bestowing enlightenment, or increasing knowledge. Although explorers may have been driven by a desire for knowledge and perhaps glory, their sponsors were certainly alive to the commercial or strategic advantages which such endeavours might deliver. In pursuing their sponsored dreams in the name of their own nation state and its own version of God, explorers also pushed back the frontiers of knowledge in the name of humanity. A Genesis-based insistence that everyone shared a common humanity as descendants of Adam may have done as little for peoples and races exploited overseas as it did for the majority at the bottom of European societies themselves. It was certainly not inconsistent with slavery, which was not formally abolished until 1807, even if, for the British, industrial development was by then more lucrative to British interests than overseas plantations.

The Atlantic slave trade

The Atlantic slave trade highlights several key aspects of European encounters with and exploitation of other peoples. Firstly, it was undertaken in competition with other operators, especially the Dutch and French in the late seventeenth century. Secondly, it could not have been established or perpetuated without the active participation of some non-Europeans whose own fortunes were affected by it (and reinforcing the point that other continents were internally at least as divided as Europe itself). British and other European traders were supplied with slaves by coastal intermediaries who raided or traded with hinterland communities on their own account. Such intermediaries became heavily militarized, and the slave trade fuelled political realignments among them and their inland partners or subsidiaries, not least because the demand for slaves impacted directly on local production, which forced suppliers to rely increasingly on European trade goods and thus on European commerce as architect of the Atlantic slave trade. Ultimately these pressures encouraged the formation of hierarchical states out of lineage-based polities. Thirdly, like most other examples of economic initiative, the slave trade was engaged in opportunistically, geared at least in part to the politics of the American

continent. The specific geographical and cultural factors behind British colonists' use of African slaves in the Americas included their use in preference to Native Americans since it was feared that adjacent groups would encourage Native slaves to escape, and that such an arrangement would threaten the loyalty of Britain's Native allies against the French or Spanish. Fourthly, state sponsorship of private enterprise can be withdrawn if justified by circumstances and incentives. Established in 1672, the London-based Royal Africa Company had by 1710 yielded in the Atlantic slave trade to private trading concerns working first out of Bristol and later Liverpool. Fifthly, the slave trade with West and Central Africa created a large new market for goods made in Britain and benefited not only manufacturers but also those who provisioned the slave ships in both their home and visiting ports. If its impact on domestic British production was insufficient to 'cause' or 'facilitate' the industrial revolution itself, the Atlantic slave trade may well have been an important contributory factor.

Yet the particular history and geography of this enterprise no more expresses some 'iron law' of economics than some flaw in so-called human nature, and arguments and principles were as integral to the whole business as profits and suffering and greed. The rhetoric which paved the way for free market capitalism – above all John Locke's works published in the 1690s – broke decisively with the principle that social fortune was given by God or nature. If against the dead hand of traditional wisdom it was now possible to argue, fiercely, that human destiny was (largely) determined by human action, then slavery, however profitable, stood condemned, with an equivalent passion, as denying the self-determination of others. Such arguments did not so much circumvent God, however, as put enlarged scope for human initiative within His remit. A state paper of 1655 (which may have been drafted by Milton) proclaimed that 'since God hath made of one blood all nations of men … on earth, … all great and extraordinary wrongs done to particular persons ought to be considered as in a manner due to all the rest of the human race'. Powerful expressions of this kind, though rooting the unity of mankind in Christian doctrine and certainly inspiring generations of anti-slavery campaigners, did not deter a host of parallel iniquities by Christians in Christian nations. Slavery would probably not have been abolished by morality if its economic attractiveness had not already been on the wane.

Cultures and understanding

To talk of a people's culture without regard to the people themselves is to misunderstand both, for there never was one without the other. Such misunderstanding is especially egregious if it sidelines people's own interpretations of the rules and apparatus by which they live; but a condition for sharing other people's assumptions is adjusting your own. The legacy of Europe's exploitative dealings with the rest of the world (notwithstanding those within its own borders or those long and still conducted by non-Europeans themselves) can be measured not only in salient disparities in the quality and quantity of life but also more subtly in misunderstanding – above all, in Europeans' almost total failure to know others on other than European terms. Above all, a culture – any culture – is a working arrangement, and not even the most exhaustive description can do full justice to its dynamic complexity. Anyone describing it from the inside is one of the interested parties on whom any outsider must depend; and no description can ever capture the culture as actually experienced, not least because how a culture is characterized for others is itself shaped by its own biases. But if a culture ultimately cannot be pinned down like a butterfly, it is usually possible to distinguish between more or less comprehensive descriptions and more or less convincing interpretations. The same applies to any attempt to evaluate cultures comparatively (or 'culture' in the abstract), independently of how people would assess their own.

No comprehensive roster of cultural achievement – such as the British Museum might claim to be – can possibly restrict itself to those cultures associated with monumental architecture, writing, durable artworks or some kind of technological progress, nor indeed to the past at the expense of the present. Not everyone has what others may regard as a 'respectable' culture, but there was never a culture that did not include language. Languages epitomize, even if they hardly encompass, the cultural differences between peoples; and although some agents of a dominant power may (need to) learn to speak with dominated others, languages in an unequal relationship generally adapt more radically upward than down. English is recognizably enriched by thousands of words and phrases lifted from the speech of imperial subjects; but it is the latter who had to adopt not just vocabulary but, in large measure also, metaphors and grammatical structures, and with these, European ideas of what it was relevant to say. If this was obviously an unequal exchange, reflecting disparities of power and wealth, it should also be clear that a Eurocentric understanding so dear to the hearts of explorers and their sponsors, and of missionaries, merchants, administrators, archaeologists, linguists, historians, geographers, anthropologists, curators, collectors and World Bank consultants, is in the long term as deficient for Europeans as it is for

everyone else. To overlook such dimensions of authentic selves as syntax, values, implicit cosmological assumptions, significances and insignificances, is inevitably to diminish understanding. When in the middle of the last century Laurens van der Post wrote in his book *Venture to the Interior* (1951) about his travels in the Kalahari Desert, the 'interior' was (he implied) that of his own mind, as well as of the African continent. But neither travelling salespeople, nor explorers, nor their successors like Laurens van der Post, ever really reached other people's minds; there was never in this sense a venture to the interior, however far they (or their bearers) penetrated inland. The world was only ever imagined even by those who thought they knew it.

To understand the interactions and iniquities that took place between dominant and dominated peoples up to and during the colonial era, it is necessary to realize that the colonial or proto-colonial process neither initiated nor ended the history of inhumanity, exploitation or ideological misrepresentation. The legacy of colonialism is a potent force in contemporary politics precisely because the distribution of power and wealth in the world is still skewed along colonial lines, now rephrased as the north–south divide. Colonial history cannot be undone by reallocating peoples, products or ideas to where they were before – even if that could be determined – because neither people, thoughts nor things remain what they were. On the contrary, people create new experiences and contexts as they shed others, producing new cultural configurations and people with new perspectives and aspirations.

No settlement of historical accounts is possible, then, outside post-colonial conditions. But to change the world without repeating past mistakes or injustices demands an understanding of everyone's past and present, not just of the West. That certainly means a – provisional – overview of the world's cultures from some inevitably privileged yet practicable vantage-point (museum, encyclopaedia, documentary television series, website); but it also means trying to learn about cultures from the inside, where culture is everyone's lived experience and as normal as breathing. Pursued as resolutely through co-operation as former ventures were competitive, that kind of learning promises forms of knowledge appropriate to present and future times – and, as Enlightenment scholars well understood in the eighteenth century, knowledge is power.

Romancing the Americas: public expeditions and private research c. 1778–1827

J. C. H. KING

Museums are slow to change, but when change occurs it happens quickly. In biological terms the late Stephen Jay Gould called this process 'punctuated evolution': changes occur swiftly but are followed by long periods of stability. At the British Museum the first collection, that of the founder Sir Hans Sloane, included two thousand items of ethnography, called 'Misceallanies'.[2] From the 1750s until 1780 these objects were displayed in a very mixed cabinet style – antiquities and ethnography (then called 'artificial curiosities') muddled and mixed without arrangement (see ch. 10). In 1780, after the death of Captain James Cook, a South Seas Room was established to display the collections, Oceanic and American, acquired during the European exploration of the Pacific during the previous fifteen years. This was the first systematic display of 'artificial curiosities' in the British Museum. By 1790, when Sir Joseph Banks was issuing these instructions to Menzies, the display of objects with those from similar, or geographically close, cultures was a given aspect of Museum display. Earlier, on the other hand, Sloane had acquired his American artefacts as marginal additions little connected to his primary interest in botany. Collector artists, such as Mark Catesby, would acquire specimens and watercolours for Sloane, and add in, perhaps as an afterthought, an article of Cherokee clothing or basketry. After this first paradigmatic change in display techniques, the aim of expeditions was to enquire into the 'degree' of civilization rather than simply obtain passively, by chance, curiosities.

In the late eighteenth and early nineteenth century the British Museum benefited from a series of official expeditions to the Americas. Almost all of these were associated with Sir Joseph Banks.[3] Banks came from a rich and intellectually independent family. From an early age he was a passionate botanist and collector. Able to afford a self-directed education at Oxford and in London, he became from the 1760s involved with the British Museum and the young Swedish scientist Daniel Solander, pupil of Carl Linnaeus.[4] In 1766 Banks left for his first field trip to North America – Newfoundland and Labrador. This only modestly successful visit was rapidly followed by his participation in Cook's First Pacific Voyage of 1768–71 (see fig. 210). Although Banks never visited the Americas again, he sat, after becoming President of the Royal Society, for the rest of his life at the centre of government scientific policy-making. He was particularly influential in encouraging exploration, economic botany and zoology. As such his office-home acted as clearing house both for ethnographic collections, a very modest adjunct to his other activities, and as a starting place for the careers of ambitious scientists. In terms of the Pacific North America he acquired important ethnography from Cook's Third Voyage (1776–80) for the British Museum. He also

218 *A View in King George's Sound* (now Nootka Sound, Vancouver Island), pen and ink and watercolour drawing by John Webber, 1778. The Mowachahts with pikes or lances are wearing twined capes and cloaks of nettle fibre and yellow cedar bark, with a dug-out canoe of red cedar alongside. P&D.

oversaw the career of the botanist Archibald Menzies in the 1780s and 1790s. In particular Banks channelled the official collection from California and the Pacific Northwest from Vancouver's voyage of 1791–5 to the British Museum. Banks's last American achievement was to foster Arctic exploration during the global warming period of the 1810s, an interest of the Admiralty which continued to result in new Arctic collections for the Museum up until the 1870s.

THE NORTHWEST COAST OF AMERICA

Cook's Third Voyage was designed to determine whether or not there existed a Northwest Passage through North America, a fabled route that would enable traders to travel rapidly to the rich markets of Asia.[5] In 1778–9 the expedition visited Vancouver Island and Alaska and reported that there was no passage through the continent. The expedition, however, recorded much valuable information, made collections and at least on Vancouver Island was remembered in Native mythology. There Cook was involved in disciplined, profitable trade with the Mowachaht people – Natives benefiting from iron and ornaments, and the Europeans from naval supplies, and sea otter pelts which were sold on with great gain, privately, in China.[6]

Cook's account is quite straightforward. He sailed from Hawai'i to the American coast and put into a large inlet off Vancouver Island in March 1778. There he replenished water and grass for the animals, and replaced a mast. The people encountered, the Mowachaht (fig. 218), 'people of the deer', greeted the European expedition effusively, ceremonially and with great respect. Dug-out canoes filled with Natives approached the ships, the Natives sang and gave speeches. They accompanied their greetings with rattles in the form of birds and with offerings of eagle down. Another very significant ritual was performed later on when a number of people visited Cook in his cabin and left him with a screen and a number of masks. These people were great, even formidable traders. Cook found he had to pay for everything: water, the new mast and fish of course. When they went to cut grass for the expedition animals he complained that he thought he was going to have to pay for each blade of grass individually. They visited the village at Yuquot, or Windy Cove, and went into one of the houses, where the Anglo-Swiss official expedition artist (John Webber) drew the scene. At the back of the house were two large screens carved with figures, probably from lineage or family mythology. These represent a category of object later misleadingly named 'totem' poles by John Muir the Scottish-American naturalist in 1879. The Natives covered up the figures, forcing Webber to pay for the privilege of depicting them with the buttons from his coat – only when he had cut them all off was he allowed to draw in peace.

The Native view of these circumstances is rather different. The Mowachaht are one of twenty or so distinct peoples, collectively called the Nuu-chah-nulth, living along the 250 miles of the west coast of Vancouver Island between Cape Cook and Point No Point. Each was originally a loose confederacy, formed through conquest and alliance, with ranked chiefs, the most senior of whom possessed distinct rights in land resources, and in non-material rights: to songs, names, dances and traditions, *tuupaati*. The great resources of the coast, including particularly different species of salmon, and other fish such as herring, provided bountiful supplies of food – access to which was owned by specific chiefs. Yuquot is a summer village used for fishing various species in season. A Native tradition recorded by Winifred David in the 1970s suggests that the explorers were seen as salmon, representatives of the salmon people from the sea, personification of fish and symbols of wealth and status. It was put like this: 'they went out to the [Cook's] ship and they thought it was a fish come alive into people ... One white man had a real hooked nose ...

one of the men was saying ... "See ... he must have been a dog salmon, that guy he's got a hooked nose".'[7]

Appropriately then the Natives treated Cook's expedition with the respect due to food resources, and also exploited these strange salmon people in trade. Traditionally the first salmon of each run every year was ceremonially treated. The whole of the first catch 'were laid on mats in the chief's house. The owner of the trap [i.e. the chief] sprinkled them with [bird] down, and "Talked" to them, saying, "We are glad you have come to visit us; we have been saving these [feathers] for you for a long time, and hope you will return to visit us soon".'[8] Of vital importance was the specific preparation of these fish for eating, and the maintenance of the head, bones, guts and tail, to be returned to the sea. If the salmon parts were not returned to the sea, then the salmon would be born deformed, and deformed salmon could not be eaten. While Cook and his men were treated like salmon, awe of white people, *maamatlini* ('those whose houses float about on the water'), soon diminished. Fur trading expeditions found that they were treated with much less respect only eight years later. There were no songs and no eagle down in the greetings and Nuu-chah-nulth would not trade sacred salmon to the Europeans – who turned out, alas, to be merely human.

Trade with the Nuu-chah-nulth and other Natives for sea otter fur continued. In this British traders were at a disadvantage compared with those from New England. From a British point of view Pacific trade constituted part of the monopoly of the East India Company, which chose not to participate in this business, thus creating difficulties for trading expeditions which set out from Britain. Americans knew no such constraints, and were known by Indians as 'Boston' men, while

219 Wood grease or feast bowl, in the form of a seal, from southern Alaska, Aluttiq or Chugach, collected on Cook's Third Voyage, 1778. In a nearly all-protein diet the consumption of fish and seal mammal grease assumes a great importance in providing protection from the cold. L 37 cm. Ethno.

British were dubbed 'King George's' men. Banks obtained collections from two of the early British entrepreneurs who braved the East India Company monopoly. One was George Dixon, amongst whose collection from the 1780s was a magic crystal collected from the Nuu-chah-nulth, crystals being used in supernatural rites for hunting sea otters.

While no longer a traveller during the 1780s and 1790s Banks remained a vital patron. He had contributed collections from Cook's Third Voyage to the Museum in 1780, including probably a fine grease bowl from the Chugach or Pacific Eskimo (fig. 219). In the longer term he identified talented young scientists whom he placed on voyages, and looked after his protégés as their careers developed. Archibald Menzies was one such; Menzies involved himself successfully in Banks's life, quickly benefiting from his patronage. From Perth, Menzies trained in Edinburgh, becoming a surgeon. In the mid-1780s he travelled, like Cook and Banks, to Atlantic Canada for his first voyage, on HMS *Assistance*, on the Halifax station from 1783 to 1786. Menzies sent botanical specimens to Banks, and then on his return visited Banks, probably in 1786 with a gift of plants. Hearing of another voyage he applied for a posting. Menzies was recommended as surgeon for the trading voyage of Richard Etches, on the *Prince of Wales*, with time allowed for scientific pursuits.

Captain George Vancouver's voyage, in which Menzies also participated, followed this up with two aims – the first was to resolve difficulties with Spain over the Nootka Sound Controversy of 1790. This arose from conflicting claims to the Pacific Northwest, and specifically over the seizure of British trading vessels by the Spanish. Secondly Vancouver was to map the Pacific coast of North America. This he did, in the voyage of 1791–5, beginning with Puget Sound and Washington state, the Inside Passage and Vancouver Island, before continuing up into southern Alaska, and, conversely, southwards down to Baja California. Many important artefacts were collected, including a slat armour cuirass from British Columbia, described by Menzies as 'Wooden War Stays from Bank's Isles' (fig. 220). While it was a remarkable, and unparalleled, achievement, Vancouver, who had travelled with Cook on his Third Voyage, was in his own personal characteristics a controversial figure. He was easily given to slights to which he regularly responded with unjustifiably brutal punishments.

Difficulties arose between Menzies and Vancouver for a number of reasons, but in particular because Menzies, although promised a copy, was never given details of Vancouver's instructions from the Admiralty. Banks had been involved in early negotiations with Vancouver over the role of voyage scientists. Cook, and other naval officers, found scientists bothersome and in this Vancouver was no exception. A 7 by 12 foot glass frame for plants was built on the deck of the *Discovery* to Banks's specification. This, while a regular scientific practice, cluttered the deck and cannot have been favoured by naval commanders. Menzies asked to be made surgeon as well

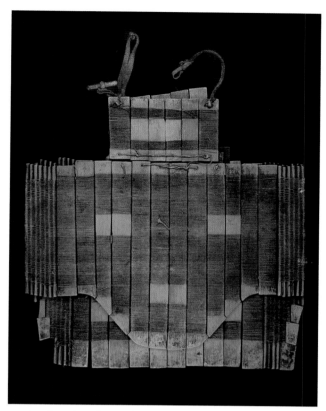

220 A cuirass from the Northwest Coast of America, c. 1790. Natives wore body armour constructed of wood slats over elk skin tunics. Heads were protected by helmets carved with animal crests, such as Raven and Killer Whale. This example was probably collected by Archibald Menzies on Vancouver's voyage. Ethno.

as naturalist. Vancouver refused, so that originally Menzies was appointed supernumerary naturalist only. Illness of the *Discovery*'s surgeon meant that Menzies became surgeon-naturalist in any case; unfortunately this was still insufficient status to ensure the protection of his plants on his way home, which perished when Menzies's servant was taken away for watch duties. Nevertheless Menzies's collection reached the British Museum via Banks and George III in 1796, only to be nearly forgotten for almost two hundred years.[9]

THE WEST INDIES

Other parts of the Americas were important at this time in England, although they were peripheral from the point of the view of the Museum. A few ethnographic objects were collected from the peoples of the southern tip of South America, for instance by Cook and Banks on the first voyage in 1769, although no objects can now be identified. Much more significant was Banks's involvement in preparing plans for the transfer of economically important botanical species to the West Indies from the Pacific: this resulted of course in Bligh's adventures on, and off, the *Bounty*, and his most remarkable survival. Both the prosperity of the West Indies and the growth of the anti-slave-trade movement were major features of economic and social life in the late eighteenth century. Few effects were felt in the Museum; families such as the Beckfords, grown rich from sugar plantations in Jamaica, did not collect American artefacts. Sloane had of course visited Jamaica in the seventeenth century, and collected information about American products such as chocolate and cochineal, acquired many thousands of natural history specimens, and published his *Natural History* (of Jamaica), 1707–25 (see ch. 6). He had also collected artefacts from an unidentified slave revolt, which have, alas, disappeared. Although no Afro-Caribbean objects have survived from this period in the Museum, earlier Native objects, from the Taino in Jamaica, were acquired both by collectors such as Sloane and by the Society of Antiquaries. These include hardwood *duhos* (fig. 221), and figurative sculpture. Therefore the contemporaneous movement towards the abolition of slavery, unique in intent through history, is best represented graphically. Most famous is the great 1791 woodcut prepared for Parliament, showing the grotesque on-board arrangement of slaves during transportation (fig. 222). Propaganda pieces, china plaques created in the factory of abolitionist Josiah Wedgwood, were mass-produced within a very discrete classical idiom (see fig. 12). These were eventually to contribute to success, with the banning of the slave trade from 1807, and the abolition of this 'peculiar institution' from 1833 (in Britain) onwards.

THE ARCTIC

Banks, in his last decade, retained an interest in exploration, and in the search for the Northwest Passage through Arctic North America. In 1817 when alerted by the whaler William Scoresby of ice-free seas in northern Greenland he instigated new expeditions. Post-Napoleonic Britain was a country of unemployed naval officers retired on half-pay, eager to be involved in expeditions to unexplored areas of the world. The first voyage of 1818, commanded by John Ross, sailed between what is now Canada and Greenland, and discovered the Inughuit or Polar Inuit, a people numbering two hundred souls who believed they lived alone in the world. A most significant feature of the voyage, which ended in scientific controversy and personality clashes, was the employment of an Inuit interpreter adviser and artist, Hans Zakaeus, who guided the expedition. This lesson was not always remembered by later explorers such as John Franklin who eschewed the full use of Native knowledge in subsistence and travel, with his consequential catastrophic disappearance in the 1840s. Ross's expedition entered Lancaster Sound in August 1818.

222 Woodcut showing details of the shipping arrangements for Africans transported into slavery in the New World, from Anon., *... evidence delivered before a Select Committee of the House of Commons ... for the abolition of the slave trade ...* (London, 1791). Anti-slavery propaganda contributed to the abolition of the trade from 1807, and of slavery in the 1830s; at about the same time, however, technical developments and the demand from Manchester mills for cotton led to the expansion of the plantation economy in the United States. Ethno Library.

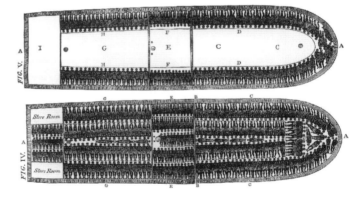

221 Taino chief's seat, *duho*, West Indies, 1600 or earlier. Fashioned from guayacán hardwood, the stool is said to have been recovered from a cave in the interior of Jamaica. The orifices and joint marks are inlaid with beaten gold. L. 44 cm. National Art Collections Fund. Ethno.

Landing the Treasures, or Results of the Polar Expedition !!!

223 Polar Inuit lance head of narwhal ivory fitted with meteoric iron from the Cape York Fall in northern Greenland. It was collected by John Ross in 1818 at the start of the final efforts to locate the Northwest Passage by the Royal Navy. Natural History Museum, Mineralogy.

224 George Cruikshank's *Landing the Treasures …* (1819) is one of the few satirical prints relating to official collecting from voyages of discovery, here the return of John Ross's controversial voyage in search of the Northwest Passage in 1818. The Inuit figure on the extreme right, wearing polar-bear-skin pants and holding a narwhal tusk and artist's portfolio, represents Hans Zakaeus, interpreter and artist on the voyage. P&D.

Ross decided, incorrectly, that this waterway was closed at the west end by mountains and turned round and came home.

But the expedition was not entirely unsatisfactory. Ross brought home a small ethnographic collection; presented to the British Museum in 1819, it was perhaps Banks's last donation. This included a unique surviving sled lashed together from bone and ivory pieces – because the Inughuit were almost entirely without drift wood from which to make tools. The Inughuit were, however, blessed with metal from a large shower of meteorites, hammered slivers of which they used on knives and harpoons for the preparation of equipment (fig. 223).[10] George Cruikshank commemorated the arrival of this collection in the British Museum with a wonderful caricature depicting the grumpy curators receiving this bounty, and an image of Zakaeus wearing nothing but polar-bear-skin pants, as might have been normal at home, and holding a folio of his

sketches (fig. 224).[11] The menagerie in the Jardin des Plantes, Paris, benefited too, for instance with the gift of a husky dog.

Ross's colleague in 1818, William Parry, captain of HMS *Alexander*, decided that the expedition commander had made a mistake and that there was a route towards the Northwest Passage through Lancaster Sound. Consequently the following year Parry was given his own expedition, and proved that Lancaster Sound did indeed lead far to the west. Parry was a Bath acquaintance of Banks, who continued to command expeditions after Banks's death through the early 1820s. At about this time the Arctic also of course entered the romantic imagination, as Ultima Thule, the end of the world, was the place to which Mary Shelley was to consign the monster from *Frankenstein* (1818). A more satisfactory series of stereotypes was to emerge after Parry's second voyage of 1821–3.[12] He overwintered twice with the Iglulingmiut, of Melville Peninsula at Winter Island and Igloolik Island. Parry's expedition benefited enormously from Inuit skills, in hunting, of course, but also in making snow goggles to prevent the Europeans developing snow blindness. Parry also recorded copious ethnographic information, and his publication was accompanied by dazzling images of Inuit life by George Lyon, his second-in-command. In this way the idea of the snow house – or *igluviga* – entered the western imagination – *iglu*, as was noted at the time, simply meaning home (figs 225–6).

The important Alaskan explorations of Frederick William Beechey on HMS *Blossom* of 1826–7 were the last to yield American collections for the Georgian British Museum.[13] Beechey, after participation in the War of 1812 on the Mississippi River,

225 'An Esquimaux creeping into the passage of a snow hut', engraving after George Lyon from William Parry's *Journal of a second voyage for the discovery of a North-West Passage …* (1824). This image probably introduced the *igluviga*, or snow house, to European audiences. Ethno Library.

226 Sketches by George Lyon of Inuit implements, in pencil, ink and watercolour, 1820s. Snow goggles were invented about two thousand years ago around the Bering Strait, and prevent snow blindness, but they also exclude much peripheral vision and make walking in rough terrain difficult. Ethno Library.

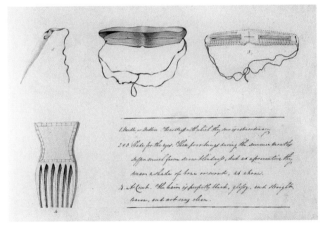

227 Arrow-shaft straightener, ivory, Inupiat, Alaska, before 1850. Such instruments were used to straighten arrows; by being carved with the head of a caribou foetus, this one propitiates caribou spirits. It is engraved with scenes of caribou and seal hunting. Ethno (Haslar Hospital Collection).

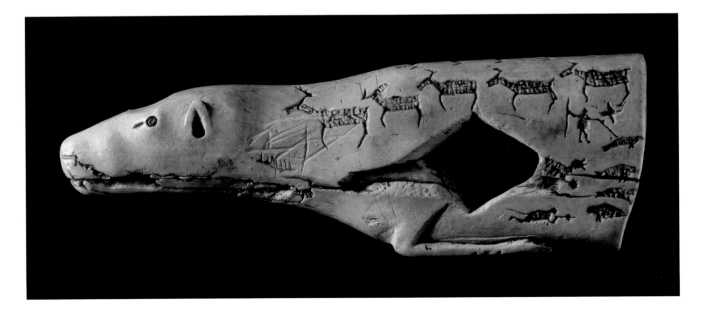

had served with Parry on his first voyage in search of the Northwest Passage. In 1825 Beechey, now captain, was directed to approach the passage from the west around Alaska. He was to meet up with Parry, travelling westwards from what is now Canada, and with John Franklin who was exploring the Western Arctic shores. Although he did not encounter either expedition Beechey, and his lieutenant Edward Belcher, mapped much of the coast of north-west Alaska and collected avidly from the Inupiat, also great traders with Siberian Eskimos. Cook had noted in the 1770s the similarity of Greenlanders to Alaskans. It was only on Beechey's expedition, however, that it was confirmed that the North American Arctic was inhabited by a series of closely related Eskimoan peoples. All, including the Inupiat and Canadian Inuit, speak related dialects stretching in a cline from the Bering Strait eastwards to Greenland. And they share many other aspects of culture, including hunting and transport technology, and cosmology. Beechey, Belcher and others recorded copious details about Inupiat life. Both officers collected examples of mammoth and walrus ivory arrow-shaft straighteners, for instance (fig. 227). These wrench-like instruments were used to straighten out heated and steamed arrow-shafts for use, particularly in caribou hunting. Shaft straighteners and other tools are sometimes decorated with engraved scenes of the seal hunt, in a decorative tradition which both no doubt recorded actual events and provided amuletic assistance to the owner, artist and hunter in his endeavours. Beechey's particular contribution was to note that the engraved designs were executed with a 'truth and character which showed the art to be common among them'. He may be suggesting that the engraved scenes were not, as it were, the chance work of an individual but part of art tradition.[14] He was observant about other material culture traditions. In California for instance he noted how sinew-backed bows were made, and particularly that they were recurved, requiring very substantial strength and skill to pull back through the vertical before release.[15]

Latin America

After 1789 European war and revolution transformed Middle and South America, both politically and scientifically: it also changed European perception of these two continents and the role of metropolitan museums. The Prado, for instance, in Madrid had its origins in the natural history cabinet founded by Carlos III in 1771. This was eventually to receive the American collections from the scientific expedition of Alejandro Malaspina – Vancouver's great Italian contemporary in the 1790s. When actually opened, after the Napoleonic wars, in 1819, the Prado featured, instead of Enlightenment science, displaced art collections from destroyed palaces. More positively the revolutionary and Napoleonic wars in Europe, which resulted in political turmoil in the West Indies and Latin America, also

permitted opportunities for travel and research. The work of Alexander von Humboldt, scientist and traveller, was seminal in transforming European perception of the region. After his expedition of 1799–1804 Humboldt, based in Paris and Berlin, wrote extensively of minerals, botanical geography, meteorology and the Native peoples of Latin America.[16] While for the British Museum his work is symbolized in his publication of a figure of the Aztec female deity Chalchiuhtlicue,[17] now in London, he was also first to note the importance of guano – from the later mines of which important wooden sculptures were to be recovered for the Museum. Humboldt also published numerous Mesoamerican manuscripts, a major concern of European collectors, particularly during the slightly later period when Jean-François Champollion was working on Egyptian hieroglyphics (see ch. 19).

British scholarly interest in Mexico was first stimulated after Independence, and the founding of the national museum in 1821, with the travels and work of William Bullock.[18] His London Museum, which was eventually placed in the Egyptian Hall, graced Piccadilly from c. 1810. Most monuments and buildings in the Aztec capital, Tenochtitlán, had been destroyed in the aftermath of the European invasion in the early sixteenth century. In 1790 in the Plaza Mayor (central square) of Mexico City in front of the cathedral a number of monuments were uncovered during drainage work. The giant figure of Coatlicue, the mother goddess, and the Stone of the Sun were described and published by Antonio de Léon y Gama in 1792. They were re-buried and excavated again to show Humboldt at the beginning of the nineteenth century. Bullock in his expedition of 1823 obtained sufficient information for large models to be made for his exhibition of *Ancient Mexico* in the Egyptian Hall (see fig. 209). He also included seventeen borrowed codices, plaster casts of monuments and Aztec antiquities. He employed an Italian draughtsman, Augustin Aglio, to depict the exhibitions and copy manuscripts. Later Aglio worked for the Irish scholar Edward King, Viscount Kingsborough, in creating his *Antiquities of Mexico* (1831–48). In a second exhibition, *Modern Mexico*, Bullock was able to describe economic possibilities in Mexico, with the help of a guide he had brought with him. He used the sketches, by William Bullock, junior, which he brought back with him, both in this exhibition and for a full-scale panorama of Mexico City which was mounted in Leicester Square in 1826. Later he combined both exhibitions together, eventually returning many of the antiquities to Mexico and auctioning the rest in 1825. William Buckland, professor of geology at Oxford, and scholar of the antediluvian (see ch. 9), purchased much of the exhibition and sold it on to the British Museum. Perhaps most importantly Bullock published a travel account, *Six Months' Residence and Travels in Mexico* (1824), so that in effect he disseminated information through all available media. A quarter of a century later another Mexican collection, made in the late eighteenth century in colonial

New Spain, came to the British Museum. This was acquired by a trader, Juan Wetherell, in the nineteenth century, but had been assembled earlier by a lawyer named Carvajal.[19] Interestingly it includes a Tlingit frontlet and other Pacific North American items no doubt obtained by Spanish explorers, perhaps Malaspina himself, in the 1790s (fig. 228).

Bullock's importance extended beyond his Mexican speculations. He flourished in London with a museum of natural history and artificial curiosities from Cook's and later voyages. His rooms were filled with arms and armour, and he and his brother George provided furniture and collections for the Gothic fantasies of Samuel Rush Meyrick, the first scholar of European arms, and for Walter Scott, and Napoleon on St Helena. This interest in arms followed the creation of a collection of arms for the Prince Regent in Carlton House. Interest in armouries signalled, perhaps, a change in collecting habits – from scientific to the romantic and decorative. Bullock had also been influential in auctioning more modest collections, for instance of exotic weapons belonging to one P. Dick, a neighbour of the adolescent Edgar Allan Poe in Sloane Street, some of which came to the British Museum with the Meyrick collection in 1878.[20]

Further to the south in Central and South America political change and scientific curiosity advanced in the same way. During and in the aftermath of the French Revolution and Peninsular War most of Spain's other American colonies also achieved independence. In London interest in the Maya area also began in the early 1820s. In 1822 Henry Berthoud published an account of the classic Maya city, Palenque, in Chiapas, Mexico, by Antonio del Río, *Descriptions of the Ruins of an Ancient City* (1822). Del Río was sent under the auspices of the Spanish Crown to describe the city in 1787. Not published at the time of receipt, somehow a copy of the report reached London from Madrid, and was made available in English. This illustrated volume inspired intense interest in the Maya for successive generations of explorers, epigraphers and archaeologists (see figs 192, 213). Perhaps most important were the travels of John Lloyd Stephens and Frederick Catherwood in Mexico and Central America in the 1830s and 1840s. Catherwood, an English traveller, artist and panorama creator, accompanied Stephens, the American lawyer and traveller, and later railroad promoter. The publication of Frederick Catherwood's exceptional lithographs of Maya monuments, *Views of Ancient Monuments ...* (1844), represents an early climax in the scholarly descriptive recording of Maya sites (fig. 229). Most significant of early Maya archaeologists from the English point of view was, however, Alfred Maudslay.[21] Maudslay spent many years at the end of the nineteenth century recording monuments, by mould and by camera, throughout the Maya area, his collection of originals and casts first being put on display in the British Museum in the early twentieth century. Most notable are the sculptures from Copán, Honduras (fig. 231).

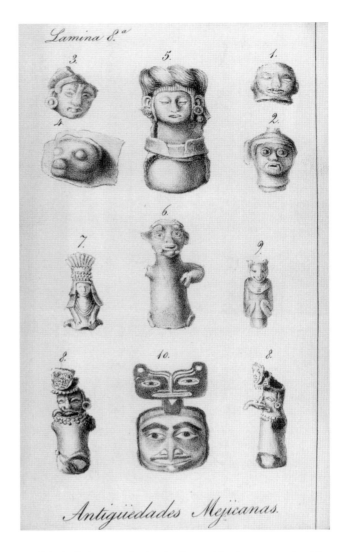

Scholarly interest in the Andes and in Andean antiquities parallels that in Mexico and the Maya area, although research did not really begin until the mid nineteenth century. From the early eighteenth century onwards, cabinets, including Sloane's and Townley's, had accessioned Peruvian ceramics casually collected from graves. These included sculpturally realistic, stirrup-spouted vessels, depicting people, plants and animals, placed in tombs to provide sustenance in the afterlife (fig. 230). Sloane's few examples date from this period, and were accorded a significant place in the British Museum on opening in the 1750s. In the Museum guide it was said that:

> AMERICAN ... idols are made of earth, and either burnt or hardened in the sun; some of them were worshipped in Peru, others in Mexico, when the Europeans discovered that part of the world: They were placed in high-ways, to be ready for the adoration of passengers.[22]

Further it was speculated that there were two gods, one of goodness, one of evil. From the resemblance of the figures to those from Egypt, it was proposed for the first time in a

228 Lithograph of Mexican ceramic figurines and a north-west coast shaman's frontlet (middle of bottom line) collected in Mexico before Independence, from Juan Wetherell *Antigüedades Mejicanas,* (Seville, 1842). Ethno Library.

229 Copán, Honduras, Stela A, lithograph by Frederick Catherwood from his and J. L. Shepherd's *Views of Ancient Monuments in Central America, Chaipas and Yucatan,* 1844. Their publications were the first major contributions to the popular knowledge of the ancient Maya in Europe and North America. Ethno Library.

Museum context that the Americas were populated from Egypt, a recurring diffusionist fantasy through much of the nineteenth century and beyond. Sloane's occasional American antiquities were, as one would expect, paralleled and exceeded by much grander continental collections. The founding of Carlos III's cabinet was followed by the despatch by the Bishop of Trujillo, Martínez Compañon, of three hundred Moche and Chimú vessels to Madrid in 1788.[23]

Although Humboldt was the first European scholar to work in the Andes, significant description and classification of South American civilizations had to wait until the mid nineteenth century. By then scholar-travellers were appreciative of monumental adobe and stone Peruvian architecture and the very occasional monumental sculpture. Pottery was, however, less highly considered. The Prussian scholar Johann Jakob von Tschudi in his *Travels in Peru* of 1838–42 (1847) stated unequivocally that most pots 'exhibit ludicrous caricatures of human figures; others are unrecognisable representations of animals or fancy features'.[24] In what is perhaps the first account of *Peruvian Antiquities* (1857) he went on to provide, critically but quite neatly, a definition of Andean abstraction in the 'plastic arts'. This could also have served also as a succinct explanation for the 'primitive' human figure for the twentieth century so beloved by collectors and western artists:

230 Selection of ritual vessels produced by the principal pre-Columbian cultures of coastal Peru and used as tomb offerings for the afterlife. First and last: Chimú AD 900–1470 (Sloane and Townley collections), Moche AD 100–700 and Nasca AD 100–700. Ethno.

231 Maize god, stone, Maya, Structure 22, from a temple (?), Copán, Honduras, AD 250–900. The maize god personifies the agricultural cycle and is associated with abundance and prosperity. Maize was the ingredient used by the gods to fashion sentient human beings. H 90 cm. Maudslay collection. Ethno.

'the artists always intended to represent a whole figure, yet, wanting the dexterity or skill and a correct execution of the exact proportions, they exaggerated the relative size of the parts'.[25]

CONCLUSION

The first display in the British Museum of American ethnography and antiquities was in the form of a traditional cabinet of curiosities, a decontextualized group of highly disparate objects. From c. 1780 to 1800 this situation was improved with a 'South Seas Room' providing groupings of objects from specific cultures of the Pacific and Pacific rim. During the first decade of the nineteenth century, rapid change to the display paradigm occurred once more. Objects came to be organized geographically from across the world. This display paradigm survived into the 1850s. Thereafter with the increasing influence of ideas of evolution, and particularly of social evolution, objects from 'higher' cultures, especially Asian, were gradually detached from world ethnography. By the first half of the twentieth century Chinese, Indian and Japanese objects came to be totally removed into a separate Department of Oriental Antiquities.

But long before then fieldwork to the Americas, by official explorers sent by the government, had ceased.

The great eighteenth-century collections in the British Museum were created through the vast network of travellers and collectors associated with Sir Joseph Banks and official expeditions to western and northern North America. This was all carried out with deliberate intent, professionalism and a high degree of success. Similar collections were made through the nineteenth century in the Arctic, but unfortunately almost nothing was obtained from the rest of the North American continent by focused government- or British-Museum-led intervention. The exploring and the boundary expeditions in Canada before confederation in 1867 acquired few objects, which in any case did not come directly to the British Museum. The Canadian confederation was in a sense created out of the lands and interests of the Hudson's Bay Company, and the Company's collection is in Winnipeg, at the Manitoba Museum of Man and Nature. No attempts were made before the 1890s to acquire North American material in the field, and so the continent was, in effect, a marginal area of interest in terms of the Museum collections.

In contrast to the early official collecting of Arctic and Pacific North American material, Latin American research was often undertaken privately. More generally, scholarship in the Americas really came to the British Museum only in the middle of the nineteenth century with the acquisition of the collection of Henry Christy, after his death in 1865, by the curator A. W. Franks.[26] It was then that the 'Esquimaux' collections made by Beechey were used as comparative material in the visualization of the Palaeolithic, or Upper Stone Age. Christy had also made field collections in Mexico in the 1850s, but it was only in the early twentieth century, with the collaborative Maya work of T. A. Joyce and Thomas Gann in Belize, that field research in the Americas became an important component of Museum activities.[27]

23 Irresistible objects: collecting in the Pacific and Australia in the reign of George III

JENNIFER NEWELL

Enlightenment Europeans were not alone in being captivated by exotic objects. From their first encounters, Pacific islanders and Europeans were fascinated by each other, and the passion for collecting the material creations of the other was mutual. A young Lieutenant with Captain Bligh's second expedition to Tahiti wrote: 'the natives laughed at the avidity with which we coveted all their household and other goods. Yet have they at *O'tahytey* their *Collectors*, and their cabinets of *European curiosities*.'[1]

Over decades of increasing contacts, from the 1760s to the early decades of the 1800s, the eagerness for collecting remained. British ships continued to return home with every available space filled with 'native manufactures'. Islanders in the eastern Pacific met each new ship with canoe-loads of fruit, carvings and barkcloth, trading before the anchor was down, then continuing on shore, obtaining European shirts, iron axes, mirrors, books and scissors. In 1807 the paramount chief of Tahiti wrote to the London Missionary Society, saying, 'I wish that you would send me all the curious things that you have in England.'[2]

Islanders and their visitors often went to exceptional lengths to obtain the exotic objects they desired. Sailors chanced a flogging for purloining ship's stores to trade privately with the islanders. Young islanders took English hats, pistols or ship's fittings knowing they risked being shot as they swam to shore, their ears lopped or their houses burnt.[3] The accounts of captains, officers, gentlemen of science, sailors and, later, islanders, were full of scenes of trade. The vibrancy of their accounts, of lavish welcoming gifts, the bartering for provisions and the company of women, the bickering and subterfuge on island shores; all reveal the key role objects took within the exchanges. When we visit museums in Britain and Europe today, we are confronted with the quiet presence of artefacts from the Pacific, sitting on shelves or under glass, labelled briefly. One cannot help but feel the extent to which their stories have leached away.

Dipping into the narratives of the voyaging era, we can make our own voyage across the time and span of the Pacific Ocean and try to uncover some of the distant meanings of collected objects. Each account reveals a little more of the techniques and struggles employed in exchanges of material creations. Also revealed is evidence of the motivations behind those exchanges. It soon becomes clear that the success of British Enlightenment projects of Pacific exploration and missionization depended on the willingness of islanders to enter into negotiations. Europeans did not by any means possess a firm grip of power over islanders. Captains and their crews were more vulnerable and anxious than has been admitted by traditional historians, with their sights firmly on the triumphs of noble navigators. Looking back to those navigators' texts, historians are now recognizing the imprint of the actions of indigenous peoples, and seeing the complex, two-way, plays of power. By re-reading the texts of varied entanglements, we can hope to recover snatches of the vivid lives behind those stilled objects under glass.

BEYOND KNOWN HORIZONS

It was 1766, six years into George III's reign. In a dock on the Thames the *Dolphin* and its consort, the *Swallow*, were being fitted up for Captain Samuel Wallis. His orders were to seek the fabled southern continent, which Enlightenment scholars reasoned must, to balance the globe, lie between the west coast of America and the spice islands of the Malaysian archipelago. Wallis set sail in August toward the southern tip of South America. After four months struggling through the Straits of Magellan, losing its consort on the way, the *Dolphin* set out alone across the expanse of the Pacific Ocean.

The prelude to this voyage lay in an earlier period of growing awareness of the Pacific. Rumours of Portuguese and Spanish discoveries of new lands and new riches on the far side of the earth had been leaking into Britain over the course of the sixteenth and seventeenth centuries. Captains Rogers, Shelvocke, and Anson were sent out from the early to mid eighteenth century, to investigate. Whatever the gentlemen of science and philosophy at home might have hoped, the captains did not compile detailed observations or form careful collections of the new flora, fauna and peoples they encountered. They were pursuing maritime glory for Britain and the gold and spices that Magellan, Mendaña, and Quirós had uncovered.[4] Steering their ships along the routes of the Spanish galleons, the British travelled north of the equator, through much open sea, and missed the major island groups. Scurvy and starvation dogged them. By 1770, K. R. Howe has noted, despite '250 years of periodic European voyaging across the ocean, only a few Islanders saw canvas sails, and even fewer actually met those who worked them'.[5]

British curiosity and avarice remained undampened, however. After an interval imposed by the Seven Years War (1756–63), the Admiralty began to plan more extensive explorations.[6] The time was opportune. Ships were now freed from warfare, the seas less troubled with privateers, John Harrison's chronometers promised to remove the guesswork from navigating, and George III, more so than his predecessors, was an active supporter. Influential men of science pressed the Admiralty to allow Britain to take the lead in 'pushing back the frontiers of human knowledge' by voyaging more systematically into this new realm. The Pacific was soon to replace America as the primary 'testing ground' for Enlightenment

ideas of the worlds of nature and humankind.[7] The potential for acquiring new lands, new resources and new knowledge were clear; so were the advantages these acquisitions would bring for the nation. John Byron's circumnavigation took the lead in 1764–6 and Wallis followed. The Royal Society petitioned for a return voyage to Tahiti to better record the region and its astronomical views, collaborating with the Admiralty to create a quintessentially Enlightenment voyage of scientific endeavour. For the first time, natural philosophers – botanist Joseph Banks and astronomer William Wales – accompanied a British maritime expedition. They set sail with James Cook in 1768. The British were startled to hear that Louis-Antoine de Bougainville, with the naturalist Philibert Commerçon, had conducted a thorough Pacific exploration in 1766–9, returning from Tahiti a few months after Wallis.[8] The quest had been nudged into a race. Cook and Bougainville were both captivated by Tahiti and, once their accounts reached booksellers, it was this island, more than any other Pacific location, that grasped the European imagination.

In the middle of the Pacific Ocean in June 1767 Captain Wallis's crewmen sighted a land of lush peaks topped with cloud. They had arrived not at the great southern continent, as they first thought, but a small island. The island was, nevertheless, bountiful. The trees were laden with food, the water was fresh and the inhabitants welcoming. The people called their island Tahiti. Their society was conveniently familiar, with an apparent royal family (a rule of title-holding lineages, the *ari'i*), a decadent aristocracy (the *arioi*), powerful priests (*tahua*), a class of landowners (*ra'atira*) and commoners (*manahune*). Wallis anchored in Matavai Bay for a month, entertained by the local chief, Tu, and his retinue. The ship's officers traded for food and tried to stave off numerous thefts of ship's property, vacillating between distributing gifts and panicky, devastating, musket fire.[9] But Wallis had to tread carefully. He was sufficiently informed of the intense spear, club and arrow attacks on other South Sea islands that had been fatal to earlier, over-confident crews. It was recognized that blazing away with muskets and cannons, as the Spanish had in the sixteenth century, was not only an unenlightened but an ineffective way of obtaining an ongoing supply of crucial provisions and valuables from island communities.

On Tahiti, as an increasing number of ships arrived, both islanders and Europeans worked to maintain amicable relations. Tahitians were experts of diplomacy and along with a consistently warm welcome, ships' crews would be given generous quantities of baked pigs, fruit and valuables such as lengths of finely beaten barkcloth (*tapa*).[10] The islanders found that some of the traditional techniques for incorporating Polynesian newcomers into their society worked just as effectively with Europeans. Friendly and lucrative relations were set up by high-ranking individuals, who adopted a member of a ship's crew as a *taio*, a ceremonially established bond friend, with whom presents were exchanged frequently and lavishly.[11] The willingness of these islanders to engage in exchanges meant that Tahiti, unlike many places in the western Pacific, was an ideal place for Europeans to refresh, as well as a rewarding place for scientific voyagers to gather material evidence for their evolving systems of classification.

ethnographic objects (see fig. 211).[14] While a shell necklace or bamboo flute was easy to accommodate, there were other items that were far more challenging: ten full-body mourners' costumes from Tahiti on the second voyage (see fig. 243),[15] long spears from Australia, heavy treasure boxes from New Zealand (fig. 232), great cloaks covered with feathers, and bales of decorated *tapa*.

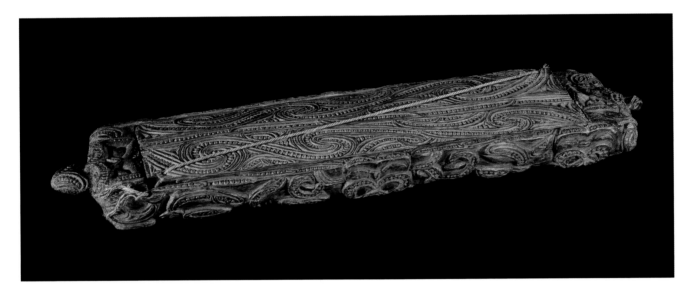

232 A New Zealand Maori treasure box (*papahou* variety), carved in Bay of Islands style. Drawings of this box by John Frederick Miller (1771–2) make it possible to identify it as one of the pieces collected during Captain Cook's first voyage. L. 65 cm. Ethno.

'CURIOUS AND COVETABLE':
THE CONTEXTS OF COLLECTING

Collecting – that is, gathering for the basic purpose of keeping – was not the exclusive preserve of Europeans. Islanders and sailors alike collected material goods from each other with great energy and persistence, despite considerable difficulties for all those involved. If an islander was resolved to obtain a pistol, jacket, or some other personal possession of a British officer, he or she would often have to agree to part with a precious – even sacred – possession of their own community in return. 'Itea, one of the most powerful women in Tahiti in the early 1790s, agreed after many days of delay to procure for her *taio*, Lt George Tobin, a warrior's potent personal chest shield (a *taumi*; a heavy gorget with rows of dark feathers and shark teeth). It was only after receiving this treasure that Tobin would agree to recommence supplying her with European goods.[12] The British surmounted another set of difficulties. Despite the limited space on Cook's ships, collectors on the three Pacific voyages he commanded (between 1768 and 1779),[13] managed to transport home in their cramped quarters an estimated total of two thousand

The collections taken back to Britain were by no means uniform representations of the broad sweep of Pacific cultures. Collecting in the central and eastern Pacific – from what are usually termed 'Polynesian' communities – was much more active than collecting in the western Pacific from Australian, 'Melanesian' and 'Micronesian' communities.

The cultural-geographical region of Polynesia forms a triangle stretching from the far east of the Pacific; from Rapa Nui (Easter Island) near Chile, up to the Hawaiian archipelago in the north, reaching down to Aotearoa/New Zealand (fig. 233). The triangle encompasses Fiji,[16] Tuvalu, Samoa, Tonga, Niue, the Cook Islands, the Society Islands (of which Tahiti is one), the Marquesas, the Tuamotus and others, all sharing a common ancestry of settlers. The people of this region provided European visitors with a rich variety of items used in everyday, ceremonial and ritual life. Fish hooks, mats, carved canoe paddles, earrings, warrior's regalia, talismans and feathered images of gods were among the things brought back to Europe. This range reveals the extent to which, in general, new arrivals were welcomed into the social, political, and sometimes spiritual workings of local communities. As we saw in the example of Tahiti, the Polynesians had a tradition of voyaging and receiving voyagers that remained a substantive part of their cultural forms.[17]

A different set of historical, cultural and political imperatives operated in Melanesia and Australia, in the western Pacific. There was a narrower range of objects collected from Vanuatu,

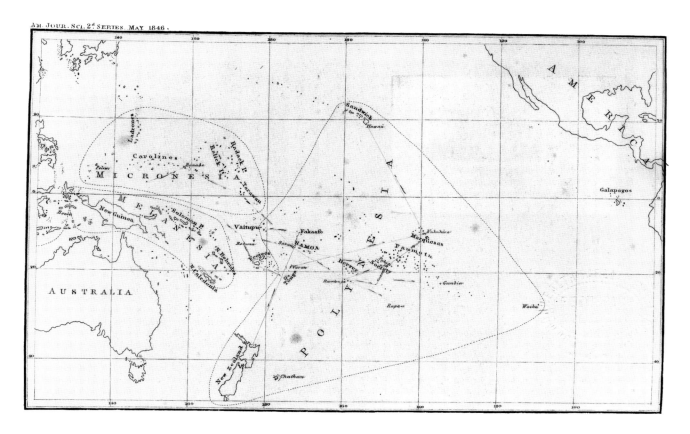

AM. JOUR. SCI. 2ª SERIES. MAY 1846.

the Solomons, New Caledonia, Papua New Guinea and Australia. Explorers and traders who stopped at these places did not come away with the locally produced decorative mats, wooden figures and vessels, or jewellery-like forms of currency typical of those regions.[18] The great majority of objects gathered in Melanesia and Australia were weapons.

Melanesians of the eighteenth century had an already long history of raiders and colonizers arriving from nearby islands, as well as sporadic, violent encounters with European sailors from the 1500s. The islanders were generally unwilling to let visitors come inland, into villages or, in some places, to land at all. Many visitors to Melanesia collected artefacts by picking up the spears and arrows that had been lobbed in their direction.

When Cook, Banks and several officers tried to go on shore in Australia for the first time, on the south-east coast on 28 March 1769, two Eora men came toward them, holding weapons, shouting and gesturing for them to leave. Sydney Parkinson, Banks's draftsman, recorded that the crew in the longboat persisted, offering 'trinkets', but the Australians were not interested.[19] So the longboat crew fired off their muskets to scare the men away. One ran back to his hut to fetch a bark shield, collecting rocks on his way back. The longboat party shot directly at the men and wounded one of them. Parkinson picked up two 'lances' from where they had landed between his feet. The shield, too, was picked up and kept. It was later given to the British Museum (fig. 234).[20] The voyagers found it an alarming incident. Without being able to spark the local population's

233 'Map of the Pacific Regions', from Horatio Hale, 'Migrations in the Pacific Ocean', *American Journal of Science* 2nd ser., vol. 1, no. 3 (May 1846). National Library of Australia, Canberra.

234 Eora bark shield, picked up by some of Cook's party after their first confrontation with indigenous Australians. The shield has been identified from drawings made by John Fredrick Miller, after a sketch by Sydney Parkinson, an artist on Cook's first voyage. L. 97 cm. Ethno.

Plate 1.

3 Feet in Length. — 1 Foot 9 Inches in Height.

235 Serving bowl, engraving by J. Kingsbury, in George Keate, *Account of the Pelew Islands* (London, 1788), a popular publication recounting Captain Wilson's shipwreck and subsequent months in Palau, Micronesia. This was one of the gifts a Palauan leader gave to his friend Wilson, whose family later presented the gifts to the British Museum. L. 92 cm. Ethno.

desire for British trade goods, how could the crew bargain for the food, fresh water and information they required?

The people of Australia had, in the end, no choice about establishing an ongoing relationship with Europeans: in 1788 an entire fleet of convicts and soldiers came to stay. The Aboriginal people discovered that British things – flour, sugar, blankets, guns – could be useful after all, seeing as their ability to support themselves from the land was being wrested away, the country cleared, fenced and patrolled by armed settlers. In the changed land, trade relations were established, along with other insidious consequences of contact with Europeans: disease, dispossession and unpredictable violence. Further afield in Melanesia, it was later in the 1800s that extensive relationships were established; most commonly with missionaries and traders.[21]

In the north-west portion of the Pacific lies Micronesia, the third cultural-geographical region of the Pacific. This region includes Kiribati near the equator, Nauru and the Marshall Islands and continues westward to the Caroline Islands. It was on scattered islands here that Spanish and Portuguese explorers and Jesuit missionaries made their presence felt throughout the sixteenth and seventeenth centuries.[22] But the small islands and atolls were thin in resources; most explorers found it more profitable elsewhere. Ships of Britain's East India Company did occasionally pass through the western Carolines. In 1783 a Company ship, the

Antelope, ran on to a reef near the island of Palau. One of the most distinctive episodes of Pacific collecting unfolded as Captain Wilson and his crew were welcomed warmly by the Palauans and assisted over the four months it took the crew to build a new ship.[23] In return the English put themselves and their salvaged weaponry at the disposal of Ibedul, the paramount chief of Koror, in his drive to overpower nearby rivals. When the English eventually made their farewells, Ibedul gave Wilson a set of ceremonial vessels and knives made of tortoiseshell and strikingly inlaid wood (fig. 235).[24] It was a rare gift and a rare experience. It was not until the 1850s that more involved relations were established in Micronesia with the arrival of whalers and sandalwood traders.

COLLECTING FROM EUROPE

It was Polynesians, then, who during our period entertained the greatest number of British visitors and encouraged the greatest number of exchanges. European objects that could be found in Polynesian households ranged from the practical to the ornamental, the intriguing and the entertaining. These things quickly became useful and potent within Polynesian communities. There were immediate practical advantages. The British could supply labour-saving, ready-made clothes, water-proof cloth, ceramic vessels and new tools. When Tongan carvers obtained iron nails and other metal implements they were able

to experiment with finer and more elaborate designs than had been possible with stone or coral gouges (fig. 236). Women in the Cook Islands, Tahiti and Niue used English scissors to create innovative, intricate edgings for their *tapa* garments, some having over-layers with minutely cut keyhole designs.[25]

Travellers in Polynesia often commented on the islanders' being: 'covetous and eager after property', or that 'they are constantly asking us for presents'.[26] While the standard trade items the British brought in their holds were quite appealing, there were some specific objects that Polynesian viewers found particularly worth bargaining for. Captain Furneaux noted, on meeting a group of Maori in Cook Strait in 1773: 'We had a catalogue of their words in their language calling several things by name which surprised them much. They wanted it much and offered a great quantity of Fish for it.'[27] George Tobin saw a Tahitian priest's drive to collect exotica mirroring his own:

old *Hammaneminhay*, the High priest was in possession of a volume of the 'Statues at large', which he procured from a vessel that had touched at the Island, on which he placed as much value as some among us do, on a petrified periwinkle or a stuffed baboon.[28]

236 A Tongan whale bone club. The sharply defined intricacy of the designs suggests the carver was working with a sharpened metal point, probably a nail or similar piece of iron collected from a visiting ship. L. 87 cm. Ethno.

237 European artists tended to depict indigenous peoples holding traditional tools and weapons. This is a rare image of a Rapa Nui couple (an unnamed man and a woman recorded to be 'Te'ree') holding a European trade axe and mirror. Drawing by Captain Charles Bishop, 1795. British Columbia Archives and Record Office Service.

The value Polynesians placed on certain objects changed as the flow of ships increased, and previously rare trade items became common. Wallis's arrival in Tahiti brought probably the first appearance of metalwork, and iron nails were highly valued there as general-purpose tools. One of the crew noted in June 1767 that 'A large Nail will Purchase a Large Hog Sufficient to Dine 20 Men'. By 1792 Matthew Flinders could record that in Tahiti 'they no longer prize small nails and scarcely large ones at this time. Scissars were a valuable Article'.[29] By 1801 nails were outclassed – an *ari'i rahi* ascending in power in the island's north-west compelled his people to surrender a pig to the British only if they could get a musket in return.[30]

In 1825 Captain Beechey prepared his cargo for a surveying voyage in the eastern Pacific (and to deliver dispatches to the British consul in Hawai'i). Knowing from earlier voyages what was likely to be most popular, he arranged for:

50 yards of blue and red broadcloth, iron in the form of hoops and bars, 500 hatchets, nails, saws, 4 cases of beads, jewellery and trinkets of different colours but mainly blue, 500 knives, 100 printed handkerchiefs, 50 kaleidoscopes, 100 bundles of needles, 40 pair of scissors, 80 looking glasses, 36 common shirts, 1,000 fish hooks of different sizes, 10 bundles of vermilion, and 2 double-barrelled guns as presents to the kings of Tahiti and the Sandwich Islands.[31]

Owning European things operated in many island societies as a claim to status (fig. 237). Possessing an officer's scarlet jacket or peaked hat, a kaleidoscope or knife was a demonstration of one's allegiance with politically powerful foreigners. These objects worked as symbols of power because they worked within pre-existing systems of status, spiritual significance, and management of authority.

Kamehameha I, the great *ali'i* (chief) of Hawai'i, was one of the Pacific's most dramatic collectors of European material culture. The arrival of the first tall ship – Cook's *Resolution* – in 1778 presented Kamehameha with a new avenue to augment his already rising status. He still displayed his power with the huge red and yellow feather cloaks and other feathered regalia his people wove for him from the plumage of thousands of birds. As he won battles and the allegiance

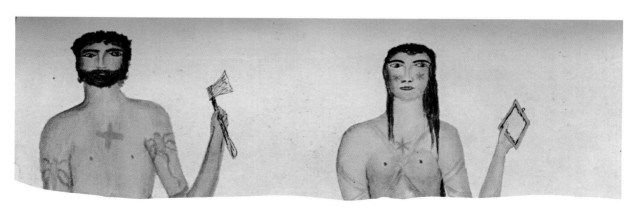

of lesser *ali'i*, he also began to stockpile European silverware, porcelain, shoes and brocades. Trading with his sandalwood forests, he secured from American and British traders a fleet of thirty ships and a cannonade. These worked to demonstrate to his subjects his growing spiritual and material power and authority – his *mana*. In the same way as his cloaks did, these showy new possessions extended Kamehameha's bodily presence and made clear his ability to maintain his people's prosperity.[32]

Kamehameha knew the ongoing value of his traditional regalia. In 1792 he sent two of his feather cloaks and several fine capes with Captain Vancouver as gifts to King George.[33] The relationship established between the two ruling families was sustained by further gifts and visits. Kamehameha's *mana* did indeed increase; with a combination of military and diplomatic successes, he was not only able to repulse two Russian attacks but was the first *ali'i* to unite the islands of the archipelago.[34]

Connections with individual Europeans could be memorialized with specific mementoes. A portrait of Cook was kept in a Tahitian cave, presented with offerings of sacred red feathers, and brought out for each English captain to record his name on the back along with the date of his stay. An iron hatchet that Captain Cook gave to a Maori community on one of his early visits was reportedly 'preserved as a relic' for generations, before being given to the British Governor of New Zealand, Sir George Grey, in the mid nineteenth century (fig. 238). As part of Joseph Banks's preparations to accompany Cook's Second Voyage, he arranged for forty replica Maori hand clubs (*mere*) to be cast in solid brass (fig.239). He had them engraved with his name, crest and the year, 1772. However, he took umbrage at the slight accommodations provided for him on the *Resolution* and instead of handing out his brass tokens himself to chiefs and other people of significance across Polynesia, he gave them to his friend, Lt Charles Clerke, to distribute. In 1801 some missionaries stopping briefly at New Zealand's North Cape saw a Maori man carrying 'a brass weapon with the name of Joseph Banks, esq engraved on it'.[35] In the early twentieth century another was

found amongst the grave valuables of a native American on the North West coast of America.[36]

The British were not the only people manufacturing objects specifically for Pacific collectors. Polynesians recognized the market potential of making surplus tools and weapons for trade. George Tobin had trouble securing 'authentic' artefacts:

> To get such articles there was no little difficulty, from the eagerness with which we sought them, and from the introduction of european implements having rendered many of them nearly useless; the stone adzes in particular, nor have I a doubt but that nine tenths of those brought home in the Providence were purposely made for sale.[37]

The officers of the *Blonde* visiting Hawai'i in 1825 were, it was reported, 'anxious to procure some ancient idols to carry home as curios', but they soon exhausted the available stock of carved figures. To 'supply the deficiency the Hawaiians made idols, and smoked them, to impart to them an appearance of antiquity'.[38] The strategy worked, an early instance of tourist art.

MANAGING THE MARKET

Those with authority in island communities worked to manage the trade in foreign objects. Unlike in Melanesia, where political leaders had to negotiate to maintain their

238 Hatchet given to the New Zealanders by Captain Cook and preserved as a relic. Iron axe on wooden handle, presented to the British Museum by Sir George Grey in 1854. L. 44 cm. Ethno.

239 Brass replica of a Maori hand club (*mere*), one of forty made in 1772 in Mrs Eleanor Gyles' brass foundry, off Fleet Street, London, for Joseph Banks. Given to the British Museum by H. G. Beasley in 1936. L. 36 cm. Ethno.

influence, the hereditary chiefs of Polynesia could more readily direct their people to trade their livestock and garden produce for European goods, then gather up the spoils for themselves. The people complied for the most part, expecting protection and favour in return. Not all foreign treasures were surrendered; one account in Tahiti tells of Tu's father quickly hiding an English shirt when he heard his son was approaching, to avoid having to give it up. For the most part, however, the *ari'i* were in a position to command the practice and products of their people's trade.

Ships' captains, too, strove to manage their crew's trading. As we have seen, visiting British crews gave and received manufactured items in exchange for other commodities: foodstuffs, timber, fresh water to provision ships; plus local knowledge and sexual services. Sailors desperate for the company of women seemed prepared, if left to their will, to give away almost all the goods from home they could lay hands on. Captains recognized that if the islanders' desire for European goods was satisfied the crucial ability to provision their ships would be jeopardized. They thus imposed strict regulations on their crews, to be enforced by floggings, restricting trade to a few officers at a designated place on shore. Despite all precautions, sailors could still be caught pulling the nails out of the ship's side or stripping themselves of their whole stock of shirts to secure a tryst.[39]

Nor could captains and chiefs entirely tailor the exchanges between them to their own desires. Throughout the voyaging era, British visitors were obliged to co-operate and negotiate

240 Carved hand from Rapa Nui (Easter Island). This hand, the only known one of its type, may represent the hand of a chief during his embodiment of the bird god, Make Make. It was collected in 1774 by Mahine, a Tahitian accompanying Cook on his Second Voyage. Mahine later gave it to one of the naturalists on the *Resolution*, J. R. Forster, who in turn presented it to the British Museum. L. 31 cm. Ethno.

with local chiefs, and sometimes admit defeat. During a night's festivities in the Gambier Islands, Captain Beechey was impressed by the tall drums being used. He bargained for some time with the chief to obtain the largest one. Beechey 'understood that he had purchased it, but', Lieutenant Peard writes, 'when our people attempted to take it away, the Natives resisted and we gave up the point'.[40] Island chiefs, with the supply of essential provisions under their control, could often command delivery of the items they wanted more effectively than the European visitors were able to. The high-ranking Tahitian 'Itea was able to convince Captain Bligh, despite his misgivings, to give her the gift she most desired: a pistol and ammunition.

The exchanges that were played out from the last part of the eighteenth and early nineteenth centuries depended on mutual agreements. The quantities and types of objects collected by Europeans and islanders were during this time shaped by what the other party was prepared to let go, and what deals could be struck. This even footing was lost from the 1840s when French and British generals, with settled outposts in the Pacific, became less vulnerable and could afford to push their newly formed colonial structures into the islands. During the reign of George III, however, before the colonial machine was fully launched and the focus of the visits remained on discovery, the islanders still possessed the power to manage the interchanges.

Polynesians were also able to find ways to negotiate the need to give away at times objects of great social or spiritual value. Members of Cook's *Resolution* voyage in 1774 found the Easter islanders' long-term shortage of plants for producing *tapa* meant that the desire to secure cloth and clothes 'prompted them to expose to sale several articles which perhaps they would not have parted with so easily under other circumstances'.[41] Mahine, a Tahitian man travelling with Cook, succeeded in trading some Tahitian *tapa* for some

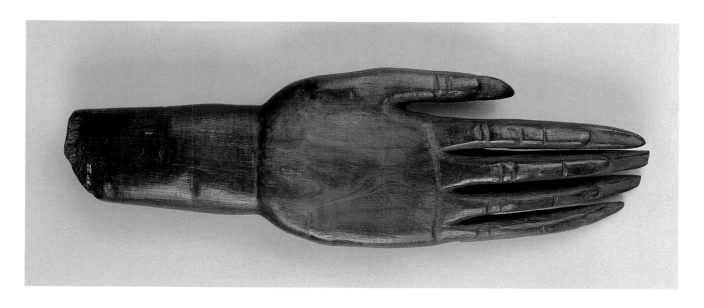

wooden human figures and a wooden hand thought to be part of a priest's or priestess' ritual equipment (fig. 241). An English traveller, Hugh Cuming, found the situation was the same in 1827. He met people who had some 'small Figures carv'd of Wood in the shape of men and Fishes' (fig.241). They would not part with them except for the handkerchiefs and shirts he had brought along. Cuming writes: 'previous to the delivery of the Idol the[y] set up a great Shout lifting up the figure above their Heads several times all joining in Chorus and when upon delivery they would prop it against their brest several times'.[42] It seems likely that the transference of the figures from one state to another was made through this ceremony, which has similarities with ceremonies for requesting forgiveness or severing sacred attachments to ritual materials recorded on other islands.

EMPLOYING THE EXOTIC:
PACIFIC OBJECTS IN BRITAIN

On arriving back in Britain, the objects voyagers had collected took on new roles. British collectors found these objects useful for similar reasons as Polynesian collectors found European objects useful.[43] They not only provided collectors with material benefits and personal mementoes but also publicly demonstrated the collectors' achievements and provided links to power.

The Pacific weapons, garments, musical instruments, ceremonial dress and tattooing tools provided returning voyagers with material proof of the extraordinary people and fabulous places they had encountered. Displayed on walls or glass-fronted cabinets, these 'curiosities' were expected to entertain and enlighten a returned voyager's friends and acquaintances. A 'South Seas' collection could also be drawn upon for effective gifts to influential patrons (fig. 242).

Different groups of collectors put their spoils to different uses. Missionaries, settling in Tahiti, the Marquesas and Tonga from 1797, had formed collections too. When Pomare II eventually decided to convert to Christianity after 1811, the London Missionary Society brothers in Tahiti were proud to report that the chief had sent them many of his sacred figures which previously had been used to contain and communicate with a range of gods and spirits. Pomare included a note: 'I wish you to send these idols to Britain for the Missionary Society, that they may know the likes of the gods that Tahiti worshipped.'[44] The sort of collecting that these missionaries carried out was as much about trophies as the voyagers' had been. Sacred objects, once relinquished, were either burnt in public ceremonies in the islands or sent back to London as clear demonstrations of the progress of the mission. These

241 *Kavakava* figure representing an ancestral being, the head carved with symbols of the birdman cult. Collected in Rapa Nui in 1827 by Hugh Cuming in exchange for some cloth items. H. 46 cm. Ethno.

242 Maori *nephrite hei tiki*, presented to George III by Captain Cook. L. 7 cm. Royal collection. Copyright HM Queen Elizabeth II.

displays promoted the missions in England and helped to raise additional funds.

Sailors returning from the Pacific expected their collections to bring personal profit, through either private sales or London auction rooms. The conflicting aims of collecting for profit and collecting for the noble improvement of human understanding created tension on board 'scientific' expeditions. J. R. Forster, government naturalist on Cook's Second Voyage, was already driven to exasperation by the sailors' gathering great quantities of artefacts and specimens before he had a chance to get ashore, and was furious when a

sailor had the audacity to offer to sell him six shabby shells in return for half a guinea's worth of brandy.[45] Natural history collections from the Pacific – shells, bird skins, pressed plants and geological specimens – attracted much attention in Britain, assisting as they did to flesh out Linnaeus's classificatory schema. Ethnographic collections, evidence of the 'customs and habits' of exotic peoples, might have been harder to pigeonhole and draw conclusions from, but they drew in plenty of curious purchasers none the less, particularly in the first flush of enthusiasm in the years following the Cook voyages.

As ship after ship returned to Europe with wondrous cargoes and stories, there was, for the last three decades of the eighteenth century, a certain vogue for the Pacific. The-atre, interior design, and garden design were richly inspired by the Eden-like South Seas. The set designer Phillipe de Loutherbourg obtained some authentic Tahitian garments from John Webber, artist on Cook's Third Voyage. These were likely to have been used in costuming the hugely successful pantomime of 1785–6 based on the story of that most famous of early Pacific visitors to England: Omai.[46]

Gossip, newspapers and published accounts of Pacific voyages abounded. Leather-bound volumes illustrated with fine engravings were bought by subscription, and cheap penny serials sold out rapidly. Violent debates erupted in the press over the moral, religious and political issues raised by what was being discovered about the radically different societies on the other side of the globe. The Pacific was seen to possess 'young' societies, still at the early stage of human development, in an innocent 'state of nature'; these societies provided the perfect illumination to throw into relief Europe's civilized, yet corrupt, social and political structures. Tahiti in particular, with its comparable social structures but radically different social mores, was a potent spark to French and British *philosophes*' musings on the condition of human-kind. The disillusionment brought by Cook's violent end in Hawai'i and the rapid 'corruption' of Tahitians with the vices of 'civilized' society stripped some of the romanticism from the discussion, but none of the vigour.

In 1776 Johann Reinhold Forster and his son George, the natural historians on Cook's Second Voyage, sent a gift of Pacific 'clothes, arms and domestic goods' to the Ashmolean Museum at Oxford. The Forsters hoped that the objects would act as a public demonstration and perpetual reminder of British advances in 'geography, astronomy, nau-tical matters and natural science, resulting from sea voyages to such scattered races'.[47] But judging from comments (at the Ashmolean and later the Pitt Rivers Museum), visitors found the greatest attraction of the objects was their association with Captain Cook.

Banks's collections from his Pacific travels were displayed in his own, crowded, premises in Soho Square. He later presented several large selections of Polynesian objects to the British Museum, in 1778 and 1780. These, along with other Cook voyage objects, were displayed in the 'Otaheiti or South Seas Room'. Featuring one of the Cook's Tahitian mourner's costumes (fig. 243), brilliant feather cloaks and helmets, clubs and carved gods 'in their hideous rudeness', it soon became one of the most popular rooms in the Museum.[48] Sir Ashton Lever and William Bullock maintained large museums in central London to which they charged admission. They purchased Pacific materials from returned voyagers directly or at auctions. By 1810 Mr Bullock's museum had 'upwards of Seven thousand Natural & Foreign Curiosities'.[49] A visitor to Lever's museum

noted that the three rooms dedicated to the Cook voyage objects presented a 'striking picture of the manner and cus-toms of many of the barbarous nations in the Southern hemisphere'.[50] Most visitors did not move beyond such per-functory reflections, and were primarily drawn in by the strangeness of the display; the novelty and scandalized fasci-nation of a 'cannibal's fork' or unseemly carving of a naked god. Despite the rhetoric, few museum operators or their visitors sought a more careful consideration of the societies creating those objects.

The Pacific became, and in many respects has remained, a symbol of exotic difference. Despite the more nuanced under-standings presented by later, longer-term visitors, Europe's initial eager delight in things Pacific remained superficial, and soon dimmed. It proved hard to shift the heady, general-ized, ill-informed views on the people of the Pacific that had been imbibed during the age of Enlightenment.

By the first decades of the nineteenth century most islands of the Pacific had witnessed sweeping changes to their ways of life. Communities were often devastated by epidemics and hemmed in by colonial structures. Exchanges were less likely to be mutual negotiations. Islander autonomy was eroded. Lively negotiations became financial transactions, the time and skills of craftspeople were now demanded for work on plantations or trading ships. The material creations of the islands and of Europe both became commodified and lost much of the appeal they had possessed when they had been vital parts of community life.

But the Pacific Ocean is a moving, shifting place. Artists, writers and others of the contemporary Pacific, living in Auckland, Apia, Sydney, San Francisco and London, are seeking out the creations of their ancestors, visiting them, giving them new roles to play, finding inspiration within them. The material of everyday life, the objects that attended the play of family, hierarchy and spirituality, have again become irresistible objects, enlivening the Pacific.

243 Tahitan costume of the chief mourner (*parae*), a highly valuable gift from the ruling family of the Matavai Bay district, probably given to Cook on 7 May 1774. The costume soon became, and remains, one of the most readily recognized pieces in the British Museum's Polynesian collection. Ethno.

24

Trade and learning: the European 'discovery' of the East

JOE CRIBB, JESSICA HARRISON-HALL
AND TIM CLARK

In the age of Enlightenment the growth of European understanding of the histories and cultures of Asia is essentially a story of trade and empire. The rounding of the Cape of Good Hope in South Africa by Vasco da Gama in 1498 opened up the rich potential of trade across the India Ocean, and the expanding commercial interests of the European powers, especially the British, the Portuguese and the Dutch, took them to countries such as India, China and Japan. Similarly, Magellan's circumnavigation in 1520–1 gave Spanish traders access to China through Manila in the Philippines. English and Dutch adventurers, such as Sir Francis Drake and later William Dampier, stimulated demand for exotic products by seizing Spanish and Portuguese cargoes. By 1660 Pepys might 'send for a cup of tee (a China drink) of which I never had drank before', and thereby enjoy one of the fruits of the enormous expansion of trade with China brought about by the Dutch. Trade was carried on in particular by the English East India Company (founded in 1600) and its Dutch equivalent, the Verenigde Oost-Indische Compagnie or VOC, the United East India Company founded in 1602. Their officials were often learned individuals, well versed in the classics, who wanted to develop a further knowledge of civilizations known only dimly through old sources or distant trading contacts. Alongside them went missionaries, particularly the Jesuits, who travelled to China to propagate their faith. Some returned and published accounts of what they found there as well as translations of Chinese texts, such as Ludovicus Magnus's 1688 translation of Confucius.[1]

But on the whole the ability to develop an understanding of the civilizations they encountered was limited by the defensive reaction of those societies to European traders and contacts. Japan was closed to foreigners from 1639, and so Japan, and indeed China, were not well understood before the late nineteenth and early twentieth centuries. And, while the recognition of the ancient civilizations of 'the Orient' and an appreciation for their products led to a revolution in taste (indeed, it might be said that one of the strongest impacts was on the visual culture of the Enlightenment), only India was open to the sort of enquiry that could revolutionize the knowledge of its past.

The information and objects that were brought back to Europe were sometimes collected by those imbued with the enthusiasms of the Enlightenment. The study of Sanskrit played its part in the understanding of different languages (see ch. 19), the collection of images of Indian deities prompted enquiry into the relationship between religions (see ch. 20), while the personal collection and study of objects such as coins in conjunction with classical texts brought a new understanding of India's past. Many of these developments were achieved by men whose minds were, characteristically for the time, active in other fields, especially natural history, and it would be a mistake to divorce these activities from their other interests.

INDIA

The growth of western understanding of the histories and cultures of south and south-east Asia during the eighteenth and early nineteenth centuries was largely driven by the needs of European powers to rule these regions, and to rule them in order to trade. Britain, in the form of the East India Company, was the strongest power in the Indian subcontinent, gradually subduing France's endeavour to take that position, but Portugal and the Netherlands also had long-standing trading enclaves securely established as well. In south-east Asia western rule was not so securely established, except for Dutch rule in the Indonesian archipelago. The Napoleonic wars briefly brought French rule into the region, but quickly gave Britain the opportunity to expand its interests beyond small trading posts in Sumatra and Penang at both French and Dutch expense.

As European contacts with south and south-east Asia grew from the time of Vasco da Gama and Magellan, traders and colonial officials gradually built a view of the region's religious, social and political life in the European mind, based on two main sources. The first was the surviving canon of western classical literature. A few of these texts remained a vital source of information for the understanding of ancient India, and were collected together, for example, by William Robertson in his *A Historical Disquisition Concerning the Knowledge which the Ancients Had of India* (1799). The second was the series of reports of the Mughal Empire written by travellers in the seventeenth century. The English ambassador to the Mughal court Sir Thomas Roe's reports of India under Jahangir were published in 1625, in Samuel Purchas's anthology of travellers' accounts of trade and exploration beyond Europe.[2] Two French travellers published accounts of their time in Mughal India: François Bernier, a doctor at the Mughal court, published his *History of the Late Revolution of the Empire of the Great Mogul* in 1670 and Jean-Baptiste Tavernier, a gem merchant, his *Six Voyages* in 1675.[3] Both appeared in numerous editions and were translated into English, Dutch, German and Italian. As well as recounting the events of their time, each of these writers included numerous observations on many aspects of everyday life in India.

Local languages were learnt by Europeans, and by the late eighteenth century the sacred language of India, Sanskrit, had begun to be studied in depth by European scholars, following the lead of Sir William Jones (see fig. 204), a judge in the East India Company's supreme court at Calcutta. With considerable difficulty Jones persuaded a Bengali doctor to teach him Sanskrit after help was refused by Hindu priests seeking to protect their sacred language from foreign contamination.

After less than a year of study, in 1786 he discovered the close relationship between Sanskrit and European languages such as Latin, ancient Greek, Celtic and German, believing them all 'to have sprung from some common source'. This had an enormous influence on studies of writing and language, and became a key part of the effort to set the rediscovery of India's history on a systematic footing. His pioneering study of Sanskrit, begun in an attempt to gain access to ancient Indian law in support of his official role, soon led Jones to discover a wealth of ancient literature and by 1788 he had completed a translation of a play by Kalidasa (India's Shakespeare).[4]

Jones had already founded the Asiatic Society in Calcutta in 1784 'to inquire into the history and antiquities, arts, science and literature of Asia'. A journal, *Asiatick Researches*, was established in 1788 and a museum in 1814. Both had a wide brief covering history, languages, technology, science and ethnography, but with a particular focus on building the repertoire of manuscripts, inscriptions and coins for use as sources in the study of Indian political, religious and cultural history. Soon correspondents of the Society were sending such materials to the museum and for publication in the journal from all over India and the other territories under the control of the East India Company. Much of the Society's museum collection was later transferred to the Indian Museum, Calcutta.

In the 1820s and 1830s the Society founded by Jones was to become an important centre for a growing understanding of India's early history. The year 1825 was a crucial turning point, with the realization that collecting coins could contribute an enormous amount to the subject. In that year two separate publications appeared in London: James Tod's *An Account of Greek, Parthian and Hindu Medals, Found in*

244 Facsimile of a gold dinar of the Kushan king of north-western India, Vasudeva I (c. AD 190–227), made in Calcutta in the 1810s by an East India Company Official, Peter Speke, 'as a curious specimen of Hindu Art' to present to fellow collectors. Sir John Anstruther, President of the Asiatic Society of Bengal, presented this gold facsimile to William Marsden. C&M.

India,[5] and William Marsden's *Numismata orientalia illustrata* (fig. 246).[6] Marsden had formerly been an East India Company official in Sumatra, while Tod was an officer in the army of the East India Company. Tod published his account in the first volume of the transactions of the newly formed Royal Asiatic Society of London. Founded as the Asiatic Society of London in 1823, it received its Charter of Incorporation as a Royal Society from George IV on 11 August 1824. Tod's article included illustrations of key coins in his collection and with them he was able to demonstrate two phases of early Indian history – Greek rule after Alexander and the Scythian conquest of the Greeks – confirming the accounts found in the classical authors.

Tod linked the Greek coins of the kings Menander and Apollodotus II with a classical reference to Menander and Apollodorus (*sic*) as kings of India, and to the recently translated text of the *Periplus of the Erythrean Sea*, which stated that 'coins with the Greek inscriptions of Menander and Apollodotus, who reigned in this country after Alexander, were still current in Barugaza'.[7] Tod had acquired the coins in northern India and was accordingly able to verify the Greek sources as a meaningful account of ancient India. He also published coins, which he referred to as Parthian or Indo-Scythian, with Greek inscriptions on them, but without Greek names. From these he inferred the accuracy of the Greek historian Strabo's account of Central Asian barbarians overthrowing Greek rule in India. Tod was also able to link this event with the account of Central Asian barbarians constructed from Chinese and classical sources by a French priest, Abbé Joseph de Guignes.[8]

Tod also contributed an account of the part of India he knew best, Rajputana, the region of his military service. He published *The Annals and Antiquities of Rajast'han*, in 1829. It was the fruit of many years studying the literary religious traditions of Indian history and observing and working with the local peoples. A work of great detail, with many comparisons drawn between classical traditions and those of India, it is a typical example of the mixture of wonder and admiration tempered with the contempt of a military conqueror to be found in many such accounts of India:

> these are the fabricated genealogies of the ancient
> families of India, the fabrication is of ancient date, and
> they are all they know themselves upon the subject …
> The Hindus, with the decrease in their intellectual
> power … lost the relish for the beauty of truth, and
> adopted the monstrous in their writings … in the East,
> in the moral decrepitude of ancient Asia … Plain
> historical truths have long ceased to interest this
> artificially-fed people.

Tod's discoveries paved the way to a new approach to Indian history, since his personal examination of coins enabled him to offer an alternative to the picture normally painted of India, based principally on classical texts and trav-

245 James Prinsep, Secretary of the Asiatic Society, Calcutta, 1832–39, first editor of the *Journal of the Asiatic Society of Bengal*. Prinsep was responsible for the decipherment of India's two ancient scripts, Brahmi and Kharoshthi. Portrait engraving by C G, 1838, P&D.

ellers' accounts. This was to add a new factual dimension into early Indian history which was soon to be a major source of enquiry. At the Asiatic Society in Calcutta the Secretary and Editor of its new *Journal of the Asiatic Society of Bengal*, James Prinsep (fig. 245), and his mentor Horace Wilson (both officials of the East Indian Company mint in Calcutta), began during the 1830s to reconstruct a chronology for ancient India, linking the classical texts with the coins to show the survival of Greek rule after Alexander, and the successive waves of Central Asian nomadic peoples, Scythians, Parthians, Kushans, Huns and Turks, who dominated North Indian history until the arrival of Islam. On James Prinsep's death in 1840 this project was continued throughout the next five decades by his young friend Alexander Cunningham. Wilson also made the first translation of an Indian historical text, the *Rajatarangini*, the chronicle of the Hindu kingdom of Kashmir, published by the Asiatic Society in 1824. Their work was greatly aided by the activities of European mercenaries serving the Sikh ruler Ranjit Singh, and other European travellers in the north-west of India and in Afghanistan collecting ancient coins and excavating ancient monuments. From the coins Prinsep was able to decipher Kharoshthi, the ancient script of the north-west. He also deciphered Brahmi, the ancient script used in the rest of India.

The decipherment of Brahmi gave ancient Indian history its first concrete datable record. The inscriptions, found in many parts of India, which gave Prinsep the incentive to decipher the script were mostly edicts erected by a king soon recognized as Ashoka, the patron of Buddhism. In one of the edicts Ashoka named four Greek kings with whom he had contacts: Antiochus (of Syria), Ptolemy (of Egypt), Alexander (of Corinth) and Magas (of Cyrene). These four kings ruled in the mid third century BC, providing a date for Ashoka and confirming that his grandfather Chandragupta was correctly identified by William Jones as the Sandracotus named by

Greek authors as an Indian king who met Alexander the Great. In the pages of the Asiatic Society's *Journal*, edited by Prinsep, the study of both inscriptions and coins combined with classical scholarship to begin the process of creating a history for India.

SUMATRA AND JAVA

In the British East India Company's trading settlements further east, the knowledge of local languages and the thirst for knowledge through collecting made possible the first understanding of the history and cultures of the islands of the East Indies. The earliest detailed account of Sumatra came from the pen of the coin collector William Marsden, who became an expert in Malay languages while serving as an official of the Company. On his return to Britain he secured the study of Malay with the publication of his *Grammar and Dictionary*

246 Plate LV from William Marsden's *Numismata orientalia illustrata* (1823–5), vol. 2, showing Javanese bronze coin-shaped religious charms (14–17th century) presented to him by Stamford Raffles (with two examples from Marsden's collection, C&M). The charms depict Javanese shadow theatre puppets of the hero Panji and his wife, and the lower part of the plate shows Japanese gold, silver and copper coins; all are now in the British Museum. C&M Library.

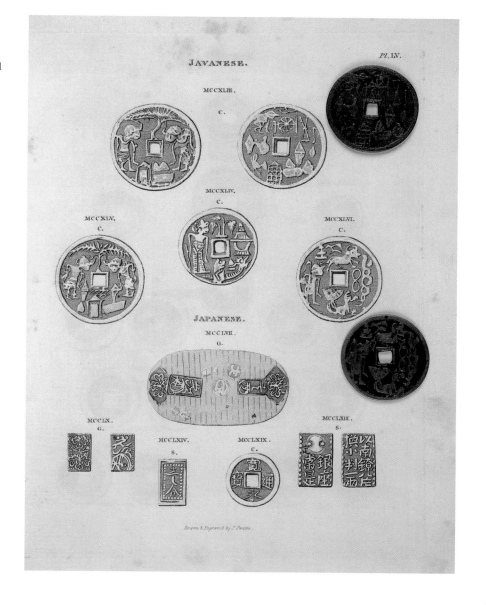

247 Miniature model of an orchestra of gamelan instruments, Javanese, collected by Sir Stamford to document Javanese society. He also collected one of the finest and oldest full-scale gamelans – tuned percussion metal and wood instruments, which accompanied voices and string instruments and flutes at traditional dramatic performances, such as the *wayang* shadow-puppet theatre. Ethno.

248 Three flat carved wood puppets for the Javanese *wayang keruchil* shadow-puppet theatre for performing plays about Javanese heroes, collected by Sir Stamford Raffles: a noble prince, a king and an evil prince. His collection, which also included leather figures and masks, is of high importance, documenting the range and variety of the puppet and dance theatre repertoire before European influence. Ethno.

of the Malay Language. Marsden also published the coins collected by both himself and Stamford Raffles, the East India Company's Governor of Java (fig. 246). Both self-taught scholars, starting their careers as minor secretarial officials in the Company, they were driven by a thirst to understand by collecting – Raffles returned to London with over a hundred cases of objects. Back in England Marsden and Raffles came under the influence of Sir Joseph Banks, who introduced them to scholarly circles in London and encouraged them to document their discoveries. Marsden wrote the detailed History of Sumatra (London, 1782), which undoubtedly in its turn inspired Raffles's remarkable History of Java (2 volumes, London, 1819), written while he was on leave in London between his governorships of Java (1811–16) and Bencoolen (1817–24).

Raffles's discoveries on Java still continue to be studied as key resources in understanding that island's culture and history. Although his main preoccupation as governor of the island was to establish British rule, Raffles devoted equal energy to collecting antiquities, manuscripts, ethnographic objects, plants and animals to illustrate the cultural and natural history of the island. He also consulted local Javanese

Raffles's researches later continued during his rule as Lieutenant-Governor of Bencoolen, Sumatra, gathering another collection, which sadly was lost in a fire on board ship off Sumatra on his way home. Back in London in 1825 he was elected the first President of the London Zoo, which he established with the help of Sir Humphry Davy, President of the Royal Society. Raffles's varied roles as political and military leader, collector, linguist, author, ethnographer, historian and naturalist single him out as the epitome of the British Enlightenment.

CHINA

Although the British were not as successful as the Dutch in terms of large-scale trade in the seventeenth century, they rose to dominate commerce in the eighteenth century. The Honourable East India Company was founded in 1708, replacing earlier English East India companies which competed for profits in trading Far Eastern goods; it later became the world's largest trading company.[10] Westerners only ever had a toehold in China first in Macao, then Canton (Guangzhou) and later Hong Kong. For most of the

249 Chinese porcelain punchbowl with en grisaille enamel and gold painting showing the European trading stations (hongs) along the Pearl River waterfront at Guangzhou (Canton). National flags identify the buildings rented by the East India companies of Holland, England, Sweden, etc. Qing dynasty, c. 1780–5. Dia. 56.5 cm. Presented by F. C. Harrison. OA.

scholars and conducted archaeological excavations in his search for information. Much of his rich Javanese collection survives today in the British Museum's Ethnography Department, including a complete orchestra of Javanese gamelan instruments (fig. 247), small-scale models of domestic objects and sets of puppets and masks (fig. 248) for the various genres of the Javanese theatrical tradition.[9]

eighteenth century, the foreign community occupied an area approximately a thousand feet long on the banks of the Pearl River, in the south-western quarter of Canton.[11] Merchants lived and conducted their business in thirteen hongs during the trading season, August to January (fig. 249). Hongs were so named after the Cantonese pronunciation for the Chinese for business, 'hang'. Until 1760 all foreign staff had to leave

250 Chinese porcelain blue-and-white openwork fruit basket and dish, recovered from the *Diana* cargo, made c. 1816. The forms of this basket and dish are entirely European, copying a silverware prototype. The landscape decoration on the dish inspired the European Willow Pattern copies. OA.

Canton during the dead season and retire to Macao. Trade was conducted between the supercargoes, commercial agents of the East India Companies, and the Chinese merchants who had purchased monopolies for trading with the Europeans through the government in Peking (Beijing). Chinese merchants fixed the prices of goods for the Europeans and were responsible for the Europeans' behaviour to the Chinese authorities. Traded goods were transported ten miles downstream to the European ships anchored in deep water at Whampoa. These ships had large holds for cargo and provisions and an armament comparable to battleships of the period. They could hold two to three hundred thousand porcelains with tea, silk and other luxury goods placed on top. Voyages from and to China were extremely risky, as salvage of wrecks in the twentiethth century has revealed.[12] Two early nineteenth-century shipwrecks testify to the continuity of this trade prior to the Opium Wars: the *Diana* wrecked in 1816 (fig. 250)[13] and the *Tek Sing*, dubbed the 'Titanic of the East', in 1822.[14]

The main object for export was porcelain: most Chinese export porcelains were everyday tablewares in blue-and-white and, to a lesser degree, coloured with overglaze enamels. However, there were also specially commissioned tablewares, commemorative wares and interior ornaments,

ordered for particular customers in western shapes, based on European ceramic or metalwork models, or painted with western designs, copied from coins, satirical cartoons, romantic prints and playing cards.[15] By the early nineteenth century approximately five thousand British families owned personalized tableware imported from China (see figs 216–17).[16] In fact there were few directors of East India companies, captains, supercargoes and their families who did not own Chinese armorial services by this time. Dinner, tea, coffee and chocolate services were commissioned to supplement silver and glass tableware. The shapes of sauce boats, tureens, salt cellars and custard cups were entirely European and would have seemed quite alien to the Chinese manufacturers in Jingdezhen. This factor was reflected in their price. Porcelain painted with specific coats of arms was ten times as expensive as ordinary blue-and-white wares. Chinese porcelain painters copied the arms, crests and mottoes from printed heraldic bookplates sent out to China for this purpose.[17] Commodore, later Admiral, Lord Anson (1697–1762) of Shugborough, Staffordshire, travelled to Canton in 1743 during his circumnavigation of the world (see fig. 142) on HMS *Centurion*. There he ordered an armorial dinner service decorated with pictures of Canton and Plymouth harbours and a breadfruit tree, copied from drawings by his draughtsman Percy Brett (fig. 251). In 1748 Anson published his *Voyage Around the World*, illustrated with engravings after Brett's drawings of the places he visited.

Chinese (and Japanese) porcelains aroused the curiosity of English collectors in the seventeenth century as interior ornaments and tablewares. Inventories of 1688 and 1690 from

251 Chinese porcelain soup plate with *famille rose* arms of Commodore, later Admiral, Lord Anson (1697–1762), c. 1743–7. Dia. 23 cm. The rim cartouches contain pictures of Canton and Plymouth harbours. The breadfruit tree in the centre and palm to the left have been copied from drawings by his draughtsman Percy Brett. Presented by the Earl of Lichfield. OA.

bright colours and rhino horn cups. Some of these were bought from missionaries or others who worked or travelled in the Far East. Porcelains with heraldic and western print designs, collected eagerly in the succeeding century for the British Museum by Sir A. W. Franks, were not collected during Sloane's lifetime but would have been present in England as modern luxury tableware.[20] Chinese graphic art is represented in the Sloane collection by fine coloured wood-block prints traditionally believed to have been brought to England by the physician Engelbert Kaempfer, who visited Japan in 1690–2.[21] Until the end of the eighteenth century few Chinese paintings were seen in Europe. Exceptional items include a set of four decorative silk paintings belonging to Archduke Ferdinand II of Austria, acquired in the late sixteenth century,[22] and one of the earliest Chinese paintings

252 Pair of porcelain phoenixes and tree peonies decorated in *famille verte* enamels. H. 10 cm. Beneath the magical birds are hinged doors which conceal erotic sculptures of couples making love. These amusing desk ornaments were made in China between 1700 and 1720 for sale to Europeans and were collected as novelties by Sir Hans Sloane. OA.

Burghley House near Stamford in Lincolnshire,[18] home to the Cecil family, testify to their popularity, as do Queen Mary II's inventories of Kensington Palace and Hampton Court.[19] They appear in still-life oil paintings and curiosity cabinets. Sir Hans Sloane collected Chinese *famille verte* figures (fig. 252) and vessels made between 1662 and 1722 as well as soap-stone, boxwood and ivory carvings of popular gods, ivory plaques, tiny bronze sculptures of boys playing, glass wares in

to reach England, a handscroll in ink and colour on silk, by Xie Chufang, *The Fascination of Nature*, dated 1321 (fig. 253). An inscription inside its outer cover is dated 1797 and signed by the then owner William Butler (1748–1822), a writing master who tutored female East Enders.[23] Lower-quality watercolours produced by Chinese for sale to foreigners illustrating costumes, trades and craft industries would have been more familiar in Britain.[24]

253 Detail of a Chinese insect and flower painting, *The Fascination of Nature*, by Xie Chufang (1321), handscroll in ink and colour on silk. An inscription inside its outer cover is dated 1797 and signed by the then owner, the writing master William Butler (1748–1822). Purchased with funds from the Brooke Sewell Permanent Fund and the National Art Collections Fund. OA.

Despite the relative lack of understanding of China in Europe and Europe in China prior to the twentieth century, Chinese ceramics, decorative arts, paintings, architecture and gardens had a tremendous impact on British visual design. Fantastical visions of China infused a style of decoration called *Chinoiserie* which drew upon Chinese, Japanese, Indian, Persian and African motifs to form a hybrid decorative style for architecture, painting and applied art.[25] China, or rather Cathay, this idealized version, was a popular subject for rococo romantic paintings by artists such as François Boucher and Antoine Watteau (1684–1721). Chinese crafts were copied in poor local materials throughout Europe, giving rise to brown stoneware teapots, blue-and-white ceramics and later on enamel decorated porcelains. Formal Italianate garden design was fundamentally altered by Chinese asymmetrical styles incorporating buildings such as pagodas. China was believed to be a state ruled by sage emperors and wise philosophers, a state lauded by learned eighteenth-century thinkers such as Voltaire. Despite the doc-

umentary paintings and eye-witness accounts of, for example, Lord Macartney's diplomatic embassy to the court of the Qianlong emperor in 1793–4 (fig. 254), this illusion was not dispersed until the mid nineteenth century. Then the coming of the European industrial revolution made mass-produced items more affordable locally than imports from China.

The First Opium War between Britain and China in 1839–42, leading to the forcible opening of treaty ports and the leasing of Hong Kong island, dispelled much of China's mystique for the British. In France the formal study of China and Chinese had begun with the establishment of a chair in Chinese and Tartar-Manchu literature and language at the Collège de France in 1814. Its first occupant was the twenty-seven-year-old Jean-Pierre Abel-Rémusat (1788–1832). In England sinologists are first described as such in English in 1838, and it was not until about 1860–80 that the study of China and its language became a recognized academic subject in Britain.[26]

JAPAN

As we have seen, there was extensive trade to and from China, but little understanding of its culture or language, even though there would have been ample opportunity to develop such studies as a result of commercial contacts and diplomatic contacts like Lord Macartney's embassy. In the case of

254 *The Approach of the Emperor of China to his Tent in Tartary to Receive the British Ambassador*, pencil and watercolour by William Alexander, 1793.The five-hour-long meeting of Lord Macartney (far right) with the Emperor of China (in sedan chair) took place in a specially erected tent in the Garden of Ten Thousand Trees near Jehol (Chengde). P&D.

Japan trade was much more restricted, and knowledge of Japanese civilization was very limited before the nineteenth century. There are only the accounts of a few officials with the Dutch East India Company (the VOC), the only Europeans permitted to dock in the single port of Nagasaki.

The English trading factory at Hirado was closed in 1623, and by 1639 Europeans were expelled from Japan and Japanese forbidden to travel abroad. Japan's ruling elite found Spanish and Portuguese Catholic missionaries to be quarrelsome and meddlesome and, bringing to an end the experiment of Japan's so-called 'Christian century' (from 1543), they persecuted and then banned the alien religion. Only merchants of the VOC and Chinese merchants were allowed to dock a limited number of trading vessels each year at the extreme western port of Nagasaki and to staff and maintain small permanent settlements there. The VOC was confined (and watched) on an artificial island, Dejima, in Nagasaki Bay, and trade was supposedly controlled by shogunal officials; however, a degree of illicit trade continued. There was a need to

prevent the undue drain from Japan of precious metal, first silver, later copper. Interstate relations with Qing China were conducted via the occasional embassies sent from Choson Korea and the Ryukyuan kingdom (also claimed by the Japanese Satsuma domain), and the Dutch Kapitan (head of the VOC factory), too, was required to offer symbolic homage to the Shogun by means of an annual 'court journey' to his great castle in distant Edo, some 600 miles from Nagasaki. Attempts by German, French, Russian, US and British vessels to land in Japan and establish new relations in the late eighteenth and early nineteenth centuries were all rebuffed, but galvanized the shogunal authorities into reconsidering both their foreign policies and the fundamental nature of the national polity. Ultimately it was US Commodore Perry's military mission of 1853–4 which forced the opening of designated 'treaty ports' to trade with the USA and Europe.

In the absence of unbridled foreign incursion and trade, the encounter between Japan and the outside world in this era has been characterized as 'an almost egalitarian cultural collision'.[27] Foreign goods imported into Japan – lenses, mercury mirrors, clockwork mechanisms, diagrams in printed books – took on magnified significance as emblems of European scientific inquiry, spawning a small but vital school of 'Dutch studies' (*Rangaku*) which in some ways served a vanguard role to the more engulfing westernization that occurred in the later nineteenth century. The process was accelerated by the personal interest in western technology of the eighth Tokugawa shogun, Yoshimune (1684–1751), who in 1721 eased restrictions on the importation of Chinese translations of western books, providing they did not deal with Christianity. The other main sources of information about Europe were the regular interviews with VOC officers and the secret debriefing of individual Japanese who were shipwrecked abroad and repatriated. In the visual arts from the late 1730s Japanese *ukiyo-e* artists copied the deep perspective systems of imported European and Chinese prints, revolutionizing the depiction of landscape.

In western Europe the most tangible arrivals from Japan were superior luxury goods – principally lacquer (which was imitated in 'Japanned' wares), porcelains and silks. Seventeenth-century Japan at first supplied Europe with imitations of Chinese porcelains, which had become temporarily available with the fall of the Ming dynasty, showy export wares ('Imari') sometimes made to order in western shapes. These and wares in more restrained styles, such as Kakiemon, spawned many European imitations.[28] Knowledge about Japan in the period was almost entirely reliant on the accounts, both manuscript and published, of certain key individuals associated with the VOC and the collections of objects they carried out of Japan.[29]

The most influential early Japanologist was the German Engelbert Kaempfer (1651–1716), who served as physician to the VOC in Japan 1690–2 and participated in two court journeys to Edo. The principal study published during his lifetime was *Amoenitatum exoticarum* (*Exotic Titbits*) about travels in Persia, Siam and Japan, but the major work *History of Japan, Together with a Description of the Kingdom of Siam* did not appear until after his death, and first in English (1727–8) (fig. 255).[30] This was because Kaempfer's oriental rarities, manuscripts and letters languished for many years before being bought up by Sir Hans Sloane in 1723–5 (fig. 256).[31] Kaempfer's eye-witness account provides a uniquely detailed and generally accurate description of Japan in the 1690s, and his admiring views about the ability of the 'absolute ruler' (i.e., the shogun) to maintain peaceful government were subsequently influential in Europe. The *History of Japan* was translated into French, Dutch and German, and a chapter of *Amoenitatum*, translated into Japanese, provoked debate back in Japan in the early years of the nineteenth century about the desirability of maintaining the policy of 'closed country' (*sakoku*), the first time that the policy was so named.[32]

Kaempfer's drawings of Japanese plants were subsequently republished by two European authorities: Carl Peter Thunberg (1743–1828), the Swedish botanist and pupil of Linnaeus, who himself visited Japan in 1775–6, collecting more than eight hundred specimens of Japanese flora and lecturing to Japanese scholars interested in European science; and Sir Joseph Banks (1743–1820). Thunberg stayed with Banks in London in 1777

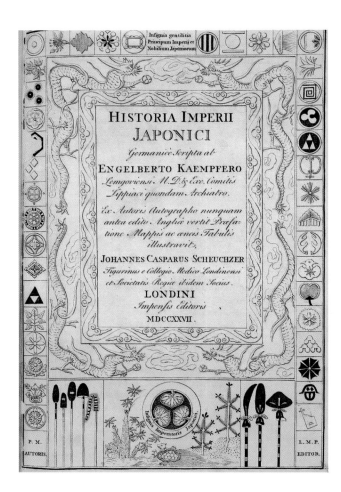

255 Frontispiece to *The History of Japan* by Engelbert Kaempfer, 1727, designed by J. C. Scheuchzer, Sloane's librarian. Kaempfer's papers and Japanese collections were purchased by Sloane in 1723–5. He had Kaempfer's manuscript *Heutiges Japan* translated and published in this book, which shaped the Enlightenment's view of Japan. JA Library.

while preparing his *Flora Japonica* (1784) and Banks later published a volume of engravings after Kaempfer's drawings in 1791. During the 1780s Banks backed several abortive attempts to open up trade in furs between the American north-west and Japan: as so often, scholarly enquiry was paralleled by schemes to expand still further the global mercantile empire.[33]

Isaac Titsingh (1744?–1812) headed the Dutch trading post in Japan almost a century after Kaempfer had been there, in 1779–80, 1781–3 and 1784. He participated in two official visits to Edo and made the acquaintance of Japanese scholars of western studies there. Following his return to England and France in 1809 he published two accounts, *Cérémonies usitées au Japon pour les mariages et les funérailles* (1819), and *Mémoires et anecdotes sur la dynastie régnante des djogouns* [*shoguns*], *souverains des Japon* (1820). Both were published in English with other writings in 1822 as illustrations of Japan.

Kutsuki Masatsuna, lord of the Fukuchiyama fief (1750–1802), was an important Japanese collaborator of Titsingh. He was a keen coin collector, and he reciprocated Titsingh's interest in Japan by an interest in things European. As well as publishing a detailed and systematic catalogue of his own Japanese and Chinese coin collection in twelve volumes, he also published Japan's first book on European coins.[34]

In the middle of the nineteenth century the most authoritative and influential sources of information on Japan were the collections and publications of Philipp Franz von Siebold (1796–1866), another German who served as VOC physician in Japan in 1823–9, returning to that country again in 1859–63. In 1824 Siebold established the Narutaki-juku school in Nagasaki and collected ethnography, art and 'dissertations' from his pupils which were later incorporated into his own publications. He also tutored an art-pupil, Kawahara Keiga (dates unknown), to provide hundreds of paintings in a novel, strongly western-influenced style of plants, animals, genre scenes and some portraits (see fig. 212). In 1826, during an official visit to Edo, Siebold befriended Takahashi Kageyasu, shogunal astronomer, who subsequently sent many maps to him in Nagasaki. This led, however, to accusations of spying, and Siebold was expelled from Japan in 1829.[35]

With the arrival in Japan of US and European diplomats in the 1850s, traders in the 1860s, tourists and 'experts' (*o-yatoi*) employed by the Japanese government in the 1870s – mirrored by the enthusiastic participation by Japan in all the international expositions from 1867 onwards – the regulated exchange outlined above became much more of a free-for-all, while Japan's punitive expedition against Taiwan in 1874 announced the rekindling of its own colonial ambitions. From that time on, there was an increased level of contact with Japan and a growing level of knowledge about its culture and history.

The patterns of European contact with the countries and cultures of the East were, as has been described, very different. The thirst for trade and empire that took Europeans to this new part of the globe brought Enlightenment scholars such as Engelbert Kaempfer, William Jones and Stamford Raffles in its wake. Though they travelled primarily in the service of governments and the great trading companies they were nevertheless in many ways true Enlightenment figures, whose ability to transmit knowledge back to Europe was constrained only by the open or closed reaction of the cultures they encountered to the European powers and ideas they brought.

256 Group of Japanese objects from Kaempfer's collection acquired by Sir Hans Sloane, including scales in a wooden box, two ceramic lidded boxes, and a tea bowl (one of three) of Utsutsugawa ware. Kaempfer also brought home natural history specimens, including shells and plants, and a pair of slippers (see fig. 70). JA.

25

Africa: in the shadow of the Enlightenment

NIGEL BARLEY

Africa was the closest of continents to Europe yet was the last to be systematically explored. In part this was due to the barrier of the Sahara that made travel to the south elementally hazardous. In part it was due to the dramatic rates of mortality from disease among Europeans who went there. The hostility of coastal polities to European interference in the hinterland markets from which they drew sustenance also entered into it. An unwritten understanding defined the interior as the exclusive concern of Africans, and European interest in matters beyond the coast was not considered necessary for trade and seen as commercial espionage. A complete reliance on African intermediaries even a few miles inland was the norm. But from the European side, it was also a metaphysical problem. Detailed research was unnecessary, for there reigned a European conviction that – beneath superficial differences – Africans were in their essentials all 'the same'.

European contact with the west coast of Africa dated back to the voyages of discovery of the fifteenth century, and a string of European trading forts was dotted along the littoral ensuring a continuity of detailed political and commercial information in that narrow region. Various English monarchs had issued charters to merchants to trade on the west coast of Africa but it was not until 1638 that the Royal Africa Company was recognized as the sole relevant body by Charles I, and it would endure until 1752. By the beginning of the eighteenth century this area was described through an established tradition of documentation that comprised some twenty major works, though many were unreliable recensions, translations and fanciful elaborations of earlier texts. The illustrations were often works of sheer fantasy and led an independent existence that rarely touched reality. The poor quality of much of this material is hardly surprising. The records of the Royal Africa Company show both a high mortality amongst its employees and their extreme youthfulness. Much of its onshore business was conducted by men scarcely out of their teens so that there was little extensive, mature exposure to Africa. And the vast interior of the continent was hardly imaginable at all. The European vision relied on rare, out-of-date, second-hand editions and versions of Arabic travellers such as the sixteenth-century Moroccan Leo Africanus. It is striking how little the heated eighteenth-century discussions about the nature of 'the African' in the context of slavery and the myriad Utopian schemes propounded for African development drew on actual reports of contemporary Africans. They functioned almost entirely in terms of myth.

257 *A View of Kamalia*, an Arcadian landscape as depicted in *Travels in the Interior Districts of Africa* by Mungo Park (1799). Engraving by J. C. Barrow after Park's original drawing. The picture includes on the left one of the very first illustrations of African iron-smelting, a skill that would largely disappear under pressure of European imports. Ethno Library.

Yet this ignorance was both an affront to Enlightenment notions of knowledge and a bar to that freedom of commerce that was increasingly considered a natural right of Europeans wherever they went. With the loss of the American colonies, moreover, there was a new and urgent incentive to find a new site to which convicts could be transported. Both governments and scholarly institutions began to recognize the need to send 'scientific' investigators to fill in the huge blanks on the map. The indefatigable Sir Joseph Banks was a vital part of this, despatching botanical researchers privately and later from his base at the Royal Botanical Gardens in Kew. Thus in 1771 he sent Henry Smeathman to the Banana Islands off the coast of Sierra Leone for several years to make a systematic collection of plant and insect specimens. Smeathman, when he returned, allocated himself a larger frame of reference and set himself up as a full-time 'expert' on all aspects of Africa, becoming a 'projector' of yet more Utopian schemes.[1]

Sir Joseph Banks worked towards an even more systematic organization of enlightened travel in Africa. An African Committee already administered the Gold Coast forts, mainly for the benefit of the slave trade, but in 1788 Banks founded the Association for promoting the Discovery of the Interior Parts of Africa, commonly called the African Association. He dominated its operation until 1805 from the post of Treasurer. An African Institution was founded in 1807 to promote humanitarian policies. These three bodies were respectively 'mercantile, scientific and Evangelical-humanitarian. Each worked within its own circle of interests, though individuals could and did belong to two or more of them.'[2] The advancement of science and increase of knowledge, the goals of the earlier Enlightenment voyages, were increasingly joined by the intention to derive benefits from them: subtle interweavings of botanical, economic and imperial purposes were at play.[3]

In 1788 the African Association sent three travellers, Ledyard, Lucas and Houghton, to penetrate the Western Sudan from three different points of departure. The association described itself explicitly as being 'desirous of rescuing the age from a charge of ignorance, which in other respects belongs so little to its character'. Yet Lucas achieved nothing and the other two died. Such results were far from unusual in the history of African exploration.

MUNGO PARK

A turning point was the journey of Mungo Park beginning in 1795. Park spent some two years wandering in the Western Sudan between the Gambia and Niger rivers, on behalf of the African Association and the Colonial Office. He was a Scottish assistant surgeon who had secured the favour of Sir Joseph Banks and thus secured an appointment in a vessel of the East India Company. In the course of his first voyage to the East, he had contributed descriptions of several new species of fish to

the Linnean Society, and it was as an expert on fish that he was held suited to exploring Africa. His *Travels in the Interior Districts of Africa* was first published in 1799 and caused a sensation. Although he failed to reach fabled Timbuktu, he confirmed the existence of the great River Niger as mentioned first by the Greek historian Herodotus. His work's rich descriptions of populous towns and prosperous agriculture opened the entire area to European speculation if not physical penetration and fired renewed interest in the region. In Britain Mungo Park became a celebrity, and tales of his sufferings, privations and imprisonment by a local leader excited the popular imagination. More than merely a curiosity, Africa even became briefly fashionable. The Duchess of Devonshire penned a pastoral poem, which was set to music, about the African ladies who were kind to Mungo Park and it was included in the published volume along with tasteful etchings of an Arcadian landscape (fig. 257).

The coastal rivers of the Gambia and Senegal were navigable for some distance inland but – as elsewhere – knowledge and navigation had tended to end together abruptly. During the Enlightenment Africa increasingly became viewed in the popular and learned mind as a limited number of geographical puzzles. What was the source of the Nile? What was the course of the Niger? Did it flow into Lake Chad? Did it join the Congo or the Nile? For some time it was unclear whether it even flowed east or west. Yet from all this confused information the notable French geographers of the period, such as d'Anville (1697–1782), pieced together much of what was then known, and their English counterpart, James Rennell, began to produce a series of maps for the African Association, beginning in 1790, only slightly vitiated by his dogged conviction that the Niger flowed into an inland sea.

Yet myth continued to flourish. James Bruce (1730–94), the former British Consul in Algiers, explored Ethiopia and left an account (published 1790) that was the last gasp of a very ancient attempt to pin down the location of the Christian kingdom of Prester John. This tradition stretched back to the twelfth century, while new entirely illusory elements made their appearance on the 'scientific' maps – such as the Mountains of Kong, north of Ouidah, invoked to explain the supposed course of the Niger. Once such features were established, it became extremely difficult to discredit and erase them, so that in the mid nineteenth century Richard Burton was still giving vivid, detailed physical descriptions of the non-existent Mountains of Kong – as seen with his own eyes. Africans too tended to approach the unknown through the known, so that in Benin Europeans were held to be messengers of a white-faced god, Olokun, who sent wealth from beyond the sea. And such views could be extremely resistant. We know from remarks made by the king when signing a treaty with the British in the 1890s that this vision still obtained some four hundred years after first contact.

Park's second expedition, in 1805, to journey up the

Gambia River as far as the Niger, was a rather different affair from the first. He was convinced that the Niger and the Congo were the same river. But whereas he had previously travelled as a private individual, very much in interaction with and at the mercy of locals, this expedition was government-sponsored, military and aggressive. By the time they reached the Niger only eleven of the original forty Europeans were alive. The party aroused hostility in the areas it passed through and the sudden cessation of Park's journals and letters, sent back to the coast, made his own fate another of the great mysteries of Africa. Only later would it become clear that he had finally come to grief at the Bussa rapids, a thousand miles downstream in what is now northern Nigeria, while once more under attack from local people. His journal was finally published by the African Association in 1815. It had been intended merely as an aide-memoire, 'to recall to his own recollection *other* particulars illustrative of the manners and customs of the natives, which would have swelled the communication to a most unreasonable size'.[4] These '*other* particulars', naturally, never appeared in print and exploration somewhat lapsed as a result. A further blow was the death of Sir Joseph Banks in 1820 and the final incorporation of the Association into the Royal Geographical Society in 1831, though the government organized two further military expeditions to the Gambia and Congo in 1816 and 1817. Both were dismal failures.

THE BEGINNINGS OF
ETHNOGRAPHIC EXPLORATION

The rise of Sierra Leone and the abolition of the Atlantic slave trade in 1807 led to an urgent review of the role of the old African forts administered by the African Committee, which now had to justify its existence within the new regime of legitimate trade. Throughout the eighteenth century the inland kingdom of Ashanti, in what is modern Ghana, had continuously expanded and provided profitable exports of slaves and gold. Now it posed a problem for British policy, since a standing Ashanti objective was to conquer a corridor to the sea to cut out the Fante middlemen who were the allies of the British. The British themselves vacillated between supporting and opposing this goal, according to the tastes of the relevant – and usually short-lived – governor. Finally, in 1817 a diplomatic expedition was organized to visit the Asantehene, supreme ruler of the Ashanti kingdom, at his capital, Kumasi. It would become known by the name of its most active member, Thomas Bowdich.

Bowdich was an amateur naturalist and ethnographer and highly ambitious. A low-ranking employee of the Royal Africa Company and only twenty-five years old, he soon saw the mission to Kumasi as the vehicle that would raise him within both the Company and the public imagination. He rapidly undermined and displaced the supposed head of the

mission and negotiated a treaty with the Ashanti that would make them allies of the British interest and a route to the interior. When the Company seemed unappreciative of his efforts, he resigned and published his *Mission from Cape Coast to Ashantee* (1819) as a private venture. It was the most vivid and detailed account of an African kingdom to date. Bowdich and his companions were dazzled by the wealth, power and pageantry of Ashanti kingship (figs 258–9).

'We entered Coomasie at 2 o'clock, passing under a fetish, or sacrifice of a dead sheep, wrapped up in red silk, and suspended between two lofty poles. Upwards of 5,000 people, the greater part warriors, met us with awful bursts of martial music, discordant only in its mixture; for horns, drums, rattles, and gong-gongs were all exerted with a zeal bordering on phenzy, to subdue us by the first impression. The smoke which encircled us from the incessant discharges of musquetry, confined our glimpses to the foreground; and we were halted whilst the captains performed their Pyrrhic dance, in the centre of a circle formed by their warriors, where a confusion of flags, English, Dutch and Danish were waved and flourished in all directions ... The dress of the captains was a war-cap, with gilded rams horns projecting in front, the sides extended beyond all proportion by immense plumes of eagles feathers, and fastened under the chin with bands of couries. Their vest was of red cloth, covered with fetishes and saphies [amulets] in gold and silver; and embroidered cases of almost every colour, which flapped against their bodies as they moved ... their black countenances heightened the effect of this attire, and completed a figure scarcely human.'[5]

The importance of the mission is that it came at a time when interest in Africa and exploration was at its lowest ebb. Nowadays, the expedition in which Bowdich began as a junior member and which he ended by leading is not remembered for the treaty it negotiated. This would rapidly be superseded. Far more important is Bowdich's book. It is a lively and colourful, first-hand account, full of accurate detail and observation, and has proved an invaluable source for both anthropologists and historians. Until recently a third aspect of Bowdich's work has been almost entirely neglected: his activities as a collector. During his stay in Kumasi Bowdich made a collection of local art and craft work, most of which survives in the British Museum's collections – 'almost certainly the earliest documented collection from Ashanti and one of the evidential treasures of the Ethnography Department'.[6]

THE BOWDICH COLLECTION

The surviving specimens number some two dozen, mostly everyday objects. We know very little of how Bowdich acquired them, yet Malcolm McLeod, author of an important study of this collection, argued cogently that it was no

258 *The king's sleeping room*, an Ashanti house as depicted in *Mission from Cape Coast to Ashantee* by Thomas Bowdich (1819). Coloured engraving from an original drawing by Bowdich. The sophisticated architectural drawings brought back from this expedition refuted the assumption that Africans all lived in simple huts and showed a society of rich sumptuary distinctions. Ethno Library.

259 *First day of the yam custom*, an Ashanti procession as depicted in *Mission from Cape Coast to Ashantee* by Thomas Bowdich (1819). Coloured engraving from an original drawing by Bowdich. The Ashanti seem to have deliberately set out to impress Bowdich by organizing his attendance at major court rituals where the king's power and wealth might be displayed. Ethno Library.

random assemblage of objects, rather a *systematic* collection. The specimens Bowdich brought back represent the main indigenous technologies available to the Ashanti and so fall naturally into several groups; goldwork (small castings of a bell, drum, sanko and two pectoral insignia) (fig. 260), woodworking and carpentry (a stool, a child's umbrella with a beautifully carved finial, and a sanko), metalworking (needles, two arrowheads, and a knife and a lock made either in Hausaland, northern Nigeria, or by Hausa working in Ashanti), textiles (a complete loom and bobbins, a painted funeral cloth, woven silk and cotton girdles), leatherwork (a cushion, sandals, a bag, a needle case, and a cow's tail fly-whisk, presumably leather-bound), and pottery (tobacco-pipes (fig. 261) and a small bowl). The Ashanti seem to have collaborated in this collecting endeavour, and Bowdich noted that the goldwork was intended by the King of Ashanti as a gift for the British Museum that Bowdich had told him about. It would be interesting to know what he said, for it is clear that the Ashanti, on their side, were also keen to learn what they

could about their foreign, unpredictable and possibly dangerous neighbours, and other gifts were said to be presents from senior Ashanti. 'Nevertheless', Macleod noted, 'the majority appear to have been collected as part of a conscious effort to produce a representative collection of Ashanti products.'[7]

And of course, as a representative of the Africa Company, Bowdich was very interested in gold, and his account of goldworking and casting was exemplary for its time. He was also careful to note the amount of gold used in lost-wax casting, the proportion wasted in the process and the amount taken by the caster as his fee. Ashanti goldwork of this period is very rare. As late as the end of the nineteenth century it was still assessed and valued in the West purely as bullion and treated accordingly.

It is striking that European imports are absent from his collection but goods from internal African trade and influences are numerous, reflecting Bowdich's interest in Ashanti as a nexus of links with the interior and across the northern desert. The most significant is perhaps the Hausa lock, show-

ing a society already very concerned with the differential control of wealth and authority over resources.

A NEW KIND OF EXPLORER — RICHARD LANDER

Those ancient trade routes across the desert had not been entirely forgotten. The indefatigable John Barrow was both Under-Secretary of State at the Admiralty from 1805 to 1845 and a founder of the Royal Geographical Society, and used his position to foster the cause of African exploration. In 1821 he arranged support for the Oudney-Clapperton-Denham expedition, bringing together both Army and Navy, that set out from Tripoli to Lake Chad and the kingdom of Bornu. Afflicted by disease, hardship and internal dissent, they nevertheless succeeded in crossing the desert. Oudney died, Denham got involved in local warfare and politics but did see Lake Chad. Clapperton visited the Hausa cities of Kano and Sokoto and contacted the expanding Fulani empire that was busily redrawing the map of the entire West African hinterland. Clapperton brought back a letter from the Fulani ruler, Muhammad Bello, offering consular relations and an end to the slave trade from his dominions. This was considered to be so important that a follow-up expedition was ordered at once.

It was this attempt to exploit these new powerful contacts that brought on stage one of the most surprising and significant figures of African exploration, Richard Lander (1804–34). Lander (fig. 262), having previously travelled to the West Indies, was hired as Clapperton's manservant on an expedition that was to approach the Fulani empire again but from the west coast, crossing the Niger at the same Bussa rapids that had claimed the life of Mungo Park. The area was in military uproar, with Fulani forces on the advance in several directions. Sultan Bello, however, proved suspicious of both Britain and Clapperton and refused to sign a preferred treaty. Clapperton perished from fever in 1827, along with all other European members of the expedition, with the exception of Richard Lander, who was thus obliged to continue

260 Group of Ashanti gold objects: small castings of a bell, drum, sanko harp and two pectoral insignia, collected by Thomas Bowdich. Much easier to transport than life-size objects, models allowed the collection both of ethnographic information and the commercially important gold mining and casting seen at their best in courtly regalia. Ethno.

261 Ashanti tobacco-pipe. Tobacco-pipes typically depict proverbs, one of the ways in which foreign artefacts could be incorporated into the Ashanti system of material culture. Ethno.

alone, wrestling pathetically with the 'scientific' paraphernalia with which the party had been encumbered. He survived, bringing out with him Clapperton's journal, and subsequently published an account of both Clapperton's journey and his own adventures that marked a major change in the nature of African exploration.

Hitherto exploration had been a task for gentlemen, especially military gentlemen, distinguished equally as seasoned travellers, masters of dealing with awkward natives and representatives of their nation. Richard Lander was lower-class, uneducated and provincial. As a mere servant, he was treated with contempt by the British government. Although the sole survivor of the original expedition, as a manservant he had no claim on official finances at all but was finally allowed the salary of a mulatto interpreter who had perished. Being self-taught, it is no surprise that in his writings Lander strove hard to comply with the demand from his readers for material that showed the bizarre and exotic in Africa. His accounts are full of rich personal detail. But what is striking in his work is the depiction of relaxed, egalitarian relationships with Africans, the frank avowal of sexual attraction across racial lines and the view that the lot of the ordinary African, when peace obtained, was not inferior to that of his or her English counterpart. All this deeply shocked John Barrow at the Royal Geographical Society. Yet he found Richard Lander useful. There was a need to be seen to be doing something in Africa at the time so, in 1830, he arranged for a commission from the Colonial Office to send Richard and his

John Lander retired to his native Cornwall, but Africa had not finished with Richard. In 1832–3 he was induced to accompany yet a third expedition, this time *up* the Niger, led by MacGregor Laird, a Liverpool shipbuilder and Africa enthusiast. Steamers and an iron-bottomed vessel were used for the first time by the African Inland Commercial Company in this bold attempt to explore and trade for ivory and other produce. The expedition was to be self-financing and blatantly centred on the search for profit. In a sense this was a return to very old ideas of how to deal with Africa, as exem-

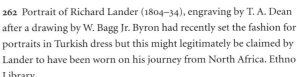

263 Two objects of Yoruba workmanship collected by the Lander brothers in the northern kingdom of Kiama before embarking on the River Niger. The actual objects were lost when the Landers were taken prisoner and their canoe overturned, but they give us some of our earliest images of what remain recognizable Yoruba carvings. Ethno Library.

262 Portrait of Richard Lander (1804–34), engraving by T. A. Dean after a drawing by W. Bagg Jr. Byron had recently set the fashion for portraits in Turkish dress but this might legitimately be claimed by Lander to have been worn on his journey from North Africa. Ethno Library.

brother, John Lander, to determine definitively the course of the Niger 'wherever that might be'. In a letter to Hay, the Colonial Under-Secretary, he remarked, 'With a bundle of beads and bafts and other trinkets, we could land him somewhere about Bonny and let him find his way'.[8] He never expected to see Richard Lander again, but the expenses and support requested by the brothers were trivial. They took the by now accustomed route from Badagery to the Niger, explored some hundred miles upstream and then, driven by necessity, descended the river by boat. On the way they industriously collected both information and objects (fig. 263). After many brushes with death, they discovered the confluence of the Niger and Benue and finally emerged in the Ibo country of southern Nigeria, where they were ransomed by King Boy of Brass but managed to escape his clutches and return to England some seventeen months later. In their *Journal of an Expedition to Explore the Course and Termination of the Niger* (1832), the path of the mighty river 'discovered' by Mungo Park was finally fixed and identified once and for all and presented as the great highway that would allow Europe to trade direct with the heart of Africa.

plified by the Royal Africa Company. But African notions of extended trust were incompatible with western ideas of shop-keeping. Traders would expect a large advance of goods on trust that would be paid for only after many months' free credit. These would be sold in the inland markets and the European supplier could hope to receive actual payment only after all manner of excuses, prevarications and renegotiation. Events followed a course curiously similar to those of Mungo Park's last voyage. Relationships with locals deteriorated and the heavily armed vessels offered the expedition the unusual temptation to use force to ensure compliance with the expedition's wishes as its financial situation became ever more desperate. Frustration and impatience led to an opening of hostilities. There were kidnappings and punitive measures and Richard Lander was finally wounded with an iron missile that had been stolen from his own vessel. He perished in Fernando Po in February 1834. Gentlemanly exploration had given way to practical trade and trade to armed conflict. It was to be the pattern of the future. Africa had indeed become the Dark Continent and the Enlightenment was over.

This table covers the period from about 1600 to about 1830. It does not include literature or music as they are not themes of this book.

BRITISH RULERS	EVENTS	BOOKS (abbreviated titles)	COLLECTORS (arranged by date of death)	SOCIETIES AND MUSEUMS	TRADE AND EXPLORATION
		William Camden, *Britannia* (1586)		Bodleian Library (1602)	East India Company (1600); Dutch East India Company (1602)
James I (1603–25)		'King James Bible' (1611)			
Charles I (1625–49)		Francis Bacon, *Novum Organum* (1620)	Robert Cotton (1571–1631)		Expulsion of Europeans from Japan (1639)
Commonwealth (1649–60)	English Civil War (1640–9)	René Descartes, *Discours de la méthode* (1637)	Earl of Arundel (1585–1646)		
	Reign of Louis XIV ('The Sun King') (1647–1715)	James Ussher, *Annales veteris testamenti* (1650)	King Charles I (1600–49)		
Charles II (1660–85)		*Musaeum Tradescantianum* (1656)		Royal Society (1660)	Hudson's Bay Company (1670)
		T. Burnet, *Telluris theoria sacra* (1681)			
James II (1685–8)		M. Lister, *Historia Conchyliorum* (1685–92)		Ashmolean Museum (1683)	Royal African Company (1672)
		Isaac Newton, *Principia* (1687)			
William III (1689–1702)	Glorious Revolution (1688)	John Ray, *Historia Plantarum* (1686–1704)			
		John Locke, *Essay Concerning Human Understanding* (1690)			Engelbert Kaempfer in Japan (1690–2)
Anne (1702–14)	War of Spanish Succession (1701–14)	H. Sloane, *Natural History of Jamaica* (1707–25)	William Courten (1642–1702)	Society of Antiquaries (1707)	
				Spalding Gentleman's Society (1710)	
George I (1714–27)	Jacobite rebellion in Britain (1715)	B. de Montfaucon, *L'Antiquité expliqué et représentée en figures* (1719–24)	Engelbert Kaempfer (1651–1716)		
		William Stukeley, *Itinerarium curiosum* (1724)	James Petiver (c. 1658–1718)		
George II (1727–60)		E. Kaempfer, *History of Japan* (1727)			
		E. Chambers, *Cyclopaedia* (1728)			
		J. Catesby, *Natural History of Carolina* (1731–43)			
		Voltaire, *Lettres philosophiques* (1734)		Society of Dilettanti (1734)	
		Carl Linnaeus, *Systema Plantarum* (1735)			
	Revolt of 'Young Pretender' and defeat at Culloden, Scotland (1745–6)	W. Warburton, *The Divine Legation of Moses* (1740)		Dresden Museum (1744)	George Anson's circumnavigation of world (1740–4)
	Treaty of Aix-la-Chapelle (1746)	J. Spence, *Polymetis* (1747)			
		D. Diderot and J. d'Alembert, *Encyclopédie* (1751–72)	Hans Sloane (1660–1753)	Society of Antiquaries, royal charter (1751)	Dawkins and Wood discover Palmyra (1751)
		Comte de Caylus, *Receuil d'antiquités* (1752–6)		British Museum Act (1753)	
	Seven Years War (1756–63)	Samuel Johnson, *Dictionary of the English Language* (1755)	Richard Mead (1673–1754)	Society of Arts (1754)	
	Clive's victory at Plassey, India (1757)	D. Hume, *Natural History of Religion* (1757)		British Museum opens to public in Montagu House (1759)	
George III (1760–1820)	British defeat of French in Canada (1760)	J. Stuart, N. Revett, *Antiquities of Athens* (1762–1816)			K. Niebuhr explores Arabia (1761)
		J. J. Winckelmann, *Geschichte der Kunst des Altertums* (1764)		Hermitage (1764)	John Harrison wins Board of Longitude's prize (1762)
		T. Pennant, *British Zoology* (1766)		Royal Academy (1768)	

BRITISH RULERS	EVENTS	BOOKS (abbreviated titles)	COLLECTORS (arranged by date of death)	SOCIETIES AND MUSEUMS	TRADE AND EXPLORATION
		Baron d'Hancarville, *Antiquités etrusques, grecques et romaines* (1767–76)			Wedgwood and Bentley open factory at Etruria (1771)
	Slaves landing in England declared free (1772)	*Encyclopaedia Britannica* (1771)		Hamilton's first vase collection acquired by British Museum (1772)	Cook's First Voyage to Pacific (1768–71)
		A. Smith, *Wealth of Nations* (1776)	Thomas Hollis (1720–74)		Cook's Second Voyage (1772–5)
	American Declaration of Independence (1776)	W. Hamilton, *Campi Phlegraei* (1776)		Ashton Lever's Museum (1775–86)	
	Gordon riots in London (1780)	Edward Gibbon, *Decline and Fall* (1776–88)	William Hunter (1718–83)		Cook's Third Voyage (1776–80)
	US constitution (1787)	Immanuel Kant, *Critik der reinen Vernunft* (1781)	Duchess of Portland (1715–85)	Asiatic Society founded by William Jones (1784)	African Association (1788)
	French Revolution (1789)	Gilbert White, *Natural History of Selborne* (1789)	Horace Walpole (1717–97)	Linnean Society (1788)	George Vancouver's voyage (1791–5)
	Nelson defeats French at Battle of Nile (1798)	J. Eckhel, *Doctrina numorum veterum* (1792–8)	Thomas Pennant (1726–98)	Musée du Louvre (1793)	Lord Macartney's embassy to China (1792)
		M. Park, *Travels in Interior Districts of Africa* (1799)	C. M. Cracherode (1730–99)	Discovery of Rosetta Stone (1799)	
	Act of Union (1801)	J. Sowerby, various books on *British Mineralogy* (1804–46)	William Hamilton (1730–1803)	Royal Institution (1800)	Mungo Park's first expedition (1795)
	Nelson defeats French at Trafalgar (1805)	R. P. Knight, *Specimens of Ancient Sculpture* (1809)	Charles Townley (1737–1805)	Hunterian Museum (1807)	Mungo Park's second expedition (1805)
	Abolition of slave trade in colonies (1807)	E. Moor, *The Hindu Pantheon* (1810)	Charles Greville (1749–1809)		
		R. C. Hoare, *The Ancient History of South Wiltshire* (1812–21)		William Bullock's Museum (1810–19)	Rich's identification of Babylon (1813)
	Defeat of Napoleon at Waterloo (1815)	W. Smith, *Map of the Strata of England and Wales* (1815)		William Smith's fossils and Elgin's antiquities acquired by British Museum (1816)	Thomas Bowdich's expedition (1817)
		S. Raffles, *History of Java* (1819)	King George III (1738–1820)		Robert Ker Porter's visit to Persepolis (1818)
		T. Bowdich, *Mission to Ashantee* (1819)			
George IV (1820–30)		J.-F. Champollion, *Précis du système hiéroglyphique* (1824)	Joseph Banks (1743–1820)	Belzoni's Egyptian Hall exhibition (1821)	
				Royal Asiatic Society (1822)	
			C. J. Rich (1787–1821)	George III's library (King's Library) to British Museum (1823)	
			Giovanni Belzoni (1778–1823)	Robert Smirke starts new British Museum building (1823)	
			Richard Payne Knight (1751–1824)	National Gallery (1824)	F. W. Beechey's voyage to Alaska (1826–7)
			Stamford Raffles (1781–1826)	William Bullock's Ancient Mexico exhibition (1824)	
			Henry Salt (1780–1827)		
William IV (1830–7)	Slavery abolished in British empire (1834) and USA (1865)	C. Lyell, *Principles of Geology* (1830–3)	Earl of Elgin (1766–1841)	Fire at Westminster destroys House of Commons Library (1834)	R. and J. Lander's expedition down the Niger (1830)

OTHER (LATER) DATES

The National Portrait Gallery was created in 1856. Like the National Gallery (1824), its collections include a number of paintings formerly in the British Museum.

The Natural History Museum. The natural history collections of the British Museum were transferred to the new building in South Kensington, London, in 1880–3 and became a separate museum in 1963.

The British Library. The library departments of the British Museum (maps, manuscripts, music and printed books including the King's Library) became part of the new British Library in 1973 and moved to the new British Library building at St Pancras, London, in 1998.

Reopening of the King's Library after restoration with the new Enlightenment exhibition, during the Museum's 250th anniversary in 2003.

277

Further reading and notes

PART I:
THE 'UNIVERSAL MUSEUM'

Chapter 1 pages 12–25

FURTHER READING

R. G. W. Anderson, M. L. Caygill,
A. G. MacGregor and L. Syson (eds),
*Enlightening the British: Knowledge,
Discovery and the Museum in the Eighteenth
Century* (London, 2004).

M. Caygill, *The Story of the British Museum*
(London, 1998)

N. Hampson, *The Enlightenment*
(Harmondsworth, 1968)

F. Haskell, *History and its Images: Art and the
Interpretation of the Past* (New Haven and
London, 1993)

I. Jenkins, *Archaeologists and Aesthetes in the
Sculpture Galleries of the British Museum
1800–1939* (London, 1992)

A. MacGregor (ed.), *Sir Hans Sloane: Collector,
Scientist, Antiquary* (London, 1994)

D. Outram, *The Enlightenment* (Cambridge,
1995)

E. Paintin, *The King's Library* (London, 1989)

R. Porter, *Enlightenment: Britain and the
Creation of the Modern World*
(Harmondsworth, 2000)

T. Rice, *Voyages of Discovery: Three Centuries of
Natural History Exploration* (London, 1999)

W. T. Stern, *The Natural History Museum at
South Kensington: A History of the Museum,
1753–1980* (London, 1998)

D. M. Wilson, *The British Museum: A History*
(London, 2002)

NOTES

1 A. Pope, *Epitaph. Intended for Sir Isaac Newton,
in Westminster Abbey* (1730). I am indebted to a
number of colleagues for their useful advice and
comments on this introduction, especially
Andrew Burnett, Frances Carey, Marjorie
Caygill, Ian Jenkins, Nina Shandloff, St John
Simpson and Luke Syson.

2 W. Doyle, *The Old European Order 1660–1800*
(Oxford, 1992), pp. 179, 180. I am greatly
indebted to this excellent account.

3 Quoted in N. Hampson, *The Enlightenment*,
p. 36.

4 *Ibid.*, p. 38.

5 Cited in 'Fontanelle, Bernard le Bovier, sieur
de', *Encyclopaedia Britannica*
http://www.search.eb.com/.

6. See P. Gay, *Age of Enlightenment* (New York,
1966), p. 11. Published by Time-Life, this book
provides a well-illustrated, good general guide
to the Enlightenment in Europe.

7. See for example T. Adorno and M.
Horkheimer, trans. J. Cumming, *Dialectic of
Enlightenment* (London, 1973). For an excellent
summary of how thinking about the
Enlightenment has changed through the
century see D. Outram, *The Enlightenment*.

8 Quoted in Porter, *Enlightenment*, p. xxi.

9 Hampson, *Enlightenment*, p. 9.

10 S. C. Bullock, 'Remapping Masonry: a
Comment', in 'Forum: Exits from the
Enlightenment', *Eighteenth-Century Studies* 33,
no. 2 (Winter 2000), p. 275.

11 Hampson, *Enlightenment*, pp. 10–11.

12 The most prominent of these societies are
the International, American, British, Scottish,
Irish and Canadian societies. There are thirty-
five other national Societies for Eighteenth-
Century Studies, with their various regional
subdivisions and producing their own
journals, newsletters and conferences; there is
also a Centre for Eighteenth-Century Studies
at the University of York and the Voltaire
Foundation at Oxford.

13 Porter, *Enlightenment*, p. xxiv.

14 Quoted in M. Caygill, 'Sloane's Will and the
Establishment of the British Museum', in
MacGregor (ed.), *Sir Hans Sloane*, p. 47.
Sloane's collection was intended as a bequest to
the nation, but he requested some payment,
much less than its true value, in order to
provide for his daughters.

15 The Cotton collection had been given to the
nation in 1700 and £10,000 of the lottery
money was used to purchase the Harleian
collection – again, much less than its true
value. For the history of the libraries see P. R.
Harris, *A History of the British Museum Library
1753–1973* (London, 1998).

16 See Caygill (n. 14 above); admission was free
but by tickets which had to be applied for in
advance (see Caygill, *The Story of the British
Museum*, pp. 12–13). Three other histories of
the Museum discuss these issues: E. Edwards,
Lives of the Founders of the British Museum
(London, 1870); E. Miller, *That Noble Cabinet:
A History of the British Museum* (London,
1974); and Wilson, *The British Museum*.

17 Solomon da Costa, 1760, in Caygill, *The
Story of the British Museum*, p. 14.

18 The House of Commons library was
destroyed in the fire of 1834 and afterwards an

effort was made to collect the type of books it
once contained, a library similar in character,
although not in size, to the King's Library. See
D. Menhennet, *The House of Commons Library:
A History* (London, 1991). There were no
comparable libraries in the British Museum
after the British Library left the site, and books
have been borrowed for the cases here in order
to echo the original character of the room as a
library and to remind visitors of the role that
such publications played in the dissemination
of Enlightenment ideas. They will be made
available to readers along the same lines as
were the books in the King's Library when they
were housed in the British Museum.

19 J. W. Yolton, *Locke: An Introduction* (Oxford,
1985), p. 1.

20 J.M. Sweet, 'Sir Hans Sloane: Life and
Mineral Collection, Part III: Mineral
Pharmaceutical Collection', *Natural History
Magazine* 5, no. 36 (October 1935), pp. 145–64.

21 Rice, *Voyages of Discovery*, p. 228.

22 See B. Woolley, *The Queen's Conjuror: The
Science and Magic of Dr Dee* (London, 2001).
Three of Dr Dee's wax disks came to the
Museum with the Cotton collection.

23 H. Tait, '"The Devil's Looking Glass": The
Magical Speculum of John Dee', in W. H. Smith
(ed.), *Horace Walpole: Writer, Politician and
Connoisseur* (London, 1967), p. 200.

24 C. Gibson-Wood, 'Classification and Value
in a Seventeenth-century Museum: William
Courten's Collection', *Journal of the History of
Collections* 9, no. 1 (1997), pp. 61–77.

25 See MacGregor (ed.), *Sir Hans Sloane*.

26 This has recently become a rapidly
expanding field of academic studies. See for
example *Journal of the History of Collections*,
several recent exhibition catalogues devoted to
individual collectors, including N. Penny and
M. Clarke, *The Arrogant Connoisseur: Richard
Payne Knight* (Manchester, 1982), and I. Jenkins
and K. Sloan, *Vases and Volcanoes: Sir William
Hamilton and his Collection* (London, 1996), a
new series of source books by S. Pearce and K.
Arnold, *Perspectives on Collecting* (Aldershot,
1999–2000), 2 vols and forthcoming, and
innumerable books on the history of
individual museums and on museology in
general.

27 See R. Altick, *The Shows of London*
(Cambridge, Mass., and London, 1978), and J.
King, 'New Evidence for the Contents of the
Leverian Museum', *Journal of the History of
Collections* 8, no. 2 (1996), pp. 167–86.

28 S. Pearce and K. Arnold, *The Collector's*

Voice, vol. 2, *Perspectives on Collecting* (Aldershot, 2000), pp. 139–46.

29 See A. B. Shteir, *Cultivating Women, Cultivating Science: Flora's Daughters and Botany in England 1760–1860* (Baltimore, 1996), and Sue Bennett, *Five Centuries of Women and Gardens*, National Portrait Gallery exhibition, 2000.

30 K. Sloan, *'A Noble Art': Amateur Artists and Drawing Masters c. 1600–1800* (London, 2000), p. 213.

31 A See S. H. Myers, *The Bluestocking Circle: Women, Friendship and the Life of the Mind in Eighteenth-century England* (Oxford, 1990).

32 Surprisingly little has been written about her collection, which was dispersed in a sale of 4,156 lots in April 1786; see D. E. Allen, *The Naturalist in Britain: A Social History* (Princeton, 1994), pp. 25–6, and Pearce and Arnold, *Collector's Voice* (n. 28 above), pp. 139–46.

33 Her collections have not been catalogued in detail, nor much written about, but see A. Griffiths and R. Williams, *Department of Prints and Drawings in the British Museum: User's Guide* (London, 1987), pp. 82–4. I am indebted to Luke Syson for this particular insight into her collecting.

34 For these see Caygill in MacGregor (n. 14 above) and other sources listed in n. 16 and M. Caygill, 'From Private Collection to Public Museum: the Sloane Collection at Chelsea and the British Museum in Montagu House', in R. Anderson *et al.*, *Enlightening the British*.

35 Jenkins, *Archaeologists and Aesthetes*, pp. 78, 102–9; see also M. Caygill and C. Date, *Building the British Museum* (London, 1999), pp. 16–19.

36 R. Porter, 'The Terraqueous Globe', in G. S. Rousseau and R. Porter (eds), *The Ferment of Knowledge: Studies in the Historiography of Eighteenth-century Science* (Cambridge, 1980), p. 308.

37 Caygill, *Story of the British Museum*, p. 25.

38 Jenkins and Sloan, *Vases and Volcanoes* (n. 26 above), Appendix, p. 305.

39 J. Thackray, '"The Modern Pliny": William Hamilton and Vesuvius', in *ibid.*, p. 68.

40 A. Momigliano, 'Ancient History and the Antiquarian', *Journal of the Warburg and Courtauld Institutes* 13 (1950), p. 299.

41 See J. M. Levine, *Dr Woodward's Shield: History, Science, and Satire in Augustan England* (Berkeley, 1977).

42 See ch. 3 and Paintin, *The King's Library*. Both the King and Queen Charlotte also maintained small private libraries for their personal use.

43 See K. D. Kriz, 'Curiosities, Commodities, and Transplanted Bodies in Hans Sloane's "Natural History of Jamaica", *William and*

Mary Quarterly 3rd ser., 57, no. 1 (January 2000), pp. 36–78, J. C. H. King, 'Ethnographic Collections', in MacGregor (ed.), *Sir Hans Sloane*, and J. Gascoigne, *Sir Joseph Banks and the English Enlightenment: Knowledge and Polite Culture* (Cambridge, 1994).

44 Doyle, *Old European Order* (n. 2 above), p. 196.

45 *Ibid.*, p. 203.

46 J. L. Abbott, 'Thomas Hollis and the Society 1756–1774', *The Royal Society of Arts Journal* 119 (1971), p. 713.

47 Even the enlightened desires for taxonomy and its scientific and aesthetic imperatives operated at times in opposition to liberal notions of equality; see D. Bindman, *Ape to Apollo: Aesthetics and the Idea of Race in the 18th Century* (Ithaca, 2002), especially p. 12 where he points out that the founding fathers of comparative racial taxonomy were fervently opposed to slavery.

Chapter 2 pages 26–37

FURTHER READING

A. Bermingham and J. Brewer (eds), *The Consumption of Culture 1600–1800: Image, Object, Text* (London, 1995)

A. Dawson, *Portrait Sculpture: A Catalogue of the British Museum Collection, c. 1675–1975* (London, 1999)

F. Haskell, *History and its Images: Art and the Interpretation of the Past* (New Haven and London, 1993)

O. Impey and A. MacGregor (eds), *The Origins of Museums: The Cabinet of Curiosities in 16th- and 17th-century Europe* (Oxford, 1985)

M. Pointon, *Hanging the Head: Portraiture and Social Formation in Eighteenth-century England* (London, 1993)

J. R. Fawcett Thompson and F. Gordon Roe, 'Some Oil Portraits in the British Museum' and 'More Paintings in the British Museum', *Connoisseur* 147, no. 592 (March 1961), pp. 114–18, and no. 593 (April 1961), pp. 189–95

NOTES

1 (London, 1770), vol. I, p. 62, letter IX, 4 June 1750, description of a visit to Lord Cobham's seat at Stow.

2 Pointon, *Hanging the Head*, p. 62; A. Martindale, *Heroes, Ancestors, Relatives and the Birth of the Portrait*, the Fourth Gerson Lecture, University of Groningen, May 1988 (The Hague, 1988), p. 33. I am most grateful to John Cherry for drawing my attention to this interesting publication.

3 L. Klinger Aleci, 'Images of Identity, Italian

Portrait Collections of the Fifteenth and Sixteenth Centuries', in N. Mann and L. Syson (eds) *The Image of the Individual: Portraits in the Renaissance* (London, 1998), pp. 67–79.

4 Haskell, *History and its Images*, pp. 61–3.

5 J. Richardson, *An Essay on the Theory of Painting* (1715), pp. 12–13, quoted in *ibid.*, p. 70.

6 J. Menzhausen, 'Elector Augustus's *Kunstkammer*: an Analysis of the Inventory of 1587', in Impey and MacGregor (eds), *The Origins of Museums*, p. 70.

7 See S. Cliff, *The French Archive of Design and Decoration* (New York, 1999), pp. 26, 30.

8 Inscribed on Courten's tomb by Sloane, transcribed in British Library Sloane MS 3515, fol. 49, quoted in Thompson and Roe, 'More Paintings in the British Museum', p. 192, caption to fig. 4.

9 Impey and MacGregor (eds), *The Origins of Museums*, p. 3. Numerous illustrations of cabinets of curiosities depict paintings and sculpture amongst naturalia and medals.

10 The manuscript is housed in the Department of Ethnography, pp. 238–71. There are bound photocopies in the register cupboards of the Departments of Medieval and Modern Europe and of Prints and Drawings.

11 For instance no. 394 'Henricus. IIII. D.G. Francorum et Navarae Rex. Round his Busto, crownd wth Laurel. At bottom: 1606. Round. Brass; no. 395 A Busto of K. Charles 2d, with an oval wreath of Flowers, Fruit &c Lead'. J. Cherry, 'Medieval and Later Antiquities, Sir Hans Sloane and the Collecting of History', in A. MacGregor (ed.), *Sir Hans Sloane: Collector, Scientist, Antiquary* (London, 1994), pp. 198–217, discusses a number of portraits in a variety of materials which belonged to Sloane, analysing them as the collector's attempt to construct a history of Britain through objects.

12 A. Griffiths, 'Sir Hans Sloane (1660–1753)', in A. Griffiths (ed.), *Landmarks in Print Collecting: Connoisseurs and Donors at the British Museum since 1753* (London, 1996), p. 22.

13 Now National Portrait Gallery (no. 563). Quoted by A. MacGregor, 'The Life, Character and Career of Sir Hans Sloane', in MacGregor (ed.), *Sir Hans Sloane* (n. 11 above), p. 33. For Sloane's collection of prints and drawings see J. Rowlands, 'Prints and Drawings', in *ibid.*, pp. 245–62, and Griffiths, 'Sir Hans Sloane', *Landmarks* (n. 12 above), pp. 21–9. Sloane also owned 'Mr Ray in crayons by Faithorn', now in the Department of Prints and Drawings, British Museum, inv. 1994,U,5, Sloane, Misc. Pic. 407.

14 Transferred to the National Portrait Gallery, 1879 (no. 538).

15 MacGregor, 'The Life, Character and Career of Sir Hans Sloane', in MacGregor (ed.), *Sir*

Hans Sloane (n. 11 above), pp. 22–3; and see C. Gibson-Wood, 'Classification and Value in a Seventeenth-century Museum: William Courten's Collection', *Journal of the History of Collections* 9:1 (1997), pp. 61–77.

16 See Thompson and Roe, 'More Paintings', p. 193.

17 Reg. no. MME SL 1985, illustrated in Dawson, *Portrait Sculpture*, no. 58.

18 Reg. no. SL 1984, illustrated in Dawson, *Portrait Sculpture*, no. 59. The choice of subject was apt: Sloane succeeded Newton as President of the Royal Society in 1727.

19 The Sloane catalogue is kept in the Department of Medieval and Modern Europe; the annotation must date from between 1753 and, at the latest, 1776 when Maty died.

20 The bust is the model for the head of the stone statue of Sloane formerly in the Chelsea Physic Garden and now on loan to the British Museum.

21 [E. Powlett], *The General Contents of the British Museum: with remarks serving as a Directory in Viewing that Noble Cabinet* (London, 1761), p. 4.

22 For an interesting account of Maty's place in intellectual life in mid eighteenth-century Britain see U. E. M. Janssens-Knorsch, *Matthieu Maty and the Journal Britannique 1750–55* (Amsterdam, 1975), and the same author's 'Matthieu Maty (1718–1776): A French "Apostle" of English Letters', *Proceedings of the Huguenot Society of London* 22 (1970–6), pp. 211–23. His certificate for election to the Royal Society was signed by Thomas Birch, Librarian of the British Museum, Richard Mead, Martin Folkes and others with close ties to the Museum.

23 Mead showed her 'a fine collection of the pictures of several different schools; a head of HOMER, saved out of the fire of Corinth [see p. 34]; Egyptian bronzes, and pictures of the greatest Poets and most eminent Philosophers of his country; ornaments worthy of the care of a good citizen', *Letters Concerning England, Holland and Italy. By the Celebrated Madam du Bocage*, vol. 1 (London, 1770), letter V, London, 25 May 1750, p. 36. For Mead's collection, see I. Jenkins, in R. G. W. Anderson, M. L. Caygill, A. G. MacGregor and L. Syson (eds), *Enlightening the British: Knowledge, Discovery and the Museum in the Eighteenth Century* (London, 2004).

24 According to G. Gill-Mark, *Une femme de lettres au XVIIIe siècle: Anne-Marie du Boccage* (Paris, 1927), p. 55, although her visit to London took place three years before the establishment of the Museum.

25 Dawson, *Portrait Sculpture*, no. 74.

26 *Ibid.*, no. 1.

27 The whereabouts of the classical busts is now uncertain.

28 Barrow and Bentley are of fired grey clay (see Dawson, *Portrait Sculpture*, nos 3, 7), which may well have been described as 'terracotta'.

29 *Book of Presents*, 28 May 1762.

30 See M. Baker, 'The Portrait Sculpture', in D. McKitterick (ed.), *The Making of the Wren Library, Trinity College, Cambridge* (Cambridge, 1995), pp. 110–37, and S. Jervis, 'The English Country House Library', in N. Barker (ed.), *Treasures from the Libraries of the National Trust Country Houses* (New York, 1999), pp. 13–43.

31 M. Maty, *Authentic Memoirs of the Life of R. Mead* (London, 1755).

32 M. Maty, *Memoirs of Lord Chesterfield* (London, 1777).

33 Maty's early poem *Vauxhall*, dated 1741 and published in the first volume of his *Journal Britannique* in April 1750, pp. 34–49, includes a passage on Roubiliac's statue of Handel commissioned by Jonathan Tyers for Vauxhall Gardens (now in the Victoria and Albert Museum), in which he uses the well-known comparison with the classical sculptor Phidias.

34 Dawson, *Portrait Sculpture*, no. 22.

35 For Cotton see C. J. Wright (ed.), *Sir Robert Cotton as Collector: Essays on an Early Stuart Courtier and his Legacy* (London, 1997).

36 D. Howarth, 'Sir Robert Cotton and the Commemoration of Famous Men', in *ibid.*, pp. 40–67.

37 Dawson, *Portrait Sculpture*, no. 33. There is no trace of this bust, and even its sculptor is unknown.

38 L. Lippincott, 'Expanding on Portraiture: The Market, the Public, and the Hierarchy of Genres in Eighteenth-century Britain', in Bermingham and Brewer (eds), pp. 75, 82.

39 Illustrated by Thompson and Roe, 'More Paintings', p. 192, fig. 3.

40 Transferred to the National Portrait Gallery, 1879 (no. 550).

41 Transferred to the National Gallery, 1879 (no. 566). Charles Marguetel de Saint-Denis, seigneur de Saint-Évremond (1613–1703) escaped imprisonment for a political offence and on coming to England found favour at Court.

42 [Powlett], *The General Contents*, pp. 4–6.

43 Department of Greek and Roman Antiquities, reg. no. GR 1760.9–19.1 (Bronze 847), illustrated in S. Walker, *Greek and Roman Portraits* (London, 1995), col. pl. 1.

44 Dawson, *Portrait Sculpture*, no. 55.

45 For the bust of Clarke see Dawson, *Portrait Sculpture*, no. 21; for this picture, now on loan to the Government Art Collection, see Dawson, fig. 56.

46 Thompson and Roe, 'More Paintings', p. 189; printed copy of Ellis's list bound into the MS Catalogue of Paintings kept with the registers in the Department of Prints and Drawings, British Museum.

47 These included portraits of Edward III, Henry VI, Lord Burghley, Lord Bacon, Henry VIII, Mary Queen of Scots, James I, Henrietta Maria and others, and an anonymous portrait of King Henry VIII, now in the Department of Medieval and Modern Europe, British Museum.

48 Presented by the Earl of Macclesfield, 1760, and by Lord Cardross, 1765; transferred to the National Portrait Gallery, 1879 (nos 542, 541).

49 Presented in 1768 by Mrs Mary Mackmorren, now Government Art Collection.

50 Government Art Collection. Presented by Mrs Elizabeth Gambarini of Golden Square in 1759.

51 The first two (presented in 1763 and 1765) are now in the Government Art Collection while the last hangs in the Director's Residence, British Museum.

52 Transferred to the National Portrait Gallery, 1879 (nos 520, 525, 574).

53 Transferred to the National Portrait Gallery, 1879 (no. 590).

54 Now on loan to the British Library, displayed in the Manuscripts Reading Room lobby.

55 Director's Residence, British Museum. The identity of the sitter is now considered doubtful.

56 Sloane Collection 183, kept in the Department of Prints and Drawings, Blythe Road store. The picture was attributed to Giorgione when purchased for £10 15s from 'Mr Cock' by Sloane and bears the seal of William Courten, father of Sloane's friend William Courten, on the reverse of the panel.

57 Presented by Mrs Wolfreys in 1757 and now in the British Museum Friends Room, East Residence, British Museum.

58 Presented in 1777; see Dawson, *Portrait Sculpture*, no. 18.

59 Presented by Henry Reene in 1756, transferred to the National Gallery, 1880 (no. 1096).

60 J. Rowlands, 'Prints and Drawings', in MacGregor (ed.), *Sir Hans Sloane* (n. 11 above), p. 245.

61 See I. Jenkins and K. Sloan, *Vases and Volcanoes: Sir William Hamilton and his Collection* (London, 1996), no. 51, p. 76 for the portrait by Reynolds; and for the portrait by David Allan see *ibid.*, no. 1, p. 106. The Allan portrait was presented by the artist and bears a dedicatory inscription. Transferred to the

National Portrait Gallery in 1879 (no. 589), it was returned on long-term loan in 1982 and is hung in the Hartwell Room.

62 Illustrated by Thompson and Roe, 'More Paintings', p. 189; referred to in Trustees' Standing Committee Minutes of 16 April 1762 when it was almost finished.

63 See p. 16. This is apparently the earliest edition of the *Synopsis* to survive in the Museum archive, but it may not be the first edition.

64 Thompson and Roe, 'More Paintings', p. 190.

65 In the 1838 list it was recorded in the Banksian Room but by 1847 it was in a basement and seems to have remained unseen until it was resurrected for display in the King's Library in 1956; see Dawson, *Portrait Sculpture*, no. 2.

66 See A. Griffiths, 'The Department of Prints and Drawings', *Burlington Magazine* 136 (August 1994), pp. 531–45, and Griffiths, *Landmarks in Print Collecting* (n. 12 above).

67 Jenkins and Sloan, *Vases and Volcanoes* (n. 61 above), pp. 81, 278–80.

68 *Ibid.*, p. 81.

69 F. Owen and D. Blayney Brown, *Collector of Genius: A Life of Sir George Beaumont* (New Haven and London, 1988), pp. 209–26.

70 *Ibid.*, p. 210.

71 The paintings were described as 'belonging to the Trustees of the British Museum' in a list produced by Henry Ellis in 1850, and as 'deposited in the National Gallery' in another by Antonio Panizzi in 1861, by which time loans had been made to South Kensington.

72 Pointon, *Hanging the Head*, p. 299.

73 *Ibid.*, pp. 229–30.

74 Thompson and Roe, 'More Paintings', p. 189. The collection has only ever to the writer's knowledge been discussed by these writers, in 'Some Oil Portraits in the British Museum', *Connoisseur* 147, no. 592 (March 1961), pp. 114–18, and in 'More Paintings', pp. 189–95.

75 Pointon, *Hanging the Head*, pp. 229–30.

76 See the leather-bound volume 'British Museum Oil Paintings Etc.' kept in the Register Cupboard, Department of Prints and Drawings, British Museum.

77 The work, which bears a long explanatory inscription, once belonged to Dr Mead, and is now in the new display in the room that once housed the King's Library in the British Museum.

78 Dawson, *Portrait Sculpture*, no. 81.

79 *Ibid.*, no. 65.

Chapter 3 pages 38–45

FURTHER READING

N. Barker, *Treasures of the British Library* (London, 1988)

P. R. Harris, *A History of the British Museum Library* (London, 1998)

E. Paintin, *The King's Library* (London, 1989)

NOTES

1 J. M. Crook, *The British Museum* (London, 1972), p. 130.

2 C. Hibbert, *George III: A Personal History* (London, 1999), pp. 14–21.

3 J. Roberts, 'Sir William Chambers and George III', in J. Harris and M. Snodin (eds), *Sir William Chambers: Architect to George III* (New Haven und London, 1996), pp. 41–5.

4 See Paintin, *The King's Library*, p. 6.

5 Dalton was said by Horace Walpole to be 'totally illiterate' and appears to have had little interest in books. He transferred to the keepership of the King's medals and drawings in 1774. See Paintin, *The King's Library*, p. 17 and L. Syson, ch. 10 below.

6 See Barker, *Treasures of the British Library*, pp. 65–7. The Thomason Tracts were purchased not for the King's own retention but for the British Museum.

7 Giovanni Battista Pasquali's catalogue *Bibliotheca Smithiana, seu Catalogus librorum D. Josephi Smithii Angli per cognomina authorum dispositus* had been published in Venice in 1755. BL: 823.h.26. See also Barker, *Treasures*, pp. 95–7.

8 J. Brooke, 'The Library of George III', *Yale University Library Gazette* 52 (1978), p. 36.

9 Barnard remained responsible for the Library until his own death, even after its incorporation into the collections of the British Museum. His portrait can be found today overlooking the King's Library Tower at St Pancras.

10 Brooke, 'The Library of George III', p. 38.

11 See Paintin, *The King's Library*, p. 15–17.

12 See Barker, *Treasures*, pp. 95–9.

13 David Paisey has pointed out, however, that German books were present in the private libraries of both the King and Queen. See 'The British Library', in G. Jefcoate, W. A. Kelly and K. Kloth (eds), *Handbuch deutscher historischer Buchbestände in Europa. Band 10: A Guide to Books Printed in German-speaking Countries (or in German Elsewhere) Held by Libraries in Great Britain and Ireland* (Hildesheim, 2000), pp. 80–1.

14 See Barker, *Treasures*, p. 97, and Paintin, *The King's Library*, pp. 7–8.

15 See Barker, *Treasures*, pp. 98–9.

16 This is now available in digital form on the British Library's web pages.

17 B. C. Bloomfield (ed.), *A Directory of Rare Book and Special Collections in the United Kingdom and the Republic of Ireland* 2nd edition (London, 1997), p. 139. A number of choice items were retained for the Royal Library at Windsor. Antonio Panizzi (1797–1879) was Keeper of Printed Books at the British Museum from 1837 and Principal Librarian from 1856 to 1866.

18 Most of the around 440 held by the Department of Manuscripts related to contemporary literature, including the autograph manuscript of Samuel Johnson's *Irene*.

19 The King's topographical collections are cared for by the British Library's Map Library; his musical scores by the British Library's Music Library; the coins and medals came to the British Museum in 1823, where they remain; and his prints and drawings remain in the Royal Library at Windsor.

20 See Brooke, 'The Library of George III', p. 36.

21 L. H. Butterfield (ed.), *Diary and Autobiography of John Adams* (Cambridge, Mass., 1961), vol. 3, p. 150, quoted in Paintin, *The King's Library*, p. 12.

22 For example, M. Robinson's *Buckingham Palace* (London, 1995), pp. 16–17, which reproduces James Stephanoff's fine watercolours. See also Paintin, *The King's Library*, p. 13, and Roberts, 'Sir William Chambers', p. 47: 'The walls were lined with books; the central octagonal desk, made for the room, survives in the royal library at Windsor.'

23 British Library: L.2.b.2.

24 Brooke, 'The Library of George III', pp. 44–5.

25 Paintin, *The King's Library*, pp. 11–12.

26 J. I. Israel, *Radical Enlightenment* (Oxford, 2001), pp. 119–27.

27 George II visited the University in 1748, the published account of his visit providing one of the first accounts of the Library itself.

28 See my 'Wilhelm Best und der Londoner Buchhandel: ein deutscher Diplomat im Dienste der Universitätsbibliothek Göttingen im 18. Jahrhundert', *Leipziger Jahrbuch zur Buchgeschichte* 6 (1996), pp. 199–210.

29 See my 'Christian Gottlob Heyne and the University Library at Göttingen as "Universalbibliothek" of the Eighteenth Century', *Library History* 14 (1998), pp. 111–16.

30 Niedersächsisches Hauptstaatsarchiv Hannover, Hann 92; XXXIV, II, 2a fols 107–9.

31 C. Kind-Doerne, *Die Niedersächsische Staats- und Universitätsbibliothek Göttingen* (Wiesbaden, 1986), pp. 27, 147.

32 See *ibid.*, p. 87.

33 *Göttingische gelehrte Anzeigen*, pp. 851 ff, quoted and translated in B. Fabian, 'An Eighteenth-century Research Collection: English Books at Göttingen University Library', *The Library*, 6th series (1979), p. 212.

34 Paintin, *The King's Library*, p. 18.

35 *Ibid.*, pp. 18–19; see also Harris, *A History of the British Museum Library*, pp. 31–3.

36 I should like to thank John Goldfinch of the British Library, Early Printed Collections, for his corrections and comments on this article.

Chapter 4 pages 46–57

FURTHER READING

J. M. Crook, *The British Museum* (London, 1972)

J. M. Crook and M. H. Port, *The History of the King's Works*, vol. 6, 1782–1851 (London, 1973)

S. Jervis, 'The English Country House Library', in N. Barker (ed.), *Treasures from the Libraries of National Trust Country Houses* (exh. cat. New York, 1999), pp. 13–43

E. Paintin, *The King's Library* (London, 1989)

J. Summerson, *Architecture in Britain, 1530–1830* (London, 1963)

NOTES

1 A. Aspinall, *The Letters of King George IV 1812–1830* (Cambridge, 1938), vol. 2, pp. 550–1.

2 *Quarterly Review* 88 (1850), p.143. The story is almost certainly untrue.

3 T. H. Shepherd, *London and its Environs in the Nineteenth Century …* (London, 1829), p. 46.

4 H. S. Peacock, *Remarks on the Present State of the British Museum* (London, 1835), p. 7.

5 Letter from King George IV to the Earl of Liverpool, 1823, British Library C.11.d.9.

6 Public Record Office. Works 1/10, fol. 337; Works 1/7, fols 213–14, 9 August and fols 348–9, 9 December 1816. Works 33/3 7 33/563–4.

7 Sir Edward Maunde-Thompson, MS 'History of the British Museum' (c. 1898), BL Add. MS. 52292, fols 1–6. *Gentleman's Magazine*, 1819, pt 1, p. 6.

8 PRO. Works 1/10, fol. 336, 13 February and fol. 339, 19 February 1821.

9 J. M. Crook and M. H. Port, *The History of the King's Works*, vol. 6, 1782–1851 (London, 1973), pp. 403–41.

10 Summerson, *Architecture in Britain, 1530–1830*, p. 305.

11 Jean-Nicholas-Louis Durand (1760–1834), a pupil of E.-L. Boullée and perhaps the most influential architectural theorist of the nineteenth-century, not only in his native France but throughout Europe, particularly Germany and even in England. His *Précis des leçons d'architecture* (1802–9) includes a design for a museum that prefigures the British Museum in some of its aspects. N. Pevsner, *A History of Building Types* (London, 1976), pp. 115–31, discusses Durand, his predecessors and heirs. See also N. Pevsner, 'The British Museum, 1753–1953', *Architectural Review* 118 (1953), p. 179.

12 J. Timbs, *The Romance of London* (London, 1865), vol. 3, p.177.

13 H. Honour, *Neo-classicism* (Harmondsworth, 1968), p. 13.

14 Smirke was interested in novel methods of heating: C. J. Richardson's *Warming and Ventilation* (London, 1837) was dedicated to him. See J. M. Crook, *The British Museum* (London, 1972), p. 142.

15 Pasley, pp. 18, 248–9, 288. This was laid by Messrs Kemp, a firm Smirke used throughout his work of rebuilding. 'The material is so rarely used', the architect later told the Commissioners of Woods and Works, 'that I do not know of any other tradesman employed in such work except on a very small scale'.

16 Crook and Port, *History*, vol. 6, pp. 414–15.

17 *Ibid.*, p. 416. Although the building was ready for occupation from September 1827, the books were not installed until nearly a year later; see P. R. Harris, *A History of the British Museum Library 1753–1973* (London, 1998), pp. 67–8.

18 PRO. Works 4/26, fol. 231, 27 November 1823; Works 1/16, fols. 234–5, 1 April 1827; Works 1/6, fols 234–5; Works 4/27, fols 351, 363.

19 *Gentleman's Magazine*, 1834, I, p. 21.

20 Dr Roger Bowdler has commented upon the similarity of this form of decoration with that of the Gilt Hall at Cobham Hall in Kent, probably added in 1792–4 by James Wyatt for the fourth Earl of Darnley. See *Cobham Hall* guidebook (English Life Publications, 1987).

21 PRO. Works 33/4-163. The effect would have been somewhat similar to the layout of the central bay of the Egyptian Gallery.

22 J. Lemprière, *A Classical Dictionary* (London, 1845), pp. 403–5. See also D. Watkin, 'Stuart, James [Athenian], Thomas', *The Grove Dictionary of Art Online*, ed. L. Macy (accessed 23 June 2002), http://www.groveart.com (reference from Jonathan Williams).

23 *Gentleman's Magazine*, 1834, I, p. 21.

24 *Ibid.*, 1834, I, pp. 16–22.

25 *Ibid.*, 1834, I, p. 21.

26 E. Edwards, *Lives of the Founders of the British Museum* (London, 1870), vol. 1, p. 48.

27 *Gentleman's Magazine*, 1834, I, p. 22.

28 Crook and Port, *History*, vol. 6, p. 412.

29 See D. Vaisey and D. McKitterick, *The Foundations of Scholarship: Libraries and Collecting 1650–1750* (Los Angeles, 1992); D. McKitterick, *Cambridge University Library: A History* (Cambridge, 1986); G. Barber, *Architecture for Learning: A Short History of Oxford Library Buildings* (Oxford, 1995) etc.

30 'Report of the Select Committee on the British Museum', *Parliamentary Papers*, 1836, vol. 10, pp. 444, 448.

31 Crook and Port, *History*, vol. 6, pp. 134–7.

32 J. Harris, *Sir William Chambers* (London, 1970), pp. 82–3.

33 H. Roberts, 'Metamorphoses in Wood: Royal Library Furniture in the Eighteenth and Nineteenth Centuries', *Apollo*, June 1990, p. 383.

34 C. Williams (ed.), *Sophie in London 1786 (being the Diary of Sophie v la Roche)*, (London, 1933), p. 145.

35 Smirke exhibited a 'Design for a National Museum' at the Royal Academy of Arts in 1799, winning a Gold medal for his performance.

36 See D. Stillman, *English Neo-classical Architecture* (London, 1988), vol. I, reproduction pp. 57–8, fig. 10 (the plan in the Accademia Parmense di Belli Arti, Parma) and fig. 12 (elevation and section, Sir John Soane's Museum, London).

37 E. Harris, *The Genius of Robert Adam: His Interiors* (London, 2001), pp. 112–31.

38 These designs are now in the Bute Archives. See F. Russell, 'The House that Became a Hostage', *Country Life*, 18 October 1998, pp. 64–7.

39 See Harris, *Genius of Robert Adam*, pp. 242–55.

40 *Ibid.*, p. 131. Shelburne's set is preserved at Sir John Soane's Museum. SM 30:59-62.

41 See Stillman, *English Neo-classical Architecture*, vol. 1, reproduction p. 78, fig. 183.

42 See Peter Meadows, *Joseph Bonomi 1739–1808* (exh. cat. Royal Institute of British Architects – Heinz gallery, London, 1998), reproduction on front cover.

43 See C. S. Sykes, *Private Palaces: Life in Great London Town Houses* (London, 1986), reproduction on p. 206.

44 'Urbane banality' is taken from Sir Howard Colvin's entry on Smirke in his *Biographical Dictionary of British Architects, 1600–1830* (London, 1978), p. 41. F. A. Barnard, *Bibliothecae Regiae Catalogus* (London, 1820–9), vol. 1, p. ix.

45 See O. Impey and A MacGregor (eds), *The Origins of Museums: the Cabinet of Curiosities in 16th- and 17th-Century Europe* (Oxford, 1985), and S. Jervis, 'The English Country House Library', in N. Barker, *Treasures from the Libraries of National Trust Country Houses* (exh. cat. New York, 1999), pp. 13–43.

Chapter 5 pages 58–67

FURTHER READING

J. Brewer, *The Pleasures of the Imagination: English Culture in the Eighteenth Century* (New York, 1997)

L. Casson, *Libraries in the Ancient World* (New Haven and London, 2001)

S. Jervis, 'The English Country House Library', in N. Barker (ed.), *Treasures from the Libraries of National Trust Country Houses* (exh. cat. New York, 1999), 12–33

A. Wilton and I. Bignamini (eds), *Grand Tour: The Lure of Italy in the Eighteenth Century* (London, 1997)

NOTES

1 Gavin Hamilton to the Earl of Shelburne, 1 July 1773. I am indebted to my colleagues Kim Sloan and Ian Jenkins for helpful discussions on this topic. The following abbreviations are used throughout the notes: *Antikensammlungen I*: H. Beck, P. C. Bol, W. Prinz, H. v. Steuben (eds), *Antikensammlungen im 18. Jahrhundert* [= *Frankfurter Forschungen zur Kunst 9*] (Berlin, 1981); *Antikensammlungen II: Antikensammlungen des europäischen Adels im 18. Jahrhundert als Ausdruck einer europäischen Identität: Internationales Kolloquium in Düsseldorf vom 7.2.–10.2.1996* [*Monumenta Artis Romanae 27*] (Mainz, 2001).

2 For a vivid account of this dynamic process and the underlying statistics see for example Brewer, *The Pleasures of the Imagination*, particularly chapters 3 ('Authors, Publishers and the Making of Literary Culture') and 4 ('Readers and the Reading Public').

3 J. Raven, 'Modes of Reading and Writing in the Eighteenth-century Private Library', in P. Goetsch (ed.), *Lesen und Schreiben im 17. und 18. Jahrhundert: Studien zu ihrer Bewertung in Deutschland, England, Frankreich* (Tübingen, 1994), pp. 49–60.

4 H. Oehler, *Foto + Skulptur: Römische Antiken in englischen Schlössern* (Cologne, 1980), p. 39.

5 On ancient libraries see L. Casson, *Libraries in the Ancient World* (New Haven and London, 2001); W. Hoepfner (ed.), *Antike Bibliotheken* (Mainz, 2001).

6 I. Favoretto and G. L. Ravagnan, *Lo statuario pubblico della Serenissima: due secoli di collezionismo di antichità 1596–1797* (Venice, 1997).

7 For a discussion of the evolution of studies and libraries in seventeenth-century Britain see P. Thornton, *Seventeenth-century Interior Decoration in England, France and Holland* (New Haven and London, 1978), pp. 303–15.

8 G. Schmook, 'Justus Lipsius' "De Bibliothecis Syntagma"', *Handelingen van het Zesde Wetenschappelijk Vlaamse Congres voor Boek en Bibliotheekwezen Gent, 31 Maart 1940* (Antwerp, 1941), pp. 35–58.

9 J. A. Clarke, *Gabriel Naudé 1600–1653* (Hamden, Conn., 1970).

10 These libraries and their contexts are admirably discussed by M. Baker, 'The Portrait Sculpture', in D. McKitterick (ed.), *The Making of the Wren Library, Trinity College, Cambridge* (Cambridge, 1995), pp. 110–37, figs 52–97.

11 The basic study on the history of British collecting remains A. Michaelis, *Ancient Marbles in Great Britain* (Cambridge, 1882), pp. 1–205. See also G. B. Waywell, 'Influences on the Formation of English Collections of Ancient Sculpture in the 18th Century', *Antikensammlungen II*, pp. 87–92. On the Grand Tour see Wilton and Bignamini (eds), *Grand Tour* with extensive bibliography; also J. Ingamells, *A Dictionary of British and Irish Travellers in Italy 1701–1800* (New Haven and London, 1997).

12 A. W. Moore, *Norfolk and the Grand Tour: Eighteenth-century Travellers Abroad and their Souvenirs* (exh. cat., Norwich, 1985). On the antiquities at Holkham Hall see most recently E. Angelicoussis, *The Holkham Collection of Classical Sculptures* [= *Monumenta Artis Romanae 30*] (Mainz, 2001).

13 J. Kenworthy-Browne, 'Designing around the Statues: Matthew Brettingham's Casts at Kedleston', *Apollo*, April 1993, pp. 248–52.

14 V. Coltman, 'Classicism in the English Library: Reading Classical Culture in the Late Eighteenth and Early Nineteenth Centuries', *Journal of the History of Collections* 11:1 (1999), pp. 35–50.

15 S. Jervis, 'The English Country House Library', in N. Barker, *Treasures from the Libraries of National Trust Country Houses* (exh. cat. New York, 1999), pp. 12–33, esp. 22.

16 P. Liverani, 'The Museo Pio-Clementino at the Time of the Grand Tour', *Journal of the History of Collections* 12:2 (2000), pp. 151–9.

17 A. Masson, *Le Décor des bibliothèques du moyen âge à la Revolution* (Geneva, 1972), p. 151, fig. 51.

18 On Townley see B. Cook, 'The Townley Marbles in Westminster and Bloomsbury', *British Museum Yearbook* 2 (London, 1977), pp. 34–78; Cook, *The Townley Marbles* (London, 1985); G. Vaughan, *The Collecting of Classical Antiquities in England in the 18th Century: A Study of Charles Townley* (unpublished D. Phil. thesis, Oxford, 1988); Vaughan, 'The Townley Zoffany: Reflections on Charles Townley and His Friends', *Apollo*, November 1996, pp. 32–5; S. Walker, 'Tenez le Vraye', *Antikensammlungen II*, pp. 93–8. The Townley Papers are now in the Central Archives of the British Museum.

19 Letter of 18 January 1772. Cf. E. Fitzmaurice, *Letters of Gavin Hamilton, edited from the mss. at Lansdowne House* (1879), p. 14.

20 On the various designs for the gallery in Lansdowne House see ch. 4 and D. Stillman, 'The Gallery for Lansdowne House: International Neoclassical Architecture in Microcosm', *Art Bulletin* 52 (1970), pp. 69–80.

21 Many country houses saw their traditional long galleries transformed into libraries during the later eighteenth century; see Jervis, 'The English Country House Library', p. 22.

22 For the early history of the Göttingen cast collection in the University library see C. Boehringer, 'Lehrsammlungen von Gipsabgüssen im 18. Jahrhundert am Beispiel der Göttinger Universitäts-sammlung', *Antikensammlungen I*, pp. 273–91; K Fittschen (ed.), *Archäologisches Institut der Georg-August-Universität Göttingen: Verzeichnis der Gipsabgüsse* (Göttingen, 1990), esp. pp. 9–12.

23 Cf. D. C. Kurtz, *The Reception of Classical Art in Britain: An Oxford Story of Plaster Casts from the Antique* (Oxford, 2000), p. 118.

24 *Ibid.*, pp. 150–3.

25 Quoted in J. M. Crook, *The British Museum* (London, 1972), pp. 40–1.

26 On the growth of the Museum's sculpture collections and its intellectual repercussions see the excellent study by I. Jenkins, *Archaeologists and Aesthetes in the Sculpture Galleries of the British Museum 1800–1939* (London, 1992).

PART II: THE NATURAL WORLD

Chapter 6 pages 70–79

FURTHER READING

W. Blunt, *The Compleat Naturalist: A Life of Linnaeus* (London, 2001)

H. B. Carter, *Sir Joseph Banks 1743–1820* (London, 1988)

M. Hunter, *Establishing the New Science: The Experience of the Royal Society* (Woodbridge, 1989)

A. MacGregor (ed.), *Sir Hans Sloane, Collector, Scientist, Antiquary* (London, 1994)

P. O'Brian, *Joseph Banks* (London, 1987)

C. E. Raven, *John Ray, Naturalist: His Life and Works* (Cambridge, 1950)

NOTES

1 Taxonomy is the science of classification, description and naming of organisms. Systematics extends this definition to take in the evolutionary history of organisms.

2 See M. Hunter, *The Royal Society and its Fellows 1660–1700: The Morphology of an Early Scientific Institution* (London, 1994).

3 R. Hooke, *Micrographia* (London, 1665), p. 154.

4 Cited in P. R. Sloane, 'John Locke, John Ray and the Problem of the Natural System', *Journal of the History of Biology* 5:1 (1972), pp. 1–53.

5 J. Ray, *Historia plantarum*, vol. 20 (1686). Cited in E. Mayr, *The Growth of Biological Thought: Diversity, Evolution and Inheritance* (Cambridge, Mass., 1982), pp. 256–7; for Ray see Raven, *John Ray*.

6 For the background to the debates on essentialism see n. 4 above.

7 For Sloane's natural history collections see ch. 7 below, and for his 'artificial rarities', ch. 10 and *passim*; see also MacGregor (ed.), *Sir Hans Sloane*.

8 Sloane's Jamaican plant collections were digitized in 2000 and can now be viewed along with a number of other significant early botanical collections on the website of the Natural History Museum, London (www.nhm.ac.uk); see also J. F. Cannon, 'Botanical Collections', in MacGregor (ed.), *Sir Hans Sloane*, pp. 136–49. Sloane's collection of wood specimens (some of them from Jamaica) are now housed in the Botany Department of the Liverpool Museum.

9 A. MacGregor, 'The Life, Character and Career of Sir Hans Sloane', in MacGregor (ed.), *Sir Hans Sloane*, p. 28.

10 C. Linnaeus, *Philosophica botanica* (Stockholm, 1751), Aph. 163, p. 101.

11 Blunt, *The Compleat Naturalist*, p. 112.

12 See E. Duyker, *Nature's Argonaut: Daniel Solander, 1733–1782. Naturalist and Voyager with Cook and Banks* (Carlton South, 1995); E. Duyker and P. Tingbrand, *Daniel Solander: Collected Correspondence 1753–1782* (Melbourne, 1995).

13 J. Stuart, *Botanical Tables* [1785?], cited in J. Gascoigne, *Joseph Banks and the English Enlightenment* (Cambridge, 1994), p. 81.

14 Gascoigne, *Joseph Banks*, p. 81.

15 T. Pennant, letter to Joseph Banks, 1767, cited in Gascoigne, *Joseph Banks*, p. 104.

16 See the judgement of Raven in *John Ray*, p. 309: 'it is one of the misfortunes in the history of botany … that the sound principles laid down by Ray should have largely been abandoned or ignored by his great successor'.

17 The Linnean Society is the oldest body in Britain exclusively devoted to natural history. It remains a highly active society promoting biology with an emphasis on the study of diversity and interrelationships of living things. See http://www.linnean.org.

Chapter 7 pages 80–91

FURTHER READING

D. E. Allen, *The Naturalist in Britain: A Social History* (London, 1976).

R. D Altick, *The Shows of London* (Cambridge, Mass., and London, 1978)

J. Gascoigne, *Joseph Banks and the English Enlightenment: Useful Knowledge and Polite Culture* (Cambridge, 1994)

O. Impey and A. MacGregor (eds), *The Origins of Museums: The Cabinet of Curiosities in 16th- and 17th-century Europe* (Oxford, 1985)

A. MacGregor (ed.), *Sir Hans Sloane, Collector, Scientist, Antiquary* (London, 1994)

T. Rice, *Voyages of Discovery: Three Centuries of Natural History Exploration* (London, 2000)

W. T. Stearn, *The Natural History Museum at South Kensington: A History of the Museum, 1753–1980* (London, 1998)

NOTES

1 John Woodward, cited by D. Price, 'John Woodward and a surviving British Geological Collection', *Journal of the History of Collections* 1:1 (1989), pp. 79–95, at p. 80.

2 Both could be found in the collection of Sir Hans Sloane: see J. F. M. Cannon, 'Botanical Collections', in MacGregor (ed.), *Sir Hans Sloane*, pp. 146–7.

3 From an account of the Tradescant collection by Georg Christoph Stirn (1638), cited on the web site of the Ashmolean Museum.

4 C. G. Wood, 'Classification and Value in a Seventeenth-century Museum', *Journal of the History of Collections* 9:1 (1997), pp. 61–77.

5 For an introduction to these collections see A. MacGregor, 'The Cabinet of Curiosities', in Impey and MacGregor, *The Origins of Museums*, pp. 147–58.

6 Mary Astell thus describes the character of a virtuoso in *An Essay in Defence of the Female Sex* (London, 1696), quoted in W. J. Houghton, 'The English Virtuoso in the Seventeenth Century', *Journal of the History of Ideas* 3:1 (January 1942), p. 53.

7 It was catalogued by the botanist Nehemiah Grew in 1681: Impey and MacGregor (eds), *The Origins of Museums*, p. 164.

8 *Philosophical Transactions* 1 (1666), p. 321, cited in M. Hunter, 'The Cabinet Institutionalised: the Royal Society's "Repository" and its Background', in Impey and. MacGregor (eds), *The Origins of Museums*, p. 163.

9 M. Hunter, *Science and Society in Restoration England* (Cambridge, 1981), cited by E. Hooper Greenhill, *Museums and the Shaping of Knowledge* (New York, 1993), p. 147.

10 P. Gay, *Age of Enlightenment* (New York, 1966), p. 17.

11 J. Gascoigne, *Joseph Banks*, p. 4.

12 For Petiver see P. I. Edwards, 'Sir Hans Sloane and his Curious Friends', in A. Wheeler and J. H. Price (eds), *History in the Service of Systematics* (London, 1981), pp. 30–1, and J. E. Dandy, *Sloane Herbarium* (London, 1958), pp. 175–82.

13 Allen, *The Naturalist in Britain*, p. 37.

14 Dandy, *Sloane Herbarium*, p. 175.

15 For a reproduction of insects from his collection, see MacGregor (ed.), *Sir Hans Sloane*, pl. 13.

16 Dandy, *Sloane Herbarium*, pp. 183–7.

17 W. Dampier, *A New Voyage Round the World: The Journal of an English Buccaneer* (1697), ed. with preface by Giles Milton (London, 1998).

18 Most of Dampier's collections are lodged in the Plant Sciences Department at Oxford, but some also came to Sir Hans Sloane and thence to the British Museum and the Natural History Museum. See K. Way, 'Invertebrate Collections', in MacGregor (ed.), *Sir Hans Sloane*, p. 108.

19 Type specimen: when a new species of plant or animal is described and named, the actual specimen used for that description is known as the type specimen. The name can be applied only to a species or other group that includes that specimen within its defining limits.

20 On Catesby see A. R. W. Meyers and M. B. Pritchard, *Empire's Nature: Mark Catesby's New World Vision* (Chapel Hill, 1998).

21 See K. Way, 'Invertebrate collections'.

22 For a history of shell collecting see S. P. Dance, *Shell Collecting: An Illustrated History* (London, 1966).

23 See J. Clutton-Brock, 'Vertebrate Collections', in MacGregor (ed.), *Sir Hans Sloane*, pp. 77–92.

24 Allen, *The Naturalist in Britain*, p. 25.

25 See G. L. Wilkins, 'The Cracherode Shell Collection', *Bulletin of the British Museum (Natural History)* Historical Series 1:4 (1957).

26 *Dictionary of National Biography* (London, 1904), s.v.

27 *Synopsis of the Contents of the British Museum* (London, 1808), p. 28.

28 Two satirical prints were issued in July 1772 labelling Banks as a 'fly-catching macaroni' and Solander as a 'simpling macaroni' ('simpling' is collecting medicinal herbs): British Museum Satires 4695 and 4696. They are reproduced in Gascoigne, *Joseph Banks*, pp. 64–5.

29 See Rice, *Voyages of Discovery*, chs 5 and 6.

30 After several abortive attempts, in the 1980s the Florilegium project was undertaken with the printing of all the surviving plates, issued

in a limited edition of hand-coloured engravings published by Alecto.

31 Cited in Gascoigne, *Joseph Banks*, p. 32.

32 Gascoigne, *Joseph Banks*, p. 7. Most of Banks's collections were to come to the British Museum at his death in 1820.

33 Allen, *The Naturalist in Britain*, p. 127.

34 Gascoigne, *Joseph Banks*, p. 66.

Chapter 8 pages 92–99

FURTHER READING

N. Cohn, *Noah's Flood: The Genesis Story in Western Thought* (New Haven, 1996)

W. N. Edwards, *The Early History of Palaeontology* (London, 1967)

S. J. Gould, *Time's Arrow. Time's Cycle. Myth and Metaphor in the Discovery of Geological Time* (Cambridge, Mass., 1987)

A. MacGregor (ed.), *Sir Hans Sloane: Collector, Scientist, Antiquary* (London, 1994)

R. Porter, *The Making of Geology: Earth Science in Britain 1660–1815* (Cambridge, 1977)

W. T. Stearn, *The Natural History Museum at South Kensington: A History of the Museum, 1753–1980* (London, 1998)

NOTES

1 N. Hampson, *The Enlightenment* (Harmondsworth, 1968), p. 78.

2 T. Burnet, *The Sacred Theory of the Earth: containing an Account of the Original of the Earth, and all the General Changes which it hath already undergone, or is to undergo, till the Consummation of all Things* (London, 1690), p. xx.

3 Cohn, *Noah's Flood*, pp. 48–57; Gould, *Time's Arrow*, pp. 21–59.

4 Gould, *Time's Arrow*, figure 2.1.

5 Also spelt LLwyd and Lhuyd.

6 R. Porter, 'Gentlemen and Geology: the Emergence of a Scientific Career, 1660–1920', *The Historical Journal* 24, no. 4 (1978), pp. 809–36.

7 Burnet, *The Sacred Theory*, Preface p. xx.

8 Woodward Collection catalogue entry f.225, Sedgwick Museum, Cambridge

9 Cohn, *Noah's Flood*, pp. 74–8; J. G. Winter, *The Prodromus of Nicolaus Steno's Dissertation Concerning a Solid Body Enclosed by a Process of Nature within a Solid. An English Version* (New York, 1968).

10 R. W. Purcell and S. J.Gould, *Finders, Keepers: Eight Collectors* (London, 1992), pp. 84–94.

11 C. C. Albritton, *The Abyss of Time: Changing Conceptions of the Earth's Antiquity after the Sixteenth Century* (San Francisco, 1980), pp. 42–57; S. Inwood, *The Man Who Knew Too Much: The Strange and Inventive Life of Robert Hooke 1635–1703* (Oxford, 2002).

12 E. T. Drake, *Restless Genius: Robert Hooke and His Earthly Thoughts* (New York, 1996).

13 M. Hellyer, 'The Pocket Museum: Edward Lhwyd's Lithophylacium', *Archives of Natural History* 23:1 (1996), pp. 43–60.

14 Cohn, *Noah's Flood*, pp. 79–93; J. M. Levine, *Dr Woodward's Shield: History, Science and Satire in Augustan England* (Berkeley, 1977), pp.18–47.

15 J. Woodward, *An Essay Towards a Natural History of the Earth and Terrestrial Bodyes especially Minerals: as also of the Sea, Rivers and Springs, with an Account of the Universal Deluge: and of the Effects that it had upon the Earth* (London, 1723), p. 22.

16 Woodward, *An Essay*, p. 27.

17 Levine, *Dr Woodward's Shield*, p. 40.

18 Woodward, *An Essay*, p.3.

19 D. Price, 'John Woodward and a Surviving British Geological Collection from the Early Eighteenth century', *Journal of the History of Collections* 1 (1989), pp. 79–95.

20 *Ibid.*

21 *Ibid.*, p. 80.

22 *Ibid.*, pp. 85–91.

23 W. C. Smith, 'History of the First Hundred Years of the Mineral Collection in the British Museum', *Bulletin of The British Museum (Natural History), Historical Series* 3:8 (1969), pp. 235–59.

24 A. MacGregor, 'The Life, Character and Career of Sir Hans Sloane', in MacGregor (ed.), *Sir Hans Sloane*, pp. 11–44, at p.20; J. Thackray, 'Mineral and Fossil Collections', in MacGregor (ed.), *Sir Hans Sloane*, pp. 123–35.

25 MacGregor (ed), *Sir Hans Sloane*, pp. 291–4.

26 J. M. Sweet, 'Sir Hans Sloane: Life and Mineral Collection. Part III Mineral Pharmaceutical Collection', *Natural History Magazine* 5:36 (1935), pp. 145–64.

27 L. Jardine, *Ingenious Pursuits* (London, 1999), pp. 280–4.

28 J. M. Sweet, 'Robert Jameson in London, 1793', *Annals of Science* 19:2 (1963), pp. 81–116, at p. 87.

29 C. Haynes, 'A "Natural" Exhibitioner: Sir Ashton Lever and his "Holophusikon"', *British Journal of Eighteenth Century Studies* 24:1 (2001), pp. 1–13.

30 C. E. Jackson, *Sarah Stone: Natural Curiosities from the New Worlds* (London, 1998).

31 R. Porter, *The Making of Geology: Earth Science in Britain 1660–1815* (Cambridge, 1977), pp. 91–3.

32 Smith, 'History of the First Hundred Years'.

33 W. E. Wilson, *The History of Mineral Collecting 1530–1799* (Tuscon, 1994), pp. 78–81.

34 W. Blunt, *The Compleat Naturalist: A Life of Linnaeus* (London, 2001); H. Goerke, *Linnaeus* (New York, 1973), pp. 104–6.

35 J. G. Burke, *Origins of the Science of Crystals* (Berkeley, 1966).

36 E. A.Eyles, 'Abraham Gottlieb Werner (1749–1817) and his Position in the History of Mineralogical and Geological Sciences', *History of Science* 3 (1964), pp. 102–15.

37 A. G. Werner, *Neue Theorie von der Entstehung der Gänge* (Freiburg, 1791).

38 Smith, 'History of the First Hundred Years', pp. 239–40.

39 F. Ellenberger, *History of Geology: Volume 2 1680–1810* (Rotterdam, 1999), pp. 273–4; 309.

40 D. R. Dean, 'The Word "Geology"', *Annals of Science* 36 (1979), pp. 35–43.

Chapter 9 pages 100–105

FURTHER READING

D. Cadbury, *The Dinosaur Hunters* (London, 2000)

S. J. Gould, *Time's Arrow, Time's Cycle: Myth and Metaphor in the Discovery of Geological Time* (Cambridge, Mass., 1987)

N. Jardine, J. A. Secord and E. C. Spray (eds), *Cultures of Natural History* (Cambridge, 1996)

I. Jenkins and K. Sloan, *Vases and Volcanoes: Sir William Hamilton and his Collection* (London, 1996)

S. Winchester, *The Map that Changed the World: The Tale of William Smith and the Birth of a Science* (London, 2001)

NOTES

1 J. Thackray, '"The Modern Pliny". Hamilton and Vesuvius', in Jenkins and Sloan, *Vases and Volcanoes*, pp. 65–74.

2 M. Rudwick, 'Minerals, Rocks and Strata', in Jardine, *et al.* (eds) *Cultures of Natural History*, pp. 266–86.

3 J. Hutton, *Theory of the Earth* (Edinburgh, 1795).

4 D. R. Dean, 'James Hutton on Religion and Geology: the Unpublished Preface to his *Theory of the Earth* (1788)', *Annals of Science* 32 (1975), pp. 187–93, at p.190.

5 D. R. Dean, 'James Hutton and his Public, 1785–1802', *Annals of Science* 30 (1973), pp. 89–105.

6 Gould, *Time's Arrow*, pp. 61–97.

7 *Ibid.*, p. 72.

8 Rudwick, 'Minerals, Rocks and Strata', p. 277.

9 J. Challinor, 'The Beginnings of Scientific Palaeontology in Britain', *Annals of Science* 6 (1948), pp. 46–53, at p. 52.

10 W. Buckland, *Geology and Mineralogy Considered with Reference to Natural Theology* (London, 1837), vol. 2, pl. 1.

11 W. Smith, *Strata Identified by Organized Fossils* (London, 1816); *Stratigraphical System of Organized Fossils, with Reference to the Original Geological Collection in the British Museum: Explaining their State of Preservation and their Use in Identifying the British Strata* (London, 1817).

12 R. J. Cleevely and J. Cooper, 'James Parkinson (1755–1824); a Significant English 18th Century Doctor and Fossil Collector', *Tertiary Research* 8:4 (1987), pp. 133–45; J. C. Thackray, 'James Parkinson's *Organic Remains of a former world (1804–1811)*', *Journal of the Society of Bibliography for Natural History* 7:4 (1976), pp. 451–66.

13 Challinor, 'The Beginnings of Scientific Palaeontology'.

14 J. Parkinson, *Organic Remains of a Former World*, vol. 2 (London, 1808), p. 127.

15 Challinor, 'The Beginnings of Scientific Palaeontology', p. 51.

16 Mr Wooller, 'A Description of the Fossil Skeleton of an Animal Found in the Alum Rock near Whitby', *Philosophical Transactions of the Royal Society* 50 (1758), pp. 786–91.

17 M. J. S. Rudwick, *The Meaning of Fossils: Episodes in the History of Palaeontology* (New York, 1976).

18 R. W. Purcell and S. J. Gould, *Finders, Keepers: Eight Collectors* (London, 1992), pp. 95–109; D. Cadbury, *The Dinosaur Hunters* (London, 2000), pp. 3–57.

19 I. Inkster, 'Science and Society in the Metropolis: a Preliminary Examination of the Social and Institutional Context of the Askesian Society of London, 1796–1807', *Annals of Science* 34 (1977), pp. 1–32.

20 J. Uglow, *The Lunar Men: The Friends Who Made the Future, 1730–1810* (London, 2002).

21 *Ibid.*, p. 141.

22 R. Porter, *The Making of Geology: Earth Science in Britain 1660–1815* (Cambridge, 1977).

23 H. B. Woodward, *The History of the Geological Society of London* (London, 1909).

24 Porter, *The Making of Geology*, p. 103.

PART III: THE ARTIFICIAL WORLD

Chapter 10 pages 108–121

FURTHER READING

T. Bennett, *The Birth of the Museum: History, Theory, Politics* (London and New York, 1995)

F. Haskell, *History and its Images: Art and the Interpretation of the Past* (New Haven and London, 1993)

D. Knight, *Ordering the World: A History of Classifying Man* (London, 1981)

A. MacGregor (ed.), *Sir Hans Sloane: Collector, Scientist, Antiquary* (London, 1994)

K. Pomian, *Collectors and Curiosities: Paris and Venice, 1500–1800* (Cambridge, 1990)

A. Potts, *Flesh and the Ideal: Winckelmann and the Origins of Art History* (New Haven and London, 1994)

NOTES

1 I. Jenkins, *Archaeologists and Aesthetes in the Sculpture Galleries of the British Museum 1800–1939* (London, 1992). I am grateful to David Bindman and Frances Carey for their critical readings of this chapter.

2 Bennett, *The Birth of the Museum*, pp. 95–7.

3 A. MacGregor, 'The Life, Character and Career of Sir Hans Sloane', in MacGregor (ed.), *Sir Hans Sloane*, pp. 11–44, esp. p. 29.

4 The contemporary accounts of these visits can be found in MacGregor (ed.), *Sir Hans Sloane*, pp. 30–5.

5 Pomian, *Collectors and Curiosities*, pp. 45–7.

6 L. Franzoni, 'Origine e storia del Museo Lapidario Maffeiano', *Il Museo Maffeiano riaperto al pubblico* (1982), pp. 29–72.

7 Jenkins, *Archaeologists and Aesthetes* (n. 1 above), p. 56.

8 Haskell, *History and its Images*, p. 162, citing J. de La Lande, *Voyage en Italie* (Yverdon, 1787–8) vol. 1, p. 98, and E. Gibbon (ed. G. A. Bonnard), *Journey from Geneva to Rome: His Journal from 20 April to 2 October 1764* (London, 1961), p. 21.

9 E. Castelnuovo and M. Rosci (eds), *Turin: cultura figurativa e architettonica negli Stati del Re di Sardegna* (Turin, 1980), vol. 1, pp. 42–3.

10 J. C. H. King, 'Ethnographic Collections: Collecting in the Context of Sloane's Catalogue of "Miscellanies"', in MacGregor (ed.), *Sir Hans Sloane*, pp. 228–44, esp. pp. 231–2.

11 I. Jenkins, 'Classical Antiquities: Sloane's "Repository of Time"', in MacGregor (ed.), *Sir Hans Sloane*, pp. 167–73, esp. p. 168.

12 T. DaCosta Kaufmann, 'From Treasury to Museum: the Collections of the Austrian Habsburgs', in J. Elsner and R. Cardinal (eds), *The Cultures of Collecting* (London, 1994), pp. 137–54, 282–5, esp. pp. 148–51.

13 D. J. Meijers, 'La Classification comme principe: la transformation de la Galerie impériale de Vienne en "histoire visible de l'art"', in E. Pommier (ed.), *Les Musées en Europe à la veille de l'ouverture du Louvre: Actes du colloque organisé par la service culturel de musée du Louvre, juin 1993* (Paris, 1995), pp. 593–613. Von Mechel's work in Vienna was preceded by similar efforts in Düsseldorf: see L. H. Wüthrich, *Christian von Mechel: Leben und Werk eines basler Kupferstechers und Kunsthändlers* (Basel and Stuttgart, 1956), pp. 119–28, and is paralleled by rearrangement and publication of the prints and paintings in Dresden by Carl Heinrich von Heinecken (1707–91): see C. Drittich, 'Heinrich von Heinecken's kunsthistorische Schriften', *Jahrbuch Staatl. Kstsamml. Dresden* 1965/6, pp. 79–85.

14 S. Bann, *The Clothing of Clio: A Study of the Representation of History in Nineteenth-century Britain and France* (Cambridge, 1984), pp. 83–8; Haskell, *History and its Images*, pp. 236–52.

15 A. Potts, 'Die Skulpturenaufstellung in der Glyptothek', in K. Vierneisel and G. Leinz (eds), *Glyptothek München, 1830–1980* (Munich, 1980), pp. 258–83.

16 MacGregor, *Sir Hans Sloane*, p. 16.

17 Pope, *Dunciad*. Quoted by R. Porter, *Enlightenment: Britain and the Creation of the Modern World* (London, 2000), p. 546, note 7.

18 A. Momigliano, 'Ancient History and the Antiquarian', *Journal of the Warburg and Courtauld Institutes* 13 (1950), pp. 295 ff; Momigliano, 'The Rise of Antiquarian Research', in *The Classical Foundations of Modern Historiography* (Berkeley and Oxford, 1990), pp. 54–79; L. Peltz and M. Myrone, 'Introduction: "Mine are the subjects rejected by the historian": Antiquarianism, History and the Making of Modern Culture', in M. Myrone and L. Peltz (eds), *Producing the Past: Aspects of Antiquarian Culture and Practice* (Aldershot, 1999), pp. 1–12.

19 Pomian, *Collectors and Curiosities*, pp. 170–1.

20 *Ibid.*, pp. 170–2.

21 *Ibid.*, pp. 56–63.

22 Porter, *Enlightenment*, pp. 56–7.

23 *Ibid.*, pp. 61–3.

24 M. Foucault, *The Order of Things* (London, 1970), pp. 144–9.

25 Knight, *Ordering the World*, pp. 58–81.

26 Haskell, *History and its Images*, pp. 131–2.

27 Addison, p. 26.

28 Haskell, *History and its Images*, pp. 174–8; G. P. Romagnani (ed.), *Scipione Maffei nell'Europa del Settecento: atti del convegno, Verona, 23–25 settembre 1996* (Verona, 1998), *passim*.

29 J. Guillerme, 'Caylus technologue: note sur les commencements d'une discipline', *Revue de l'Art* 60 (1983), pp. 47–50; R. T. Ridley, 'A Pioneer Art Historian and Archaeologist of the Eighteenth Century: the Comte de Caylus and his Recueil', *Storia dell'Arte* 76 (1992), pp. 362–75; Haskell, *History and its Images*, pp. 179–85.

30 A. Momigliano, 'The Origins of Universal History', in *On Pagans, Jews and Christians* (Hanover, NH, 1987), pp. 31–57.

31 W. H. Youngren, 'Addison and the Birth of Eighteenth-century Aesthetics', *Modern Philology* 79 (1982), pp. 267–83.

32 D. Townsend, 'Shaftesbury's Aesthetic Theory', *Journal of Aesthetics and Art Criticism* 41 (1982), pp. 206–13.

33 C. Gibson-Wood, 'Jonathan Richardson and the Rationalisation of Connoisseurship', *Art History* 7 (1984), pp. 38–56; Gibson-Wood, 'Jonathan Richardson, Lord Somers's Collection of Drawings and Early Art-historical Writing in England', *Journal of the Warburg and Courtauld Institutes* 52 (1989), pp. 167–87.

34 *The Works of Jonathan Richardson* (London, 1792), p. 194.

35 *Ibid.*, p. 200.

36 *Ibid.*, p. 201.

37 F. Haskell, 'Gibbon and the History of Art', *Daedalus* 105:3 (1976), pp. 217–29; Haskell, *History and its Images*, pp. 163–4, 187.

38 A. Potts, *Flesh and the Ideal: Winckelmann and the Origins of Art History* (New Haven and London, 1994), *passim*, but esp. p. 33. See also F. Testa, *Winckelmann e l'invenzione della storia dell'arte: i modelli e la mimesi* (Bologna, 1999), *passim*.

39 A. Potts, 'The Verbal and the Visual in Winckelmann's Analysis of Style', *Word and Image* 6 (1990), pp. 226–40.

40 Potts, *Flesh and the Ideal*, pp. 33–4.

41 W. Lepenies, 'Johann Joachim Winckelmann: Kunst- und Naturgeschichte in achtzehn Jahrhundert', in *Johann Joachim Winckelmann, 1717–1768* (Hamburg, 1986), pp. 221–37.

42 J. Wiesner, 'Winckelmann und Hippokrates: zu Winckelmanns naturwissenschaftlich-medizinischen Schriften', *Gymnasium* 60 (1951), pp. 149–67.

43 W. Sauerländer, 'From Stilus to Style: Reflections on the Fate of a Notion', *Art History* 6 (1983), pp. 253–70, esp. p. 256.

44 Haskell, *History and its Images*, pp. 218–20.

45 S. Howard, 'Albani, Winckelmann and Cavaceppi: the Transition from Amateur to Professional Antiquarianism', *Journal of the History of Collections* 4:1 (1992), pp. 27–38.

Chapter 11 pages 122–131

FURTHER READING

F. Bassoli, *Monete e medaglie nel libro antico dal xv al xix secolo* (Florence, 1985); English translation (by E. Saville), *Antiquarian Books on Coins and Medals* (London, 2001)

M. Crawford, J. Trapp and C. R. Ligota (eds), *Medals and Coins from Budé to Mommsen* (London, 1990)

J. Cunally, *Images of the Illustrious: The Numismatic Presence in the Renaissance* (Princeton, 1999)

M. Grant, 'A Great Age of Numismatics', *Numismatic Chronicle*, 1954, proceedings iii–xv

O. Mørkholm, '200 Years of Greek Numismatics', *Nordisk Numismatisk Årsskrift*, 1979–80, pp. 5–21, and 1982, pp. 7–26

H. Pagan, 'Presidential Address', *British Numismatic Journal* 57 (1987), pp. 173–80

NOTES

1 H. Walpole, *Correspondence*, ed. W. S. Lewis, vol. 21 (London, 1960), p. 449, cited in the exhibition catalogue *George III Collector and Patron: The Queen's Gallery, Buckingham Palace 1974–75* (London, 1974), p. 3. Thanks to Luke Syson, Kim Sloan, Hugh Pagan, Jonathan Kagan and Christian Dekesel for their help with this chapter.

2 F. Haskell, *History and its Images* (New Haven and London, 1993), p. 14.

3 C. E. Dekesel, *Hubertus Goltzius: The Father of Ancient Numismatics* (Ghent, 1988), pp. 5–7. See also C. E. Dekesel, *A Bibliography of 16th Century Numismatic Books* (London, 1997), and J. Cunally, J. H. Kagan and S. K. Scher, *Numismatics in the Age of Grolier* (New York, 2001).

4 In this chapter all quotations are translated into English.

5 For example, J. Foy-Vaillant in his books on *Numismata aerea imperatorum, augustarum et caesarum in coloniis, municipiis, et urbibus jure latio donatis, ex omni modulo percussa* (Paris, 1688) and *Numismata imperatorum, augustarum et caesarum a populis romanae ditionis graece loquentibus* (Paris, 1698).

6 The quotation is from T. E. Mionnet, *Description de médailles antiques, grecques et romaines* (Paris, 1806), p. 7; the debt is explicitly acknowledged in the first *British Museum Catalogue of Greek Coins*, published in 1863.

7 See A. Momigliano, 'Ancient History and the Antiquarian', *Journal of the Warburg and Courtauld Institutes* 13 (1950), pp. 285–315; Haskell, *History and its Images*, p. 188.

8 H. Walpole, *Anecdotes of Painting in England*, with additions by J. Dallaway, revised with additional notes by R. N. Wornum (London, 1862), vol. 1, p. 262.

9 N. Haym, *Tesoro Britannico, overo il museo nummario &c.* (London, 1719), p. ii.

10 H. Pagan, 'Martin Folkes', in R. G. W. Anderson, M. L. Caygill, A. G. MacGregor and L. Syson (eds), *Enlightening the British: Knowledge, Discovery and the Museum in the Eighteenth Century* (London, 2004).

11 Many thanks to John Goldfinch for information about the numismatic section of the George III library.

12 D. Shrub, 'The Vile Problem', *Victoria and Albert Museum Bulletin* 4 (October 1965), pp. 26–35.

13 M. M. Archibald, 'Coins and Medals', in A. MacGregor (ed.), *Sir Hans Sloane: Collector, Scientist, Antiquary* (London, 1994), pp. 150–66.

14 T. Combe, *Veterum populorum et regum numi qui in Museo Britannico adservantur* (London, 1814), pp. v–viii. We don't know why Cracherode collected coins – perhaps the coins and the gems (see ch. 12) were a natural complement to his library of 4,500 very fine books. He also collected minerals, shells (see ch. 7) and, especially, prints and drawings. His coins remain some of the finest pieces in the British Museum collection. See A. Mallinson, 'CMC – an Eighteenth-century Coin Collector', *Seaby's Coin and Medal Bulletin* 694 (June 1976), pp. 193–5.

15 J. Millingen, *Receuil de quelques médailles grecques inédites* (Rome, 1812).

Chapter 12 pages 132–139

FURTHER READING

Y. Kagan and O. Neverov, *Treasures of Catherine the Great*, exh. cat. Hermitage Rooms at Somerset House (London, 2000)

J. Rudoe, 'The Faking of Gems in the Eighteenth Century', in M. Jones (ed.), *Why Fakes Matter: Essays on the Problems of Authenticity* (London, 1992), pp. 23–30

D. Scarisbrick, 'English Collectors of Engraved Gems: Aristocrats, Antiquaries and Aesthetes', in M. Henig, *Classical Gems: Ancient and Modern Intaglios and Cameos in the Fitzwilliam Museum Cambridge* (Cambridge, 1994), pp. xiii–xxiii

G. Seidmann, 'Nathaniel Marchant, Gem-Engraver 1729–1816', *The Walpole Society* 53 (1987)

J. Smith, *James Tassie (1735–99): Modeller in Glass* (London, 1995)

P. and H. Zazoff, *Gemmensammler und Gemmenforscher* (Munich, 1983)

NOTES

1 For Consul Smith's collection see *A King's Purchase: King George III and the Collection of Consul Smith*, exh. cat. London, The Queen's Gallery (London, 1993). For the gems see K. Piacenti in *Connoisseur* (June 1977), pp. 79–83. A full catalogue of the engraved gems in the royal collection is currently being prepared by Kirsten Piacenti: see K. Piacenti, *Catalogue of Gems and Jewellery in the Royal Collection* (London, forthcoming).

2 Both were by A. F. Gori: *Gemmae antiquae Antonii Mariae Zanetti* (1750) and *Dactiliotheca Smithiana* (1767). Zanetti's gems were purchased by the Duke of Marlborough in 1762, Smith's by George III in the same year.

3 *Gemmae antiquae caelatae [Ancient Carved Gems]*.

4 For the Stosch collection see P. and H. Zazoff. It was sold after his death to Frederick the Great of Prussia and is today in Berlin.

5 Winckelmann's catalogue of the Stosch collection and its influence is fully discussed by Ian Jenkins in I. Jenkins and K. Sloan, *Vases and Volcanoes: Sir William Hamilton and his Collection* (London, 1996), pp. 94–6.

6 Mariette's treatise was in two parts: the first looked at the technique and existing literature; the second was an illustrated catalogue of intaglios in the French royal gem cabinet. This is still an essential reference because there is to date no illustrated catalogue of intaglios (as opposed to cameos) in the French royal gem collection.

7 L. Réau, 'Correspondance artistique de Grimm avec Catherine II', *Archives de l'Art Français* 17 (1932), p. 166. Much of what we know about Catherine's gem collecting comes from this correspondence with her agent, Melchior Grimm, in Paris. Further letters are quoted in Kagan and Neverov, *Treasures of Catherine the Great*, pp. 94–102.

8 Sulphur is actually much stronger than sealing wax or plaster, but it ruined the lungs and the practice did not last into the nineteenth century. For more on sulphur casts see J. Smith, *James Tassie (1735–99): Modeller in Glass* (London, 1995), pp. 23 and 36.

9 She had a pair of special cabinets made to house them. See Kagan and Neverov, *Treasures of Catherine the Great*.

10 Tassie's casts were catalogued in 1791 by Rudolph Erich Raspe, mineralogist and author of Baron Munchhausen's *Travels*; although largely unillustrated, Raspe's volume is still indispensable today.

11 See D. Jaffé, *Rubens's Self-Portrait in Focus*, exh. cat. Australian National Gallery (Canberra, 1988). Rubens also collected cameos; a large classical cameo from his collection was acquired by the British Museum in 1956: GR 1956.5–17.1.

12 For Cassiano's drawings of engraved gems see I. Jenkins, 'Newly Discovered Drawings from the Museo Cartaceo in the British Museum', in F. Solinas (ed.), *Cassiano Dal Pozzo: Atti del Seminario Internazionale di Studi* (Rome, 1989), pp. 131–5.

13 For the gem collections of Sir William Hamilton (1730–1803) see Jenkins and Sloan, *Vases and Volcanoes*, chapter 6. After 1772 when the gems entered the British Museum, Hamilton formed a second collection, which was largely sold to Sir Richard Worsley in 1792, and from him it descended to the Earls of Yarborough. This second collection included contemporary works by Pichler, Rega and Marchant.

14 For the most recent biography of Sloane see A. Griffiths, 'Sir Hans Sloane', in *Landmarks of Print Collecting* (London, 1996), pp. 21–42; see also A. MacGregor (ed.), *Sir Hans Sloane: Collector, Scientist, Antiquary* (London, 1994).

15 There are some fifty of these tiny animals. For the classical cameos see H. B. Walters, *Catalogue of the Engraved Gems and Cameos, Greek, Etruscan and Roman, in the British Museum* (London, 1926), nos 2336, 2519, 2528–9, 2545, 2553, 2579, 2583, 3678, 3690. For the post-classical examples see O. M. Dalton, *Catalogue of the Engraved Gems of the Post-classical Periods in the British Museum* (London, 1915), nos 277–306. The 'African' heads are Dalton, nos 215 and 218.

16 For Sloane's layered stones see his 'Moncalis', a female head with veil cut in the black layer (Dalton, *Engraved Gems*, no. 406), his 'Mulior Africana in achate varie' (Dalton, no. 66, as Minerva) and his head of Socrates (Dalton, no. 316).

17 For agates see H. G. Macpherson, *Agates* (London, 1989). See also R. Webster, *Gems: Their Sources, Descriptions and Identification*, 3rd edn (London, 1975).

18 Sloane List B. 269.

19 P. von Stosch, *Gemmae antiquae caelatae* (Amsterdam, 1724).

20 For an account of the fourth Earl of Carlisle's gem collecting see D. Scarisbrick, 'Gem Connoisseurship – the 4th Earl of Carlisle's Correspondence with Francesco de Ficoroni and Antonio Maria Zanetti', *Burlington Magazine*, February 1987, pp. 90–104. Ficoroni, like Zanetti, was also a collector, and his gems were published in 1757 by Nicolao Galeotti.

21 For a biography of Cracherode see Griffiths, 'The Reverend Clayton Mordaunt Cracherode', in *Landmarks of Print Collecting*, pp. 43–64.

22 The lion is Dalton, *Engraved Gems*, no. 232, but Dalton did not identify it as a Cracherode gem. It has only recently been matched up with no. 57 in the manuscript inventory. This inventory is a confusing document because the order is completely different from that of the

set of numbered casts that accompanied the gems when they entered the museum. Possibly the manuscript inventory, with its prices against each item, relates to the order in which the gems were acquired.

23 For Cracherode's 'modern' gems see Dalton, *Engraved Gems*, nos 776 (intaglio of Urania by Pichler), 371 (cameo of Vespasian by Pichler) and 1132 (intaglio with female head by Burch). For the six gems by Marchant see Dalton, nos 584, 694, 700, 742, 817, 1117.

24 One of his Marchants, Bacchus and a Bacchante, was purchased in 1785 at the sale of the late Matthew Duane for £24 3s 6d. See the annotated Duane sale catalogue in the British Library: *A Catalogue of the Entire Valuable Museum of the Late Matthew Duane*: Gerard, London, 13 June 1785, lot 96.

25 Sadly this gem was destroyed by enemy action in 1941.

26 The information on Townley's purchasing of gems comes from G. Vaughan, *The Collecting of Classical Antiquities in England in the 18th Century: A Study of Charles Townley* (unpublished D. Phil. thesis, Oxford, 1988), pp. 237, 116–17, note 103, and 424.

27 Both gems in fig. 122 were subsequently catalogued as neoclassical by Dalton, *Engraved Gems*, cat. 663 and 643. The Venus and Cupid has recently been reassessed and is now thought ancient: see Rudoe, 'The Faking of Gems in the Eighteenth Century'. For a discussion of gems with false Greek signatures see M. Jones (ed.), *Fake? The Art of Deception*, exh. cat. (London, 1990), p. 147 and no. 151a.

28 Townley 378; this gem was included in the 1830 catalogue of gems but not in Dalton's *Engraved Gems*. It seems that it was already missing by then.

29 The Girometti head is Payne Knight no. 109, Dalton, *Engraved Gems* no. 500 (destroyed in the Blitz); the Pistrucci Augustus is Payne Knight no. 110, This gem was wrongly numbered and has only recently been matched up with the manuscript catalogue: see J. Rudoe, 'Eighteenth and Nineteenth-century Engraved Gems in the British Museum; Collectors and Collections from Sir Hans Sloane to Anne Hull Grundy', *Zeitschrift für Kunstgeschichte* 59:2 (1996), pp. 198–213, fig. 6. Dalton catalogued it as sixteenth century (*Engraved Gems*, no. 321).

30 Dalton, *Engraved Gems*, no. 176.

31 See A. Billing, *The Science of Gems, Jewels, Coins and Medals* (London, 1875), pp. 182–90; M. Clarke and N. Penny, *The Arrogant Connoisseur: Richard Payne Knight 1751–1824*, exh. cat. Manchester, Whitworth Art Gallery (Manchester, 1982), pp. 74–5; Jones, *Fake?*, cat. 152.

32 It would have remained longer, but for a series of thefts of the Cracherode prints,

following which the collections were redistributed.

33 A. H. Smith, *Catalogue of Engraved Gems in the British Museum (Department of Greek & Roman Antiquities)* (London, 1888).

34 A full catalogue of Greek and Roman gems appeared in 1926: see Walters, *Engraved Gems*.

35 The Townley papers have yet to be fully researched. Cracherode left no papers, and a full correlation between the manuscript inventory and the Cracherode set of casts, arranged in a completely different order, is still to be done.

Chapter 13 pages 140–149

FURTHER READING

L. Burn, 'Sir William Hamilton and the Greekness of Greek Vases', *Journal of the History of Collections* 9:2 (1997), pp. 241–52

I. Jenkins and K. Sloan, *Vases and Volcanoes: Sir William Hamilton and his Collection* (London, 1996)

C. Lyons, 'The Museo Mastrilli and the Culture of Collecting in Naples, 1700–1755', *Journal of the History of Collections* 4:1 (1992), pp. 1–26

C. Lyons, 'The Neapolitan context of Hamilton's Antiquities Collection', *Journal of the History of Collections* 9:2 (1997), pp. 229–40

P. Rouet, *Approaches to the Study of Attic Vases, Beazley and Pottier* (Oxford, 2001), pp. 7–24

B. A. Sparkes, *The Red and the Black* (London and New York, 1996), pp. 34–63

NOTES

1 For a brief account of the discoveries at Vulci see Sparkes, *The Red and the Black*, pp. 58–60.

2 For an excellent overview of the evidence see *ibid.*, pp. 34–63, with earlier bibliography; C. Lyons, in the earlier part of her paper 'The Museo Mastrilli', pp. 1–26, also offers a useful survey of evidence for interest in vases before the eighteenth century.

3 See J. Chamay in M. Flashar (ed.), *Europe à la Grecque* (Freiburg, 1999), pp. 11–15.

4 See D. M. Bailey, 'Small Objects in the dal Pozzo-Albani Drawings: Early Gatherings', in I. Jenkins (ed.), *Cassiano dal Pozzo's Paper Museum*, 1 (Milan, 1992), pp. 3–30.

5 Lyons, 'The Museo Mastrilli'; also in 'The Neapolitan Context of Hamilton's Antiquities Collection', pp. 229–40.

6 For Sloane's antiquities see I. Jenkins in A MacGregor (ed.), *Sir Hans Sloane: Collector, Scientist, Antiquary* (London, 1994), pp. 167–73.

7 For eyewitness accounts of the collections see

MacGregor, *Sir Hans Sloane*, pp. 30–5: the quotation is taken from the account of Sauveur Morand, who visited in 1729.

8 See Lyons, 'The Museo Mastrilli'.

9 For the gradual progress towards realization that most of the painted vases found in Italy and Sicily were Greek, rather than Etruscan see L. Burn, 'Sir William Hamilton and the Greekness of Greek Vases', pp. 241–52.

10 For Hamilton's life, interests and achievements see Jenkins and Sloan, *Vases and Volcanoes*, with full bibliography to 1996, L. Burn (ed.), *Sir William Hamilton: Collector and Connoisseur, Journal of the History of Collections* 9:2 (1997), and D. Constantine, *Fields of Fire: A Life of Sir William Hamilton* (London, 2001).

11 See I. Jenkins, *Archaeologists and Aesthetes* (London, 1992), p. 103.

12 See W. Hamilton, *Collection of Engravings from Ancient Vases* (W. Tischbein, Naples, 1791–5), vol. 1, pp. 20–2, 156–8, and vol. 2, 96, with pls 61–2.

13 V. Smallwood, introduction to *Greek Vases from HMS Colossus* (London, forthcoming); I am very grateful to Mrs Smallwood for kindly allowing me to read the Introduction before publication.

14 See Smallwood; the question is also discussed by Ian Jenkins, *Vases and Volcanoes*, p. 57.

15 *Vases and Volcanoes*, p. 61.

16 *Ibid.*, p. 184.

17 I. Jenkins, 'Adam Buck and the Vogue for Greek Vases', *Burlington Magazine* 130 (June 1988), pp. 448–57.

18 For Thomas Hope see D. Watkin, *Thomas Hope, 1769–1831, and the Neo-Classical Idea* (London, 1968).

19 See *ibid.*

20 R. Westmacott, *British Galleries of Painting and Sculpture* (London, 1824), pp. 229–30.

21 *Monthly Review* 58 (1809), p. 180 (quoted by Watkin, *Thomas Hope*).

22 See I. Jenkins, 'La Vente des vases Durand (Paris 1836) et leur réception en Grand-Bretagne', in A.-F. Laurens and K. Pomian (eds), *L'Anticomanie (int. colloquium Montpellier-Lattes, 9–12 Juin 1988)* (Paris, 1992), pp. 269–78.

23 See I. Jenkins in D. E. Ostergard (ed.), *William Beckford 1760–1844: An Eye for the Magnificent* (New Haven and London, 2001), p. 367.

24 For these two initiatives see the recent discussion of P. Rouet, *Approaches to the Study of Attic Vases*.

Chapter 14 pages 150–157

FURTHER READING

R. G. W. Anderson, 'Early Scientific Instruments and Horology', in M. Caygill and J. Cherry (eds), *A. W. Franks: Nineteenth-century Collecting and the British Museum* (London, 1997), pp. 286–95

T. Birch, *The History of the Royal Society of London …* (Facsimile of first edition 1756/7, New York and London, 1968)

P. Blom, 'A Curious Old Gentleman', *To Have and to Hold* (London, 2002), pp. 77–91

P. de Clercq, 'A Musschenbroek Trade Catalogue in the Library of Sir Hans Sloane', *Bulletin of the Scientific Instrument Society* 70 (2001), 10–13

A. E. Gunther, *The Founders of Science at the British Museum 1753–1900* (Halesworth, 1986)

M. Boas Hall, *Promoting Experimental Learning: Experiment and the Royal Society* (Cambridge, 1991)

M. Hunter, *Establishing the New Science: The Experience of the Early Royal Society* (Woodbridge, 1989)

L. Jardine, *Ingenious Pursuits: Building the Scientific Revolution* (London, 1999)

A. MacGregor (ed.), *Sir Hans Sloane: Collector, Scientist, Antiquary* (London, 1994)

A. Q. Morton, *Science in the 18th Century: The King George III Collection* (London, 1993)

A. Q. Morton and J. A. Wess, *Public and Private Science: The King George III Collection* (Oxford, 1993)

S. Shapin, *The Scientific Revolution* (Chicago, 1996)

L. Stewart, *The Rise of Public Science: Rhetoric, Technology, and Natural Philosophy in Newtonian Britain, 1660–1750* (Cambridge, 1992)

Chapter 15 pages 158–165

FURTHER READING

P. M. Barber, 'Maps and Monarchs in Europe 1500–1800', in R. Oresko, G. C. Gibbs and H. M. Scott (eds), *Royal and Republican Sovereignty in Early Modern Europe* (Cambridge, 1997), pp. 75–124

J. Brooke, 'The Library of King George III', *Yale University Library Gazette* 52 (1978), pp. 33–45

P. R. Harris, *A History of the British Museum Library* (London, 1998)

Y. Hodson, 'Prince William, Royal Map Collector', *The Map Collector* 44 (Autumn 1988), pp. 2–12

R. A. Skelton, 'The Royal Map Collections of England', *Imago Mundi* 13 (1956), pp. 81–3

H. M. Wallis, *The Royal Map Collections of England* (Coimbra, Antiga, 1981)

NOTES

1 This chapter is based on and partly extracted from a more extensive treatment of King George III's geographical collections that is under active preparation. Unless otherwise stated, all references are to items from the British Library's collections.

2 The Wilson portrait hangs with the National Portrait Gallery collection at Beningborough Hall, Yorkshire, and the Knapton, which shows him with his mother and siblings, is in the Royal Collection.

3 A set of cartographic jigsaw puzzles supposedly used by their governess, Lady Charlotte Finch, came on to the market at Christie's London on 5 June 2000 and is described and illustrated in *Imago Mundi* 53 (2001), pp. 176–7, plate 12.

4 I. Cobbin, *Georgiana: or Anecdotes of George the Third* (London, 1820), p. 16. I am most grateful to Tony Campbell for bringing this quotation to my attention.

5 Maps 4 Tab. 48 formerly K. Top. 102.21; Maps 6 Tab. 4 and 5 formerly K. Top. 78.30 – a and b. All contain Sloane's pressmarks.

6 K. Top. 49.23-a-3-6; 49.23-b.

7 K. Top. 31.42 – b-h.

8 Printed in F. A. Barnard, *Bibiliothecae regiae catalogus*, vol. 1 (London, 1820), pp. v–vi.

9 The hostility of the ruling Whig oligarchy to central government interference, however, outweighed their Enlightened principles and meant that the detailed mapping of England by the Ordnance Survey at a scale of one inch to the mile was long delayed. Commenced in the 1790s as a response to the threat of invasion by Revolutionary France, it was completed only in 1869 – eighty years after the completion of the mapping of France at a similar scale. See Barber, 'Maps and Monarchs', pp. 94–6, 105–6.

10 Now K. Top. 80.21 – a-e. F. J. B. Watson, 'A Group of Views of Lucca by Bellotto', *Burlington Magazine*, 1953, pp. 166–9; Hugh Honour discusses the drawings and related painting of the Piazza San Martino in Lucca (now in the York City Art Gallery) in S. Marinelli (ed.), *Bernardo Bellotto: Verona e le città europee*, exh. cat. Verona, 1990 (Milan, 1990), pp. 64–5.

11 Aaron Lambe (auctioneer), *A Catalogue of a Curious Collection of Original Pictures . . . of that well known architect Nicholas Hawksmoor deceased . . . 21 April 1740*. Reproduced in full in D. J. Wilkin, *Sale Catalogues of Eminent Persons*, vol. 4 (London, 1974). K. Downes, *Hawksmoor* (2nd ed., London 1979), pp. 286–7.

12 K. Top. 119.111. The remaining surveys of Newfoundland are now in the archives of the Hydrographic Office in Taunton.

13 The Brambila views are K. Top. 124 Supp. 43, 44, 45. And see P. Barber, 'Malaspina and George III, Brambila and Watling: Three Discovered Drawings of Sydney and Parramatta by Fernando Brambila', *Australian Journal of Art* 11 (1993), pp. 31–56.

14 K. Top. 118.49b.

15 K. Top. 17.43.

16 E. Miller, *That Noble Cabinet* (London, 1973), p. 124. The enormously increased budget could well have been, in part, a response to the urgent need to catalogue and to house the enormous backlogs that had been allowed to build up since 1790.

17 The boxes continued to be used until the mid-1950s when they were replaced by the large guardbooks that are currently in use.

18 'Compte Rendu à S. E. Le Ministre de l'Intérieur', *Le Moniteur*, 28 July 1824, pp. 11–24.

19 Barnard to the Earl of Buchan, 3 October 1786, printed in *The R. B. Adam Library Relating to Dr. Samuel Johnson and his Era* (London and Oxford, 1929), p. 15.

20 *Catalogue of the King's Topographical Collection* (London, 1829). It is a sign of the ambiguous position of the King's Topographical Collection that while it was mentioned in the introduction to the catalogue of the King's Library, which appeared in 1820, with the room accommodating much of it in the Queen's House being illustrated, the collection itself became the subject of a special catalogue. Because the Military and Maritime Collections were not made available to the public and did not reach the British Museum, neither received a printed catalogue at the time – or after.

21 For this craze see J. Brewer, *The Pleasures of the Imagination: English Culture in the Eighteenth Century* (London, 1997), pp. 450–1, 458–9, 461.

22 The Gough collection is now divided up into 61 guardbooks and portfolios, while 770 pieces of the 'Frog Service' (which takes its name from the Russian palace for which the service was intended) with 1,025 views still survive. See L. Voronikhina, 'The Green Frog Service and its History in Russia', in L. Voronikhina and A. Nurnberg (eds), *The Green Frog Service* (London, 1995), p. 9. The Innys collection, containing approximately twenty thousand items, is currently being listed by the Earl of Leicester's librarian, Dr Matlock.

23 M. Raeburn, 'The Frog Service and its Sources', in H. Young (ed.), *The Genius of Wedgwood* (London, 1995), pp. 134–48, and M. Raeburn and L.Voronikhina, 'List of the Views' (i.e. *catalogue raisonné*), in *The Green Frog Service*, pp. 235–406. The Innys collection, which seems to have been in Holkham Hall

since at least the mid-1750s (and which may have been the inspiration for the Duke of Cumberland's collection), also shares many similar sources for material created before 1749.

24 Brewer, *Pleasures*, pp. 452–3; M. Pedley (ed.), *The Map Trade in the Late Eighteenth Century: Letters to the London Map Sellers Jefferys and Faden* (Oxford, 2000).

25 Brewer, *Pleasures*, passim, and M. Raeburn, 'Catherine the Great and the Image of Britain', in *The Green Frog Service*, pp. 42–56; S. Daniels, *Humphrey Repton: Landscape Gardening and Geography in Georgian England* (New Haven, 1999), especially pp. 7–8.

26 Raeburn, 'The Frog Service and its Sources', p. 136.

27 See, for instance, K. Top. 85.69-a&b.

PART IV: ANCIENT CIVILIZATIONS

Chapter 16 pages 169–177

FURTHER READING

I. Jenkins, *Archaeologists and Aesthetes in the Sculpture Galleries of the British Museum 1800–1939* (London, 1992)

I. Jenkins, 'Classical Antiquities. Sloane's Repository of Time', in A. MacGregor (ed.), *Sir Hans Sloane: Collector, Scientist, Antiquary* (London, 1994)

I. Jenkins and K. Sloan, *Vases and Volcanoes: Sir William Hamilton and his Collection* (London, 1996)

A. Michaelis, *Ancient Marbles in Great Britain* (London, 1882)

K. Pomian, *Collectors and Curiosities: Paris and Venice, 1500–1800* (Cambridge, 1990)

A. Schnapp, *The Discovery of the Past* (London, 1996)

NOTES

1 See L. Patrice, *Sister Republics: The Origins of French and American Republicanism.* (Cambridge, 1988). For further reading on the Classical origins of the American Enlightenment see 'American Political Thought and the Classics: a Bibliography', in S. F. Wiltshire, *Greece, Rome and the Bill of Rights* (Norman, Oklahoma and London, 1992), pp. 229–38.

2 I. Jenkins, 'Athens Rising near the Pole' – London, Athens and the Idea of Freedom', in C. Fox (ed.), *London World City 1800–1840*, exh. cat. (London, 1992), pp. 143–54.

3 See, for example, the *Roman Antiquities* of Dionysius of Halicarnassus.

4 See A. Momigliano, 'Ancient History and the Antiquarian', *Journal of the Warburg and Courtauld Institutes* 13 (1950), pp. 288–9.

5 E. Mandowsky and C. Mitchell, 'Pirro Ligorio's Roman Antiquities', *Studies of the Warburg Institute* 28 (London, 1963), *passim*. For more recent studies see B. Palma Venetucci (ed.), *Pirro Ligorio e le erme Tiburtine* (Rome, 1992); and *Pirro Ligorio e le erme di Roma* (Rome, 1998).

6 F. Haskell *et al.*, *The Paper Museum of Cassiano dal Pozzo*, Quaderni Puteani 4 (Olivetti, 1993); I. Herklotz, *Cassiano dal Pozzo und die Archäologie des 17. Jahrhunderts* (Munich, 1999).

7 The drawings are now the subject of a cataloguing project. Some volumes of this catalogue have already appeared under the title *The Paper Museum of Cassiano dal Pozzo*, general editors the late Francis Haskell and Jennifer Montagu.

8 F. Haskell, *History and its Images* (New Haven and London, 1993), pp. 31 ff.

9 Haskell, *ibid.*, pp. 26 ff.

10 Jenkins, 'Classical Antiquities', p. 171.

11 Schnapp, *Discovery of the Past*, pp. 139–219.

12 Pomian, *Collectors and Curiosities*, pp. 169–84; Haskell, *History and its Images*, pp. 180–6; Jenkins, 'Classical Antiquities', p. 171; Schnapp, *Discovery*, pp. 238–42.

13 Le Comte de Caylus, *Recueil d'antiquités égyptiennes, étrusques, grecques et romaines*, 7 vols (Paris, 1752–67), vol. 1, Preface, pp. 1–2.

14 Jenkins, *Archaeologists and Aesthetes*, p. 60.

15 Michaelis, *Ancient Marbles in Great Britain*, pp. 5 ff.

16 R. Stoneman, *Land of Lost Gods* (London, 1987), pp. 110–35.

17 K. Justi, *Winckelmann und seine Zeitgenossen* (Leipzig, 1932); A. Potts, *Flesh and the Ideal* (New Haven and London, 1994).

18 R. Payne Knight, *Specimens of Ancient Sculpture*, vol. 1 (London, 1809); M. Clarke and N. Penny, *The Arrogant Connoisseur: Richard Payne Knight 1751–1824*, exh. cat. Whitworth Art Gallery, Manchester (Manchester, 1982).

19 F. Haskell, 'The Baron d'Hancarville: an Adventurer and Art Historian in Eighteenth-century Europe', in *Past and Present in Art and Taste* (New Haven and London, 1987), pp. 30–45; Jenkins and Sloan, *Vases and Volcanoes*, pp. 45 ff.

20 Jenkins, 'Classical Antiquities'.

21 Jenkins, *Archaeologists and Aesthetes*, pp. 19–29, 56–74; I. Jenkins, '"Gods Without Altars": the Belvedere in Paris', in M. Winner *et al.* (eds), *Il cortile delle statue* (Mainz, 1998), pp. 459–74.

22 E. Gombrich, *The Ideas of Progress and their Impact on Art* (New York, 1971).

23 I. Jenkins, 'Greek and Roman Life at the BM', *Museums Journal* 86:2 (1986), pp. 67–9.

24 Pomian, *Collectors and Curiosities*, p. 32.

Chapter 17 pages 178–191

FURTHER READING

G. Daniel, *150 Years of Archaeology* (London, 1975)

D. K. Grayson, *The Establishment of Human Antiquity* (New York, 1983)

S. Piggott, *Ruins in Landscape: Essays in Antiquarianism* (Edinburgh, 1976)

S. Piggott, *Ancient Britons and the Antiquarian Imagination* (London, 1989)

A. Schnapp, *The Discovery of the Past* (London, 1996)

S. Smiles, *The Image of Antiquity: Ancient Britain and the Romantic Imagination* (New Haven and London, 1994)

NOTES

1 Daniel, *150 Years of Archaeology*; Piggott, *Ruins in Landscape*; Piggott, *Ancient Britons and the Antiquarian Imagination*; Schnapp, *The Discovery of the Past*. For their patient help and for encouragement with this chapter my thanks are due to the editors of this volume, Mr Bernard Nurse and Mr Adrian James, librarians at the Society of Antiquaries, as well as my colleagues Catherine Johns, Ralph Jackson, Stuart Needham, Ian Jenkins and Leslie Webster.

2 A. Gordon, *Itinerarium Septentrionale; or a Journey thro' Most of the Counties in Scotland, and those in the North of England* (London, 1726), Preface.

3 Daniel, *150 Years of Archaeology*, pp. 27–8; Daniel, *The Idea of Prehistory* (London, 1962), pp. 23–30.

4 D. Outram, *The Enlightenment* (Cambridge, 1995), pp. 47–62.

5 M. C. W. Hunter, 'The Royal Society and the Origins of British Archaeology', *Antiquity* 65 (1971), pp. 113–21; M. Purver, *The Royal Society: Concept and Creation* (London, 1967).

6 E. Cassirer, *The Philosophy of the Enlightenment* (Princeton, 1952), p.42; Outram, *Enlightenment*, pp. 1–13.

7 Burial mounds or graves.

8 R. Plot, *The Natural History of Stafford-shire* (Oxford, 1686), p. 392.

9 M. Lister, 'A Letter from Dr Lister of York, Containing an Account of Several Curious Observations Made by him about Antiquities &c.', *Philosophical Collections of the Royal Society of London* 4 (1682), pp. 87–97.

10 Cassirer, *Philosophy*, p. 47.

11 W. Stukeley, *Itinerarium Curiosum or an Account of the Antiquities and Remarkable Curiosities in Nature or Art Observed in Travels through Great Britain* (London, 1724), Preface.

12 M. Hunter, *John Aubrey and the Realm of Learning* (London, 1975).

13 John Aubrey, ed. J. Britton, *Natural History of Wiltshire* (London, 1847), Preface.

14 Piggott, *Ruins in Landscape*.

15 D. K. Grayson, *The Establishment of Human Antiquity* (New York, 1983), pp. 17–20.

16 A late Roman illustrated document, surviving in medieval copies, which outlines the order of battle and administrative structure, as well as listing the high officers of state, military units and forts in Britain.

17 J. Woodward, 'An Account of some Roman Urns and other Antiquities Lately Digg'd up near Bishops-gate', in a Letter to Sir Christopher Wren included in T. Hearne (ed.), *Johannis Lelandi antiquarii de rebus britannicis collectanea* (Oxford, 1715), p. 25.

18 Daniel, *The Idea of Prehistory*.

19 J. Barr, 'Why the World was Created in 4004 BC: Archbishop Ussher and the Biblical Chronology', *Bulletin of the John Rylands University Library* 67 (1985), pp. 575–608.

20 J. Ussher, *Annales veteris testamenti, a prima mundi origine deducti [Annals of the Old Testament, Deduced from the First Origin of the World]* (Geneva, 1650).

21 S. J. Gould, 'Fall in the House of Ussher', in S. J. Gould, *Eight Little Piggies* (New York, 1993), pp. 181–93.

22 Daniel, *The Idea of Prehistory*.

23 Grayson, *Human Antiquity*, pp. 27–42.

24 Burnet in C. Blount *et al.*, *The Oracles of Reason* (London, 1693), p. 32.

25 E. Halley, 'A Short Account of the Saltness of the Ocean, and of Several Lakes that Emit to Rivers; With a Proposal, by Help Thereof, to Discover the Age of the Earth', *Philosophical Transactions of the Royal Society of London* 29 (1715), pp. 296–300.

26 Grayson, *Human Antiquity*, pp. 38–40; S. Winchester, *The Map that Changed the World: The Tale of William Smith and the Birth of Science* (London, 2000).

27 R. Jessup, *Man of Many Talents: An Informal Biography of James Douglas 1753–1819* (London, 1975).

28 Daniel, *150 Years of Archaeology*, pp. 115–16.

29 Jessup, *James Douglas*, p. 82.

30 W. Buckland, *Reliquiae Diluvianae or Observations on the Organic Remains*

Contained in Caves, Fissures and Diluvial Gravel, and on Other Geological Phenomena, Attesting the Action of the Universal Deluge (London, 1823), p. 97.

31 W. Buckland, *Geology and Mineralogy: Considered with Reference to Natural Theology*, Bridgewater Treatises 6 (London, 1837), p. 85.

32 Grayson, *Human Antiquity*, pp. 46–54.

33 Buckland, *Geology and Mineralogy*, p. 103.

34 C. Lyell, *Principles of Geology, being an Attempt to Explain the Former Changes of the Earth's Surface by Reference to Causes now in Operation*, vol. 2 (London, 1832), pp. 225–7.

35 Exodus 4.25.

36 Piggott, *Ruins in Landscape*, pp. 10, 66–7.

37 U. Aldrovandi, *Musaeum metallicum in libros III distributum* (Bologna, 1648), pp. 606–12.

38 *Ibid.*, p. 604.

39 Sir William Dugdale (1605–86). Studied law at Oxford and later became a Herald in 1638. In addition to his the study of his home county, he published several volumes on the monasteries and cathedrals of England. He bequeathed his manuscripts to the Ashmolean Museum, Oxford, founded by his son-in-law Elias Ashmole in 1683. See also note 41.

40 W. Dugdale, *The Antiquities of Warwickshire* (London, 1656), p. 778.

41 M. Hunter, *Elias Ashmole 1617–1692: The Founder of the Ashmolean Museum and his World* (Oxford, 1983), pp. 20, 48.

42 G. Daniel, 'Edward Lhwyd: Antiquary and Archaeologist', *Welsh Historical Review* 3 (1967), pp. 345–59.

43 Plot, *Stafford-shire*, p. 397.

44 J. Bagford, 'Mr Bagford's Letter Relating to the Antiquities of London', in T. Hearne (ed.), *Johannis Lelandi antiquarii de rebus britannicis collectanea*, pp. lxiii–lxv; MacGregor (ed.), *Sir Hans Sloane: Collector, Scientist, Antiquary* (London, 1994), pp. 24, 89, 180–2.

45 Hunter, 'The Royal Society', p. 115.

46 Bagford, 'Mr Bagford's Letter'.

47 J. Frere, 'Account of Flint Weapons Discovered at Hoxne in Suffolk', *Archaeologia* 13 (1800), pp. 204–5.

48 Bishop Lyttelton, 'Observations on a Stone Hatchet', *Archaeologia* 2 (1773), pp. 118–23; Mr Pegge, 'Observations on Stone Hammers', *Archaeologia* 2 (1773), esp. pp. 124–6.

49 N. Mahudel, 'Sur les prétendues pierres de foudre', *Histoire de l'Académie Royale des Inscriptions et Belles Lettres* 12 (1740), pp. 163–9.

50 P. A. S. Pool, *William Borlase* (Truro, 1986).

51 W. Borlase, *The Antiquities of Cornwall* (London, 1754), pp. 289–90.

52 Lyttelton, 'Observations on a Stone Hatchet', p. 122.

53 Daniel, *150 Years of Archaeology*, pp. 40–52.

54 T. Kendrick, *British Antiquity* (London, 1950), pp. 45–64.

55 *Ibid.*

56 *Ibid.*, pp. 134–67; Piggott, *150 Years of Archaeology*, pp. 33–53.

57 R. J. C. Atkinson, *Stonehenge* (London, 1951).

58 J. Aubrey, ed. by J. Fowles and annotated by R. Legg, *Monumenta Britannica or A Miscellany of British Antiquities* (Milbourne Port, 1980; original publication: London, 1665–93).

59 P. Ucko et al., *Avebury Reconsidered from the 1660s to the 1990s* (London, 1991), pp. 42–8.

60 Daniel, 'Edward Lhwyd'.

61 S. Piggott, *William Stukeley: An Eighteenth Century Antiquary* (Oxford, 1950). It was revised in 1985.

62 *Ibid.*, p. 110.

63 Ucko et al., *Avebury Reconsidered*, pp. 5, 3.

64 Piggott, *150 Years of Archaeology*, pp. 116–18.

65 Piggott, *William Stukeley*, pp. 27–9.

66 Outram, *Enlightenment*, pp. 31–46.

67 Freemasonry was one of the many sociable fraternities which developed in Britain in the late seventeenth century. It was particularly fashionable among those with interests in antiquities, architecture and geometry and numbered several Fellows of the Royal Society as members. It was established by the merger of four London lodges into The Grand Lodge in 1717 although there were many earlier speculative lodges such as that which Elias Ashmole joined in Warrington in 1649.

68 Stukeley became an associate member of the newly formed Egyptian Society in 1742. Piggott, *William Stukeley*, p. 144.

69 Quoted in Ucko et al., *Avebury Reconsidered*.

70 W. Stukeley, *Stonehenge a Temple Restor'd to the Druids* (London, 1740), p. 2.

71 Smiles, *The Image of Antiquity*, pp. 85–95; Ucko et al., *Avebury Reconsidered*, pp. 53–7.

72 *Ibid.*, p. 55.

73 *Ibid.* p. 54.

74 S. Piggott, *The Druids* (London, 1968); Piggott, *Ancient Britons*.

75 Aubrey, ed. Britton, *Natural History of Wiltshire*, p. 5.

76 Piggott, *Ruins in Landscape*, p. 113.

77 *Ibid.*, p. 81.

78 *Ibid.*, pp. 92–6.

79 *Ibid.*, pp. 194–217.

80 M. Hunter, *The Royal Society and its Fellows 1660–1700: The Morphology of an Early*

Scientific Institution, British Society for the History of Science monograph 4 (Chalfont St Giles, 1982).

81 J. Horsley, *Britannia Romana or the Roman Antiquities of Britain* (London, 1732), p. ii.

82 Anon., 'An Historical Account of the Origin and Establishment of the Society of Antiquaries', *Archaeologia* 1 (1770), pp. i–xxxix; J. Evans, *History of the Society of Antiquaries* (Oxford, 1956).

83 P. Clark, *British Clubs and Societies, 1580–1800: The Origins of the Associational World* (Oxford, 2000), p. 85.

84 *Ibid.*, p. 90.

85 Evans, *History of the Society of Antiquaries*, pp. 105–6.

86 Piggott, *Ancient Britons*, pp. 123–59.

87 D. C. Douglas, *English Scholars, 1660–1730*, 2nd ed. (London, 1951), pp. 273–5; Piggott, *Ruins in Landscape*, pp. 118–19.

88 R. Sweet, 'Antiquaries and Antiquities in Eighteenth Century England', *Journal of Eighteenth Century Studies* 34:2 (2001), pp. 181–206.

89 Borlase, *The Antiquities of Cornwall*, p. v.

90 *Ibid.*, plates xx–xxii opposite pp. 219, 223–4.

91 *Ibid.*, plate xxiii; pp. 259–74.

92 Horsley, *Britannia Romana*.

93 Y. O'Donoghue, *William Roy 1726–1790: Pioneer of the Ordnance Survey* (London, 1977).

94 W. Roy, *The Military Antiquities of the Romans in Britain* (London, 1793).

95 Jessup, *James Douglas*.

96 J. Douglas, *Nenia Britannica* (London, 1786), title page.

97 Aubrey, ed. Britton, *Natural History of Wiltshire*, Preface, p. 6.

98 S. Piggott, *Antiquity Depicted: Aspects of Archaeological Illustration* (London, 1978).

99 R. H. Cunnington, *From Antiquary to Archaeologist: A Biography of William Cunnington 1754–1810* (Aylesbury, 1975).

100 R. C. Hoare, *The Ancient History of Wiltshire* (London, 1812–19), Preface.

101 C. Johns, 'Samuel Lysons: a Founding Father of Romano-British Archaeology', *Mosaic* 27 (2000), pp. 8–10.

102 D. and S. Lysons, *Magna Britannia: Being a Concise Topographical Account of the Several Counties of Great Britain* (London, 1806–22).

103 S. Lysons, *An Account of Roman Discoveries at Woodchester in the County of Gloucestershire* (London, 1797).

104 S. Lysons, *Reliquae Britannico-romanae* (London, 1813).

105 Johns, 'Samuel Lysons', p. 10.

106 Piggott, *Ruins in Landscape*, p. 52.

107 Sweet, 'Antiquaries and Antiquities', pp. 181–2.

Chapter 18 pages 192–201

FURTHER READING

F. Beaucour, Y. Laissus and C. Orgogozo, *The Discovery of Egypt: Artists, Travellers and Scientists* (Paris, 1990)

S. Lloyd, *Foundations in the Dust: The Story of Mesopotamian Exploration* (London, 1980)

NOTES

1 A. H. Layard, *Nineveh and its Remains* (London, 1849), vol. 1, pp. 16–17. I am grateful to Kim Sloan, Richard Parkinson and Terence Mitchell for their helpful comments on this chapter, Erika Ingham of the National Portrait Gallery for information relating to Ker Porter, and Barbara Winter for the photography.

2 A. Wild, *The East India Company: Trade and Conquest from 1600* (London, 1999), pp. 122–7.

3 Beaucour, Laissus and Orgogozo, *The Discovery of Egypt*; I. A. Ghali, *Vivant Denon ou la conquête du bonheur* (Cairo, 1986); A. Siliotti (ed.), *Belzoni's Travels* (London, 2001).

4 There is an abundant literature on these early travellers; for instance J. Sancisi-Weerdenburg and J. W. Drijvers (eds), *Achaemenid History VII: Through Travellers' Eyes* (Leiden, 1991).

5 W. Francklin, *Observations Made on a Tour from Bengal to Persia, in the Years 1786–7* (London, 1790), p. 220.

6 However, it was not until the publication in 1837 of Henry Creswicke Rawlinson's hand copies (followed by paper squeezes made in 1847) of the much longer trilingual Achaemenid inscription at Bisitun that scholars – notably Edward Hincks (1792–1866), William Fox Talbot (1800–77), Jules Oppert (1825–1905) and Rawlinson (1810–95) himself – were able to present a full decipherment of cuneiform.

7 R. D. Barnett, 'Sir Robert Ker Porter – Regency Artist and Traveller', *Iran* 10 (1972), pp. 19–24; N. Vasilieva, 'About the History of Sir Robert Ker Porter's Album with his Sketches of Achaemenid and Sassanian Monuments', *Archaeologische Mitteilungen aus Iran* 27 (1994), pp. 339–48.

8 R. Ker Porter, *Travels in Georgia* (London, 1822), vol. 1, p. 641.

9 St J. Simpson, 'Bushire and Beyond: Some Early Archaeological Discoveries in Iran', in E. Errington and V. S. Curtis (eds), *From Persepolis to the Punjab: 19th-century Discoveries* (London, in press).

10 J. C. Simmons, *Passionate Pilgrims: English Travelers to the World of the Desert Arabs* (New York, 1987).

11 C. J. Rich, ed. M. Rich, [1] *Narrative of a Journey to the Site of Babylon in 1811, now First Published:* [2] *Memoir on the Ruins; with Engravings from the Original Sketches by the Author:* [3] *Remarks on the Topography of Ancient Babylon, by Major Rennell; in Reference to the Memoir* [reprinted from *Archaeologia* 18]: [4] *Second Memoir on the Ruins; in Reference to Major Rennell's Remarks:* [5] *With Narrative of a Journey to Persepolis: now First Printed, with Hitherto Unpublished Cuneiform Inscriptions Copied at Persepolis,* (London, 1839), part [2], p. 44.

12 P. Della Valle, *Voyages de Pietro Della Valle* (Paris, 1664), pp. 465–6; A. Invernizzi (ed.), *In viaggio per l'Oriente: Le Mummie, Babilonia, Persepoli* (Turin, 2001), pp. 208–10.

13 This identification was criticized by J. B. Tavernier, *Les Six Voyages* (Paris, 1676) and K. Niebuhr, *Voyage en Arabie & en d'autres pays circonvoisins* (Amsterdam/Utrecht, 1776–80), vol. 2, pp. 248–9, who visited in 1643 and 1766 respectively, on the grounds that the site was closer to the Tigris than to the Euphrates.

14 K. Niebuhr, *Voyage*, vol. 2, pp. 235–6.

15 Nevertheless, Rennell's identification of the Birs Nimrud continued to influence some later scholars and travellers, including G. Keppel, *Personal Narrative of a Journey from India to England* (London, 1827), pp. 100–5.

16 R. Byron, 'Don Juan', canto 5, stanza 62; cf. C. J. Rich, 'Memoir on the Ruins of Babylon', *Les Mines de l'Orient* (1813, republished 1815 and again with new engravings in Rich 1839, part [1]); J. Rennell, *Remarks on the Topography of Ancient Babylon* (London, 1816) (reprinted in Rich, *Remarks on the Topography*); C. J. Rich, *Second Memoir on Babylon* (London, 1818).

17 Lloyd, *Foundations in the Dust*, pp. 12–42; J. S. Buckingham, *Travels in Mesopotamia* (London, 1827), p. 390.

18 J. R. F. Thompson, 'The Rich Manuscripts', *The British Museum Quarterly* 27 (1963/4), pp. 18–23.

19 A cylinder seal which formerly belonged to Hine was presented to the British Museum by C. D. Cobham (ANE 89126), as was an Achaemenid contract tablet (ANE 47340).

20 Rich, *Narrative*, p. 8; Rich, *Memoir on the Ruins*, p. 199.

21 Rich, *Narrative*, p. 21; *Second Memoir*, pp. 70–1; Buckingham, *Travels*, p. 426. Rich's report prompted R. Mignan, *Travels in Chaldaea* (London, 1829), pp. 171–2, to re-investigate the site in November 1827; cf. also Keppel, *Personal Narrative*, pp. 108–9; E. L. Mitford, *A Land March from England to Ceylon* (London, 1884), vol. 1, p. 321.

22 Rich, *Memoir on the Ruins*, p. 199, fig. 8; Rich, *Narrative*, p. 26; *Memoir on the Ruins*, pp. 70–2; *Second Memoir on the Ruins*, pp. 186–7. The neo-Babylonian Pazuzu head (ANE 91874 = R90) must have been reused in antiquity as the grave appears to have been Parthian or Sasanian.

23 Rich, *Memoir on the Ruins*, pp. 68–72; reiterated by Buckingham, *Travels*, pp. 418–26. Later excavations confirmed that the palace of Nebuchadnezzar was succeeded by Hellenistic, Parthian and Sasanian constructions.

24 Rich, *Narrative of a Journey*, p. 36; *Memoir on the Ruins*, p. 64 but cf. Keppel, *Personal Narrative*, p. 111.

25 Rich, *Narrative of a Journey*, pp. 31–2; cf. Niebuhr, *Voyage en Arabie*, vol. 2, pp. 236–7.

26 The first recorded excavation in Mesopotamia was in c.1782 by the Papal Vicar-General in Babylonia, the Abbé J. de Beauchamp, who cleared the so-called 'Lion of Babylon', and who recorded pottery, terracottas, a large statue and neo-Babylonian glazed brick façades uncovered by local brick-robbers at the Kasr (E. A. W. Budge, *By Nile and Tigris* (London, 1920), vol. 1, p. 286, where it is misattributed to 1784).

27 Rich, *Second Memoir on the Ruins*, p. 181; reiterated by W. K. Loftus, *Travels and Researches in Chaldaea and Susiana* (London, 1857), p. 26; cf. A. D. H. Bivar, 'A Sasanian Hoard from Hilla', *Numismatic Chronicle*, 1963, pp. 157–78. The scale of brick robbing at the Kasr is described by Rich (*Memoir on the Ruins*, pp. 62–3) as causing 'great confusion, and contributing much to increase the difficulty of deciphering the original design of this mound'. The mound of Amran likewise was quarried at this date (*ibid.*, p. 61).

28 Rich, *Memoir on the Ruins*.

29 G. K. Jenkins, 'Coins from the Collection of C. J. Rich', *The British Museum Quarterly* 28 (1964), pp. 88–95; for more details on the circumstances of discovery, see Mignan, *Travels in Chaldaea*, pp. 52–4.

30 Rich, *Memoir on the Ruins* (republished 1815 and again with new engravings in Rich, *Narrative of a Journey*, p. 19).

31 *Ibid.*, pp. 199.

32 R. D. Barnett, 'Charles Bellino and the Beginnings of Assyriology', *Iraq* 36 (1974), pp. 5–28.

33 C. J. Rich, M. Rich (ed.), *Narrative of a Residence in Koordistan* (London, 1836), vol. 2, p. 345.

34 Rich, *Koordistan*, vol. 1, pp. 19–21; a sherd of this type exists in the Rich collection (ANE R98).

35 Most early travellers agreed that the mound of Kuyunjik, unlike Babylon, marked the centre of ancient Nineveh although many considered, as did Rich himself, that the

biblical references (Jonah 1.2, 3.3, 4.11) to it being an 'exceeding great city of three days' journey' with a reputed population of 'six score thousand persons' (120,000) could not be accommodated within the surviving city walls and thus the city must have extended a considerable distance beyond.

36 Rich, *Koordistan*, vol. 2, p. 39.

37 Described thus in a letter from Rich to von Hammer: Barnett, 'Charles Bellino', p. 21; The British Museum: central archives, *Original Papers* V, December 1824.

38 Rich, *Koordistan*, vol. 2, pp. 131–2.

39 Rich, *Memoir on the Ruins*.

40 Buckingham, *Travels*; R. E. Turner, *James Silk Buckingham 1786–1855: A Social Biography* (London, 1934).

41 Burckhardt described the Hama inscription as 'a stone with a number of small figures and signs which appears to be a kind of hieroglyphic writing, though it does not resemble that of Egypt'; it was recorded in 1870 along with others covered 'with a number of small figures and signs' by J. Augustus Johnson, the American Consul-General, and the Reverend S. Jessup; the original inscriptions were removed and sent to Istanbul but two sets of gypsum plaster casts were made by William Wright, an Irish missionary, and sent to London in 1872 (W. Wright, *The Empire of the Hittites* (London, 1886), pp. 1–12).

42 Rich presented some objects to the Archduke John of Austria through his friend the Austrian historian and Orientalist Joseph von Hammer (1774–1856) (E. Unger, *Der Beginn der altmesopotamischen Siegelbildforschung* (Vienna, 1958); S. A. Pallis, *The Antiquity of Iraq: A Handbook of Assyriology* (Copenhagen, 1956), p. 68) and at least part of his seal collection was acquired by Claude Scott Steuart and thence entered the British Museum.

43 Buckingham, *Travels*, p. 530; cf. Keppel, *Personal Narrative*, pp. 66–8 = ANE 1903-10-12, 3.

44 R. Ker Porter, *Travels in Georgia* (London, 1822).

45 *Ibid.*, vol. 1, p. 278. A complete mudbrick from this monument was presented to the British Museum by Gustavus Brander in 1768 and registered as 1768-5-13,1 but this brick had already disintegrated by 1791 when it was illustrated by J. and A. Van Rymsdyk (revised by P. Boyle), *Museum Britannicum* (London, 1791), pl. 34; see J.-C. Klamt, *Sternwarte und Museum im Zeitalter der Aufklärung: Der Mathematische Turm zu Kremsmunster (1749–1758)* (Mainz, 1999), p. 304, fig. 152.

46 Rich, *Second Memoir on the Ruins*, p. 185; *Narrative of a Journey to Persepolis*, pp. 248–9; cf. Keppel, *Personal Narrative*, p. 97.

47 Rich, *Narrative of a Journey to Persepolis*.

48 J. B. Fraser, *Travels in Koordistan, Mesopotamia, etc.* (London, 1840).

49 Mignan, *Travels in Chaldaea*, p. 74; R. Mignan, *A Winter Journey through Russia, the Caucasian Alps, and Georgia* (London, 1839), vol. 2, pp. 26–8; see also note 34.

50 E. Robinson, *Biblical Researches* (London 1867).

51 Reprinted in six volumes in 1855/6.

52 I. Jenkins, *Archaeologists and Aesthetes in the Sculpture Galleries of the British Museum 1800–1939* (London, 1992), pp. 114, 240 note 48.

53 C. W. Meade, *Road to Babylon* (Leiden, 1974); M. T. Larsen, *The Conquest of Assyria* (London and New York, 1994).

54 W. H. Ward, *Report on the Wolfe Expedition to Babylonia 1884–85*, Papers of the Archaeological Institute of America (Boston, 1886), pp. 6–7.

Chapter 19 pages 202–211

FURTHER READING

G. Boas, *The Hieroglyphics of Horapollo* (new edn, Princeton, 1993)

J. Drucker, *The Alphabetic Labyrinth: The Letters in History and Imagination* (London, 1995)

U. Eco, *The Search for the Perfect Language*, translated by James Fentress (London, 1995)

R. Parkinson, *Cracking Codes: The Rosetta Stone and Decipherment* (London, 1999)

M. Pope, *The Story of Decipherment from Egyptian Hieroglyphs to Maya Script* (London, revised edn, 1999)

NOTES

1 Plotinus, *Ennead* 5.8.6.

2 See Boas, *The Hieroglyphics of Horapollo*.

3 On Kircher see J. Goodwin, *Athanasius Kircher: A Renaissance Man and the Quest for Lost Knowledge* (London, 1979).

4 After Pope, *The Story of Decipherment*, pp. 31–2.

5 T. Herbert, *A Description of the Persian Monarchy and Other Parts of the Greater Asia and Africa* (London, 1634; enlarged 3rd edn, 1677).

6 T. Hyde, *Historia Religionis Veterum Persarum* (Oxford, 1700).

7 Le Chevalier de Jaucourt, s.v. 'Écriture', in D. Diderot and J. d'Alembert (eds), *Encyclopédie*, vol. 5 (1755), pp. 358–60.

8 W. Warburton, *Divine Legation* (3rd ed., 1758), vol. 2, part 1, pp. 65–220.

9 A. R. Pagden (ed. and transl.), *The Maya: Diego de Landa's Account of the Affairs of Yucatan* (Chicago, 1975). For a brief account, with an explanation of how Landa's work, rediscovered only in 1862, eventually helped the decipherment of Maya glyphs see M. D. Coe, *Breaking the Maya Code* (rev. edn, London, 2000), esp. pp. 92–7.

10 The theory of a universally comprehensible writing system was a fundamental part of thought about writing in this period, dating back to Descartes, Mersenne and Leibniz; many attempts were made to devise a system in practice, the most ambitious being that of John Wilkins, Bishop of Chester, in 1668. See Pope, *Story*, pp. 39–42; Drucker, *The Alphabetic Labyrinth*, pp. 176–88; M. Yaguello, *Lunatic Lovers of Language* (London, 1991), esp. pp. 31–40; U. Eco, *La ricerca della lingua perfetta nella cultura europea* (Rome, 3rd edn 2002), chapters 11–14; also 1995 English ed. cited above.

11 Among those cited by Warburton as holding a different view were the French scholar Nicolas Freret (1688–1749) and the Jesuits Antoine Gaubil (1688–1759) and Domenique Parennin, who were long resident in China. Writing in the *Encyclopédie* Jaucourt resolved the difference by positing two sorts of character.

12 R. Pococke, *A Description of the East and Some Other countries* (London, 1743–5), pp. 228–9; Warburton, *Divine Legation*, pp. 75–80.

13 Warburton, *Divine Legation*, pp. 145–7. The ancient view of Cadmus as the father of Greek letters is given by Herodotus, 5.60. See M. Bernal, *Cadmean Letters: The Transmission of the Alphabet to the Aegean and Further West before 1400 BC* (Winona Lake, 1990) for a nuanced but interesting account of how the 'ancient model' has fared in modern times.

14 Barthélemy's work on non-hieroglyphic Egyptian writing is in his publication of the collections of the Comte de Caylus: *Recueil d'antiquités égyptiennes, étrusques, grecques et romaines* (7 vols, Paris, 1752–67).

15 Barthélemy, *Reflexions sur l'alphabet et sur la langue dont on se servoit autrefois à Palmyre* (Paris, 1754); J. Swinton, 'Letters to the Royal Society on the Palmyra Alphabet', *Philosophical Transactions* 48 (1754), p. 690.

16 *Corpus inscriptionum semiticarum* 11, 141; M. Lidzbarski, *Handbuch der nordsemitischen Epigraphik* (Weimar, 1898), pl. xxviii, 3 and p. 448; G. A. Cooke, *A Text-book of North-Semitic Inscriptions* (Oxford, 1903), no. 75.

17 E. de Rougé, *Mémoire sur l'origine égyptienne de l'alphabet phénicien* (Paris, 1874: a belated and posthumous publication of a paper delivered to the Académie des Inscriptions in 1859); I. Taylor, *The History of the Alphabet* (London, 1883; enlarged 2nd edn 1899).

18 W. Gesenius, *Scripturae linguaeque phoeniciae monumenta* (Leipzig, 1837).

19 G. Garbini, 'La questione dell'alfabeto', in S. Moscati *et al.* (eds), *I Fenici* (Milan, 1988), pp. 86–103; P. T. Daniels and W. Bright, *The World's Writing Systems* (Oxford, 1996). The Semitic consonantal alphabet is sometimes called the *ab-jad*, from the names of its first two characters.

20 C. Niebuhr, *Reisebeschreibung nach Arabien und andern umliegendem Ländern* (Copenhagen, 1774; English translation, 1792).

21 The work of creating the science of comparative philology out of Jones's insight was largely carried out by Bopp and Rask. Jones was also responsible for pioneering work on the scripts of ancient and modern Asia: see Daniels and Bright, *Writing Systems*, section 9.

22 S. de Sacy, *Mémoires sur diverses antiquités de la Perse* (Paris, 1792).

23 See Parkinson, *Cracking Codes*, pp. 19–24.

24 See Pope, *Story*, pp. 60–84; Parkinson, *Cracking Codes*, passim.

25 Sacy, in *Magasin Encyclopédique* 4 (1811), 184, note 2, quoted by Pope, *Story*, p. 66. On Zoëga and his *De origine et usu obeliscorum* (Rome, 1792) see Pope, *Story*, pp. 55–9.

26 J. P. Abel-Rémusat, *Essai sur la langue et la littérature chinoises* (Paris, 1811); 'Utrum lingua sinica sit vere monosyllabica', *Fundgraben des Orients* 3 (1813), pp. 279–88; *Élemens de la grammaire chinoise* (Paris, 1822).

27 Pope, *Story*, pp. 65–8. For a biography, mainly covering Young's work in the natural sciences, see A. Wood and F. Oldham, *Thomas Young: Natural Philosopher* (Cambridge, 1954).

28 On Champollion see the several biographies and studies listed in the bibliography of Parkinson, *Cracking Codes*, p. 202. Note especially the exhibition catalogue, *Mémoires d'Egypte: hommage de l'Europe à Champollion* (ed. E. Le Roy Ladurie *et al.*, Strasbourg 1990).

29 Grotefend's work was initially delivered as a lecture to the Göttingen Literary Society in 1802, and then published as an appendix to A. H. L. Heeren, *Ideen über die Politik, den Verkehr, und den Handel der vornehmster Völker der Alten Welt* (Göttingen, 1805). The latter is usually cited in its third edition, 1815.

30 R. C. Rask, *Über das Alter und die Echtheit der Zend-Sprache und des Zend-Avesta: und Herstellung des Zend-Alphabets; nebst einer Übersicht des gesammten Sprachstammes* (Berlin, 1826).

31 C. Lassen, *Die Altpersischen Keil-Inschriften von Persepolis: Entzifferung des Alphabets und Erklärung des Inhalts* (Bonn, 1836).

32 On Rawlinson see Pope, *Story*, pp. 106–10.

33 See Coe, *Breaking*, passim.

Chapter 20 pages 212–221

FURTHER READING

G. R. Cragg, *The Church and the Age of Reason, 1648–1789* (Cambridge, new edn, 1991)

B. Feldman and R. D. Richardson, Jr (eds), *The Rise of Modern Mythology, 1680–1860* (Bloomington, 1972)

A. D. Momigliano, 'Historiography of Religion: the Western Tradition', in *The Encyclopaedia of Religion*, vol. 6 (New York and London, 1987), pp. 383–90

S. Piggott, *William Stukeley: An Eighteenth-century Antiquary* (Oxford, 2nd edn, 1985)

S. Piggott, *Ancient Britons and the Antiquarian Imagination: Ideas from the Renaissance to the Regency* (London, 1989)

NOTES

1 Invaluable in the writing of this chapter have been the following: Feldman and Richardson Jr (eds), *The Rise of Modern Mythology, 1680–1860*, and Momigliano, 'Historiography of Religion: the Western Tradition', pp. 383–90. I should like to thank Michael Morse, Ian Jenkins, Clive Cheesman and the editors for their help and advice in the writing of this chapter.

2 [Edmund Powlett], *The General Contents of the British Museum* (London, 1761), pp. 29–33; compare the slightly amended second edition of 1762, pp. 54–62. See also J. C. H. King 'Ethnographic Collections' in A. MacGregor (ed.), *Sir Hans Sloane. Collector, Scientist, Antiquary* (London, 1994), pp. 228–44, at p. 231.

3 In the catalogue of the collection of Leeds antiquarian Ralph Thoresby (1658–1725) a Japanese pagoda, Jamaican idols and 'adder bead' amulets from Britain are listed together with rings and amulets 'which in the dark Days of Popery were eagerly sought after by poor deluded People'. See *Musaeum Thoresbyanum or, a Catalogue of the Antiquities, and of the Natural and Artificial Rarities Preserved in the Repository of Ralph Thoresby , Gent. F.R.S. at Leedes in Yorkshire: A.D. MDCCXII* (London, 1713), pp. 493–5.

4 John Toland, *Letters to Serena* (London, 1704), Letter III, 'The Origin of Idolatry, and Reasons of Heathenism', para. 22.

5 In his *Stonehenge: A Temple Restor'd to the British Druids* (London, 1740).

6 John Locke, *Essay Concerning Human Understanding* (London, 1690), Book I, chapter 2, section 9.

7 See R. Porter, *Enlightenment: Britain and the Creation of the Modern World* (Harmondsworth, 2000), chapter 5, and D. Outram, *The Enlightenment* (Cambridge, 1995), chapter 3.

8 David Hume, *The Natural History of Religion* (London, 1757), chapter 1.

9 *Ibid.*, chapter 15.

10 J. Lafitau, *Moeurs des sauvages amériquains comparées aux moeurs des premiers temps* (Paris, 1724).

11 See P. Mitter, *Much Maligned Monsters: A History of European Reactions to Indian Art* (Chicago, 2nd edn, 1992), chapter 2.

12 R. Payne Knight, *An Account of the Remains of the Worship of Priapus lately existing at Isernia, in the Kingdom of Naples, to which is added A Discourse on the Worship of Priapus and its connection with the mystic theology of the Ancients* (London, 1786), p. 34. On which see further M. Clarke and N. Penny, *The Arrogant Connoisseur: Richard Payne Knight 1751–1824*, exh. cat. Whitworth Art Gallery, University of Manchester (Manchester, 1982), chapter 4. For Hamilton's letter to Banks and his gifts of wax votives to the museum, see I. Jenkins and K. Sloan, *Vases and Volcanoes: Sir William Hamilton and His Collection* (London, 1996), pp. 45.

13 See Knight, *Worship of Priapus*, pp. 35–6.

14 Knight also referred to and illustrated Indian sculptures, in drawing parallels between Greek, Egyptian and Indian religious traditions. See *Worship of Priapus*, pp. 80 ff., and plate X, fig. 1.

15 *Zend-Avesta, ouvrage de Zoroastre* (Paris, 1771).

16 *The Bhagvat-geeta, or Dialogues of Kreeshna and Arjoon* (London, 1785).

17 W. Jones, 'On the Gods of Greece, Italy and India', *Asiatick Researches or Transactions of the Society Instituted in Bengal for Inquiry into the History and Antiquities, the Arts, Sciences and Literatures of Asia* vol. 1 (1801, London reprint), pp. 221–2.

18 On Moor see Mitter, *Much Maligned Monsters*, pp. 178–80.

19 F. Schlegel, *Über die Sprache und Weisheit der Inder* (Heidelberg, 1808). His brother August (1767–1845) was also an eminent orientalist, and established a Sanskrit printing press at Bonn in 1818.

20 F. Majer, *Allgemeines mythologisches Lexicon* (Weimar, 1803).

21 P. H. Mallet, *Monumens de la mythologie et de la poésie des celtes, et particulièrement des anciens scandinaves* (Copenhagen, 1756).

22 For the Ossianic texts see James Macpherson, *Fragments of Ancient Poetry Collected in the Highlands of Scotland* (London, 1760); *Fingal* (London, 1762); *Temora* (London, 1763).

23 See A. L. Owen, *The Famous Druids* (Oxford, 1962), pp. 194–211, S. Piggott, *The Druids* (London, 1968), pp. 142–6, and P. Morgan, 'From a Death to a View: the Hunt for the Welsh Past in the Romantic Period', in E.

Hobsbawn and T. Ranger (eds), *The Invention of Tradition* (Cambridge, 1983), pp. 43–100, and S. Smiles, *Ancient Britain and the Romantic Imagination* (New Haven and London, 1994).

24 On Goerres and Creuzer see Feldman and Richardson, *Rise of Modern Mythology*, pp. 381–96.

25 See especially his *Prolegomena zu einer wissenschaftlichen Mythologie* (Göttingen, 1825; English translation, *Introduction to a Scientific System of Mythology*, 1844).

26 T. Keightley, *Tales and Popular Fictions: Their Resemblance, and Transmission from Country to Country* (London, 1834), pp. 1–5.

27 Cited by J. M. Crook, *The British Museum* (London, 1972), p. 127.

28 See, e.g., T. Heyerdahl, *The Kon-Tiki Expedition: By Raft Across the South Seas* (London, 1950); G. Hancock and S. Faiia, *Heaven's Mirror: Quest for the Lost Civilization* (New York, 1998), and G. Hancock, *Underworld: The Mysterious Origins of Civilization* (London, 2002). The titles alone are sufficiently revealing.

PART V: VOYAGES OF DISCOVERY

Chapter 21 pages 224–233

FURTHER READING

P. D. Curtin, *Cross-cultural Trade in World History* (Cambridge, 1984)

J. Diamond, *Guns, Germs and Steel: A Short History of Everybody for the Last 13,000 Years* (London, 1997)

P. J. Marshall and G. Williams, *The Great Map of Mankind: British Perceptions of the World in the Age of Enlightenment* (London, 1982)

R. Robert, *Chartered Companies and their Role in the Development of Overseas Trade* (London, 1969)

E. R. Wolf, *Europe and the People Without History* (Berkeley, 1982)

NOTE

1 H. Morley (ed.), *The Earlier Life and the Chief Earlier Works of Daniel Defoe* (London, 1889), pp. 189–95.

Chapter 22 pages 234–245

FURTHER READING

H. B. Carter, *Sir Joseph Banks 1743–1820* (London, 1988)

I. Graham, *Alfred Maudslay and the Maya: A Biography* (London, 2002)

J. C. H. King, *Artificial Curiosities from the Northwest Coast of America: Native American Artefacts in the British Museum collected on the Third Voyage of Captain James Cook and acquired through Sir Joseph Banks* (London, 1981)

J. C. H. King, *First Peoples, First Contacts: Native Peoples of North America* (London, 1999)

NOTES

1 King, *Artificial Curiosities from the Northwest Coast of America*, p. 25.

2 See 'Ethnographic Collections: Collecting in the Context of Sloane's Catalogue of "Miscellanies"', in A. MacGregor (ed.), *Sir Hans Sloane: Collector, Scientist, Antiquary* (London, 1994), pp. 228–44.

3 For Banks's life see Carter, *Sir Joseph Banks*.

4 R. A. Rauschenberg, 'Daniel Carl Solander Naturalist on the *Endeavour*', *Transactions of the American Philosophical Society*, N.S. 58:8 (1968).

5 King, *First Peoples, First Contacts*, pp. 122–45.

6 For the Native/British/Chinese trade in sea otter skins see R. Fisher, *Contact and Conflict: Indian-European Relations in British Columbia, 1774–1890*, 2nd edn (Vancouver, 1992), and B. M. Gough, *The Northwest Coast: British Navigation, Trade and Discoveries to 1812* (Vancouver, 1992).

7 Barbara S. Efrat and W. J. Langlois, 'The Contact Period as Recorded by Indian Oral Tradition', in 'NU.TKA. Captain Cook and the Spanish Explorers on the Coast', *Sound Heritage* 7:1 (1978), pp. 54–62, at p. 54.

8 P. Drucker, 'The Northern and Central Nootkan Tribes', *Bureau of American Ethnology* 144 (1951), p. 175.

9 See J. C. H. King, 'Vancouver's Ethnography: A Preliminary Description of Five Inventories from the Voyage of 1791–95', *Journal of the History of Collections* 6:1 (1994), pp. 35–58.

10 M. L. Wayman, J. C. H. King and P. T. Craddock, 'Aspects of Early North American Metallurgy', *British Museum Occasional Paper* 79 (London, 1992).

11 King, *First Peoples, First Contacts*, pp. 196–7.

12 William Edward Parry, *Journal of a Second Voyage for the Discovery of a North-west Passage* (London, 1824).

13 Frederick William Beechey, *Narrative of a Voyage to the Pacific and Beering's Strait* (London, 1831).

14 *Ibid.*, p. 251.

15 *Ibid.*, pp. 401–2.

16 Alexander von Humboldt and Aimé Bonpland, *Personal Narrative of Travels to the Equinoctial Regions of the New Continent* (London, 1814).

17 H. B. Nicholson, *Art of Aztec Mexico: Treasures of Tenochtitlan* (Washington, 1983), pp. 70–1.

18 J. C. H. King, 'William Bullock Showman', in Pablo Diener (ed.), *European Traveller-Artists in Nineteenth Century Mexico* (Mexico, 1996), pp. 116–25.

19 Juan Wetherell, *Catalogo de una coleccion de antigüedades Mejicanas* (Seville, n.d. [1842]), pl. 8 (10).

20 For Meyrick's collection see King, *Artificial Curiosities*, pp. 36, 37.

21 Graham, *Alfred Maudslay and the Maya*.

22 R. and J. Dodsley, *The General Contents of the British Museum*, 2nd edn, (London, 1762), p. 54.

23 G. Bankes, 'Museums, Exhibitions and Collections', in 'South-America, Pre-Columbian Art; Study and Excavation', in Jane Turner (ed.), *The Dictionary of Art* (London, 1996), vol. 29, pp. 220–2, at p. 220.

24 J. J. von Tschudi, *Travels in Peru, during the Years 1838–1842* (London, 1847), p. 501.

25 Mario Edward Rivero and John James von Tschudi, *Peruvian Antiquities* (New York, 1857), p. 225.

26 For Franks and Christy see J. C. H. King, 'Franks and Ethnography', in M. Caygill and J. Cherry (eds), *A. W. Franks* (London, 1997), pp. 136–59.

27 E. Carmichael, *The British and the Maya* (London, 1973), pp. 34–40.

Chapter 23 pages 246–257

FURTHER READING

A. Calder, J. Lamb and B. Orr (eds), *Voyages and Beaches: Pacific Encounters, 1769–1840* (Honolulu, 1999)

D. Denoon, S. Firth and J. Linneken (eds), *The Cambridge History of the Pacific Islanders* (Cambridge, 1997)

D. Howse (ed.), *Background to Discovery: Pacific Exploration from Dampier to Cook* (Berkeley, 1990)

A. Kaeppler, *'Artificial Curiosities': An Exposition of Native Manufactures Collected on the Three Pacific Voyages of Captain James Cook, R. N.* (Honolulu, 1978)

T. C. Mitchell (ed.), *Captain Cook and the South Pacific* (London, 1979)

D. Oliver, *Oceania: The Native Cultures of Australia and the Pacific Islands* (Honolulu, 1989)

N. Thomas, *Entangled Objects: Exchange, Material Culture, and Colonialism in the Pacific* (Cambridge, Mass., 1991)

NOTES

1 George Tobin, 'Journal on H.M.S. Providence 1791–1793', manuscript journal, Mitchell Library, Sydney, 1797, p. 162.

2 Pomare II, Letter to the London Missionary Society, from 'Pomare King of Tahete', Youl Family Papers, National Library of Australia, Canberra, 1807, p. 1.

3 J. C. Beaglehole (ed.) The Journals of Captain Cook, vols 1–4 (Cambridge, 1961–7), and W. K. Lamb (ed.) George Vancouver. 'A Voyage of Discovery ... 1791–5' (London, 1984), for examples of such reprisals.

4 See G. Williams, The Great South Sea: English Voyages and Encounters 1570–1750 (New Haven and London, 1997); P. Edwards, The Story of the Voyage: Sea-narratives in Eighteenth-century England (Cambridge, 1994).

5 K. R. Howe, Where the Waves Fall: A New South Sea Islands History from First Settlement to Colonial Rule, Pacific Islands Monograph Series (Honolulu, 1984), p. 81.

6 See G. Williams, 'The Achievement of the English Voyages 1650–1800', in Howse (ed.), Background to Discovery, pp. 56 f.

7 P. Hulme and L. Jordanova (eds), The Enlightenment and its Shadows (London, 1990), p.10.

8 Bougainville touched at Tahiti, nine months after Samuel Wallis, and then went on to Samoa, Vanuatu and New Ireland. His account appeared in English translation in 1772: L. A. de Bougainville, A Voyage Round the World: Performed by Order of His Most Christian Majesty, in the Years 1766, 1767, 1768 and 1769, trans. J. F. Forster (London, 1772).

9 George Robertson recorded their frequent, fatal shootings of the Tahitians. At one point the English fired a canon at a crowd on the beach and 'cut a poor fellow in two'. H. Carrington (ed.), The Discovery of Tahiti: The Journal ... of George Robertson (London, 1948).

10 Carrington, The Discovery of Tahiti, p.165.

11 See, for example, 'Journal of Arthur Bowes, Surgeon of the Convict Transport Lady Penrhyn on a Voyage from Portsmouth to Botany Bay', manuscript journal, 1787–9, British Library, London, Add. MS 47966, p. 105.

12 Tobin, 'Journal', p. 161.

13 Cook's First Voyage set off to the Pacific in 1768, to record the transit of the planet Venus from the vantage point of Tahiti. He returned to England in 1771. The Second, from 1772 to 1775, searched for the southern continent down into Antarctic waters. The last embarked in 1776, to explore further in the Pacific and look, fruitlessly, for a north-west passage above Canada. The ship returned to England in 1780, without Cook – he had been killed in Hawai'i in 1779.

14 J. Tanner, From Pacific Shores: Eighteenth-century Ethnographic Collections at Cambridge: The Voyages of Cook, Vancouver and the First Fleet (Cambridge, 1999), p. 3.

15 Kaeppler, 'Artificial Curiosities', p. 37.

16 The Fijian islands are in many ways a place of cultural cross-over between Melanesian and Polynesian regions. The terms are a convenient shorthand, but are becoming less appropriate now as the migration of people and ideas increases.

17 Thomas, 'Epilogue', in Michael O'Hanlon and Robert Welsch (eds), Hunting the Gatherers: Ethnographic Collectors, Agents and Agency in Melanesia, 1870s–1930s (New York and Oxford, 2000), pp. 273–7, at p. 275.

18 Thomas, 'Epilogue', p. 275.

19 Sydney Parkinson, Journal of a Voyage to the South Seas in His Majesty's Ship the Endeavour (London, 1784), p. 134.

20 See entry in the 'Compass' database (www.thebritishmuseum.ac.uk/compass) for more details on this shield, along with many of the other items featured in this chapter.

21 B. Lawson, Collected Curios: Missionary Tales from the South Seas (Montreal, 1994).

22 The Spanish first found succour in the atolls and islands of Micronesia at the end of their tortuous, empty voyages across the Pacific from South America. Spain then annexed not just the Philippines but also Guam in 1565. Jesuit missionaries made a forceful entry into Guam in 1668, which the people resented – their rebellion was not quelled for twenty-seven years. I. C. Campbell, A History of the Pacific Islands (Christchurch, 1992), chapter 9.

23 K. Nero and N. Thomas (eds), An Account of the Pelew Islands, by George Keate (London, 2003).

24 Ibedul also entrusted his adopted son Libuu to Wilson's care, so he could learn the crafts, agriculture and other ways of England. He did learn much in England, but died there of smallpox. The Ibedul's gifts were handed down through Wilson's family and donated to the British Museum in 1875.

25 As can be seen in a tiputa (poncho) from the Cook Islands, British Museum Oc9955a, collected by the Reverend Wyatt Gill, c. 1876.

26 'Rev Elder & Wilson's Journal Round Tyerrabboo, 28th June–1st August 1803', manuscript, SOAS CWM Archives, London, South Seas Journals, Box 1 folio 14, 1803, p. 73.

27 Captain Furneaux, narrative, BL Add. MS 27809, fols 2v–20, quoted in J.C. Beaglehole, The Journals of Captain Cook, vol. 2, The Voyage of the Resolution and Adventure 1772–1775 (Cambridge, 1961), p. 738.

28 Tobin, 'Journal', 5 May 1792, p. 162.

29 Lt Matthew Flinders, manuscript notes

(1792), quoted in A. D'Alleva, 'Continuity and Change in Decorated Barkcloth from Bligh's Second Breadfruit Voyage, 1791–1793', Pacific Arts 11–12 (July 1995).

30 C. Newbury, Tahiti Nui: Change and Survival in French Polynesia 1767–1945 (Honolulu, 1980), p.9.

31 The Sandwich Islands was Cook's name for the Hawaiian archipelago. F. W. Beechey, Narrative of a Voyage to the Pacific and Beering's Strait ... in the Years 1825, 26, 27, 28 (London, 1831), p. 22.

32 P. V. Kirch and M. Sahlins, Anahulu: The Anthropology of History in the Kingdom of Hawaii: Historical Ethnography, vol. 1 (Chicago and London, 1992).

33 These capes and cloaks are still part of the collection of the Royal family and housed at the British Museum. In regard to one of them, Vancouver reported that Kamehameha: 'very carefully folded it up, and desired, that on my arrival in England, I would present it in his name to His Majesty, King George, saying, that it was the most valuable thing in the island of Owhyhee, and for that reason he had sent it to so great a monarch, and so good a friend, as he considered the King of England.' Lamb (ed.), Voyage of Discovery, pp. 839–40.

34 Kamehameha died in May 1819 but his dynasty was to last until 1872. A. Grove Day, History Makers of Hawaii: A Biographical Dictionary (Honolulu, 1984).

35 'The Missionaries Journale in the Royal Admiral from Port Jackson to Matavai, Taheite', manuscript, SOAS Church World Mission Archives, London, South Seas Journals Box 1 fol. 11, 1801, p.12. See also H. Beasley, 'Metal Mere', Journal of the Polynesian Society (1925).

36 Found near the Columbia River, Washington State. With thanks to Richard Wells, Sooke, B.C., Canada.

37 Tobin, 'Journal', 5 May 1792, p. 162.

38 Ruscenberger, 1838, quoted in A. Kaeppler, Eleven Gods Assembled: An Exhibition of Hawaiian Wooden Images, Bernice Pauahi Bishop Museum, Honolulu, Hawaii, April 6–June 10 1979 (Honolulu, 1979).

39 Carrington, The Discovery of Tahiti, and John Jefferson, 'Journal of the Missionaries Proceedings on Otaheite', manuscript, SOAS Church World Mission Archives, London, South Seas Journals, Box 2 fol. 22, 1804, p. 11.

40 B. M. Gough (ed.), To the Pacific and Arctic with Beechey: The Journal of Lieutenant George Peard of H.M.S. 'Blossom', 1825–1828 (Cambridge, 1973), p. 98.

41 Carrington, The Discovery of Tahiti, p. 312.

42 S. R. Fischer, 'Hugh Cuming's Account of an Anchorage at Rapanui (Easter Island) November 27–28, 1827', Journal of the

Polynesian Society 100:3 (1991), p. 304. With thanks to Jill Hasell, British Museum, for alerting me to this, and other object histories which have helped form this chapter. Similar ceremonies to this one were recorded in Tahiti. See D. Oliver, *Ancient Tahitian Society*, 3 vols (Canberra, 1974).

43 Nicholas Thomas has used the idea of 'a kind of symmetry of collecting between indigenous appropriations of European artefacts and the colonial collecting of indigenous goods' as an attractive but, he suggests, somewhat optimistic image of the exchanges of objects in the Pacific from the mid eighteenth century. Thomas, *Entangled Objects*, p. 5. I am making a more definite claim for symmetry.

44 London Missionary Society, 'Draft Catalogue of the London Missionary Society Collection at the British Museum', British Museum (London), n.d.

45 M. Hoare (ed.), *The Resolution Journal of Johann Reinhold Forster, 1772–1775* (London, 1982), vol. 4, pp. 555–7.

46 The pantomime, *Omai: or a Trip Round the World*, ran for seventy shows in 1785–6. I. McCalman, 'Spectacles of Knowledge: Omai as Ethnographic Travelogue', in F. Rendle-Short (ed.), *Cook and Omai: The Cult of the South Seas* (Canberra, 2001). For more on Omai (properly Mai) of Raiatea, the Society Islands, see E. H. McCormick, *Omai: Pacific Envoy* (Auckland, 1977).

47 From the Forsters' letter accompanying their gift, in J. Coote, P. Gathercole, and N. Meister, '"Curiosities sent to Oxford": The Original Documentation of the Forster Collection at the Pitt Rivers Museum', *Journal of the History of Collections* 12:2 (2000), pp. 177–92.

48 E. Miller, *That Noble Cabinet: A History of the British Museum* (Ohio, 1974), p. 75; H. Cobbe (ed.), *Cook's Voyages and Peoples of the Pacific* (London, 1979), p. 139, and see N. Chambers on Cook and Banks material in the British Museum, in R. G. W. Anderson, M. L. Caygill, A. G. MacGregor and L. Syson (eds), *Enlightening the British: Knowledge, Discovery and the Museum in the Eighteenth Century* (London, 2004).

49 William Bullock, *A Companion to Mr Bullock's Museum, Containing a Brief Description of Upwards of Seven Thousand Natural & Foreign Curiosities*, 9th edn (London, 1810). See also R. D. Altick, *The Shows of London* (Cambridge, 1978).

50 C. Haynes, 'A "Natural" Exhibitioner: Sir Ashton Lever and his Holosphusikon', *British Journal for Eighteenth-century Studies* 24:1 (Spring 2001), p. 7.

Chapter 24 pages 258–269

FURTHER READING

SOUTH AND SOUTH-EAST ASIA

N. Barley, *The Duke of Puddle Duck: Travels in the Footsteps of Stamford Raffles* (London, 1991)

D. K. Chakrabarti, *A History of Indian Archaeology from the Beginning to 1947* (New Delhi, 1988)

D. K. Chakrabarti, *Colonial Indology* (New Delhi, 1997)

J. Keay, *India Discovered: The Recovery of a Lost Civilization* (London, 1981)

P. Mitter, *Much Maligned Monsters: A History of European Reactions to Indian Art* (Chicago, 1977)

CHINA

F. and N. Hervouet and Y. Bruneau, *La Porcelaine des compagnies des Indes à décor occidental* (Paris, 1986)

D. S. Howard, *The Choice of the Private Trader: The Private Market in Chinese Export Porcelain Illustrated from the Hodroff Collection* (London, 1994)

R. Krahl and J. Harrison-Hall, *Ancient Chinese Trade Ceramics in the British Museum, London* (Taipei, 1994)

D. F. Lach, *Asia in the Making of Europe*, vol. 1: *The Century of Discovery* (Chicago and London, 1965)

JAPAN

J. Ayers *et al.*, *Porcelain for Palaces: The Fashion for Japan in Europe, 1650–1750* (London, 1990)

B. M. Bodart-Bailey, *Kaempfer's Japan: Tokugawa Culture Observed* (Honolulu, 1999)

A. Farrer (ed.), *A Garden Bequest: Plants from Japan Portrayed in Books, Paintings and Decorative Art of 300 Years* (London, 2001)

A. Kouwenhoven and M. Forrer, *Siebold and Japan: His Life and Work* (Leiden, 2000)

T. Screech, *The Western Scientific Gaze and Popular Imagery in Later Edo Japan* (Cambridge, 1996)

NOTES

1 Magnus's translation was into Latin but an English version was available from 1691. Matteo Ricci (1552–1610), a Chinese-speaking Italian missionary, wrote a first-hand account of China which was one of the best available in Europe at that time. It was translated into Latin and published in 1615.

2 Samuel Purchas, *Purchas His Pilgrimes: A History of the World in Sea Voyages and Lande Travells* (London, 1625).

3 Jean-Baptiste Tavernier, *Six Voyages de Jean-Baptiste Tavernier qu'il fait en Turquie, en Perse et aux Indes* (Paris, 1675–6).

4 For Jones see Keay, *India Discovered*; see also ch. 19.

5 'An Account of Greek, Parthian and Hindu Medals, Found in India', by Major James Tod, MRAS, read 18 June 1825, *Transactions of the Royal Asiatic Society of Great Britain and Ireland* 1 (1824–5), pp. 313–42.

6 W. Marsden, *Numismata orientalia illustrata* (London, 1823–5).

7 W. Vincent, *The Commerce and Navigation of the Ancients in the Indian Ocean, vol. II. The Periplus of the Erythraean Sea* (London, 1807).

8 Abbé Joseph de Guignes, *Histoire générale des Huns, des Turcs, de Mongols et des autres tartares occidentaux* (Paris, 1756).

9 Barley, *The Duke of Puddle Duck*; J. Cribb, *Magic Coins of Java, Bali and the Malay Peninsula* (London, 1999).

10 Other western trading companies followed suit. For example the French traded in China 1699–1769, the Danish 1731–1800 and the Americans from 1784.

11 For a full account of the appearance of these trading stations over the century see C. L. Crossman, *The Decorative Arts of the China Trade* (Woodbridge, 1991).

12 Captain Michael Hatcher, the salvage expert, recovered over 23,000 'new' Chinese porcelains from an unnamed junk which sank in the South China Sea on its way to the VOC headquarters in Jakarta in the mid-1640s. See C. Sheaf and R. Kilburn, *The Hatcher Porcelain Cargoes: The Complete Record* (Oxford, 1988). Another ship, bound for Jakarta, was wrecked 100 nautical miles off Vung Tau, on the southern coast of Vietnam, in the 1690s: from this 48,288 porcelains and other artefacts were recovered. See C. J.A. Jörg and M.Flecker, *Porcelain from the Vung Tau Wreck: The Hallstrom Excavation* (London, 2001). Salvage experts retrieved more than 140,000 whole porcelains and 125 gold ingots from the wreck of the Dutch ship *Geldermalsen* which sank in 1752. See C. J. A. Jörg, *The Geldermalsen* (Groningen, 1986).

13 Dorian Ball, *The Diana Adventure* (Groningen, 1995).

14 N. Pickford and M. Hatcher, *The Legacy of the Tek Sing, China's Titanic: its Tragedy and its Treasure* (Cambridge, 2000).

15 Krahl and Harrison-Hall, *Ancient Chinese Trade Ceramics*.

16 D. S. Howard, *Chinese Armorial Porcelain* (London, 1974).

17 Occasionally enamelling instructions were also copied by the decorators, and services exist with the names of the colours, 'red' and 'green',

mistakenly copied next to the colours themselves.

18 G. Lang, *The Wrestling Boys: An Exhibition of Chinese and Japanese Ceramics from the 16th to the 18th Century in the Collection at Burghley House*, exh. cat. (Stamford, 1983); J. Ayers, O. Impey and J. V. G. Mallet, *Porcelain for Palaces: The Fashion for Japan in Europe 1650–1750*, exh. cat. (London, 1990).

19 A. Lane, 'Queen Mary II's Porcelain Collection at Hampton Court', *Transactions of the Oriental Ceramic Society* 25 (1949–50), pp. 21–31.

20 D. Wilson, *The Forgotten Collector: Augustus Wollaston Franks of the British Museum* (Wisbech, 1984).

21 For Kaempfer see Y. Bruun, 'Japanese Books and Manuscripts', in A. MacGregor (ed.), *Sir Hans Sloane: Collector, Scientist, Antiquary* (London, 1994), pp. 284–5, pl. 21; see also below on Japan.

22 R. Whitfield, 'Chinese Paintings from the Collection of Archduke Ferdinand II', *Oriental Art* 22:4 (Winter 1976), pp. 406–16.

23 R. Whitfield, 'Landmarks in the Collection and Study of Chinese Art in Great Britain: Reflections on the Centenary of the birth of Sir Percival David, Baronet (1892–1967)', in M. Wilson and J. Cayley (eds), *Europe Studies China: Papers from an International Conference on the History of European Sinology* (London, 1995), pp. 202–14.

24 C. Clunas, *Chinese Export Watercolours* (London, 1984).

25 Ayers *et al.*, *Porcelain for Palaces*; O. Impey, *Chinoiserie: The Impact of Oriental Styles on Western Art and Decoration* (London, 1977).

26 H. Franke, 'In Search of China: Some General Remarks on the History of European Sinology', in Wilson and Cayley (eds), *Europe Studies China*, pp. 11–23. Former diplomats Sir Thomas Wade (1818–95) and Herbert Allen Giles (1845–1935) were not selected for professorships of Chinese at Oxford and Cambridge until the second half of the nineteenth century.

27 See T. Screech, *The Western Scientific Gaze and Popular Imagery in Later Edo Japan* (Cambridge, 1996).

28 Ayers *et al.*, *Porcelain for Palaces*.

29 Modern knowledge of Dutch–Japanese relations in the period has been much enhanced by the recent ongoing publication of the *Dejima Daily Registers* (*Deshima Dagregisters*), translations of the records of the VOC station in Nagasaki. L. Blussé *et al.* (eds), *The Deshima Dagregisters*, 10 vols (Leiden, 1986–97).

30 For a new translation see Bodart-Bailey, *Kaempfer's Japan*.

31 They therefore became part of the British Museum collection, and are distributed among the Departments of Japanese Antqiuities, Oriental Antiquities and Ethnography, as well as now, of course, the British Library and the Natural History Museum; and see Y. Bruun, 'Japanese Books and Manuscripts'.

32 H. D. Smith II, 'Five Myths about Early Modern Japan', in A. Embree and C. Gluck (eds), *Asia in Western and World History* (Armonk, NY, 1997), p. 520.

33 Farrer (ed.), *A Garden Bequest*.

34 *Wakan koku senkakan* (A Survey of the Ancient and Modern Coins of Japan and China) (Edo, 1798); *Seiyō senpu* (Western Coin Catalogue) (Edo, 1780). About 2,500 coins from Masatsuna's coin collection were acquired by the British Museum in 1844 (where they were known as the 'Tamba collection') and are now its most important resource for the study of the monetary systems of China, Japan, Vietnam and Korea.

35 Kouwenhoven and Forrer, *Siebold and Japan*. Nevertheless, the extensive collections of botanical, zoological, ethnographic items, paintings, prints and books that Siebold was able to bring out of Japan were purchased by the Dutch state in 1837, and are now mainly in Leiden. Siebold's major publications on Japan were *Nippon: Archiv zur Beschreibung von Japan* (1832–58), *Fauna Japonica* (1833–50) and *Flora Japonica* (1835–70).

Chapter 25 pages 270–275

FURTHER READING

P. Curtin, *The Image of Africa* (Madison, 1963)

R. Hallett, *The Penetration of Africa: European Enterprise and Exploration Principally in Northern and Western Africa up to 1830* (London, 1965)

R. Lander, *Records of Captain Clapperton's Last Expedition to Africa*, vols 1, 2. (London, 1830)

R. and J. Lander, *The Niger Journal of Richard and John Lander*, ed. R. Hallett (London, 1965)

M. McLeod, 'T. E. Bowdich, an Early Collector in West Africa', in R. Camber (ed.), *Collectors and Collecting: British Museum Yearbook* (London, 1977)

M. Park, *The Journal of a Mission to the Interior of Africa in the Year 1805* (London, 1815)

M. Park, *Travels in the Interior Districts of Africa Performed in the Years 1795, 1796 and 1797 with an Account of a Subsequent Mission to that Country in 1805*, 2 vols (London, 1816)

S. Schaffer, 'Visions of Empire: Afterwards', in D. P. Miller and P. H. Reill (eds), *Visions of Empire: Voyages, Botany and Representations of Nature* (Cambridge, 1996)

NOTES

1 C. Fyfe, *A History of Sierra Leone* (London, 1962), p. 14.

2 Curtin, *The Image of Africa*, p. 17.

3 S. Schaffer, 'Visions of empire: afterward', in D. P. Miller and P. H. Reill, *Visions of Empire: Voyages, Botany and Representations of Nature* (Cambridge, 1996), p. 339.

4 Park, *Travels in the Interior Districts of Africa*, introduction.

5 T. Bowdich, *Mission from Cape Coast Castle to Ashantee* (London, 1819), p. 32.

6 M. McLeod, 'T.E. Bowdich', p. 83.

7 *Ibid.*, p. 93.

8 C.O 2/18 Public Record Office, London.

Picture credits

Further details about many of the British Museum objects described and illustrated in this book can be found on the Compass database on the British Museum's website: www.thebritishmuseum.ac.uk/compass. We have noted in the captions which curatorial department is responsible for each object illustrated, but have provided dimensions only where we felt it would be useful to judge the scale.

The British Museum's curatorial departments have been abbreviated as below although, shortly before going to press, several departments were amalgamated: MME and PEE joined to form the Department of Prehistory and Europe, and OA and JA combined to form the Department of Asia.

AES	Department of Ancient Egypt and Sudan
ANE	Department of the Ancient Near East
Archives	Central Archives
C&M	Department of Coins and Medals
Ethno	Department of Ethnography
GR	Department of Greek and Roman Antiquities
JA	Department of Japanese Antiquities
MME	Department of Medieval and Modern Europe
OA	Department of Oriental Antiquities
P&D	Department of Prints and Drawings
PEE	Department of Prehistory and Early Europe

All the photographs in this book are © The Trustees of The British Museum, with the exception of the following figures:
Berlin, Bildarchiv Kulturbesitz 48 (Jörg P. Anders); Burnley, Lancashire, Townley Hall 51; Canberra, National Library of Australia 233; Farmington, The Lewis Walpole Print Collection, Yale University 50; Göttingen, Stadtisches Museum 34; London: The British Library 29 (139.g.13), 33, 88 (Tab 435.a.15), 134 (1261.f.23, pl. 3), 145 (K Top L-83-2), 146 (K Top CXXIV (Supp.) 45), 147, 148 (K Top XLVII-37-c), 149 (K Top XCV-13-b), 150 (K Top XLVII-41-d), 151 (K Top Wrest), English Heritage, National Monument Record 47, National Portrait Gallery Picture Library 71, 144, 161, National Trust Photographic Library (John Hammond) 49, Natural History Museum, 59–61, 63–6, 69, 72, 74, 77, 80–5, 87, 89, 90, 223, Public Record Office Image Library 43, Royal Collection Picture Library © HM Queen Elizabeth II 242, Royal Institute of British Architects 44, Museum of Science and Industry, Science and Society Picture Library 138–43, Sir John Soane's Museum 45, 46 (Geremy Butler), 133 (Richard Bryant/Arcaid), Society of Antiquaries, Library, 166, Victoria and Albert Museum Picture Library 28, 112; Manchester, Whitworth Art Gallery, University of Manchester 201; Montpellier, Musée Fabre 155 (cliché Frédéric Jaulmes); New Haven, Yale Center for British Art 132 (Bridgeman Art Library); New York, Metropolitan Museum of Art 99 (photo ©1999); Victoria, British Columbia Archives and Record Office Service 237; Vienna, Kunsthistorisches Museum 102; Worcester Art Museum, Massachusetts 114.

Index